ROTHMANS RUGBY LEAGUE YEARBOOK 1992-93

**Raymond Fletcher
and David Howes**

ROTHMANS

HEADLINE

© **Rothmans Publications Ltd 1992**

First published in 1992
by HEADLINE BOOK PUBLISHING PLC

10 9 8 7 6 5 4 3 2 1

COVER PHOTOGRAPHS

Front Cover: Two of the outstanding prop forwards of the 1991-92 season, Kevin Ward of St. Helens being tackled by Castleford skipper Lee Crooks. *Back Cover:* Shaun Edwards on Test duty as skipper of Great Britain against France at Hull in March 1992.

ACKNOWLEDGEMENTS

The compilers would like to acknowledge the assistance of the Rugby League Record Keepers' Club, club secretaries and individuals in providing material as a further source of reference for accuracy.

PHOTOGRAPHS

Modern day domestic photographs in this *Rothmans Rugby League Yearbook* are mainly from the files of the *Rugby Leaguer.* The compilers acknowledge the co-operation of Chief Photographer Gerald Webster and his staff.
The colour photographs on the front and back covers, plus a number of black-and-white contributions, are by freelance photographer Andrew Varley.

British Library Cataloguing in Publication Data

Rothmans Rugby League Yearbook — 1992-93
  1. Rugby football — Great Britain —
  Periodicals
  796.33.3.0941 GV945.9.G7

ISBN 0 7472 7906 3

Photoset by New Rush Filmsetters, London

Reproduced, printed and bound in Great Britain by
Clay Ltd, St. Ives plc

HEADLINE BOOK PUBLISHING PLC
Headline House
79 Great Titchfield Street
London W1P 7FN

Rothmans Rugby League Yearbook 1992-93

CONTENTS

EDITORIAL PREFACE

Since the launch of the bestselling *Rothmans Rugby League Yearbook* back in 1980, there has been a deliberate policy of adopting a familiar layout for the compilation of the statistics of both the past season and yesteryear.

For this 12th edition, the emphasis is transformed to be club orientated. The traditional service of honours, records and the previous season's players' summary and match analysis has been extended to feature individual club registers of transfers, representative honours and coaching appointments.

The advent of computerisation at Chapeltown Road has improved the League's registration system, but the player personnel department still has a number of problems to solve regarding signing and qualification of players. With regret, we would issue a disclaimer regarding London Crusaders' registration of players and their 1991-92 scoring records, the club affairs being subject to a League inquiry at the publication deadline.

Wigan, inevitably, dominate the review of the 1991-92 season and while congratulating the Riversiders for their record-breaking feats, we would endorse the view that Wigan's setting of high standards should set a challenge for others to emulate and surpass.

For the 12th season, sincere thanks go to our wives for their continuing understanding and patience, despite their being resigned to a role of *Rothmans Rugby League Yearbook* "widows". Ian Marshall has been a supportive and meticulous house editor and we look forward to an excellent relationship with new publishers, Headline.

● Facts and figures in this *Rothmans Rugby League Yearbook* as at 1 June 1992.

RAYMOND FLETCHER, of the *Yorkshire Post*

DAVID HOWES, Rugby League Public Affairs Executive

COACHES SELECT XIII

For the fourth time, the coaches of the 14 clubs in the Stones Bitter Championship were invited to select their form team of the season as an exclusive feature of the 1992-93 *Rothmans Rugby League Yearbook.*

The coaches were asked not to include members of their own club sides and to base their choice on opposition performances during the 1991-92 campaign, while taking general form into account. It is based on individual form and does not necessarily represent their best team.

A total of 47 players were nominated by the 13 coaches taking part, St. Helens supremo Mike McClennan having returned to New Zealand for a summer break. David Hobbs represented Bradford Northern as Peter Fox again declined the invitation to select a team.

Wigan provided a record 14 nominees, the next best being arch-rivals St. Helens with seven. Seven players were named in more than one position, the largest category nomination being 11 for the two second row spots, followed by nine for the centre duo.

In the Coaches Select XIII, a record nine selections came from Wigan, the quartet of outsiders being Graham Steadman (Castleford), John Devereux (Widnes), Kevin Ward (St. Helens) and Gary Mercer (Warrington).

The only players to have achieved a 100 per cent appearance record in the Coaches Select XIII over the four years are Martin Offiah and Andy Gregory. Phil McKenzie and Ellery Hanley failed to make the 1991-92 line-up after a hat-trick of appearances.

After increasing to five nominees in the previous poll, the number of overseas inclusions reverted to three, as in the first two polls. The successful trio were Kiwi Mercer, fellow countryman Dean Bell — the newly crowned Stones Bitter Man of Steel — and Australian Gene Miles.

Of the remaining 10 British players in the Coaches Select XIII, only Ward did not represent Great Britain on the 1992 British Coal tour Down Under, having retired from international football.

There was only one tie, between Phil Clarke, Ellery Hanley and Kiwi Tawera Nikau at loose forward. The vote went to Great Britain Under-21 skipper Clarke as he also collected a nomination for a second row berth.

Unlike previous polls, no one received 100 per cent support. Denis Betts and Andy Gregory each received 10 of a possible 12 votes; Shaun Edwards and Martin Offiah, nine; and Dean Bell, Martin Dermott and Andy Platt, eight.

Castleford full back Graham Steadman, voted Stones Bitter First Division Player of the Year.

COACHES SELECT XIII

1. **Graham Steadman** (Castleford)
2. **John Devereux** (Widnes)
3. **Dean Bell** (Wigan)
4. **Gene Miles** (Wigan)
5. **Martin Offiah** (Wigan)
6. **Shaun Edwards** (Wigan)
7. **Andy Gregory** (Wigan)
8. **Kevin Ward** (St. Helens)
9. **Martin Dermott** (Wigan)
10. **Andy Platt** (Wigan)
11. **Denis Betts** (Wigan)
12. **Gary Mercer** (Warrington)
13. **Phil Clarke** (Wigan)

Widnes threequarter John Devereux, capped in 1991-92 for Great Britain and Wales.

Wigan skipper Dean Bell, Stones Bitter Man of Steel 1992.

ALLAN AGAR, Featherstone R.

1. Steadman (Castleford)
2. Devereux (Widnes)
3. Bell (Wigan)
4. Connolly (St. Helens)
5. Botica (Wigan)
6. Edwards (Wigan)
7. Mackey (Hull)
8. Crooks (Castleford)
9. Dermott (Wigan)
10. Platt (Wigan)
11. Betts (Wigan)
12. P. Fletcher (Hull K.R.)
13. Nikau (Castleford)

TONY BARROW, Swinton

1. Lyon (Warrington)
2. Devereux (Widnes)
3. Schofield (Leeds)
4. Miles (Wigan)
5. Offiah (Wigan)
6. Edwards (Wigan)
7. Gregory (Wigan)
8. Ward (St. Helens)
9. Jackson (Hull)
10. Platt (Wigan)
11. Betts (Wigan)
12. Nickle (St. Helens)
13. Hanley (Leeds)

STEVE CROOKS, Hull

1. Steadman (Castleford)
2. Myers (Wigan)
3. Bell (Wigan)
4. Newlove (Featherstone R.)
5. Offiah (Wigan)
6. Powell (Sheffield E.)
7. Gregory (Wigan)
8. Crooks (Castleford)
9. Dermott (Wigan)
10. Platt (Wigan)
11. Betts (Wigan)
12. Mercer (Warrington)
13. Clarke (Wigan)

GEORGE FAIRBAIRN, Hull K.R.

1. Steadman (Castleford)
2. Bentley (Leeds)
3. Schofield (Leeds)
4. Davies (Widnes)
5. Offiah (Wigan)
6. Edwards (Wigan)
7. Gregory (Wigan)
8. Crooks (Castleford)
9. Dermott (Wigan)
10. Lucas (Wigan)
11. Betts (Wigan)
12. Dixon (Leeds)
13. Hanley (Leeds)

Wigan's Australian import, Gene Miles.

Wigan's world record signing, Test winger Martin Offiah.

DAVID HOBBS, Bradford N.

1. Steadman (Castleford)
2. Botica (Wigan)
3. Bell (Wigan)
4. Newlove (Featherstone R.)
5. Preston (Halifax)
6. Edwards (Wigan)
7. Gregory (Wigan)
8. Harrison (Halifax)
9. Lee (Salford)
10. Skerrett (Wigan)
11. Sharp (Hull)
12. Mercer (Warrington)
13. Clarke (Wigan)

BRIAN JOHNSON, Warrington

1. Steadman (Castleford)
2. Myers (Wigan)
3. Ropati (St. Helens)
4. Newlove (Featherstone R.)
5. Devereux (Widnes)
6. Edwards (Wigan)
7. Gregory (Wigan)
8. Ward (St. Helens)
9. Jackson (Hull)
10. Platt (Wigan)
11. Betts (Wigan)
12. Jackson (Wakefield T.)
13. Busby (Hull)

DOUG LAUGHTON, Leeds

1. Steadman (Castleford)
2. Devereux (Widnes)
3. Bell (Wigan)
4. Miles (Wigan)
5. Offiah (Wigan)
6. Edwards (Wigan)
7. Gregory (Wigan)
8. Skerrett (Wigan)
9. Dermott (Wigan)
10. Fairbank (Bradford N.)
11. Betts (Wigan)
12. Mercer (Warrington)
13. Nikau (Castleford)

Top tryscorer, Wigan half back Shaun Edwards.

Wigan and Great Britain scrum half Andy Gregory.

ROGER MILLWARD, Halifax

1. Lyon (Warrington)
2. Hunte (St. Helens)
3. Loughlin (St. Helens)
4. Miles (Wigan)
5. Offiah (Wigan)
6. Edwards (Wigan)
7. Gregory (Wigan)
8. Ward (St. Helens)
9. Dermott (Wigan)
10. Platt (Wigan)
11. Betts (Wigan)
12. Mercer (Warrington)
13. Clarke (Wigan)

JOHN MONIE, Wigan

1. Lyon (Warrington)
2. Devereux (Widnes)
3. Ropati (St. Helens)
4. Schofield (Leeds)
5. Bentley (Leeds)
6. Steadman (Castleford)
7. Ellis (Warrington)
8. Ward (St. Helens)
9. Jackson (Hull)
10. Mann (St. Helens)
11. Fairbank (Bradford N.)
12. Mercer (Warrington)
13. Hanley (Leeds)

FRANK MYLER, Widnes

1. Lyon (Warrington)
2. Myers (Wigan)
3. Bell (Wigan)
4. Miles (Wigan)
5. Offiah (Wigan)
6. Powell (Sheffield E.)
7. Gregory (Wigan)
8. Ward (St. Helens)
9. Dermott (Wigan)
10. Platt (Wigan)
11. Fairbank (Bradford N.)
12. Fogerty (Halifax)
13. Nikau (Castleford)

St. Helens' blockbusting prop forward Kevin Ward.

Great Britain and Wigan hooker Martin Dermott.   *Wigan and Great Britain second row man Denis Betts.*

Wigan's Test prop Andy Platt, 1992 Harry Sunderland Trophy winner.

11

KEVIN TAMATI, Salford

1. Lydon (Wigan)
2. Devereux (Widnes)
3. Bell (Wigan)
4. Miles (Wigan)
5. Offiah (Wigan)
6. Edwards (Wigan)
7. Gregory (Wigan)
8. Ward (St. Helens)
9. Dermott (Wigan)
10. Platt (Wigan)
11. Betts (Wigan)
12. Clarke (Wigan)
13. Hanley (Leeds)

DAVID TOPLISS, Wakefield T.

1. Steadman (Castleford)
2. Devereux (Widnes)
3. Bell (Wigan)
4. Ropati (St. Helens)
5. Offiah (Wigan)
6. Edwards (Wigan)
7. Gregory (Wigan)
8. Ward (St. Helens)
9. Dermott (Wigan)
10. Crooks (Castleford)
11. Betts (Wigan)
12. Mann (St. Helens)
13. Nikau (Castleford)

Gary Mercer, Warrington's Kiwi second row import.

DARRYL VAN DE VELDE, Castleford

1. Connolly (St. Helens)
2. Botica (Wigan)
3. Bell (Wigan)
4. Devereux (Widnes)
5. Offiah (Wigan)
6. Schofield (Leeds)
7. Fox (Featherstone R.)
8. Skerrett (Wigan)
9. Jackson (Hull)
10. Platt (Wigan)
11. Betts (Wigan)
12. Mercer (Warrington)
13. Clarke (Wigan)

Great Britain Under-21 skipper Phil Clarke, Wigan's replacement for Ellery Hanley.

Offiah runs in ten tries

MEMORIES

Hanley goes to Leeds for £¼m

Wigan kings of the world

Hard-up Leigh are rescued by player

Try spree for Welsh

Pier-fect as Wigan treble it

Wigan sign Offiah in world record transfer

Wigan dominate tour party

MEMORIES

1991-92 HEADLINES

Behind the scoring feats and records of the 1991-92 season were a number of stories which made the headlines:

TRANSFER RECORD SMASHED .... TWICE

The world record transfer fee of £170,000 was smashed and then more than doubled after Britain's two greatest players and biggest attractions were transferred during the season.

Wigan captain Ellery Hanley was the first to go when, after weeks of haggling, Leeds paid out £250,000 for the Great Britain loose forward. Although Hanley was not on the transfer list, Wigan had been asking as much as £450,000 for Hanley after he rejected a new contract at Central Park. Hanley signed for Leeds on 6 September and made his debut at home to Hull two days later.

Within four months, the record transfer fee soared to an astonishing £440,000 when Wigan signed Martin Offiah from Widnes. The Great Britain winger had been on the list at £700,000 since November, after seeking a move before the start of the season and refusing to play for Widnes again. Offiah signed for Wigan on 3 January and made his debut at home to Wakefield Trinity two days later. Including his four-year contract, the deal was reckoned to have cost Wigan £1m.

Before last season the record transfer fee was £170,000 for Featherstone Rovers stand off Graham Steadman's move to Castleford in 1989.

HANLEY JAW-BREAKER

Ellery Hanley suffered a broken jaw in only his ninth match for Leeds following an incident which remained in the headlines for nearly three weeks until Hull's Andy Dannatt was banned for eight matches. Hanley's jaw was broken in three places after a 22nd-minute off-the-ball tackle by Dannatt in the Regal Trophy second round tie at Hull on 23 November.

Bradford referee Brian Galtress did not award a penalty but Leeds official Joe Warham, acting as an RL Council member, called for the Rugby League to study a video of the incident. After viewing the tape, the Board of Directors forwarded the case to the Disciplinary Committee who dealt with it on 12 December after the High Court rejected Hull's move to prevent the *trial by video*.

Dannatt's eight-match suspension included three reserve team matches, while Hanley's injury ruled him out of 12 first team games, plus another with a calf strain.

PRO-AM PEACE MOVE

The Rugby Football League and the British Amateur Rugby League Association had "reached agreement on unification", it was announced on 21 January. League Chief Executive David Oxley proclaimed: "It is one of the most momentous decisions since the breakaway from the English Rugby Union in 1895 and certainly the most important policy-making decision."

BARLA was formed as an independent body in 1973 following a breakaway from the League, whom they believed were hampering the amateurs' development.

Last season began with increased acrimony when the RFL introduced an Academy League for youth rugby. BARLA claimed it was nothing but the old semi-professional Colts League in disguise, which they said was in direct opposition to their own youth rugby plans. A series of retaliatory moves then followed:

● BARLA threatened to suspend any player who joined the Academy, the League banning amateur clubs from entering the Silk Cut Challenge Cup and Regal Trophy.
● BARLA "locked out" Phil Larder from his office after he quit as Director of Coaching to join the Academy and top BARLA official Maurice Oldroyd was ejected when he attempted to attend a National Coaching Scheme meeting at

League headquarters.

With the dispute at its height, both bodies then had a series of peace talks which led to the "agreement on unification". There remained some uncertainty about what it meant exactly, with BARLA denying it was a merger, while many believed it was the first move in the League regaining control of amateur rugby.

WIGAN SEVENS ROW

Wigan ran into a controversy when they were nominated as Britain's entry into the first Nissan World Sevens in Sydney and left for a week in Australia during the busiest League, Cup and representative period of the season.

With many clubs struggling to fit in Cup ties postponed by frost and snow, Wigan were allowed to play their second round match a week later than the rest. That meant no Wigan players would be available for Great Britain's British Coal Test in France on 16 February.

On the positive side, Wigan proved great British ambassadors by winning the sevens tournament and a £50,000 prize. Wigan winger Martin Offiah was named man of the tournament after scoring 10 tries in five matches, including all four in the 18-6 final defeat of Brisbane Broncos at Sydney Football Stadium on 9 February.

SUPER LEAGUE TALKS AGAIN

The now almost annual talk of a *Super League* was raised again following a meeting of "Top 16" clubs in February. All 14 Division One clubs, plus Division Two's Sheffield Eagles and Oldham, were invited to the meeting and a six-man committee was formed. Leigh joined the group soon after.

They planned moves to give the top clubs a greater say in the running of the game by giving them more voting power, which is currently restricted to one per club. They also sought a bigger share of television money and a reduction in the eight per cent levy Division One clubs pay to the League.

Gary Hetherington of Sheffield emerged as the spokesman of the committee which also included Alf Davies (Leeds), Peter Higham (Warrington), Eric Gardiner (Featherstone R.), John Wilkinson (Salford) and Steve Watson (Hull). The meeting was declared illegal by the uninvited lower clubs and they expressed their discontent at a Rugby League Council meeting on 4 March. Later, the League's Board of Directors said they would examine key features in the top clubs' proposals.

THREE DIVISIONS RETAINED

The "Top 17" clubs caused further controversy with their plan to scrap three divisions after only one season and replace them with a revolutionary two division system. They also called for the scrapping of the County Cups and for Division One clubs to be exempt from the preliminary stages of the Silk Cut Challenge Cup and Regal Trophy.

The two division plan called for 16 clubs in each with four others losing their senior status and forming a subsidiary league including amateur and development area clubs. The bottom two clubs in Division Two would apply for re-election and not face automatic relegation.

The Council discussed the proposals on 1 April and decided against them. Then the League's Board of Directors came up with their own revolutionary and controversial plan. It called for Division One reverting to 16 clubs, Division Two increasing to 14 and a third tier of 12 consisting of the remaining six senior clubs and six top reserve teams from the Alliance, who could not be promoted. They also planned to abolish the County Cups to ease the fixture congestion. All the proposals were to take effect immediately.

The plan was discussed by the Council on 6 May when yet another fixture formula was mooted and clubs were given a day to put forward other ideas. But at a special general meeting on 12 May the clubs voted narrowly to leave things as they were. And, though the meeting was instigated by the Board of Directors' controversial plan, it was withdrawn before being put to the vote. The proposal to revert to two divisions of 16 and 20 clubs fell only three votes short of the necessary three-fifths majority.

TV DEALS

Friday night became Rugby League TV night when BSkyB announced a new four-year deal on 11 May to cover top Stones Bitter Championship matches from the start of 1992-93. The satellite TV station would also cover four Premiership matches, including the double-header final, the Charity Shield and European international matches. In addition they would replace their live Sunday matches with recorded highlights of games. They had already agreed live coverage of 1992 British Lions tour matches, including the Tests against Australia and New Zealand.

Sky also led the way in February 1992 with the game's first regular magazine-style programme, *Boots 'n' All*, on Thursday nights.

Although no fee was revealed for the new contract, it was said to be worth more than the BBC's new four-year £2.5m deal signed four days earlier. The BBC package included continued live coverage of Regal Trophy and Silk Cut Challenge Cup matches plus incoming Test series.

Sky's exclusive deal meant the end of Yorkshire TV's *Scrumdown* programme which had televised recorded matches late on Sunday nights for the past five years. Granada TV's live Saturday afternoon matches also ended.

Another TV outlet to end came with the sudden collapse of the satellite channel Sportscast, which relayed live and recorded Division Two and Three matches to pubs and clubs. The British Aerospace-owned company, which also covered other sports, folded on 11 March after only 18 months. It meant the League would not receive the £500,000

due for 1992-93 as they were only two-thirds through a three-year £1.5m contract.

CRUSADERS OVERSEAS ROW

Huddersfield protested over London Crusaders allegedly fielding double their allotted number of overseas players in the Stones Bitter Divisional Premiership match on 26 April. The home side beat Huddersfield 14-4 to book a semi-final place, but the Yorkshire club claimed they should be awarded the tie because London fielded eight — and possibly nine — overseas players. The League's Board of Directors rejected Huddersfield's claim because they "presented insufficient evidence". But the Board said they would continue the inquiry into London's overseas players. See TRANSFERS section.

RUSSIAN INVASION

Moscow Magicians and Tiraspol of Moldavia became the first clubs from the old Soviet Union to face senior teams in Britain when they made a brief tour in December.

Both matches were played on 22 December, with Moscow losing 58-12 at Huddersfield, while Tiraspol went down 34-14 to Batley.

Earlier, Moscow had begun the week-long trip with a 16-12 defeat against a North East Academy youth side, Tiraspol going down 30-19 to North West Academy.

After the tour, four Moscow players became the first Russian players to sign for a British team when Oleg Zotov, Alexander Diatlov, Valerie Medwedj and Valerie Savikhine joined Trafford Borough for a brief spell. Zotov was the first to play and scored a try at prop in the Division Three 26-18 home defeat by Chorley Borough on 26 December. In the same match Diatlov made a substitute appearance. All four eventually played for the first team but never more than three in the same match.

WIGAN — THE GREATEST?

Wigan laid claim to being the greatest British club side of all time after completing a Challenge Cup and League title double for an extended record third successive season and adding the Premiership Trophy to become the first club to complete the big Spring treble.

They won their last 25 matches of the season including a record 71-10 Challenge Cup semi-final defeat of Bradford Northern and a record 74-6 Premiership competition defeat of Leeds in the semi-final.

Wigan completed their remarkable season by winning the Premiership Trophy with a 48-16 defeat of second-placed St. Helens that was the highest score in any Cup final during the game's near 100-year history.

Wigan's success resulted in them providing a record 13 players for Great Britain's 1992 Down Under tour.

OFFIAH SCORES 10 TRIES

Martin Offiah produced one of the most astonishing individual performances of all time when he scored a Wigan club record 10 tries in the 74-6 Stones Bitter Premiership semi-final home defeat of Leeds on 10 May. The Great Britain winger scored all but four of Wigan's 14 tries with five in each half. None of them was presented to Offiah, as he roamed the field to support attacking moves and touch down left, right and centre of the posts.

It was only the third time in the game's history that a player had scored 10 or more tries. Hull Kingston Rovers winger George West set the record with 11 against Brookland Rovers amateurs in 1905 and Australian winger Lionel Cooper got 10 for Huddersfield against Keighley in 1951.

FRANCE v RUSSIA

The Soviet Union made their international match debut when they lost 26-6 to France on 27 October, unrecognised as a Test as they were not yet members of the International Board. The historic match was played at the Stade Georges Lyvet, Villeurbanne, near Lyon, before a crowd of about 2,000.

The teams for the international match were:

France 26: Fages; Garcia (1t), Despin (1t), Bienes, Sirvent; Dumas (Capt) (5g), Entat (1t); Calvo, Torreilles, Ruiz, Grandjean, Storer (1t), Divet. Subs: Romano, Chamorin, Bonnet, Frison.

Soviet Union 6: Otkadnov; Savikhine, Vynokhodov, Piskunov, Korsakov; Olar (1t, 1g), Osadekiv; Liukianichev, Zotov, Koriubin, Pareshin (Capt), Lizov, P. Sokolow. Subs: A. Sokolow, Senin, Sapega, Netchaiv.

Referee: Claude Alba (France).

Earlier, a French President's XIII had beaten them 60-10 at Corbeil, near Paris.

JUNE

Widnes target Wigan scrum half Andy Gregory as player-coach .... Batley line up David Ward as their new coach pending a dismissal settlement with Leeds .... Oldham cut the asking price for scrum half Mike Ford from £150,000 to £95,000 .... Andy Gregory agrees a new one-year contract with Wigan .... Runcorn Highfield change their official title to Highfield .... Doncaster transfer list their entire register of 36 players .... Hall of Fame member Brian Bevan dies .... Australia arrange first-ever Friday night Test series for the 1992 British Lions .... Whitehaven appoint Jackie Davidson as coach .... Administrator warns that Leigh have only days left to find a buyer .... Halifax recruit Allan Agar as assistant to coach Roger Millward .... Veteran prop forward Jeff Grayshon signs for Batley .... Halifax prop forward Peter Brown charged with bringing the game into disrepute for being involved in a melee in the Stones Bitter Second Division Premiership final .... Widnes duo Martin Offiah and Andy Currier reprimanded for not receiving their runners-up medals in the Stones Bitter Premiership final .... Salford sign Australian scrum half David Cruickshank from Fulham .... Halifax pay Wigan £60,000 for winger Mark Preston .... Castleford lose interest in South Sydney scrum half Craig Coleman .... Widnes fail to land Australian scrum half Peter Sterling as player-coach .... Leigh fans launch a petition to the local council urging them to save the club .... Bradford Northern offer Henderson Gill at £20,000 and Simon Tuffs at £10,000 .... Rochdale Hornets list Steve Turner at £15,000 .... Wigan nominated as the British representatives in the first-ever international sevens to be staged in Sydney in February 1992 .... Salford sign Wigan forward Ged Stazicker for £30,000 .... Oldham reject Halifax bid for Mike Ford .... Australian Test star Wally Lewis turns down the player-coach role at Widnes .... Featherstone Rovers sign Richard Agar, 19-year-old son of former coach Allan .... Great Britain coach Malcolm Reilly awarded the OBE .... The Board of Directors project a £17 million sponsorship and television bonanza over the next five years .... Swinton offer of ground sharing at Station Road turned down by Leigh .... Huddersfield offer packman Chris Parr at £100,000 .... Former Australian Test forward Paul Vautin applies for the vacant Widnes coaching job .... Australian Test skipper Mal Meninga rejects the player-coach position at Widnes .... Rochdale Hornets offer forward Mike O'Neill at £75,000 .... Oldham scrum half Mike Ford moves to Castleford for £77,500 .... Warrington claim to sign New Zealand Test stand off Kelly Shelford .... The League sanction the formation of the South African Rugby Football League .... Gary Stephens leaves Ryedale-York to become assistant coach at Leeds .... St. Helens launch determined bid to land Australian captain Mal Meninga .... Australian Steve Blakeley turns down a return to Ryedale-York as player-coach .... Widnes appoint Frank Myler for a second stint as coach .... Wigan scrum half Bobby Goulding at the centre of a contractual row after quitting Australian club Eastern Suburbs .... Wigan offer Bobby Goulding at £120,000 .... Trafford Borough give player-coach job to Norman Turley .... Wigan sell Bobby Goulding to Leeds for £90,000 .... Sheffield Eagles and Warrington fail to get necessary support at League AGM for First Division clubs to be exempt from cup preliminary rounds .... Widnes appoint George Nicholls as assistant coach.

JULY

Australian back row forward Jeff Hardy prefers Sydney club St. George to a further spell at Castleford .... Southern club Hemel Hempstead elected as the first-ever amateur members of the Youngers Alliance .... Great Britain Under-21 forward Sonny Nickle joins St. Helens after being listed at £195,000 by Sheffield Eagles .... The League launch a five-year fund-raising programme for National Children's Home .... Jim Mills appointed manager of Wales, with Clive Griffiths as coach .... Bob Ashby gives year's notice of stepping down as Chairman of the League, Maurice Lindsay being named as Chairman-Designate .... Jim Crellin resigns as coach of promoted Swinton .... Workington Town's Ray Ashton appointed as coach of Lancashire for the 1991 Rodstock War of the Roses .... Halifax chase Wigan loose forward Mike Forshaw .... The League encourage the signing of Russians as a development-aid by lifting quota restrictions for the 1991-92 season .... St. Helens offer a two-year £250,000 deal to Mal Meninga .... Warrington offer Billy McGinty at £95,000, with Mark Roberts and Mark Thomas priced at £30,000 .... Australian Test back Laurie Daley agrees to join Wakefield Trinity on a short-term contract .... Oldham forward John Fieldhouse turns down the Swinton player-coach role and is approached by Wakefield Trinity .... Test prop forward Andy Dannatt listed by Hull at £200,000 ....

Castleford ask £25,000 for prop Andy Clarke .... Prop Tony Humphries valued at £55,000 by Rochdale Hornets .... St. Helens put price tag of £50,000 on Welsh packman Stuart Evans .... Jonathan Davies named as captain of Wales .... Hunslet reject Halifax bid of £50,000 for back row forward Michael Jackson .... Assistant Derek Foster promoted to coach of Ryedale-York .... Scarborough Pirates sign scrum half Steve Robinson from Hull K.R. .... Warrington list full back David Lyon at £135,000 .... Tribunal fixes transfer fee on Sonny Nickle's move from Sheffield Eagles to St. Helens at £80,000, plus £25,000 after two Tests against Australia or New Zealand .... Australian half back Chris O'Sullivan leaves Warrington to join Swinton as player-coach .... Castleford sign New Zealand Test winger Richard Blackmore .... Bradford Northern claim the signing of Kiwi Kelly Shelford .... Swinton sign Canberra utility back Craig Bellamy .... Halifax ask £150,000 for 12 players headed by centre Rob Hutchinson .... Hull cut Andy Dannatt's fee from £200,000 to £150,000 .... BARLA closes ranks on youth issue as the League prepare to launch an under-18 set-up .... The League rule that Kelly Shelford is a Warrington player.

AUGUST

Winger Tex Evans valued at £90,000 by Salford .... Former chairman Bobby Hope steps in with a bid to save Leigh .... Leeds open contract talks with Wigan skipper Ellery Hanley .... Veteran forward Tony Cottrell heads a successful consortium bid to save Leigh .... Auckland forward Se'e Solomona joins Widnes .... Halifax pay a club record £120,000 for Hull Test prop Karl Harrison .... Ex-Great Britain captain David Watkinson appointed assistant coach of Ryedale-York .... Kevin Ashcroft joins Alex Murphy on the coaching staff at Leigh .... Halifax pay Leeds £30,000 for scrum half Paul Harkin .... Trafford Borough list centre Paul

Reynolds at £45,000 .... Welshman Gary Pearce leaves Hull for Scarborough Pirates in £18,000 deal .... Wakefield Trinity sign Michael Jackson from Hunslet .... CIS Insurance agree a new £80,000 three-year deal for the Charity Shield .... Leigh offer full back Paul Topping at £150,000 .... Swinton sign Oldham duo Neil Clawson and John Fairbank in exchange for Tim Street .... Wigan fail to tempt Australian tourist Des Hasler away from Manly .... The League forced to move the Foster's World Club Challenge from Old Trafford to Liverpool's Anfield because of European soccer commitments .... St. Helens centre Tony Kay returns to Barrow for £8,000 fee .... Australian stand off Wayne Portlock joins Hull .... Oldham sign Rochdale Hornets half back Neil Holding in exchange for Brett Clark and Ronnie Duane .... Leeds swap Mike Kuiti for Rochdale Hornets forward Mike O'Neill .... Wigan reject a Leeds bid of £200,000 for Ellery Hanley .... Hull recruit Manly centre David Ronson .... Workington Town sign Kiwi centre Ben Lia, formerly with Widnes .... Sports Council offer to mediate in the youth rugby row .... The League refuse permission for a change of official title to Bramley Marketmen .... The 1992 Stones Bitter Champions to receive a record £45,000, the first-ever Third Division title-winners to be awarded £10,500 .... Colin Hutton appointed as the inaugural chairman of the Academy .... Wigan sign Auckland Test back Sam Panapa .... Wigan beat Hull 22-8 to lift the 1991 CIS Insurance Charity Shield .... Halifax list utility back Warren Wilson at £50,000 .... The League launch a pilot apprenticeship scheme in the Leeds area .... Hunslet sign loose forward Paul Carr from South Sydney .... Sheffield Eagles swap winger David Nelson for Castleford Test man David Plange .... Wakefield Trinity overcome threat of closure with the formation of a first-ever board of directors .... Wigan hand over £60,000 for Warrington's Billy McGinty

19

.... New Leeds coach Doug Laughton drops former New Zealand RU international full back John Gallagher for the opening match of the season .... Fulham retitled London Crusaders .... Scarborough Pirates offered a sponsorship prize of £1 million for promotion.

SEPTEMBER

Wigan sign £200,000-rated prop forward Neil Cowie from Rochdale Hornets .... Salford swap Tony Conroy for Oldham's Trevor Croston .... Wigan offer Ellery Hanley another chance to stay at Central Park .... Leeds recruit New Zealand full back Morvin Edwards .... BARLA ban young players who join the League's new Academy under-18 set-up .... Australian Test star Laurie Daley confirms that he will not be signing for Wakefield Trinity because of injury .... Oldham reject £12,500 Doncaster bid for winger Paul Lord .... Leigh part company with team manager Alex Murphy, upgrading Kevin Ashcroft .... Keighley sack coach Tony Fisher .... Ellery Hanley joins Leeds in record £250,000 deal .... St. Helens forward Roy Haggerty moves to Barrow for £15,000 .... Warrington packman Bob Jackson returns to native Australia for personal reasons .... The League withdraw invitation for amateur clubs to take part in the two major knockout tournaments as youth football row escalates .... Sheffield Eagles sign New Zealand back Iva Ropati .... Huddersfield sack joint coaches Mick Blacker and Francis Jarvis .... Wigan fill third overseas quota place with former Australian Test player Gene Miles on a one-year contract .... Oldham's John Fieldhouse joins Halifax .... Huddersfield and Keighley chase Alex Murphy .... Leeds skipper Garry Schofield upset as Ellery Hanley is given the captaincy in his second match .... Halifax sign loose forward Greg Pearce from London Crusaders .... Widnes order stay-away Martin Offiah to visit a specialist for a fitness report .... Yorkshire extend their unbeaten record in the Rodstock

War of the Roses series with a 17-12 defeat of Lancashire at Leeds .... Hull K.R. winger Garry Clark moves to Scarborough Pirates .... Alex Murphy turns down Keighley job offer .... Bob Jackson arrives back at Warrington after 12 days Down Under .... The League and BARLA declare peace, lift respective bans and set up unification talks .... London Crusaders offer Australian skipper Mal Meninga £3,000 a match for a short-term contract .... Peter Roe returns to Keighley for a second stint as coach .... Alex Murphy takes over at Huddersfield with Terry Flanagan as assistant .... Great Britain to play second Test against Australia in 1992 in Melbourne, their debut in the Victorian capital .... Scarborough Pirates hand over £7,000 to Leigh for scrum half Bob Beardmore .... Welsh prop forward Stuart Evans walks out on St. Helens .... Penrith's bid to lift the Foster's World Club Challenge title boosted by 11th-hour availability of skipper Greg Alexander and Test colleague John Cartwright .... Bob Eccles resigns as coach of Chorley and joins Rochdale Hornets.

OCTOBER

Widnes turn down an approach from Wigan for winger Martin Offiah .... Rochdale Hornets sign New Zealander Paul Okesene .... Wigan lift the Foster's World Club Challenge title at Anfield, beating Australian Premiers Penrith 21-4 .... Castleford swoop to sign Penrith centre Graeme Bradley .... Keighley recruit Halifax loose forward Mick Keebles .... Scarborough Pirates and Huddersfield chase Leeds' Kenyan winger Eddie Rombo .... Wakefield Trinity offer centre Ged Byrne at £70,000 .... Hull K.R. sign Gold Coast centre Troy McCarthy .... Rochdale Hornets list utility forward Ian Gormley at £65,000 .... The League clamp down on clubs introducing an away strip rather than an alternative .... Martin Offiah threatens to quit Rugby League and switch to American football .... Wakefield Trinity prop Adrian Shelford and Hull centre Brian Blacker cleared of drug charges after being unable to provide a sample for testing .... The League introduce a fourth official to cater for substitutions, sin bins and blood bins .... Sydney referee Bill Harrigan appointed for the British Coal series against Papua New Guinea .... Tribunal value Wigan prop Neil Cowie's move from Rochdale Hornets at £65,000, plus £15,000 on Test debut .... Wigan coach John Monie advocates the introduction of four substitutes in domestic football .... Featherstone Rovers sign Leeds reserve forward Tony Butt .... Peter Fox resigns as coach of Featherstone Rovers .... Whitehaven recruit New Zealand stand off Steve Carey and Australian Jason Charlton .... The League announce backing for the introduction of an eight-club South African league within two years .... Leeds ask Hull to pay £80,000 for Test forward Roy Powell .... Peter Fox returns to Bradford Northern as team manager .... Oldham duo Paul Round and Paul Lord join Wakefield Trinity in straight swap for Ged Byrne .... Halifax hand over £27,500 to Leeds for utility player Gary Lord .... Leeds forward Richard Gunn rejects a move to Scarborough Pirates .... Leeds put price tag of £80,000 on loose forward Gary Divorty .... Featherstone Rovers fail to agree terms with Widnes forward Kurt Sorensen for the coaching job .... New Zealander Jason Gilbert joins Huddersfield .... Hull K.R. offer hooker Chris Rudd at £20,000 .... Castleford beat Bradford Northern 28-6 to lift the John Smiths Yorkshire Cup .... Battling Second Division Rochdale Hornets go down 24-14 to St. Helens in the Greenalls Lancashire Cup final .... Jonathan Davies signs a new three-year contract at Widnes .... Rochdale Hornets list captain Colin Whitfield at £30,000 .... New Zealander Tony Tuimavave joins Sheffield Eagles .... Test full back Alan Tait puts in a shock transfer request at Widnes .... Dewsbury offer forward Andy

Dickinson at £15,000 .... Sheffield Eagles ask £18,000 for packman Nick Grimoldby .... Alan Tait makes his peace at Widnes .... Scotland B RU prop forward George Graham signs for Carlisle .... Allan Agar appointed coach of Featherstone Rovers for a second stint .... Wales beat Papua New Guinea 68-0 in the opening fixture of a five-match tour of Britain .... Buoyant Wales request future fixtures against France and England .... Great Britain Under-21s defeat Papua New Guinea 58-0.

NOVEMBER
Martin Offiah returns to training at Naughton Park .... Oldham sell winger Norman Francis to Bramley for £5,000 .... Swinton fine Welshman Paul Kennett and list him at £25,000 for disciplinary reasons .... Keighley Cougars sign Otley RU winger Johnny Walker .... Martin Offiah plays 30 minutes of Youngers Alliance football, scoring a try .... The League confirm Wales v France at Swansea in March .... Tribunal prices Dave Kendall's move from Carlisle to Barrow at £16,500 .... Humberside XIII snatch last-minute 16-14 victory over Papua New Guinea .... Great Britain select trio of new caps, Anthony Sullivan, Paul Moriarty and Michael Jackson .... Papua New Guinea beaten 34-12 by Cumbria at Workington .... Peace talks take place between the League and BARLA .... Leigh criticise the Board of Directors for not referring Workington Town centre Ben Lia to the Disciplinary Committee after an incident in which Andy Collier's jaw was broken .... Salford exchange prop Ian Sherratt for Oldham's Austin Donegan .... Garry Schofield named as British captain for the first time after the withdrawal of injured Ellery Hanley .... Great Britain gain two World Cup points in 56-4 defeat of Papua New Guinea .... Widnes take court action to prevent Martin Offiah playing American football .... Huddersfield sign Hungarian RU player and sprinter Bela Varga on trial ....

January... Garry Schofield led Leeds into the Regal Trophy final, their first major final for four years.

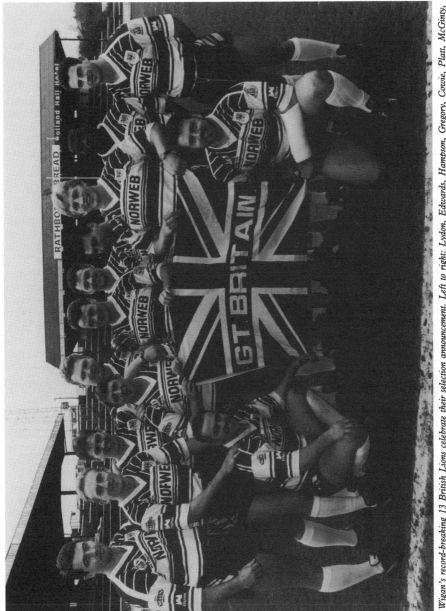

Wigan's record-breaking 13 British Lions celebrate their selection announcement. Left to right: Lydon, Edwards, Hampson, Gregory, Cowie, Platt, McGinty, Skerrett, Betts, Offiah and Clarke. Kneeling: Dermott and Lucas.

Huddersfield and Batley selected to host Russian clubs' visit in December .... Trafford Borough offer Ken Jones at £8,000 .... Hunslet's Under-21 half back Tim Lumb asks for a move .... Keighley list former captain Andy Gascoigne after his refusal to act as substitute .... Hull scrum half Phil Windley joins Scarborough Pirates in £10,000 deal .... Widnes reveal that Martin Offiah was seeking £600,000 for a three-and-a-half-year contract .... Widnes place a £700,000 price tag on Martin Offiah .... Tribunal fixes £40,000 fee on Greg Pearce's move from London Crusaders to Halifax .... Leeds reject London Crusaders' overtures for the loan of former All Black John Gallagher .... Castleford list centre Ian Bragger at £40,000 .... Bradford Northern fail to persuade stand off Bob Grogan to return for a further spell at Odsal .... Wigan part company with assistant coach Harry Pinner .... Great Britain management duo Maurice Lindsay and Malcolm Reilly demand close-season steroid testing for Australian Test players .... Leeds release Kenyan winger Eddie Rombo .... Oldham swoop to land New Zealander Logan Edwards, formerly with Swinton and Rochdale Hornets .... Ellery Hanley breaks his jaw in three places in Leeds' Regal Trophy tie at Hull .... Oldham fail in a move for Widnes Under-21 international packman Jason Critchley .... Highfield list Sean Dolan at £10,000 .... Scrum half Paul Kay offered at £25,000 by Batley .... Wigan offer of £250,000 for Martin Offiah turned down by Widnes .... The League rule that comments to referee Ian Ollerton by Leeds coach Doug Laughton did not affect the result against Featherstone Rovers .... Workington Town sign Halifax utility back Dave Needham .... Kenyan winger Eddie Rombo joins Dewsbury.

DECEMBER
Hull join Leeds and Wigan in the chase for Martin Offiah .... Bradford Northern protest as the League choose Bradford City FC's Valley Parade for the Regal Trophy semi-final between Leeds and Salford .... The Board of Directors refer Andy Dannatt to the Disciplinary Committee for trial by video following Ellery Hanley broken jaw incident .... Norman Turley resigns as coach of Trafford Borough .... Leigh list winger Barry Ledger at £10,000 .... Huddersfield hand over £18,000 for St. Helens wingman Brimah Kebbie .... Castleford referee Ray Tennant resigns .... Oldham sign Wigan full back Sean Tyrer for £8,000 .... Workington Town part company with player-coach Ray Ashton .... Altrincham-based Trafford Borough propose a move to Blackpool .... Hull fail in a High Court injunction bid to prevent the Andy Dannatt case being heard by the League's Disciplinary Committee .... The police eight-day roster programme forces changes to Rugby League fixture arrangements .... Workington Town appoint New Zealander Dean Williams as caretaker coach .... Hull recruit Ian Stevens, ex-Wales Under-21 stand off .... Hull prop Andy Dannatt suspended for eight matches in trial by video .... Leigh fail to get Leeds full back John Gallagher on loan .... Leeds talk to All Black RU centre Craig Innes .... Silk Cut announce new five-year sponsorship of the Challenge Cup worth £2,325,000 .... Former Highfield player-coach Chris Arkwright rejoins the club as a player .... Widnes forward Paul Moriarty ruled out of further Great Britain and Wales honours for the rest of the season with a shoulder injury .... Widnes turn down a Trafford Borough move from Kiwi prop Joe Grima .... Castleford offer centre Graeme Bradley and packman Martin Ketteridge in exchange for Oldham's Charlie McAlister .... Hull put in offer of £350,000 for Martin Offiah .... Cash crisis club Swinton sever contracts with Australian trio, player-coach Chris O'Sullivan, Craig Bellamy and Mark Lowry .... Wigan raise their bid for Martin Offiah to £400,000.

JANUARY

Len Casey sacked as coach of Scarborough Pirates .... Castleford list utility man Terry McAllister at £10,000 .... Leigh and Salford show interest in Leeds full back John Gallagher .... Swinton appoint Tony Barrow as coach after failing to tempt Alex Murphy to move from Huddersfield .... Wigan hand over world record £440,000 to Widnes for Martin Offiah .... Leeds capture New Zealand All Black RU centre Craig Innes .... The League reschedule Wigan's potential second round Silk Cut Challenge Cup tie to accommodate their trip to Australia to represent Britain in the inaugural World Sevens .... Welsh RU international centre Scott Gibbs backs out of a £200,000 deal with Hull on the eve of the Silk Cut Challenge Cup deadline .... Scarborough Pirates promote Trevor Bailey to coaching role .... Doncaster sack coach Dave Sampson and upgrade assistant Geoff Morris, John Sheridan returning to the club as manager .... Former British heavyweight boxing champion Gary Mason has trials with London Crusaders .... Widnes lift the Regal Trophy by beating Leeds 24-0, a record winning margin .... Widnes list winger Steve Wynne at £45,000 .... Huddersfield pay club record £20,000 for Doncaster back row forward Gary Coulter .... Warrington offer prop Tony Burke at £35,000 after his refusal to play Alliance football .... Ryedale-York sign Scarborough Pirates' Welsh international Gary Pearce on loan .... Boxer Adam Fogerty signs a 16-month contract with Halifax .... Workington Town confirm Dean Williams' appointment as coach .... BARLA and the League announce a declaration of unification .... Freezing conditions cause havoc with the first round of the Silk Cut Challenge Cup, with only half the ties being played .... Widnes chairman Jim Mills flies to South Africa on a scouting mission .... Great Britain skipper Garry Schofield ruled out of the French series with a broken cheekbone ....

Salford win appeal to retain home advantage in first round Silk Cut Challenge Cup tie with Wigan after League suggest a move to an undersoil heated neutral venue to help ease Wigan's fixture congestion .... The League rule Wigan players out of the British Coal Test in France to accommodate their World Sevens and Challenge Cup commitments.

FEBRUARY

Swinton winger Martin Leyland put on critical list after an accidental clash of heads with a teammate in the Silk Cut Challenge Cup tie at Doncaster .... England RU second row man Wade Dooley turns down an approach from Trafford Borough .... Reconstruction work on the Stretford Road end of Old Trafford reduces the capacity for the Stones Bitter Premiership from 48,000 to 33,000 .... Jonathan Davies named as captain of Great Britain for the first time .... BSkyB announce live and exclusive coverage of Great Britain's Test series in both Australia and New Zealand .... Swinton swap winger Scott Ranson for Oldham trio Simon Longstaff, Richard Irving and Tony Barrow, son of the Swinton coach .... Martin Offiah scores all four tries in Wigan's 18-6 defeat of Brisbane Broncos in the final of the first-ever Nissan World Sevens .... The League release Alan Hunte from Great Britain travelling reserve duty in France after protest from St. Helens, due to play Bradford Northern on the same day .... Rochdale Hornets offer centre Darren Abram at £80,000 .... Great Britain Academy beat France 28-7 in their first-ever international encounter .... Substitute Graham Steadman comes on to score two tries in Great Britain's 30-12 victory over France in Perpignan .... France propose six-team European tournament involving two teams from France, England and Russia .... Sydney club Manly target Wigan second row man Denis Betts .... Swinton winger Martin Leyland given all-clear to return home from hospital .... Wigan ask £125,000 for want-away winger David Myers .... Bradford Northern manager Peter Fox banned from the touchline for six weeks after admitting encroachment of the pitch at Halifax .... Mike McClennan signs up for another season as coach of St. Helens .... Mike Round priced at £50,000 by Leigh .... Hull K.R. sign ex-Workington Town player-coach Ray Ashton on loan .... Caretaker coach Geoff Morris put in charge of Doncaster until the end of 1992-93 season .... Great Britain coach Malcolm Reilly makes 12 squad changes for the return British Coal Test with France .... Great Britain Academy draw 14-14 with France at Wigan .... Leigh half back Jason Donohue, banned sine die 16 months earlier, selected in the Great Britain Under-21 squad to meet France .... Leeds packman Roy Powell moves to Bradford Northern for £80,000.

MARCH
Batley sign half back Lee Hanlan from Hull .... Castleford offer utility man Neil Roebuck at £55,000 .... Halifax recruit half back Mark Bailey from St. Helens for £25,000 .... Whitehaven sign full back David Lightfoot from Hull K.R. after a five-month loan period .... Shaun Edwards confirmed as captain of Great Britain for the return British Coal Test at Hull .... Private meeting of top clubs instructed to refer their findings to the Board of Directors .... A dispute over World Cup table policy between Great Britain and New Zealand to be referred to the May meeting of the International Board .... The League turn down a Trafford Borough proposal to move to the Blackpool Mechanics soccer ground for their last four matches of the season .... Salford offer back row forward Mick Worrall at £85,000 .... St. Helens seek £35,000 for packman Paul Jones .... Great Britain Under-21s beat their French counterparts 56-2 at Halifax .... Great Britain collect two World Cup points with a 36-0 British Coal Test victory over France at Hull .... A knee

injury rules Mike Gregory out of the summer tour Down Under, and possibly until Christmas .... The League give Trafford Borough permission to complete their match programme at Huddersfield .... Leeds back row forward Gary Divorty refuses to join hooker Richard Gunn in a transfer move to Featherstone Rovers, preventing an Ian Smales move to Headingley in exchange .... Fighting on the terraces mars the first Silk Cut Challenge Cup semi-final as Castleford beat Hull 8-4 .... The Welsh RU turn down a request from the Wales RL squad for the purchase of tickets for the Wales-Scotland RU Cardiff international on the eve of the Wales-France 13-a-side clash at Swansea .... Salford forward Mick Worrall announces agreement of terms with Leeds for the next season .... St. Helens skipper Shane Cooper fined £400 and given a four-match suspended ban for "wilfully introducing a second ball into play" .... Trafford Borough fined £4,000 for postponing a fixture without permission .... Hunslet ordered to improve their hooter system after a Doncaster protest over a drop goal which gave Hunslet a 33-32 success .... Further meeting of the top clubs advocates the scrapping of four clubs to pave way for a return to two divisions of 16 clubs .... Wales beat France 35-6 at Swansea .... The League make a provisional booking for the World Cup final at Wembley on 24 October .... Workington Town advertise for a coach from the start of the next season .... Skipper Colin Armstrong listed at £35,000 by Workington Town .... New Zealand Test prop Adrian Shelford joins Sheffield Eagles .... Major matches at Headingley, Leeds, to have a new police control box for crowd surveillance and no swapping of ends following Silk Cut Challenge Cup semi-final trouble .... Wigan coach John Monie signs up for a fourth season .... Wigan rewrite the record books with a 71-10 trouncing of Bradford Northern in the Silk Cut Challenge Cup semi-final at Bolton .... New Zealand centre Iva Ropati moves from

Sheffield Eagles to Oldham, fellow-countryman Charlie McAlister transferring in part-exchange .... Tony Burke returns to Bramley on loan after a 10-year break.

APRIL
Trafford Borough sign centre David Wood and scrum half Tony Hewitt from Chorley Borough .... Rugby League Council reaffirms official policy of aiming for three divisions, each of 14 clubs .... Salford list want-away Welsh winger Adrian Hadley at £120,000 .... Jonathan Davies declares himself doubtful for the tour Down Under .... Wigan's Andy Gregory makes himself available for the Australasian tour after announcing his international retirement in 1990 .... Hull K.R. offer Welshman David Bishop for an undisclosed sum .... Workington Town agree fee of £18,000 for Carlisle's Brad Hepi .... Biggest-ever Great Britain 32-man touring squad, skippered by Ellery Hanley, features a record 13 from Wigan .... Workington Town appoint Australian Peter Walsh as coach for next season .... Barrow list Neil Shaw at £50,000 .... Wigan lift a record third consecutive Stones Bitter Championship Trophy with a 50-8 home victory over Bradford Northern .... Hull sack coach Noel Cleal with only two league games left .... Castleford veteran John Joyner announces his retirement as a player from the end of the season .... Oldham recruit Widnes forward Se'e Solomona .... Huddersfield clinch the first-ever Third Division title, Bramley being promoted as runners-up .... Sheffield Eagles lift the Second Division title, with Leigh also being promoted .... Dramatic last-day contests see Featherstone Rovers join Swinton in demotion from the Stones Bitter Championship .... Great Britain name a 13-man training squad for tour stand-by duty .... Scarborough Pirates appoint Trevor Bailey as coach for the 1992-93 campaign .... The League turns down a request from Queensland for a five-match autumn tour .... London Crusaders and Huddersfield fail to get League permission to switch their Stones Bitter Divisional Premiership tie to Huddersfield Town's soccer ground .... Jonathan Davies withdraws from the British Coal tour with a pelvic bone injury .... Huddersfield allege that London Crusaders played more than their permitted four overseas players in their 14-4 home success .... The Board of Directors release a policy document advocating a three-division system of 16-14-12, the third division including six leading Alliance sides.

MAY
Wigan lift their fifth successive Silk Cut Challenge Cup with a 28-12 triumph over Castleford .... Martin Offiah awarded the Lance Todd Trophy for two spectacular tries, plus a superb try-saving chase .... The League allow London Crusaders to play in the semi-finals of the Stones Bitter Divisional Premiership, despite demanding a second hearing for alleged breaches of the import quota system .... Huddersfield manager Alex Murphy fined £250 and banned from the touchline for a month for verbal abuse .... Scarborough Pirates hold a finance crisis meeting .... Wakefield Trinity and Swinton each fined £1,000 for brawling .... Sheffield Eagles recruit Hunslet's Australian loose forward Paul Carr .... St. Helens threequarter Alan Hunte drafted in by Great Britain to replace injured tourist Jonathan Davies .... Bradford Council refuse to help finance Bradford Northern and Bradford City's desire to share City's Valley Parade soccer ground .... The League sign a four-year £2.5m deal with BBC TV for the Regal Trophy, Silk Cut Challenge Cup and incoming Test series .... Martin Offiah scores a club record 10 tries in Wigan's 74-6 rout of Leeds, one short of the League's all-time record .... The League agree a record £3m-plus four-year deal with BSkyB for exclusive coverage of the Stones Bitter Championship and Premiership featuring

27

Friday night football .... Special general meeting fails to gain sufficient support for a move from the present 14-8-14 three-division system to return to two divisions of 16 and 20 or a three-tier format of 16-14-12, the third division including six Alliance sides .... Wakefield Trinity's Michael Jackson loses disciplinary appeal and misses opening four matches of the tour .... Leeds announce that record RU recruit John Gallagher can leave Headingley .... Swinton centre Ian Pickavance put on offer at £100,000 .... Wigan skipper Dean Bell named as Stones Bitter Man of Steel, with category awards going to Graham Steadman, Iva Ropati, Wally Gibson, Gary Connolly, John Monie and Robin Whitfield .... Phil Larder appointed coach of Widnes, Frank Myler moving up to manager .... Leeds scrum half Bobby Goulding banned for four matches and axed from the tour squad .... Wigan lift the first-ever end-of-season treble with a record-breaking 48-16 Stones Bitter Premiership success over St. Helens .... Sheffield Eagles pull off a Second Division double by beating Oldham 34-20 in the Stones Bitter Divisional Premiership final .... England B and Bath RU winger Jim Fallon signs for Leeds on a five-year £200,000 contract .... Featherstone Rovers skipper Deryck Fox called up to replace Bobby Goulding on the tour Down Under .... Wigan named as Stones Bitter Team of the Year .... Widnes list want-away full back Alan Tait at £230,000 .... Maurice Lindsay steps down as chairman of Wigan, Jack Robinson taking over the helm .... Swinton sell Station Road ground and move in with soccer neighbours Bury .... Oldham offer

Neil Holding and Shaun Allen at £10,000 each, Steve Robinson at £5,000, while halving the £25,000 fees on centres Des Foy and John Henderson .... GB management reveal that tour skipper Ellery Hanley is sidelined with a stress fracture of the foot .... Relegated Featherstone Rovers turn down transfer requests from skipper Deryck Fox and prop Leo Casey .... Welsh RU mastermind a financial package to match Wigan's offer to international centre Scott Gibb .... Great Britain open their tour Down Under with a 24-15 defeat of Highlands Zone, despite the sending off of Sonny Nickle .... Australian coach Darryl Van de Velde signs up for another season at Castleford .... Britain record 38-20 victory over Islands Zone after being kept waiting in searing heat for 20 minutes .... Castleford sign Swinton skipper Tony Morrison for a bargain £30,000, the maximum fee permitted in his contract .... The International Board, meeting in Papua New Guinea, clamp down on high tackles, introduce grid iron-style 10-metre pitch markings and rule that the World Cup table will be determined on points average .... Twin boost for the North East with the appointment of a development officer and the staging of the 1992 CIS Insurance Charity Shield between Wigan and St. Helens at Gateshead .... Britain trail 14-12 to Papua New Guinea at Port Moresby with only 10 minutes left before two Martin Offiah tries save embarrassment in a 20-14 success .... Hull appoint newly-retired Penrith Panthers hooker Royce Simmons as coach, succeeding fellow Australians Noel Cleal and, previously, Brian Smith.

New Zealander Brad Hepi, scorer of 10 tries in 27 games for Second Division Carlisle in 1991-92.

CLUBS

Scarborough Pirates' Brendan Carlyle on the burst with half back Steve Robinson in support.

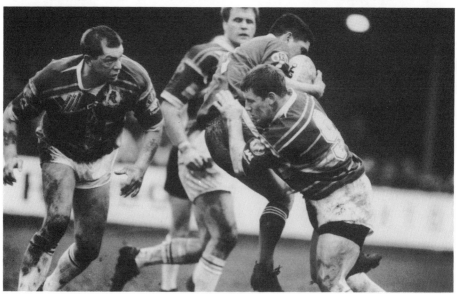

Scarborough Pirates defensive trio, left to right, Ian Douglas, Gary Van Bellen and Ken Hill, in action against Trafford Borough.

The following is a focus on the 36 professional Rugby League clubs, the section providing each club with a profile and an analysis of their 1991-92 campaign on a match-by-match basis with a summary for each first team player.

KEY

In the individual club profiles the following headings are featured:

First season refers to when the club gained senior league status. In some instances clubs have disbanded and re-formed, sometimes under different titles. For record purposes these changes are ignored except where there has been a break of more than one full season.

Honours. Until they were scrapped in 1970, the Yorkshire and Lancashire Leagues were among the honours in the professional game. Before 1903 they operated under the title of the Yorkshire and Lancashire Senior Competitions. Winners of these senior competitions are listed under Yorkshire and Lancashire League Champions. The pre-1903 Yorkshire Senior Competition should not be confused with the league operating for A-teams in Yorkshire which had the same title.

Regal Trophy is the new title for the John Player/Player's No. 6 Trophy competition.

Coaches. Changes in the appointment of a club's coach since 1 June 1991 are shown in brackets. The clubs' individual coaching register is from the start of the 1974-75 season.

Attendances. Crowds in brackets are at neutral venues.

Appearances. Players' totals are based on official teamsheets submitted to the League after each first team match. + indicates playing substitute appearance.

Great Britain Register. The figure in brackets after a player's name is the number of Great Britain appearances he made while serving the club under whose entry he is listed, and the number after the + sign indicates playing substitute. This is followed by the time span between his first and last British cap while at that club.

In the match-by-match review for each club the following abbreviations are used:

YC	—	Yorkshire Cup	A	—	Away
LC	—	Lancashire Cup	W	—	Won
SBC	—	Stones Bitter Championship	L	—	Lost
SD	—	Second Division	D	—	Drawn
TD	—	Third Division	dg	—	Drop goal
RT	—	Regal Trophy	Fr	—	France
CC	—	Challenge Cup	Aus	—	Australia
PT	—	Premiership Trophy	NZ	—	New Zealand
DP	—	Divisional Premiership	PNG	—	Papua New Guinea
P	—	Preliminary Round	Pr	—	Probationer
H	—	Home			

BARROW

Ground: Craven Park (0229-820273)
Colours: Royal blue
First Season: 1900-01
Nickname: Shipbuilders
Chairman: John Gilbert
Secretary: Les Kirkham
Coach: Paul Kavanagh (Feb 1991-)
Honours: **Division Two** Champions, 1975-76,
             1983-84
             Challenge Cup Winners, 1954-55
             Beaten finalists, 1937-38, 1950-51,
             1956-57, 1966-67
             Regal Trophy Beaten finalists,
             1980-81
             Lancashire Cup Winners, 1954-55,
             1983-84
             Beaten finalists, 1937-38

RECORDS
Match
Goals: 12 by Frank French v. Maryport,
        19 Feb 1938
        Willie Horne v. Cardiff, 8 Sep 1951
        Steve Tickle v. Kent Invicta,
        8 Apr 1984
Tries: 6 by Val Cumberbatch v. Batley,
        21 Nov 1936
        Jim Thornburrow v. Maryport,
        19 Feb 1938
        Frank Castle v. York, 29 Sep 1951

Neil Shaw, Barrow's top points-scorer in 1991-92.

Points: 28 by Keith Jarrett v. Doncaster,
        25 Aug 1970
        Steve Tickle v. Kent Invicta,
        8 Apr 1984
        Dean Marwood at Runcorn H.,
        16 Apr 1989

Season
Goals: 135 by Joe Ball, 1956-57
Tries: 50 by Jim Lewthwaite, 1956-57
Points: 305 by Ian Ball, 1979-80
Career
Goals: 741 by Willie Horne, 1943-58
Tries: 352 by Jim Lewthwaite, 1943-57
Points: 1,818 by Willie Horne, 1943-58
Appearances: 500 by Jim Lewthwaite, 1943-57
Highest score: 83-3 v. Maryport, 19 Feb 1938
Highest against: 90-0 at Leeds, 11 Feb 1990
Attendance: 21,651 v. Salford (League),
             15 Apr 1938

COACHING REGISTER
● **Since 1974-75**

Frank Foster	May 73 - Apr 83
Tommy Dawes	May 83 - Feb 85
Tommy Bishop	Feb 85 - Apr 85
Ivor Kelland	May 85 - Feb 87
Dennis Jackson	Feb 87 - Nov 87
Rod Reddy	Nov 87 - Nov 89
Dennis Jackson	Nov 89 - Apr 90
Steve Norton	May 90 - Feb 91
Paul Kavanagh	Feb 91 -

GREAT BRITAIN REGISTER
(19 players)

W. Burgess	(16)	1924-29
W. Burgess	(13)	1962-68
D. Cairns	(2)	1984
C. Camilleri	(2)	1980
C. Carr	(7)	1924-26
F. Castle	(4)	1952-54
R. Francis	(1)	1947
H. Gifford	(2)	1908
D. Goodwin	(5)	1957-58
J. Grundy	(12)	1955-57
P. Hogan	(4 + 1)	1977-78
W. Horne	(8)	1946-52

P. Jackson	(27)	1954-58
J. Jones	(1)	1946
B. Knowelden	(1)	1946
E. Szymala	(1 + 1)	1981
E. Toohey	(3)	1952
L. A. Troup	(2)	1936
J. Woods	(1)	1933

1991-92 SIGNINGS REGISTER

Signed	Player	Club From
17.6.91	Wassell, Colin	Barrow Island ARL
17.6.91	Westwood, Gary	Barrow Island ARL
26.6.91	Wild, John	Walney Central ARL
26.6.91	Petcher, Graham	Barrow Island ARL
3.7.91	Morrow, Shaun	Walney Central ARL
24.7.91	Marwood, Stephen	Walney Central ARL
8.8.91	Lupton, Paul	Millom ARL
1.9.91	*Pollard, Damien	Carlisle
1.9.91	*Rae, Steve	Carlisle
1.9.91	*Kendall, Dave	Carlisle
3.9.91	Fell, Ian	Barrow Island ARL
23.9.91	Conlon, Aaron	Glenora Bears, NZ
26.9.91	Honey, Chris	Thatto Heath ARL

1991-92 PLAYERS' SUMMARY

	App	Tries	Goals	Dr	Pts
Archer, Darren	2	—	—	—	—
Brown, Ralph	0 + 1	—	—	—	—
Burns, Paul	21 + 4	12	3	—	54
Cairns, David	32	5	—	—	20
Cartmel, Ian	1 + 1	—	—	—	—
Clayton, Steve	1 + 2	—	—	—	—
Conlon, Aaron	24	11	—	—	44
Crarey, Paul	30	3	—	—	12
Dunn, Reg	3 + 5	1	—	—	4
Fell, Ian	2 + 1	—	—	—	—
Hadley, Derek	2	—	—	—	—
Haggerty, Roy	25 + 3	1	—	3	7
Honey, Chris	26	7	—	1	29
Jackson, Wayne	1	—	—	—	—
James, Mick	21	8	—	—	32
Kay, Tony	25 + 1	20	2	—	84
Kendall, Dave	30	7	—	—	28
Kendall, Gary	20	2	—	—	8
Keresoma, Moses	19 + 6	8	—	—	32
Lupton, Graham	7	—	5	—	10
Marwood, Dean	4	1	13	—	30
Middleton, Glen	3	2	—	—	8
Morrison, Steve	2 + 2	—	—	—	—
Morrow, Shaun	17 + 10	5	—	—	20
Mossop, Steve	8 + 3	1	—	—	4
Payne, Darren	1	—	—	—	—
Pemberton, Keith	5 + 3	—	—	—	—
Petcher, Graham	8 + 3	—	—	—	—
Rea, Steve	1 + 1	1	—	—	4
Rhodes, Stuart	4 + 4	—	—	—	—
Rowan, Steve	1 + 3	1	—	—	4
Shaw, Neil	28	18	75	2	224
Thompson, Phil	0 + 1	—	—	—	—
Trainor, Pat	25 + 1	6	—	1	25
Wassell, Colin	1 + 1	—	—	—	—
Westwood, Gary	18 + 3	6	—	—	24
Wild, John	11 + 1	4	—	—	16

TOTALS:

37 players		130	98	7	723

Representative Appearances 1991-92
Kay — Cumbria (1)
D. Kendall — Cumbria (1)

New Zealander Moses Keresoma, scorer of eight tries in 25 games.

Prop forward Dave Kendall, who touched down seven times in 30 appearances.

33

BARROW 1991-92 MATCH ANALYSIS

Date	Competition	H/A	Opponent	Rlt	Score	Tries	Goals	Attendance	Referee
1.9.91	TD	A	Hunslet	L	22-30	Burns (2), Cairns, Rea	Burns (2), Lupton	—	—
8.9.91	TD	H	Doncaster	L	8-12	Dunn, Kay	—	1112	Burke
15.9.91	LC(1)	A	Workington T.	L	6-12	Morrow	Marwood	—	—
22.9.91	TD	A	Chorley B.	W	54-8	D. Kendall (2), Middleton, Burns, Morrow, Kay, Wild, Westwood, Marwood	Marwood (9)	—	—
30.9.91	TD	H	Highfield	W	18-10	Wild, Kay, Middleton	Marwood (3)	1021	Gilmour
6.10.91	TD	A	Batley	W	19-10	Conlon, Burns, Wild	Lupton (2), Shaw, Haggerty (dg)	—	—
13.10.91	TD	H	Bramley	L	16-24	Morrow, Kay, Keresoma	Lupton (2)	1029	Tidball
20.10.91	TD	A	Keighley C.	W	12-6	Kay, D. Kendall	Shaw (2)	—	—
27.10.91	TD	H	Scarborough P.	W	11-10	Cairns, D. Kendall	Shaw (1, 1dg)	699	J. Connolly
3.11.91	TD	A	Trafford B.	W	18-14	Cairns, Keresoma, Wild	Shaw (3)	—	—
10.11.91	TD	H	Hunslet	L	12-22	Keresoma	Shaw (4)	799	Cummings
17.11.91	RT(1)	A	Halifax	L	4-46	Burns	—	—	—
1.12.91	TD	A	Highfield	W	26-14	Shaw (2), Keresoma, Kay, Haggerty	Shaw (3)	—	—
8.12.91	TD	H	Trafford B.	W	45-8	Shaw (2), Kay (2), Keresoma, Conlon, Honey, Crarey	Shaw (6, 1dg)	453	Kershaw
15.12.91	TD	A	Bramley	L	6-24	G. Kendall	Shaw	—	—
26.12.91	TD	H	Whitehaven	W	48-6	Conlon (2), Honey (2), Shaw (2), Westwood, Kay, Trainor	Shaw (6)	914	Crashley
12.1.92	TD	H	Chorley B.	W	50-11	James (3), Conlon (2), Kay, Trainor, Cairns, Westwood	Shaw (7)	730	Whitelam
19.1.92	TD	H	Nottingham C.	W	78-8	D. Kendall (2), Shaw (2), Burns (2), Westwood (2), Trainor (2), Conlon (2), G. Kendall, Honey, Crarey	Shaw (9)	731	Ollerton
26.1.92	CC(1)	H	Keighley C.	D	7-7	Shaw	Shaw, Haggerty (dg)	1730	Tidball
2.2.92	CC(1) Replay	A	Keighley C.	D	14-14	Kay (2), Conlon	Shaw	—	—
4.2.92	CC(1) 2nd Replay	N[1]	Keighley C.	W	16-0	Keresoma, Trainor, James	Shaw (2)	(872)	Tidball
10.2.92	CC(2)	H	Bradford N.	L	13-30	Shaw (2)	Shaw (2), Haggerty (dg)	3414	Cummings
16.2.92	TD	H	Huddersfield	W	12-10	Kay, James	Shaw (2)	1887	Allatt
23.2.92	TD	A	Dewsbury	W	24-6	Kay (2), Keresoma, Burns, Cairns	Burns, Shaw	—	—
1.3.92	TD	A	Nottingham C.	W	54-1	Morrow, Shaw (2), Westwood, Kay, D. Kendall, Crarey, Honey, James	Shaw (7)	—	—
4.3.92	TD	A	Whitehaven	W	30-4	Conlon (2), Honey, Kay, James	Shaw (3), Kay (2)	—	—
8.3.92	TD	H	Dewsbury	L	4-28	Trainor	—	1672	Crashley
15.3.92	TD	A	Doncaster	D	11-11	Shaw, James	Shaw, Trainor (dg)	—	—
22.3.92	TD	H	Batley	L	13-22	Shaw, Burns	Shaw (2), Honey (dg)	991	Campbell
5.4.92	TD	A	Huddersfield	L	10-42	Rowan, Kay	Shaw	—	—
12.4.92	TD	H	Keighley C.	W	38-2	Burns (2), Kay (2), Honey, Mossop, Keresoma	Shaw (5)	1021	J. Smith
17.4.92	TD	A	Scarborough P.	W	24-12	Shaw (3), Burns	Shaw (4)	—	—
20.4.92	DP(1)	A	Batley	L	0-46	—	—	—	—

N[1] at Widnes

BATLEY

Ground: Mount Pleasant (0924-472208)
Colours: Cerise and fawn
First Season: 1895-96
Nickname: Gallant Youths
Chairman: Stephen Ball
Secretary: Richard Illingworth
Coach: David Ward (May 1991-)
Honours: **Championship** Winners, 1923-24
Challenge Cup Winners, 1896-97,
1897-98, 1900-01
Yorkshire Cup Winners, 1912-13
Beaten finalists, 1909-10, 1922-23,
1924-25, 1952-53
Yorkshire League Winners,
1898-99, 1923-24

RECORDS

Match
Goals: 10 by Steve Parrish at Nottingham C.,
10 Nov 1991
Tries: 5 by Joe Oakland v. Bramley,
19 Dec 1908
Tommy Brannan v. Swinton,
17 Jan 1920
Jim Wale v. Bramley, 4 Dec 1926
Jim Wale v. Cottingham,
12 Feb 1927
Points: 26 by Jack Perry v. Liverpool C.,
16 Sep 1951

Season
Goals: 120 by Stan Thompson, 1958-59
Tries: 29 by Jack Tindall, 1912-13
Points: 281 by Jack Perry, 1950-51

Career
Goals: 463 by Wharton "Wattie" Davies,
1897-1912
Tries: 123 by Wharton "Wattie" Davies,
1897-1912
Points: 1,297 by Wharton "Wattie" Davies,
1897-1912
Appearances: 421 by Wharton "Wattie" Davies,
1897-1912
Highest score: 64-0 at Nottingham C.,
10 Nov 1991
Highest against: 78-9 at Wakefield T.,
26 Aug 1967
Attendance: 23,989 v. Leeds (RL Cup),
14 Mar 1925

COACHING REGISTER
● **Since 1974-75**

Don Fox	Nov 72 - Oct 74
Alan Hepworth	Nov 74 - Apr 75
Dave Cox	May 75 - June 75
Trevor Walker	June 75 - June 77
Albert Fearnley	June 77 - Oct 77
Dave Stockwell	Oct 77 - June 79
*Tommy Smales	June 79 - Oct 81
Trevor Lowe	Oct 81 - May 82
Terry Crook	June 82 - Nov 84
George Pieniazek	Nov 84 - Nov 85
Brian Lockwood	Nov 85 - May 87
Paul Daley	July 87 - Apr 90
Keith Rayne	May 90 - Apr 91
David Ward	May 91 -

Ex-forward

GREAT BRITAIN REGISTER
(4 players)

N. Field	(1)	1963
F. Gallagher	(8)	1924-26
C. Gibson	(+1)	1985
J. Oliver	(4)	1928

Brian Lockwood, an 18-month coaching stint at Mount Pleasant.

1991-92 SIGNINGS REGISTER

Signed	Player	Club From
20.6.91	Robinson, Simon	Bramley
28.6.91	Kellett, Neil	Sheffield E.
20.7.91	Holdsworth, Alan	Batley Victoria ARL
2.8.91	*Harcombe, Kevin	Wakefield T.
11.8.91	Grayshon, Jeff	Featherstone R.
29.8.91	Dyson, Jeremy	Thornhill ARL
29.8.91	Krause, Michael	Brible Island, Aus
29.8.91	Tomlinson, Glen	Caboolture, Aus
29.8.91	Wilkinson, Shaun	Hunslet
18.9.91	Edghill, Richard	Saddleworth R. ARL
29.10.91	Cook, Mark	Hunslet
7.11.91	Heron, Wayne	Bradford N.
22.11.91	*Spooner, Chris	Dewsbury
5.12.91	Hindricks, Andy	Tugun, Aus
19.12.91	Mahmood, Rashid	Hemel Hempstead ARL
9.2.92	*Rawlinson, Scott	Halifax
29.2.92	Hanlan, Lee	Hull
29.2.92	*Cass, Mark	Hull
18.3.92	*Gumbs, Hugh	Bradford N.
28.3.92	*Bragger, Ian	Castleford

1991-92 PLAYERS' SUMMARY

	App	Tries	Goals	Dr	Pts
Bargate, Lee	2 + 1	—	—	—	—
Booth, Michael	33	7	—	—	28
Bownass, Mark	11 + 1	4	—	—	16
Bragger, Ian	5	2	—	—	8
Cass, Mark	2	1	—	—	4
Child, Darren	9	1	—	—	4
Craven, Nigel	2 + 1	—	—	—	—
Dyson, Jeremy	10 + 1	2	1	—	10
Edghill, Richard	3 + 1	—	—	—	—
Fortis, Mark	0 + 6	—	—	—	—
Gearey, Paul	6 + 4	1	—	—	4
Grayshon, Jeff	29 + 1	1	—	—	4
Gumbs, Hugh	7	5	6	—	32
Hamill, James	15 + 3	1	—	—	4
Hanlan, Lee	9	5	8	—	36
Hartley, Neil	2 + 1	—	—	—	—
Heron, Wayne	19 + 1	1	—	—	4
Hindricks, Andy	14 + 6	9	—	—	36
Kay, Paul	0 + 1	—	—	—	—
Kellett, Neil	7 + 7	1	—	—	4
Krause, Michael	0 + 2	—	—	—	—
Marshall, Paul	6	2	—	—	8
Parkinson, Andy	15 + 3	1	—	—	4
Parrish, Steve	32	10	104	2	250
Rawlinson, Scott	3 + 7	1	—	—	4
Redick, Paul	6	2	—	—	8
Scott, Mark	28	10	—	—	40
Speight, Mark	0 + 2	—	—	—	—
Spendler, Mark	14 + 5	3	—	—	12
Spooner, Chris	1 + 2	—	—	—	—
Stainburn, John	1 + 2	—	3	—	6
Thornton, Gary	30	16	—	—	64
Tomlinson, Glen	28	17	—	1	69
Wilkinson, Shaun	31	16	—	—	64
Williams, Andy	17 + 3	4	—	—	16
Wilson, Simon	32 + 1	14	2	1	61
TOTALS:					
36 players		137	124	4	800

Veteran Jeff Grayshon, scorer of one try in a 30-match debut campaign for Batley.

BATLEY 1991-92 MATCH ANALYSIS

Date	Competition	H/A	Opponent	Rlt	Score	Tries	Goals	Attendance	Referee
1.9.91	TD	H	Whitehaven	W	22-12	Parrish, Tomlinson, Hamill, Wilson	Parrish (3)	825	Ollerton
9.9.91	TD	A	Huddersfield	W	20-19	Thornton (2), Child, Williams	Parrish (2)	—	—
15.9.91	YC(1)	H	Castleford	L	12-36	Wilson, Booth	Parrish (2)	3089	Whitelam
22.9.91	TD	H	Nottingham C.	W	48-4	Parrish (2), Wilson (2), Williams (2), Thornton, Scott, Tomlinson	Parrish (6)	703	Cummings
29.9.91	TD	A	Keighley C.	D	2-2	—	Parrish	—	—
6.10.91	TD	H	Barrow	L	10-19	Wilkinson	Parrish (3)	1009	Redfearn
13.10.91	TD	A	Chorley B.	W	46-6	Thornton (3), Wilkinson, Wilson, Scott, Booth	Parrish (6), Stainburn (3)	—	—
20.10.91	TD	H	Huddersfield	W	28-12	Tomlinson (2), Scott (2), Redick	Parrish (4)	1908	Cross
27.10.91	TD	A	Highfield	W	16-11	Parrish (2)	Parrish (4)	—	—
10.11.91	TD	A	Nottingham C.	W	64-0	Tomlinson (3), Thornton (2), Wilson (2), Kellett, Scott, Dyson, Parrish	Parrish (10)	—	—
18.11.91	RT(1)	A	Hull	L	8-12	Tomlinson	Parrish (2)	—	—
24.11.91	TD	H	Chorley B.	W	38-2	Marshall (2), Booth, Tomlinson, Bownass, Heron, Thornton, Wilkinson	Parrish (2), Wilson	721	Tidball
1.12.91	TD	H	Keighley C.	L	8-23	Tomlinson	Parrish (2)	1027	Whitelam
8.12.91	TD	H	Doncaster	W	15-0	Parrish, Thornton, Wilkinson	Dyson, Tomlinson (dg)	1068	J. Smith
26.12.91	TD	H	Dewsbury	D	16-16	Wilson, Booth	Parrish (3, 1dg), Wilson (dg)	4119	Cross
1.1.92	TD	A	Dewsbury	L	12-18	Williams, Tomlinson	Parrish (2)	—	—
8.1.92	CC(P)	A	Nottingham C.	W	36-0	Parrish (2), Hindricks, Grayshon, Wilson, Booth	Parrish (6)	—	—
12.1.92	TD	H	Highfield	W	22-0	Gearey, Wilkinson, Bownass	Parrish (5)	609	Crashley
19.1.92	TD	A	Whitehaven	L	4-11	—	Parrish (2)	—	—
26.1.92	CC(1)	H	Featherstone R.	L	20-36	Hindricks, Bownass, Tomlinson	Parrish (4)	2039	Steele
2.2.92	TD	H	Trafford B.	W	40-0	Hindricks (3), Spendler (2), Bownass, Dyson, Wilkinson	Parrish (4)	509	Redfearn
12.2.92	TD	A	Doncaster	L	10-20	Thornton (2)	Parrish	—	—
16.2.92	TD	H	Bramley	L	4-6	—	Parrish (2)	826	Tidball
23.2.92	TD	A	Scarborough P.	W	32-14	Thornton (2), Spendler, Parkinson, Parrish, Tomlinson	Parrish (3), Wilson	—	—
2.3.92	TD	A	Hunslet	W	22-13	Tomlinson, Booth, Hindricks, Hanlan	Parrish (3)	—	—
8.3.92	TD	H	Scarborough P.	W	36-18	Tomlinson, Booth, Wilkinson, Thornton, Scott, Hanlan	Parrish (6)	737	Allatt
22.3.92	TD	A	Barrow	W	22-13	Gumbs, Tomlinson, Hindricks, Bragger	Parrish (3)	—	—
29.3.92	TD	H	Hunslet	W	34-14	Wilkinson (3), Wilson, Gumbs, Rawlinson, Hindricks	Parrish (3)	827	Morris
5.4.92	TD	A	Bramley	W	12-6	Thornton, Tomlinson	Parrish (2)	—	—
12.4.92	TD	A[1]	Trafford B.	W	58-12	Wilkinson (3), Gumbs (3), Scott, Cass, Redick, Wilson	Hanlan (4), Parrish (3), Gumbs (2)	—	—
20.4.92	DP(1)	H	Barrow	W	46-0	Scott (3), Wilkinson (2), Hanlan, Wilson, Hindricks	Hanlan (4), Gumbs (3)	679	Burke
26.4.92	DP(2)	A	Leigh	W	15-6	Wilkinson, Hanlan	Parrish (2,1dg), Gumbs	—	—
10.5.92	DP(SF)	A	Sheffield E.	L	22-36	Wilson (2), Bragger, Hanlan	Parrish (3)	—	—

[1] at Huddersfield

BRADFORD NORTHERN

Ground: Odsal Stadium (0274-733899)
Colours: White, red, amber and black
First Season: 1895-96 as "Bradford". Disbanded and became Bradford Northern in 1907-08. Disbanded during 1963-64 and re-formed for start of 1964-65
Nickname: Northern
Chairman: Chris Caisley
Coach: David Hobbs (Mar 1990-Oct 1991) Peter Fox (Oct 1991-)
Honours: **Championship** Beaten finalists, 1947-48, 1951-52
War-time Emergency League Championship winners, 1939-40, 1940-41, 1944-45
Beaten finalists, 1941-42
Division One Champions, 1903-04, 1979-80, 1980-81
Division Two Champions, 1973-74
Challenge Cup Winners, 1905-06, 1943-44, 1946-47, 1948-49
Beaten finalists, 1897-98, 1944-45, 1947-48, 1972-73
Regal Trophy Winners, 1974-75, 1979-80
Beaten finalists, 1990-91
Premiership Winners, 1977-78
Beaten finalists, 1978-79, 1979-80, 1989-90
Yorkshire Cup Winners, 1906-07, 1940-41, 1941-42, 1943-44, 1945-46, 1948-49, 1949-50, 1953-54, 1965-66, 1978-79, 1987-88, 1989-90
Beaten finalists, 1913-14, 1981-82, 1982-83, 1991-92
Yorkshire League Winners, 1899-1900, 1900-01, 1939-40, 1940-41, 1947-48

RECORDS

Match
Goals: 14 by Joe Phillips v. Batley, 6 Sep 1952
Tries: 7 by Joe Dechan v. Bramley, 13 Oct 1906
Points: 36 by John Woods v. Swinton, 13 Oct 1985

Season
Goals: 173 by Eddie Tees, 1971-72
Tries: 63 by Jack McLean, 1951-52
Points: 364 by Eddie Tees, 1971-72
Career
Goals: 775 by Keith Mumby, 1973-90
Tries: 261 by Jack McLean, 1950-56
Points: 1,820 by Keith Mumby, 1973-90
Appearances: 574+4 by Keith Mumby, 1973-90
Highest score: 76-0 v. Leigh East, 17 Nov 1991
Highest against: 75-18 at Leeds, 14 Sep 1931
Attendance: 102,569 Warrington v. Halifax (RL Cup final replay), 5 May, 1954
Home match: 69,429 v. Huddersfield (RL Cup), 14 Mar 1953

Half back Neil Summers, who recorded a 1991-92 tally of 13 tries in 34 appearances.

COACHING REGISTER
● Since 1974-75

Ian Brooke	Jan 73 - Sep 75
Roy Francis	Oct 75 - Apr 77
Peter Fox	Apr 77 - May 85
Barry Seabourne	May 85 - Sep 89
Ron Willey	Oct 89 - Mar 90
David Hobbs	Mar 90 - Oct 91
Peter Fox	Oct 91 -

GREAT BRITAIN REGISTER
(31 players)

D. Barends	(2)	1979
E. Batten	(4)	1946-47
I. Brooke	(5)	1966
L. Casey	(5)	1979
G. Cordle	(1)	1990
W. T. H. Davies	(3)	1946-47
K. Fairbank	(5+4)	1987-92
A. Fisher	(8)	1970-78
P. Ford	(7)	1987-88
T. Foster	(3)	1946-48
J. Grayshon	(11)	1979-82
E. Hanley	(10+1)	1984-85
D. Hobbs	(1+1)	1989
R. Jasiewicz	(1)	1984
J. Kitching	(1)	1946
A. Mann	(2)	1908
K. Mumby	(11)	1982-84
B. Noble	(11)	1982-84
T. Price	(1)	1970
J. Rae	(1)	1965
W. Ramsey	(+1)	1974
A. Rathbone	(4+1)	1982-85
A. Redfearn	(1)	1979
D. Redfearn	(6+1)	1972-74
K. Skerrett	(8)	1989-90
T. Smales	(3)	1965
H. Smith	(2)	1926
J. Thompson	(1)	1978
K. Traill	(8)	1950-54
E. Ward	(20)	1946-52
F. Whitcombe	(2)	1946

David Hobbs, coach of Northern for 19 months, collecting two Great Britain caps while at Odsal.

The irrepressible Peter Fox, who returned to Odsal in October 1991 for a second spell in charge, having previously served Northern for eight years.

1991-92 SIGNINGS REGISTER

Signed	Player	Club From
10.6.91	Hardwick, Phillip	Middleton ARL
13.8.91	Turpin, David	Dudley Hill ARL
4.9.91	Anderson, Tony	Oldham
6.9.91	Holroyd, Robert	Siddal ARL
27.1.92	Greenwood, Adam	Calder Valley ARL
28.2.92	Powell, Roy	Leeds
18.2.92	Johnson, Marc	Oulton ARL

Test forward Roy Powell, a February 1992 recruit from Leeds.

1991-92 PLAYERS' SUMMARY

	App	Tries	Goals	Dr	Pts
Anderson, Tony	25 + 1	5	—	—	20
Barnett, Steve	8 + 5	—	—	—	—
Barraclough, Glenn	8	—	—	—	—
Cooper, David	3 + 3	3	—	—	12
Cordle, Gerald	11 + 1	8	—	—	32
Croft, David	3 + 10	—	—	—	—
Fairbank, Karl	34	14	—	—	56
Francis, Richard	16 + 1	2	—	—	8
Gill, Henderson	16 + 1	9	1	—	38
Grayshon, Paul	12 + 10	—	—	—	—
Green, Alex	6 + 2	1	3	—	10
Greenwood, Adam	2 + 1	—	—	—	—
Gumbs, Hugh	3	1	2	—	8
Hamer, Jon	34 + 1	4	—	—	16
Hellewell, Phil	3	—	—	—	—
Hobbs, David	35 + 1	2	105	5	223
Iti, Brett	6 + 14	5	—	—	20
McGowan, Steve	21 + 1	11	—	—	44
Marchant, Tony	22 + 1	16	—	—	64
Medley, Paul	31 + 1	15	—	—	60
Moxon, Darren	1 + 1	—	—	—	—
Noble, Brian	28	3	—	—	12
Pendlebury, John	14 + 1	1	1	—	6
Powell, Daio	11	7	—	—	28
Powell, Roy	7	—	—	—	—
Richards, Craig	9 + 10	1	—	—	4
Shelford, Darrall	32	12	—	—	48
Simpson, Roger	29 + 1	5	—	—	20
Summers, Neil	31 + 3	13	—	—	52
Wilkinson, Ian	20	1	—	—	4

TOTALS:

30 players		139	112	5	785

Representative Appearances 1991-92
Cordle — Wales (+1)
Fairbank — Britain (2 + 1, 1t); Yorkshire (1)

Nine tries and a goal in 17 appearances for wingman Henderson Gill.

BRADFORD NORTHERN 1991-92 MATCH ANALYSIS

Date	Competition	H/A	Opponent	Rlt	Score	Tries	Goals	Attendance	Referee
1.9.91	SBC	H	Hull K.R.	L	10-18	Shelford, McGowan	Hobbs	4103	Carter
8.9.91	SBC	A	Wakefield T.	L	18-22	Gill, Medley, McGowan	Hobbs (3)	—	—
16.9.91	YC(1)	A	Sheffield E.	W	15-13	Powell, Summers	Hobbs (3, 1dg)	—	—
22.9.91	SBC	H	Salford	W	48-24	McGowan (2), Hamer (2), Medley (2), Gill, Green, Summers	Hobbs (6)	3310	Holdsworth
25.9.91	YC(2)	A	Bramley	W	38-15	Shelford (2), Powell (2), Noble (2), Fairbank	Hobbs (5)	—	—
29.9.91	SBC	A	Featherstone R.	L	8-22	Powell	Hobbs (2)	—	—
6.10.91	SBC	H	Leeds	L	14-48	Powell, Anderson	Green (3)	8796	Tennant
9.10.91	YC(SF)	H	Wakefield T.	W	14-10	Simpson	Hobbs (5)	4173	Tennant
13.10.91	SBC	A	St. Helens	L	12-30	Powell, Iti	Hobbs (2)	—	—
20.10.91	YC(F)	N[1]	Castleford	L	6-28	Powell	Hobbs	(8916)	Holdsworth
23.10.91	SBC	A	Hull	L	14-40	Anderson, Shelford, Marchant	Hobbs	—	—
3.11.91	SBC	H	Castleford	L	12-18	Gill, Fairbank	Hobbs (2)	3663	Ollerton
10.11.91	SBC	A	Warrington	L	8-12	Marchant	Hobbs (2)	—	—
17.11.91	RT(1)	H	Leigh East	W	76-0	Gill (4), Marchant (2), Fairbank (2), Wilkinson, Shelford, Anderson, Simpson, Summers, Hobbs, Iti	Hobbs (7), Gill	1613	Burke
24.11.91	RT(2)	H	Sheffield E.	W	44-10	Fairbank (2), Hobbs, Anderson, McGowan, Hamer, Pendlebury	Hobbs (8)	3118	Campbell
1.12.91	RT(3)	A	St. Helens	L	12-30	McGowan (2)	Hobbs (2)	—	—
4.12.91	SBC	H	Widnes	W	36-14	Summers (2), McGowan (2), Marchant, Fairbank	Hobbs (6)	3151	J. Connolly
18.12.91	SBC	A	Leeds	L	12-22	Gumbs, Anderson	Gumbs (2)	—	—
22.12.91	SBC	H	Warrington	W	16-10	Cooper (2), Medley	Hobbs (2)	3600	Whitfield
26.12.91	SBC	H	Halifax	W	14-8	Medley (2)	Hobbs (3)	8252	Burke
1.1.92	SBC	A	Halifax	W	26-18	Marchant, Richards, Cooper, McGowan	Hobbs (5)	—	—
7.1.92	SBC	H	Hull	L	10-14	Shelford, Fairbank	Hobbs	3465	R. Smith
12.1.92	SBC	H	Wigan	L	22-28	Medley (2), Cordle, Shelford, Marchant	Hobbs	8757	Cummings
19.1.92	SBC	A	Castleford	L	10-24	Marchant (2)	Hobbs	—	—
2.2.92	CC(1)	A	Scarborough P.	W	52-4	Marchant (3), Fairbank (2), Cordle (2), Summers, McGowan, Medley	Hobbs (6)	—	—
10.2.92	CC(2)	A	Barrow	W	30-13	Hamer, Medley, Noble, Shelford, Cordle	Hobbs (4), Pendlebury	—	—
16.2.92	SBC	H	St. Helens	L	8-20	Francis, Medley	—	3956	Morris
23.2.92	CC(3)	A	Halifax	W	12-4	Cordle	Hobbs (3, 2dg)	—	—
28.2.92	SBC	A	Salford	L	6-23	Medley	Hobbs	—	—
11.3.92	SBC	H	Featherstone R.	W	22-4	Marchant (2), Shelford (2), Medley	Hobbs	4529	Carter
15.3.92	SBC	A	Swinton	W	42-14	Cordle (3), Medley (2), Shelford, Iti, Simpson	Hobbs (5)	—	—
22.3.92	SBC	A	Widnes	W	17-10	Summers (2), Iti	Hobbs (2, 1dg)	—	—
28.3.92	CC(SF)	N[2]	Wigan	L	10-71	Shelford, Gill	Hobbs	(18,027)	Whitfield
5.4.92	SBC	H	Wakefield T.	W	9-8	Fairbank	Hobbs (2, 1dg)	5114	Cummings
11.4.92	SBC	A	Wigan	L	8-50	Gill, Summers	—	—	—
17.4.92	SBC	H	Swinton	W	60-0	Summers (3), Marchant (2), Fairbank (2), Francis, Iti, Simpson	Hobbs (10)	2936	R. Smith
20.4.92	SBC	A	Hull K.R.	W	14-12	Summers, Simpson, Fairbank	Hobbs	—	—

N[1] at Elland Road, Leeds
N[2] at Bolton W. FC

BRAMLEY

Ground: McLaren Field (0532-564842)
Colours: Amber and black
First Season: 1896-97
Nickname: Villagers
Chairman: Jeff Wine
General
  Manager: Maurice Bamford
Coach: Roy Dickinson (Jan 1991-Apr 1992)
  Maurice Bamford (Apr 1992-)
Honours: **BBC2 Floodlit Trophy** Winners,
  1973-74

RECORDS

Match
Goals: 11 by Bernard Ward v. Doncaster,
  1 Sep 1974
Tries: 7 by Joe Sedgewick v. Normanton,
  16 Apr 1906
Points: 28 by Bernard Ward v. Doncaster,
  1 Sep 1974

Season
Goals: 138 by Steve Carroll, 1991-92
Tries: 34 by Peter Lister, 1985-86
Points: 288 by Steve Carroll, 1991-92

Career
Goals: 926 by John Wilson, 1953-64
Tries: 140 by Peter Lister, 1982-91
Points: 1,903 by John Wilson, 1953-64
Appearances: 406 + 4 by John Wolford, 1962-76
Highest score: 62-14 v. Dewsbury, 30 Oct 1988
Highest against: 92-7 v. Australia, 9 Nov 1921
Attendance: 12,600 v. Leeds (League),
  7 May 1947 — at Barley Mow
  7,500 v. Bradford N. (RL Cup),
  17 Feb 1972 — at McLaren Field

COACHING REGISTER ● Since 1974-75

Arthur Keegan	May 73 - Sep 76
Peter Fox	Sep 76 - Apr 77
*Tommy Smales	May 77 - Dec 77
Les Pearce	Jan 78 - Oct 78
Don Robinson	Oct 78 - May 79
Dave Stockwell	June 79 - June 80
Keith Hepworth	June 80 - May 82
Maurice Bamford	May 82 - Oct 83
Peter Jarvis	Oct 83 - Apr 85

Ken Loxton	Apr 85 - Dec 85
Allan Agar	Dec 85 - Apr 87
Chris Forster	June 87 - Nov 87
Tony Fisher	Nov 87 - Feb 89
Barry Johnson	Mar 89 - Dec 90
John Kear	Dec 90 - Jan 91
Roy Dickinson	Jan 91 - Apr 92
Maurice Bamford	Apr 92 -

*Ex-forward

1991-92 SIGNINGS REGISTER

Signed	Player	Club From
4.6.91	Agar, Andrew	Pudsey ARL
4.6.91	Eccles, Adam	Pudsey ARL
4.6.91	Freeman, Glen	Pudsey ARL
18.6.91	Smith, Michael	Middleton ARL
21.6.91	McLeary, Jack	Batley
1.7.91	Neave, Mark	Stanningley ARL
1.7.91	Freeman, Wayne	Pudsey ARL
2.7.91	Bell, Kevin	Wakefield Red'bles ARL
9.8.91	Coen, Darren	Dewsbury
12.8.91	Lyons, Paddy	Hunslet
12.8.91	Marson, Andy	Hunslet
21.8.91	Entwhistle, Steve	Oldham
30.8.91	Hall, Gary	Featherstone R.
3.9.91	Pilmoor, Shaun	Normanton ARL
3.9.91	Cain, Michael	Normanton ARL
6.9.91	Morrisey, Gary	Nottingham C.
21.9.91	May, Paul	Aus
22.9.91	Trayhurn, Rodney	Cambridge Park, Aus
22.9.91	Wrice, Alan	Penhurst, Aus
11.10.91	Francis, Norman	Oldham
24.10.91	Whakarau, Sonny	Batley
14.11.91	Butterfield, Lee	Normanton ARL
27.11.91	Langi, Markish	NZ
17.12.91	Creasser, Dean	Bison Sports ARL
24.12.91	Whitehead, Craig	Dewsbury
3.1.92	*Gregg, Carl	Huddersfield
6.1.92	Nickle, Vince	W. Yorks Fire ARL
11.2.92	Potter, Ian	Leigh
19.3.92	Durnin, Paul	Dewsbury
30.3.92	*Burke, Tony	Warrington
9.4.92	Toole, Tim	Nottingham C.
9.4.92	Haigh, Chris	Nottingham C.

1991-92 PLAYERS' SUMMARY

	App	Tries	Goals	Dr	Pts
Barnett, Gary	1 + 1	—	—	—	—
Bell, Kevin	30 + 1	17	—	—	68
Blankley, Dean	23 + 8	3	—	—	12
Brentley, Gary	33	9	—	—	36
Brier, Simon	1	—	—	—	—
Burke, Tony	3	—	—	—	—
Carroll, Steve	33	5	130	8	288
Charles, Marquis	13 + 1	7	—	—	28
Coen, Darren	33	7	—	—	28
Connell, Phil	0 + 1	—	—	—	—
Creasser, Dean	13 + 1	3	—	—	12
Devine, Paul	0 + 1	—	—	—	—
Dickinson, Roy	5	—	—	—	—
Durnin, Paul	3	1	—	—	4
Edmondson, Steve	20 + 1	2	—	—	8
Francis, Norman	24 + 1	15	—	—	60
Hall, Gary	19 + 9	6	—	—	24
Harker, Keith	12	10	—	—	40

42

Harwood, Dean	4 + 1	1	—	—	4
Jones, Keith	4 + 4	—	—	—	—
Langi, Markish	16	7	—	—	28
Lyons, Paddy	32	11	—	1	45
McLeary, Jack	1	—	—	—	—
Marson, Andy	23 + 5	6	—	—	24
May, Paul	2 + 1	—	—	—	—
Morrisey, Gary	9 + 5	3	—	—	12
Ngataki, Shane	1 + 1	—	—	—	—
Nickle, Vince	1	—	—	—	—

Potter, Ian	6 + 2	—	—	—	—
Sharp, Roy	31	8	—	—	32
Trayhurn, Rodney	0 + 1	1	—	—	4
Whakarau, Sonny	21	7	—	—	28
Whitehead, Craig	11 + 2	—	—	—	—
Wrice, Alan	1	1	—	—	4
TOTALS:					
34 players		130	130	9	789

1991-92 MATCH ANALYSIS

Date	Competition	H/A	Opponent	Rlt	Score	Tries	Goals	Attendance	Referee
1.9.91	TD	H	Keighley C.	W	41-12	Harker (2), Marson, Charles, Edmondson, Blankley, Sharp	Carroll (6, 1dg)	782	Steele
6.9.91	TD	A	Trafford B.	W	20-6	Bell, Edmondson, Harker	Carroll (4)	—	—
15.9.91	YC(1)	A	Keighley C.	W	20-8	Bell, Charles, Sharp	Carroll (4)	—	—
22.9.91	TD	H	Huddersfield	L	9-14	Blankley	Carroll (2, 1dg)	879	Asquith
25.9.91	YC(2)	H	Bradford N.	L	15-38	Charles, Harker	Carroll (3, 1dg)	2009	Crashley
29.9.91	TD	A	Dewsbury	L	12-26	Wrice, Harker	Carroll (2)	—	—
6.10.91	TD	H	Nottingham C.	W	54-0	Harker (2), Bell (2), Brentley, Lyons, Trayhurn, Morrisey, Coen, Charles	Carroll (7)	497	Gilmour
13.10.91	TD	A	Barrow	W	24-16	Charles, Lyons, Sharp, Morrisey	Carroll (4)	—	—
20.10.91	TD	H	Chorley B.	W	52-0	Charles (2), Hall (2), Lyons, Harwood, Marson, Harker, Carroll, Brentley	Carroll (6)	464	J. Connolly
27.10.91	TD	A	Doncaster	W	19-10	Harker (2), Francis	Carroll (3), Lyons (dg)	—	—
3.11.91	TD	H	Dewsbury	W	20-10	Brentley (2), Hall	Carroll (4)	1255	Carter
10.11.91	TD	A	Huddersfield	L	6-21	—	Carroll (3)	—	—
19.11.91	RT(1)	H	Featherstone R.	D	18-18	Sharp, Brentley	Carroll (4, 2dg)	1643	J. Smith
21.11.91	RT(1) Replay	A	Featherstone R.	L	8-44	Morrisey	Carroll (2)	—	—
1.12.91	TD	H	Whitehaven	W	20-17	Carroll, Sharp	Carroll (6)	517	Redfearn
8.12.91	TD	A	Chorley B.	W	36-0	Lyons (2), Francis, Langi, Whakarau, Brentley	Carroll (6)	—	—
15.12.91	TD	H	Barrow	W	24-6	Bell (2), Francis, Carroll, Langi	Carroll (2)	734	Cross
27.12.91	TD	H	Hunslet	W	22-20	Lyons, Francis, Bell, Coen	Carroll (3)	1750	J. Smith
1.1.92	TD	A	Hunslet	L	18-23	Brentley, Langi, Whakarau	Carroll (3)	—	—
8.1.92	TD	H	Trafford B.	W	44-6	Whakarau (2), Creasser (2), Marson, Francis, Langi, Hall	Carroll (6)	350	Tidball
12.1.92	TD	A	Keighley C.	W	10-7	Francis	Carroll (3)	—	—
19.1.92	TD	H	Scarborough P.	W	47-0	Coen (2), Lyons (2), Whakarau, Bell, Francis, Langi	Carroll (7, 1dg)	778	Steele
21.1.92	CC(P)	H	Leeds	L	12-36	Carroll, Lyons	Carroll (2)	3484	J. Connolly
29.1.92	TD	A	Nottingham C.	W	34-4	Francis, Hall, Langi, Bell, Marson, Sharp	Carroll (5)	—	—
16.2.92	TD	A	Batley	W	6-4	Coen	Carroll	—	—
1.3.92	TD	H	Doncaster	W	38-8	Bell (2), Whakarau (2), Coen, Carroll	Carroll (7)	1053	Ollerton
8.3.92	TD	A	Highfield	W	36-6	Lyon (2), Francis (2), Langi, Sharp	Carroll (6)	—	—
16.3.92	TD	A	Scarborough P.	W	29-14	Bell (2), Brentley, Marson	Carroll (6, 1dg)	—	—
22.3.92	TD	H	Highfield	W	28-6	Bell (2), Francis (2), Marson	Carroll (4)	734	Allatt
29.3.92	TD	A	Whitehaven	W	20-10	Bell, Brentley, Francis, Blankley	Carroll (2)	—	—
5.4.92	TD	H	Batley	L	6-12	Francis	Carroll	1523	Steele
21.4.92	DP(1)	H	Keighley C.	D	18-18	Bell, Creasser, Hall	Carroll (3)	810	J. Smith
23.4.92	DP(1) Replay	A	Keighley C.	L	23-26	Sharp, Durnin, Coen, Francis	Carroll (3, 1dg)	—	—

43

CARLISLE

Ground: Gillford Park (0228-401212)
Colours: Blue, red and white
First Season: 1981-82. Carlisle City entered the
              League in 1928-29 but withdrew
              after 10 matches, winning one
Chairman: Alan Tucker
Secretary: Miriam Lewis
Coach: Cameron Bell (Feb 1990-)

RECORDS

Match
Goals: 10 by Barry Vickers at Nottingham C.,
       11 Mar 1990
Tries: 4 by Gary Peacham v. Workington T.,
       25 Jan 1987
       Kevin Pape v. Rochdale H.,
       11 Feb 1987
Points: 24 by Barry Vickers at Nottingham C.,
       11 Mar 1990

Season
Goals: 113 by Steve Ferres, 1981-82
Tries: 25 by Mick Morgan, 1981-82
       Gary Peacham, 1984-85
Points: 242 by Steve Ferres, 1981-82

Career
Goals: 352 by Barry Vickers, 1988-
Tries: 141 by Kevin Pape, 1984-
Points: 733 by Barry Vickers, 1988-
Appearances: 252 by Kevin Pape, 1984-
Highest score: 60-0 v. Nottingham C.,
       11 Mar 1990
Highest against: 112-0 at St. Helens, 14 Sep 1986
Attendance: 5,903 v. Workington T. (League),
       6 Sep 1981 — at Brunton Park
       1,874 v. Widnes (Regal Trophy),
       24 Nov 1991 — at Gillford Park

COACHING REGISTER
● **Since formation in 1981**

Allan Agar	May 81 - June 82
Mick Morgan	July 82 - Feb 83
John Atkinson	Feb 83 - Feb 86
Alan Kellett	Feb 86 - May 86
Roy Lester	June 86 - Nov 88
Tommy Dawes	Dec 88 - Jan 90
Cameron Bell	Feb 90 -

44

1991-92 SIGNINGS REGISTER

Signed	Player	Club From
1.8.91	Tait, Alan	Carlisle RU
1.8.91	Thomas, Phillip	Carlisle RU
20.8.91	Findlay, Carl	Carlisle RU
29.8.91	Kolose, Chris	Manakau, NZ
29.8.91	Okesene, Hitro	Manakau, NZ
1.9.91	*Riley, Steve	Barrow
5.9.91	Georgallis, Steve	Eastern Suburbs, Aus
11.10.91	Black, Jamie	St. George Dragons, Aus
18.10.91	Alberts, Wayne	Yeppoon, Aus
22.10.91	Graham, George	Stirling County RU
8.11.91	Johnston, Robert	Glasson ARL
1.12.91	Knox, Simon	Hensingham ARL
6.12.91	Armstrong, Malcolm	Workington T.
2.1.92	Cowgill, David	Aspatria ARL
3.1.92	Paxton, Colin	Hawick RU
23.1.92	Harris, Grant	Hawick RU
14.2.92	Reid, Anthony	Huddersfield
20.4.92	Armstrong, Derek	Hawick RU

1991-92 PLAYERS' SUMMARY

	App	Tries	Goals	Dr	Pts
Ackerman, Rob	31	4	—	—	16
Alberts, Wayne	5 + 1	1	—	—	4
Armstrong, Ian	17 + 5	—	—	—	—
Armstrong, Malcolm	3	—	—	—	—
Black, James	2	—	—	—	—
Bowness, Chris	0 + 1	—	—	—	—
Brierley, Steve	31 + 1	3	—	—	12
Charlton, Gary	22	5	—	—	20
Doyle, Mark	0 + 1	—	—	—	—
Findlay, Carl	10 + 4	2	—	—	8
Friend, Clayton	30	17	2	3	75
Georgallis, Steve	18	8	—	—	32
Graham, George	21 + 1	3	1	1	15
Harris, Grant	8	6	—	—	24
Hepi, Brad	27	10	—	—	40
Johnston, Robert	1 + 1	—	—	—	—
Kavanagh, Mike	7 + 5	2	—	—	8
Knox, Simon	10 + 3	3	—	—	12
Lithgow, Paul	12 + 3	4	—	—	16
Lunt, Peter	0 + 1	—	—	—	—
Manning, Phil	3	1	—	—	4
Murdock, Gary	18 + 9	2	—	—	8
Okesene, Hitro	31	4	3	—	22
Pape, Kevin	27	9	—	—	36
Paxton, Colin	8 + 1	—	—	—	—
Pollard, Damian	7 + 1	3	—	—	12
Robinson, Paul	6 + 9	—	—	—	—
Scott, Tony	9 + 9	—	—	—	—
Southwell, Eddie	3 + 1	—	—	—	—
Thomason, Malcolm	25 + 3	2	—	—	8
Vickers, Barry	24 + 1	3	63	1	139
White, Nigel	1	1	—	—	4
Williams, Barry	25 + 2	10	18	8	84

TOTALS:
33 players		103	87	13	599

Representative Appearances 1991-92
Ackerman — Wales (2, 1t)
Williams — Wales (2, 1t)

1991-92 MATCH ANALYSIS

Date	Competition	H/A	Opponent	Rlt	Score	Tries	Goals	Attendance	Referee
2.9.91	SD	A	Rochdale H.	D	18-18	Pape, Charlton, Brierley	Vickers (3)	—	—
8.9.91	SD	H	Sheffield E.	W	23-12	Hepi, Friend	Vickers (7), Williams (dg)	850	J. Smith
15.9.91	LC(1)	A	Whitehaven	W	44-12	Brierley (2), Georgallis, Charlton, Williams, Friend, Lithgow, Murdock	Vickers (6)	—	—
22.9.91	SD	A	Leigh	L	22-32	Ackerman (2), Okesene, Hepi	Vickers (3)	—	—
26.9.91	LC(2)	A	Workington T.	W	11-2	Friend	Vickers (2), Williams (3dg)	—	—
29.9.91	SD	H	Workington T.	W	39-10	Lithgow (2), Friend (2), Thomason, Williams, Murdock, Georgallis	Vickers (3), Williams (dg)	1700	Galtress
6.10.91	SD	A	Ryedale-York	W	26-6	Vickers, Georgallis, Pollard, Friend, Hepi	Vickers (3)	—	—
10.10.91	LC(SF)	A	Rochdale H.	L	6-19	Pollard	Vickers	—	—
13.10.91	SD	H	London C.	W	12-4	Friend, Pape	Vickers (2)	696	Cross
20.10.91	SD	H	Oldham	L	10-30	Okesene	Vickers (3)	1185	Tidball
6.11.91	SD	A	Sheffield E.	L	6-12	Georgallis	Vickers	—	—
10.11.91	SD	H	Leigh	L	12-16	Hepi, Williams	Vickers (2)	825	Redfearn
17.11.91	RT(1)	A	Highfield	W	28-10	Vickers, Lithgow, Georgallis, Williams, Hepi	Vickers (4)	—	—
24.11.91	RT(2)	H	Widnes	L	16-30	Okesene, Vickers, Georgallis	Vickers, Williams	1874	J. Connolly
1.12.91	SD	A	Workington T.	W	17-11	Friend, Pollard	Vickers (4), Friend (dg)	—	—
8.12.91	SD	H	Ryedale-York	W	28-10	Williams (3), Manning, Georgallis	Vickers (4)	598	R. Smith
22.12.91	SD	A	London C.	L	8-12	Ackerman	Williams (2)	—	—
26.12.91	SD	H	Workington T.	W	25-6	Pape, Georgallis, Alberts, Graham	Vickers (4), Williams (dg)	1098	Volante
5.1.92	SD	A	Oldham	L	4-14	Pape	—	—	—
13.1.92	CC(P)	A	Workington T.	L	4-11	—	Williams (2)	—	—
19.1.92	SD	H	Sheffield E.	L	22-25	Friend (2), Ackerman, Okesene	Williams (3)	610	Whitfield
2.2.92	SD	A	Leigh	L	18-19	Charlton (2), Pape	Vickers (3)	—	—
9.2.92	SD	H	Rochdale H.	L	0-5	—	—	615	Ollerton
16.2.92	SD	A	Ryedale-York	L	1-22	—	Friend (dg)	—	—
23.2.92	SD	H	London C.	W	28-24	Hepi (3), Kavanagh (2)	Vickers (4)	495	Morris
1.3.92	SD	A	Rochdale H.	L	14-44	Pape (2), Friend	Vickers	—	—
8.3.92	SD	A	Oldham	L	17-20	Harris (2), Friend	Vickers (1, 1dg), Friend	—	—
15.3.92	SD	H	Leigh	W	19-11	Findlay (2), Hepi	Okesene (2), Vickers, Graham (dg)	867	Steele
22.3.92	SD	A	London C.	L	15-20	Friend (2), Harris	Okesene, Friend (dg)	—	—
29.3.92	SD	H	Oldham	L	10-23	Graham, Hepi	Williams	849	Cross
5.4.92	SD	A	Sheffield E.	L	14-32	Friend (2), Harris	Graham	—	—
12.4.92	SD	H	Rochdale H.	W	20-8	Knox (2), Pape, Harris	Friend, Williams (2dg)	468	Asquith
17.4.92	SD	H	Ryedale-York	W	22-8	Williams, Charlton, Harris, Graham	Williams (3)	482	Crashley
20.4.92	SD	A	Workington T.	W	40-12	Williams (2), Knox, White, Pape, Thomason, Friend	Williams (6)	—	—

CASTLEFORD

Ground: Wheldon Road (0977-552674)
Colours: Yellow, black and white
First Season: 1926-27. There was also a
Castleford team from 1896-97 to
1905-06 inclusive
Nickname: Tigers
Chairman: David Poulter
Secretary: Denise Cackett
Coach: Darryl Van de Velde (July 1988-)
Honours: **Championship** Beaten finalists,
1938-39, 1968-69
Challenge Cup Winners, 1934-35,
1968-69, 1969-70, 1985-86
Beaten finalists, 1991-92
Regal Trophy Winners, 1976-77
Premiership Beaten finalists,
1983-84
Yorkshire Cup Winners, 1977-78,
1981-82, 1986-87, 1990-91, 1991-92
Beaten finalists, 1948-49, 1950-51,
1968-69, 1971-72, 1983-84,
1985-86, 1987-88, 1988-89
Yorkshire League Winners,
1932-33, 1938-39, 1964-65
Eastern Division Championship
Beaten finalists, 1963-64
Charity Shield Beaten finalists,
1986-87
BBC2 Floodlit Trophy Winners,
1965-66, 1966-67, 1967-68, 1976-77

RECORDS

Match
Goals: 17 by Geoff "Sammy" Lloyd v. Millom,
16 Sep 1973
Tries: 5 by Derek Foster v. Hunslet, 10 Nov 1972
John Joyner v. Millom, 16 Sep 1973
Steve Fenton v. Dewsbury,
27 Jan 1978
Ian French v. Hunslet, 9 Feb 1986
St. John Ellis at Whitehaven,
10 Dec 1989
Points: 43 by Geoff "Sammy" Lloyd v. Millom,
16 Sep 1973

Season
Goals: 158 by Geoff "Sammy" Lloyd, 1976-77
Tries: 36 by Keith Howe, 1963-64
Points: 334 by Bob Beardmore, 1983-84
Career
Goals: 875 by Albert Lunn, 1951-63
Tries: 206 by Alan Hardisty, 1958-71
Points: 1,870 by Albert Lunn, 1951-63
Appearances: 585 + 28 by John Joyner, 1973-92
Highest score: 94-12 v. Huddersfield,
18 Sep 1988
Highest against: 62-12 at St. Helens,
16 Apr 1986
Attendance: 25,449 v. Hunslet (RL Cup),
9 Mar 1935

*Stand off Grant Anderson, who contributed
12 touchdowns in 29 appearances during 1991-92.*

COACHING REGISTER
- **Since 1974-75**

Dave Cox	Apr 74 - Nov 74
*Malcolm Reilly	Dec 74 - May 87
Dave Sampson	May 87 - Apr 88
Darryl Van de Velde	July 88 -

Shortly after his appointment Reilly returned to Australia to fulfil his contract before resuming at Castleford early the next season.

GREAT BRITAIN REGISTER
(27 players)

A. Atkinson	(11)	1929-36
K. Beardmore	(13 + 1)	1984-90
W. Bryant	(4 + 1)	1964-67
L. Crooks	(2)	1992
A. Croston	(1)	1937
B. Cunniffe	(1)	1937
W. J. Davies	(1)	1933
D. Edwards	(3 + 2)	1968-71
S. Ellis	(+ 2)	1991
K. England	(6 + 5)	1987-91
A. Hardisty	(12)	1964-70
D. Hartley	(9)	1968-70
K. Hepworth	(11)	1967-70
S. Irwin	(+ 4)	1990
J. Joyner	(14 + 2)	1978-84
B. Lockwood	(7)	1972-74
A. Marchant	(3)	1986
R. Millward	(1)	1966
S. Norton	(2 + 1)	1974
D. Plange	(1)	1988
M. Reilly	(9)	1970
P. Small	(1)	1962
G. Steadman	(2 + 1)	1990-92
G. Stephens	(5)	1979
D. Walton	(1)	1965
J. Ward	(3)	1963-64
K. Ward	(14)	1984-89

Australian centre Graeme Bradley, converted to the second row by Castleford after an October 1991 signing from Penrith Panthers.

1991-92 SIGNINGS REGISTER

Signed	Player	Club From
24.6.91	Ford, Mike	Oldham
17.7.91	Blackmore, Richard	Otahuhu, NZ
19.8.91	Nikau, Tawera	Ryedale-York
27.8.91	Nelson, David	Sheffield E.
30.8.91	*Starbuck, Jason	Ryedale-York
14.9.91	Sykes, Nathan	Moldgreen ARL
14.9.91	Price, Simon	East Leeds ARL
27.9.91	Bradley, Adam	Jubilee ARL
3.10.91	Bradley, Graeme	Penrith, Aus
15.11.91	Watson, Chris	Cutsyke ARL
24.1.92	*Jones, Gary	Leeds

1991-92 PLAYERS' SUMMARY

	App	Tries	Goals	Dr	Pts
Anderson, Grant	28 + 1	12	—	—	48
Atkins, Gary	1 + 3	—	—	—	—
Battye, Neil	10 + 2	3	—	—	12
Beardmore, Kevin	1	—	—	—	—
Blackmore, Richard	16 + 2	9	—	—	36
Boothroyd, Giles	0 + 1	—	—	—	—
Bradley, Graeme	29 + 4	4	—	—	16
Bragger, Ian	2	—	—	—	—
Clarke, Andy	10 + 2	1	—	—	4
Crooks, Lee	31 + 1	5	111	—	242
Ellis, St. John	39 + 1	15	4	—	68
England, Keith	28 + 1	4	—	—	16
Fletcher, Paul	5 + 3	—	—	—	—
Ford, Mike	39	8	—	—	32
Irwin, Shaun	12 + 1	4	—	—	16
Joyner, John	4 + 6	1	—	—	4
Ketteridge, Martin	28 + 7	—	27	—	54
Middleton, Simon	27 + 6	14	—	—	56
Nelson, David	38	13	—	—	52
Nikau, Tawera	37 + 1	6	—	—	24
Roebuck, Neil	9 + 8	3	—	—	12
Sampson, Dean	19 + 11	1	—	—	4
Smith, Tony	29 + 8	12	—	—	48
Southernwood, Graham	31	4	—	—	16
Steadman, Graham	35 + 1	29	4	1	125
Sykes, Nathan	1	—	—	—	—
Watson, Chris	1	—	—	—	—
Whitehead, Paul	0 + 1	—	—	—	—
Wray, Jon	10	3	—	—	12

TOTALS:

	App	Tries	Goals	Dr	Pts
29 players		151	146	1	897

Representative Appearances 1991-92
Crooks — Britain (2); Yorkshire (1, 2g)
Southernwood — GB Under-21 (2)
Steadman — Britain (1 + 1, 2t); Yorkshire (+ 1)

Winger David Nelson, an August 1991 capture from Sheffield Eagles.

Prop Dean Sampson, who touched down once in 30 games during 1991-92.

1991-92 MATCH ANALYSIS

Date	Competition	H/A	Opponent	Rlt	Score	Tries	Goals	Attendance	Referee
1.9.91	SBC	H	Wigan	W	38-26	Ellis (2), Anderson (2), Smith, Steadman, Nelson	Crooks (5)	4103	Morris
8.9.91	SBC	A	Salford	W	18-10	Steadman, Ellis	Crooks (5)	—	—
15.9.91	YC(1)	A	Batley	W	36-12	Smith (2), Nikau, Ford, Steadman, Irwin	Crooks (6)	—	—
22.9.91	SBC	H	Leeds	L	8-13	Middleton	Crooks (2)	11,539	R. Connolly
25.9.91	YC(2)	H	Hull K.R.	W	34-12	Ford (2), Nikau, Nelson, Steadman	Crooks (7)	4953	Galtress

(Continued)

CASTLEFORD 1991-92 MATCH ANALYSIS (continued)

Date	Competition	H/A	Opponent	Rlt	Score	Tries	Goals	Attendance	Referee
29.9.91	SBC	A	St. Helens	L	14-25	Irwin, Steadman, England	Crooks	—	—
6.10.91	SBC	H	Widnes	L	20-22	Anderson, Battye, Ellis	Crooks (4)	6216	Kershaw
9.10.91	YC(SF)	H	Featherstone R.	W	18-10	Southernwood, Irwin, Smith	Crooks (3)	8890	Holdsworth
13.10.91	SBC	A	Hull K.R.	W	22-14	Blackmore (2), Steadman, Anderson, Ellis	Crooks	—	—
20.10.91	YC(F)	N[1]	Bradford N.	W	28-6	Steadman (2), Ford, Smith, Battye	Steadman (4)	(8916)	Holdsworth
23.10.91	SBC	A	Warrington	L	6-23	Nelson	Ketteridge	—	—
27.10.91	SBC	H	Featherstone R.	W	22-20	Sampson, Nikau, Roebuck, Smith	Ketteridge (3)	6819	Cross
3.11.91	SBC	A	Bradford N.	W	18-12	Steadman, Middleton, Nelson	Ketteridge (3)	—	—
10.11.91	SBC	H	Halifax	L	16-22	Steadman, Middleton	Ketteridge (4)	7659	Campbell
17.11.91	RT(1)	A	Hull K.R.	W	22-10	Middleton, Smith, Southernwood	Ketteridge (5)	—	—
25.11.91	RT(2)	H	Doncaster	W	38-6	Steadman (3), Clarke, Ellis, Middleton, Bradley	Ketteridge (5)	4145	Cross
1.12.91	RT(3)	A	Leeds	L	4-24	Nikau	—	—	—
15.12.91	SBC	A	Swinton	W	40-4	Steadman (2), Crooks, Middleton, Anderson, Nelson, Ford	Crooks (6)	—	—
22.12.91	SBC	A	Wigan	L	6-10	Anderson	Crooks	—	—
26.12.91	SBC	H	Hull	W	30-8	Roebuck (2), Crooks, Smith, Middleton	Crooks (5)	6587	Morris
1.1.92	SBC	A	Wakefield T.	D	14-14	Anderson, Steadman, Middleton	Crooks	—	—
5.1.92	SBC	A	Widnes	W	14-4	Battye, Anderson, Nelson	Crooks	—	—
12.1.92	SBC	H	Salford	W	26-12	Middleton, Crooks, Ellis, Steadman	Crooks (5)	4598	Campbell
19.1.92	SBC	H	Bradford N.	W	24-10	Nikau, Ellis, Irwin, Anderson	Crooks (4)	4814	J. Smith
26.1.92	CC(1)	A[1]	Trafford B.	W	50-0	Steadman (4), Nelson (2), Ellis, Anderson, Blackmore	Crooks (7)	—	—
2.2.92	SBC	A	Leeds	W	18-4	Steadman (2), Nelson	Crooks (3)	—	—
9.2.92	CC(2)	A	Hunslet	W	28-12	Steadman (3), Nelson	Crooks (6)	—	—
23.2.92	CC(3)	H	Featherstone R.	W	19-12	Steadman, Blackmore, Nelson	Crooks (3), Steadman (dg)	10,440	Whitfield
1.3.92	SBC	H	Warrington	W	40-8	Southernwood (2), Nikau, Anderson, Steadman, Blackmore, Nelson	Crooks (6)	5456	Volante
8.3.92	SBC	H	St. Helens	D	8-8	Crooks	Crooks (2)	8135	Cummings
14.3.92	CC(SF)	N[2]	Hull	W	8-4	Ford	Crooks (2)	(14,636)	Morris
17.3.92	SBC	A	Featherstone R.	L	16-24	Smith (2), Joyner	Crooks (2)	—	—
22.3.92	SBC	H	Hull K.R.	L	18-28	Nelson, Smith, Crooks	Crooks (2), Ellis	5366	Galtress
29.3.92	SBC	H	Swinton	W	56-2	Middleton (3), Blackmore (2), Ford, Wray, Anderson, Ellis	Crooks (8), Ketteridge (2)	3556	Carter
12.4.92	SBC	A	Halifax	L	8-24	England	Crooks (2)	—	—
17.4.92	SBC	H	Wakefield T.	W	28-4	Ellis (2), England, Middleton, Smith, Wray	Ketteridge (2)	6299	Holdsworth
20.4.92	SBC	A	Hull	W	30-14	Steadman, Blackmore, Ellis, Middleton, Bradley	Crooks (5)	—	—
26.4.92	PT(1)	H	Wakefield T.	W	28-18	Ellis (2), Bradley (2)	Crooks (6)	6616	Morris
2.5.92	CC(F)	N[3]	Wigan	L	12-28	Blackmore, England	Ketteridge (2)	(77,386)	Whitfield
10.5.92	PT(SF)	A	St. Helens	L	14-30	Ford, Wray	Ellis (3)	—	—

N[1] at Elland Road, Leeds
N[2] at Leeds
N[3] at Wembley
A[1] at Leeds

CHORLEY BOROUGH

Ground:	Victory Park, Chorley, before moving to Grundy Hill, Horwich (0204-696908) for the 1992-93 season
Colours:	Black and white
First Season:	1989-90 as Chorley. Officially became Chorley Borough in 1991-92
Chairman:	Mike Livesey
Secretary:	Brian Green
Coach:	Bob Eccles (May 1990-Sep 1991) John Taylor (Sep 1991-)

RECORDS

Match
Goals: No player has scored more than 6
Tries: No player has scored more than 3
Points: No player has scored more than 12

Season
Goals: 73 by Mike Smith, 1989-90
Tries: 10 by David Bacon, 1989-90
Points: 142 by Mike Smith, 1989-90

Career
Goals: 181 by Mike Smith, 1989-
Tries: No player has scored 20 or more
Points: 372 by Mike Smith, 1989-
Appearances: 84 + 2 by Mike Smith, 1989-
Highest score: 46-12 v. Runcorn H., 1 Jan 1990
Highest against: 66-16 at Oldham, 18 Feb 1990
Attendance: 2,851 v. Oldham (League), 21 Jan 1990 — at Victory Park
5,026 v. Wigan (Lancs Cup), 15 Sep 1989 — at Leigh

COACHING REGISTER
● **Since formation in 1989**

Stan Gittins	June 89 - Apr 90
Bob Eccles	May 90 - Sep 91
John Taylor	Sep 91 -

1991-92 SIGNINGS REGISTER

Signed	Player	Club From
17.7.91	Ramsden, Dennis	Wigan
18.7.91	Lee, Andrew	ARL
18.7.91	Brooks, David	Adlington ARL
18.7.91	Bullough, Steve	Crown Springs ARL
18.7.91	Hewitt, Tony	Swinton
23.7.91	Baker, Gary	Shevington ARL
6.8.91	Berry, John	Swinton
22.8.91	Bentham, Stephen	Orrell St. James ARL
3.9.91	*Capewell, Phil	Swinton
3.9.91	Sephton, Rob	Tarleton ARL
12.9.91	Borowski, Nigel	Tarleton ARL
12.9.91	Crook, Lee	St. Patricks ARL
19.9.91	Johnson, Steve	St. Patricks ARL
24.9.91	Gibbons, David	Bolton ARL
24.9.91	Gilligan, Paul	St. Patricks ARL
24.9.91	Green, Tony	St. Patricks ARL
2.10.91	Roberts, David	St. Patricks ARL
3.10.91	Whittle, Jason	St. Patricks ARL
7.10.91	Watene, Vaughan	Coburg, NZ
7.10.91	Benson, Karl	Coburg, NZ
13.10.91	Painter, Trevor	St. Patricks ARL
24.10.91	Gregory, Bryn	Orrell RU
7.11.91	McTigue, Mick	Huddersfield
8.11.91	Ashcroft, Steve	Leigh Miners ARL
17.11.91	Carney, John	St. Patricks ARL
27.11.91	Fletcher, Darren	St. Patricks ARL
10.12.91	Moore, Jim	Leigh
1.1.92	Matauesi, Sireli	Camborne RU, Fiji
23.2.92	Dutson, Neil	St. Judes ARL
11.3.92	Marsh, Peter	Leigh Miners ARL

1991-92 PLAYERS' SUMMARY

	App	Tries	Goals	Dr	Pts
Ainscough, Steve	0 + 1	—	—	—	—
Ashcroft, Steve	16	5	—	—	20
Baker, Gary	0 + 2	—	—	—	—
Benson, Karl	15 + 4	1	—	—	4
Berry, John	15 + 1	2	—	—	8
Bimson, Jeff	14 + 2	1	—	—	4
Borowski, Nigel	2 + 1	—	—	—	—
Briscoe, Carl	24	3	—	—	12
Brooks, David	2	1	—	—	4
Broxton, Paul	3 + 2	—	—	—	—
Carney, John	10 + 4	1	—	—	4
Clayton, Richard	9 + 3	1	—	—	4
Crook, Lee	20	1	—	—	4
Duffy, John	3	1	—	—	4
Dutson, Neil	0 + 3	—	—	—	—
Eccles, Bob	4	2	—	—	8
Edwards, Mark	20 + 1	1	—	—	4
Evans, Andy	7 + 1	3	—	—	12
Fletcher, Darren	13	—	—	1	—
Gibbons, David	0 + 1	—	—	—	—
Green, Tony	4 + 1	—	—	—	—
Hankey, Steve	24 + 3	7	—	—	28
Hewitt, Tony	3	—	—	—	—
Hodson, Tony	11 + 5	2	—	—	8
Johnson, Steve	5 + 2	—	—	—	—
Knight, Mark	5 + 2	—	—	—	—
McTigue, Mick	18	4	—	—	16
Marsh, Peter	3	—	—	—	—
Mayo, John	22 + 1	2	—	—	8
Meadows, Kevin	26	3	—	—	12
Moore, Jim	2	—	—	—	—
Painter, Trevor	5	2	—	—	8
Price, Billy	15 + 4	2	4	3	19
Roberts, Paul	4	—	1	—	2
Sephton, Rob	1	—	—	—	—
Smith, Mike	27	5	46	3	115
Watene, Vaughan	10 + 4	1	—	—	4
Wood, David	15 + 5	3	—	—	12
TOTALS:					
38 players		54	51	7	325

1991-92 MATCH ANALYSIS

Date	Com-petition	H/A	Opponent	Rlt	Score	Tries	Goals	Atten-dance	Referee
1.9.91	TD	H	Dewsbury	L	12-62	Mayo, Duffy	Smith (2)	501	Campbell
8.9.91	TD	A	Keighley C.	L	12-52	Edwards, Eccles	Smith (2)	—	—
15.9.91	LC(1)	A	Leigh	L	12-59	Hankey, Wood	Smith (2)	—	—
22.9.91	TD	H	Barrow	L	8-54	Eccles, Evans	—	429	R. Smith
29.9.91	TD	A	Whitehaven	L	12-44	Bimson, Evans	Smith (2)	—	—
6.10.91	TD	A	Scarborough P.	L	10-28	Hankey, Evans	Roberts	—	—
13.10.91	TD	H	Batley	L	6-46	Smith	Smith	464	R. Smith
20.10.91	TD	A	Bramley	L	0-52	—	—	—	—
27.10.91	TD	H	Hunslet	L	16-48	Hankey, Watene, Brooks	Price (2)	265	Ollerton
4.11.91	RT(P)	A	Leigh East	L	10-20	Meadows, Crook	Smith	—	—
10.11.91	TD	H	Scarborough P.	L	7-12	Price	Price (1, 1dg)	268	Carter
24.11.91	TD	A	Batley	L	2-38	—	Price	—	—
1.12.91	TD	A	Doncaster	L	1-19	—	Price (dg)	—	—
8.12.91	TD	H	Bramley	L	0-36	—	—	279	Gilmour
15.12.91	TD	A	Dewsbury	L	0-38	—	—	—	—
26.12.91	TD	A	Trafford B.	W	26-18	Hankey (2), Briscoe, Wood	Smith (5)	—	—
1.1.92	TD	H	Trafford B.	W	36-18	McTigue (2), Benson, Mayo, Smith, Hankey, Carney	Smith (4)	382	Redfearn
9.1.92	CC(P)	H	Salford	L	13-64	Smith (2)	Smith (2), Fletcher (dg)	932	Ollerton
12.1.92	TD	A	Barrow	L	11-50	Hankey	Smith (3, 1dg)	—	—
19.1.92	TD	H	Keighley C.	L	13-28	Wood, Ashcroft	Smith (2), Price (dg)	541	Cross
2.2.92	TD	A	Huddersfield	L	8-46	McTigue	Smith (2)	—	—
5.2.92	TD	H	Huddersfield	L	9-26	Meadows	Smith (2, 1dg)	686	R. Connolly
16.2.92	TD	H	Nottingham C.	W	22-7	Smith, Ashcroft, Hodson, Price	Smith (3)	253	Gilmour
23.2.92	TD	A	Highfield	L	8-14	Briscoe	Smith (2)	—	—
1.3.92	TD	H	Whitehaven	L	10-16	Ashcroft	Smith (3)	303	J. Connolly
8.3.92	TD	A	Hunslet	L	10-28	Meadows, Berry	Smith	—	—
15.3.92	TD	A	Nottingham C.	W	24-16	Ashcroft (2), McTigue, Berry	Smith (4)	—	—
22.3.92	TD	H	Doncaster	L	17-30	Clayton, Painter, Briscoe	Smith (2, 1dg)	442	Crashley
29.3.92	TD	H	Highfield	L	10-16	Hodson, Painter	Smith	316	Asquith

Richard Clayton, scoring his only try of the 1991-92 campaign at home to Doncaster.

Chorley Borough stalwart Mike Smith, holder of five club records.

DEWSBURY

Ground: Moved to Mqunt Pleasant,
           Batley (0924-472208) for 1991-92
           and 1992-93 seasons from Crown
           Flatt
Colours: Red, amber and black
First Season: 1901-02
Chairman: Rodney Hardcastle
Secretary: Ian Clough
Coach: Jack Addy (Dec 1990-)
Honours: **Championship** Winners, 1972-73
           Beaten finalists, 1946-47
           War League Championship
           Winners, 1941-42 (1942-43 won
           final but championship declared
           null and void because Dewsbury
           played an ineligible player.)
           Beaten finalists, 1943-44
           Division Two Champions, 1904-05
           Challenge Cup Winners, 1911-12,
           1942-43
           Beaten finalists, 1928-29
           Yorkshire Cup Winners, 1925-26,
           1927-28, 1942-43
           Beaten finalists, 1918-19, 1921-22,
           1940-41, 1972-73
           Yorkshire League Winners, 1946-47
           BBC2 Floodlit Trophy Beaten
           finalists, 1975-76

RECORDS

Match

Goals: 10 by Jim Ledgard v. Yorkshire Amateurs,
       13 Sep 1947
       Nigel Stephenson v. Blackpool B.,
       28 Aug 1972
       Chris Wilkinson v. Huddersfield,
       27 Mar 1989
Tries: 8 by Dai Thomas v. Liverpool C.,
       13 Apr 1907
Points: 29 by Joe Lyman v. Hull, 22 Apr 1919

Season

Goals: 145 by Nigel Stephenson, 1972-73
Tries: 40 by Dai Thomas, 1906-07
Points: 368 by Nigel Stephenson, 1972-73

Career

Goals: 863 by Nigel Stephenson, 1967-78 &
          1984-86
Tries: 144 by Joe Lyman, 1913-31
Points: 2,082 by Nigel Stephenson, 1967-78 &
          1984-86
Appearances: 454 by Joe Lyman, 1913-31
Highest score: 72-0 v. Doncaster, 7 Oct 1984
Highest against: 82-0 at Widnes, 30 Nov 1986
Attendance: 26,584 v. Halifax (Yorks Cup),
          30 Oct 1920 — at Crown Flatt

COACHING REGISTER

● **Since 1974-75**

Maurice Bamford	June 74 - Oct 74
Alan Hardisty	Oct 74 - June 75
Dave Cox	June 75 - July 77
Ron Hill	July 77 - Dec 77
Lewis Jones	Dec 77 - Apr 78
Jeff Grayshon	May 78 - Oct 78
Alan Lockwood	Oct 78 - Oct 80
Bernard Watson	Oct 80 - Oct 82
Ray Abbey	Nov 82 - Apr 83
★Tommy Smales	May 83 - Feb 84
Jack Addy	Feb 84 - Jan 87
Dave Busfield	Jan 87 - Apr 87
Terry Crook	Apr 87 - Dec 88
Maurice Bamford	Dec 88 - Dec 90
Jack Addy	Dec 90 -

★Ex-forward

GREAT BRITAIN REGISTER

(6 players)

A. Bates	(2 + 2)	1974
F. Gallagher	(4)	1920-21
J. Ledgard	(2)	1947
R. Pollard	(1)	1950
M. Stephenson	(5 + 1)	1971-72
H. Street	(4)	1950

1991-92 SIGNINGS REGISTER

Signed	Player	Club From
17.6.91	Cocks, Mark	Redhill ARL
10.8.91	Bell, Glen	NZ
27.8.91	Sidebottom, Gary	Nottingham C.
19.9.91	Fleary, Darren	Moldgreen ARL

19.9.91	James, Sean	Moldgreen ARL
28.11.91	Rombo, Eddie	Leeds
29.11.91	*Russell, Julian	Wakefield T.
24.12.91	Charles, Marquis	Bramley
2.1.92	Bastian, John	Featherstone R.
5.5.92	Wright, Paul	Redhill ARL
16.5.92	Hardy, Ryan	Redhill ARL
26.5.92	Collins, Darren	Clayton ARL

Kenyan wingman Eddie Rombo, scorer of 22 tries in 20 games after being signed from Leeds in November 1991.

1991-92 PLAYERS' SUMMARY

	App	Tries	Goals	Dr	Pts
Bailey, Denis	30	22	—	—	88
Bastian, John	5 + 8	1	—	—	4
Bell, Glen......................	30	5	—	—	20
Charles, Marquis..............	10 + 1	6	—	—	24
Cocks, Gary....................	18 + 11	7	—	—	28
Coughlan, Glen................	27 + 3	7	—	—	28
Delaney, Paul..................	30	15	—	—	60
Dickinson, Andy...............	2 + 4	1	—	—	4
Drummond, Barry	0 + 1	1	—	—	4
Garforth, David...............	2 + 1	—	—	—	—
Graham, Nathan	30	6	13	—	50
Haigh, Chris...................	0 + 1	—	—	—	—
Haigh, Mark...................	9 + 1	2	—	—	8
Hall, Dean	16 + 3	9	—	—	36
Hindricks, Andrew...........	4	2	—	—	8
Hughes, Lee	8 + 1	3	—	—	12
Hughes, Paul	29 + 2	6	—	—	24
Kelly, Neil	31 + 1	6	—	—	24
Labourn, Terry	13 + 3	4	2	—	20
Rombo, Eddie.................	20	22	—	—	88
Russell, Julian................	4	1	—	—	4
Shuttleworth, Paul	28 + 1	7	—	7	35
Sidebottom, Gary............	13 + 2	9	—	—	36
Squires, Chris	8 + 7	4	—	—	16
Vasey, Chris	25 + 2	7	109	—	246
Worthy, Paul	24 + 5	3	—	—	12

TOTALS:

26 players......................		156	124	7	879

1991-92 MATCH ANALYSIS

Date	Competition	H/A	Opponent	Rlt	Score	Tries	Goals	Attendance	Referee
1.9.91	TD	A	Chorley B.	W	62-12	Sidebottom (2), Delaney (2), Labourn, Cocks, Bailey, Squires, Hall, Vasey, Kelly	Vasey (9)	—	—
8.9.91	TD	H	Hunslet	W	42-9	Bailey (4), Vasey, Labourn	Vasey (9)	1004	Tidball
15.9.91	YC(1)	A	Hull K.R.	L	5-18		Vasey (2), Shuttleworth (dg)	—	—
22.9.91	TD	A	Doncaster	L	12-22	Coughlan, Labourn	Vasey (2)	—	—
29.9.91	TD	H	Bramley	W	26-12	Bailey (2), Graham, Hall	Vasey (5)	764	R. Smith
6.10.91	TD	A	Highfield	W	38-14	Kelly (2), Bell, Sidebottom, Hall, Labourn, Coughlan	Vasey (5)	—	—
13.10.91	TD	H	Scarborough P.	W	24-2	Shuttleworth, Hall, P. Hughes, Coughlan	Vasey (4)	931	Ollerton

(Continued)

DEWSBURY 1991-92 MATCH ANALYSIS (continued)

Date	Com-petition	H/A	Opponent	Rlt	Score	Tries	Goals	Atten-dance	Referee
20.10.91	TD	A	Trafford B.	W	48-13	Delaney (2), Sidebottom (2), Bailey (2), Hall, Bell, Vasey	Vasey (6)	—	—
27.10.91	TD	H	Whitehaven	W	48-8	Bailey (2), Hindricks (2), Delaney, P. Hughes, Coughlan, Shuttleworth	Vasey (7), Labourn	762	Steele
29.10.91	RT(P)	A	Wigan	L	14-34	Shuttleworth, Drummond, Hall	Labourn	—	—
3.11.91	TD	A	Bramley	L	10-20	Delaney (2)	Vasey	—	—
10.11.91	TD	H	Doncaster	W	24-2	Vasey, Hall, Shuttleworth, Delaney, Dickinson	Vasey (2)	1155	Steele
2.12.91	TD	A	Scarborough P.	W	17-16	Rombo (2), Sidebottom	Vasey (2), Shuttleworth (dg)	—	—
8.12.91	TD	A	Huddersfield	L	4-13	Rombo	—	—	—
15.12.91	TD	H	Chorley B.	W	38-0	Rombo, Kelly, Russell, Delaney, Sidebottom, P. Hughes, Bailey	Graham (5)	702	R. Connolly
26.12.91	TD	A	Batley	D	16-16	Shuttleworth, Bailey	Graham (3), Shuttleworth (2dg)	—	—
1.1.92	TD	H	Batley	W	18-12	Kelly, Cocks, Sidebottom, Bailey	Vasey	2876	Whitelam
12.1.92	TD	A	Nottingham C.	W	58-0	Rombo (3), Bailey (2), Cocks (2), Sidebottom, Delaney, Coughlan, Bastian	Vasey (7)	—	—
19.1.92	TD	H	Trafford B.	W	34-6	Hall (2), Delaney, Graham, Coughlan, L. Hughes	Vasey (5)	784	Asquith
25.1.92	CC(1)	H	Leigh	W	14-2	Shuttleworth, Charles	Vasey (2), Shuttleworth (2dg)	1811	Burke
9.2.92	CC(2)	H	Featherstone R.	L	10-23	Delaney, Rombo	Vasey	3460	J. Connolly
16.2.92	TD	A	Whitehaven	W	42-18	Vasey, Charles, Rombo, Worthy, Bailey, Graham, Delaney	Vasey (7)	—	—
23.2.92	TD	H	Barrow	L	6-24	Charles	Vasey	1036	Burke
1.3.92	TD	H	Highfield	W	48-6	Rombo (5), Delaney, P. Hughes, Graham, Bailey	Vasey (6)	788	Whitelam
8.3.92	TD	A	Barrow	W	28-4	M. Haigh, Bailey, Kelly, Charles, Rombo	Vasey (4)	—	—
22.3.92	TD	H	Nottingham C.	W	66-6	Rombo (2), Cocks (2), Charles (2), L. Hughes, Bell, Bailey, Squires, P. Hughes, Worthy	Vasey (9)	712	Ollerton
29.3.92	TD	A	Keighley C.	L	13-14	Bell, L. Hughes	Vasey (2), Shuttleworth (dg)	—	—
5.4.92	TD	A	Hunslet	W	40-8	Rombo (2), Vasey (2), Squires, Shuttleworth, Coughlan	Vasey (6)	—	—
12.4.92	TD	H	Huddersfield	L	6-15	Cocks	Vasey	2184	Galtress
17.4.92	TD	H	Keighley C.	W	26-7	Rombo (2), Delaney, Bailey, Bell	Graham (3)	1002	Redfearn
21.4.92	DP(1)	H	Doncaster	W	24-6	Graham (2), Worthy, P. Hughes, Squires	Graham, Vasey	1283	Carter
26.4.92	DP(2)	A	Oldham	L	18-36	M. Haigh, Bailey, Rombo	Vasey (2), Graham	—	—

DONCASTER

Ground: Tattersfield (0302-390150)
Colours: Blue and yellow
First Season: 1951-52
Nickname: Dons
Chairman: John Desmond
Secretary: Ray Green
Coach: Dave Sampson (May 1989-Jan 1992)
Geoff Morris (Jan 1992-)

RECORDS

Match
Goals: 12 by Tony Zelei v. Nottingham C.,
1 Sep 1991
Tries: 4 by Vernon Grace v. Rochdale H.,
4 Oct 1952
Brian Tasker v. Leeds, 26 Oct 1963
John Buckton v. Rochdale H.,
30 Aug 1981
Tony Kemp v. Carlisle,
23 Nov 1986
Neil Turner v. Keighley,
22 Nov 1989
Mark Roache v. Nottingham C.,
1 Sep 1991
Points: 32 by Tony Zelei v. Nottingham C.,
1 Sep 1991

Season
Goals: 118 by David Noble, 1985-86
Tries: 21 by Mark Roache, 1989-90
Points: 250 by David Noble, 1986-87

Career
Goals: 850 by David Noble, 1976-77, 1980-89
& 1992
Tries: 83 by Mark Roache, 1985-
Points: 1,751 by David Noble, 1976-77, 1980-89
& 1992
Appearances: 305 + 15 by David Noble, 1976-77,
1980-89 & 1992
Highest score: 88-6 v. Nottingham C., 1 Sep 1991
Highest against: 75-3 v. Leigh, 28 Mar 1976
Attendance: 5,274 v. Wigan (RL Cup),
29 Jan 1989 — at Tattersfield
10,000 v. Bradford N. (RL Cup),
16 Feb 1952 — at York Road Stadium

COACHING REGISTER
● **Since 1974-75**

Ted Strawbridge	Feb 73 - Apr 75
Derek Edwards	July 75 - Nov 76
Don Robson	Nov 76 - Sep 77
Trevor Lowe	Sep 77 - Apr 79
*Tommy Smales	Feb 78 - Apr 79
Billy Yates	Apr 79 - May 79
Don Vines	Sep 79 - Jan 80
Bill Kenny	June 80 - May 81
Alan Rhodes	Aug 81 - Mar 83
Clive Sullivan	Mar 83 - May 84
John Sheridan	June 84 - Nov 87
Graham Heptinstall	Nov 87 - Jan 88
John Sheridan	Jan 88 - Apr 89
Dave Sampson	May 89 - Jan 92
Geoff Morris	Jan 92 -

*Ex-forward, who shared the coaching post
with Trevor Lowe for just over a year.*

*Clive Sullivan, coach at Doncaster for 14 months
to May 1984.*

1991-92 SIGNINGS REGISTER

Signed	Player	Club From
13.8.91	Coulter, Gary	Keighley C.
15.8.91	*Francis, Norman	Oldham
15.8.91	*Lord, Paul	Oldham
20.8.91	Walton, Tony	Ossett ARL
23.8.91	Smith, Mike	Hull K.R.
25.8.91	*Eden, Phil	Wakefield T.
30.8.91	*Hill, Simon	Leeds
30.8.91	Rowse, Martin	Leeds
5.9.91	Rayne, Keith	Batley
6.9.91	*Horton, Stewart	Ryedale-York
17.9.91	Hermansson, Terry	NZ
24.10.91	*Grimoldby, Nick	Sheffield E.
24.10.91	*Smithson, Martin	Leeds
1.11.91	Wilkinson, Tony	Brodsworth ARL
1.11.91	Briggs, Carl	Oulton ARL
1.11.91	Brown, Paul	Oulton ARL
1.11.91	Denton, Lee	Oulton ARL
1.11.91	Smith, Gary	Oulton ARL
15.11.91	*Rudd, Neil	Nottingham C.
15.11.91	Shackleton, Michael	Kippax ARL
15.11.91	Shackleton, Robert	Kippax ARL
18.12.91	Armstrong, Mick	ARL
27.12.91	Briggs, Trevor	Keighley C.
3.1.92	Bowes, Tony	Walnut Warriors ARL
3.1.92	Evans, David	ARL
3.1.92	Mycock, Shaun	Bentley ARL
3.1.92	Heptinstall, Jason	Doncaster Colts ARL
3.1.92	Pell, Richard	Cutstyke ARL
17.1.92	*Jones, Kevin	Dewsbury
14.2.92	*Amman, David	Leeds
15.2.92	Holmes, Gary	Oulton ARL

Kevin Rayne, a non-scorer in 18 appearances in 1991-92.

1991-92 PLAYERS' SUMMARY

	App	Tries	Goals	Dr	Pts
Amman, David	0 + 1	—	—	—	—
Armstrong, Mick	17 + 3	5	—	—	20
Bowes, Tony	7 + 1	5	—	—	20
Carr, Allan	5 + 2	2	—	—	8
Carroll, Dean	8 + 1	—	9	2	20
Coulter, Gary	11 + 2	3	—	—	12
Eden, Phil	4	3	—	—	12
Ellis, Mark	18 + 3	5	—	—	20
Ellison, Mark	5	—	—	—	—
Evans, David	13	5	—	—	20
Evans, John	22 + 2	2	—	—	8
Firth, Steve	2 + 5	—	—	—	—
Fletcher, Ian	0 + 1	—	—	—	—
Grimoldby, Nick	4	—	—	—	—
Hall, Carl	11 + 3	6	—	—	24
Heptinstall, Jason	1 + 1	—	—	—	—
Hermansson, Terry	21 + 1	5	—	—	20
Holmes, David	5 + 2	—	—	—	—
Horton, Stewart	4	1	—	—	4
Idle, Graham	16 + 1	—	—	—	—
Jasiewicz, Dick	8 + 3	3	—	—	12
Jones, Kevin	2 + 1	1	4	—	12
Lord, Paul	3	3	—	—	12
Matautia, Vila	17 + 2	7	—	—	28
Miller, Tony	21 + 5	4	—	—	16
Noble, David	1 + 3	—	5	—	10
O'Hara, Dane	7	3	—	—	12
Pell, Richard	7	1	4	—	12
Pennant, Audley	27	8	—	—	32
Price, Darren	1	—	—	—	—
Rayne, Keith	7 + 2	—	—	—	—
Rayne, Kevin	16 + 2	—	—	—	—
Roache, Mark	20 + 3	12	—	—	48
Rowse, Martin	26	8	2	1	37
Sheldon, Ian	8 + 3	1	—	—	4
Smith, Mike	15	3	—	—	12
Tomlinson, Paul	1	—	—	—	—
Walton, Tony	17 + 7	4	—	—	16
Watkins, Darren	13	1	—	—	4
Zelei, Tony	25 + 2	10	68	1	177
TOTALS:					
40 players		111	92	4	632

*Long-serving Hull K.R. utility man Mike Smith,
who joined the Dons in August 1991 and scored three tries
in 15 appearances.*

DONCASTER 1991-92 MATCH ANALYSIS

Date	Competition	H/A	Opponent	Rlt	Score	Tries	Goals	Attendance	Referee
25.8.91	YC(P)	H	Scarborough P.	L	10-14	Lord, Smith	Carroll	1080	Volante
1.9.91	TD	H	Nottingham C.	W	88-6	Roache (4), Zelei (2), Eden (2), Lord (2), Miller, Rowse, Coulter, Bowes, Ellis, Walton	Zelei (12)	1049	J. Connolly
8.9.91	TD	A	Barrow	W	12-8	Zelei (2)	Carroll (2)	—	—
22.9.91	TD	H	Dewsbury	W	22-12	Bowes (2), Eden	Zelei (5)	1584	Redfearn
29.9.91	TD	A	Huddersfield	L	0-14	—	—	—	—
6.10.91	TD	H	Trafford B.	W	68-7	Matautia (3), Zelei (2), Coulter, Rowse, Hermansson, Miller, Bowes, Horton, Pennant	Zelei (10)	1127	Campbell
13.10.91	TD	A	Keighley C.	D	10-10	Pennant, Bowes	Zelei	—	—
20.10.91	TD	A	Whitehaven	W	16-12	J. Evans, Pennant	Zelei (4)	—	—
27.10.91	TD	H	Bramley	L	10-19	Walton	Zelei (3)	1571	Cummings
3.11.91	TD	H	Huddersfield	L	16-25	Pennant (2), Coulter	Zelei (2)	1725	Volante
10.11.91	TD	A	Dewsbury	L	2-24	—	Zelei	—	—
17.11.91	RT(1)	H	Whitehaven	W	21-20	Hall (2), Roache (2)	Carroll (2, 1dg)	693	Kershaw
25.11.91	RT(2)	A	Castleford	L	6-38	Hall	Carroll	—	—
1.12.91	TD	H	Chorley B.	W	19-1	Hermansson, Rowse, Hall	Carroll (3, 1dg)	1068	Crashley
8.12.91	TD	A	Batley	L	0-15	—	—	—	—
15.12.91	TD	H	Whitehaven	W	50-14	Hermansson (2), Smith, Sheldon, Roache, O'Hara, Pennant, Ellis, Armstrong, Miller	Zelei (5)	664	Whitelam
22.12.91	TD	A	Scarborough P.	L	6-14	Hermansson	Zelei	—	—
29.12.91	TD	A	Nottingham C.	W	42-20	O'Hara (2), Matautia, Walton, J. Evans, Zelei, Roache	Zelei (7)	—	—
5.1.92	TD	H	Keighley C.	L	12-14	Matautia, Ellis	Zelei (2)	1013	Gilmour
12.1.92	TD	A	Trafford B.	W	18-14	Jasiewicz, Matautia, Armstrong, D. Evans	Zelei	—	—
19.1.92	TD	H	Highfield	W	17-10	Ellis, Matautia, Hall	Zelei (2), Rowse (dg)	1048	Volante
2.2.92	CC(1)	H	Swinton	W	14-4	Pennant, Jasiewicz, Rowse	Zelei	1000	Carter
9.2.92	CC(2)	A	Halifax	L	8-66	Jasiewicz	Pell (2)	—	—
12.2.92	TD	H	Batley	W	20-10	Rowse (2), Pennant, Pell	Pell (2)	1047	Galtress
16.2.92	TD	A	Hunslet	L	32-33	D. Evans (2), Jones, Hall, Walton, Zelei	Jones (4)	—	—
1.3.92	TD	A	Bramley	L	8-38	Carr, Watkins	—	—	—
15.3.92	TD	H	Barrow	D	11-11	Zelei, Rowse	Zelei (1, 1dg)	1118	Gilmour
22.3.92	TD	A	Chorley B.	W	30-17	Roache, Rowse, Armstrong, Smith, D. Evans	Zelei (5)	—	—
29.3.92	TD	H	Scarborough P.	W	10-2	Carr	Rowse (2), Noble	1073	Tidball
5.4.92	TD	A	Highfield	W	28-8	Armstrong (2), D. Evans, Roache, Zelei	Noble (3), Zelei	—	—
12.4.92	TD	H	Hunslet	W	20-4	Ellis, Roache, Miller	Zelei (4)	968	Whitelam
21.4.92	DP(1)	A	Dewsbury	L	6-24	Roache	Noble	—	—

57

FEATHERSTONE ROVERS

Points: 2,654 by Steve Quinn, 1975-88
Appearances: 440 by Jim Denton, 1921-34
Highest score: 86-18 v. Keighley, 17 Sep 1989
Highest against: 70-2 at Halifax, 14 Apr 1941
Attendance: 17,531 v. St. Helens (RL Cup),
21 Mar 1959

Ground: Post Office Road (0977-702386)
Colours: Blue and white
First Season: 1921-22
Nickname: Colliers
Chairman: Eric Gardner
Secretary: Terry Jones
Coach: Peter Fox (May 1987-Oct 1991)
Allan Agar (Oct 1991-)
Honours: **Championship** Beaten finalists,
1927-28
Division One Champions, 1976-77
Division Two Champions, 1979-80
Challenge Cup Winners, 1966-67,
1972-73, 1982-83
Beaten finalists, 1951-52, 1973-74
Second Division Premiership
Beaten finalists, 1987-88
Yorkshire Cup Winners, 1939-40,
1959-60
Beaten finalists, 1928-29, 1963-64,
1966-67, 1969-70, 1970-71,
1976-77, 1977-78, 1989-90
Captain Morgan Trophy Beaten
finalists, 1973-74

RECORDS

Match
Goals: 13 by Mark Knapper v. Keighley,
17 Sep 1989
Tries: 6 by Mike Smith v. Doncaster,
13 Apr 1968
Chris Bibb v. Keighley, 17 Sep 1989
Points: 30 by Mark Knapper v. Keighley,
17 Sep 1989

Season
Goals: 163 by Steve Quinn, 1979-80
Tries: 31 by Cyril Woolford, 1958-59
Points: 375 by Steve Quinn, 1979-80

Career
Goals: 1,210 by Steve Quinn, 1975-88
Tries: 162 by Don Fox, 1953-66

COACHING REGISTER
● **Since 1974-75**

*Tommy Smales	July 74 - Sep 74
Keith Goulding	Sep 74 - Jan 76
†Tommy Smales	Feb 76 - May 76
Keith Cotton	June 76 - Dec 77
Keith Goulding	Dec 77 - May 78
Terry Clawson	July 78 - Nov 78
†Tommy Smales	Nov 78 - Apr 79
Paul Daley	May 79 - Jan 81
Vince Farrar	Feb 81 - Nov 82
Allan Agar	Dec 82 - Oct 85
George Pieniazek	Nov 85 - Nov 86
Paul Daley	Nov 86 - Apr 87
Peter Fox	May 87 - Oct 91
Allan Agar	Oct 91 -

Ex-forward
†*Ex-scrum half*

GREAT BRITAIN REGISTER
(15 players)

T. Askin	(6)	1928
C. Bibb	(1)	1990
K. Bridges	(3)	1974
T. Clawson	(2)	1962
M. Dixon	(2)	1962-64
S. Evans	(5 + 3)	1979-80
Deryck Fox	(9 + 4)	1985-92
Don Fox	(1)	1963
D. Hobbs	(7 + 1)	1984
G. Jordan	(2)	1964-67
A. Morgan	(4)	1968
S. Nash	(16)	1971-74
P. Newlove	(3 + 1)	1989-91
P. Smith	(1 + 5)	1977-84
J. Thompson	(19 + 1)	1970-77

1991-92 SIGNINGS REGISTER

Signed	Player	Club From
13.6.91	Agar, Richard	Travellers ARL
13.6.91	Bradbrook, Neil	Travellers ARL
1.7.91	Goulbourne, Alex	Northern Dairies ARL
1.7.91	Minter, Steve	Travellers ARL
1.7.91	Dickinson, Robert	Travellers ARL
1.7.91	Smelt, Roger	Travellers ARL
22.7.91	Wilson, Mark	Bradford N.
25.7.91	Child, Simon	Travellers ARL
7.9.91	*Moore, Darren	Halifax
1.10.91	Wilkinson, Darren	Cutsyke ARL
11.10.91	Butt, Tony	Leeds
28.12.91	Evans, Daniel	Travellers ARL
5.1.92	Fox, Martin	Dewsbury Albion ARL
5.3.92	Akaidere, Paul	Dewsbury Celtic ARL

1991-92 PLAYERS' SUMMARY

	App	Tries	Goals	Dr	Pts
Bastian, John	4	—	—	—	—
Bibb, Chris	36	11	—	—	44
Bonson, Paul	0 + 2	—	—	—	—
Booth, Craig	0 + 2	—	—	—	—
Booth, Glen	2 + 7	1	—	—	4
Burton, Chris	23 + 4	1	—	—	4
Butt, Ikram	36	21	—	—	84
Butt, Tony	1 + 1	—	—	—	—
Casey, Leo	18 + 3	—	—	—	—
Clark, Trevor	28	5	—	—	20
Fisher, Andy	25 + 4	6	—	—	24
Fox, Deryck	36	1	109	5	227
Gibbon, Mark	2 + 3	—	—	—	—
Goulbourne, Alex	2 + 1	—	—	—	—
Iti, Clarry	3	—	—	—	—
Jepson, John	1	—	—	—	—
Longstaff, Spencer	4 + 5	2	—	—	8
Manning, Terry	34 + 1	6	—	—	24
Newlove, Paul	32	25	—	—	100
Newlove, Shaun	0 + 1	—	—	—	—
Pearson, Martin	22 + 6	9	1	—	38
Price, Gary	14 + 6	2	—	—	8
Rose, Gary	35 + 1	—	—	—	—
Sharp, Tim	24 + 12	6	—	—	24
Simpson, Owen	36	23	—	—	92
Smales, Ian	26	6	—	—	24
Tuuta, Brendon	31 + 1	4	—	—	16
Whiteley, Lee	6	1	—	—	4

TOTALS:

	App	Tries	Goals	Dr	Pts
28 players		130	110	5	745

Representative Appearances 1991-92
Bibb — Yorkshire (1, 1t)
Bonson — GB Under-21 (2)
Fox — Britain (+2, 1t); Yorkshire (1, 1t, 1dg)
P. Newlove — Britain (1, 1t); GB Under-21 (3, 2t)
Pearson — GB Under-21 (3, 4t, 19g)
Smales — Yorkshire (1, 1t)

New Zealand Test import Brendon Tuuta, four tries in 32 games in 1991-92.

1990 British Lion Ian Smales, whose 26 games in 1991-92 produced six tries.

FEATHERSTONE ROVERS 1991-92 MATCH ANALYSIS

Date	Competition	H/A	Opponent	Rlt	Score	Tries	Goals	Attendance	Referee
1.9.91	SBC	A	Halifax	W	40-12	Simpson (2), I. Butt (2), Newlove, Bibb, Sharp	Fox (6)	—	—
8.9.91	SBC	H	Swinton	W	22-20	I. Butt, Clark, Sharp	Fox (5)	3273	Morris
15.9.91	YC(1)	H	Scarborough P.	W	30-7	Clark, Manning, Burton, Smales, Sharp	Fox (5)	2761	Asquith
22.9.91	SBC	A	Warrington	L	24-42	Clark, Tuuta, I. Butt, Manning	Fox (4)	—	—
25.9.91	YC(2)	A	Hull	D	16-16	Manning, I. Butt	Fox (4)	—	—
29.9.91	SBC	H	Bradford N.	W	22-8	Sharp, Fisher, Bibb	Fox (5)	3645	Carter
1.10.91	YC(2) Replay	H	Hull	W	21-18	Newlove (2), Simpson, I. Butt	Fox (2, 1dg)	3751	J. Smith
6.10.91	SBC	A	Wigan	L	10-52	Pearson, Fisher	Pearson	—	—
9.10.91	YC(SF)	A	Castleford	L	10-18	Bibb, I. Butt	Fox	—	—
13.10.91	SBC	H	Hull	L	12-40	Simpson, Newlove	Fox (2)	3641	Morris
20.10.91	SBC	A	Widnes	L	20-34	Simpson (2), Newlove, Bibb	Fox (2)	—	—
27.10.91	SBC	A	Castleford	L	20-22	Newlove (2), Booth	Fox (4)	—	—
3.11.91	SBC	H	Salford	L	22-27	Newlove, Simpson, I. Butt, Clark	Fox (3)	3280	Whitfield
10.11.91	SBC	A	Leeds	L	20-26	Simpson, I. Butt, Clark, Newlove	Fox (2)	—	—
19.11.91	RT(1)	A	Bramley	D	18-18	I. Butt, Pearson, Tuuta, Simpson	Fox	—	—
21.11.91	RT(1) Replay	H	Bramley	W	44-8	I. Butt (2), Pearson, Bibb, Longstaff, Sharp, Newlove, Fisher	Fox (6)	1617	J. Smith
24.11.91	RT(2)	H	Halifax	W	64-18	Pearson (4), Simpson (3), Newlove (2), Bibb, Tuuta	Fox (10)	5462	Whitfield
1.12.91	RT(3)	A	Widnes	L	22-34	Fox, Newlove, Simpson, I. Butt	Fox (3)	—	—
4.12.91	SBC	H	St. Helens	W	8-6	Newlove	Fox (2)	3473	Burke
8.12.91	SBC	A	Hull	L	14-30	I. Butt, Smales, Simpson	Fox	—	—
26.12.91	SBC	H	Wakefield T.	L	10-18	Simpson, I. Butt	Fox	5227	Holdsworth
5.1.92	SBC	H	Halifax	W	26-14	Price (2), Fisher, Simpson	Fox (5)	3458	Galtress
12.1.92	SBC	A	St. Helens	L	10-28	Newlove	Fox (3)	—	—
19.1.92	SBC	A	Hull K.R.	L	6-24	Smales	Fox	—	—
26.1.92	CC(1)	A	Batley	W	36-20	Newlove (3), Sharp, Bibb, Simpson	Fox (6)	—	—
9.2.92	CC(2)	A	Dewsbury	W	23-10	Bibb (2), Longstaff, Newlove	Fox (3, 1dg)	—	—
16.2.92	SBC	A	Salford	L	4-26	Simpson	—	—	—
23.2.92	CC(3)	A	Castleford	L	12-19	I. Butt (2)	Fox (2)	—	—
26.2.92	SBC	H	Warrington	W	29-6	Simpson, Newlove, Fisher, Smales, I. Butt	Fox (4, 1dg)	3310	J. Smith
1.3.92	SBC	H	Hull K.R.	W	12-7	Manning, Bibb	Fox (2)	3837	Morris
11.3.92	SBC	A	Bradford N.	L	4-22	Manning	—	—	—
17.3.92	SBC	H	Castleford	W	24-16	Simpson (2), Newlove, Bibb, I. Butt	Fox (2)	5235	Campbell
22.3.92	SBC	A	Swinton	W	18-6	Simpson (2), I. Butt	Fox (3)	—	—
29.3.92	SBC	H	Widnes	W	28-2	Newlove (2), Pearson (2), Smales, I. Butt	Fox (2)	3438	Holdsworth
5.4.92	SBC	H	Wigan	L	13-34	Manning, Fisher	Fox (2, 1dg)	5096	Galtress
12.4.92	SBC	H	Leeds	W	21-20	Newlove (2), Smales	Fox (4, 1dg)	5113	Cummings
20.4.92	SBC	A	Wakefield T.	L	10-28	Whiteley, Tuuta	Fox	—	—

HALIFAX

Ground: Thrum Hall (0422-361026)
Colours: Blue and white
First Season: 1895-96
Nickname: Thrum Hallers
Secretary: David Fleming
Coach: Roger Millward (May 1991-)
Honours: **Championship** Winners, 1906-07,
               1964-65
               Beaten finalists, 1952-53, 1953-54,
               1955-56, 1965-66
               War League Beaten finalists,
               1942-43, 1944-45
               Division One Champions, 1902-03,
               1985-86
               Challenge Cup Winners, 1902-03,
               1903-04, 1930-31, 1938-39, 1986-87
               Beaten finalists, 1920-21, 1940-41,
               1941-42, 1948-49, 1953-54, 1955-56,
               1987-88
               Regal Trophy Winners, 1971-72
               Beaten finalists, 1989-90
               Premiership Trophy Beaten
               finalists, 1985-86
               Second Division Premiership
               Beaten finalists, 1990-91
               Yorkshire Cup Winners, 1908-09,
               1944-45, 1954-55, 1955-56, 1963-64
               Beaten finalists, 1905-06, 1907-08,
               1941-42, 1979-80
               Yorkshire League Winners,
               1908-09, 1920-21, 1952-53, 1953-54,
               1955-56, 1957-58
               Eastern Division Championship
               Winners, 1963-64
               Charity Shield Winners, 1986-87
               Beaten finalists, 1987-88

RECORDS

Match
Goals: 14 by Bruce Burton v. Hunslet, 27 Aug 1972
Tries: 8 by Keith Williams v. Dewsbury,
         9 Nov 1957
Points: 31 by Bruce Burton v. Hunslet, 27 Aug 1972

Season
Goals: 147 by Tysul Griffiths, 1955-56
Tries: 48 by Johnny Freeman, 1956-57
Points: 298 by Colin Whitfield, 1986-87

Career
Goals: 1,028 by Ron James, 1960-72
Tries: 290 by Johnny Freeman, 1954-67
Points: 2,191 by Ron James, 1960-72
Appearances: 481 by Stan Kielty, 1946-58
Highest score: 82-8 v. Runcorn H., 14 Oct 1990
Highest against: 64-0 at Wigan, 7 Mar 1923
Attendance: 29,153 v. Wigan (RL Cup),
               21 Mar 1959

COACHING REGISTER
● **Since 1974-75**

Derek Hallas	Aug 74 - Oct 74
Les Pearce	Oct 74 - Apr 76
Alan Kellett	May 76 - Apr 77
Jim Crellin	June 77 - Oct 77
Harry Fox	Oct 77 - Feb 78
Maurice Bamford	Feb 78 - May 80
Mick Blacker	June 80 - June 82
Ken Roberts	June 82 - Sep 82
Colin Dixon	Sep 82 - Nov 84
Chris Anderson	Nov 84 - May 88
Graham Eadie	May 88 - Aug 88
Ross Strudwick	Aug 88 - Feb 89
Alan Hardisty	Feb 89 - Apr 89
John Dorahy	June 89 - Aug 90
Peter Roe	Aug 90 - May 91
Roger Millward	May 91 -

GREAT BRITAIN REGISTER
(30 players)

A. Ackerley	(2)	1952-58
A. Bassett	(2)	1946
J. Beames	(2)	1921
N. Bentham	(2)	1929
H. Beverley	(2)	1937
O. Burgham	(1)	1911
A. Daniels	(3)	1952-55
W. T. Davies	(1)	1911

C. Dixon	(1)	1968
P. Dixon	(3+3)	1987-88
P. Eccles	(1)	1907
T. Fogerty	(+1)	1966
A. Halmshaw	(1)	1971
K. Harrison	(1)	1991
N. James	(1)	1986
R. Lloyd	(1)	1920
A. Milnes	(2)	1920
S. Prosser	(1)	1914
D. Rees	(1)	1926

C. Renilson	(7+1)	1965-68
J. Riley	(1)	1910
K. Roberts	(10)	1963-66
A. Robinson	(3)	1907-08
D. Schofield	(1)	1955
J. Shaw	(5)	1960-62
J. C. Stacey	(1)	1920
J. Thorley	(4)	1954
J. Wilkinson	(6)	1954-55
F. Williams	(2)	1914
D. Willicombe	(1)	1974

Irish-born hooker Seamus McCallion, only two appearances in 1991-92.

New Zealand Test star Dave Watson, scorer of 16 tries in 32 games in 1991-92.

HALIFAX

1991-92 SIGNINGS REGISTER

Signed	Player	Club From
11.6.91	Preston, Mark	Wigan
13.6.91	Rhodes, Paul	Bradford N.
8.8.91	Harrison, Karl	Hull
12.8.91	Harkin, Paul	Leeds
20.8.91	Boston, William	St. Patricks ARL
5.9.91	Fogerty, Adam	—
12.9.91	Fieldhouse, John	Oldham
18.9.91	Perrett, Mark	Ovenden ARL
20.9.91	Pearce, Greg	London C.
1.10.91	*Roberts, Mark	Warrington
10.10.91	Pickles, Damien	Siddal ARL
15.10.91	Lord, Gary	Leeds
5.12.91	*Warrener, Stan	Hunslet
20.12.91	*Mountain, Gary	Huddersfield
17.1.92	Turner, Craig	Siddal ARL
28.2.92	Cooper, David	Bradford N.
4.3.92	Bailey, Mark	St. Helens
25.3.92	Tiffany, Richard	Dudley Hill ARL
9.4.92	Platt, Carl	Seddon Panthers ARL

1991-92 PLAYERS' SUMMARY

	App	Tries	Goals	Dr	Pts
Austin, Greg	33	33	1	—	134
Bailey, Mark	4 + 1	2	—	—	8
Bell, Peter	9 + 4	1	—	—	4
Brooke-Cowden, Mark	0 + 1	—	—	—	—
Cooper, David	8	2	22	1	53
Fieldhouse, John	24	5	—	—	20
Fogerty, Adam	21 + 2	5	—	—	20
George, Wilf	3	—	—	—	—
Hancock, Andy	0 + 2	—	—	—	—
Harkin, Paul	28	1	—	—	4
Harrison, Karl	32	2	—	—	8
Hill, Brendan	10 + 2	1	—	—	4
Hutchinson, Rob	21 + 9	6	—	—	24
Irvine, Jimmy	16 + 10	5	—	—	20
Keebles, Mick	0 + 2	—	—	—	—
Lord, Gary	27	3	—	—	12
McCallion, Seamus	2	—	—	—	—
Milner, Richard	19 + 13	4	4	—	24
Pearce, Greg	21 + 2	5	81	—	182
Perrett, Mark	0 + 1	—	—	—	—
Preston, Mark	32	27	—	—	108
Ramshaw, Jason	1 + 3	—	—	—	—
Rhodes, Paul	2 + 1	—	—	—	—
Richardson, Gary	9	3	—	—	12
Robinson, Chris	4	—	—	—	—
Sharp, Henry	17 + 2	7	—	—	28
Silva, Matthew	1 + 1	—	1	—	2
Smith, Steve	4 + 1	1	—	—	4
Southernwood, Roy	25	4	—	1	17
Turner, Craig	0 + 2	1	—	—	4
Watson, Dave	32	16	—	—	64
Wilson, Warren	22	7	—	—	28
Wood, Martin	2 + 1	—	2	—	4

TOTALS:

33 players		141	111	2	788

Representative Appearances 1991-92
Harrison — Britain (1)
Silva — Wales (+1)

Scrum half Paul Harkin, recruited from Leeds in August 1991, appointed skipper and scorer of one try in 28 outings.

HALIFAX 1991-92 MATCH ANALYSIS

Date	Competition	H/A	Opponent	Rlt	Score	Tries	Goals	Attendance	Referee
1.9.91	SBC	H	Featherstone R.	L	12-40	Preston, Austin	Wood (2)	7894	Galtress
8.9.91	SBC	A	Hull K.R.	L	16-24	Preston, Irvine, Southernwood	Milner (2)	—	—
15.9.91	YC(1)	H	Wakefield T.	L	18-24	Milner, Fieldhouse, Bell, Watson	Milner	6132	Holdsworth
22.9.91	SBC	H	Wakefield T.	W	28-18	Hutchinson, Harrison, Preston, Austin, Irvine	Pearce (4)	6514	Carter
6.10.91	SBC	H	St. Helens	W	26-6	Austin (2), Wilson, Watson	Pearce (5)	7931	Holdsworth
13.10.91	SBC	A	Salford	L	14-34	Preston, Watson	Pearce (2), Silva	—	—
20.10.91	SBC	H	Hull K.R.	W	76-8	Austin (5), Preston (4), Hutchinson (2), Southernwood, Watson, Sharp	Pearce (10)	6019	Tennant
27.10.91	SBC	A	Wigan	L	18-40	Sharp, Preston, Austin	Pearce (3)	—	—
3.11.91	SBC	H	Widnes	W	28-14	Austin (2), Watson, Preston, Southernwood	Pearce (4)	7376	Galtress
10.11.91	SBC	A	Castleford	W	22-16	Southernwood, Pearce, Austin, Preston	Pearce (3)	—	—
17.11.91	RT(1)	H	Barrow	W	46-4	Austin (3), Lord (2), Preston, Hill, Wilson	Pearce (7)	4791	Kendrew
24.11.91	RT(2)	A	Featherstone R.	L	18-64	Hutchinson, Austin, Preston	Pearce (3)	—	—
1.12.91	SBC	H	Hull	L	10-20	Watson	Pearce (3)	6359	Ollerton
8.12.91	SBC	A	Warrington	L	14-38	Preston, Wilson, Richardson	Milner	—	—
15.12.91	SBC	H	Salford	W	29-12	Pearce (2), Harrison, Sharp, Hutchinson, Richardson	Pearce (2), Southernwood (dg)	5573	J. Connolly
26.12.91	SBC	A	Bradford N.	L	8-14	Fogerty, Austin	—	—	—
1.1.92	SBC	H	Bradford N.	L	18-26	Pearce, Preston, Fogerty	Pearce (3)	9490	Campbell
5.1.92	SBC	A	Featherstone R.	L	14-26	Richardson, Watson, Preston	Pearce	—	—
12.1.92	SBC	A	Swinton	W	32-4	Austin (3), Watson, Fogerty, Irvine	Pearce (4)	—	—
19.1.92	SBC	H	Wigan	L	10-30	Preston, Smith	Austin	9742	Holdsworth
26.1.92	CC(1)	H	Hull K.R.	W	12-8	Preston, Watson	Pearce (2)	5982	Whitfield
9.2.92	CC(2)	H	Doncaster	W	66-8	Fieldhouse (2), Irvine (2), Austin (2), Pearce, Watson, Fogerty, Wilson, Preston	Pearce (11)	5962	R. Smith
16.2.92	SBC	H	Swinton	W	58-10	Watson (4), Austin (3), Preston (2), Milner	Pearce (9)	4937	Cummings
23.2.92	CC(3)	H	Bradford N.	L	4-12	Wilson	—	9537	R. Smith
26.2.92	SBC	A	Hull	L	10-34	Preston, Turner	Pearce	—	—
1.3.92	SBC	A	Widnes	L	8-18	Wilson	Cooper (2)	—	—
8.3.92	SBC	A	Wakefield T.	W	19-14	Preston, Austin, Wilson	Cooper (3, 1dg)	—	—
15.3.92	SBC	H	Warrington	W	38-20	Austin (2), Lord, Watson, Sharp, Fogerty, Hutchinson	Cooper (5)	6163	Galtress
22.3.92	SBC	A	St. Helens	L	28-30	Fieldhouse (2), Austin, Milner, Bailey	Cooper (4)	—	—
12.4.92	SBC	H	Castleford	W	24-8	Austin (2), Sharp, Watson, Bailey	Cooper (2)	6506	Volante
17.4.92	SBC	A	Leeds	W	24-16	Preston (2), Cooper, Sharp	Pearce (3), Cooper	—	—
20.4.92	SBC	H	Leeds	L	34-46	Preston (2), Cooper, Milner, Sharp, Austin	Cooper (5)	9016	Whitfield
26.4.92	PT(1)	A	St. Helens	L	6-52	Harkin	Pearce	—	—

HIGHFIELD

Ground: Hoghton Road (0744-812817)
Colours: Yellow, red, green and black
First Season: 1922-23 as Wigan Highfield.
Became London Highfield in
1933-34. Became Liverpool Stanley
in 1934-35 and changed to
Liverpool City in 1951-52. Became
Huyton in 1968-69 and changed to
Runcorn Highfield in 1984-85.
Became Highfield in 1991-92.
Chairman: Terry Hughes
Secretary: Phil Thomas
Coach: Chris Arkwright (Apr 1991-Aug 1991)
Willie Johnson (Aug 1991-)
Honours: **Lancashire League** Winners,
1935-36

RECORDS

Match
Goals: 11 by Peter Wood v. Batley, 21 Oct 1984
Tries: 5 by John Maloney v. Bramley,
25 Apr 1931
Points: 30 by Norman Barrow v. Keighley,
31 Mar 1991

Season
Goals: 126 by Peter Wood, 1984-85
Tries: 28 by John Maloney, 1930-31
Points: 240 by Peter Wood, 1984-85

Career
Goals: 304 by Wilf Hunt, 1955-66
Tries: 204 by John Maloney, 1926-45
Points: 731 by Wilf Hunt, 1955-66
Appearances: 413 by John Maloney, 1926-45
Highest score: 59-11 v. Bramley, 4 May 1934
Highest against: 92-2 v. Wigan, 13 Nov 1988
92-0 v. Rochdale H., 5 Nov 1989
Attendance: 18,000 v. Wigan (League),
2 Sep 1922 — at Tunstall Lane,
Pemberton
1,600 v. Halifax (League),
6 Jan 1991 — at Hoghton Road

COACHING REGISTER
● **Since 1974-75**

Terry Gorman	Aug 74 - May 77
Geoff Fletcher	Aug 77 - June 86
Frank Wilson	July 86 - Nov 86
Arthur Daley ⎫	Nov 86 - Apr 87
Paul Woods ⎭	
Bill Ashurst	Apr 87 - Jan 89
John Cogger	Jan 89 - Feb 89
Geoff Fletcher	Feb 89 - Apr 89
Dave Chisnall	June 89 - Oct 90
Alan Bishop	Oct 90 - Apr 91
Chris Arkwright	Apr 91 - Aug 91
Willie Johnson	Aug 91 -

GREAT BRITAIN REGISTER
(4 players)

R. Ashby	(1)	1964
W. Belshaw	(6)	1936-37
N. Bentham	(6)	1928
H. Woods	(5)	1936

Welsh international Frank Wilson, coach of Runcorn Highfield for four months during 1986.

1991-92 SIGNINGS REGISTER

Signed	Player	Club From
25.7.91	Chappell, Simon	Aus
29.8.91	Burrows, Alan	St. Helens
1.9.91	*Haggerty, Gary	Wakefield T.
22.9.91	Fanning, Sean	Hare and Hounds ARL
10.10.91	Litherland, Roy	Pilkington Recs. ARL
29.10.91	Twist, Bobby	Leigh Victoria ARL
6.12.91	*Frodsham, Tommy	St. Helens
31.12.91	Tuavao, Harmon	Tonga
2.1.92	Hulse, John	Ashton Fleece ARL
28.2.92	Rushton, Andy	St. Cuthberts ARL
12.3.92	Atherton, Darren	Smithy Manor ARL
12.3.92	Pimblett, Brian	St. Anne ARL
12.3.92	Hancock, Mick	Swinton
20.3.92	Langley, Tony	Clock Face ARL
20.3.92	Pojunas, David	Parkside ARL

1991-92 PLAYERS' SUMMARY

	App	Tries	Goals	Dr	Pts
Arkwright, Chris	1 + 1	—	—	—	—
Ashcroft, Simon	27	20	—	—	80
Atherton, Darren	0 + 1	—	—	—	—
Barrow, Norman	20 + 3	6	33	—	90
Barrow, Shaun	25	7	—	—	28
Beckett, Peter	2 + 5	—	—	—	—
Burrows, Alan	20 + 2	3	—	—	12
Chappell, Simon	29	14	—	—	56
Cooney, Paul	23 + 3	2	24	1	57
Dean, Geoff	20 + 1	1	—	—	4
Dolan, Shaun	26 + 1	5	—	—	20
Frodsham, Tommy	4	—	—	—	—
Goodier, Frank	7 + 1	1	—	—	4
Goulding, Dean	7 + 8	—	1	—	2
Haggerty, Gary	10	1	—	—	4
Hancock, Mick	1	—	—	—	—
Hine, David	11	—	—	—	—
Hulse, John	0 + 2	—	—	—	—
Johnson, Willie	26	3	1	2	16
Langley, Tony	3	—	—	—	—
Latu, Patelesio	8 + 2	5	—	—	20
Litherland, Roy	0 + 1	—	—	—	—
Littler, Paul	20 + 5	2	—	—	8
Pimblett, Brian	1 + 1	1	—	—	4
Platt, Brian	7 + 3	1	—	—	4
Rawlinson, Tommy	11	—	—	—	—
Rushton, Andy	2 + 2	—	—	—	—
Southward, Phil	18 + 7	—	—	—	—
Tinsley, Eddie	18 + 4	—	—	—	—
Tuavao, Bob	19 + 3	4	—	—	16
Tuavao, Harmon	6	—	—	—	—
Twist, Bobby	18	6	—	—	24

TOTALS:

	App	Tries	Goals	Dr	Pts
32 players		82	59	3	449

Highfield's Eddie Tinsley powers towards the Dewsbury rearguard, supported by Gary Haggerty in the October 1991 Third Division clash at Hoghton Road.

HIGHFIELD 1991-92 MATCH ANALYSIS

Date	Competition	H/A	Opponent	Rlt	Score	Tries	Goals	Attendance	Referee
1.9.91	TD	H	Trafford B.	W	29-14	S. Barrow (3), Latu	Cooney (6), Johnson (dg)	380	Redfearn
8.9.91	TD	A	Whitehaven	W	24-12	Latu (2), Ashcroft	Cooney (6)	—	—
15.9.91	LC(1)	H	Rochdale H.	L	11-34	Johnson, Ashcroft	Cooney (1, 1dg)	700	Cummings
22.9.91	TD	H	Keighley C.	L	18-28	Dolan, Chappell, Dean	Cooney (3)	350	Allatt
30.9.91	TD	A	Barrow	L	10-18	Chappell, Burrows	N. Barrow	—	—
6.10.91	TD	H	Dewsbury	L	14-38	Ashcroft (2), Latu	N. Barrow	350	Steele
13.10.91	TD	A	Huddersfield	L	16-32	Ashcroft (2), Chappell	Cooney, N. Barrow	—	—
23.10.91	TD	A	Hunslet	L	10-36	Ashcroft, S. Barrow	N. Barrow	—	—
27.10.91	TD	H	Batley	L	11-16	S. Barrow, Dolan	N. Barrow, Johnson (dg)	330	Allatt
3.11.91	TD	H	Nottingham C.	W	36-10	B. Tuavao, Chappell, Twist, Ashcroft, Cooney, N. Barrow, Latu	N. Barrow (4)	175	J. Connolly
10.11.91	TD	A	Keighley C.	L	14-42	Twist, Dolan, S. Barrow	Goulding	—	—
17.11.91	RT(1)	H	Carlisle	L	10-28	Ashcroft (2)	Cooney	180	Volante
1.12.91	TD	H	Barrow	L	14-26	Burrows (2), Ashcroft	Johnson	175	Tidball
8.12.91	TD	A	Nottingham C.	W	20-13	Chappell, Ashcroft, N. Barrow, Goodier	Cooney (2)	—	—
15.12.91	TD	H	Huddersfield	L	12-46	B. Tuavao, S. Barrow	Cooney (2)	803	Carter
5.1.92	TD	H	Scarborough P.	L	12-22	Ashcroft (2), Twist	—	193	Kendrew
12.1.92	TD	A	Batley	L	8-22	Chappell	N. Barrow (2)	—	—
19.1.92	TD	A	Doncaster	L	10-17	Chappell (2)	N. Barrow	—	—
2.2.92	CC(1)	H	London C.	D	12-12	Twist, Ashcroft	N. Barrow (2)	230	Gilmour
4.2.92	CC(1) Replay	A	London C.	L	10-24	Twist, Chappell	N. Barrow	—	—
9.2.92	TD	H	Whitehaven	W	34-26	Ashcroft (3), Chappell (2), N. Barrow	N. Barrow (5)	235	Kershaw
16.2.92	TD	A	Trafford B.	W	20-8	Ashcroft, B. Tuavao, Johnson	N. Barrow (4)	—	—
23.2.92	TD	H	Chorley B.	W	14-8	Chappell, N. Barrow, Ashcroft	N. Barrow (2)	293	Cross
1.3.92	TD	A	Dewsbury	L	6-48	Chappell	Cooney	—	—
8.3.92	TD	H	Bramley	L	6-36	Littler	N. Barrow	269	Redfearn
15.3.92	TD	H	Hunslet	L	20-48	N. Barrow, Dolan, B. Tuavao, Haggerty	N. Barrow (2)	300	Burke
22.3.92	TD	A	Bramley	L	6-28	Johnson	N. Barrow	—	—
29.3.92	TD	A	Chorley B.	W	16-10	Pimblett, Twist, Dolan	N. Barrow (2)	—	—
5.4.92	TD	H	Doncaster	L	8-28	Cooney, Platt	—	300	Cross
12.4.92	TD	A	Scarborough P.	W	18-14	N. Barrow, Littler, Chappell	N. Barrow (2), Cooney	—	—

Simon Chappell touches down against Keighley Cougars in September 1991, one of his season's tally of 14 in 29 games.

HUDDERSFIELD

Ground:	Fartown (0484-530710)
Colours:	Claret and gold
First Season:	1895-96; added Barracudas to title from 1984-85 to 1987-88 inclusive
Nickname:	Fartowners
Chairman:	Joe Bramley
Secretary:	David Parker
Coach:	Mick Blacker and Francis Jarvis (Feb 1991-Sep 1991)
	Alex Murphy (Sep 1991-)
Honours:	**Championship** Winners, 1911-12, 1912-13, 1914-15, 1928-29, 1929-30, 1948-49, 1961-62

Championship Winners, 1911-12, 1912-13, 1914-15, 1928-29, 1929-30, 1948-49, 1961-62
Beaten finalists, 1913-14, 1919-20, 1922-23, 1931-32, 1945-46, 1949-50
Division Two Champions, 1974-75
Division Three Champions, 1991-92
Challenge Cup Winners, 1912-13, 1914-15, 1919-20, 1932-33, 1944-45, 1952-53
Beaten finalists, 1934-35, 1961-62
Yorkshire Cup Winners, 1909-10, 1911-12, 1913-14, 1914-15, 1918-19, 1919-20, 1926-27, 1931-32, 1938-39, 1950-51, 1952-53, 1957-58
Beaten finalists, 1910-11, 1923-24, 1925-26, 1930-31, 1937-38, 1942-43, 1949-50, 1960-61
Yorkshire League Winners, 1911-12, 1912-13, 1913-14, 1914-15, 1919-20, 1921-22, 1928-29, 1929-30, 1948-49, 1949-50, 1951-52
Eastern Division Beaten finalists, 1962-63

RECORDS

Match
Goals: 18 by Major Holland v. Swinton Park, 28 Feb 1914
Tries: 10 by Lionel Cooper v. Keighley, 17 Nov 1951
Points: 39 by Major Holland v. Swinton Park, 28 Feb 1914

Season
Goals: 147 by Ben Gronow, 1919-20
Tries: 80 by Albert Rosenfeld, 1913-14
Points: 332 by Pat Devery, 1952-53
Career
Goals: 958 by Frank Dyson, 1950-63
Tries: 420 by Lionel Cooper, 1947-55
Points: 2,072 by Frank Dyson, 1950-63
Appearances: 485 by Doug Clark, 1909-29
Highest score: 119-2 v. Swinton Park, 28 Feb 1914
Highest against: 94-12 at Castleford, 18 Sep 1988
Attendance: 35,136 Leeds v. Wakefield T. (RL Cup SF), 19 Apr 1947
Home match: 32,912 v. Wigan (League), 4 Mar 1950

COACHING REGISTER
● **Since 1974-75**

Brian Smith	Jan 73 - Mar 76
Keith Goulding	Mar 76 - Dec 76
Bob Tomlinson	Jan 77 - May 77
Neil Fox	June 77 - Feb 78
★Roy Francis	-
Keith Goulding	May 78 - July 79
Ian Brooke	July 79 - Mar 80
Maurice Bamford	May 80 - May 81
Les Sheard	June 81 - Nov 82
Dave Mortimer	Nov 82 - Aug 83
Mel Bedford	Aug 83 - Nov 83
Brian Lockwood	Nov 83 - Feb 85
Chris Forster	Feb 85 - Dec 86
Jack Addy	Jan 87 - Mar 88
Allen Jones ⎱ Neil Whittaker ⎰	Mar 88 - Nov 88
Nigel Stephenson	Nov 88 - Mar 90
Barry Seabourne	Mar 90 - Feb 91
Mick Blacker ⎱ Francis Jarvis ⎰	Feb 91 - Sep 91
Alex Murphy	Sep 91 -

★Although Roy Francis was appointed he was unable to take over and Dave Heppleston stood in until the next appointment.

GREAT BRITAIN REGISTER
(24 players)

J. Bowden	(3)	1954
K. Bowman	(3)	1962-63
B. Briggs	(1)	1954
S. Brogden	(9)	1929-33
J. Chilcott	(3)	1914
D. Clark	(11)	1911-20
D. Close	(1)	1967
R. Cracknell	(2)	1951
J. Davies	(2)	1911
F. Dyson	(1)	1959
B. Gronow	(7)	1911-20
F. Longstaff	(2)	1914
K. Loxton	(1)	1971
S. Moorhouse	(2)	1914
R. Nicholson	(3)	1946-48
J. Rogers	(7)	1914-21
K. Senior	(2)	1965-67
T. Smales	(5)	1962-64
M. Sullivan	(16)	1954-57
G. Thomas	(8)	1920-21
D. Valentine	(15)	1948-54
R. Valentine	(1)	1967
H. Wagstaff	(12)	1911-21
H. Young	(1)	1929

Huddersfield packman Chris Parr in action for Great Britain Under-21s against Papua New Guinea at Leeds in November 1991.

1991-92 SIGNINGS REGISTER

Signed	Player	Club From
25.6.91	Darkes, Richard	Deighton ARL
8.8.91	*Kemp, Martin	Halifax
20.8.91	Roe, Dean	Green Man ARL
20.8.91	Southern, Roy	Jubilee ARL
22.8.91	*Willis, Chris	Nottingham C.
6.9.91	Westbury, Mark	Dewsbury
6.9.91	Smith, Jonathan	Idle ARL
7.9.91	Walker, Paul	Greetland ARL
26.9.91	Fogerty, Jason	—
10.10.91	Wilde, Darran	St. Patricks ARL
18.10.91	Gilbert, Jason	Wainuiemata, NZ
31.10.91	Pearson, Richard	Ovenden ARL
2.11.91	Lomax, Arnold	Wainuiemata, NZ
5.12.91	Kebbie, Brimah	St. Helens
12.12.91	Marriott, John	Underbank ARL
30.1.92	Maders, Martin	Saddleworth R. ARL
11.2.92	Walton, Dean	Wakefield T.
5.3.92	*Stewart, Michael	Trafford B.

1991-92 PLAYERS' SUMMARY

	App	Tries	Goals	Dr	Pts
Boothroyd, Alan	19	2	—	—	8
Chapman, Chris	30	17	—	—	68
Cocker, Stuart	22	22	—	—	88
Coulter, Gary	10 + 1	3	—	—	12
Darkes, Richard	2 + 1	—	—	—	—
Edwards, Anthony	21 + 5	8	—	—	32
Fogerty, Jason	18 + 1	2	—	—	8
Gibson, Wally	26	20	—	1	81
Gilbert, Jason	16 + 1	5	70	—	160
Huck, Phil	30 + 1	4	—	—	16
Jowett, Bob	3 + 1	—	—	—	—
Kebbie, Brimah	17	16	—	—	64
Kenworthy, Simon	31 + 2	6	70	1	165
Lomax, Arnold	16	5	—	—	20
Maskery, Mark	4 + 1	—	1	—	2
Meillam, Paul	3 + 1	1	—	—	4
Naidole, Joe	14 + 14	8	—	—	32
Neilson, Scott	3	—	—	—	—
Oates, David	14 + 14	7	3	—	34
Parr, Chris	17 + 2	2	—	—	8
Royston, Paul	0 + 2	—	—	—	—
St. Hilaire, Lee	0 + 1	—	—	—	—
Scholes, Damon	1 + 2	—	—	—	—
Senior, Gary	33	12	—	—	48
Sewell, Andy	1 + 7	—	—	—	—
Shuttleworth, Greg	33	13	—	5	57
Simpson, Frank	0 + 1	—	—	—	—
Southern, Roy	0 + 2	—	—	—	—
Stewart, Michael	5	1	—	—	4
Thomas, Ian	24 + 2	18	—	—	72
Walker, Stuart	3 + 1	—	—	—	—
White, Brendan	9 + 2	—	—	—	—
Wilde, Darran	1	1	—	—	4
Willis, Chris	3 + 1	—	—	—	—

TOTALS:					
34 players		173	144	7	987

Representative Appearances 1991-92
Parr — GB Under-21 (1)

HUDDERSFIELD 1991-92 MATCH ANALYSIS

Date	Com- petition	H/A	Opponent	Rlt	Score	Tries	Goals	Atten- dance	Referee
25.8.91	YC(P)	A	Nottingham C.	W	36-7	Kenworthy (3), Parr, Edwards, Naidole	Kenworthy (6)	—	—
1.9.91	TD	A	Scarborough P.	W	22-18	Thomas (2), Chapman, Oates	Oates (2), Kenworthy	—	—
9.9.91	TD	H	Batley	L	19-20	Shuttleworth, Thomas, Chapman	Kenworthy (2), Oates, Shuttleworth (dg)	2117	Kendrew
15.9.91	YC(1)	H	Ryedale-York	W	28-10	Thomas (2), Boothroyd, Naidole, Meillam	Kenworthy (4)	1387	Tennant
22.9.91	TD	A	Bramley	W	14-9	Gibson, Naidole	Kenworthy (3)	—	—
25.9.91	YC(2)	H	Wakefield T.	L	9-52	Thomas, Chapman	Shuttleworth (dg)	4799	Kershaw
29.9.91	TD	H	Doncaster	W	14-0	Edwards, Gibson	Kenworthy (2), Maskery	1489	Whitelam
6.10.91	TD	A	Whitehaven	W	36-18	Naidole (2), Edwards, Cocker, Chapman, Gibson, Oates	Kenworthy (4)	—	—
13.10.91	TD	H	Highfield	W	32-16	Senior (2), Chapman, Naidole, Wilde, Kenworthy	Kenworthy (4)	1429	Burke
20.10.91	TD	A	Batley	L	12-28	Thomas (2)	Gilbert (2)	—	—
27.10.91	TD	H	Trafford B.	W	70-0	Gibson (4), Shuttleworth (2), Senior (2), Huck, Chapman, Lomax, Thomas	Gilbert (11)	1311	R. Smith
3.11.91	TD	A	Doncaster	W	25-16	Gibson, Edwards, Gilbert	Gilbert (6), Gibson (dg)	—	—
10.11.91	TD	H	Bramley	W	21-6	Shuttleworth (2), Senior	Gilbert (4), Shuttleworth (dg)	1837	Tidball
17.11.91	RT(1)	H	St. Helens	L	10-32	Shuttleworth, Gibson	Gilbert	4239	Whitfield
1.12.91	TD	A	Trafford B.	W	78-4	Cocker (4), Lomax (2), Shuttleworth (2), Edwards (2), Chapman (2), Senior, Naidole, Huck	Gilbert (9)	—	—
8.12.91	TD	H	Dewsbury	W	13-4	Chapman, Senior	Gilbert (2), Shuttleworth (dg)	3263	Volante
15.12.91	TD	A	Highfield	W	46-12	Chapman (2), Gibson (2), Kebbie, Parr, Fogerty, Naidole, Thomas, Gilbert	Gilbert (3)	—	—
29.12.91	TD	H	Scarborough P.	W	36-9	Shuttleworth (2), Cocker (2), Senior, Huck	Kenworthy (4), Gilbert (2)	3489	Kershaw
12.1.92	CC(P)	A	Wakefield T.	L	18-32	Cocker, Kebbie, Gibson	Gilbert (3)	—	—
20.1.92	TD	A	Hunslet	W	30-6	Gilbert, Cocker, Senior, Kebbie	Gilbert (7)	—	—
2.2.92	TD	H	Chorley B.	W	46-8	Cocker (3), Kebbie (2), Gilbert, Senior, Gibson, Lomax	Gilbert (5)	1891	R. Connolly
5.2.92	TD	A	Chorley B.	W	26-9	Thomas, Kebbie, Lomax, Oates	Gilbert (5)	—	—
9.2.92	TD	H	Nottingham C.	W	78-0	Cocker (4), Kebbie (4), Coulter (2), Thomas (2), Kenworthy, Senior, Gibson	Gilbert (9)	1524	Allatt
16.2.92	TD	A	Barrow	L	10-12	Shuttleworth, Cocker	Gilbert	—	—
1.3.92	TD	H	Keighley C.	W	18-14	Shuttleworth, Gilbert, Gibson	Kenworthy (3)	2581	Carter
8.3.92	TD	A	Keighley C.	W	30-6	Chapman (3), Kebbie, Edwards	Kenworthy (5)	—	—
15.3.92	TD	H	Whitehaven	W	24-6	Oates (2), Chapman, Thomas	Kenworthy (4)	1882	Cross

(Continued)

1991-92 MATCH ANALYSIS (continued)

Date	Competition	H/A	Opponent	Rlt	Score	Tries	Goals	Attendance	Referee
29.3.92	TD	A	Nottingham C.	W	82-0	Gibson (3), Cocker (2), Huck, Chapman, Kebbie, Boothroyd, Stewart, Kenworthy, Thomas, Fogerty, Oates, Edwards	Kenworthy (11)	—	—
5.4.92	TD	H	Barrow	W	42-10	Kebbie (2), Gibson (2), Chapman, Cocker, Oates, Thomas	Kenworthy (5)	2908	Whitfield
12.4.92	TD	A	Dewsbury	W	15-6	Kebbie, Shuttleworth	Kenworthy (3, 1dg)	—	—
17.4.92	TD	H	Hunslet	W	30-20	Cocker (2), Senior, Kebbie, Thomas, Coulter	Kenworthy (3)	3811	Gilmour
21.4.92	DP(1)	H	Hunslet	W	13-6	Thomas	Kenworthy (4), Shuttleworth (dg)	2178	J. Connolly
26.4.92	DP(2)	A	London C.	L	4-14	—	Kenworthy (2)	—	—

Huddersfield's Australian skipper Greg Shuttleworth (right) leads the Stones Bitter Third Division Championship celebrations.

71

HULL

Ground: The Boulevard (0482-29040)
Colours: Black, white and purple
First Season: 1895-96
Nickname: Airlie Birds
Chairman: Steve Watson
Secretary: Brian Johnson
Coach: Noel Cleal (Sep 1990-Apr 1992)
Royce Simmons (May 1992-)
Honours: **Championship** Winners, 1919-20, 1920-21, 1935-36, 1955-56, 1957-58
Beaten finalists, 1956-57
Division One Champions, 1982-83
Division Two Champions, 1976-77, 1978-79
Challenge Cup Winners, 1913-14, 1981-82
Beaten finalists, 1907-08, 1908-09, 1909-10, 1921-22, 1922-23, 1958-59, 1959-60, 1979-80, 1982-83, 1984-85
Regal Trophy Winners, 1981-82
Beaten finalists, 1975-76, 1984-85
Premiership Winners, 1990-91
Beaten finalists, 1980-81, 1981-82, 1982-83, 1988-89
Yorkshire Cup Winners, 1923-24, 1969-70, 1982-83, 1983-84, 1984-85
Beaten finalists, 1912-13, 1914-15, 1920-21, 1927-28, 1938-39, 1946-47, 1953-54, 1954-55, 1955-56, 1959-60, 1967-68, 1986-87
Yorkshire League Winners, 1918-19, 1922-23, 1926-27, 1935-36
Charity Shield Beaten finalists, 1991-92
BBC2 Floodlit Trophy Winners, 1979-80

RECORDS

Match
Goals: 14 by Jim Kennedy v. Rochdale H., 7 Apr 1921
Geoff "Sammy" Lloyd v. Oldham, 10 Sep 1978
Tries: 7 by Clive Sullivan at Doncaster, 15 Apr 1968
Points: 36 by Jim Kennedy v. Keighley, 29 Jan 1921

Treble record-holder Sammy Lloyd, set in 1978-79.

Season
Goals: 170 by Geoff "Sammy" Lloyd, 1978-79
Tries: 52 by Jack Harrison, 1914-15
Points: 369 by Geoff "Sammy" Lloyd, 1978-79

Career
Goals: 687 by Joe Oliver, 1928-37 & 1943-45
Tries: 250 by Clive Sullivan, 1961-74 & 1981-85
Points: 1,842 by Joe Oliver, 1928-37 & 1943-45
Appearances: 501 by Edward Rogers, 1906-25
Highest score: 86-0 v. Elland, 1 Apr 1899
Highest against: 64-2 at St. Helens, 17 Feb 1988
Attendance: 28,798 v. Leeds (RL Cup), 7 Mar 1936

COACHING REGISTER
● **Since 1974-75**

David Doyle-Davidson	May 74 - Dec 77
Arthur Bunting	Jan 78 - Dec 85
Kenny Foulkes	Dec 85 - May 86
Len Casey	June 86 - Mar 88
Tony Dean	} Mar 88 - Apr 88
Keith Hepworth	
*Brian Smith	July 88 - Jan 91
*Noel Cleal	Sep 90 - Apr 92
Royce Simmons	May 92-

*Joint coaches Sep 90 - Jan 91.

GREAT BRITAIN REGISTER
(35 players)

W. Batten	(1)	1921
H. Bowman	(8)	1924-29
F. Boylen	(1)	1908
R. Coverdale	(4)	1954
M. Crane	(1)	1982
L. Crooks	(11 + 2)	1982-87
A. Dannatt	(3)	1985-91
G. Divorty	(2)	1985
J. Drake	(1)	1960
W. Drake	(1)	1962
P. Eastwood	(8)	1990-92
S. Evans	(2)	1982
V. Farrar	(1)	1978
R. Gemmell	(2)	1968-69
T. E. Gwynne	(3)	1928-29
T. Harris	(25)	1954-60
K. Harrison	(3)	1990
M. Harrison	(7)	1967-73
W. Holder	(1)	1907
L. Jackson	(9)	1990-92
M. Jones	(+ 1)	1992
A. Keegan	(9)	1966-69
S. McNamara	(+ 1)	1992
E. Morgan	(2)	1921
S. Norton	(9)	1978-82
W. Proctor	(+ 1)	1984
P. Rose	(1)	1982
G. Schofield	(15)	1984-87
T. Skerrett	(6)	1980-82
W. Stone	(8)	1920-21
C. Sullivan	(17)	1967-73
H. Taylor	(3)	1907
R. Taylor	(2)	1921-26
D. Topliss	(1)	1982
J. Whiteley	(15)	1957-62

Lee Jackson, Hull's Test hooker and double tourist.

Back row forward Steve McNamara, a Great Britain debutant at the Boulevard in March 1992.

73

1991-92 SIGNINGS REGISTER

Signed	Player	Club From
23.7.91	Lawson, Ian	Telephones ARL
23.7.91	O'Donnell, Craig	Hull Boys ARL
23.7.91	Sullivan, Scott	Crown Malet ARL
13.8.91	Wilson, Rob	West Hull ARL
15.8.91	Drushton, Nick	Barrow Island ARL
29.8.91	Smirk, Terry	Hull Dockers ARL
30.8.91	Danby, Robert	Hull Boys ARL
11.9.91	Ronson, Dave	Manly, Aus
12.9.91	Portlock, Wayne	Young, Aus
18.9.91	Cochrane, Gareth	Northern Dairies ARL
5.11.91	Boulter, Lee	Northern Dairies ARL
11.12.91	Stevens, Ian	Swansea Police RU
12.12.91	Spring, Peter	St. George, Aus

1991-92 PLAYERS' SUMMARY

	App	Tries	Goals	Dr	Pts
Blacker, Brian	23 + 5	4	—	—	16
Busby, Dean	10 + 11	6	—	—	24
Crooks, Steve	2	—	—	—	—
Dannatt, Andy	21	1	—	—	4
Dixon, Mike	4 + 16	2	—	—	8
Durham, Steve	9 + 1	—	—	—	—
Eastwood, Paul	32	14	101	—	258
Feather, Steve	1	—	—	—	—
Gay, Richard	33	14	—	—	56
Hanlan, Lee	1	—	—	—	—
Harrison, Paul	22 + 9	5	—	—	20
Hick, Steve	1	—	—	—	—
Jackson, Anthony	15 + 2	3	—	—	12
Jackson, Lee	34 + 2	6	—	—	24
Jones, Mark	19 + 9	2	—	—	8
Mackey, Greg	37	6	—	—	24
McNamara, Steve	29	—	2	—	4
Marlow, Ian	7 + 1	—	—	—	—
Mighty, Andrew	12	2	—	—	8
Nolan, Gary	7 + 4	2	—	—	8
Nolan, Rob	5 + 8	2	—	—	8
Portlock, Wayne	13	6	—	—	24
Ronson, Dave	24 + 2	10	—	—	40
Sharp, Jon	25	4	—	1	17
Smirk, Terry	7	1	—	—	4
Spring, Peter	18	—	—	—	—
Stevens, Ian	8 + 1	1	6	—	16
Turner, Neil	22	8	—	—	32
Walker, Russ	34	4	—	—	16
Welham, Paul	5	—	—	—	—
Wilson, Rob	1 + 1	1	—	—	4

TOTALS:

	App	Tries	Goals	Dr	Pts
31 players		104	109	1	635

Representative Appearances 1991-92
Busby — GB Under-21 (2 + 1)
Dixon — GB Under-21 (1)
Eastwood — Britain (1, 1t, 6g)
L. Jackson — Britain (1); Yorkshire (1)
Jones — Britain (+ 1); Wales (2)
McNamara — Britain (+ 1); GB Under-21 (2)
Marlow — Wales (1)
Walker — Cumbria (1)

Other Match
Humberside XIII v Papua New Guinea: Eastwood (1g), Blacker, Portlock, Dannatt, L. Jackson (1t), Sharp, Busby. Subs: Ronson, Jones

Hull skipper Greg Mackey, the Australian half back scoring six tries in 37 appearances for the Airlie Birds in 1991-92.

HULL 1991-92 MATCH ANALYSIS

Date	Com-petition	H/A	Opponent	Rlt	Score	Tries	Goals	Atten-dance	Referee
25.8.91	CS	N[1]	Wigan	L	8-22	G. Nolan	Eastwood (2)	(10,248)	Whitfield
1.9.91	SBC	H	St. Helens	L	10-31	Blacker	Eastwood (3)	6525	J. Smith
8.9.91	SBC	A	Leeds	L	14-20	Smirk, Walker	Eastwood (3)	—	—
15.9.91	YC(1)	H	Leeds	W	16-11	Walker, Mackey	Eastwood (4)	8255	Morris
22.9.91	SBC	H	Wigan	L	4-30	Busby	—	8151	Galtress
25.9.91	YC(2)	H	Featherstone R.	D	16-16	Busby, Portlock	Eastwood (4)	6437	J. Smith
29.9.91	SBC	A	Wakefield T.	W	28-14	Gay (2), Eastwood, Walker, Blacker	Eastwood (4)	—	—
1.10.91	YC(2) Replay	A	Featherstone R.	L	18-21	Harrison, R. Nolan, Turner, L. Jackson	Eastwood	—	—
6.10.91	SBC	H	Salford	L	12-24	Ronson	Eastwood (4)	4254	J. Smith
13.10.91	SBC	A	Featherstone R.	W	40-12	Busby, Ronson, Portlock, Eastwood, L. Jackson, Walker	Eastwood (8)	—	—
23.10.91	SBC	H	Bradford N.	W	40-14	Sharp (3), Eastwood (2), Gay, Mackey	Eastwood (6)	4629	Crashley
27.10.91	SBC	A	Salford	L	8-26	Eastwood	Eastwood (2)	—	—
31.10.91	RT(P)	H	Leigh	W	22-7	Mighty, Portlock, Blacker, Eastwood	Eastwood (3)	2219	Gilmour
10.11.91	SBC	H	Swinton	W	22-4	Dannatt, Portlock, Mackey	Eastwood (5)	4242	Morris
18.11.91	RT(1)	H	Batley	W	12-8	Portlock	Eastwood (4)	2149	R. Smith
23.11.91	RT(2)	H	Leeds	L	4-12	Mighty	—	4359	Galtress
1.12.91	SBC	A	Halifax	W	20-10	Portlock, Busby, Dixon	Eastwood (4)	—	—
8.12.91	SBC	H	Featherstone R.	W	30-14	Harrison, A. Jackson, Gay, Blacker	Eastwood (7)	5109	Holdsworth
15.12.91	SBC	A	Wigan	L	12-24	Mackey (2)	Eastwood (2)	—	—
26.12.91	SBC	A	Castleford	L	8-30	Gay, R. Nolan	—	—	—
1.1.92	SBC	H	Hull K.R.	L	12-15	Gay, Turner	Stevens (2)	11,128	J. Connolly
7.1.92	SBC	A	Bradford N.	W	14-10	Ronson, Turner	Stevens (3)	—	—
12.1.92	SBC	H	Warrington	L	6-32	Jones	Stevens	5319	Allatt
19.1.92	SBC	A	Widnes	L	20-22	Sharp, Harrison, Dixon, Mackey	McNamara (2)	—	—
2.2.92	CC(1)	A	Rochdale H.	W	32-28	Gay (3), Eastwood (2), Turner, Harrison	Eastwood (2)	—	—
9.2.92	CC(2)	A	Sheffield E.	W	11-6	Gay, Jones	Eastwood, Sharp (dg)	—	—
23.2.92	CC(3)	A	Workington T.	W	24-8	Eastwood (2), Turner (2)	Eastwood (4)	—	—
26.2.92	SBC	H	Halifax	W	34-10	Ronson (2), Harrison, A. Jackson, L. Jackson, Gay	Eastwood (5)	5267	J. Connolly
1.3.92	SBC	H	Wakefield T.	L	14-15	Stevens, L. Jackson	Eastwood (3)	5809	Holdsworth
8.3.92	SBC	A	Warrington	W	22-12	Busby (2), Turner	Eastwood (5)	—	—
14.3.92	CC(SF)	N[2]	Castleford	L	4-8	Eastwood	—	(14,636)	Morris
22.3.92	SBC	H	Leeds	W	22-14	Ronson, Gay, Wilson	Eastwood (5)	6126	Carter
29.3.92	SBC	A	St. Helens	L	12-42	Eastwood, L. Jackson	Eastwood (2)	—	—
5.4.92	SBC	A	Swinton	L	18-27	L. Jackson, Eastwood, Ronson, Turner	Eastwood	—	—
12.4.92	SBC	H	Widnes	L	20-36	Gay (2), G. Nolan, Eastwood	Eastwood (2)	4450	R. Smith
17.4.92	SBC	A	Hull K.R.	W	12-8	Ronson (2)	Eastwood (2)	—	—
20.4.92	SBC	H	Castleford	L	14-30	Ronson, A. Jackson	Eastwood (3)	5587	Cummings

N[1] at Gateshead International Stadium
N[2] at Leeds

HULL KINGSTON ROVERS

Ground: Craven Park (0482-74648)
Colours: Red, blue and white
First Season: 1899-1900
Nickname: Robins
Chairman: Phil Love
Secretary: Ron Turner
Coach: George Fairbairn (May 1991-)
Honours: **Championship** Winners, 1922-23, 1924-25
Beaten finalists, 1920-21, 1967-68
First Division Champions, 1978-79, 1983-84, 1984-85
Second Division Champions, 1989-90
Challenge Cup Winners, 1979-80
Beaten finalists, 1904-05, 1924-25, 1963-64, 1980-81, 1985-86
Regal Trophy Winners, 1984-85,
Beaten finalists, 1981-82, 1985-86
Premiership Winners, 1980-81, 1983-84
Beaten finalists, 1984-85
Second Division Premiership
Beaten finalists, 1989-90
Yorkshire Cup Winners, 1920-21, 1929-30, 1966-67, 1967-68, 1971-72, 1974-75, 1985-86
Beaten finalists, 1906-07, 1911-12, 1933-34, 1962-63, 1975-76, 1980-81, 1984-85
Yorkshire League Winners, 1924-25, 1925-26
Eastern Division Championship Winners, 1962-63
Charity Shield Beaten finalists, 1985-86
BBC2 Floodlit Trophy Winners, 1977-78
Beaten finalists, 1979-80

RECORDS

Match
Goals: 14 by Alf Carmichael v. Merthyr Tydfil, 8 Oct 1910
Mike Fletcher v. Whitehaven, 18 Mar 1990
Colin Armstrong v. Nottingham C. (at Doncaster), 19 Aug 1990
Tries: 11 by George West v. Brookland R., 4 Mar 1905
Points: 53 by George West v. Brookland R., 4 Mar 1905

Season
Goals: 199 by Mike Fletcher, 1989-90
Tries: 45 by Gary Prohm, 1984-85
Points: 450 by Mike Fletcher, 1989-90

Career
Goals: 1,192 by Cyril Kellett, 1956-67
Tries: 207 by Roger Millward, 1966-80
Points: 2,489 by Cyril Kellett, 1956-67
Appearances: 481 + 8 by Mike Smith, 1974-91
Highest score: 100-6 v. Nottingham C. (at Doncaster), 19 Aug 1990
Highest against: 76-8 at Halifax, 20 Oct 1991
Attendance: 27,670 v. Hull (League), 3 Apr 1953 — at Boothferry Park, Hull C. AFC
8,557 v. Hull (League), 1 Jan 1991 — at new Craven Park

Utility man Paul Lyman, who contributed seven tries in 21 appearances during 1991-92.

COACHING REGISTER
● **Since 1974-75**

Arthur Bunting	Feb 72 - Nov 75
Harry Poole	Dec 75 - Mar 77
Roger Millward	Mar 77 - May 91
George Fairbairn	May 91 -

GREAT BRITAIN REGISTER
(26 players)

D. Bishop	(+1)	1990
C. Burton	(8+1)	1982-87
A. Burwell	(7+1)	1967-69
L. Casey	(7+2)	1977-83
G. Clark	(3)	1984-85
A. Dockar	(1)	1947
G. Fairbairn	(3)	1981-82
J. Feetham	(1)	1929
P. Flanagan	(14)	1962-70
F. Foster	(1)	1967
D. Hall	(2)	1984
P. Harkin	(+1)	1985
S. Hartley	(3)	1980-81
P. Hogan	(2+2)	1979
R. Holdstock	(2)	1980
W. Holliday	(8+1)	1964-67
D. Laws	(1)	1986
B. Lockwood	(1+1)	1978-79
P. Lowe	(12)	1970-78
R. Millward	(27+1)	1967-78
H. Poole	(1)	1964
P. Rose	(1+3)	1974-78
M. Smith	(10+1)	1979-84
B. Tyson	(3)	1963-67
D. Watkinson	(12+1)	1979-86
C. Young	(5)	1967-68

1991-92 SIGNINGS REGISTER

Signed	Player	Club From
1.6.91	Chamberlain, Richard	Greatfield ARL
22.7.91	Leighton, Jamie	Crown Malet ARL
25.7.91	Wesson, Gavin	Crown Malet ARL
7.8.91	Busby, David	—
9.8.91	Richardson, Stephen	Greatfield ARL
11.8.91	Power, Bryan	Greatfield ARL
11.9.91	Barkworth, Julian	Hull Ionians RU
19.9.91	Anderson, Peter	Stanthorpe, Aus
23.9.91	Harrison, Chris	Ureka ARL
3.10.91	McCarthy, Troy	Gold Coast, Aus
10.1.92	Clark, Dean	Scarborough P.
21.2.92	*Ashton, Ray	Workington T.

1991-92 PLAYERS' SUMMARY

	App	Tries	Goals	Dr	Pts
Anderson, Peter	0 + 2	—	—	—	—
Barkworth, Julian	26	6	—	—	24
Bibby, Mike	1	—	—	—	—
Bishop, David	4 + 2	1	—	—	4
Chamberlain, Richard	2	—	—	—	—
Chatfield, Gary	13 + 1	1	—	3	7
Clark, Dean	6 + 1	1	—	—	4
Cook, Graham	10 + 3	1	—	—	4
Crane, Mike	16 + 6	4	—	1	17
Ema, Zook	11 + 7	—	—	—	—
Fletcher, Mike	30	2	71	—	150
Fletcher, Paul	27 + 2	1	—	—	4
Gotts, Andy	0 + 1	—	—	—	—
Hallas, Graham	27 + 1	7	1	—	30
Harrison, Chris	19 + 3	—	—	—	—
Harrison, Des	18 + 2	1	—	—	4
Hoe, Sean	3 + 11	—	—	—	—
Jackson, Wayne	5 + 1	—	—	—	—
Leighton, Jamie	1	—	—	—	—
Lydiat, John	13 + 3	4	—	—	16
Lyman, Paul	18 + 3	7	—	—	28
McCarthy, Troy	12 + 1	4	—	—	16
O'Brien, Craig	0 + 1	—	—	—	—
Parker, Wayne	15 + 1	1	—	1	5
Richardson, Lee	26	2	—	—	8
Sodje, Bright	30	20	—	—	80
Speckman, Paul	20 + 4	1	—	2	6
Thompson, Andy	28	5	—	—	20
Vannett, Paul	9 + 1	—	—	—	—

TOTALS:

29 players		69	72	7	427

Representative Appearances 1991-92
Bishop — Wales (2, 1t)
Hallas — GB Under-21 (1+2)

Other Match
Humberside XIII v Papua New Guinea: M. Fletcher (1g), McCarthy, Sodje (1t), Bishop, Vannett, P. Fletcher (1t). Subs: Lyman, Chatfield

HULL KINGSTON ROVERS 1991-92 MATCH ANALYSIS

Date	Com-petition	H/A	Opponent	Rlt	Score	Tries	Goals	Atten-dance	Referee
1.9.91	SBC	A	Bradford N.	W	18-10	Hallas, Sodje, Crane	M. Fletcher (3)	—	—
8.9.91	SBC	H	Halifax	W	24-16	Sodje (3), Hallas	M. Fletcher (4)	6267	Whitfield
15.9.91	YC(1)	H	Dewsbury	W	18-5	Hallas, Lyman	M. Fletcher (5)	3060	Kendrew
22.9.91	SBC	A	Widnes	L	6-24	Cook	M. Fletcher	—	—
25.9.91	YC(2)	A	Castleford	L	12-34	Barkworth	M. Fletcher (4)	—	—
29.9.91	SBC	H	Warrington	L	9-14	Sodje, Lyman	Speckman (dg)	3382	R. Connolly
6.10.91	SBC	A	Swinton	W	17-6	Lyman, Barkworth, Lydiat	M. Fletcher (2), Chatfield (dg)	—	—
13.10.91	SBC	H	Castleford	L	14-22	M. Fletcher, Lyman	M. Fletcher (3)	4791	Carter
20.10.91	SBC	A	Halifax	L	8-76	Sodje	M. Fletcher (2)	—	—
27.10.91	SBC	H	Wakefield T.	W	23-4	Barkworth, Sodje, Crane, Lyman	M. Fletcher (3), Chatfield (dg)	4300	Whitfield
10.11.91	SBC	A	St. Helens	L	15-38	D. Harrison, McCarthy, Sodje	M. Fletcher, Chatfield (dg)	—	—
17.11.91	RT(1)	H	Castleford	L	10-22	McCarthy, Sodje	M. Fletcher	3406	Morris
15.12.91	SBC	H	St. Helens	W	24-14	Hallas (2), Sodje (2)	M. Fletcher (4)	3479	R. Smith
22.12.91	SBC	H	Salford	W	28-7	Sodje (2), Lyman, Bishop, Thompson	M. Fletcher (4)	3460	Campbell
26.12.91	SBC	A	Leeds	L	8-22	Thompson	M. Fletcher (2)	—	—
1.1.92	SBC	A	Hull	W	15-12	Sodje, McCarthy	M. Fletcher (3), Speckman (dg)	—	—
6.1.92	SBC	H	Swinton	W	18-6	Lydiat, Parker, Crane	M. Fletcher (3)	3253	Allatt
19.1.92	SBC	H	Featherstone R.	W	24-6	Hallas, McCarthy, P. Fletcher, Thompson	M. Fletcher (4)	4322	Campbell
26.1.92	CC(1)	A	Halifax	L	8-12	Lydiat	M. Fletcher (2)	—	—
9.2.92	SBC	A	Warrington	L	12-23	Hallas, Thompson	M. Fletcher (2)	—	—
23.2.92	SBC	A	Wakefield T.	W	25-22	Sodje (3), Lyman	M. Fletcher (4), Crane (dg)	—	—
1.3.92	SBC	A	Featherstone R.	L	7-12	M. Fletcher	M. Fletcher, Parker (dg)	—	—
8.3.92	SBC	A	Wigan	L	10-28	Barkworth, Crane	M. Fletcher	—	—
15.3.92	SBC	H	Widnes	W	10-8	Richardson	M. Fletcher (3)	3744	Volante
22.3.92	SBC	A	Castleford	W	28-18	Sodje, Barkworth, Clark, Thompson, Speckman	M. Fletcher (4)	—	—
1.4.92	SBC	H	Wigan	L	2-17	—	M. Fletcher	7610	Cummings
5.4.92	SBC	H	Leeds	L	4-13	Lydiat	—	4831	Campbell
12.4.92	SBC	A	Salford	L	10-22	Chatfield, Richardson	M. Fletcher	—	—
17.4.92	SBC	H	Hull	L	8-12	Barkworth	M. Fletcher (2)	8422	J. Connolly
20.4.92	SBC	H	Bradford N.	L	12-14	Sodje (2)	M. Fletcher, Hallas	3919	Volante

Hull K.R.'s record RU recruit David Bishop touches down for Wales at Swansea in October 1991, one of only eight first-class matches during the season.

HUNSLET

Ground: Elland Road (0532-711675)
Colours: Green and white
First Season: 1895-96. Disbanded at end of 1972-73. Re-formed as New Hunslet in 1973-74. Retitled Hunslet from start of 1979-80
Chairman: Graham Lisle
Secretary: Mabel Grainger
Coach: Paul Daley (May 1990-)
Honours: **Championship** Winners, 1907-08, 1937-38
Beaten finalists, 1958-59
Division Two Champions, 1962-63, 1986-87
Challenge Cup Winners, 1907-08, 1933-34
Beaten finalists, 1898-99, 1964-65
Second Division Premiership
Beaten finalists, 1986-87
Yorkshire Cup Winners, 1905-06, 1907-08, 1962-63
Beaten finalists, 1908-09, 1929-30, 1931-32, 1944-45, 1956-57, 1965-66
Yorkshire League Winners, 1897-98, 1907-08, 1931-32

RECORDS

Match
Goals: 12 by Billy Langton v. Keighley, 18 Aug 1959
Tries: 7 by George Dennis v. Bradford N., 20 Jan 1934
Points: 28 by Tim Lumb v. Runcorn H., 7 Oct 1990

Season
Goals: 181 by Billy Langton, 1958-59
Tries: 34 by Alan Snowden, 1956-57
Points: 380 by Billy Langton, 1958-59

Career
Goals: 1,044 by Billy Langton, 1955-66
Tries: 154 by Fred Williamson, 1943-55
Points: 2,202 by Billy Langton, 1955-66
Appearances: 569 + 10 by Geoff Gunney, 1951-73
572 by Jack Walkington, 1927-48
Highest score: 75-5 v. Broughton Rec., 20 Mar 1897
Highest against: 76-8 v. Halifax, 27 Aug 1972
Attendance: 54,112 v. Leeds (Championship final), 30 Apr 1938
Home match: 14,004 v. Castleford (RL Cup), 13 Mar 1983

Former Great Britain Under-21 half back Tim Lumb, who scored 18 points in six games for Hunslet before moving to Sheffield Eagles on loan.

COACHING REGISTER
● **Since 1974-75**

Paul Daley	Apr 74 - Aug 78
Bill Ramsey	Aug 78 - Dec 79
Drew Broatch	Dec 79 - Apr 81
Paul Daley	Apr 81 - Nov 85
*Peter Jarvis	Nov 85 - Apr 88
*David Ward	July 86 - Apr 88
Nigel Stephenson	June 88 - Oct 88
Jack Austin ⎫ John Wolford ⎭	Oct 88 - Jan 89
David Ward	Jan 89 - May 89
Graeme Jennings	Sep 89 - Apr 90
Paul Daley	May 90 -

Joint coaches from July 1986.

GREAT BRITAIN REGISTER
(23 players)

W. Batten	(9)	1907-11
H. Beverley	(4)	1936-37
A. Burnell	(3)	1951-54
H. Crowther	(1)	1929
J. Evans	(4)	1951-52
K. Eyre	(1)	1965
B. Gabbitas	(1)	1959
G. Gunney	(11)	1954-65
D. Hartley	(2)	1964
J. Higson	(2)	1908
D. Jenkins	(1)	1929
A. Jenkinson	(2)	1911
W. Jukes	(6)	1908-10
B. Prior	(1)	1966
W. Ramsey	(7)	1965-66
B. Shaw	(5)	1956-60
G. Shelton	(7)	1964-66
F. Smith	(9)	1910-14
S. Smith	(4)	1954
C. Thompson	(2)	1951
L. White	(7)	1932-33
R. Williams	(3)	1954
H. Wilson	(3)	1907

1991-92 SIGNINGS REGISTER

Signed	Player	Club From
8.8.91	Cook, Mark	Batley
15.8.91	Simpson, Andrew	Huddersfield
12.9.91	Carr, Paul	South Sydney, Aus
17.9.91	McKelvie, Daniel	Newcastle, Aus
19.9.91	Campling, Steve	Travellers Rest ARL
9.10.91	Bartliff, Andrew	Queenswood ARL
20.1.92	*Seabourne, Peter	Bradford N.
17.3.92	*Moore, Thomas	Sheffield E.

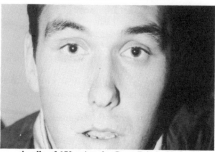

A tally of 172 points for Great Britain Under-21 debutant Andy Precious.

1991-92 PLAYERS' SUMMARY

	App	Tries	Goals	Dr	Pts
Bartliff, Andrew	25	3	9	—	30
Bell, Keith	19 + 2	1	—	2	6
Bowden, Chris	1 + 1	—	—	—	—
Brook, David	29	13	—	1	53
Burrow, Paul	9 + 4	1	—	—	4
Campling, Steve	10	1	1	—	6
Carr, Paul	28	22	—	1	89
Coates, Jed	1	—	—	—	—
Cook, Mark	3	—	—	—	—
Coyle, Mick	27	4	—	—	16
Daniel, Alan	28 + 1	17	—	—	68
Davies, Alec	1 + 1	—	—	—	—
King, Graham	3	1	—	—	4
Lay, Steve	18 + 2	1	—	—	4
Liles, Richard	1 + 3	—	—	—	—
Lowes, James	23 + 1	10	18	—	76
Lumb, Tim	2 + 4	2	5	—	18
McKelvie, Daniel	19 + 4	2	—	—	8
Mitchell, Keith	16 + 1	2	—	—	8
Moore, Thomas	1 + 1	1	—	—	4
Morgan, Paul	8 + 1	2	—	—	8
Petch, Andrew	4	—	—	—	—
Petch, Richard	0 + 1	—	—	—	—
Precious, Andy	17 + 14	3	77	6	172
Raw, Andrew	28	15	—	—	60
Sampson, Roy	29	7	—	—	28
Simpson, Andrew	7 + 10	2	—	—	8
Steele, Matthew	8 + 1	—	—	—	—
Taylor, David	0 + 1	—	—	—	—
Waites, Brian	29	13	—	—	52
Wilson, Sean	1	—	—	—	—
Wood, Mark	5 + 4	—	—	—	—
Wright, Jason	3 + 2	—	—	—	—

TOTALS:
33 players		123	110	10	722

Representative Appearances 1991-92
Precious — GB Under-21 (+1)

HUNSLET 1991-92 MATCH ANALYSIS

Date	Com-petition	H/A	Opponent	Rlt	Score	Tries	Goals	Atten-dance	Referee
25.8.91	YC(P)	A	Ryedale-York	L	8-36	Raw (2)	—	—	—
1.9.91	TD	H	Barrow	W	30-22	Morgan, Raw, Sampson, King, Lowes	Precious (5)	483	R. Smith
8.9.91	TD	A	Dewsbury	L	9-42	Waites	Precious (2, 1dg)	—	—
22.9.91	TD	H	Trafford B.	W	40-6	Carr (2), Lowes (2), Brook, Morgan, Waites, Daniel	Lowes (3), Precious	387	Burke
29.9.91	TD	A	Nottingham C.	W	44-11	Carr (2), Waites (2), Raw, Lowes, Bell, Sampson, Precious	Precious (2), Lowes, Bartliff	—	—
6.10.91	TD	H	Keighley C.	W	25-22	Lowes, Waites, Carr, Brook	Precious (4, 1dg)	658	J. Connolly
14.10.91	TD	A	Trafford B.	W	24-20	Campling, Sampson, Simpson, Daniel	Precious (3, 2dg)	—	—
23.10.91	TD	H	Highfield	W	36-10	Brook (2), Raw, Daniel, Lowes	Precious (8)	561	Cummings
27.10.91	TD	A	Chorley B.	W	48-16	Raw (2), Brook, Bartliff, Waites, Daniel, Carr, Lowes	Precious (8)	—	—
3.11.91	TD	H	Whitehaven	W	24-12	Brook (2), Coyle, Waites	Precious (3), Bartliff	454	Allatt
10.11.91	TD	A	Barrow	W	22-12	Waites, Sampson, Carr	Precious (4), Campling	—	—
17.11.91	RT(1)	A	Keighley C.	L	10-25	Carr, Sampson	Lowes	—	—
1.12.91	TD	H	Nottingham C.	W	52-4	Raw (3), Carr, Sampson, McKelvie, Bartliff, Lowes, Daniel, Waites	Lowes (3), Precious (3)	440	Asquith
8.12.91	TD	H	Scarborough P.	W	25-14	Carr (2), Sampson (2), Raw	Precious (2, 1dg)	626	R. Connolly
16.12.91	TD	A	Keighley C.	L	8-40	Precious	Precious (2)	—	—
27.12.91	TD	A	Bramley	L	20-22	Lowes, Carr, Brook	Lowes (4)	—	—
1.1.92	TD	H	Bramley	W	23-18	McKelvie, Carr, Brook	Lowes (3), Precious (2, 1dg)	860	Carter
12.1.92	TD	A	Scarborough P.	W	24-12	Daniel (3), Brook	Lowes (3), Brook (dg), Bell (dg)	—	—
20.1.92	TD	H	Huddersfield	L	6-30	Raw	Bartliff	2227	Burke
29.1.92	CC(1)	A[1]	Kells	W	32-14	Brook (2), Lumb, Carr, Waites	Lumb (5), Precious	—	—
9.2.92	CC(2)	H	Castleford	L	12-28	Carr, Lumb	Bartliff, Precious	3182	Campbell
16.2.92	TD	H	Doncaster	W	33-32	Daniel (2), Carr, Waites, Raw	Bartliff (5), Precious, Carr (dg)	922	Kershaw
23.2.92	TD	A	Whitehaven	L	26-32	Daniel (2), Waites, Coyle	Precious (5)	—	—
2.3.92	TD	H	Batley	L	13-22	Carr, Daniel	Precious (2), Bell (dg)	926	Cummings
8.3.92	TD	H	Chorley B.	W	28-10	Carr (3), Mitchell, Coyle, Daniel	Precious (2)	496	Ollerton
15.3.92	TD	A	Highfield	W	48-20	Daniel (3), Raw (2), Brook, Bartliff, Mitchell, Burrow	Precious (6)	—	—
29.3.92	TD	A	Batley	L	14-34	Carr, Lay	Precious (3)	—	—
5.4.92	TD	H	Dewsbury	L	8-40	Waites	Precious (2)	968	R. Connolly
12.4.92	TD	A	Doncaster	L	4-20	Moore	—	—	—
17.4.92	TD	A	Huddersfield	L	20-30	Precious, Lowes, Carr	Precious (4)	—	—
21.4.92	DP(1)	A	Huddersfield	L	6-13	Coyle	Precious	—	—

[1] at Whitehaven

KEIGHLEY COUGARS

Ground: Lawkholme Lane (0535-602602)
Colours: Green, scarlet and white
First Season: 1901-02. Added Cougars to title at start of 1991-92.
Nickname: Cougars
Chairman: Ian Mahady
Secretary: Graham Heap
Coach: Tony Fisher (June 1990-Sep 1991)
Peter Roe (Sep 1991-)
Honours: **Division Two** Champions, 1902-03
Challenge Cup Beaten finalists, 1936-37
Yorkshire Cup Beaten finalists, 1943-44, 1951-52

RECORDS

Match
Goals: 11 by Robert Walker v. Castleford, 13 Jan 1906
Bert Cook v. Hull K.R., 31 Oct 1953
John Wasyliw v. Nottingham C., 23 Feb 1992
Tries: 5 by Ike Jagger v. Castleford, 13 Jan 1906
Sam Stacey v. Liverpool C., 9 Mar 1907
Points: 26 by John Wasyliw v. Highfield, 10 Nov 1991

Season
Goals: 155 by Brian Jefferson, 1973-74
Tries: 30 by Joe Sherburn, 1934-35
Points: 331 by Brian Jefferson, 1973-74

Career
Goals: 967 by Brian Jefferson, 1965-77
Tries: 155 by Sam Stacey, 1904-20
Points: 2,116 by Brian Jefferson, 1965-77
Appearances: 372 by Hartley Tempest, 1902-15
David McGoun, 1925-38
Highest score: 70-0 v. Nottingham C., 23 Feb 1992
Highest against: 92-2 at Leigh, 30 Apr 1986
Attendance: 14,500 v. Halifax (RL Cup), 3 Mar 1951

COACHING REGISTER
● **Since 1974-75**

Alan Kellett	Jan 73 - May 75
Roy Sabine	Aug 75 - Oct 77
Barry Seabourne	Nov 77 - Mar 79
Albert Fearnley (Mgr)	Apr 79 - Aug 79
Alan Kellett	Apr 79 - Apr 80
Albert Fearnley	May 80 - Feb 81
Bakary Diabira	Feb 81 - Sep 82
Lee Greenwood	Sep 82 - Oct 83
Geoff Peggs	Nov 83 - Sep 85
Peter Roe	Sep 85 - July 86
Colin Dixon	July 86 - June 89
Les Coulter	July 89 - Apr 90
Tony Fisher	June 90 - Sep 91
Peter Roe	Sep 91 -

GREAT BRITAIN REGISTER
(1 player)

T. Hollindrake	(1)	1955

Packman Mark Fairbank, touching down once in 21 appearances in 1991-92.

1991-92 SIGNINGS REGISTER

Signed	Player	Club From
13.7.91	Hall, Steve	Dudley Hill ARL
27.7.91	Boyle, Hamish	Kippax Welfare ARL
27.7.91	Handford, Colin	Magnet ARL
13.8.91	Race, Wayne	Doncaster
14.8.91	*Chick, Stuart	Workington T.
15.8.91	McLean, Brian	RU
15.8.91	Plath, Andre	St. Marys College ARL
20.9.91	St. Hilaire, Lee	Huddersfield
3.10.91	Keebles, Mick	Halifax
25.10.91	Johnson, Arthur	RU
29.10.91	Walker, Johnny	Otley RU
21.11.91	Hinchliffe, Andy	RU
12.12.91	Brooke-Cowden, Mark	Halifax
12.12.91	Machon, John	Milton Ulloaulla, Aus
13.12.91	*Cass, Mark	Hull
17.1.92	Wood, Martin	Scarborough P.
6.2.92	Reeves, Bob	Mayfield ARL
19.3.92	Bailey, Mark	Ovenden ARL

1991-92 PLAYERS' SUMMARY

	App	Tries	Goals	Dr	Pts
Bailey, Mark	1	—	—	—	—
Brooke-Cowden, Mark	12 + 3	1	—	—	4
Butterfield, Jeff	29	4	—	—	16
Chick, Stuart	2	1	—	—	4
Cox, Dave	2 + 1	—	—	—	—
Dixon, Keith	21 + 3	10	19	4	82
Eyres, Andy	35	17	—	1	69
Fairbank, Mark	17 + 4	1	—	—	4
Farrell, Carlton	31	8	—	—	32
Gascoigne, Andy	10	2	—	—	8
Godfrey, Heath	5 + 3	1	—	—	4
Hall, Steve	33 + 2	1	—	—	4
Handford, Colin	6 + 4	—	—	—	—
Hiley, Greg	23	4	4	—	24
Hinchliffe, Andy	16 + 2	8	—	—	32
James, Tony	7	3	7	—	26
Keebles, Mick	26 + 2	1	—	—	4
McLean, Brian	1	1	—	—	4
Machon, John	1 + 1	—	—	—	—
Moses, Paul	29 + 1	1	—	6	10
Palelei, Aaron	5 + 3	1	—	—	4
Plath, Andre	2	1	—	—	4
Priestley, Ray	1 + 3	—	—	—	—
Race, Wayne	25 + 2	9	—	—	36
Reeves, Bob	3 + 9	1	—	—	4
Roe, Peter	0 + 1	—	—	—	—
Roiall, Matthew	4 + 1	2	—	—	8
Rose, Kevin	12 + 2	1	—	—	4
St. Hilaire, Darren	0 + 1	—	—	—	—
St. Hilaire, Lee	3 + 3	2	—	—	8
Stephenson, Andy	13 + 3	1	—	—	4
Stephenson, Phil	18 + 6	4	—	—	16
Summerscales, Damien	0 + 2	—	—	—	—
Walker, Johnny	25	13	—	—	52
Wasyliw, John	25	14	80	—	216
Winterbottom, Ricky	1 + 2	—	—	—	—
Wood, Martin	11	6	—	—	24

TOTALS:
37 players		119	110	11	707

Prop Kevin Rose, who crossed the line once in 14 appearances in 1991-92.

KEIGHLEY COUGARS 1991-92 MATCH ANALYSIS

Date	Com-petition	H/A	Opponent	Rlt	Score	Tries	Goals	Atten-dance	Referee
1.9.91	TD	A	Bramley	L	12-41	McLean, Dixon, Eyres	—	—	—
8.9.91	TD	H	Chorley B.	W	52-12	Eyres (2), Farrell (2), Chick, Godfrey, Race, James, Rose	Dixon (8)	777	Cross
15.9.91	YC(1)	H	Bramley	L	8-20	Eyres, James	—	1204	Redfearn
22.9.91	TD	A	Highfield	W	28-12	Gascoigne (2), James, Hiley, Dixon	Hiley (4)	—	—
29.9.91	TD	H	Batley	D	2-2	—	Dixon	1139	Steele
6.10.91	TD	A	Hunslet	L	22-25	St. Hilaire (2), Roiall (2)	James (3)	—	—
13.10.91	TD	H	Doncaster	D	10-10	Race	James (3)	1347	Tennant
20.10.91	TD	H	Barrow	L	6-12	—	James, Dixon, Moses (2dg)	811	Allatt
27.10.91	TD	A	Nottingham C.	W	42-4	Farrell (2), Plath, Walker, Dixon, Race, P. Stephenson	Dixon (7)	—	—
7.11.91	TD	A	Scarborough P.	L	13-38	Palelei, Walker, Eyres	Dixon (dg)	—	—
10.11.91	TD	H	Highfield	W	42-14	Wasyliw (3), Hiley (2), Walker, Eyres	Wasyliw (7)	701	R. Connolly
17.11.91	RT(1)	H	Hunslet	W	25-10	Walker (3), Keebles	Wasyliw (4), Dixon (dg)	1155	Crashley
24.11.91	RT(2)	A	Wigan	L	8-32	Eyres	Wasyliw (2)	—	—
1.12.91	TD	A	Batley	W	23-8	Wasyliw (2), Dixon, Eyres	Wasyliw (3), Moses (dg)	—	—
8.12.91	TD	A	Whitehaven	W	11-7	Wasyliw (2)	Wasyliw, Moses (dg)	—	—
16.12.91	TD	H	Hunslet	W	40-8	Dixon (3), A. Stephenson, Hall, Farrell	Wasyliw (8)	1181	Redfearn
5.1.92	TD	A	Doncaster	W	14-12	Farrell, Dixon	Dixon (2), Wasyliw	—	—
12.1.92	TD	H	Bramley	L	7-10	Butterfield	Wasyliw, Dixon (dg)	1241	Asquith
19.1.92	TD	A	Chorley B.	W	28-13	Wasyliw, Fairbank, Race, Eyres, Hiley	Wasyliw (4)	—	—
26.1.92	CC(1)	A	Barrow	D	7-7	—	Wasyliw (3), Eyres (dg)	—	—
2.2.92	CC(1) Replay	H	Barrow	D	14-14	Wasyliw, Butterfield, Race	Wasyliw	2127	Tidball
4.2.92	CC(1) 2nd Replay	N[1]	Barrow	L	0-16	—	—	(872)	Tidball
17.2.92	TD	H	Scarborough P.	W	18-16	Eyres, Butterfield, Brooke-Cowden	Wasyliw (3)	1128	Volante
23.2.92	TD	H	Nottingham C.	W	70-0	P. Stephenson (2), Race (2), Eyres (2), Wood (2), Butterfield, Hinchliffe, Reeves, Farrell	Wasyliw (11)	844	Crashley
1.3.92	TD	A	Huddersfield	L	14-18	Eyres, Wasyliw	Wasyliw (3)	—	—
8.3.92	TD	H	Huddersfield	L	6-30	Walker	Wasyliw	2142	Tidball
15.3.92	TD	H	Trafford B.	W	28-14	Eyres (2), Wasyliw, Wood, Race	Wasyliw (4)	1163	Whitelam
22.3.92	TD	A	Trafford B.	W	30-7	Wood (2), Hinchliffe, Walker, Eyres	Wasyliw (5)	—	—
29.3.92	TD	H	Dewsbury	W	14-13	P. Stephenson, Eyres	Wasyliw (3)	1081	Gilmour
5.4.92	TD	H	Whitehaven	W	46-24	Hinchliffe (3), Walker, Wood, Farrell, Race, Wasyliw	Wasyliw (7)	2002	Redfearn
12.4.92	TD	A	Barrow	L	2-38	—	Wasyliw	—	—
17.4.92	TD	A	Dewsbury	L	7-26	Dixon	Wasyliw, Moses (dg)	—	—
21.4.92	DP(1)	A	Bramley	D	18-18	Dixon, Moses, Walker	Wasyliw (3)	—	—
23.4.92	DP(1) Replay	H	Bramley	W	26-23	Walker (3), Wasyliw, Hinchliffe	Wasyliw (2), Moses (dg), Dixon (dg)	1092	J. Smith
25.4.92	DP(2)	A	Sheffield E.	L	14-72	Hinchliffe (2), Wasyliw	Wasyliw	—	—

N[1] at Widnes

LEEDS

Ground: Headingley (0532-786181)
Colours: Blue and amber
First Season: 1895-96
Nickname: Loiners
Chairman: Dennis Greenwood
Chief Exec: Alf Davies
Coach: Doug Laughton (May 1991-)
Honours: **Championship** Winners, 1960-61, 1968-69, 1971-72
Beaten finalists, 1914-15, 1928-29, 1929-30, 1930-31, 1937-38, 1969-70, 1972-73
League Leaders Trophy Winners, 1966-67, 1967-68, 1968-69, 1969-70, 1971-72
Challenge Cup Winners, 1909-10, 1922-23, 1931-32, 1935-36, 1940-41, 1941-42, 1956-57, 1967-68, 1976-77, 1977-78
Beaten finalists, 1942-43, 1946-47, 1970-71, 1971-72
Regal Trophy Winners, 1972-73, 1983-84
Beaten finalists, 1982-83, 1987-88, 1991-92
Premiership Winners, 1974-75, 1978-79
Yorkshire Cup Winners, 1921-22, 1928-29, 1930-31, 1932-33, 1934-35, 1935-36, 1937-38, 1958-59, 1968-69, 1970-71, 1972-73, 1973-74, 1975-76, 1976-77, 1979-80, 1980-81, 1988-89
Beaten finalists, 1919-20, 1947-48, 1961-62, 1964-65
Yorkshire League Winners, 1901-02, 1927-28, 1930-31, 1933-34, 1934-35, 1936-37, 1937-38, 1950-51, 1954-55, 1956-57, 1960-61, 1966-67, 1967-68, 1968-69, 1969-70
BBC2 Floodlit Trophy Winners, 1970-71

RECORDS

Match

Goals: 13 by Lewis Jones v. Blackpool B., 19 Aug 1957
Tries: 8 by Fred Webster v. Coventry, 12 Apr 1913
Eric Harris v. Bradford N., 14 Sep 1931
Points: 31 by Lewis Jones v. Bradford N., 22 Aug 1956

Season

Goals: 166 by Lewis Jones, 1956-57
Tries: 63 by Eric Harris, 1935-36
Points: 431 by Lewis Jones, 1956-57

Career

Goals: 1,244 by Lewis Jones, 1952-64
Tries: 391 by Eric Harris, 1930-39
Points: 2,920 by Lewis Jones, 1952-64
Appearances: 608 + 18 by John Holmes, 1968-89
Highest score: 102-0 v. Coventry, 12 Apr 1913
Highest against: 74-6 at Wigan, 10 May 1992
Attendance: 40,175 v. Bradford N. (League), 21 May 1947

COACHING REGISTER

● **Since 1974-75**

Roy Francis	June 74 - May 75
Syd Hynes	June 75 - Apr 81
Robin Dewhurst	June 81 - Oct 83
Maurice Bamford	Nov 83 - Feb 85
Malcolm Clift	Feb 85 - May 85
Peter Fox	May 85 - Dec 86
Maurice Bamford	Dec 86 - Apr 88
Malcolm Reilly	Aug 88 - Sep 89
David Ward	Sep 89 - May 91
Doug Laughton	May 91 -

Doug Laughton, appointed coach of Leeds in May 1991.

GREAT BRITAIN REGISTER
(70 players)

L. Adams	(1)	1932
J. Atkinson	(26)	1968-80
J. Bacon	(11)	1920-26
R. Batten	(3)	1969-73
J. Bentley	(1)	1992
J. Birch	(1)	1907
S. Brogden	(7)	1936-37
J. Brough	(5)	1928-36
G. Brown	(6)	1954-55
M. Clark	(5)	1968
T. Clawson	(3)	1972
D. Creasser	(2+2)	1985-88
L. Crooks	(1)	1989
W. A. Davies	(2)	1914
K. Dick	(2)	1980
R. Dickinson	(2)	1985
P. Dixon	(8+1)	1990-92
L. Dyl	(11)	1974-82
A. Fisher	(3)	1970-71
P. Ford	(5)	1989
R. Gemmell	(1)	1964
C. Gibson	(10)	1990-91
R. Goulding	(1)	1992
J. Grayshon	(2)	1985
R. Haigh	(3+1)	1970-71
D. Hallas	(2)	1961
F. Harrison	(3)	1911
D. Heron	(1+1)	1982
J. Holmes	(14+6)	1971-82
S. Hynes	(12+1)	1970-73
J. W. Jarman	(2)	1914
D. Jeanes	(3)	1972
D. Jenkins	(1)	1947
B. L. Jones	(15)	1954-57
K. Jubb	(2)	1937
J. Lowe	(1)	1932
P. Medley	(3+1)	1987-88
I. Owens	(4)	1946
S. Pitchford	(4)	1977
H. Poole	(2)	1966
R. Powell	(13+6)	1985-91
D. Prosser	(1)	1937
Keith Rayne	(4)	1984
Kevin Rayne	(1)	1986
B. Risman	(5)	1968
D. Robinson	(5)	1956-60
D. Rose	(4)	1954
G. Schofield	(17)	1988-91
B. Seabourne	(1)	1970
B. Shaw	(1)	1961
M. Shoebottom	(10+2)	1968-71
B. Simms	(1)	1962
A. Smith	(10)	1970-73
S. Smith	(10)	1929-33
D. Stephenson	(4+1)	1988
J. Stevenson	(15)	1955-58
S. Stockwell	(3)	1920-21
A. Terry	(1)	1962
A. Thomas	(4)	1926-29
P. Thomas	(1)	1907
J. Thompson	(12)	1924-32
A. Turnbull	(1)	1951
H. Waddell	(1)	1989
D. Ward	(12)	1977-82
W. Ward	(1)	1910
F. Webster	(3)	1910
R. Williams	(9)	1948-51
H. Woods	(1)	1937
G. Wriglesworth	(5)	1965-66
F. Young	(1)	1908

Utility forward Paul Dixon, capped nine times for Great Britain while serving Leeds.

LEEDS 1991-92 SIGNINGS REGISTER

Signed	Player	Club From
17.6.91	Barrett, Anthony	Middleton ARL
20.6.91	Pickles, Steve	Middleton ARL
8.7.91	Goulding, Bobby	Wigan
9.8.91	Deakin, Leigh	Heworth ARL
9.8.91	Anderson, John	Redhill ARL
16.8.91	*Pearce, Greg	London C.
21.8.91	O'Neill, Mike	Rochdale H.
6.9.91	Hanley, Ellery	Wigan
12.9.91	Edwards, Morvin	Upper Hutt, NZ
11.10.91	*Wilby, Andrew	Ryedale-York
24.10.91	Shaw, Matthew	Ryedale-York
31.10.91	Render, Nick	Ryedale-York
22.11.91	Harrison, Mark	Stanningley ARL
12.12.91	Arundel, Stuart	Lock Lane ARL
14.12.91	Child, Lee	Stanningley ARL
4.1.92	Innes, Craig	Ponsonby RU, NZ
24.2.92	Pearson, Carl	BP ARL
26.3.92	*Hall, John	Dewsbury
27.3.92	*Petch, Andrew	Hunslet

1991-92 PLAYERS' SUMMARY

	App	Tries	Goals	Dr	Pts
Anderson, Paul	1 + 6	—	—	—	—
Arundel, Stuart	1 + 2	—	—	—	—
Bentley, John	30 + 3	19	—	—	76
Creasser, David	30 + 1	11	—	—	44
Deakin, Leigh	3 + 1	1	—	—	4
Divorty, Gary	28 + 2	5	—	—	20
Dixon, Paul	27 + 6	14	—	—	56
Edwards, Morvin	32	7	—	—	28
Fawcett, Vince	9 + 1	3	—	—	12
Ford, Phil	25 + 1	12	—	—	48
Gallagher, John	7 + 1	1	26	—	56
Gibson, Carl	27 + 6	5	—	—	20
Goulding, Bobby	32 + 3	7	14	5	61
Gunn, Richard	12 + 1	1	—	—	4
Hanley, Ellery	19	9	—	—	36
Heron, David	5 + 7	1	—	—	4
Heugh, Cavill	25 + 1	2	—	—	8
Innes, Craig	16	4	—	—	16
Irving, Simon	17 + 2	1	49	—	102
James, Neil	1 + 1	—	—	—	—
Maloney, Francis	0 + 1	—	—	—	—
Maskill, Colin	26	2	18	—	44
Molloy, Steve	18 + 8	2	—	—	8
O'Neill, Mike	27	4	—	—	16
Powell, Roy	16 + 5	2	—	—	8
Schofield, Garry	32 + 1	13	2	8	64
Shaw, Matt	3	—	—	—	—
Stephens, Gareth	6 + 6	—	—	—	—
Wane, Shaun	19 + 7	2	—	—	8

TOTALS:

29 players		128	109	13	743

Representative Appearances 1991-92
Anderson — GB Under-21 (1)
Bentley — Britain (1, 1t)
Dixon — Britain (1); Yorkshire (1)
Ford — Wales (2, 4t)
Gibson — Yorkshire (1)
Goulding — Britain (1); GB Under-21 (1, 1t, 1g); Lancashire (1)
Hanley — Yorkshire (1)
Powell — Yorkshire (+1)
Schofield — Britain (1, 1t); Yorkshire (1)
Wane — Lancashire (1)

New Zealand Test back Morvin Edwards, recruited by Leeds in September 1991, scoring seven tries in 32 games.

Two tries in 26 games in 1991-92 for Australian packman Cavill Heugh.

LEEDS 1991-92 MATCH ANALYSIS

Date	Competition	H/A	Opponent	Rlt	Score	Tries	Goals	Attendance	Referee
1.9.91	SBC	A	Widnes	L	10-12	Wane, Dixon	Irving	—	—
8.9.91	SBC	H	Hull	W	20-14	Bentley (2), Goulding	Irving (4)	15,101	Crashley
15.9.91	YC(1)	A	Hull	L	11-16	Schofield	Maskill (3), Goulding (dg)	—	—
22.9.91	SBC	A	Castleford	W	13-8	Creasser (2), Schofield	Schofield (dg)	—	—
29.9.91	SBC	H	Swinton	W	46-8	Hanley (3), Ford (2), Schofield, Bentley, Goulding	Maskill (6), Schofield	9517	Kershaw
6.10.91	SBC	A	Bradford N.	W	48-14	Dixon (4), Edwards, Ford, Creasser, Gibson, Hanley	Maskill (6)	—	—
13.10.91	SBC	H	Warrington	L	13-22	Edwards, Ford	Maskill (2), Schofield (dg)	11,056	Whitfield
20.10.91	SBC	A	Wakefield T.	L	20-22	O'Neill, Dixon, Ford, Irving	Irving (2)	—	—
27.10.91	SBC	H	St. Helens	D	8-8	Edwards, Divorty	—	12,020	Galtress
3.11.91	SBC	A	Wigan	W	19-0	Ford (2), Bentley	Irving (3), Schofield (dg)	—	—
10.11.91	SBC	H	Featherstone R.	W	26-20	Dixon (2), Bentley, Edwards	Irving (5)	10,882	Ollerton
16.11.91	RT(1)	A	Warrington	W	17-8	Goulding, Hanley	Irving (4), Schofield (dg)	—	—
23.11.91	RT(2)	A	Hull	W	12-4	Divorty, Schofield	Irving (2)	—	—
1.12.91	RT(3)	H	Castleford	W	24-4	Dixon (2), Divorty, Powell	Irving (3), Schofield (2dg)	15,409	Campbell
7.12.91	RT(SF)	N1	Salford	W	22-15	Schofield, O'Neill, Dixon	Irving (5)	(7275)	Whitfield
18.12.91	SBC	H	Bradford N.	W	22-12	Edwards, Schofield, Gunn, Goulding	Irving (3)	8084	Campbell
22.12.91	SBC	A	Swinton	W	18-10	Molloy, Powell, Ford, Bentley	Irving	—	—
26.12.91	SBC	H	Hull K.R.	W	22-8	Goulding, O'Neill, Maskill, Creasser	Irving (3)	14,023	Whitfield
1.1.92	SBC	H	Salford	W	36-10	Bentley (2), Dixon, Ford, Gibson, Schofield, Creasser	Irving (4)	12,519	Galtress
11.1.92	RT(F)	N2	Widnes	L	0-24	—		(15,070)	Galtress
18.1.92	SBC	A	Salford	W	27-10	Ford (2), Divorty, Wane, Goulding	Irving (3), Goulding (dg)	—	—
21.1.92	CC(P)	A	Bramley	W	36-12	Creasser (3), Bentley, O'Neill, Schofield, Edwards	Irving (4)	—	—
25.1.92	CC(1)	H	Ryedale-York	W	48-6	Bentley (3), Edwards (2), Creasser (2), Gallagher	Gallagher (8)	5080	Morris
2.2.92	SBC	H	Castleford	L	4-18	—	Irving (2)	14,227	Cummings
8.2.92	CC(2)	H	St. Helens	L	12-32	Gibson, Molloy	Goulding (1, 2dg)	9610	Whitfield
23.2.92	SBC	A	Warrington	L	6-17	Bentley	Goulding	—	—
1.3.92	SBC	A	St. Helens	L	8-19	Innes, Heugh	—	—	—
8.3.92	SBC	H	Widnes	W	40-28	Bentley (2), Dixon, Creasser, Schofield, Maskill, Heugh	Goulding (6)	9799	J. Connolly
15.3.92	SBC	H	Wigan	L	0-24	—	—	20,821	Whitfield
22.3.92	SBC	A	Hull	L	14-22	Hanley, Schofield, Bentley	Gallagher	—	—
29.3.92	SBC	H	Wakefield T.	L	0-17	—	—	10,100	J. Connolly
5.4.92	SBC	A	Hull K.R.	W	13-4	Bentley, Hanley	Gallagher (2), Schofield (dg)	—	—
12.4.92	SBC	A	Featherstone R.	L	20-21	Innes, Bentley, Hanley	Gallagher (4)	—	—
17.4.92	SBC	H	Halifax	L	16-24	Hanley, Gibson	Gallagher (4)	9983	Carter
20.4.92	SBC	A	Halifax	W	46-34	Fawcett (2), Innes (2), Bentley, Deakin, Heron, Gibson	Gallagher (7)	—	—
26.4.92	PT(1)	A	Warrington	D	18-18	Divorty, Goulding	Goulding (3, 1dg), Schofield (1, 1dg)	—	—
29.4.92	PT(1) Replay	H	Warrington	W	22-8	Schofield (2), Fawcett, Ford	Goulding (3)	8221	Cummings
10.5.92	PT(SF)	A	Wigan	L	6-74	Dixon	Maskill	—	—

N1 at Bradford C. FC
N2 at Wigan

LEIGH

Ground: Hilton Park (0942-674437)
Colours: Red and white
First Season: 1895-96
General
Manager: John Stringer
Coach: Alex Murphy (Mar 1990-Aug 1991)
Kevin Ashcroft (Sep 1991-)
Honours: **Championship** Winners, 1905-06
Division One Champions, 1981-82
Division Two Champions, 1977-78, 1985-86, 1988-89
Challenge Cup Winners, 1920-21, 1970-71
Lancashire Cup Winners, 1952-53, 1955-56, 1970-71, 1981-82
Beaten finalists, 1905-06, 1909-10, 1920-21, 1922-23, 1949-50, 1951-52, 1963-64, 1969-70
BBC2 Floodlit Trophy Winners, 1969-70, 1972-73
Beaten finalists, 1967-68, 1976-77

RECORDS

Match
Goals: 15 by Mick Stacey v. Doncaster, 28 Mar 1976
Tries: 6 by Jack Wood v. York, 4 Oct 1947
Points: 38 by John Woods v. Blackpool B., 11 Sep 1977
John Woods v. Ryedale-York, 12 Jan 1992

Season
Goals: 173 by Chris Johnson, 1985-86
Tries: 49 by Steve Halliwell, 1985-86
Points: 400 by Chris Johnson, 1985-86

Career
Goals: 1,043 by Jim Ledgard, 1948-58
Tries: 189 by Mick Martyn, 1954-67
Points: 2,450 by John Woods, 1976-85 & 1990-
Appearances: 503 by Albert Worrall, 1921-35 & 1936-38
Highest score: 92-2 v. Keighley, 30 Apr 1986
Highest against: 60-8 at Salford, 25 May 1940
Attendance: 31,324 v. St. Helens (RL Cup), 14 Mar 1953

COACHING REGISTER
● **Since 1974-75**

Eddie Cheetham	May 74 - Mar 75
Kevin Ashcroft	June 75 - Jan 77
Bill Kindon	Jan 77 - Apr 77
John Mantle	Apr 77 - Nov 78
Tom Grainey	Nov 78 - Dec 80
★Alex Murphy	Nov 80 - June 82
★Colin Clarke	June 82 - Dec 82
Peter Smethurst	Dec 82 - Apr 83
Tommy Bishop	June 83 - June 84
John Woods	June 84 - May 85
Alex Murphy	Feb 85 - Nov 85
Tommy Dickens	Nov 85 - Dec 86
Billy Benyon	Dec 86 - Mar 90
Alex Murphy	Mar 90 - Aug 91
Kevin Ashcroft	Sep 91 -

★From Dec 80 to June 82 Clarke was officially appointed coach and Murphy manager.

GREAT BRITAIN REGISTER
(19 players)

K. Ashcroft	(5)	1968-70
J. Cartwright	(7)	1920-21
D. Chisnall	(2)	1970
J. Darwell	(5)	1924
S. Donlan	(+2)	1984
D. Drummond	(22)	1980-86
P. Foster	(3)	1955
C. Johnson	(1)	1985
F. Kitchen	(2)	1954
J. Ledgard	(9)	1948-54
G. Lewis	(1)	1965
M. Martyn	(2)	1958-59
W. Mooney	(2)	1924
S. Owen	(1)	1958
C. Pawsey	(7)	1952-54
W. Robinson	(2)	1963
Joe Walsh	(1)	1971
W. Winstanley	(2)	1910
J. Woods	(7+3)	1979-83

1991-92 SIGNINGS REGISTER

Signed	Player	Club From
25.8.91	Ake, Basil	Ryedale-York
28.8.91	Collier, Andrew	Wigan
28.8.91	Rodgers, Craig	Wigan
29.8.91	Ruane, Andy	Oldham
6.9.91	Costello, John	Leigh Miners ARL
1.10.91	Hansen, Lee	Orange United, Aus
1.10.91	Moran, Peter	Wigan
13.10.91	Dainty Mark	Leigh East ARL
13.10.91	Hayes, Tommy	Leigh East ARL
13.10.91	Johnson, Kevin	Golbourne ARL
13.10.91	Pendlebury, Gary	Wigan
2.11.91	*Platt, Alan	Halifax
28.11.91	Barrett, David	Langworthy ARL
13.12.91	*Shaw, David	Salford
29.12.91	Martin, Scott	Leigh East ARL
2.1.92	Tanner, David	St. Helens
2.1.92	*McCormack, Kevin	St. Helens
25.1.92	*Viller, Paul	Rochdale H.
29.3.92	Rowley, Paul	Leigh Miners ARL
31.3.92	Baldwin, Simon	Leigh East ARL
5.4.92	Fanning, Sean	Hare and Hounds ARL

1991-92 PLAYERS' SUMMARY

	App	Tries	Goals	Dr	Pts
Ake, Basil	6 + 2	4	—	—	16
Barrett, David	1 + 1	—	—	—	—
Blakeley, Mike	0 + 1	—	1	—	2
Booth, Simon	26 + 1	9	—	—	36
Bridge, Russ	18 + 5	1	—	—	4
Collier, Andrew P.	14	2	—	—	8
Collier, Andy	8 + 3	4	—	—	16
Costello, John	22 + 2	3	—	—	12
Cottrell, Tony	3 + 1	—	—	—	—
Dainty, Mark	13 + 5	3	—	—	12
Donohue, Jason	30 + 1	11	7	—	58
Dunn, Brian	9 + 1	1	—	—	4
Earner, Adrian	11 + 4	—	—	—	—
Fanning, Sean	1	—	—	—	—
Hansen, Lee	16 + 6	1	—	—	4
Hayes, Tommy	12 + 6	3	—	—	12
Hill, David	26 + 3	15	—	—	60
Jeffrey, Ian	31 + 1	8	—	1	33
Johnson, Kevin	1 + 2	—	—	—	—
Johnson, Phil	0 + 1	—	—	—	—
Ledger, Barry	9 + 2	6	—	—	24
McCulloch, Neil	7	4	—	—	16
Mellor, Terry	0 + 1	—	—	—	—
Moore, Jim	6 + 1	—	—	—	—
Pendlebury, Gary	4 + 4	—	—	—	—
Potter, Ian	10	—	—	—	—
Rodgers, Craig	1 + 4	—	—	—	—
Round, Mick	4	1	—	—	4
Ruane, Andy	32 + 1	5	2	17	41
Ruane, David	16 + 1	6	—	—	24
Sheals, Mark	27 + 1	3	—	—	12
Standish, Wayne	3	1	—	—	4
Tanner, David	13	5	2	—	24
Topping, Paul	26	16	17	1	99
Valentine, Peter	1 + 1	—	—	—	—
Woods, John	22 + 2	8	72	2	178

TOTALS:
	App	Tries	Goals	Dr	Pts
36 players		120	101	21	703

Representative Appearances 1991-92
Donohue — GB Under-21 (+1)
Topping — Lancashire (1)

Great Britain Under-21 debutant Jason Donohue, scorer of 11 tries and seven goals for Leigh in 1991-92.

Veteran John Woods, who contributed 178 points in 24 outings in 1991-92.

LEIGH 1991-92 MATCH ANALYSIS

Date	Com-petition	H/A	Opponent	Rlt	Score	Tries	Goals	Atten-dance	Referee
1.9.91	SD	H	Ryedale-York	W	26-10	D. Ruane (2), Topping (2), Andy Collier	Topping (3)	3090	Tidball
8.9.91	SD	A	Oldham	L	19-46	Topping, Donohue, Andy Collier, Round	Topping, A. Ruane (dg)	—	—
15.9.91	LC(1)	H	Chorley B.	W	59-12	D. Ruane (3), McCulloch (2), Andrew Collier (2), Standish, Andy Collier, Donohue, Jeffrey, Booth	Topping (4), Donohue, A. Ruane (dg)	2415	Gilmour
22.9.91	SD	H	Carlisle	W	32-22	Jeffrey (2), Booth, Donohue, McCulloch, Topping	Topping (4)	2822	Campbell
26.9.91	LC(1)	A	Wigan	L	12-42	McCulloch, Ledger	Topping (2)	—	—
29.9.91	SD	A	London C.	L	18-20	Topping (2), Jeffrey (2)	Topping	—	—
7.10.91	SD	A	Rochdale H.	W	19-10	Hayes, Ake, Andy Collier	Woods (3), A. Ruane (dg)	—	—
13.10.91	SD	H	Sheffield E.	L	13-14	Booth, Topping	Woods (2), A. Ruane (dg)	3064	Whitelam
20.10.91	SD	H	Workington T.	W	10-5	Booth	Woods (3)	2754	Whitfield
28.10.91	SD	A	Ryedale-York	W	22-7	Booth, Hill, Sheals, Bridge	Donohue (3)	—	—
31.10.91	RT(P)	A	Hull	L	7-22	Ake	Donohue, A. Ruane (dg)	—	—
6.11.91	SD	H	Oldham	W	20-4	A. Ruane, Ake, Hill, Donohue	Donohue (2)	2550	Crashley
10.11.91	SD	A	Carlisle	W	16-12	Hill, Donohue, Ake	A. Ruane (2)	—	—
24.11.91	SD	A	London C.	L	4-14	—	Topping (2)	—	—
15.12.91	SD	A	Sheffield E.	W	16-10	Woods, D. Ruane	Woods (3, 1dg), Topping (2)	—	—
22.12.91	SD	H	Rochdale H.	W	24-22	Topping, Woods, Jeffrey, Hansen	Woods (4)	2942	Kendrew
26.12.91	SD	H	London C.	W	13-6	Booth	Woods (4, 1dg)	2888	J. Connolly
1.1.92	SD	H	Oldham	W	23-12	Dunn, Hill, Topping	Woods (5), A. Ruane (dg)	4560	Ollerton
5.1.92	SD	A	Workington T.	W	15-9	Topping, Hayes	Tanner, Woods, A. Ruane (2dg), Jeffrey (dg)	—	—
12.1.92	SD	H	Ryedale-York	W	70-0	Woods (4), Topping (3), Hill (2), Dainty, A. Ruane, Tanner	Woods (11)	2685	Redfearn
25.1.92	CC(1)	A	Dewsbury	L	2-14	—	A. Ruane (2dg)	—	—
2.2.92	SD	H	Carlisle	W	19-18	Woods, Tanner, Hayes	Woods (3), A. Ruane (dg)	2420	Cross
16.2.92	SD	A	Rochdale H.	W	27-14	Donohue, Topping, Tanner, Sheals	Woods (5), A. Ruane (dg)	—	—
23.2.92	SD	H	Sheffield E.	W	26-24	Hill (2), Donohue, Topping	Woods (4), A. Ruane (2dg)	4059	Steele
1.3.92	SD	A	Ryedale-York	W	21-4	Hill (3)	Woods (4), A. Ruane (dg)	—	—
8.3.92	SD	H	Workington T.	W	68-6	Ledger (4), Dainty (2), Costello (2), A. Ruane, Hill, Sheals, Tanner, Donohue	Woods (8)	2713	Kershaw
15.3.92	SD	A	Carlisle	L	11-19	Donohue, Topping	Woods, A. Ruane (dg)	—	—
22.3.92	SD	A	Sheffield E.	L	6-51	Hill	Woods	—	—
29.3.92	SD	H	London C.	W	30-8	Booth (2), Hill, Jeffrey, Costello, A. Ruane	Woods (3)	2307	R. Smith
5.4.92	SD	H	Rochdale H.	L	0-12	—	—	3351	J. Smith
12.4.92	SD	A	Workington T.	W	34-8	A. Ruane, Donohue, Jeffrey, Hill, Tanner, Ledger	Woods (5)	—	—
20.4.92	SD	A	Oldham	W	15-14	Woods, Donohue	Woods (2), Tanner, A. Ruane (dg)	—	—
26.4.92	DP(2)	H	Batley	L	6-15	Booth	Blakeley	2320	Burke

LONDON CRUSADERS

Ground: Crystal Palace National Sports
Centre (081-659-4241)
Colours: Black, red and white
First Season: 1980-81. Began as Fulham and
became London Crusaders at start
of 1991-92
General
Manager: Ross Strudwick
Coach: Ross Strudwick (June 1989-)
Honours: **Division Two** Champions, 1982-83

RECORDS

Match

Goals: 11 by Steve Guyett v. Huddersfield,
23 Oct 1988
Greg Pearce v. Runcorn H.,
26 Aug 1990
Tries: No player has scored more than 3
Points: 22 by Alan Platt v. Mansfield M.,
10 May 1986
Greg Pearce v. Runcorn H.,
26 Aug 1990

Season

Goals: 136 by Steve Diamond, 1982-83
Tries: 27 by John Crossley, 1982-83
Points: 308 by Steve Diamond, 1982-83

Career

Goals: 309 by Steve Diamond, 1981-84
Tries: 74 by Hussein M'Barki, 1981-84 & 1988-
Points: 691 by Steve Diamond, 1981-84
Appearances: 148 + 14 by Hussein M'Barki,
1981-84 & 1988-
Highest score: 61-22 v. Huddersfield, 23 Oct 1988
Highest against: 72-6 v. Whitehaven, 14 Sep 1986
Attendance: 2,324 v. Hull (John Player Trophy),
18 Nov 1984 — at Crystal Palace
15,013 v. Wakefield T. (RL Cup),
15 Feb 1981 — at Craven Cottage

COACHING REGISTER

● **Since formation in 1980**

Reg Bowden	July 80 - June 84
Roy Lester	June 84 - Apr 86
Bill Goodwin	Apr 86 - May 88
⋆Bev Risman	May 88 - Feb 89
Phil Sullivan	Feb 89 - Mar 89
Bill Goodwin	Mar 89 - Apr 89
Ross Strudwick	June 89 -

⋆Team manager

GREAT BRITAIN REGISTER
(1 player)

J. Dalgreen	(1)	1982

1991-92 SIGNINGS REGISTER

Signed	Player	Club From
14.8.91	Olsen, Ben	Beaudesert, Aus
30.8.91	Atkinson, Colin	Halifax
30.8.91	Beevers, Ben	Halifax
30.8.91	Ovens, Ray	Beaudesert, Aus
31.8.91	Smith, Chris	Twickenham RU
	Workman, Glen	Aus
3.9.91	Why, Adrian	Fulham
12.9.91	Rolls, Francis	Valleys, Aus
18.10.91	Plath, Johnny	Brisbane B., Aus
6.12.91	Halafihi, Nick	Sheffield E.
6.12.91	Wilby, Tim	Sheffield E.
2.1.92	Berney, Gary	Hemel Hempstead ARL
2.1.92	Boyle, Wayne	Fulham
2.1.92	Cartwright, John	London Colonials ARL
2.1.92	Deaker, Gary	Fulham
2.1.92	Dray, Matt	Batley
2.1.92	Gilbert, Bernie	Bath RU
2.1.92	Heisner, Ross	Villefranche, Fr
2.1.92	Mulkerin, Danny	Peckham ARL
2.1.92	Rosolen, Steve	—
2.1.91	Stevens, Andy	—
2.1.92	Tuson, Lee	Essex RU
10.3.92	Mason, Gary	—
27.3.92	Ashman, Thomas	Herne Hill ARL
27.3.92	Poletti, Nick	Oxford Univ. ARL
27.3.92	Shaw, Andy	Oxford Univ. ARL
27.3.92	Welsh, Matthew	—
27.3.92	Wood, John	Oxford Univ. ARL

1991-92 PLAYERS' SUMMARY

	App	Tries	Goals	Dr	Pts
Abderaman, Dazi	1	—	—	—	—
Atkinson, Colin	26	5	—	—	20
Beevers, Ben	8 + 1	—	—	—	—
Berney, Gary	4 + 1	2	—	—	8
Boyle, Wayne	1	—	—	—	—
Browning, Russell	3	—	—	—	—
Buckley, Shane	34	17	—	—	68
Churchill, Lachlan	26 + 7	7	—	—	28

Corcoran, Colin	6 + 4	—	—	—	—	Scott, Conrad	2	—	—	—	—
Crompton	0 + 1	—	—	—	—	Shaw, Andy	2 + 2	—	—	—	—
Deaker, Gary	24	5	—	—	20	Simpson, Ian	1	—	—	—	—
Dray, Matt	23	1	—	—	4	Smith, Chris	29 + 2	3	78	—	168
Gilbert, Bernie	14 + 2	2	—	—	8	Taylor, Mick	24 + 3	2	—	—	8
Halafihi, Nick	10 + 8	3	—	—	12	Why, Adrian	0 + 1	—	—	—	—
Holderness, Kevin	0 + 1	—	—	—	—	Wilby, Tim	24 + 2	—	—	—	—
M'Barki, Hussein	2 + 2	1	—	—	4	Wilkins, Brett	4	—	—	—	—
Olsen, Ben	27 + 3	3	—	—	12	Wilkinson, Bernie	26 + 1	7	—	—	28
Ovens, Ray	4	1	—	—	4	Winbourne, Doug	0 + 4	—	—	—	—
Pitt, Darryl	33	12	11	—	70	Wing, Jason	12	2	—	—	8
Plath, Johnny	15 + 1	5	—	—	20	Winstanley, Chris	7 + 1	—	—	—	4
Roberts, Steve	0 + 2	—	—	—	—	Workman, Glen	11 + 16	—	—	—	—
Rolls, Francis	2	—	—	—	—						
Rosolen, Steve	26 + 1	5	—	—	20	TOTALS:					
Rotheram, Dave	24 + 2	—	—	—	—	38 players		84	89	—	514
Scarlett, Richard	0 + 1	—	—	—	—						

1991-92 MATCH ANALYSIS

Date	Competition	H/A	Opponent	Rlt	Score	Tries	Goals	Attendance	Referee
1.9.91	SD	A	Workington T.	L	8-12	Buckley	Smith (2)	—	—
8.9.91	SD	A	Rochdale H.	W	28-26	Pitt (2), Olsen, Ovens, Wing	Smith (4)	—	—
15.9.91	LC(1)	H	Wigan	L	10-38	Buckley, Wing	Smith	1893	Campbell
22.9.91	SD	H	Sheffield E.	L	22-44	Buckley (2), M'Barki, Pitt	Pitt (3)	1220	Morris
29.9.91	SD	H	Leigh	W	20-18	Pitt (2), Buckley	Smith (3), Pitt	1090	Asquith
6.10.91	SD	H	Oldham	L	20-23	Churchill, Halafihi	Smith (6)	1102	Volante
13.10.91	SD	A	Carlisle	L	4-12	Halafihi	—	—	—
20.10.91	SD	H	Ryedale-York	W	20-10	Buckley, Churchill, Pitt	Smith (3), Pitt	526	R. Connolly
27.10.91	SD	A	Workington T.	W	10-4	Wilkinson	Smith (3)	—	—
3.11.91	SD	H	Rochdale H.	L	14-22	Smith, Rosolen, Buckley	Smith	750	Harrigan (Aus)
10.11.91	SD	H	Sheffield E.	L	12-29	Buckley, Deaker	Smith (2)	820	R. Smith
17.11.91	RT(1)	A	Oldham	L	10-16	Buckley (2)	Pitt	—	—
24.11.91	SD	H	Leigh	W	14-4	Churchill (2)	Pitt (3)	500	Cummings
8.12.91	SD	A	Oldham	W	10-0	Wilkinson, Atkinson	Pitt	—	—
22.12.91	SD	H	Carlisle	W	12-8	Wilkinson, Plath, Rosolen	—	350	Crashley
26.12.91	SD	A	Leigh	L	6-13	Olsen	Pitt	—	—
5.1.92	SD	H	Ryedale-York	W	18-6	Plath, Buckley, Deaker, Rosolen	Smith	376	R. Connolly
12.1.92	SD	A	Rochdale H.	W	32-12	Taylor (2), Buckley, Pitt, Rosolen	Smith (6)	—	—
19.1.92	SD	H	Rochdale H.	W	20-18	Dray, Wilkinson, Pitt	Smith (4)	700	Cummings
2.2.92	CC(1)	A	Highfield	D	12-12	Plath, Deaker	Smith (2)	—	—
4.2.92	CC(1) Replay	H	Highfield	W	24-10	Wilkinson, Buckley, Plath, Gilbert	Smith (4)	245	Gilmour
9.2.92	CC(2)	A	Workington T.	L	2-9	—	Smith	—	—
16.2.92	SD	H	Oldham	L	8-12	Rosolen	Smith (2)	900	J. Smith
23.2.92	SD	A	Carlisle	L	24-28	Pitt (2), Smith, Plath	Smith (4)	—	—
27.2.92	SD	A	Sheffield E.	L	12-36	Pitt, Wilkinson	Smith (2)	—	—
1.3.92	SD	H	Workington T.	W	28-7	Gilbert, Churchill, Winstanley, Wilkinson	Smith (6)	600	Ward
8.3.92	SD	A	Ryedale-York	W	14-8	Atkinson, Churchill	Smith (3)	—	—
15.3.92	SD	A	Oldham	L	4-16	Pitt	—	—	—
22.3.92	SD	H	Carlisle	W	20-15	Atkinson, Olsen, Buckley	Smith (4)	450	Steele
29.3.92	SD	A	Leigh	L	8-30	Smith	Smith (2)	—	—
5.4.92	SD	A	Ryedale-York	L	4-16	Churchill	—	—	—
12.4.92	SD	A	Sheffield E.	L	4-38	Berney	—	—	—
17.4.92	SD	H	Workington T.	W	32-16	Atkinson (2), Deaker, Berney, Buckley	Smith (6)	750	Asquith
26.4.92	DP(2)	H	Huddersfield	W	14-4	Buckley, Deaker	Smith (3)	561	Volante
10.5.92	DP(SF)	A	Oldham	L	14-22	Halafihi, Buckley	Smith (3)	—	—

93

NOTTINGHAM CITY

Ground: Harvey Hadden Stadium
             (0602-691666)
Colours: Green and yellow
First Season: 1984-85 as Mansfield Marksman.
             Moved and became Nottingham
             City at start of 1989-90.
Nickname: Outlaws
Chairman: Paul Tomlinson
Secretary: Joan Tomlinson
Coach: Arnold Hema (Feb 1991-June 1991)
             Mark Burgess (June 1991-Apr 1992)
             Dave Sampson (May 1992-)

RECORDS

Match

Goals: 7 by Barry Holden v. Keighley,
         10 Mar 1985
         Wayne Sanchez v. Hunslet,
         2 Oct 1988
Tries: 4 by Keith Whiteman v. Doncaster,
         4 Nov 1984
Points: 18 by Barry Holden v. Keighley,
         10 Mar 1985
         Mick Howarth v. Dewsbury,
         17 Jan 1988

Season

Goals: 63 by Carl Sanderson, 1984-85
Tries: 13 by Steve Nicholson, 1984-85
         Keith Whiteman, 1984-85
Points: 136 by Carl Sanderson, 1984-85

Career

Goals: 79 by Carl Sanderson, 1984-86
Tries: 26 by Chris Willis, 1984-91
Points: 195 by David Oates, 1986-91
Appearances: 103 + 12 by Chris Willis, 1984-91
Highest score: 54-10 v. Doncaster, 4 Nov 1984
Highest against: 100-6 v. Hull K.R.
          (at Doncaster), 19 Aug 1990
Attendance: 2,545 v. Halifax (Div. 2), 1 Oct 1989

COACHING REGISTER
● **Since formation in 1984**

Mick Blacker	May 84 - Oct 85
Bill Kirkbride	Nov 85 - Mar 86
Steve Dennison	Apr 86 - Dec 86
Jim Crellin	Dec 86 - June 88
Billy Platt	July 88 - Dec 88
Steve Nash	Dec 88 - Feb 89
Lee Greenwood	Feb 89 - Mar 90
Mel Wibberley	Mar 90 - Feb 91
Arnold Hema	Feb 91 - June 91
Mark Burgess	June 91 - Apr 92
Dave Sampson	May 92 -

1991-92 SIGNINGS REGISTER

Signed	Player	Club From
11.6.91	Cartwright, Steve	Bradley Arms ARL
12.7.91	Dakin, Heath	Hunslet Junction ARL
13.7.91	Francis, Danny	Derby RU
20.7.91	Cooper, Paul	Dewsbury
20.7.91	Moore, John	Dewsbury
26.7.91	Milton, Roy	Hunslet
26.7.91	Haines, Andy	Oulton ARL
5.8.91	Morrisey, Gary	Brisbane Souths, ARL
6.8.91	Hare, Tyrone	Notts Crusaders ARL
25.8.91	Taylor, Steve	Notts Crusaders ARL
25.8.91	Okiwe, Andy	—
28.8.91	*McCabe, Martin	Dewsbury
28.8.91	*Howley, Pat	Dewsbury
17.9.91	Richardson, Tony	Airedale & Wharfedale ARL
17.9.91	Cooper, Gary	Shaws ARL
18.9.91	McDaid, Gary	Shaws ARL
20.9.91	Dawson, Terry	Bradley Arms ARL
1.10.91	Greenwood, Ian	BBA ARL
8.10.91	Dibb, Graham	BBA ARL
8.10.91	Maxwell, Terry	Bradley Arms ARL
11.10.91	May, Paul	Bramley
15.10.91	Hodson, Justin	Kinsley Grey'ds ARL
16.10.91	Madden, Shaun	Batley
8.11.91	Trayhurn, Rod	Bramley
11.11.91	Ellis, Ian	Bradley Arms ARL
22.11.91	Williams, Gerald	Kinsley Grey'ds ARL
29.11.91	*Tyers, Andy	Keighley C.
2.2.92	Paige, Darren	Leeds Supporters ARL
7.2.92	Wilkinson, Mark	Bison Sports ARL
11.2.92	*Gregg, Carl	Huddersfield
12.2.92	Idle, Graham	Doncaster
21.2.92	Corion, Rudi	Huddersfield
2.4.92	Haigh, Chris	Dewsbury
2.4.92	Toole, Tim	Dewsbury
1.5.92	Ventola, Roy	Huddersfield

1991-92 PLAYERS' SUMMARY

	App	Tries	Goals	Dr	Pts
Burgess, Mark	15 + 1	—	—	—	—
Cartwright, Steve	24	5	12	1	45
Chappell, Tony	25	4	14	4	48
Cooper, Gary	6 + 7	—	—	—	—
Cooper, Paul	28	1	—	—	4
Corion, Rudi	2	—	—	—	—
Dakin, Heath	1	—	—	—	—
Dawson, Terry	13	—	—	—	—
Edridge, Lee	12 + 4	1	—	—	4
Fletcher, Andy	3	—	—	—	—
Francis, Danny	0 + 1	—	—	—	—
Greenwood, Ian	23	—	—	—	—
Gregg, Carl	8	—	—	1	1
Gregoire, Donn	17 + 1	3	—	—	12
Haines, Andy	8 + 1	—	—	—	—
Handley, Geoff	1 + 3	—	—	—	—
Hare, Tyrone	2 + 1	—	—	—	—
Harrold, Brian	9 + 5	2	—	—	8
Hodson, Justin	2 + 1	—	—	—	—
Howley, Pat	2	—	—	—	—
Idle, Graham	9	—	—	—	—
Jackson, Darryl	21 + 1	2	—	—	8
Jackson, Dean	24 + 3	4	—	—	16
McCabe, Martin	4 + 1	—	—	—	—
McDaid, Gary	0 + 1	—	—	—	—
Maxwell, Tony	0 + 2	—	—	—	—
May, Paul	2 + 3	—	—	—	—
Milton, Roy	17 + 3	4	—	—	16
Moore, Gary	21	1	—	—	4
Moore, John	25	2	—	—	8
Morrisey, Gary	1	—	—	—	—
Paige, Darren	1	—	—	—	—
Richardson, Tony	2	—	—	—	—
Riley, Malcolm	3 + 1	—	—	—	—
Roberts, Howard	2	—	—	—	—
Rudd, Neil	7	1	—	—	4
Taylor, Adrian	2 + 4	—	—	—	—
Toder, Jai	1 + 1	—	—	—	—
Trayhurn, Rod	4 + 1	—	—	—	—
Tyers, Andy	12 + 3	—	—	—	—
Vale, Andy	1	—	—	—	—
Ventola, Roy	8	—	—	—	—
Wilder, Peter	1	—	—	—	—
Wilkinson, Mark	6 + 1	1	—	—	4
Wood, Richard	2 + 3	—	—	—	—
TOTALS: 45 players		31	26	6	182

1991-92 MATCH ANALYSIS

Date	Competition	H/A	Opponent	Rlt	Score	Tries	Goals	Attendance	Referee
25.8.91	YC(P)	H	Huddersfield	L	7-36	—	Cartwright (3), Chappell (dg)	176	Tidball
1.9.91	TD	A	Doncaster	L	6-88	P. Cooper	Cartwright	—	—
8.9.91	TD	H	Scarborough P.	L	4-54	Milton	—	201	R. Smith
22.9.91	TD	A	Batley	L	4-48	Dean Jackson	—	—	—
29.9.91	TD	H	Hunslet	L	11-44	Milton, Gregoire	Cartwright (1, 1dg)	233	Ollerton
6.10.91	TD	A	Bramley	L	0-54	—	—	—	—
13.10.91	TD	H	Whitehaven	L	8-32	Harrold	Cartwright (2)	360	Volante
20.10.91	TD	A	Scarborough P.	L	10-36	J. Moore, Dean Jackson	Cartwright	—	—
27.10.91	TD	H	Keighley C.	L	4-42	Dean Jackson	—	220	Redfearn
3.11.91	TD	A	Highfield	L	10-36	Cartwright, Gregoire	Cartwright	—	—
10.11.91	TD	H	Batley	L	0-64	—	—	401	J. Smith
17.11.91	RT(1)	H	Wakefield T.	L	11-42	Darryl Jackson, Milton	Cartwright, Chappell (dg)	916	Ollerton
1.12.91	TD	A	Hunslet	L	4-52	Cartwright	—	147	Redfearn
8.12.91	TD	H	Highfield	L	13-20	Milton, Edridge	Cartwright (2), Chappell (dg)	147	Redfearn
22.12.91	TD	H	Trafford B.	L	14-50	Darryl Jackson, Chappell	Chappell (3)	148	Tidball
29.12.91	TD	H	Doncaster	L	20-42	Cartwright (2), Harrold, Dean Jackson	Chappell (2)	398	R. Connolly
8.1.92	CC(P)	H	Batley	L	0-36	—	—	168	Asquith
12.1.92	TD	H	Dewsbury	L	0-58	—	—	357	Kershaw
19.1.92	TD	A	Barrow	L	8-78	Chappell	Chappell (2)	—	—
2.2.92	TD	H	Bramley	L	4-34	Gregoire	—	155	Burke
9.2.92	TD	A	Huddersfield	L	0-78	—	—	—	—
16.2.92	TD	A	Chorley B.	L	7-22	Cartwright	Chappell (1, 1dg)	—	—
23.2.92	TD	A	Keighley C.	L	0-70	—	—	—	—
1.3.92	TD	H	Barrow	L	1-54	—	Gregg (dg)	150	R. Connolly
15.3.92	TD	H	Chorley B.	L	16-24	Rudd, J. Moore, G. Moore	Chappell (2)	198	Tidball
22.3.92	TD	A	Dewsbury	L	6-66	Chappell	Chappell	—	—
29.3.92	TD	H	Huddersfield	L	0-82	—	—	548	Steele
7.4.92	TD	A[1]	Trafford B.	L	8-15	Chappell	Chappell (2)	—	—
12.4.92	TD	A	Whitehaven	L	6-80	Wilkinson	Chappell	—	—

[1] at Huddersfield

OLDHAM

Ground: Watersheddings (061-624-4865)
Colours: Red and white
First Season: 1895-96
Nickname: Roughyeds
Chairman: John Chadwick
Chief Exec: Ian Carr
Coach: Peter Tunks (Apr 1991-)
Honours: **Championship** Winners, 1909-10,
               1910-11, 1956-57
               Beaten finalists, 1906-07, 1907-08,
               1908-09, 1921-22, 1954-55
               Division One Champions, 1904-05
               Division Two Champions, 1963-64,
               1981-82, 1987-88
               Challenge Cup Winners, 1898-99,
               1924-25, 1926-27
               Beaten finalists, 1906-07, 1911-12,
               1923-24, 1925-26
               Second Division Premiership
               Winners, 1987-88, 1989-90
               Divisional Premiership Beaten
               finalists, 1991-92
               Lancashire Cup Winners, 1907-08,
               1910-11, 1913-14, 1919-20, 1924-25,
               1933-34, 1956-57, 1957-58, 1958-59
               Beaten finalists, 1908-09, 1911-12,
               1918-19, 1921-22, 1954-55, 1966-67,
               1968-69, 1986-87, 1989-90
               Lancashire League Winners,
               1897-98, 1900-01, 1907-08, 1909-10,
               1921-22, 1956-57, 1957-58

RECORDS

Match
Goals: 14 by Bernard Ganley v. Liverpool C.,
       4 Apr 1959
Tries: 7 by James Miller v. Barry, 31 Oct 1908
Points: 30 by Abe Johnson v. Widnes, 9 Apr 1928

Season
Goals: 200 by Bernard Ganley, 1957-58
Tries: 49 by R. Farrar, 1921-22
Points: 412 by Bernard Ganley, 1957-58

Career
Goals: 1,365 by Bernard Ganley, 1951-61
Tries: 173 by Alan Davies, 1950-61
Points: 2,775 by Bernard Ganley, 1951-61
Appearances: 626 by Joe Ferguson, 1899-1923
Highest score: 67-6 v. Liverpool C., 4 Apr 1959
Highest against: 67-11 at Hull K.R., 24 Sep 1978
Attendance: 28,000 v. Huddersfield (League),
               24 Feb 1912

COACHING REGISTER
● **Since 1974-75**

Jim Challinor	Aug 74 - Dec 76
Terry Ramshaw	Jan 77 - Feb 77
Dave Cox	July 77 - Dec 78
Graham Starkey (Mgr)	Jan 79 - May 81
Bill Francis	June 79 - Dec 80
Frank Myler	May 81 - Apr 83
Peter Smethurst	Apr 83 - Feb 84
Frank Barrow	Feb 84 - Feb 84
Brian Gartland	Mar 84 - June 84
Frank Myler	June 84 - Apr 87
*Eric Fitzsimons	June 87 - Nov 88
*Mal Graham	June 87 - Apr 88
Tony Barrow	Nov 88 - Jan 91
John Fieldhouse	Jan 91 - Apr 91
Peter Tunks	Apr 91 -

Joint coaches June 87 - Apr 88

GREAT BRITAIN REGISTER
(40 players)

A. Avery	(4)	1910-11
C. Bott	(1)	1966
A. Brough	(2)	1924
T. Clawson	(9)	1973-74
A. Davies	(20)	1955-60
E. Davies	(3)	1920
T. Flanagan	(4)	1983-84
D. Foy	(3)	1984-85
B. Ganley	(3)	1957-58
A. Goodway	(11)	1983-85
W. Hall	(4)	1914
H. Hilton	(7)	1920-21

D. Hobbs	(2)	1987
D. Holland	(4)	1914
R. Irving	(8+3)	1967-72
K. Jackson	(2)	1957
E. Knapman	(1)	1924
S. Little	(10)	1956-58
T. Llewellyn	(2)	1907
J. Lomas	(2)	1911
W. Longworth	(3)	1908
L. McIntyre	(1)	1963
T. O'Grady	(5)	1954
J. Oster	(1)	1929
D. Parker	(2)	1964
D. Phillips	(3)	1946
F. Pitchford	(2)	1958-62
T. Rees	(1)	1929
S. Rix	(9)	1924-26
R. Sloman	(5)	1928
A. Smith	(6)	1907-08
I. Southward	(7)	1959-62
L. Thomas	(1)	1947
D. Turner	(11)	1956-58
G. Tyson	(4)	1907-08
H. Waddell	(4)	1988
T. White	(1)	1907
C. Winslade	(1)	1959
A. Wood	(4)	1911-14
M. Worrall	(3)	1984

1991-92 SIGNINGS REGISTER

Signed	Player	Club From
2.8.91	Philips, Abraham	Moldgreen ARL
7.8.91	Burns, Gary	Widnes Tigers ARL
15.8.91	Bradbury, David	Leigh Miners ARL
15.8.91	Christie, Gary	Widnes Tigers ARL
15.8.91	Green, Jake	St. Annes ARL
15.8.91	McDermott, Barrie	Waterhead ARL
15.8.91	Pitts, David	Bramley
15.8.91	Rogers, Darrell	Waterhead ARL
15.8.91	Street, Tim	Swinton
19.8.91	Holding, Neil	Rochdale H.
19.8.91	Nicklin, Vince	Limoux, Fr
28.8.91	Eckersley, Chris	Saddleworth R. ARL
2.9.91	Hourigan, Paul	Leigh Miners ARL
4.9.91	Conroy, Tony	Salford
13.9.91	Tupaea, Shane	Swinton
17.9.91	Barrow, Paul	—
7.10.91	*Grima, Joe	Widnes

16.10.91	Byrne, Ged	Wakefield T.
6.11.91	Faimalo, Joe	Workington T.
8.11.91	Sherratt, Ian	Salford
29.11.91	Edwards, Logan	NZ
6.12.91	Tyrer, Sean	Wigan
28.12.91	*Hetherington, Gary	Whitehaven
1.1.92	*Bimson, Jeff	Chorley B.
21.1.92	Bardsley, Michael	—
21.1.92	Yeomans, Richard	Kirkholt ARL
3.2.92	Stephenson, David	Queens Park ARL
11.3.92	Edwards, Michael	Parkside ARL
13.3.92	Buckley, Paul	Golbourne ARL
30.3.92	Ropati, Iva	Sheffield E.
30.3.92	Hudspith, Mark	Leigh East ARL

1991-92 PLAYERS' SUMMARY

	App	Tries	Goals	Dr	Pts
Allen, Shaun	3 + 1	—	—	—	—
Atkinson, Keith	2 + 2	—	—	—	—
Barrow, Tony	2	—	—	—	—
Bates, Ian	12 + 1	—	—	1	1
Bimson, Jeff	1	—	—	—	—
Bradbury, David	1 + 6	—	—	—	—
Buckley, Paul	0 + 1	—	—	—	—
Byrne, Ged	26	6	—	—	24
Christie, Gary	16 + 3	6	—	—	24
Clements, Mike	1	—	—	—	—
Conroy, Tony	5 + 2	—	—	—	—
Donegan, Austin	6	1	—	—	4
Edwards, Logan	13 + 1	5	—	—	20
Faimalo, Joe	0 + 1	—	—	—	—
Flanagan, Neil	28	4	—	2	18
Grima, Joe	3	—	—	—	—
Henderson, John	5 + 1	2	—	—	8
Holding, Neil	4	—	1	—	2
Irving, Richard	16	4	—	—	16
Jones, Brett	1	—	—	—	—
Joynt, Chris	23 + 3	10	—	—	40
Longstaff, Simon	5 + 4	1	—	—	4
Lord, Paul	4	2	—	—	8
McAlister, Charlie	18 + 4	4	10	—	36
McDermott, Barrie	4 + 10	3	—	—	12
Martyn, Tommy	24 + 1	13	34	5	125
Maxwell, John	1 + 1	—	—	—	—
Mulligan, Mark	2	—	—	—	—
Newton, Keith	11 + 3	2	—	—	8
Nicklin, Vince	34	8	—	—	32
Pachnuik, Richard	27 + 2	12	7	—	62
Platt, Duncan	20	6	25	—	74
Ranson, Scott	9	8	—	—	32
Robinson, Steve	1	—	—	—	—
Ropati, Iva	7 + 1	3	—	—	12
Round, Paul	6	2	—	—	8
Russell, Richard	20 + 2	1	—	—	4
Sherratt, Ian	24 + 1	2	—	—	8
Stephenson, David	1	—	—	—	—
Street, Tim	25 + 2	5	—	—	20
Tupaea, Shane	19 + 1	—	—	—	—
Tyrer, Sean	20	7	29	1	87
Warburton, Steve	18 + 11	8	—	—	32
TOTALS:					
43 players		125	106	9	721

Representative Appearances 1991-92
Joynt — GB Under-21 (2+1, 1t)
Martyn — GB Under-21 (+2, 1g)

OLDHAM 1991-92 MATCH ANALYSIS

Date	Com-petition	H/A	Opponent	Rlt	Score	Tries	Goals	Atten-dance	Referee
1.9.91	SD	A	Sheffield E.	D	16-16	Martyn, Warburton, Irving	Holding, McAlister	—	—
8.9.91	SD	H	Leigh	W	46-19	Henderson (2), Martyn, Pachnuik, Longstaff, Irving, Donegan, McDermott	McAlister (4), Martyn (3)	3503	Galtress
15.9.91	LC(1)	A	Swinton	W	22-21	McAlister, Martyn, Pachnuik, Nicklin	Martyn (3)	—	—
23.9.91	SD	A	Workington T.	D	6-6	Street	Martyn	—	—
26.9.91	LC(2)	A	St. Helens	L	26-39	McAlister, Round, Lord, Joynt, Flanagan	Martyn (2), McAlister	—	—
29.9.91	SD	H	Rochdale H.	L	18-26	Round, Flanagan, Warburton	McAlister (3)	3822	Cross
6.10.91	SD	A	London C.	W	23-20	Pachnuik, Lord, Martyn	Martyn (4, 1dg), Pachnuik	—	—
13.10.91	SD	H	Ryedale-York	W	52-18	Pachnuik (2), Christie (2), Nicklin, Irving, Newton, Flanagan, McAlister, Joynt	Martyn (3), Pachnuik (3)	3064	Allatt
20.10.91	SD	A	Carlisle	W	30-10	Byrne, Nicklin, Flanagan, Christie, Joynt	Martyn (4), McAlister	—	—
27.10.91	SD	H	Sheffield E.	L	12-38	Christie, Pachnuik	Martyn (2)	3352	Gilmour
6.11.91	SD	A	Leigh	L	4-20	Martyn	—	—	—
10.11.91	SD	H	Workington T.	L	14-15	Warburton, Joynt	Martyn (2), Pachnuik	2536	Whitelam
17.11.91	RT(1)	H	London C.	W	16-10	Christie, Pachnuik, Street	Pachnuik, Martyn	2182	Carter
24.11.91	RT(2)	H	St. Helens	L	18-24	McAlister, Nicklin, Joynt, Irving	Platt	5814	Holdsworth
1.12.91	SD	A	Rochdale H.	W	20-10	Sherratt, Joynt, Christie	Platt (4)	—	—
8.12.91	SD	H	London C.	L	0-10	—	—	3115	Steele
15.12.91	SD	A	Ryedale-York	W	22-16	Platt, Nicklin, Martyn	Platt (5)	—	—
26.12.91	SD	H	Rochdale H.	W	26-18	Edwards (2), Joynt, Street, Nicklin	Tyrer (3)	4091	Cummings
1.1.92	SD	A	Leigh	L	12-23	Martyn, Warburton	Tyrer (2)	—	—
5.1.92	SD	H	Carlisle	W	14-4	Warburton, Byrne	Tyrer (3)	2020	Carter
12.1.92	SD	H	Sheffield E.	L	18-44	Byrne, Nicklin, Martyn	Tyrer (3)	3091	Tidball
3.2.92	CC(1)	H	Warrington	L	3-8	—	Tyrer, Martyn (dg)	4090	Allatt
12.2.92	SD	A	Workington T.	W	5-0	—	Tyrer (2, 1dg)	—	—
16.2.92	SD	A	London C.	W	12-8	Tyrer, Joynt	Tyrer (2)	—	—
24.2.92	SD	H	Ryedale-York	W	30-6	Russell, Tyrer, Byrne, Sherratt, Edwards	Tyrer (5)	2794	J. Smith
1.3.92	SD	A	Sheffield E.	W	14-10	Warburton, Nicklin, Martyn	Tyrer	—	—
8.3.92	SD	H	Carlisle	W	20-17	Pachnuik (2), Platt, Byrne	Tyrer (2)	2595	Asquith
15.3.92	SD	H	London C.	W	16-4	Edwards, Joynt, McDermott	Tyrer (2)	2829	Holdsworth
29.3.92	SD	A	Carlisle	W	23-10	Edwards, Ranson, Tyrer, Ropati	Platt (3), Flanagan (dg)	—	—
5.4.92	SD	H	Workington T.	W	44-10	Ranson (4), Martyn (3), McDermott	Martyn (5), Pachnuik	2622	Crashley
12.4.92	SD	A	Ryedale-York	W	26-18	Tyrer (2), Street (2), Ropati	Tyrer (3)	—	—
17.4.92	SD	A	Rochdale H.	W	21-10	Tyrer (2), Platt, Ropati	Platt (2), Bates (dg)	—	—
20.4.92	SD	H	Leigh	L	14-15	Warburton (2)	Martyn (2, 1dg), Flanagan (dg)	4678	Carter
26.4.92	DP(2)	H	Dewsbury	W	36-18	Platt (2), Pachnuik (2), Ranson, Joynt	Platt (6)	2514	Whitfield
10.5.92	DP(SF)	H	London C.	W	22-14	Martyn, Joynt, Ranson	Platt (4), Martyn (2dg)	2893	R. Smith
17.5.92	DP(F)	N[1]	Sheffield E.	L	20-34	Platt, Byrne, Newton, Ranson	Martyn (2)	(—)	Cummings

N[1] at Manchester U. FC

ROCHDALE HORNETS

Ground: Spotland (0706-48004)
Colours: White, blue and red
First Season: 1895-96
Nickname: Hornets
Chairman: Dick Bonser
Secretary: Paul Reynolds
Coach: Stan Gittins (Apr 1991-)
Honours: **Challenge Cup** Winners, 1921-22
            Regal Trophy Beaten finalists,
            1973-74
            Lancashire Cup Winners, 1911-12,
            1914-15, 1918-19
            Beaten finalists, 1912-13, 1919-20,
            1965-66, 1991-92
            Lancashire League Winners,
            1918-19
            BBC2 Floodlit Trophy Beaten
            finalists, 1971-72

RECORDS

Match
Goals: 14 by Steve Turner v. Runcorn H.,
        5 Nov 1989
Tries: 5 by Jack Corsi v. Barrow, 31 Dec 1921
        Jack Corsi v. Broughton Moor,
        25 Feb 1922
        Jack Williams v. St. Helens,
        4 Apr 1933
        Norman Brelsford v. Whitehaven,
        3 Sep 1972
Points: 32 by Steve Turner v. Runcorn H.,
         5 Nov 1989

Season
Goals: 115 by Kevin Harcombe, 1985-86
Tries: 30 by Jack Williams, 1934-35
Points: 243 by Steve Turner, 1988-89

Career
Goals: 741 by Walter Gowers, 1922-46
Tries: 103 by Jack Williams, 1931-37
Points: 1,497 by Walter Gowers, 1922-46
Appearances: 456 by Walter Gowers, 1922-46
Highest score: 92-0 v. Runcorn H., 5 Nov 1989
Highest against: 79-2 at Hull, 7 Apr 1921

Attendance: 8,150 v. Oldham (Div. 2),
       26 Dec 1989 — at Spotland
       26,664 v. Oldham (RL Cup),
       25 Mar 1922 — at Athletic Grounds

COACHING REGISTER
● **Since 1974-75**

Frank Myler	May 71 - Oct 74
Graham Starkey	Oct 74 - Nov 75
Henry Delooze	Nov 75 - Nov 76
Kel Coslett	Nov 76 - Aug 79
Paul Longstaff	Sep 79 - May 81
Terry Fogerty	May 81 - Jan 82
Dick Bonser	Jan 82 - May 82
Bill Kirkbride	June 82 - Sep 84
Charlie Birdsall	Sep 84 - Apr 86
Eric Fitzsimons	June 86 - June 87
Eric Hughes	June 87 - June 88
Jim Crellin	June 88 - June 89
Allan Agar	July 89 - Jan 91
Neil Holding	Jan 91 - Apr 91
Stan Gittins	Apr 91 -

GREAT BRITAIN REGISTER
(8 players)

J. Baxter	(1)	1907
J. Bennett	(6)	1924
J. Bowers	(1)	1920
T. Fogerty	(1)	1974
E. Jones	(4)	1920
M. Price	(2)	1967
J. Robinson	(2)	1914
T. Woods	(2)	1911

1991-92 SIGNINGS REGISTER

Signed	Player	Club From
16.8.91	Clark, Brett	Oldham
16.8.91	Duane, Ronnie	Oldham
2.9.91	Kuiti, Mike	Leeds
19.9.91	Eccles, Cliff	Trafford B.
26.9.91	Eccles, Bob	Chorley B.
9.10.91	Okesene, Paul	Manakau, NZ
25.10.91	*Bimson, Jeff	Chorley B.
31.10.91	Viller, Jason	Folly Lane ARL
1.11.91	*Ellis, Jeff	Chorley B.
6.12.91	*Large, David	St. Helens
15.12.91	O'Keefe, Paul	—
26.12.91	Reddican, Mal	Langworthy ARL
2.1.92	*Platt, Alan	Halifax
27.3.92	*Green, Andrew	Trafford B.

1991-92 PLAYERS' SUMMARY

	App	Tries	Goals	Dr	Pts
Abram, Darren	32	24	7	1	111
Bamber, Simon	19 + 9	5	—	—	20
Belle, Adrian	10	3	—	—	12
Bimson, Jeff	3	—	—	—	—
Calland, Matt	22 + 3	12	—	—	48
Clark, Brett	32	11	—	—	44
Duane, Ronnie	23 + 2	7	—	—	28
Eccles, Bob	7 + 12	5	15	—	50
Eccles, Cliff	26 + 3	3	—	—	12
Fox, Phil	24	15	—	—	60
Garritty, Brian	23	10	—	—	40
Gartland, Steve	17 + 2	9	—	—	36
Gormley, Ian	7 + 3	1	—	—	4
Hall, Martin	25 + 1	3	—	—	12
Hall, Rob	0 + 2	—	—	—	—
Humphries, Tony	13 + 8	4	—	—	16
Kay, Martin	9	1	—	—	4
Kuiti, Mike	32 + 1	7	—	—	28
Lord, Mark	1	—	—	—	—
Marriott, Karl	8	—	—	—	—
Marsden, Robert	31 + 1	8	—	—	32
Okesene, Paul	19 + 3	2	—	—	8
Pitt, Darren	3 + 2	—	—	—	—
Platt, Alan	1	—	—	—	—
Reddican, Mal	3 + 4	1	—	—	4
Sullivan, Andy	1 + 4	—	—	—	—
Turner, Steve	2 + 2	—	7	1	15
Viller, Mark	3	—	3	—	6
Webster, David	21 + 2	2	—	—	8
Whitfield, Colin	24	—	75	5	155
Williams, Mike	1	—	—	—	—

TOTALS:
| 31 players | | 133 | 107 | 7 | 753 |

Neil Holding, Rochdale Hornets player-coach in a four-month stint.

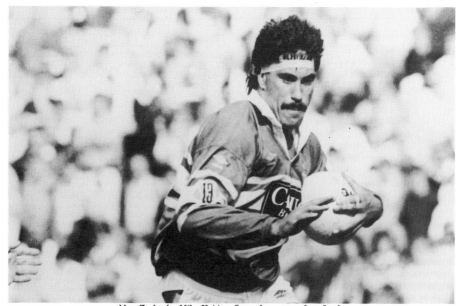

New Zealander Mike Kuiti, a September capture from Leeds.

ROCHDALE 1991-92 MATCH ANALYSIS

Date	Competition	H/A	Opponent	Rlt	Score	Tries	Goals	Attendance	Referee
2.9.91	SD	H	Carlisle	D	18-18	Humphries, Gartland	Whitfield (5)	1216	Crashley
8.9.91	SD	H	London C.	L	26-28	Garritty (2), Humphries, Abram, Kuiti	Whitfield (3)	903	Whitelam
15.9.91	LC(1)	A	Highfield	W	34-11	Clark (2), Fox (2), Garritty, Calland	Whitfield (5)	—	—
22.9.91	SD	H	Ryedale-York	W	66-14	Fox (2), Gartland (2), Abram (2), Duane (2), Calland, Clark, Kuiti, Garritty, M. Hall	Whitfield (7)	1003	Steele
26.9.91	LC(2)	H	Salford	W	25-18	Abram (2), Gartland, Kuiti	Whitfield (4, 1dg)	1829	Gilmour
29.9.91	SD	A	Oldham	W	26-18	Calland, Gartland, R. Eccles, Clark	Whitfield (5)	—	—
7.10.91	SD	H	Leigh	L	10-19	Fox, Clark	R. Eccles	1659	R. Connolly
10.10.91	LC(SF)	H	Carlisle	W	19-6	Calland, Abram, Duane, Marsden	Whitfield, Turner (dg)	1842	Carter
13.10.91	SD	A	Workington T.	W	48-12	Fox (4), Garritty (2), R. Eccles, C. Eccles, Clark	Turner (6)	—	—
20.10.91	LC(F)	N[1]	St. Helens	L	14-24	Duane, Abram, Kuiti	Whitfield	(9269)	Campbell
23.10.91	SD	A	Sheffield E.	L	14-35	Abram, R. Eccles, Garritty	Turner	—	—
29.10.91	RT(P)	H	Widnes	L	14-24	Abram (2)	R. Eccles (3)	2278	Whitelam
3.11.91	SD	A	London C.	W	22-14	Abram, R. Eccles, Clark	R. Eccles (5)	—	—
10.11.91	SD	A	Ryedale-York	D	12-12	Marsden (2)	R. Eccles (2)	—	—
1.12.91	SD	H	Oldham	L	10-20	Kuiti, Gartland	R. Eccles	3235	J. Connolly
15.12.91	SD	H	Workington T.	W	42-8	Fox (2), Abram (2), Okesene, C. Eccles, Kuiti, Clark	Abram (5)	1092	Morris
22.12.91	SD	A	Leigh	L	22-24	Gartland (2), Calland, Humphries	R. Eccles (3)	—	—
26.12.91	SD	A	Oldham	L	18-26	Marsden, Clark, Calland	Viller (3)	—	—
12.1.92	SD	H	London C.	L	12-32	Abram (2)	Whitfield (2)	1014	R. Smith
15.1.92	SD	H	Sheffield E.	L	12-26	Duane, Abram	Whitfield (2)	748	Kershaw
19.1.92	SD	A	London C.	L	18-20	Gormley, Marsden, C. Eccles	Whitfield (3)	—	—
2.2.92	CC(1)	H	Hull	L	28-32	Marsden (2), Clark, M. Hall	Whitfield (6)	1419	Kershaw
6.2.92	SD	H	Ryedale-York	L	14-18	Garritty, Kuiti	Whitfield (2), Abram	776	Allatt
9.2.92	SD	A	Carlisle	W	5-0	Belle	Whitfield (dg)	—	—
16.2.92	SD	H	Leigh	L	14-27	Fox, Bamber, Garritty	Whitfield	1787	Holdsworth
26.2.92	SD	A	Workington T.	W	5-4	—	Whitfield (1, 2dg), Abram (dg)	—	—
1.3.92	SD	H	Carlisle	W	44-14	Duane (2), Bamber (2), Garritty, Kay, Calland, Reddican	Whitfield (5), Abram	1014	Asquith
9.3.92	SD	A	Sheffield E.	L	17-23	Abram (2), Calland	Whitfield (2, 1dg)	—	—
15.3.92	SD	A	Ryedale-York	W	30-4	Abram, Gartland, M. Hall, Bamber, Humphries	Whitfield (5)	—	—
22.3.92	SD	H	Workington T.	W	50-14	Abram (2), Calland (2), Fox (2), Marsden, Webster, Bamber, Clark	Whitfield (5)	1035	Volante
29.3.92	SD	H	Sheffield E.	W	34-18	Calland (2), Abram (2), Okesene, R. Eccles	Whitfield (5)	1258	Burke
5.4.92	SD	A	Leigh	W	12-0	Fox, Belle	Whitfield (2)	—	—
12.4.92	SD	A	Carlisle	L	8-20	Abram	Whitfield (2)	—	—
17.4.92	SD	H	Oldham	L	10-21	Belle, Webster	Whitfield	3098	Allatt

N[1] at Warrington

RYEDALE-YORK

Ground: Ryedale Stadium (0904-634636)
Colours: Amber and black
First Season: 1901-02 as York. Moved and became
Ryedale-York at start of 1989-90
Nickname: Wasps
Chairman: John Stabler
Secretary: Sue Pysanczyn
Coach: Gary Stephens (Apr 1988-June 1991)
Derek Foster (July 1991-)
Honours: **Division Two** Champions, 1980-81
Challenge Cup Beaten finalists,
1930-31
Yorkshire Cup Winners, 1922-23,
1933-34, 1936-37
Beaten finalists, 1935-36, 1957-58,
1978-79

RECORDS

Match
Goals: 11 by Vic Yorke v. Whitehaven,
6 Sep 1958
Chris Gibson v. Dewsbury,
28 Sep 1980
Tries: 6 by Roy Hardgrave v. Bramley,
5 Jan 1935
David Kettlestring at Keighley,
11 Mar 1990
Points: 26 by Graham Steadman v. Batley,
25 Nov 1984
Graham Sullivan v. Keighley,
11 Mar 1990

Season
Goals: 146 by Vic Yorke, 1957-58
Tries: 35 by John Crossley, 1980-81
Points: 318 by Graham Steadman, 1984-85

Career
Goals: 1,060 by Vic Yorke, 1954-67
Tries: 167 by Peter Foster, 1955-67
Points: 2,159 by Vic Yorke, 1954-67
Appearances: 449 by Willie Hargreaves, 1952-65
Highest score: 70-8 v. Keighley, 11 Mar 1990
Highest against: 75-3 at Warrington, 23 Sep 1950
Attendance: 14,689 v. Swinton (RL Cup),
10 Feb 1934 — at Clarence Street
4,977 v. Halifax (Div. 2),
5 Jan 1990 — at Ryedale Stadium

COACHING REGISTER
● **Since 1974-75**

Keith Goulding	Nov 73 - Sep 74
Gary Cooper	Dec 74 - Sep 76
Mal Dixon	Sep 76 - Dec 78
Paul Daley	Jan 79 - May 79
David Doyle-Davidson	July 79 - July 80
Bill Kirkbride	Aug 80 - Apr 82
Alan Hardisty	May 82 - Jan 83
Phil Lowe	Mar 83 - Mar 87
Danny Sheehan	Mar 87 - Apr 88
Gary Stephens	Apr 88 - June 91
Derek Foster	July 91 -

GREAT BRITAIN REGISTER
(7 players)

E. Dawson	(1)	1956
H. Field	(3)	1936
G. Smith	(3)	1963-64
J. Stevenson	(4)	1959-60
M. Sullivan	(1)	1963
B. Watts	(5)	1954-55
L. White	(4)	1946

1991-92 SIGNINGS REGISTER

Signed	Player	Club From
1.6.91	Ramsden, Mick	York Civil Service ARL
30.8.91	*Pagdin, Wayne	Castleford
3.9.91	Steele, Matthew	South Sydney, Aus
4.9.91	Revell, Dean	Redcliffe, Aus
4.9.91	Marshall, Tony	Redcliffe, Aus
13.9.91	*Proctor, Wayne	Doncaster
13.9.91	*Dickinson, Andy	Sheffield E.
24.10.91	*Deakin, Leigh	Leeds
12.11.91	Hopcutt, Chris	Scarborough P.
3.12.91	Clements, Mike	Oldham
27.12.91	*Drummond, Barry	Dewsbury
14.1.92	Lockwood, Peter	Acorn ARL
14.1.92	Blower, Brian	York All Blacks ARL
4.2.92	*Bragger, Ian	Castleford
4.2.92	*Pearce, Gary	Scarborough P.
26.3.92	*Connell, Phil	Bramley

1991-92 PLAYERS' SUMMARY

	App	Tries	Goals	Dr	Pts
Blower, Brian	2	—	—	—	—
Bragger, Ian	4	—	—	—	—
Clements, Mike	0 + 1	—	—	—	—
Connell, Phil	1	—	—	—	—
Craven, Steve	18 + 1	—	—	—	—
Deakin, Leigh	4	2	—	—	8
Dobson, Steve	20 + 1	4	3	3	25
Drummond, Barry	3	—	—	—	—
Fellows, Darren	1	—	—	—	—
Fowler, Richard	1	—	—	—	—
Hammerton, Chris	11 + 5	4	—	—	16
Hayes, Richard	27 + 2	1	—	—	4
Holt, Richard	1 + 2	—	—	—	—
Hopcutt, Chris	13 + 1	1	—	—	4
Horton, Stuart	19	—	—	1	1
Hutchinson, Paul	28	5	—	—	20
Kettlestring, David	13	2	—	—	8
Laws, Mark	3 + 10	1	—	—	4
Lockwood, Peter	2 + 4	—	—	—	—
Marshall, Tony	10	—	—	—	—
Maxwell, Paul	1 + 1	—	—	—	—
Mieckle, David	0 + 1	—	—	—	—
Morris, Stuart	23	3	—	—	12
Pagdin, Wayne	3 + 1	2	—	—	8
Pallister, Alan	9	3	—	—	12
Paver, Ian	24 + 1	—	—	—	—
Pearce, Gary	9	2	15	4	42
Pinkney, Nick	29	13	—	—	52
Proctor, Wayne	1 + 1	—	—	—	—
Pryce, Geoff	17 + 3	3	—	—	12
Pryce, Steve	16 + 5	—	—	—	—
Ramsden, Mick	16 + 5	3	2	—	16
Render, Nick	3 + 1	—	—	—	—
Revell, Dean	6	—	—	—	—
Shaw, Matthew	2 + 5	—	—	—	—
Smith, Adrian	14	1	—	—	4
Steele, Matthew	4	—	—	—	—
Sullivan, Graham	27 + 2	7	42	—	112
Warters, Nick	1	—	—	—	—
Wheatley, Steve	2	1	—	—	4
White, Paul	26	7	—	—	28
Wigglesworth, Ian	2 + 5	1	—	—	4

TOTALS:

	App	Tries	Goals	Dr	Pts
42 players		66	62	8	396

Representative Appearances 1991-92
Pearce — Wales (+1)
Pinkney — GB Under-21 (+1)

1991-92 MATCH ANALYSIS

Date	Competition	H/A	Opponent	Rlt	Score	Tries	Goals	Attendance	Referee
25.8.91	YC(P)	H[1]	Hunslet	W	36-8	Hammerton (2), Morris, White, Ramsden, Laws	Sullivan (6)	707	R. Smith
1.9.91	SD	A	Leigh	L	10-26	Pinkney, Pallister	Sullivan	—	—
8.9.91	SD	H	Workington T.	L	18-42	Pinkney, Pagdin, Sullivan	Sullivan (3)	1564	Volante
15.9.91	YC(1)	A	Huddersfield	L	10-28	Pinkney, Pagdin	Ramsden	—	—
22.9.91	SD	A	Rochdale H.	L	14-66	Pinkney, Hammerton, Kettlestring	Sullivan	—	—
29.9.91	SD	H	Sheffield E.	L	22-26	Pinkney, Hutchinson, White, Pallister	Sullivan (3)	1155	Burke
6.10.91	SD	H	Carlisle	L	6-26	Pinkney	Sullivan	591	Kendrew
13.10.91	SD	A	Oldham	L	18-52	Pallister, Hayes	Sullivan (5)	—	—
20.10.91	SD	A	London C.	L	10-20	Dobson	Sullivan (3)	—	—
28.10.91	SD	H	Leigh	L	7-22	Hutchinson	Sullivan, Dobson (dg)	1165	Burke
10.11.91	SD	H	Rochdale H.	D	12-12	Sullivan, Morris	Sullivan (2)	1405	Gilmour
17.11.91	RT(1)	H	Sheffield E.	L	6-13	Deakin	Sullivan	1138	Cross
24.11.91	SD	A	Workington T.	L	16-20	Pinkney, Dobson, Deakin	Dobson, Sullivan	—	—
8.12.91	SD	A	Carlisle	L	10-28	Sullivan (2)	Sullivan	—	—
15.12.91	SD	H	Oldham	L	16-22	Pinkney, Hutchinson	Sullivan (3), Dobson	1222	J. Smith
26.12.91	SD	H	Sheffield E.	W	8-6	Kettlestring	Sullivan (2)	1318	Kendrew
29.12.91	SD	A	Sheffield E.	L	4-58	Ramsden	—	—	—
5.1.92	SD	A	London C.	L	6-18	Hammerton	Ramsden	—	—
12.1.92	SD	A	Leigh	L	0-70	—	—	—	—
19.1.92	SD	H	Workington T.	W	31-12	White (2), Smith, Hutchinson, Dobson	Sullivan (4), Dobson (1, 1dg)	1249	Crashley
25.1.92	CC(1)	A	Leeds	L	6-48	Sullivan	Sullivan	—	—
6.2.92	SD	A	Rochdale H.	W	18-14	Hutchinson, Wigglesworth, White	Pearce (2, 1dg), Dobson (dg)	—	—
16.2.92	SD	H	Carlisle	W	22-1	Pearce, Dobson, G. Pryce	Pearce (5)	1187	Whitelam
24.2.92	SD	A	Oldham	L	6-30	G. Pryce	Sullivan	—	—
1.3.92	SD	H	Leigh	L	4-21	G. Pryce	—	1431	Gilmour
8.3.92	SD	H	London C.	L	8-14	Pinkney (2)	—	951	Campbell
15.3.92	SD	H	Rochdale H.	L	4-30	Sullivan	—	1120	Carter
29.3.92	SD	A	Workington T.	D	19-19	Morris, White, Hopcutt	Sullivan (2), Pearce (2dg), Horton (dg)	—	—
5.4.92	SD	H	London C.	W	16-4	Pinkney (2), Sullivan	Pearce (2)	706	Allatt
12.4.92	SD	H	Oldham	L	18-26	Pearce, Pinkney, Ramsden	Pearce (3)	1657	Campbell
17.4.92	SD	A	Carlisle	L	8-22	Wheatley	Pearce (2)	—	—
19.4.92	SD	A	Sheffield E.	L	7-42	White	Pearce (1, 1dg)	—	—

[1] at Heworth ARL

ST. HELENS

Ground: Knowsley Road (0744-23697)
Colours: Red and white
First Season: 1895-96
Nickname: Saints
Chairman: Eric Latham
Secretary: Geoff Sutcliffe
Coach: Mike McClennan (Feb 1990-)
Honours: **Championship** Winners, 1931-32, 1952-53, 1958-59, 1965-66, 1969-70, 1970-71
Beaten finalists, 1964-65, 1966-67, 1971-72
League Leaders Trophy Winners, 1964-65, 1965-66
Club Championship (Merit Table) Beaten finalists, 1973-74
Division One Champions, 1974-75
Challenge Cup Winners, 1955-56, 1960-61, 1965-66, 1971-72, 1975-76
Beaten finalists, 1896-97, 1914-15, 1929-30, 1952-53, 1977-78, 1986-87, 1988-89, 1990-91
Regal Trophy Winners, 1987-88
Premiership Winners, 1975-76, 1976-77, 1984-85
Beaten finalists, 1974-75, 1987-88, 1991-92
Lancashire Cup Winners, 1926-27, 1953-54, 1960-61, 1961-62, 1962-63, 1963-64, 1964-65, 1967-68, 1968-69, 1984-85, 1991-92
Beaten finalists, 1932-33, 1952-53, 1956-57, 1958-59, 1959-60, 1970-71, 1982-83
Lancashire League Winners, 1929-30, 1931-32, 1952-53, 1959-60, 1964-65, 1965-66, 1966-67, 1968-69
Western Division Championship Winners, 1963-64
BBC2 Floodlit Trophy Winners, 1971-72, 1975-76
Beaten finalists, 1965-66, 1968-69, 1970-71, 1977-78, 1978-79

RECORDS

Match
Goals: 16 by Paul Loughlin v. Carlisle, 14 Sep 1986
Tries: 6 by Alf Ellaby v. Barrow, 5 Mar 1932
Steve Llewellyn v. Castleford, 3 Mar 1956
Steve Llewellyn v. Liverpool C., 20 Aug 1956
Tom Van Vollenhoven v. Wakefield T., 21 Dec 1957
Tom Van Vollenhoven v. Blackpool B., 23 Apr 1962
Frank Myler v. Maryport, 1 Sep 1969
Shane Cooper v. Hull, 17 Feb 1988
Points: 40 by Paul Loughlin v. Carlisle, 14 Sep 1986

Season
Goals: 214 by Kel Coslett, 1971-72
Tries: 62 by Tom Van Vollenhoven, 1958-59
Points: 452 by Kel Coslett, 1971-72

Career
Goals: 1,639 by Kel Coslett, 1962-76
Tries: 392 by Tom Van Vollenhoven, 1957-68
Points: 3,413 by Kel Coslett, 1961-76
Appearances: 519 + 12 by Kel Coslett, 1961-76
Highest score: 112-0 v. Carlisle, 14 Sep 1986
Highest against: 78-3 at Warrington, 12 Apr 1909
Attendance: 35,695 v. Wigan (League), 26 Dec 1949

COACHING REGISTER
● **Since 1974-75**

Eric Ashton	May 74 - May 80
Kel Coslett	June 80 - May 82
Billy Benyon	May 82 - Nov 85
Alex Murphy	Nov 85 - Jan 90
Mike McClennan	Feb 90 -

GREAT BRITAIN REGISTER
(51 players)

C. Arkwright	(+2)	1985
L. Aston	(3)	1947
W. Benyon	(5+1)	1971-72
T. Bishop	(15)	1966-69
F. Carlton	(1)	1958

E. Chisnall	(4)	1974
G. Connolly	(2 + 1)	1991-92
E. Cunningham	(1)	1978
R. Dagnall	(4)	1961-65
D. Eckersley	(2 + 2)	1973-74
A. Ellaby	(13)	1928-33
L. Fairclough	(6)	1926-29
J. Fieldhouse	(1)	1986
A. Fildes	(4)	1932
A. Frodsham	(3)	1928-29
P. Gorley	(2 + 1)	1980-81
D. Greenall	(6)	1951-54
J. Griffiths	(1)	1992
P. Groves	(1)	1987
R. Haggerty	(2)	1987
M. Hicks	(1)	1965
N. Holding	(4)	1984
R. Huddart	(12)	1959-63
A. Hunte	(1)	1992
L. Jones	(1)	1971
A. Karalius	(4 + 1)	1971-72
V. Karalius	(10)	1958-61
K. Kelly	(2)	1972
B. Ledger	(2)	1985-86
P. Loughlin	(12 + 1)	1988-91
S. McCormick	(1)	1948
T. McKinney	(1)	1957
J. Mantle	(13)	1966-73
R. Mathias	(1)	1979
G. Moses	(9)	1955-57
A. Murphy	(26)	1958-66
F. Myler	(9)	1970
G. Nicholls	(22)	1973-79
H. Pinner	(5 + 1)	1980-86
A. Platt	(4 + 3)	1985-88
A. Prescott	(28)	1951-58
A. Rhodes	(4)	1957-61
J. Stott	(1)	1947
A. Sullivan	(1)	1991
M. Sullivan	(10)	1961-62
J. Tembey	(2)	1963-64
A. Terry	(10)	1958-61
John Walsh	(4 + 1)	1972
K. Ward	(+ 2)	1990
J. Warlow	(3 + 1)	1964-68
C. Watson	(29 + 1)	1963-71

1991-92 SIGNINGS REGISTER

Signed	Player	Club From
24.6.91	Marsh, Paul	Nutgrove ARL
3.7.91	Nickle, Sonny	Sheffield E.
16.12.91	Casey, Sean	Blackbrook ARL
16.12.91	Davies, Glyn	—
16.12.91	Fenlon, Tony	Widnes Tigers ARL
16.12.91	Morley, Chris	Woolston Rovers ARL
12.3.92	Cannon, Peter	Crosfields ARL

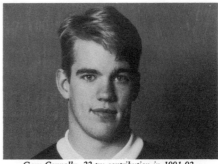

Gary Connolly, 22-try contribution in 1991-92.

1991-92 PLAYERS' SUMMARY

	App	Tries	Goals	Dr	Pts
Bailey, Mark	7 + 13	2	—	—	8
Bishop, Paul	33 + 1	11	57	7	165
Casey, Sean	0 + 1	—	—	—	—
Connolly, Gary	34 + 2	22	—	—	88
Connor, Ian	0 + 1	—	—	—	—
Cooper, Shane	36 + 2	13	—	1	53
Cosgrove, David	0 + 3	—	—	—	—
Dwyer, Bernard	30 + 1	6	12	—	48
Fenlon, Tony	1 + 1	—	1	—	2
Forber, Paul	22 + 11	4	—	1	17
Griffiths, Jonathan	18 + 1	6	—	—	24
Groves, Paul	25 + 5	7	—	—	28
Harrison, John	28 + 1	2	—	—	8
Hodkinson, Tom	0 + 1	—	—	—	—
Hunte, Alan	31	24	—	—	96
Jones, Paul	0 + 3	—	—	—	—
Lever, David	0 + 2	1	—	—	4
Loughlin, Paul	11	6	40	—	104
Mann, George	34 + 2	7	—	—	28
Neill, Jonathan	14	—	—	—	—
Nickle, Sonny	20 + 4	5	—	—	20
O'Brien, Darren	0 + 3	2	—	—	8
Quirk, Les	16 + 3	9	—	—	36
Riley, Mike	18 + 9	6	—	—	24
Ropati, Tea	36 + 1	17	—	—	68
Sullivan, Anthony	27 + 1	13	—	—	52
Tanner, David	9	1	19	—	42
Veivers, Phil	35 + 2	13	—	—	52
Ward, Kevin	35	3	—	—	12

TOTALS:

29 players		180	129	9	987

Representative Appearances 1991-92
Connolly — Britain (2 + 1); GB Under-21 (2, 2t)
Griffiths — Britain (1, 1t); Wales (2, 1t)
Hunte — Britain (1, 1t)
Quirk — Cumbria (1)
Riley — GB Under-21 (2)
Sullivan — Britain (1, 1t); Wales (2, 2t); Yorkshire (1)

ST. HELENS 1991-92 MATCH ANALYSIS

Date	Competition	H/A	Opponent	Rlt	Score	Tries	Goals	Attendance	Referee
1.9.91	SBC	A	Hull	W	31-10	Griffiths, Veivers, Hunte, Connolly, Ropati, Groves	Loughlin (3), Cooper (dg)	—	—
8.9.91	SBC	H	Warrington	W	27-20	Hunte (2), Nickle, Veivers	Bishop (3, 1dg), Loughlin (2)	10,277	Tennant
15.9.91	LC(1)	H	Trafford B.	W	104-12	Hunte (3), Sullivan (3), Quirk (3), Groves (2), Ropati (2), Connolly (2), Ward, Cooper, Mann, Bailey, Lever	Dwyer (12)	4550	J. Connolly
22.9.91	SBC	A	Swinton	W	16-12	O'Brien, Ropati, Bishop	Bishop (2)	—	—
26.9.91	LC(2)	H	Oldham	W	39-26	Bishop (2), Harrison, Dwyer, Connolly, Ropati, O'Brien	Bishop (3, 1dg), Tanner (2)	7025	Ollerton
29.9.91	SBC	H	Castleford	W	25-14	Quirk, Forber, Cooper, Riley	Tanner (4), Bishop (dg)	6843	J. Smith
6.10.91	SBC	A	Halifax	L	6-26	Veivers	Tanner	—	—
10.10.91	LC(SF)	H	Wigan	W	28-16	Forber, Connolly, Sullivan, Riley, Dwyer	Tanner (3), Bishop (dg), Forber (dg)	17,125	Whitfield
13.10.91	SBC	H	Bradford N.	W	30-12	Connolly (2), Mann, Groves, Sullivan, Riley	Tanner (3)	7591	J. Smith
20.10.91	LC(F)	N[1]	Rochdale H.	W	24-14	Veivers (2), Mann (2), Bishop	Bishop (2)	(9269)	Campbell
23.10.91	SBC	H	Salford	W	25-16	Connolly, Ropati, Veivers, Tanner, Groves	Tanner (2), Bishop (dg)	6955	Kershaw
27.10.91	SBC	A	Leeds	D	8-8	Hunte	Tanner (2)	—	—
3.11.91	SBC	A	Wakefield T.	L	12-20	Quirk, Veivers	Tanner (2)	—	—
10.11.91	SBC	H	Hull K.R.	W	38-15	Veivers, Dwyer, Hunte, Cooper, Bailey, Harrison, Connolly	Bishop (5)	6865	Galtress
17.11.91	RT(1)	A	Huddersfield	W	32-10	Sullivan, Riley, Connolly, Bishop, Hunte, Dwyer	Bishop (4)	—	—
24.11.91	RT(2)	A	Oldham	W	24-18	Hunte (2), Ropati (2), Quirk	Bishop (2)	—	—
1.12.91	RT(3)	H	Bradford N.	W	30-12	Hunte (3), Cooper (2)	Bishop (5)	8641	Morris
4.12.91	SBC	A	Featherstone R.	L	6-8	Quirk	Bishop	—	—
8.12.91	SBC	H	Swinton	W	28-4	Veivers (2), Sullivan, Groves, Ropati	Bishop (4)	6087	Allatt
15.12.91	SBC	A	Hull K.R.	L	14-24	Veivers, Sullivan, Dwyer	Fenlon	—	—
21.12.91	RT(SF)	N[2]	Widnes	L	10-18	Connolly (2)	Bishop	(6376)	Holdsworth
26.12.91	SBC	A	Wigan	L	6-16	Griffiths	Bishop	—	—
1.1.92	SBC	H	Widnes	W	24-22	Ropati, Hunte, Ward, Bishop	Bishop (4)	13,012	Burke
5.1.92	SBC	A	Salford	W	15-6	Mann, Ropati, Hunte	Bishop (1, 1dg)	—	—
12.1.92	SBC	H	Featherstone R.	W	28-10	Ropati, Connolly, Bishop, Nickle, Forber	Bishop (4)	7070	Morris
19.1.92	SBC	H	Wakefield T.	W	40-12	Cooper (2), Veivers (2), Bishop, Griffiths, Hunte	Bishop (6)	7328	Galtress
2.2.92	CC(1)	A	Widnes	W	10-2	Bishop, Riley	Bishop	—	—
8.2.92	CC(2)	A	Leeds	W	32-12	Cooper (2), Connolly (2), Sullivan (2), Hunte	Bishop (2)	—	—
16.2.92	SBC	A	Bradford N.	W	20-8	Ropati (2), Forber, Dwyer	Bishop (2)	—	—
22.2.92	CC(3)	H	Wigan	L	6-13	Connolly	Bishop	16,018	Holdsworth
1.3.92	SBC	H	Leeds	W	19-8	Hunte (2), Connolly	Bishop (3, 1dg)	7450	R. Smith
8.3.92	SBC	A	Castleford	D	8-8	Sullivan, Connolly	—	—	—
22.3.92	SBC	H	Halifax	W	30-28	Cooper (2), Loughlin, Quirk, Hunte	Loughlin (5)	8625	Whitfield
29.3.92	SBC	H	Hull	W	42-12	Griffiths (2), Ropati (2), Quirk, Groves, Cooper	Loughlin (7)	7136	Volante

(Continued)

1991-92 MATCH ANALYSIS (continued)

Date	Com-petition	H/A	Opponent	Rlt	Score	Tries	Goals	Atten-dance	Referee
4.4.92	SBC	A	Warrington	L	18-30	Mann, Ropati, Bishop	Loughlin (3)	—	—
17.4.92	SBC	H	Wigan	L	6-16	Bishop	Loughlin	14,701	J. Smith
20.4.92	SBC	A	Widnes	W	28-23	Loughlin (2), Connolly (2), Nickle	Loughlin (4)	—	—
26.4.92	PT(1)	H	Halifax	W	52-6	Hunte (3), Nickle (2), Connolly (2), Loughlin, Cooper, Riley	Loughlin (6)	9146	Holdsworth
10.5.92	PT(SF)	H	Castleford	W	30-14	Loughlin, Mann, Ward, Griffiths	Loughlin (7)	9843	Volante
17.5.92	PT(F)	N³	Wigan	L	16-48	Sullivan (2), Loughlin	Loughlin (2)	(33,157)	Holdsworth

N¹ at Warrington
N² at Wigan
N³ at Manchester U. FC

Great Britain and Wales debutant Jonathan Griffiths, scorer of six tries in 19 games in 1991-92.

SALFORD

Ground: The Willows (061-737-6363)
Colours: Red and white
First Season: 1896-97
Nickname: Red Devils
Chairman: John Wilkinson
Secretary: Graham McCarty
Coach: Kevin Tamati (Oct 1989-)
Honours: **Championship** Winners, 1913-14, 1932-33, 1936-37, 1938-39
Beaten finalists, 1933-34
Division One Champions, 1973-74, 1975-76
Division Two Champions, 1990-91
Challenge Cup Winners, 1937-38
Beaten finalists, 1899-1900, 1901-02, 1902-03, 1905-06, 1938-39, 1968-69
Regal Trophy Beaten finalists, 1972-73
Premiership Beaten finalists, 1975-76
Second Division Premiership Winners, 1990-91
Lancashire Cup Winners, 1931-32, 1934-35, 1935-36, 1936-37, 1972-73
Beaten finalists, 1929-30, 1938-39, 1973-74, 1974-75, 1975-76, 1988-89, 1990-91
Lancashire League Winners, 1932-33, 1933-34, 1934-35, 1936-37, 1938-39
BBC2 Floodlit Trophy Winners, 1974-75

RECORDS

Match
Goals: 13 by Gus Risman v. Bramley, 5 Apr 1933
Gus Risman v. Broughton R., 18 May 1940
David Watkins v. Keighley, 7 Jan 1972
Steve Rule v. Doncaster, 4 Sep 1981
Tries: 6 by Frank Miles v. Lees, 5 Mar 1898
Ernest Bone v. Goole, 29 Mar 1902
Jack Hilton v. Leigh, 7 Oct 1939
Points: 39 by Jim Lomas v. Liverpool C., 2 Feb 1907

Season
Goals: 221 by David Watkins, 1972-73
Tries: 46 by Keith Fielding, 1973-74
Points: 493 by David Watkins, 1972-73

Career
Goals: 1,241 by David Watkins, 1967-79
Tries: 297 by Maurice Richards, 1969-83
Points: 2,907 by David Watkins, 1967-79
Appearances: 496 + 2 by Maurice Richards, 1969-83
Highest score: 78-0 v. Liverpool C., 2 Feb 1907
Highest against: 65-0 at Castleford, 1 Apr 1990
Attendance: 26,470 v. Warrington (RL Cup), 13 Feb 1937

Adrian Hadley, second top tryscorer for Salford in 1991-92.

COACHING REGISTER
- **Since 1974-75**

Les Bettinson	Dec 73 - Mar 77
Colin Dixon	Mar 77 - Jan 78
Stan McCormick	Feb 78 - Mar 78
Alex Murphy	May 78 - Nov 80
Kevin Ashcroft	Nov 80 - Mar 82
Alan McInnes	Mar 82 - May 82
Malcolm Aspey	May 82 - Oct 83
Mike Coulman	Oct 83 - May 84
Kevin Ashcroft	May 84 - Oct 89
Kevin Tamati	Oct 89 -

GREAT BRITAIN REGISTER
(28 players)

W. Burgess	(1)	1969
P. Charlton	(17+1)	1970-74
M. Coulman	(2+1)	1971
G. Curran	(6)	1946-48
E. Curzon	(1)	1910
T. Danby	(3)	1950
C. Dixon	(11+2)	1969-74
A. Edwards	(7)	1936-37
J. Feetham	(7)	1932-33
K. Fielding	(3)	1974-77
K. Gill	(5+2)	1974-77
J. Gore	(1)	1926
C. Hesketh	(21+2)	1970-74
B. Hudson	(8)	1932-37
E. Jenkins	(9)	1933-37
J. Lomas	(5)	1908-10
T. McKinney	(7)	1951-54
A. Middleton	(1)	1929
S. Nash	(8)	1977-82
M. Richards	(2)	1974
A. Risman	(17)	1932-46
J. Spencer	(1)	1907
J. Ward	(1)	1970
S. Warwick	(2)	1907
D. Watkins	(2+4)	1971-74
W. Watkins	(7)	1933-37
P. Williams	(1+1)	1989
W. Williams	(2)	1929-32

Salford prop David Young on his debut for Wales against Papua New Guinea at Swansea FC in October 1991.

1991-92 SIGNINGS REGISTER

Signed	Player	Club From
8.7.91	Stazicker, Ged	Wigan
5.8.91	O'Connor, Terry	Widnes Tigers ARL
15.8.91	Cruickshank, David	London C.
28.8.91	Reid, Wayne	Wigan
4.9.91	Croston, Trevor	Oldham
11.9.91	*Reynolds, Paul	Trafford B.
24.10.91	Subritzky, Peter	Huddersfield
8.11.91	Donegan, Austin	Oldham
11.2.92	Coussons, Phil	Salford U-18s ARL
20.2.92	Skaite, Robert	Salford Academy ARL
29.4.92	Smith, Paul	Eccles ARL

Stand off Wayne Reid, a bargain buy from Wigan in August 1991.

1991-92 PLAYERS' SUMMARY

	App	Tries	Goals	Dr	Pts
Birkett, Martin	32 + 1	15	70	—	200
Blease, Ian	26 + 1	3	—	—	12
Bradshaw, Arthur	14 + 16	8	—	—	32
Brown, Shaun	2	—	—	1	1
Burgess, Andy	20 + 1	2	—	—	8
Cassidy, Frank	5 + 7	2	—	—	8
Cruickshank, David	16 + 1	2	—	—	8
Donegan, Austin	4 + 3	—	—	—	—
Evans, Tex	31	20	—	—	80
Fell, David	12 + 6	5	—	—	20
Fox, Kevin	0 + 1	1	—	—	4
Gibson, Steve	32	15	—	—	60
Gilfillan, John	13 + 8	5	—	—	20
Hadley, Adrian	17	16	—	—	64
Hansen, Shane	18 + 4	3	—	—	12
Howard, Tony	4	—	—	—	—
Kerry, Steve	14 + 2	3	36	—	84
Lee, Mark	30	3	—	4	16
O'Connor, Terry	0 + 3	—	—	—	—
O'Neill, Paul	2	—	—	—	—
Randall, Craig	1 + 4	—	—	—	—
Reid, Wayne	29	10	—	—	40
Reynolds, Paul	6 + 1	3	—	—	12
Sherratt, Ian	7	2	—	—	8
Stazicker, Ged	31 + 2	3	—	—	12
Subritzky, Peter	0 + 2	—	—	—	—
Williams, Peter	27	3	—	—	12
Worrall, Mick	20 + 4	4	—	—	16
Young, David	29	1	—	—	4
TOTALS:					
29 players		129	106	5	733

Representative Appearances 1991-92
Birkett — Cumbria (1, 1t)
Blease — Lancashire (1)
Hadley — Wales (+2, 1t)
Kerry — Lancashire (+1)
Young — Wales (2)

Australian full back Steve Gibson, contributor of 15 tries in 1991-92.

SALFORD 1991-92 MATCH ANALYSIS

Date	Competition	H/A	Opponent	Rlt	Score	Tries	Goals	Attendance	Referee
1.9.91	SBC	A	Warrington	L	20-22	Birkett, Gibson, Kerry	Kerry (4)	—	—
8.9.91	SBC	H	Castleford	L	10-18	Burgess, Hadley	Kerry	4022	Kershaw
15.9.91	LC(1)	H	Warrington	W	22-16	Hadley (2), Reid, Stazicker	Kerry (3)	3656	Carter
22.9.91	SBC	A	Bradford N.	L	24-48	Gibson (2), Fell, Reid	Birkett (4)	—	—
26.9.91	LC(2)	A	Rochdale H.	L	18-25	Birkett, Gibson, Evans	Kerry (3)	—	—
29.9.91	SBC	H	Widnes	L	10-18	Sherratt, Stazicker	Kerry	4124	Morris
6.10.91	SBC	A	Hull	W	24-12	Evans, Worrall, Birkett, Hadley	Kerry (4)	—	—
13.10.91	SBC	H	Halifax	W	34-14	Evans (2), Hadley (2), Birkett, Bradshaw	Kerry (5)	5356	Crashley
23.10.91	SBC	A	St. Helens	L	16-25	Sherratt, Birkett, Williams	Kerry (2)	—	—
27.10.91	SBC	H	Hull	W	26-8	Fell, Blease, Evans, Gibson	Birkett (5)	3128	Holdsworth
3.11.91	SBC	A	Featherstone R.	W	27-22	Evans, Gibson, Fell, Blease, Hadley	Birkett (3), Lee (dg)	—	—
13.11.91	SBC	H	Wigan	W	24-10	Reid (2), Hadley, Evans	Birkett (4)	5377	Cross
17.11.91	RT(1)	H	Trafford B.	W	74-10	Gibson (4), Hadley (2), Worrall (2), Gilfillan (2), Evans, Lee, Cruickshank, Bradshaw	Birkett (9)	1783	Allatt
23.11.91	RT(2)	A	Wakefield T.	W	30-10	Evans, Hadley, Stazicker, Reynolds, Reid, Gibson	Birkett (3)	—	—
30.11.91	RT(3)	H	Wigan	W	24-14	Evans (2), Birkett, Hadley, Cruickshank	Birkett (2)	4608	Holdsworth
7.12.91	RT(SF)	N[1]	Leeds	L	15-22	Birkett (2), Gilfillan	Birkett, Lee (dg)	(7275)	Whitfield
15.12.91	SBC	A	Halifax	L	12-29	Evans, Cassidy	Birkett (2)	—	—
22.12.91	SBC	A	Hull K.R.	L	7-28	Evans	Birkett, Brown (dg)	—	—
26.12.91	SBC	H	Swinton	W	48-4	Bradshaw (3), Birkett (2), Cassidy, Evans, Gibson	Birkett (8)	4280	R. Smith
1.1.92	SBC	A	Leeds	L	10-36	Evans, Reynolds	Birkett	—	—
5.1.92	SBC	H	St. Helens	L	6-15	Evans	Birkett	3680	Cummings
9.1.92	CC(P)	A	Chorley B.	W	64-13	Gibson (2), Birkett (2), Bradshaw (2), Reynolds, Reid, Lee, Young, Gilfillan, Williams	Birkett (8)	—	—
12.1.92	SBC	A	Castleford	L	12-26	Bradshaw, Birkett	Birkett (2)	—	—
18.1.92	SBC	H	Leeds	L	10-27	Birkett (2)	Birkett	2913	R. Smith
2.2.92	CC(1)	H	Wigan	L	6-22	Williams	Birkett	11,173	J. Smith
9.2.92	SBC	A	Wakefield T.	L	10-27	Evans, Fell	Birkett	—	—
16.2.92	SBC	H	Featherstone R.	W	26-4	Kerry, Fell, Lee, Reid	Kerry (5)	3232	J. Connolly
28.2.92	SBC	H	Bradford N.	W	23-6	Kerry, Evans, Burgess, Blease	Kerry (3), Lee (dg)	3743	Whitfield
15.3.92	SBC	H	Wakefield T.	L	12-18	Hansen	Kerry (4)	3349	Cummings
22.3.92	SBC	A	Wigan	L	7-28	Worrall	Kerry, Lee (dg)	—	—
29.3.92	SBC	H	Warrington	L	10-14	Reid, Hansen	Birkett	3130	Campbell
5.4.92	SBC	A	Widnes	W	24-20	Fox, Reid, Evans, Hadley	Birkett (4)	—	—
12.4.92	SBC	H	Hull K.R.	W	22-10	Evans, Gibson, Hansen, Reid	Birkett (3)	2880	Whitfield
20.4.92	SBC	A	Swinton	W	26-18	Hadley (3), Gilfillan	Birkett (5)	—	—

N[1] at Bradford C. FC

111

SCARBOROUGH PIRATES

Ground: McCain Stadium (0723-375094)
Colours: Royal, purple and gold
First Season: 1991-92
Secretary: Roland Davis
Coach: Len Casey (Feb 1991-Dec 1991)
             Trevor Bailey (Dec 1991-)

RECORDS

Match
Goals: 7 by Gary Pearce at Nottingham C.,
         8 Sep 1991
Tries: No player has scored more than 3
Points: 20 by Mark Knapper v. Trafford B.,
         1 Mar 1992

Season
Goals: 48 by Gary Pearce, 1991-92
Tries: 11 by Garry Clark, 1991-92
Points: 104 by Gary Pearce, 1991-92

Highest score: 54-4 at Nottingham C., 8 Sep 1991
Highest against: 52-4 v. Bradford N., 2 Feb 1992
Attendance: 1,427 v. Bradford N. (RL Cup),
2 Feb 1992

1991-92 SIGNINGS REGISTER

Signed	Player	Club From
11.6.91	Patrick, Shaun	Hull
11.6.91	Smith, Peter	Featherstone R.
24.6.91	Beall, Malcolm	Hull K.R.
24.6.91	Knapper, Mark	Featherstone R.
24.6.91	Mirfin, Phil	Castleford
25.6.91	Carlyle, Brendan	Ryedale-York
25.6.91	Olsen, Steve	Ryedale-York
1.7.91	Corban, Dean	Kellingley Welfare ARL
1.7.91	Ellis, Ian	Heworth ARL
1.7.91	Ward, Sean	Pointer Panthers ARL
1.7.91	Rowbottom, Tony	Featherstone R.
5.7.91	Barnett, Karl	Scarb'gh All Blacks ARL
5.7.91	Ash, David	Scarb'gh All Blacks ARL
5.7.91	Ash, Kevin	Scarborough RU
16.7.91	Hadi, Steve	Hull K.R.
18.7.91	Lidbury, Steve	Sheffield E.
28.7.91	Booker, Andrew	Askern M.W. ARL
30.7.91	Beaumont, Craig	Telephones ARL
30.7.91	Stead, Ray	Hull K.R.
31.7.91	Robinson, Steve	Hull K.R.
12.8.91	Pearce, Gary	Hull

15.8.91	Potts, Steve	Wakefield T.
15.8.91	Moules, Rob	Wakefield T.
15.8.91	Kelly, Richard	Dewsbury
15.8.91	*Langley, Paul	Bramley
23.8.91	Tomlinson, Alan	Hull
6.9.91	*Harcombe, Kevin	Wakefield T.
7.9.91	Larvin, Stephen	Stelrod ARL
13.9.91	Fairbank, Dick	Halifax
19.9.91	Clark, Garry	Hull K.R.
27.9.91	Beardmore, Bob	Castleford
27.9.91	McCabe, Red	S. London Wand's ARL
20.10.91	Roockley, David	Castleford
1.11.91	Noble, Dean	Otahuhu, NZ
1.11.91	Clark, Dean	Otahuhu, NZ
15.11.91	Windley, Phil	Hull
2.12.91	Wood, Martin	Halifax
4.12.91	Forsyth, Craig	Heworth ARL
29.12.91	Wright, Chris	Streethouse ARL
29.12.91	Lingard, Glyn	—
10.2.92	Van Bellen, Gary	Sheffield E.
27.3.92	Branton, Richard	Sheffield E.
10.4.92	Taylor, Steve	Streethouse ARL

1991-92 PLAYERS' SUMMARY

	App	Tries	Goals	Dr	Pts
Beall, Malcolm	9 + 2	—	—	—	—
Beardmore, Bob	1	1	—	—	4
Booker, Andrew	10 + 2	1	—	—	4
Branton, Richard	2	—	—	—	—
Carlyle, Brendan	18 + 1	4	16	—	48
Clark, Dean	7	2	—	—	8
Clark, Garry	25	11	—	—	44
Daniels, Jamie	4 + 2	—	—	—	—
Douglas, Ian	4 + 1	1	—	—	4
Fairbanks, Dick	18 + 4	1	—	—	4
Forsyth, Craig	9 + 6	1	—	—	4
Hadi, Steve	11	3	—	—	12
Harcombe, Kevin	1	1	—	—	4
Hill, Ken	19 + 3	2	—	—	8
Knapper, Mark	9 + 1	4	12	—	40
Lidbury, Steve	15 + 1	4	—	—	16
Lingard, Glyn	20 + 1	1	—	—	4
McCabe, Red	7	5	—	—	20
Mirfin, Phil	0 + 1	—	—	—	—
Moules, Robert	6	—	—	—	—
Noble, Dean	15 + 2	2	—	—	8
Olsen, Steve	1 + 1	1	—	—	4
Palmer, Craig	7 + 1	4	—	—	16
Patrick, Shaun	22	4	—	—	16
Pearce, Gary	16 + 1	3	44	4	104
Potts, Steve	0 + 7	2	—	—	8
Ramshaw, Jason	3 + 1	—	—	—	—
Robinson, Steve	15 + 4	1	—	—	4
Roockley, David	22	5	4	—	28
Rowbotton, Tony	0 + 4	—	—	—	—
Smith, Peter	12 + 1	2	—	—	8
Stead, Ray	30	8	—	—	32
Taylor, Steve	2	2	—	—	8
Tomlinson, Alan	11	3	—	—	12
Van Bellen, Gary	9	—	—	—	—
Ward, Sean	6	2	—	—	8
Windley, Phil	9	—	—	—	—
Wood, Martin	5 + 1	5	—	—	20
Wright, Chris	10 + 6	4	—	—	16

TOTALS:					
39 players		90	76	4	516

Representative Appearances 1991-92
Pearce — Wales (+1)

1991-92 MATCH ANALYSIS

Date	Competition	H/A	Opponent	Rlt	Score	Tries	Goals	Attendance	Referee
25.8.91	YC(P)	A	Doncaster	W	14-10	Tomlinson, Robinson	Pearce (3)	—	—
1.9.91	TD	H	Huddersfield	L	18-22	Pearce, Lidbury	Pearce (4, 2dg)	1402	Cummings
8.9.91	TD	A	Nottingham C.	W	54-4	Palmer (3), McCabe (2), Lidbury, Patrick, Hadi, Olsen, Harcombe	Pearce (7)	—	—
15.9.91	YC(1)	A	Featherstone R.	L	7-30	Stead	Pearce (1, 1dg)	—	—
22.9.91	TD	H	Whitehaven	W	16-14	Pearce, Ward	Pearce (4)	1038	Kendrew
29.9.91	TD	A	Trafford B.	W	34-16	Ward, G. Clark, Beardmore, McCabe, Palmer, Smith	Carlyle (5)	—	—
6.10.91	TD	H	Chorley B.	W	28-10	Patrick, G. Clark, Hill, Stead, McCabe	Pearce (4)	752	Crashley
13.10.91	TD	A	Dewsbury	L	2-24	—	Pearce	—	—
20.10.91	TD	H	Nottingham C.	W	36-10	Carlyle, G. Clark, Fairbank, Tomlinson, Lidbury, Wright	Carlyle (6)	723	Asquith
27.10.91	TD	A	Barrow	L	10-11	McCabe, Patrick	Carlyle	—	—
3.11.91	RT(P)	A	Sheffield E.	L	8-36	Patrick, Smith	—	—	—
7.11.91	TD	H	Keighley C.	W	38-13	Carlyle (2), Stead, Roockley, G. Clark, Wright, Noble	Pearce (5)	733	Kershaw
10.11.91	TD	A	Chorley B.	W	12-7	Pearce, Tomlinson	Pearce (2)	—	—
2.12.91	TD	H	Dewsbury	L	16-17	Wood (2), D. Clark	Pearce (2)	1377	R. Smith
8.12.91	TD	A	Hunslet	L	14-25	D. Clark, G. Clark, Carlyle	Pearce	—	—
22.12.91	TD	H	Doncaster	W	14-6	Noble, Forsyth	Pearce (3)	811	Ollerton
29.12.91	TD	A	Huddersfield	L	9-36	Roockley	Pearce (1, 1dg), Carlyle	—	—
5.1.92	TD	A	Highfield	W	22-12	Wood (2), Stead	Pearce (5)	—	—
12.1.92	TD	H	Hunslet	L	12-24	Wood, G. Clark	Pearce, Carlyle	812	Gilmour
19.1.92	TD	A	Bramley	L	0-47	—	—	—	—
2.2.92	CC(1)	H	Bradford N.	L	4-52	Hill	—	1427	Crashley
17.2.92	TD	A	Keighley C.	L	16-18	Lidbury, Stead, Douglas	Carlyle (2)	—	—
23.2.92	TD	H	Batley	L	14-32	G. Clark, Stead, Wright	Roockley	615	Volante
1.3.92	TD	H	Trafford B.	W	48-22	Knapper (3), G. Clark (2), Roockley, Lingard, Stead, Wright, Booker	Knapper (4)	406	Cross
8.3.92	TD	A	Batley	L	18-36	Hadi (2), Stead	Knapper (3)	—	—
16.3.92	TD	H	Bramley	L	14-29	Roockley, Potts	Knapper (3)	424	Kershaw
22.3.92	TD	A	Whitehaven	L	10-12	Knapper, Roockley	Knapper	—	—
29.3.92	TD	A	Doncaster	L	2-10	—	Knapper	—	—
12.4.92	TD	H	Highfield	L	14-18	G. Clark, Taylor, Potts	G. Clark	424	Atkin (Pr)
17.4.92	TD	H	Barrow	L	12-24	Taylor, G. Clark	Roockley (2)	463	R. Connolly

Garry Clark, former Great Britain and England winger, top scorer with 11 Pirates tries.

Ray Stead, Pirates' only ever-present in 30 games in 1991-92, scoring eight tries.

SHEFFIELD EAGLES

Ground: Don Valley Stadium (0742-610326)
Colours: Red, white, gold and black
First Season: 1984-85
Nickname: Eagles
Chairman: Gary Hetherington
Secretary: Julie Bush
Coach: Gary Hetherington (July 1986-)
Honours: **Division Two** Champions, 1991-92
Second Division Premiership Winners, 1988-89
Divisional Premiership Winners, 1991-92

RECORDS

Match
Goals: 12 by Roy Rafferty at Fulham, 21 Sep 1986
Mark Aston v. Keighley C., 25 Apr 1992
Tries: 5 by Daryl Powell at Mansfield M., 2 Jan 1989
Points: 32 by Roy Rafferty at Fulham, 21 Sep 1986

Season
Goals: 148 by Mark Aston, 1988-89
Tries: 30 by Iva Ropati, 1991-92
Points: 307 by Mark Aston, 1988-89

Career
Goals: 437 by Mark Aston, 1986-
Tries: 95 by Daryl Powell, 1984-
Points: 936 by Mark Aston, 1986-
Appearances: 238+3 by Daryl Powell, 1984-
Highest score: 80-8 v. Wigan St. Patricks, 13 Nov 1988
Highest against: 62-11 at Warrington, 9 Feb 1986
Attendance: 8,000 v. Wakefield T. (Div. 1), 26 Sep 1990 — at Don Valley
8,636 v. Widnes (Div. 1), 8 Oct 1989 — at Bramall Lane, Sheffield U. FC

COACHING REGISTER
● **Since formation in 1984**

Alan Rhodes   Apr 84 - May 86
Gary Hetherington   July 86 -

GREAT BRITAIN REGISTER
(2 players)

M. Aston	(+1)	1991
D. Powell	(11+3)	1990-92

1991-92 SIGNINGS REGISTER

Signed	Player	Club From
1.7.91	Thompson, Alex	Crown Malet ARL
1.7.91	Hughes, Ian	East Leeds ARL
1.7.91	Mowthorpe, Lee	Crown Malet ARL
10.7.91	Sheridan, Ryan	Dewsbury Moor ARL
17.7.91	Foster, Michael	Dewsbury Celtic ARL
17.7.91	Robertson, Craig	Paddock ARL
28.7.91	Boyer, Alan	Kippax ARL
26.8.91	Price, Chris	Kippax ARL
1.9.91	Ropati, Iva	Mangere East, NZ
10.9.91	Van Bellen, Gary	Dewsbury
11.9.91	Crowther, Matthew	Kippax ARL
20.9.91	Simpson, Anthony	Paddock ARL
1.10.91	Okiwe, Anderson	Nottingham C.
1.10.91	Salmon, Robert	Moldgreen ARL
21.10.91	Tuimavave, Tony	Northcote, NZ
3.12.91	Clarke, David	Sheffield Polyt'ic ARL
13.12.91	Reilly, Glen	—
1.1.92	Turner, Darren	Leeds Academy ARL
2.3.92	*Lumb, Tim	Hunslet
23.3.92	Shelford, Adrian	Wakefield T.
30.3.92	McAlister, Charlie	Oldham

1991-92 PLAYERS' SUMMARY

	App	Tries	Goals	Dr	Pts
Aston, Mark	31 + 1	2	98	6	210
Broadbent, Paul	36	9	—	—	36
Close, David	9 + 3	—	19	2	40
Cook, Mick	33	3	—	—	12
Farrell, Anthony	11 + 2	2	—	—	8
Gamson, Mark	16 + 14	6	1	—	26
Grimoldby, Nick	5	3	—	—	12
Halafihi, Nick	0 + 3	—	—	—	—
Hughes, Ian	18 + 8	2	—	—	8
Johnson, Dean	0 + 1	—	—	—	—
Laughton, Dale	21 + 6	1	—	—	4
Lumb, Tim	2 + 3	3	—	—	12
McAlister, Charlie	6 + 1	10	—	—	40
Maea, Des	13 + 2	8	—	—	32
Mumby, Keith	20 + 9	3	3	—	18
Mycoe, David	31 + 2	16	44	—	152
Okiwe, Anderson	1	—	—	—	—
Picksley, Richard	30 + 3	10	—	—	40
Plange, David	35	24	1	—	98
Powell, Daryl	26 + 1	13	—	2	54
Price, Richard	33 + 2	17	—	—	68
Robertson, Craig	1 + 4	—	—	—	—
Ropati, Iva	27	30	—	—	120
Shelford, Adrian	3 + 1	—	—	—	—
Sheridan, Ryan	2 + 2	1	—	—	4
Simpson, Anthony	3	1	—	—	4
Tuimavave, Tony	21	13	—	2	54
Waddell, Hugh	31 + 3	4	—	—	16
Young, Andy	16 + 1	6	—	—	24

TOTALS:
29 players		187	166	12	1,092

Representative Appearances 1991-92
Mycoe — GB Under-21 (3)
Picksley — GB Under-21 (1)
Powell — Britain (2+1, 1t)

1991-92 MATCH ANALYSIS

Date	Competition	H/A	Opponent	Rlt	Score	Tries	Goals	Attendance	Referee
1.9.91	SD	H	Oldham	D	16-16	Grimoldby, Gamson, Cook	Aston (2)	3454	Kershaw
8.9.91	SD	A	Carlisle	L	12-23	Price, Mumby	Aston (2)	—	—
16.9.91	YC(1)	H	Bradford N.	L	13-15	Price (2)	Aston (2, 1dg)	2012	Cross
22.9.91	SD	A	London C.	W	44-22	Plange (3), Ropati (2), Farrell, Picksley, Mycoe, Grimoldby	Close (4)	—	—
29.9.91	SD	A	Ryedale-York	W	26-22	Ropati, Mycoe, Grimoldby, Young	Close (5)	—	—
6.10.91	SD	H	Workington T.	W	28-14	Price, Mycoe, Ropati, Cook, Young	Close (4)	1488	Carter
13.10.91	SD	A	Leigh	W	14-13	Broadbent, Plange	Close, Aston, Mycoe	—	—
23.10.91	SD	H	Rochdale H.	W	35-14	Plange (2), Powell, Price, Picksley, Mycoe	Close (4, 1dg), Plange	1645	J. Smith
27.10.91	SD	A	Oldham	W	38-12	Ropati, Price, Waddell, Powell, Maea, Picksley	Mycoe (7)	—	—
3.11.91	RT(P)	H	Scarborough P.	W	36-8	Price (2), Ropati, Plange, Powell, Tuimavave	Mycoe (6)	1226	Tidball
6.11.91	SD	H	Carlisle	W	12-6	Young, Waddell	Mycoe (2)	1228	Asquith
10.11.91	SD	A	London C.	W	29-12	Price, Picksley, Ropati, Mycoe, Powell	Mycoe (4), Close (dg)	—	—
17.11.91	RT(1)	A	Ryedale-York	W	13-6	Picksley, Maea	Mycoe (2), Aston (dg)	—	—
24.11.91	RT(2)	A	Bradford N.	L	10-44	Ropati, Gamson	Aston	—	—
8.12.91	SD	A	Workington T.	W	35-2	Ropati (2), Aston, Plange, Tuimavave, Picksley	Aston (5, 1dg)	—	—
15.12.91	SD	H	Leigh	W	10-16	Ropati, Maea	Aston	1913	Asquith
26.12.91	SD	A	Ryedale-York	L	6-8	Ropati	Close	—	—
29.12.91	SD	H	Rydeale-York	W	58-4	Ropati (2), Maea (2), Plange (2), Mycoe, Young, Sheridan	Mycoe (9), Mumby, Gamson	1702	Allatt
12.1.92	SD	A	Oldham	W	44-18	Powell (3), Ropati (2), Picksley, Cook, Maea	Mycoe (6)	—	—
15.1.92	SD	A	Rochdale H.	W	26-12	Ropati (2), Young, Tuimavave	Aston (4, 1dg), Powell (dg)	—	—
19.1.92	SD	A	Carlisle	W	25-22	Ropati (2), Price, Plange, Broadbent	Aston (2), Powell (dg)	—	—
28.1.92	CC(1)	A	Whitehaven	W	56-4	Plange (3), Tuimavave (2), Powell, Price, Gamson, Picksley	Aston (9), Mumby	—	—
9.2.92	CC(2)	H	Hull	L	6-11	Tuimavave	Aston	3227	Holdsworth
16.2.92	SD	H	Workington T.	W	48-8	Ropati (2), Plange (2), Young, Price, Hughes, Laughton, Tuimavave	Aston (6)	1531	R. Smith
23.2.92	SD	A	Leigh	L	24-26	Tuimavave (2), Ropati, Waddell	Aston (3, 2dg)	—	—
27.2.92	SD	H	London C.	W	36-12	Ropati (4), Mycoe, Price, Plange	Aston (4)	1315	J. Smith
1.3.92	SD	H	Oldham	L	10-14	Tuimavave	Mumby, Mycoe, Aston	2529	Allatt
9.3.92	SD	H	Rochdale H.	W	23-17	Lumb, Mycoe, Aston, Simpson	Aston (3), Tuimavave (dg)	3849	Galtress
15.3.92	SD	A	Workington T.	W	36-18	Tuimavave (2), Plange, Ropati, Lumb, Broadbent	Mycoe (6)	—	—
22.3.92	SD	H	Leigh	W	51-6	Ropati (2), Maea (2), Powell, Broadbent, Waddell, Hughes, Tuimavave	Aston (7), Tuimavave (dg)	3228	Redfearn
29.3.92	SD	A	Rochdale H.	L	18-34	Powell, Mycoe, Broadbent	Aston (3)	—	—
5.4.92	SD	H	Carlisle	W	32-14	Broadbent (2), Plange (2), Price, McAlister	Aston (4)	6393	Morris

(Continued)

115

SHEFFIELD EAGLES 1991-92 MATCH ANALYSIS (continued)

Date	Com-petition	H/A	Opponent	Rlt	Score	Tries	Goals	Atten-dance	Referee
12.4.92	SD	H	London C.	W	38-4	Price (2), Mycoe, Picksley, Plange, McAlister	Aston (7)	1940	Redfearn
19.4.92	SD	H	Ryedale-York	W	42-7	McAlister (3), Mycoe, Gamson, Broadbent, Farrell	Aston (7)	2872	Nicholson (Pr)
25.4.92	DP(2)	H	Keighley C.	W	72-14	Mycoe (3), McAlister (3), Gamson (2), Price, Plange, Mumby, Picksley	Aston (12)	1225	J. Connolly
10.5.92	DP(SF)	H	Batley	W	36-22	Plange (2), McAlister (2), Mycoe, Broadbent	Aston (6)	2512	Whitfield
17.5.92	DP(F)	N[1]	Oldham	W	34-20	Powell (3), Mycoe, Lumb, Mumby	Aston (5)	(—)	Cummings

N[1] at Manchester U. FC

Nine-try prop Paul Broadbent, the Eagles' top appearance maker with 36 games.

New Zealander Charlie McAlister, a March recruit from Oldham, scoring 10 tries in seven games.

SWINTON

Ground: Station Road, Swinton, moving to Gigg Lane, Bury (061-764-4881) for the 1992-93 season
Colours: Blue and white
First Season: 1896-97
Nickname: Lions
Chairman: Malcolm White
Secretary: Wayne Dore
Coach: Jim Crellin (July 1989-July 1991)
Chris O'Sullivan (July 1991-Dec 1991)
Tony Barrow (Jan 1992-)
Honours: **Championship** Winners, 1926-27, 1927-28, 1930-31, 1934-35
Beaten finalists, 1924-25, 1932-33
War League Beaten finalists, 1939-40
Division One Champions, 1962-63, 1963-64
Division Two Champions, 1984-85
Challenge Cup Winners, 1899-1900, 1925-26, 1927-28
Beaten finalists, 1926-27, 1931-32
Second Division Premiership Winners, 1986-87
Beaten finalists, 1988-89
Lancashire Cup Winners, 1925-26, 1927-28, 1939-40, 1969-70
Beaten finalists, 1910-11, 1923-24, 1931-32, 1960-61, 1961-62, 1962-63, 1964-65, 1972-73
Lancashire League Winners, 1924-25, 1927-28, 1928-29, 1930-31, 1960-61
Lancashire War League Winners, 1939-40
Western Division Championship Beaten finalists, 1963-64
BBC2 Floodlit Trophy Beaten finalists, 1966-67

RECORDS

Match

Goals: 12 by Ken Gowers v. Liverpool C., 3 Oct 1959
Tries: 5 by Morgan Bevan v. Morecambe, 10 Sep 1898
Billy Wallwork v. Widnes, 15 Dec 1900
Jack Evans v. Bradford N., 30 Sep 1922
Hector Halsall v. St. Helens, 24 Jan 1925
Dick Cracknell v. Whitehaven Rec., 11 Feb 1928
Randall Lewis v. Keighley, 12 Jan 1946
John Stopford v. Bramley, 22 Dec 1962
Alan Buckley v. Salford, 8 Apr 1964
Joe Ropati v. Nottingham C., 21 Jan 1990
Points: 29 by Bernard McMahon v. Dewsbury, 15 Aug 1959

Season

Goals: 128 by Albert Blan, 1960-61
Tries: 42 by John Stopford, 1963-64
Points: 283 by Albert Blan, 1960-61

Career

Goals: 970 by Ken Gowers, 1954-73
Tries: 197 by Frank Evans, 1921-31
Points: 2,105 by Ken Gowers, 1954-73
Appearances: 593 + 8 by Ken Gowers, 1954-73
Highest score: 76-4 v. Pontefract, 8 Sep 1906
Highest against: 76-3 at Huddersfield, 20 Apr 1946
76-16 at Castleford, 6 Mar 1988
Attendance: 44,621 Wigan v. Warrington (RL Cup SF), 7 Apr 1951
Home match: 26,891 v. Wigan (RL Cup), 12 Feb 1964

COACHING REGISTER
- ### Since 1974-75

Austin Rhodes	June 74 - Nov 75
Bob Fleet	Nov 75 - Nov 76
John Stopford	Nov 76 - Apr 77
Terry Gorman	June 77 - Nov 78
Ken Halliwell	Nov 78 - Dec 79
Frank Myler	Jan 80 - May 81
Tom Grainey	May 81 - Oct 83
Jim Crellin	Nov 83 - May 86
Bill Holliday	
Mike Peers	} June 86 - Oct 87
Frank Barrow	Oct 87 - June 89
Jim Crellin	July 89 - July 91
Chris O'Sullivan	July 91 - Dec 91
Tony Barrow	Jan 92 -

GREAT BRITAIN REGISTER
(15 players)

T. Armitt	(8)	1933-37
A. Buckley	(7)	1963-66
F. Butters	(2)	1929
W. Davies	(1)	1968
B. Evans	(10)	1926-33
F. Evans	(4)	1924
J. Evans	(3)	1926
K. Gowers	(14)	1962-66
H. Halsall	(1)	1929
M. Hodgson	(16)	1929-37
R. Morgan	(2)	1963
W. Rees	(11)	1926-29
D. Robinson	(12)	1965-67
J. Stopford	(12)	1961-66
J. Wright	(1)	1932

1991-92 SIGNINGS REGISTER

Signed	Player	Club From
15.8.91	Clawson, Neil	Oldham
15.8.91	Fairbank, John	Oldham
15.8.91	Garner, Steve	Trafford B.
25.8.91	Lowry, Mark	Canberra, Aus
28.8.91	Hewitt, David	St. Annes ARL
5.9.91	Bellamy, Craig	Turvey Park, Aus
2.1.92	Ngataki, Shane	Bramley
6.1.92	Faimalo, Joe	—
13.1.92	*Whitfield, Darren	Widnes
23.1.92	Cooper, Carl	St. Helens
23.1.92	Kay, Paul	Batley
6.2.92	Barrow, Tony	Oldham
6.2.92	Longstaff, Simon	Oldham
10.3.92	Wilson, Barry	Swinton Victoria ARL
12.3.92	Whittle, Danny	Nutgrove ARL
12.3.92	Roberts, Paul	Nutgrove ARL

1991-92 PLAYERS' SUMMARY

	App	Tries	Goals	Dr	Pts
Allan, John	2 + 2	1	—	—	4
Ashall, Barry	12 + 2	2	3	—	14
Barratt, Dave	0 + 1	—	—	—	—
Barrow, Tony	10	—	—	—	—
Bellamy, Craig	14	—	—	—	—
Clark, Jason	0 + 6	—	—	—	—
Clawson, Neil	9 + 1	—	—	—	—
Cooper, Carl	4 + 1	—	—	—	—
Daintith, Ian	4 + 2	—	—	—	—
Faimalo, Joe	4 + 1	—	—	—	—
Fairbank, John	1	—	—	—	—
Garner, Steve	23	5	—	—	20
Graziano, Joe	6	1	—	—	4
Griffiths, Danny	0 + 3	—	—	—	—
Hudson, Julian	5	—	—	—	—
Irving, Richard	10	—	—	—	—
Kay, Paul	10	1	—	—	4
Kennett, Paul	10 + 4	2	—	—	8
Kerr, John	5	2	—	—	8
Leyland, Martin	6	1	—	—	4
Longstaff, Simon	6	—	—	—	—
Lowry, Mark	15	1	—	—	4
Melling, Alex	2	—	—	—	—
Morrison, Tony	18 + 1	3	—	—	12
Ngataki, Shane	0 + 2	—	—	—	—
O'Sullivan, Chris	11	1	—	1	5
Partington, Carl	11 + 4	—	—	—	—
Peters, Barry	5	—	—	—	—
Pickavance, Ian	26 + 1	8	—	—	32
Prince, Glen	13 + 1	2	—	—	8
Pucill, Andy	29	2	—	—	8
Rabbit, Jacent	2 + 4	—	—	—	—
Ranson, Scott	15	6	—	—	24
Ratu, Emon	23	4	3	—	22
Roberts, Paul	2	—	—	—	—
Skeech, Ian	16 + 3	—	—	—	—
Snape, Steve	16 + 1	3	—	—	12
Whitfield, Darren	7	1	—	—	4
Whittle, Danny	0 + 1	—	—	—	—
Wilkinson, Chris	25 + 1	1	42	2	90

TOTALS:
40 players		47	48	3	287

SWINTON 1991-92 MATCH ANALYSIS

Date	Com-petition	H/A	Opponent	Rlt	Score	Tries	Goals	Atten-dance	Referee
1.9.91	SBC	H	Wakefield T.	W	17-8	Ashall, Pucill	Wilkinson (4), O'Sullivan (dg)	2851	Holdsworth
8.9.91	SBC	A	Featherstone R.	L	20-22	Pickavance, Leyland, Allan	Wilkinson (4)	—	—
15.9.91	LC(1)	H	Oldham	L	21-22	Ranson (2), Graziano	Wilkinson (4, 1dg)	3285	Steele
22.9.91	SBC	H	St.Helens	L	12-16	Ranson, Garner	Wilkinson (2)	4217	Crashley
29.9.91	SBC	A	Leeds	L	8-46	Morrison	Wilkinson (2)	—	—
6.10.91	SBC	H	Hull K.R.	L	6-17	Garner	Wilkinson	1678	Galtress
13.10.91	SBC	A	Widnes	L	12-44	Prince, Pickavance	Ashall (2)	—	—
20.10.91	SBC	H	Wigan	L	14-26	Ranson, Snape, Ashall	Ratu	4929	Morris
3.11.91	SBC	H	Warrington	W	10-8	Ranson, Lowry	Wilkinson	3375	Campbell
10.11.91	SBC	A	Hull	L	4-22	—	Wilkinson (2)	—	—
17.11.91	RT(1)	H	Wigan	L	8-34	Morrison	Wilkinson (2)	4676	Galtress
8.12.91	SBC	A	St. Helens	L	4-28	—	Wilkinson (2)	—	—
15.12.91	SBC	H	Castleford	L	4-40	Garner	—	1526	Cummings
22.12.91	SBC	H	Leeds	L	10-18	Snape, Ranson	Ratu	2668	Morris
26.12.91	SBC	A	Salford	L	4-48	O'Sullivan	—	—	—
6.1.92	SBC	A	Hull K.R.	L	6-18	Prince	Wilkinson	—	—
12.1.92	SBC	H	Halifax	L	4-32	Morrison	—	3013	Whitfield
19.1.92	SBC	A	Warrington	L	8-62	Garner	Wilkinson (2)	—	—
2.2.92	CC(1)	A	Doncaster	L	4-14	Snape	—	—	—
16.2.92	SBC	A	Halifax	L	10-58	Ratu, Pucill	Ashall	—	—
23.2.92	SBC	H	Widnes	L	14-38	Pickavance, Wilkinson, Kerr	Ratu	1980	Ward
1.3.92	SBC	A	Wigan	L	12-38	Ratu (2), Pickavance	—	—	—
15.3.92	SBC	H	Bradford N.	L	14-42	Kay, Pickavance	Wilkinson (3)	2187	J. Connolly
22.3.92	SBC	H	Featherstone R.	L	6-18	Pickavance	Wilkinson	1850	Cummings
29.3.92	SBC	A	Castleford	L	2-56	—	Wilkinson	—	—
5.4.92	SBC	H	Hull	W	27-18	Whitfield, Garner, Ratu, Kerr	Wilkinson (5, 1dg)	1374	Holdsworth
12.4.92	SBC	A	Wakefield T.	L	8-44	Kennett	Wilkinson (2)	—	—
17.4.92	SBC	A	Bradford N.	L	0-60	—	—	—	—
20.4.92	SBC	H	Salford	L	18-26	Pickavance (2), Kennett	Wilkinson (3)	3487	J. Connolly

TRAFFORD BOROUGH

Ground: Played at Moss Lane, Altrincham, for most of 1991-92
Colours: Blue and crimson
First Season: 1954-55 as Blackpool Borough; changing to Springfield Borough in 1987-88; Chorley Borough in 1988-89; Trafford Borough from 1989-90; and Blackpool Gladiators from 1992-93
Nickname: Griffins
Chairman: Fred Wood
Secretary: Alan Sherratt
Coach: Norman Turley (June 1991-Dec 1991) Gary Ainsworth (Dec 1991-May 1992)
Honours: **Regal Trophy** Beaten finalists, 1976-77

RECORDS

Match

Goals: 11 by Norman Turley v. Carlisle, 26 Apr 1984
Tries: 4 by Tony Wilkshire v. Bradford N., 14 Jan 1961
John Stockley v. Doncaster, 1 Apr 1984
Tommy Frodsham v. Bridgend, 14 Apr 1985
Tommy Frodsham v. Mansfield M., 30 Nov 1986
Points: 27 by Norman Turley v. Carlisle, 26 Apr 1984

Season

Goals: 98 by Mike Smith, 1987-88
Tries: 30 by Tommy Frodsham, 1985-86
Points: 201 by Peter Fearis, 1957-58

Career

Goals: 334 by Terry McCarrick, 1963-69
Tries: 82 by Jimmy Johnson, 1969-76
Points: 689 by Terry McCarrick, 1963-69
Appearances: 322 + 18 by Paul Gamble, 1973-88
Highest score: 56-2 v. Runcorn H., 1 Jan 1989
Highest against: 104-12 at St. Helens, 15 Sep 1991
Attendance: 21,000 v. Leigh (RL Cup), 9 Mar 1957 — at Blackpool AFC

COACHING REGISTER

● **Since 1974-75**

Tommy Blakeley	Aug 74 - Apr 76
Jim Crellin	May 76 - Mar 77
Joe Egan Jnr	Mar 77 - Oct 77
Albert Fearnley (Mgr)	Nov 77 - Apr 79
Bakary Diabira	Nov 78 - June 79
Graham Rees	June 79 - Mar 80
Geoff Lyon	July 80 - Aug 81
Bob Irving	Aug 81 - Feb 82
John Mantle	Feb 82 - Mar 82
Tommy Dickens	Mar 82 - Nov 85
★Stan Gittins	Nov 85 - June 88
★Mike Peers	Aug 87 - May 91
Norman Turley	June 91 - Dec 91
Gary Ainsworth	Dec 91 - May 92

★Joint coaches Aug 87 - June 88

1991-92 SIGNINGS REGISTER

Signed	Player	Club From
18.8.91	★Johnson, Chris	Swinton
18.8.91	★Kerr, John	Swinton
27.8.91	Ainsworth, Gary	Workington T.
19.9.91	★Myler, Chris	Rochdale H.
20.9.91	Hulme, Andrew	Fitton Hill ARL
22.9.91	Bloor, Andy	Dewsbury
27.9.91	★Shaw, Dave	Salford
30.9.91	Grande, Dane	South Sydney, Aus
4.10.91	★Duffy, John	Chorley Borough
14.10.91	Turley, Norman	Whitehaven
18.10.91	★Simpson, Colin	Workington T.
1.11.91	Barber, Tommy	Crosfields ARL
1.11.91	Carey, Brendan	South Sydney, Aus
1.11.91	Clucas, Neil	Crosfields ARL
1.11.91	Cullen, Steve	Crosfields ARL
1.11.91	Farrell, Lee	Crosfields ARL
10.11.91	Harris, Eddie	Crosfields ARL
10.11.91	Kenyon, Ian	Golbourne ARL
15.11.91	★Hulmes, Mike	Rochdale H.
29.11.91	Clarke, Wayne	Winwick ARL
29.11.91	Pugh, Dean	Spring View ARL
1.12.91	Williams, Paul	Winwick ARL
8.12.91	★Brown, Dave	Whitehaven
13.12.91	★Chick, Stuart	Workington T.
13.12.91	Garnett, Paul	Dewsbury
26.12.91	Blackman, Richard	Oldham
26.12.91	Diatlov, Alexander	Moscow Magicians
26.12.91	Medwedj, Valeri	Moscow Magicians
26.12.91	Savikhine, Valeri	Moscow Magicians
27.12.91	Zotov, Oleg	Moscow Magicians
8.1.92	Galbraith, Glen	Oldham St. Annes ARL
28.2.92	★Frodsham, Tommy	St. Helens
28.2.92	Lennox, Paul	—
13.3.92	★Goodier, Frank	Highfield
20.3.92	★Bacon, David	Chorley B.
20.3.92	Cheetham, Mike	Irlam Hornets ARL
6.4.92	Elseworth, Steve	Chadderton ARL

1991-92 PLAYERS' SUMMARY

	App	Tries	Goals	Dr	Pts
Ainsworth, Gary	13 + 5	2	—	—	8
Bacon, David	4	—	—	—	—
Barber, Tommy	2	—	—	—	—
Bent, Peers	0 + 3	—	—	—	—
Bigg, Paul	1 + 1	—	—	—	—
Blackman, Richard	6	1	—	—	4
Bloor, Andy	11 + 1	2	—	—	8
Brown, Dave	8 + 3	—	—	—	—
Carey, Brendan	5	—	—	—	—
Cheetham, Mike	1	—	—	—	—
Chick, Stuart	3	2	—	—	8
Clarke, Wayne/Neil	0 + 2	—	—	—	—
Clucas, Neil	2	2	—	—	8
Cullen, Steve	3	—	—	—	—
Diatlov, Alexander	6 + 1	2	—	—	8
Duffy, John	4 + 2	—	—	—	—
Eccles, Cliff	2	—	—	—	—
Elseworth, Steve	2	2	2	—	12
Farrell, Lee	1 + 1	—	—	—	—
Flannery, Steve	21 + 3	1	—	—	4
Frodsham, Tommy	6	3	—	—	12
Galbraith, Glen	1	—	—	—	—
Garnett, Paul	11	—	—	—	—
Goodier, Frank	5	—	—	—	—
Grande, Dane	14	1	—	—	4
Green, Andy	16 + 3	3	—	1	13
Hall, Robert	4	1	—	—	4
Harris, Eddie	1 + 1	—	—	—	—
Hewitt, Dave	28	7	—	—	28
Hewitt, Tony	1	—	—	—	—
Honey, Chris	3	—	—	—	—
Hulme, Andy	1 + 2	—	—	—	—
Hulmes, Mike	2	—	—	—	—
Iddon, Tim	21 + 2	6	—	—	24
Johnson, Chris	25	2	37	2	84
Jones, Ken	4	1	—	—	4
Kenyon, Ian	1	—	—	—	—
Kerr, John	6	1	—	—	4
Lennox, Paul	1 + 1	—	—	—	—
McCall, Rowan	1	—	—	—	—
McKay, Rowan	0 + 1	—	—	—	—
Maloney, David	2	—	—	—	—
Meadows, Mark	21 + 1	2	—	—	8
Medwedj, Valeri	2	—	—	—	—
Myler, Chris	4	1	—	—	4
Ngataki, Shane	2	—	—	—	—
Reid, Terry	11 + 4	1	—	—	4
Rippon, Andy	19 + 3	2	11	—	30
Savikhine, Valeri	4	1	—	—	4
Shaw, Dave	4	—	—	—	—
Simpson, Colin	3	—	—	—	—
Slater, Neil	3	—	—	—	—
Smith, Graham	21 + 4	4	1	—	18
Solomona, Mani	1 + 2	—	—	—	—
Stewart, Mike	14 + 1	3	1	—	14
Summer, Richard	3 + 2	—	—	—	—
Tahaito, Brad	1	—	—	—	—
Turk, Tony	3 + 1	1	—	—	4
Turley, Norman	2	—	—	1	1
Williams, Paul	5	—	—	—	—
Zotov, Oleg	5	1	—	—	4
TOTALS:					
61 players		55	52	4	328

1991-92 MATCH ANALYSIS

Date	Competition	H/A	Opponent	Rlt	Score	Tries	Goals	Attendance	Referee
1.9.91	TD	A	Highfield	L	14-29	Green, Kerr	Johnson (3)	—	—
6.9.91	TD	H	Bramley	L	6-20	Meadows	Johnson	204	Gilmour
15.9.91	LC(1)	A	St. Helens	L	12-104	Jones, Rippon	Johnson, Rippon	—	—
22.9.91	TD	A	Hunslet	L	6-40	Iddon	Smith	138	Volante
29.9.91	TD	H	Scarborough P.	L	16-34	Stewart (2)	Rippon (4)	138	Volante
6.10.91	TD	A	Doncaster	L	7-68	Bloor	Stewart, Green (dg)	—	—
14.10.91	TD	H	Hunslet	L	20-24	Myler, Green, Ainsworth	Johnson (4)	188	Gilmour
20.10.91	TD	H	Dewsbury	L	13-48	Iddon, Reid	Johnson (2), Turley (dg)	223	Whitelam
27.10.91	TD	A	Huddersfield	L	0-70	—	—	—	—
3.11.91	TD	H	Barrow	L	14-18	Clucas (2)	Johnson (3)	178	R. Connolly
11.11.91	TD	A	Whitehaven	L	0-30	—	—	—	—
17.11.91	RT(1)	A	Salford	L	10-74	Hewitt, Johnson	Johnson	—	—
1.12.91	TD	H	Huddersfield	L	4-78	Iddon	—	638	J. Smith
8.12.91	TD	A	Barrow	L	8-45	Flannery	Johnson, Rippon	—	—
22.12.91	TD	A	Nottingham C.	W	50-14	Meadows, Grande, Stewart, Green, Chick, Hewitt, Iddon, Smith	Johnson (9)	—	—
26.12.91	TD	H	Chorley B.	L	18-26	Hewitt, Chick, Blackman, Zotov	Johnson	341	Asquith
1.1.92	TD	A	Chorley B.	L	18-36	Rippon, Iddon, Diatlov, Bloor	Johnson	—	—
8.1.92	TD	A	Bramley	L	6-44	Savikhine	Rippon	—	—
12.1.92	TD	H	Doncaster	L	14-18	Smith, Hewitt	Johnson (3)	498	Ollerton
19.1.92	TD	A	Dewsbury	L	6-34	Smith	Johnson	—	—
26.1.92	CC(1)	H[1]	Castleford	L	0-50	—	—	1630	Volante
2.2.92	TD	A	Batley	L	0-40	—	—	—	—
16.2.92	TD	H	Highfield	L	8-20	Diatlov	Johnson (2)	243	R. Connolly
1.3.92	TD	A	Scarborough P.	L	22-48	Iddon, Hewitt, Smith, Ainsworth	Rippon (3)	—	—
15.3.92	TD	A	Keighley C.	L	14-28	Johnson, Turk	Johnson (3)	—	—
22.3.92	TD	H	Keighley C.	L	7-30	Frodsham	Rippon, Johnson (dg)	456	R. Connolly
31.3.92	TD	H[2]	Whitehaven	L	8-33	Hewitt (2)	—	222	Asquith
7.4.92	TD	H[2]	Nottingham C.	W	15-8	Frodsham, Elseworth, Hall	Johnson (1, 1dg)	212	Kershaw
12.4.92	TD	H[2]	Batley	L	12-58	Elseworth, Frodsham	Elseworth (2)	481	Wood (Pr)

[1] at Leeds [2] at Huddersfield

WAKEFIELD TRINITY

Ground: Belle Vue (0924-372445)
Colours: Red, white and blue
First Season: 1895-96
Nickname: Dreadnoughts
Chairman: Rodney Walker
Secretary: Ken Dipple
Coach: David Topliss (May 1987-)
Honours: **Championship** Winners, 1966-67, 1967-68
              Beaten finalists, 1959-60, 1961-62
              Division Two Champions, 1903-04
              Challenge Cup Winners, 1908-09, 1945-46, 1959-60, 1961-62, 1962-63
              Beaten finalists, 1913-14, 1967-68, 1978-79
              Regal Trophy Beaten finalists, 1971-72
              Yorkshire Cup Winners, 1910-11, 1924-25, 1946-47, 1947-48, 1951-52, 1956-57, 1960-61, 1961-62, 1964-65
              Beaten finalists, 1926-27, 1932-33, 1934-35, 1936-37, 1939-40, 1945-46, 1958-59, 1973-74, 1974-75, 1990-91
              Yorkshire League Winners, 1909-10, 1910-11, 1945-46, 1958-59, 1959-60, 1961-62, 1965-66

RECORDS

Match
Goals: 12 by Neil Fox v. Batley, 26 Aug 1967
        Neil Fox v. Workington T., 19 Sep 1970
        Bernard Ward v. Hunslet, 6 Feb 1971
Tries: 7 by Fred Smith v. Keighley, 25 Apr 1959
         Keith Slater v. Hunslet, 6 Feb 1971
Points: 33 by Neil Fox v. Batley, 26 Aug 1967

Season
Goals: 163 by Neil Fox, 1961-62
Tries: 38 by Fred Smith, 1959-60
         David Smith, 1973-74
Points: 407 by Neil Fox, 1961-62

Career
Goals: 1,836 by Neil Fox, 1956-69 & 1970-74
Tries: 272 by Neil Fox, 1956-69 & 1970-74
Points: 4,488 by Neil Fox, 1956-69 & 1970-74
Appearances: 605 by Harry Wilkinson, 1930-49
Highest score: 78-9 v. Batley, 26 Aug 1967
Highest against: 72-6 v. Wigan, 29 Mar 1987
Attendance: 37,906 Leeds v. Huddersfield (RL Cup SF), 21 Mar 1936
Home match: 30,676 v. Huddersfield (RL Cup), 26 Feb 1921

Great Britain Test debutant Gary Price, scorer of one try in 32 games for Trinity in 1991-92.

COACHING REGISTER
● **Since 1974-75**

Peter Fox	June 74 - May 76
Geoff Gunney	June 76 - Nov 76
Brian Lockwood	Nov 76 - Jan 78
Ian Brooke	Jan 78 - Jan 79
Bill Kirkbride	Jan 79 - Apr 80
Ray Batten	Apr 80 - May 81
Bill Ashurst	June 81 - Apr 82
Ray Batten	May 82 - July 83
Derek Turner	July 83 - Feb 84
Bob Haigh	Feb 84 - May 84
Geoff Wraith	May 84 - Oct 84
David Lamming	Oct 84 - Apr 85
Len Casey	Apr 85 - June 86
Tony Dean	June 86 - Dec 86
Trevor Bailey	Dec 86 - Apr 87
David Topliss	May 87 -

GREAT BRITAIN REGISTER
(24 players)

I. Brooke	(8)	1967-68
N. Fox	(29)	1959-69
R. Haigh	(2)	1968-70
W. Horton	(14)	1928-33
M. Jackson	(2)	1991-92
D. Jeanes	(5)	1971-72
B. Jones	(3)	1964-66
H. Kershaw	(2)	1910
F. Mortimer	(2)	1956
H. Murphy	(1)	1950
H. Newbould	(1)	1910
J. Parkin	(17)	1920-29
C. Pollard	(1)	1924
E. Pollard	(2)	1932
H. Poynton	(3)	1962
G. Price	(+1)	1991
D. Robinson	(5)	1954-55
G. Round	(8)	1959-62
T. Skerrett	(4)	1979
S. Smith	(1)	1929
D. Topliss	(3)	1973-79
D. Turner	(13)	1959-62
D. Vines	(3)	1959
J. Wilkinson	(7)	1959-62

1991-92 SIGNINGS REGISTER

Signed	Player	Club From
29.8.91	Jackson, Michael	Hunslet
26.9.91	Clements, Mike	Erina, Aus
17.10.91	Round, Paul	Oldham
17.10.91	Lord, Paul	Oldham
14.11.91	Myers, David	Middleton ARL
15.11.91	*Bowie, Ian	Nottingham C.
3.1.92	Bagnall, Jeff	Gold Coast, Aus
4.1.92	Flynn, Adrian	Dewsbury Moor ARL
4.1.92	Watson, Ian	Cutsyke ARL
24.1.92	Mosley, James	Moldgreen ARL
8.4.92	Knighton, Adam	Crigglestone ARL

1991-92 PLAYERS' SUMMARY

	App	Tries	Goals	Dr	Pts
Bagnall, Jeff	15 + 1	4	1	—	18
Bell, Nigel	28 + 5	5	—	—	20
Byrne, Ged	4	2	—	—	8
Carter, Darren	3	—	2	—	4
Clements, Mike	4 + 2	—	—	—	—
Colbeck, Mark	0 + 4	—	—	—	—
Conway, Billy	23 + 3	5	—	—	20
Conway, Mark	30	6	77	1	179
Eden, Phil	19 + 4	5	—	—	20
Glancy, John	33 + 1	1	—	—	4
Goddard, Richard	4 + 4	2	—	—	8
Jackson, Michael	22 + 3	9	—	—	36
Jones, David	24 + 1	4	—	—	16
Kelly, Andy	12 + 1	3	—	—	12
Lazenby, Tracy	21 + 4	4	5	5	31
Lord, Paul	5 + 2	4	—	—	16
Mason, Andy	30	10	—	—	40
Myers, David	2	2	—	—	8
Perry, Chris	23 + 5	9	2	—	40
Price, Gary	32	1	—	—	4
Round, Paul	25 + 1	4	—	—	16
Shelford, Adrian	8	—	—	—	—
Slater, Richard	13 + 12	1	—	—	4
Spencer, Gary	30	5	—	—	20
Thompson, John	3 + 3	1	—	—	4
Webster, Mark	6 + 1	—	—	—	—
Wilson, Andy	35	17	—	—	68
Wright, Nigel	1 + 2	—	—	—	—

TOTALS:					
28 players		104	87	6	596

Representative Appearances 1991-92
Jackson — Britain (2, 2t)
Jones — Lancashire (1, 1t)
Mason — Yorkshire (1)
Price — Britain (+1)
Slater — GB Under-21 (+1)

WAKEFIELD TRINITY 1991-92 MATCH ANALYSIS

Date	Competition	H/A	Opponent	Rlt	Score	Tries	Goals	Attendance	Referee
1.9.9!	SBC	A	Swinton	L	8-17	Spencer	M. Conway (2)	—	—
8.9.91	SBC	H	Bradford N.	W	22-18	Byrne, Wilson, Lazenby, Jones	M. Conway (3)	4666	R. Connolly
15.9.91	YC(1)	A	Halifax	W	24-18	Jackson (2), B. Conway, Slater	M. Conway (4)	—	—
22.9.91	SBC	A	Halifax	L	18-28	Wilson (2), B. Conway	M. Conway (3)	—	—
25.9.91	YC(2)	A	Huddersfield	W	52-9	Wilson (3), Spencer (2), Jackson, Glancy, Lazenby, M. Conway	M. Conway (8)	—	—
29.9.91	SBC	H	Hull	L	14-28	B. Conway, Byrne	M. Conway (3)	4181	Tennant
6.10.91	SBC	A	Warrington	W	16-14	Mason, Wilson, Eden	M. Conway, Lazenby (2dg)	—	—
9.10.91	YC(SF)	A	Bradford N.	L	10-14	Perry	M. Conway (3)	—	—
13.10.91	SBC	H	Wigan	W	13-6	Jackson, Mason	M. Conway (2), Lazenby (dg)	6160	Galtress
20.10.91	SBC	H	Leeds	W	22-20	Mason, Eden, Jones, Jackson	M. Conway (3)	8114	Carter
27.10.91	SBC	A	Hull K.R.	L	4-23	M. Conway	—	—	—
3.11.91	SBC	H	St. Helens	W	20-12	Jackson (2), Lazenby, M. Conway	M. Conway (2)	5560	Cross
10.11.91	SBC	A	Widnes	L	0-34	—	—	—	—
17.11.91	RT(1)	A	Nottingham C.	W	42-11	Bell (2), Myers (2), Kelly, Eden, Lord, Goddard	M. Conway (4), Perry	—	—
24.11.91	RT(2)	H	Salford	L	10-30	Mason, Round	M. Conway	4577	R. Connolly
1.12.91	SBC	H	Warrington	L	8-12	Round	Carter (2)	3421	Cross
15.12.91	SBC	H	Widnes	Aban.	0-8	—	—	3920	Burke
26.12.91	SBC	A	Featherstone R.	W	18-10	Kelly, M. Conway, Perry	M. Conway (3)	—	—
1.1.92	SBC	H	Castleford	D	14-14	M. Conway, Bell, Wilson	M. Conway	6851	Whitfield
5.1.92	SBC	A	Wigan	L	2-20	—	M. Conway	—	—
12.1.92	CC(P)	H	Huddersfield	W	32-18	Jackson, Jones, Mason, Wilson, Perry, Eden	M. Conway (4)	3886	Cross
19.1.92	SBC	A	St. Helens	L	12-40	Kelly, Thompson	M. Conway (2)	—	—
26.1.92	CC(1)	A	Workington T.	L	8-13	Wilson	M. Conway (2)	—	—
9.2.92	SBC	H	Salford	W	27-10	Lord (2), Perry, Wilson, Eden	Lazenby (3, 1dg)	3647	J. Smith
19.2.92	SBC	H	Widnes	W	12-4	Wilson, Lord	Lazenby (2)	3509	Morris
23.2.92	SBC	H	Hull K.R.	L	22-25	Price, Bell, Bagnall, Perry, Lazenby	Bagnall	4116	Galtress
1.3.92	SBC	A	Hull	W	15-14	Bagnall, B. Conway	M. Conway (3), Lazenby (dg)	—	—
8.3.92	SBC	H	Halifax	L	14-19	Round (2), Wilson	M. Conway	6527	Morris
15.3.92	SBC	A	Salford	W	18-12	Bell, M. Conway, Spencer	M. Conway (3)	—	—
29.3.92	SBC	A	Leeds	W	17-0	Perry, Spencer, Jackson	M. Conway (2, 1dg)	—	—
5.4.92	SBC	A	Bradford N.	L	8-9	Wilson (2)	—	—	—
12.4.92	SBC	H	Swinton	W	44-8	Mason (3), Perry, Jones, B. Conway, Bagnall	M. Conway (8)	3339	Burke
17.4.92	SBC	A	Castleford	L	4-28	—	M. Conway (2)	—	—
20.4.92	SBC	H	Featherstone R.	W	28-10	Perry (2), Mason (2), Goddard	M. Conway (4)	6300	J. Smith
26.4.92	PT(1)	A	Castleford	L	18-28	Wilson (2), Bagnall	M. Conway (2), Perry	—	—

WARRINGTON

Ground: Wilderspool (0925-35338)
Colours: Primrose and blue
First Season: 1895-96
Nickname: Wire
Chairman: Peter Higham
General
  Manager: Ron Close
Coach: Brian Johnson (Nov 1988-)
Honours: **Championship** Winners, 1947-48, 1953-54, 1954-55
Beaten finalists, 1925-26, 1934-35, 1936-37, 1948-49, 1950-51, 1960-61
League Leaders Trophy Winners, 1972-73
Club Championship (Merit Table) Winners, 1973-74
Challenge Cup Winners, 1904-05, 1906-07, 1949-50, 1953-54, 1973-74
Beaten finalists, 1900-01, 1903-04, 1912-13, 1927-28, 1932-33, 1935-36, 1974-75, 1989-90
Regal Trophy Winners, 1973-74, 1977-78, 1980-81, 1990-91
Beaten finalists, 1978-79, 1986-87
Premiership Trophy Winners, 1985-86
Beaten finalists, 1976-77, 1986-87
Lancashire Cup Winners, 1921-22, 1929-30, 1932-33, 1937-38, 1959-60, 1965-66, 1980-81, 1982-83, 1989-90
Beaten finalists, 1906-07, 1948-49, 1950-51, 1967-68, 1985-86, 1987-88
Lancashire League Winners, 1937-38, 1947-48, 1948-49, 1950-51, 1953-54, 1954-55, 1955-56, 1967-68
BBC2 Floodlit Trophy Beaten finalists, 1974-75
Captain Morgan Trophy Winners, 1973-74

RECORDS

Match
Goals: 14 by Harold Palin v. Liverpool C., 13 Sep 1950
Tries: 7 by Brian Bevan v. Leigh, 29 Mar 1948
Brian Bevan v. Bramley, 22 Apr 1953

Points: 33 by George Thomas v. St. Helens, 12 Apr 1909

Season
Goals: 170 by Steve Hesford, 1978-79
Tries: 66 by Brian Bevan, 1952-53
Points: 363 by Harry Bath, 1952-53

Career
Goals: 1,159 by Steve Hesford, 1975-85
Tries: 740 by Brian Bevan, 1945-62
Points: 2,416 by Steve Hesford, 1975-85
Appearances: 620 by Brian Bevan, 1945-62
Highest score: 78-3 v. St. Helens, 12 Apr 1909
Highest against: 68-14 at Hunslet, 10 Apr 1928
Attendance: 34,304 v. Wigan (League), 22 Jan 1949

COACHING REGISTER
● **Since 1974-75**

Alex Murphy	May 71 - May 78
Billy Benyon	June 78 - Mar 82
Kevin Ashcroft	Mar 82 - May 84
Reg Bowden	June 84 - Mar 86
Tony Barrow	Mar 86 - Nov 88
Brian Johnson	Nov 88 -

Warrington centre Allan Bateman on his Great Britain debut against France at Hull in March 1992.

GREAT BRITAIN REGISTER
(45 players)

J. Arkwright	(6)	1936-37
K. Ashcroft	(+1)	1974
W. Aspinall	(1)	1966
A. Bateman	(1)	1992
W. Belshaw	(2)	1937
N. Bentham	(2)	1929
J. Bevan	(6)	1974-78
T. Blinkhorn	(1)	1929
E. Brooks	(3)	1908
J. Challinor	(3)	1958-60
N. Courtney	(+1)	1982
W. Cunliffe	(11)	1920-26
G. Dickenson	(1)	1908
W. Dingsdale	(3)	1929-33
D. Drummond	(2)	1987-88
R. Duane	(3)	1983-84
R. Eccles	(1)	1982
K. Ellis	(+1)	1991
J. Featherstone	(6)	1948-52
M. Forster	(2)	1987
E. Fraser	(16)	1958-61
L. Gilfedder	(5)	1962-63
R. Greenough	(1)	1960
A. Gregory	(1)	1986
M. Gregory	(19+1)	1987-90
G. Helme	(12)	1948-54
K. Holden	(1)	1963
A. Johnson	(6)	1946-47
K. Kelly	(2)	1980-82
T. McKinney	(3)	1955
J. Miller	(6)	1933-36
A. Murphy	(1)	1971
A. Naughton	(2)	1954
T. O'Grady	(1)	1961
H. Palin	(2)	1947
K. Parr	(1)	1968
A. Pimblett	(3)	1948
R. Price	(9)	1954-57
R. Ryan	(5)	1950-52
R. Ryder	(1)	1952
F. Shugars	(1)	1910
G. Skelhorne	(7)	1920-21
G. Thomas	(1)	1907
D. Whitehead	(3)	1971
J. Woods	(+1)	1987

1991-92 SIGNINGS REGISTER

Signed	Player	Club From
15.8.91	Dusher, Mark	Hull Boys ARL
3.9.91	Ross, Richard	Woolston R. ARL
5.10.91	Shelford, Kelly	Otauru, NZ
16.10.91	Penny, Lee	Orrell St. James ARL
1.2.92	Moxham, Barry	Orrell St. James ARL

1991-92 PLAYERS' SUMMARY

	App	Tries	Goals	Dr	Pts
Bateman, Allan	22 + 1	5	—	—	20
Burke, Tony	4 + 1	—	—	—	—
Chambers, Gary	9 + 1	2	—	—	8
Crompton, Martin	16 + 8	7	—	1	29
Cullen, Paul	12 + 8	—	—	—	—
Darbyshire, Paul	4	2	—	—	8
Drummond, Des	29	8	—	—	32
Duffy, Don	2 + 3	—	—	—	—
Dusher, Mark	0 + 1	—	—	—	—
Elliott, David	1 + 1	—	—	—	—
Ellis, Kevin	24 + 1	10	—	—	40
Forster, Mark	9 + 1	5	2	—	24
Gregory, Mike	8	1	—	—	4
Harmon, Neil	17 + 1	1	—	—	4
Jackson, Robert	28	5	—	—	20
Kenyon, Neil	17	10	—	—	40
Lyon, David	25	7	37	—	102
Mann, Duane	32	2	—	4	12
Mercer, Gary	30	4	—	—	16
Muller, Roby	0 + 1	—	—	—	—
Myler, Robert	12 + 1	6	—	—	24
Phillips, Rowland	5 + 4	1	—	—	4
Rea, Kevin	0 + 1	—	—	—	—
Richards, Basil	2 + 6	—	—	—	—
Rudd, Chris	23	11	29	—	102
Sanderson, Gary	13 + 6	—	—	—	—
Shelford, Kelly	24 + 1	4	—	—	16
Sumner, Phil	20 + 1	1	—	—	4
Tees, Gary	3 + 4	—	—	—	—
Thomas, Mark	1	—	—	—	—
Thorniley, Tony	17 + 4	7	—	—	28
Turner, Robert	7 + 4	—	14	—	28
Williamson, Paul	1	—	—	—	—

TOTALS:					
33 players		99	82	5	565

Representative Appearances 1991-92
Bateman — Britain (1); Wales (2, 2t)
Chambers — Cumbria (1)
Cullen — Lancashire (+1)
Ellis — Wales (2, 1t)
Lyon — Lancashire (1)
Phillips — Wales (+2, 1t)
Rudd — Cumbria (1, 1t)
Sumner — GB Under-21 (2, 1t)

WARRINGTON 1991-92 MATCH ANALYSIS

Date	Com-petition	H/A	Opponent	Rlt	Score	Tries	Goals	Atten-dance	Referee
1.9.91	SBC	H	Salford	W	22-20	Drummond, Rudd, Lyon, Ellis	Lyon (3)	5032	Whitfield
8.9.91	SBC	A	St. Helens	L	20-27	Chambers, Myler, Drummond	Lyon (4)	—	—
15.9.91	LC(1)	A	Salford	L	16-22	Myler (2), Lyon	Lyon (2)	—	—
22.9.91	SBC	H	Featherstone R.	W	42-24	Darbyshire (2), Myler (2), Rudd, Ellis, Thorniley, Sumner	Rudd (5)	4557	Kershaw
29.9.91	SBC	A	Hull K.R.	W	14-9	Thorniley (2), Crompton	Rudd	—	—
6.10.91	SBC	H	Wakefield T.	L	14-16	Ellis, Jackson	Rudd (3)	4726	Morris
13.10.91	SBC	A	Leeds	W	22-13	Drummond, Gregory, Thorniley, Crompton	Rudd (3)	—	—
23.10.91	SBC	H	Castleford	W	23-6	Rudd, Jackson, Drummond, Mercer	Lyon (3), Mann (dg)	4792	Holdsworth
3.11.91	SBC	A	Swinton	L	8-10	Ellis	Lyon (2)	—	—
10.11.91	SBC	H	Bradford N.	W	12-8	Lyon, Rudd	Lyon (2)	4675	Whitfield
16.11.91	RT(1)	H	Leeds	L	8-17	Thorniley	Lyon (2)	4353	Campbell
1.12.91	SBC	A	Wakefield T.	W	12-8	Ellis, Rudd	Lyon (2)	—	—
8.12.91	SBC	H	Halifax	W	38-14	Rudd (2), Jackson (2), Drummond (2), Ellis	Lyon (3), Rudd (2)	5345	Campbell
22.12.91	SBC	A	Bradford N.	L	10-16	Rudd, Crompton	Lyon	—	—
26.12.91	SBC	A	Widnes	L	8-20	Thorniley, Rudd	—	—	—
1.1.92	SBC	H	Wigan	L	6-24	Kenyon	Rudd	10,793	Holdsworth
12.1.92	SBC	A	Hull	W	32-6	Crompton, Ellis, Bateman, Mann, Mercer	Rudd (6)	—	—
19.1.92	SBC	H	Swinton	W	62-8	Kenyon (3), Shelford (2), Crompton (2), Drummond, Chambers, Mercer, Bateman	Rudd (7), Lyon (2)	4213	Morris
3.2.92	CC(1)	A	Oldham	W	8-3	Ellis	Lyon (2)	—	—
9.2.92	SBC	H	Hull K.R.	W	23-12	Rudd (2), Bateman, Kenyon	Lyon (3), Crompton (dg)	4175	Morris
16.2.92	CC(2)	A	Wigan	L	0-14	—	—	—	—
23.2.92	SBC	H	Leeds	W	17-6	Kenyon, Crompton, Bateman	Lyon (2), Mann (dg)	5636	J. Connolly
26.2.92	SBC	A	Featherstone R.	L	6-29	Phillips	Rudd	—	—
1.3.92	SBC	A	Castleford	L	8-40	Shelford	Lyon (2)	—	—
8.3.92	SBC	H	Hull	L	12-22	Kenyon (2), Drummond	—	4053	Whitfield
15.3.92	SBC	A	Halifax	L	20-38	Shelford, Mann, Myler, Forster	Turner (2)	—	—
29.3.92	SBC	A	Salford	W	14-10	Lyon (2), Forster	Turner	—	—
4.4.92	SBC	H	St. Helens	W	30-18	Kenyon, Jackson, Harmon, Mercer, Forster	Turner (5)	4529	R. Smith
17.4.92	SBC	H	Widnes	W	19-8	Thorniley, Bateman, Kenyon	Turner (3), Mann (dg)	6187	Burke
20.4.92	SBC	A	Wigan	L	13-19	Ellis, Lyon	Turner (2), Mann (dg)	—	—
26.4.92	PT(1)	H	Leeds	D	18-18	Forster, Lyon, Ellis	Lyon (2), Turner	4937	Cummings
29.4.92	PT(1) Replay	A	Leeds	L	8-22	Forster	Forster (2)	—	—

WHITEHAVEN

Eric Fitzsimons	Oct 89 - Mar 90
Norman Turley	June 90 - Apr 91
Jackie Davidson	May 91 -

Ground: Recreation Ground (0946-692915)
Colours: Chocolate, blue and gold
First Season: 1948-49
Nickname: Haven
Chairman: Keith Irving
Secretary: Keith Nelson
Coach: Jackie Davidson (May 1991-)

RECORDS

Match

Goals: 12 by Steve Maguire v. Nottingham C.,
        12 Apr 1992
Tries: 6 by Vince Gribbin v. Doncaster,
         18 Nov 1984
Points: 25 by Bill Holliday v. Hunslet,
        31 Mar 1962

Season

Goals: 141 by John McKeown, 1956-57
Tries: 31 by Vince Gribbin, 1991-92
Points: 291 by John McKeown, 1956-57

Career

Goals: 1,050 by John McKeown, 1948-61
Tries: 148 by Bill Smith, 1950-62
Points: 2,133 by John McKeown, 1948-61
Appearances: 417 by John McKeown, 1948-61
Highest score: 80-6 v. Nottingham C.,
        12 Apr 1992
Highest against: 92-10 at Hull K.R., 18 Mar 1990
Attendance: 18,500 v. Wakefield T. (RL Cup),
        19 Mar 1960

COACHING REGISTER

● **Since 1974-75**

Jeff Bawden	May 72 - May 75
Ike Southward	Aug 75 - June 76
Bill Smith	Aug 76 - Oct 78
Ray Dutton	Oct 78 - Oct 79
Phil Kitchin	Oct 79 - Jan 82
Arnold Walker	Jan 82 - May 82
Tommy Dawes	June 82 - May 83
Frank Foster	June 83 - June 85
Phil Kitchin	June 85 - Oct 87
John McFarlane	Oct 87 - May 88
Barry Smith	July 88 - Sep 89

GREAT BRITAIN REGISTER
(5 players)

V. Gribbin	(1)	1985
W. Holliday	(1)	1964
R. Huddart	(4)	1958
P. Kitchin	(1)	1965
A. Walker	(1)	1980

1991-92 SIGNINGS REGISTER

Signed	Player	Club From
29.8.91	Sanders, Kevin	Hensingham ARL
19.9.91	Lightfoot, David	Hull K.R.
9.10.91	Charlton, Jason	Canterbury Bankstown, Aus
10.10.91	Carey, Steve	Ponsonby, NZ
10.10.91	*Riley, Stephen	Barrow
18.10.91	Toomata, Mike	Highfield
27.11.91	Saltoon, Danny	St. Kilba, Aus
13.12.91	*Lunt, Peter	Carlisle
3.1.92	Lia, Ben	Workington T.
28.1.92	Dunn, Reg	Barrow
14.2.92	Howarth, Jason	Netherall ARL
10.4.92	Lewthwaite, Graeme	Lowca ARL

1991-92 PLAYERS' SUMMARY

	App	Tries	Goals	Dr	Pts
Amor, Martin	6	1	—	—	4
Beckwith, Mark	29	11	—	—	44
Blaney, Ged	8 + 4	2	—	—	8
Branthwaite, Steve	28 + 1	2	—	—	8
Brown, Dave	2 + 1	—	—	—	—
Burns, David	1 + 4	—	—	—	—
Burns, Williams	4 + 1	—	—	—	—
Cameron, Graham	22	2	1	—	10
Carey, Steve	1	—	—	—	—
Charlton, Jason	9 + 1	2	—	—	8
Davidson, Alan	2 + 4	—	—	—	—
D'Leny, Tony	5 + 2	—	—	—	—
Dover, Peter	2	—	—	—	—
Dunn, Reg	8	2	—	—	8
Fisher, Billy	7	1	—	—	4
Fryer, Steve	2 + 2	—	—	—	—
Gaffney, Mike	6 + 10	—	—	—	—
Gribbin, Vince	27	31	—	—	124
Hetherington, Gary	17 + 1	—	—	—	—
Hewer, Gary	20	6	—	—	24
Howland, Ken	0 + 4	—	—	—	—
Howse, Steve	6 + 1	2	—	—	8
Huddart, Milton	0 + 1	—	—	—	—
Lewthwaite, Graeme	1	3	—	—	12
Lia, Ben	7	—	—	—	—
Lightfoot, David	25	3	—	2	14
Lofthouse, Norman	8 + 2	—	3	—	6
Lunt, Peter	3 + 1	—	—	—	—
McCartney, Duncan	10 + 1	—	—	—	—
Maguire, Steve	27	4	62	2	142

(continued)

128

1991-92 PLAYERS' SUMMARY (continued)

	App	Tries	Goals	Dr	Pts
Mounsey, Gary	10	3	—	—	12
Pugsley, Stewart	0 + 2	—	—	—	—
Richardson, Willie	22	7	9	—	46
Routledge, John	6 + 1	6	—	—	24
Ryan, Mark	2	—	—	—	—
Saltoon, Danny	1	—	—	—	—
Sanders, Kevin	5 + 4	3	—	—	12
Short, Tom	1	—	—	—	—
Solarie, Tony	14	6	—	—	24
Telford, Robert	5 + 3	1	—	—	4
Toomata, Mike	18 + 1	—	—	—	—

TOTALS:

41 players		98	75	4	546

Representative Appearances 1991-92
Beckwith — Cumbria (+1)
Cameron — Cumbria (1)
Gribbin — Cumbria (+1)
Maguire — Cumbria (1, 1t)

1991-92 MATCH ANALYSIS

Date	Com-petition	H/A	Opponent	Rlt	Score	Tries	Goals	Atten-dance	Referee
1.9.91	TD	A	Batley	L	12-22	Sanders (2)	Richardson (2)	—	—
8.9.91	TD	H	Highfield	L	12-24	Gribbin (3)	—	743	Asquith
15.9.91	LC(1)	H	Carlisle	L	12-44	Beckwith, Mounsey	Richardson (2)	873	Whitfield
22.9.91	TD	A	Scarborough P.	L	14-16	Beckwith (2), Hewer	Richardson	—	—
29.9.91	TD	H	Chorley B.	W	44-12	Solarie (2), Lightfoot, Gribbin, Branthwaite, Hewer, Mounsey, Richardson	Maguire (6)	642	Redfearn
6.10.91	TD	H	Huddersfield	L	18-36	Gribbin (2), Solarie	Richardson (3)	908	Cummings
13.10.91	TD	A	Nottingham C.	W	32-8	Gribbin (2), Routledge, Branthwaite, Sanders, Charlton	Maguire (4)	—	—
20.10.91	TD	H	Doncaster	L	12-16	Gribbin (2)	Maguire (2)	737	R. Smith
27.10.91	TD	A	Dewsbury	L	8-48	Mounsey, Gribbin	—	—	—
3.11.91	TD	A	Hunslet	L	12-24	Routledge (2)	Maguire (2)	—	—
11.11.91	TD	H	Trafford B.	W	30-0	Solarie (3), Gribbin (2), Cameron	Lofthouse (2), Cameron	670	Volante
17.11.91	RT(1)	A	Doncaster	L	20-21	Routledge (3), Beckwith	Lofthouse, Richardson	—	—
1.12.91	TD	A	Bramley	L	17-20	Gribbin (2)	Maguire (4, 1dg)	—	—
8.12.91	TD	H	Keighley C.	L	7-11	Hewer	Maguire (1, 1dg)	640	Ollerton
15.12.91	TD	A	Doncaster	L	14-50	Telford, Maguire, Charlton	Maguire	—	—
26.12.91	TD	A	Barrow	L	6-48	Gribbin	Maguire	—	—
19.1.92	TD	H	Batley	W	11-4	Gribbin	Maguire (3), Lightfoot (dg)	660	J. Connolly
28.1.92	CC(1)	H	Sheffield E.	L	4-56	Maguire	—	852	Whitelam
9.2.92	TD	A	Highfield	L	26-34	Beckwith (2), Blaney, Gribbin, Lightfoot	Maguire (3)	—	—
16.2.92	TD	H	Dewsbury	L	18-42	Beckwith (2), Gribbin	Maguire (3)	514	Carter
23.2.92	TD	H	Hunslet	W	32-26	Maguire (2), Beckwith, Richardson, Dunn	Maguire (6)	428	Redfearn
1.3.92	TD	A	Chorley B.	W	16-10	Richardson (3), Amor	—	—	—
4.3.92	TD	H	Barrow	L	4-30	Gribbin	—	869	Burke
15.3.92	TD	A	Huddersfield	L	6-24	Gribbin	Maguire	—	—
22.3.92	TD	H	Scarborough P.	W	12-10	Dunn, Richardson	Maguire (2)	502	J. Smith
29.3.92	TD	H	Bramley	L	10-20	Hewer	Maguire (3)	482	Whitelam
31.3.92	TD	A[1]	Trafford B.	W	33-8	Gribbin (2), Howse, Lightfoot, Blaney, Hewer	Maguire (4), Lightfoot (dg)	—	—
5.4.92	TD	A	Keighley C.	L	24-46	Gribbin (3), Cameron	Maguire (4)	—	—
12.4.92	TD	H	Nottingham C.	W	80-6	Gribbin (5), Lewthwaite (3), Beckwith (2), Howse, Fisher, Richardson, Hewer	Maguire (12)	420	Steele

[1] at Huddersfield

WIDNES

Ground: Naughton Park (051-495-2250)
Colours: Black and white
First Season: 1895-96
Nickname: Chemics
Chairman: Jim Mills
General
  Manager: Peter Dickinson
Coach: Frank Myler (June 1991-May 1992)
Phil Larder (May 1992-)
Honours: **Championship** Beaten finalists,
1935-36
Division One Champions, 1977-78,
1987-88, 1988-89
Challenge Cup Winners, 1929-30,
1936-37, 1963-64, 1974-75, 1978-79,
1980-81, 1983-84
Beaten finalists, 1933-34, 1949-50,
1975-76, 1976-77, 1981-82
Regal Trophy Winners, 1975-76,
1978-79, 1991-92
Beaten finalists, 1974-75, 1977-78,
1979-80, 1983-84, 1988-89
Premiership Winners, 1979-80,
1981-82, 1982-83, 1987-88, 1988-89,
1989-90
Beaten finalists, 1977-78, 1990-91
Lancashire Cup Winners, 1945-46,
1974-75, 1975-76, 1976-77, 1978-79,
1979-80, 1990-91
Beaten finalists, 1928-29, 1939-40,
1955-56, 1971-72, 1981-82, 1983-84
Lancashire League Winners,
1919-20
Western Division Championship
Beaten finalists, 1962-63
Charity Shield Winners, 1988-89,
1989-90, 1990-91
World Club Challenge Winners,
1989-90
BBC2 Floodlit Trophy Winners,
1978-79
Beaten finalists, 1972-73, 1973-74

RECORDS

Match
Goals: 11 by Robin Whitfield v. Oldham,
28 Oct 1965
Tries: 5 by Eddie Cunningham v. Doncaster,
15 Feb 1981
John Basnett at Hunslet,
17 Oct 1981
John Basnett v. Hull K.R.,
2 Nov 1986
David Hulme v. Dewsbury,
30 Nov 1986
Andy Currier v. Featherstone R.,
25 Sep 1988
Martin Offiah v. Warrington,
15 Mar 1989
Points: 34 by Andy Currier v. Featherstone R.,
25 Sep 1988
Jonathan Davies v. Whitehaven,
26 Aug 1990

Season
Goals: 140 by Mick Burke, 1978-79
Tries: 58 by Martin Offiah, 1988-89
Points: 342 by Jonathan Davies, 1990-91

Career
Goals: 1,083 by Ray Dutton, 1966-78
Tries: 234 by Mal Aspey, 1964-80
Points: 2,195 by Ray Dutton, 1966-78
Appearances: 587+4 by Keith Elwell, 1970-86
Highest score: 82-0 v. Dewsbury, 30 Nov 1986
Highest against: 60-5 at Oldham, 9 Apr 1928
Attendance: 24,205 v. St. Helens (RL Cup),
16 Feb 1961

COACHING REGISTER
● **Since 1974-75**

Vince Karalius	Jan 72 - May 75
Frank Myler	May 75 - May 78
Doug Laughton	May 78 - Mar 83
Harry Dawson Colin Tyrer	} Mar 83 - May 83
*Vince Karalius Harry Dawson	} May 83 - May 84
Eric Hughes	June 84 - Jan 86
Doug Laughton	Jan 86 - May 91
Frank Myler	June 91 - May 92
Phil Larder	May 92 -

*Dawson quit as coach in Mar 1984 with
Karalius continuing as team manager.*

GREAT BRITAIN REGISTER
(44 players)

M. Adams	(11+2)	1979-84
J. Basnett	(2)	1984-86
K. Bentley	(1)	1980
M. Burke	(14+1)	1980-86
F. Collier	(1)	1964
A. Currier	(1)	1989
J. Davies	(7+1)	1990-92
J. Devereux	(1)	1992
R. Dutton	(6)	1970
K. Elwell	(3)	1977-80
R. Eyres	(1+3)	1989-91
J. Fieldhouse	(6)	1985-86
R. French	(4)	1968
L. Gorley	(4+1)	1980-82
A. Gregory	(8+1)	1981-84
I. Hare	(1)	1967
F. Higgins	(6)	1950-51
H. Higgins	(2)	1937
L. Holliday	(3)	1991-92
E. Hughes	(8)	1978-82
D. Hulme	(7+1)	1988-89
P. Hulme	(3+2)	1988-89
A. Johnson	(4)	1914-20
V. Karalius	(2)	1963
G. Kemel	(2)	1965
D. Laughton	(4)	1973-79
J. Lydon	(9+1)	1983-85
T. McCue	(6)	1936-46
J. Measures	(2)	1963
J. Mills	(6)	1974-79
P. Moriarty	(1)	1991
A. Myler	(14)	1983-86
F. Myler	(14+1)	1960-67
G. Nicholls	(7)	1971-72
M. Offiah	(20)	1988-91
D. O'Neill	(2+1)	1971-72
M. O'Neill	(3)	1982-83
H. Pinner	(1)	1986
G. Shaw	(1)	1980
N. Silcock	(12)	1932-37
A. Tait	(9)	1989-92
J. Warlow	(3)	1971
D. Wright	(+1)	1988
S. Wright	(7)	1977-78

1991-92 SIGNINGS REGISTER

Signed	Player	Club From
28.6.91	Holden, Graham	Blackbrook ARL
24.7.91	Ireland, Andrew	Golbourne ARL
28.8.91	Solomona, Se'e	Glenora, NZ
6.9.91	Smith, Peter	Widnes Tigers ARL
8.10.91	*Holding, Neil	Oldham
23.10.91	Wilson, Colin	St. Patricks ARL
10.1.92	Makin, Craig	St. James ARL
8.2.92	Walker, Scott	Hensingham ARL
6.3.92	Carbert, Brian	Warrington

1991-92 PLAYERS' SUMMARY

	App	Tries	Goals	Dr	Pts
Atcheson, Paul	1 + 4	—	—	—	—
Carbert, Brian	3	1	—	—	4
Critchley, Jason	6 + 1	1	—	—	4
Currier, Andy	29	9	7	—	50
Davidson, Paul	2	—	—	—	—
Davies, Jonathan	24	13	73	1	199
Devereux, John	27	33	20	—	172
Dowd, Barry	17 + 4	2	—	—	8
Eyres, Richard	26 + 3	6	—	—	24
Faimalo, Esene	24	4	—	—	16
Grima, Joe	9 + 5	—	—	—	—
Holding, Neil	1 + 2	—	—	—	—
Holliday, Les	27 + 1	3	4	2	22
Howard, Harvey	12 + 5	1	—	—	4
Hulme, David	25	8	—	—	32
Hulme, Paul	25 + 2	2	—	—	8
Kelly, Chris	2	—	—	—	—
Koloto, Emosi	15 + 4	1	—	—	4
McCurrie, Steve	3 + 3	—	—	—	—
McKenzie, Phil	20 + 2	3	—	—	12
Marsh, David	0 + 3	—	—	—	—
Moriarty, Paul	12	—	—	—	—
Myler, Tony	8	2	—	—	8
Sarsfield, Mark	21 + 2	3	—	—	12
Smith, David	14 + 8	1	—	—	4
Solomona, Se'e	12 + 2	2	—	—	8
Sorensen, Kurt	18 + 4	1	—	—	4
Spruce, Stuart	10 + 4	2	—	—	8
Tait, Alan	29 + 1	9	—	—	36
Wright, Darren	35	12	—	—	48
Wynne, Steve	11 + 2	6	—	—	24

TOTALS:
31 players		125	104	3	711

Representative Appearances 1991-92
Currier — Lancashire (1, 1t)
Davies — Britain (2, 11g); Wales (2, 3t, 13g, 1dg)
Devereux — Britain (1, 1t); Wales (2, 1t)
Eyres — Britain (+1, 1t); Lancashire (1)
Holliday — Britain (2, 1t)
McCurrie — GB Under-21 (1+1, 3t)
Moriarty — Britain (1, 2t); Wales (1)
Tait — Britain (1); Cumbria (1, 2t)

Widnes back row forward Les Holliday on Great Britain Test duty against France in Perpignan in February 1992.

Widnes record beneficiary David Hulme, scorer of eight tries in 25 games in 1991-92.

WIDNES 1991-92 MATCH ANALYSIS

Date	Competition	H/A	Opponent	Rlt	Score	Tries	Goals	Attendance	Referee
25.8.91	LC(P)	A	Workington T.	L	18-27	Koloto, Eyres, Spruce	Currier (3)	—	—
1.9.91	SBC	H	Leeds	W	12-10	Wright, Devereux	Currier (2)	9966	Tennant
8.9.91	SBC	A	Wigan	L	18-26	Devereux, Tait, Davies, Myler	Davies	—	—
22.9.91	SBC	H	Hull K.R.	W	24-6	Davies, D. Hulme, Myler, Currier	Davies (4)	5650	J. Smith
29.9.91	SBC	A	Salford	W	18-10	Davies (2), Faimalo	Davies (3)	—	—
6.10.91	SBC	A	Castleford	W	22-20	Davies, Wright, Devereux	Davies (5)	—	—
13.10.91	SBC	H	Swinton	W	44-12	Devereux (2), Davies, Solomona, D. Hulme, Wright, Eyres	Davies (8)	5330	R. Connolly
20.10.91	SBC	H	Featherstone R.	W	34-20	Wright (3), Devereux (2), Solomona	Davies (5)	5323	Galtress
29.10.91	RT(P)	A	Rochdale H.	W	24-14	Dowd, Currier, Davies, Tait, Devereux	Davies (2)	—	—
3.11.91	SBC	A	Halifax	L	14-28	Devereux (2), D. Hulme	Currier	—	—
10.11.91	SBC	H	Wakefield T.	W	34-0	Devereux (2), Eyres, Faimalo, McKenzie, Wright	Davies (5)	4626	Burke
17.11.91	RT(1)	H	Workington T.	W	26-8	Currier, Devereux, D. Hulme, Wright	Davies (4), Currier	4917	Asquith
23.11.91	RT(2)	A	Carlisle	W	30-16	Tait (2), Faimalo, Sarsfield, Wright, Davies	Davies (3)	—	—
1.12.91	RT(3)	H	Featherstone R.	W	34-22	Davies (2), Sarsfield, Holliday, Tait, D. Hulme	Davies (5)	6551	Galtress
4.12.91	SBC	A	Bradford N.	L	14-36	Wynne (3)	Davies	—	—
8.12.91	SBC	H	Wigan	L	14-23	Wynne, D. Hulme	Davies (3)	7664	Morris
15.12.91	SBC	A	Wakefield T.	Aban.	8-0	Wynne, Sarsfield	—	—	—
21.12.91	RT(SF)	N[1]	St. Helens	W	18-10	Wright, Currier, Faimalo	Davies (3)	(6376)	Holdsworth
26.12.91	SBC	H	Warrington	W	20-8	Devereux (2), Davies, Eyres, Smith	—	9287	Galtress
1.1.92	SBC	A	St. Helens	L	22-24	Devereux (2), Currier, Dowd, Eyres	Davies	—	—
5.1.92	SBC	H	Castleford	L	4-14	Wynne	—	7446	Holdsworth
11.1.92	RT(F)	N[1]	Leeds	W	24-0	Davies, Holliday, Tait, Sorensen	Davies (3, 1dg), Holliday (dg)	(15,070)	Galtress
19.1.92	SBC	H	Hull	W	22-20	Devereux, Tait, Currier	Davies (5)	5559	Kendrew
2.2.92	CC(1)	H	St. Helens	L	2-10	—	Davies	12,741	Holdworth
19.2.92	SBC	A	Wakefield T.	L	4-12	—	Davies (2)	—	—
23.2.92	SBC	A	Swinton	W	38-14	Currier (2), Davies, Wright, Devereux, D. Hulme	Davies (7)	—	—
1.3.92	SBC	H	Halifax	W	18-8	Devereux (3), D. Hulme	Davies	5417	Galtress
8.3.92	SBC	A	Leeds	L	28-40	Devereux (3), Tait (2)	Devereux (4)	—	—
15.3.92	SBC	A	Hull K.R.	L	8-10	P. Hulme	Devereux (2)	—	—
22.3.92	SBC	H	Bradford N.	L	10-17	Spruce	Holliday (3)	4500	J. Connolly
29.3.92	SBC	A	Featherstone R.	L	2-28	—	Davies	—	—
5.4.92	SBC	H	Salford	L	20-24	Devereux (2), Critchley, P. Hulme	Devereux, Holliday	3800	Volante
12.4.92	SBC	A	Hull	W	36-20	Devereux (4), Howard, Wright, Holliday	Devereux (4)	—	—
17.4.92	SBC	A	Warrington	L	8-19	Devereux	Devereux (2)	—	—
20.4.92	SBC	H	St. Helens	L	23-28	McKenzie (2), Devereux	Devereux (5), Holliday (dg)	7227	Morris
26.4.92	PT(1)	A	Wigan	L	16-42	Eyres, Currier, Carbert	Devereux (2)	—	—

N[1] at Wigan

WIGAN

Ground: Central Park (0942-31321)
Colours: Cherry and white
First Season: 1895-96
Nickname: Riversiders
Chairman: Jack Robinson
Secretary: Mary Charnock
Coach: John Monie (Sep 1989-)
Honours: **Championship** Winners, 1908-09, 1921-22, 1925-26, 1933-34, 1945-46, 1946-47, 1949-50, 1951-52, 1959-60 Beaten finalists, 1909-10, 1910-11, 1911-12, 1912-13, 1923-24, 1970-71 **War League Championship** Winners, 1943-44 Beaten finalists, 1940-41 **League Leaders Trophy** Winners, 1970-71 **Division One** Champions, 1986-87, 1989-90, 1990-91, 1991-92 **Challenge Cup** Winners, 1923-24, 1928-29, 1947-48, 1950-51, 1957-58, 1958-59, 1964-65, 1984-85, 1987-88, 1988-89, 1989-90, 1990-91, 1991-92 Beaten finalists, 1910-11, 1919-20, 1943-44, 1945-46, 1960-61, 1962-63, 1965-66, 1969-70, 1983-84 **Regal Trophy** Winners, 1982-83, 1985-86, 1986-87, 1988-89, 1989-90 **Premiership** Winners, 1986-87, 1991-92 **Lancashire Cup** Winners, 1905-06, 1908-09, 1909-10, 1912-13, 1922-23, 1928-29, 1938-39, 1946-47, 1947-48, 1948-49, 1949-50, 1950-51, 1951-52, 1966-67, 1971-72, 1973-74, 1985-86, 1986-87, 1987-88, 1988-89 Beaten finalists, 1913-14, 1914-15, 1925-26, 1927-28, 1930-31, 1934-35, 1935-36, 1936-37, 1945-46, 1953-54, 1957-58, 1977-78, 1980-81, 1984-85 **Lancashire League** Winners, 1901-02, 1908-09, 1910-11, 1911-12, 1912-13, 1913-14, 1914-15, 1920-21, 1922-23, 1923-24, 1925-26, 1945-46, 1946-47, 1949-50, 1951-52, 1958-59, 1961-62, 1969-70

Lancashire War League Winners, 1940-41 **Charity Shield** Winners, 1985-86, 1987-88, 1991-92 Beaten finalists, 1988-89, 1989-90, 1990-91 **World Club Challenge** Winners, 1987-88, 1991-92 **BBC2 Floodlit Trophy** Winners, 1968-69 Beaten finalists, 1969-70

RECORDS

Match
Goals: 22 by Jim Sullivan v. Flimby & Fothergill, 14 Feb 1925
Tries: 10 by Martin Offiah v. Leeds, 10 May 1992
Points: 44 by Jim Sullivan v. Flimby & Fothergill, 14 Feb 1925

Season
Goals: 176 by Fred Griffiths, 1958-59
Tries: 62 by Johnny Ring, 1925-26
Points: 394 by Fred Griffiths, 1958-59

Career
Goals: 2,317 by Jim Sullivan, 1921-46
Tries: 478 by Billy Boston, 1953-68
Points: 4,883 by Jim Sullivan, 1921-46
Appearances: 774 by Jim Sullivan, 1921-46
Highest score: 116-0 v. Flimby & Fothergill, 14 Feb 1925
Highest against: 58-3 at Leeds, 14 Oct 1972
Attendance: 47,747 v. St. Helens (League), 27 Mar 1959

COACHING REGISTER
● **Since 1974-75**

Ted Toohey	May 74 - Jan 75
Joe Coan	Jan 75 - Sep 76
Vince Karalius	Sep 76 - Sep 79
Kel Coslett	Oct 79 - Apr 80
George Fairbairn	Apr 80 - May 81
Maurice Bamford	May 81 - May 82
Alex Murphy	June 82 - Aug 84
Colin Clarke	
Alan McInnes	} Aug 84 - May 86
Graham Lowe	Aug 86 - June 89
John Monie	Sep 89 -

GREAT BRITAIN REGISTER
(79 players)

R. Ashby	(1)	1965
E. Ashcroft	(11)	1947-54
E. Ashton	(26)	1957-63
W. Ashurst	(3)	1971-72
F. Barton	(1)	1951
J. Barton	(2)	1960-61
J. Bennett	(1)	1926
D. Betts	(12 + 1)	1990-92
D. Bevan	(1)	1952
W. Blan	(3)	1951
D. Bolton	(23)	1957-63
W. Boston	(31)	1954-63
T. Bradshaw	(6)	1947-50
F. Carlton	(1)	1962
B. Case	(6 + 1)	1984-88
N. Cherrington	(1)	1960
C. Clarke	(7)	1965-73
P. Clarke	(+1)	1990
A. Coldrick	(4)	1914
F. Collier	(1)	1963
J. Cunliffe	(4)	1950-54
M. Dermott	(4)	1990-92
S. Edwards	(18 + 3)	1985-92
J. Egan	(14)	1946-50
R. Evans	(4)	1961-62
G. Fairbairn	(14)	1977-80
T. Fogerty	(1)	1967
P. Ford	(1)	1985
W. Francis	(4)	1967-77
D. Gardiner	(1)	1965
K. Gee	(17)	1946-51
H. Gill	(14 + 1)	1981-88
A. Goodway	(12)	1985-90
R. Goulding	(5)	1990
J. Gray	(5 + 3)	1974
A. Gregory	(15)	1987-90
S. Hampson	(10 + 1)	1987-91
E. Hanley	(23)	1985-91
C. Hill	(1)	1966
D. Hill	(1)	1971
J. Hilton	(4)	1950
T. Howley	(6)	1924
W. Hudson	(1)	1948
D. Hurcombe	(8)	1920-24
B. Jenkins	(12)	1907-14
K. Jones	(2)	1970
R. Kinnear	(1)	1929
N. Kiss	(1)	1985
D. Laughton	(11)	1970-71
J. Lawrenson	(3)	1948
J. Leytham	(5)	1907-10
I. Lucas	(1)	1991
J. Lydon	(13 + 1)	1986-90
B. McTigue	(25)	1958-63
J. Miller	(1)	1911
J. Morley	(2)	1936-37
A. Platt	(9)	1989-92
I. Potter	(7 + 1)	1985-86
J. Price	(4)	1924
R. Ramsdale	(8)	1910-14
G. Ratcliffe	(3)	1947-50
J. Ring	(2)	1924-26
D. Robinson	(1)	1970
M. Ryan	(4)	1947-50
W. Sayer	(7)	1961-63
J. Sharrock	(4)	1910-11
N. Silcock	(3)	1954
R. Silcock	(1)	1908
K. Skerrett	(1)	1992
D. Stephenson	(5)	1982-87
J. Sullivan	(25)	1924-33
M. Sullivan	(19)	1957-60
G. Thomas	(1)	1914
J. Thomas	(8)	1907-11
S. Wane	(2)	1985-86
E. Ward	(3)	1946-47
L. White	(2)	1947
D. Willicombe	(2)	1974
W. Winstanley	(3)	1911

1991-92 SIGNINGS REGISTER

Signed	Player	Club From
31.7.91	Robinson, Jason	Hunslet Parkside ARL
14.8.91	Mather, Barrie-Jon	—
14.8.91	McRae, Ian	Greatfield ARL
20.8.91	Williams, Darren	Woolston R. ARL
29.8.91	McGinty, Billy	Warrington
30.8.91	Panapa, Sam	Sheffield E.
3.9.91	Cowie, Neil	Rochdale H.
6.9.91	Turner, Stuart	Widnes
24.9.91	Stoop, Andre	Wanderers RU, SA
4.10.91	Miles, Gene	Brisbane B., Aus
10.10.91	Melling, Chris	St. Patricks ARL
18.10.91	Dean, Mike	Salford
29.12.91	Ellison, Daniel	Golbourne ARL
3.1.92	Farrell, Andrew	Orrell St. James ARL
3.1.92	Offiah, Martin	Widnes
20.5.92	Griffiths, Mark	Eastmoor ARL

Representative Appearances 1991-92
Betts — Britain (2, 1t); Lancashire (1)
Clarke — GB Under-21 (2, 2t)
Dermott — Britain (2, 1t); Lancashire (1)
Edwards — Britain (2); Lancashire (1)
Hampson — Britain (1)
Mather — GB Under-21 (+1)
Myers — Lancashire (1, 1t); GB Under-21 (3, 9t)
O'Donnell — GB Under-21 (2, 1t, 1g)
Platt — Britain (1+1, 1t); Lancashire (1)
Skerrett — Britain (1); Yorkshire (1)

1991-92 PLAYERS' SUMMARY

	App	Tries	Goals	Dr	Pts
Ball, Phil	2	—	—	—	—
Bell, Dean	32 + 1	13	—	—	52
Betts, Denis	42 + 1	19	—	—	76
Blakeley, Steve	0 + 6	2	3	—	14
Botica, Frano	34	11	159	2	364
Cassidy, Mike	1	—	—	—	—
Clarke, Phil	24 + 2	2	—	—	8
Cowie, Neil	22 + 15	—	—	—	—
Dean, Mike	2	1	—	—	4
Dermott, Martin	33 + 1	5	—	—	20
Edwards, Shaun	37	40	2	—	164
Farrell, Andrew	0 + 2	—	—	—	—
Forshaw, Mike	6 + 10	2	—	—	8
Gildart, Ian	9 + 7	1	—	—	4
Goodway, Andy	1	—	—	—	—
Gregory, Andy	35	1	—	1	5
Hampson, Steve	29 + 1	5	3	—	26
Lucas, Ian	12 + 7	1	—	—	4
Lydon, Joe	31 + 7	16	18	4	104
McGinty, Billy	36 + 3	7	—	—	28
Mather, Barrie-Jon	2 + 1	—	—	—	—
Miles, Gene	29	8	—	—	32
Myers, Dave	25 + 6	19	—	—	76
Naylor, Scott	1	—	—	—	—
O'Donnell, Augustine	7 + 3	2	5	1	19
Offiah, Martin	15 + 1	30	—	—	120
Panapa, Sam	25 + 9	11	—	—	44
Platt, Andy	34 + 1	2	—	—	8
Skerrett, Kelvin	24 + 3	3	—	—	12
Stoop, Andre	6 + 1	—	3	—	6
Turner, Stuart	3	3	—	—	12

TOTALS:
31 players		204	193	8	1,210

1991-92 MATCH ANALYSIS

Date	Competition	H/A	Opponent	Rlt	Score	Tries	Goals	Attendance	Referee
25.8.91	CS	N[1]	Hull	W	22-8	Bell (2), Myers, Edwards	Botica (3)	(10,248)	Whitfield
1.9.91	SBC	A	Castleford	L	26-38	Betts (2), Hampson, Dermott	Botica (5)	—	—
8.9.91	SBC	H	Widnes	W	26-18	Lydon, Myers, Forshaw, Botica	Botica (5)	15,964	Holdsworth
15.9.91	LC(1)	A	London C.	W	38-10	Lydon (2), Edwards (2), Myers, Gregory, Betts	Botica (5)	—	—
22.9.91	SBC	A	Hull	W	30-4	Betts (2), Myers, Botica	Botica (7)	—	—
26.9.91	LC(2)	H	Leigh	W	42-12	Edwards (2), Myers, Gildart, Botica, Betts, Platt	Botica (7)	11,153	Burke
2.10.91	WCC	N[2]	Penrith	W	21-4	Panapa, Myers	Botica (6), Lydon (dg)	(20,152)	Sablayrolles (Fr)
6.10.91	SBC	H	Featherstone R.	W	52-10	Edwards (3), Panapa (2), Myers, McGinty, Dermott, Miles	Lydon (3), O'Donnell (2), Edwards	12,154	Whitfield
10.10.91	LC(SF)	A	St. Helens	L	16-28	Panapa, O'Donnell, McGinty	Lydon (2)	—	—
13.10.91	SBC	A	Wakefield T.	L	6-13	Myers	Stoop	—	—
20.10.91	SBC	A	Swinton	W	26-14	Panapa (2), Forshaw, Blakeley	O'Donnell (3), Stoop (2)	—	—
27.10.91	SBC	H	Halifax	W	40-18	Lydon (2), Betts (2), Miles, Panapa, Myers	Lydon (5), Blakeley	14,325	Campbell

(Continued)

WIGAN 1991-92 MATCH ANALYSIS (continued)

Date	Com-petition	H/A	Opponent	Rlt	Score	Tries	Goals	Atten-dance	Referee
29.10.91	RT(P)	H	Dewsbury	W	34-14	Edwards (2), Hampson, Lydon, Betts, Bell, Blakeley	Blakeley (2), Lydon	5020	R. Smith
3.11.91	SBC	H	Leeds	L	0-19	—	—	14,874	Morris
13.11.91	SBC	A	Salford	L	10-24	Panapa	Hampson (3)	—	—
17.11.91	RT(1)	A	Swinton	W	34-8	Edwards (2), Lydon, Betts, Dermott, Miles	Lydon (5)	—	—
24.11.91	RT(2)	H	Keighley C.	W	32-8	Turner (3), McGinty (2), Bell, Myers	Lydon (2)	6052	Steele
30.11.91	RT(3)	A	Salford	L	14-24	Edwards, Bell	Botica (3)	—	—
8.12.91	SBC	A	Widnes	W	23-14	Betts, Edwards, Myers	Botica (5, 1dg)	—	—
15.12.91	SBC	H	Hull	W	24-12	Edwards (2), Panapa	Botica (6)	10,916	Galtress
22.12.91	SBC	H	Castleford	W	10-6	Lydon	Botica (3)	10,933	Burke
26.12.91	SBC	H	St. Helens	W	16-6	Edwards (2), Hampson	Botica (2)	26,307	Campbell
1.1.92	SBC	A	Warrington	W	24-6	Skerrett, Edwards, Lydon, Myers	Botica (4)	—	—
5.1.92	SBC	H	Wakefield T.	W	20-2	Edwards, Betts, Myers, Lydon	Botica (2)	17,014	Morris
12.1.92	SBC	A	Bradford N.	W	28-22	Edwards (2), Offiah, Betts, McGinty	Botica (4)	—	—
19.1.92	SBC	A	Halifax	W	30-10	Offiah (3), Clarke, McGinty, Edwards	Botica (3)	—	—
2.2.92	CC(1)	A	Salford	W	22-6	Botica, Edwards, Betts, Lydon	Botica (3)	—	—
16.2.92	CC(2)	H	Warrington	W	14-0	Skerrett, Offiah	Botica (3)	21,736	Galtress
22.2.92	CC(3)	A	St. Helens	W	13-6	Hampson, Edwards	Botica (2, 1dg)	—	—
1.3.92	SBC	H	Swinton	W	38-12	Botica, Dean, McGinty, Myers, Lydon, Bell, Edwards	Botica (5)	10,490	Campbell
8.3.92	SBC	H	Hull K.R.	W	28-10	Panapa, Botica, Betts, O'Donnell	Botica (6)	11,517	R. Smith
15.3.92	SBC	A	Leeds	W	24-0	Myers, Clarke, Edwards, Bell	Botica (4)	—	—
22.3.92	SBC	H	Salford	W	28-7	Lydon (2), Edwards (2), Botica	Botica (4)	13,231	Holdsworth
28.3.92	CC(SF)	N³	Bradford N.	W	71-10	Offiah (5), Miles (2), Botica, Betts, Lucas, Lydon, Edwards, Bell	Botica (9), Gregory (dg)	(18,027)	Whitfield
1.4.92	SBC	A	Hull K.R.	W	17-2	Panapa, Miles	Botica (4), Lydon (dg)	—	—
5.4.92	SBC	A	Featherstone R.	W	34-13	Botica, Edwards, Offiah, Myers, Skerrett, Bell	Botica (4), Edwards	—	—
11.4.92	SBC	H	Bradford N.	W	50-8	Edwards (4), Offiah (2), Bell (2), Botica	Botica (7)	12,392	Morris
17.4.92	SBC	A	St. Helens	W	16-6	Offiah, Edwards, Miles	Botica (2)	—	—
20.4.92	SBC	H	Warrington	W	19-13	Edwards (2), Lydon	Botica (3), O'Donnell (dg)	12,406	Holdsworth
26.4.92	PT(1)	H	Widnes	W	42-16	Offiah (2), Botica, Betts, Edwards, Dermott	Botica (9)	12,547	R. Smith
2.5.92	CC(F)	N⁴	Castleford	W	28-12	Offiah (2), Edwards, Hampson	Botica (5), Lydon (2dg)	(77,386)	Whitfield
10.5.92	PT(SF)	H	Leeds	W	74-6	Offiah (10), Bell (2), Dermott, Myers	Botica (9)	18,261	Morris
17.5.92	PT(F)	N⁵	St. Helens	W	48-16	Offiah (2), Betts (2), Platt, Myers, Miles	Botica (10)	(33,157)	Holdsworth

N¹ at Gateshead International Stadium
N² at Liverpool FC
N³ at Bolton W. FC
N⁴ at Wembley
N⁵ at Manchester U. FC

137

WORKINGTON TOWN

Ground: Derwent Park (0900-603609)
Colours: Blue and white
First Season: 1945-46
Nickname: Town
Chairman: Kevan Gorge
Secretary: John Bell
Coach: Ray Ashton (June 1990-Dec 1991)
Dean Williams (Dec 1991-Apr 1992)
Peter Walsh (May 1992-)
Honours: **Championship** Winners, 1950-51
Beaten finalists, 1957-58
Challenge Cup Winners, 1951-52
Beaten finalists, 1954-55, 1957-58
Lancashire Cup Winners, 1977-78
Beaten finalists, 1976-77, 1978-79,
1979-80
Western Division Championship
Winners, 1962-63

RECORDS

Match
Goals: 11 by Iain MacCorquodale v. Blackpool B.,
6 Jan 1973
Tries: 7 by Ike Southward v. Blackpool B.,
17 Sep 1955
Points: 33 by Ike Southward v. Blackpool B.,
17 Sep 1955

Season
Goals: 186 by Lynn Hopkins, 1981-82
Tries: 49 by Johnny Lawrenson, 1951-52
Points: 438 by Lynn Hopkins, 1981-82

Career
Goals: 809 by Iain MacCorquodale, 1972-80
Tries: 274 by Ike Southward, 1952-59 &
1960-68
Points: 1,800 by Iain MacCorquodale, 1972-80
Appearances: 415 + 4 Paul Charlton, 1961-69 &
1975-80
Highest score: 62-15 v. Hunslet, 20 Apr 1964
Highest against: 68-0 at Wigan, 18 Jan 1987
68-6 at Leigh, 8 Mar 1992
Attendance: 17,741 v. Wigan (RL Cup),
3 Mar 1965 — at Derwent Park
20,403 v. St. Helens (RL Cup),
8 Mar 1952 — at Borough Park

COACHING REGISTER
● **Since 1974-75**

Ike Southward	Aug 73 - June 75
Paul Charlton	June 75 - June 76
Ike Southward	June 76 - Feb 78
Sol Roper	Feb 78 - Apr 80
Keith Irving	Aug 80 - Oct 80
Tommy Bishop	Nov 80 - June 82
Paul Charlton	July 82 - Dec 82
Dave Cox	Mar 83 - Mar 83
Harry Archer/Bill Smith	May 83 - June 84
Bill Smith	June 84 - Apr 85
Jackie Davidson	Apr 85 - Jan 86
Keith Davies	Feb 86 - Mar 87
Norman Turley	Mar 87 - Apr 88
Maurice Bamford	July 88 - Dec 88
Phil Kitchin	Dec 88 - May 90
Ray Ashton	June 90 - Dec 91
Dean Williams	Dec 91 - Apr 92
Peter Walsh	May 92 -

GREAT BRITAIN REGISTER
(9 players)

E. Bowman	(4)	1977
P. Charlton	(1)	1965
B. Edgar	(11)	1958-66
N. Herbert	(6)	1961-62
V. McKeating	(2)	1951
W. Martin	(1)	1962
A. Pepperell	(2)	1950-51
I. Southward	(4)	1958
G. Wilson	(3)	1951

Half back Dean Marwood, signed from Barrow in December 1991, scoring 31 points in 14 outings.

1991-92 SIGNINGS REGISTER

Signed	Player	Club From
9.8.91	Schubert, Gary	Carlisle
19.8.91	Buglass, Barry	Cockermouth ARL
23.8.91	Patterson, Gary	Broughton Moor ARL
23.8.91	Wilson, Mark	Glasson ARL
24.8.91	Wilkes, Mark	Carlisle
29.8.91	Kirkwood, Ken	Seaton ARL
11.9.91	Faimalo, Joe	Eastern Suburbs, NZ
28.9.91	Lia, Ben	Upper Hutt, NZ
4.10.91	*Mort, Craig	Oldham
10.10.91	Lord, Mark	Rochdale H.
10.10.91	Green, Jason	Seddon Atkinson ARL
17.10.91	Lomax, John	Wainuiemata, NZ
30.11.91	Needham, David	Halifax
6.12.91	Coles, Colin	Carlisle
23.12.91	*Marwood, Dean	Barrow

1991-92 PLAYERS' SUMMARY

	App	Tries	Goals	Dr	Pts
Armstrong, Colin	31	6	11	—	46
Ashton, Ray	13 + 1	1	—	2	6
Beattie, John	12 + 2	3	—	—	12
Buglass, Barry	3 + 3	—	—	—	—
Burgess, Glen	4 + 4	—	—	—	—
Coles, Colin	8	—	—	—	—
Faimalo, Joe	1 + 4	—	—	—	—
Gorge, Paul	4 + 1	—	—	—	—
Graham, John	1 + 1	—	—	—	—
Green, Jason	5 + 1	—	—	—	—
Kerr, Ken	10 + 1	—	—	—	—
Kirkwood, Ken	2	—	—	—	—
Kitchin, Wayne	15 + 1	3	4	1	21
Law, Andrew	0 + 1	—	—	—	—
Lia, Ben	4 + 1	—	—	—	—
Lomax, John	17 + 1	1	—	—	4
Lord, Mark	12 + 2	3	—	—	12
Lowden, David	22 + 1	3	—	2	14
McGuirk, Gary	7 + 6	—	—	—	—
McLean, Ian	22	4	—	—	16
McMullen, Alan	19 + 6	—	—	—	—
Marwood, Dean	13 + 1	1	12	3	31
Mawson, Mark	16 + 2	5	—	—	20
Mort, Craig	3 + 2	2	—	—	8
Needham, David	10 + 1	—	—	—	—
Oglanby, Martin	21 + 1	4	—	—	16
Penman, Danny	1 + 1	—	—	—	—
Penrice, Paul	11 + 1	6	—	—	24
Phillips, Graeme	2 + 3	—	—	—	—
Pickering, Brendan	2 + 1	—	—	—	—
Riley, Peter	27 + 7	—	—	—	—
Rooney, Neil	30	6	—	—	24
Roskell, Mark	16 + 1	—	—	—	—
Schubert, Gary	31	3	—	—	12
Scott, Ian	13 + 4	1	—	—	4
Smith, Gary	18	2	—	—	8
Stansfield, Ivan	5 + 4	—	—	—	—
Tubman, Keith	0 + 1	—	—	—	—
Wear, Steve	28 + 1	3	64	4	144
Wilkes, Mark	3	2	—	—	8
Williams, Dean	19 + 5	—	—	—	—
Trialist	0 + 1	—	—	—	—
TOTALS:					
42 players		59	91	12	430

Representative Appearances 1991-92
Armstrong — Cumbria (1, 1t)
Oglanby — Cumbria (+1)
Riley — Cumbria (+1)
Roskell — Cumbria (1)
Wear — Cumbria (1, 5g)

Town's Steve Wear on Cumbrian County duty in November 1991, kicking one of five goals against the Papua New Guinea tourists.

WORKINGTON TOWN 1991-92 MATCH ANALYSIS

Date	Competition	H/A	Opponent	Rlt	Score	Tries	Goals	Attendance	Referee
25.8.91	LC(P)	H	Widnes	W	27-18	Penrice, Ashton, McLean	Wear (7), Ashton (dg)	3499	Burke
1.9.91	SD	H	London C.	W	12-8	Oglanby, Penrice	Wear (2)	2039	R. Connolly
8.9.91	SD	A	Ryedale-York	W	42-18	Penrice, Armstrong, Rooney, Schubert, McLean, Mawson, Kitchin	Wear (7)	—	—
15.9.91	LC(1)	H	Barrow	W	12-6	Kitchin, Oglanby	Kitchin, Wear	2721	Ollerton
23.9.91	SD	H	Oldham	D	6-6	Mawson	Armstrong	3213	J. Connolly
26.9.91	LC(2)	H	Carlisle	L	2-11	—	Wear	4278	R. Connolly
29.9.91	SD	A	Carlisle	L	10-39	Mawson, Beattie	Armstrong	—	—
6.10.91	SD	A	Sheffield E.	L	14-28	Armstrong, Mort	Armstrong (2), Lowden (2dg)	—	—
13.10.91	SD	H	Rochdale H.	L	12-48	Mawson, McLean	Armstrong (2)	2311	Kershaw
20.10.91	SD	A	Leigh	L	5-10	—	Wear (2), Ashton (dg)	—	—
27.10.91	SD	H	London C.	L	4-10	—	Armstrong (2)	1755	Tennant
3.11.91	RT(P)	A	Saddleworth R.	W	30-0	Lowden, Penrice, Mort, Oglanby, Mawson	Wear (5)	—	—
10.11.91	SD	A	Oldham	W	15-14	Penrice, Lomax	Wear (3, 1dg)	—	—
17.11.91	RT(1)	A	Widnes	L	8-26	Oglanby	Wear (2)	—	—
24.11.91	SD	H	Ryedale-York	W	20-16	Armstrong, Lord, Penrice	Wear (4)	1468	Allatt
1.12.91	SD	H	Carlisle	L	11-17	Armstrong	Wear (2, 1dg), Armstrong	2654	Kershaw
8.12.91	SD	H	Sheffield E.	L	2-35	—	Armstrong	1690	Carter
15.12.91	SD	A	Rochdale H.	L	8-42	Smith	Wear (2)	—	—
26.12.91	SD	A	Carlisle	L	6-25	Wear	Wear	—	—
5.1.92	SD	H	Leigh	L	9-15	Lord	Wear (2), Marwood (dg)	1911	Cross
13.1.92	CC(P)	H	Carlisle	W	11-4	Schubert	Wear (3), Marwood (dg)	2695	Kendrew
19.1.92	SD	A	Ryedale-York	L	12-31	Schubert, Marwood	Marwood (2)	—	—
26.1.92	CC(1)	H	Wakefield T.	W	13-8	Armstrong	Wear (4), Kitchin (dg)	2837	Cummings
9.2.92	CC(2)	H	London C.	W	9-2	Lowden	Wear (2), Marwood (dg)	2656	Carter
12.2.92	SD	H	Oldham	L	0-5	—	—	2310	Asquith
16.2.92	SD	A	Sheffield E.	L	8-48	Rooney	Marwood (2)	—	—
23.2.92	CC(3)	H	Hull	L	8-24	Lowden	Wear (2)	5298	Campbell
26.2.92	SD	H	Rochdale H.	L	4-5	—	Wear (2)	1686	Redfearn
1.3.92	SD	A	London C.	L	7-28	Smith	Wear (1, 1dg)	—	—
8.3.92	SD	A	Leigh	L	6-68	Wear	Wear	—	—
15.3.92	SD	H	Sheffield E.	L	18-36	Beattie (2), Wear	Wear (3)	1410	R. Smith
22.3.92	SD	A	Rochdale H.	L	14-50	Rooney, Kitchin	Kitchin (3)	—	—
29.3.92	SD	H	Ryedale-York	D	19-19	Rooney (2), Scott	Wear (3, 1dg)	1082	Galtress
5.4.92	SD	A	Oldham	L	10-44	Armstrong, Lord	Armstrong	—	—
12.4.92	SD	H	Leigh	L	8-34	Wilkes	Wear (2)	1290	R. Connolly
17.4.92	SD	A	London C.	L	16-32	Wilkes, Rooney	Marwood (4)	—	—
20.4.92	SD	H	Carlisle	L	12-40	McLean	Marwood (4)	1427	Ollerton

Wigan half back Shaun Edwards, top tryscorer for 1991-92.

RECORDS

LEADING SCORERS FOR 1991-92

TOP TEN TRIES

1. Shaun Edwards (Wigan) 40
2. John Devereux (Widnes)............................. 35
3. Iva Ropati (Oldham)................................. 33
   Greg Austin (Halifax)................................ 33
5. Vince Gribbin (Whitehaven) 31
   Graham Steadman (Castleford) 31
7. Martin Offiah (Wigan) 30
8. David Myers (Wigan)................................ 29
9. Paul Newlove (Featherstone R.) 28
10. Mark Preston (Halifax).............................. 27
● Others with 20 or more: Alan Hunte (St. Helens) 25;
Darren Abram (Rochdale H.), Gary Connolly (St.
Helens), David Plange (Sheffield E.) 24; Owen Simpson
(Featherstone R.) 23; Dennis Bailey (Dewsbury), Paul
Carr (Hunslet), Stuart Cocker (Huddersfield), Eddie
Rombo (Dewsbury) 22; Ikram Butt (Featherstone R.),
Bright Sodje (Hull K.R.) 21; Simon Ashcroft
(Highfield), John Bentley (Leeds), Denis Betts (Wigan),
Tex Evans (Salford), Wally Gibson (Huddersfield), Tony
Kay (Barrow) 20.

TOP TEN GOALS
(Including drop goals)

1. Frano Botica (Wigan) 161
2. Steve Carroll (Bramley)............................ 138
3. Deryck Fox (Featherstone R.) 115
4. Lee Crooks (Castleford) 113
5. David Hobbs (Bradford N.)........................ 110
6. Chris Vasey (Dewsbury)............................ 109
7. Paul Eastwood (Hull) 108
8. Steve Parrish (Batley) 106
9. Mark Aston (Sheffield E.) 104
10. Jonathan Davies (Widnes) 99

TOP FIVE DROP GOALS

1. Andy Ruane (Leigh) 17
2. Steve Carroll (Bramley) 8
   Garry Schofield (Leeds)............................... 8
   Barry Williams (Carlisle)............................. 8
   Gary Pearce (Ryedale-York)......................... 8

TOP FIVE POINTS

		T	G	DG	Pts
1.	Frano Botica (Wigan)........	11	159	2	364
2.	Steve Carroll (Bramley)	5	130	8	288
3.	Paul Eastwood (Hull)........	15	108	0	276
4.	Jonathan Davies (Widnes)..	16	97	2	260
5.	Steve Parrish (Batley)........	10	104	2	250

Key:
SBC .... Stones Bitter Championship
SD.............. Second Division
TD .... Third Division
PT.............. Premiership Trophy
DP .... Divisional Premiership
LC.............. Lancashire Cup
YC.............. Yorkshire Cup
RT .... Regal Trophy
CC.............. Challenge Cup
CS .... Charity Shield
NA .... Non-appearance

OUTSTANDING SCORING FEATS IN 1991-92

INDIVIDUAL

Most tries in a match:
10 by Martin Offiah (Wigan) v. Leeds .... PT
 5 by Martin Offiah (Wigan) v. Bradford N....... CC
    Greg Austin (Halifax) v. Hull K.R. .... SBC
    Eddie Rombo (Dewsbury) v. Highfield..... TD
    Vince Gribbin (Whitehaven) v.
    Nottingham C. .... TD

Most goals in a match:
12 by Tony Zelei (Doncaster) v. Nottingham C. . TD
    Bernard Dwyer (St. Helens)
    v. Trafford B. LC
    Steve Maguire (Whitehaven)
    v. Nottingham C..................................TD
    Mark Aston (Sheffield E.) v. Keighley C. . DP
11 by Jason Gilbert (Huddersfield)
    v. Trafford B. .... TD
    John Woods (Leigh) v. Ryedale-York....... SD
    Greg Pearce (Halifax) v. Doncaster CC
    John Wasyliw (Keighley C.)
    v. Nottingham C................................... TD
    Simon Kenworthy (Huddersfield) at
    Nottingham C. .... TD
10 by Greg Pearce (Halifax) v. Hull K.R.......... SBC
    Steve Parrish (Batley) at Nottingham C..... TD
    Deryck Fox (Featherstone R.) v. Halifax .. RT
    Tony Zelei (Doncaster) v. Trafford B....... TD
    David Hobbs (Bradford N.) v. Swinton .... SBC
    Frano Botica (Wigan) v. St. Helens .... PT

Most points in a match:
40 by Martin Offiah (Wigan) v. Leeds .... PT
38 by John Woods (Leigh) v. Ryedale-York....... SD
32 by Tony Zelei (Doncaster) v. Nottingham C. . TD

TEAM

Highest score:
St. Helens 104 v. Trafford B. 12 LC
● There was a total of 56 matches in which a team scored 50 points or more, compared with 40 in the previous season. The other 60-plus scores were:

Home:
Doncaster 88 v. Nottingham C. 6 .... TD
Whitehaven 80 v. Nottingham C. 6 .... TD
Huddersfield 78 v. Nottingham C. 0 .... TD
Barrow 78 v. Nottingham C. 8 .... TD
Halifax 76 v. Hull K.R. 8 .... SBC
Bradford N. 76 v. Leigh East 0 .... RT
Wigan 74 v. Leeds 6 .... PT
Salford 74 v. Trafford B. 0 .... RT
Sheffield E. 72 v. Keighley C. 14 .... DP
Wigan 71 v. Bradford N. 10 (at Bolton W. FC) . CC
Leigh 70 v. Ryedale-York 0 .... SD
Keighley C. 70 v. Nottingham C. 0 .... TD
Huddersfield 70 v. Trafford B. 0 .... TD
Leigh 68 v. Workington T. 6 .... SD
Dewsbury 66 v. Nottingham C. 6 .... TD
Halifax 66 v. Doncaster 8 CC
Featherstone R. 64 v. Halifax 18 .... RT
Bradford N. 60 v. Swinton 0 .... SBC

Away:
Nottingham C. 0 v. Huddersfield 82 .... TD
Trafford B. 4 v. Huddersfield 78 .... TD
Nottingham C. 0 v. Batley 64 .... TD
Chorley B. 13 v. Salford 64 CC
Chorley B. 12 v. Dewsbury 62 .... TD

Highest score by losing team:
Halifax 34 v. Leeds 46 .... SBC
● There was a total of 54 matches in which a team scored 20 points or more and lost, the same number as the previous season.

High-scoring draws:
There were no draws in which both teams scored 20 points or more, compared with two in the previous season.

● From the start of the 1983-84 season, the value of a try was raised from three points to four. It was decided officially that records for most points in a match, season or career would subsequently include the four-point try and that no attempt would be made to adjust existing records featuring the three-point try.
● Substitute appearances do not count towards players' full appearance records.
● Points and appearances in abandoned matches are included in records, except in League matches which are replayed. Although the abandoned League match points and appearances are included in players' overall totals they do not count towards League records.

RECORD-BREAKING FEATS 1991-92

STEVE CARROLL of Bramley achieved club records of 138 goals and 288 points in a season after scoring in every match.

IVA ROPATI scored a Sheffield Eagles record of 30 tries in a season.

VINCE GRIBBIN of Whitehaven scored a club record 31 tries in a season.

JOHN WOODS of Leigh equalled the club and Division Two record of 38 points in a match.

JOHN WASYLIW of Keighley Cougars scored club records of 11 goals and 26 points in a match.

FRANO BOTICA of Wigan scored Premiership final records of 10 goals and 20 points.

MARTIN OFFIAH of Wigan scored a club and Premiership competition record of 10 tries in a match. His 40 points were also a Premiership record.

MARK ROACHE of Doncaster finished the season with a club career record of 83 tries, including a club best of four in a match when TONY ZELEI scored records of 12 goals and 32 points.

JONATHAN DAVIES of Widnes broke two Wales records with eight goals and 24 points in a match and then achieved Great Britain records against Papua New Guinea of eight goals and 16 points.

MARTIN PEARSON of Featherstone Rovers achieved three Great Britain Under-21 match records with three tries, eight goals and 24 points.

DAVID MYERS of Wigan thrice equalled the Great Britain Under-21s record of three tries in a match.

GRAHAM STEADMAN of Castleford scored a Yorkshire Cup final record of 16 points.

STEVE PARRISH of Batley kicked a club record 10 goals in a match.

MARK ASTON of Sheffield Eagles kicked a club record-equalling 12 goals in a match.

STEVE MAGUIRE of Whitehaven kicked a club record 12 goals in a match.

BRADFORD NORTHERN scored a club record 76-0 victory over Leigh East amateurs.

DONCASTER scored a club and Third Division record 88-6 win against Nottingham City.

BATLEY gained a club record 64-0 win at Nottingham City.

KEIGHLEY COUGARS ran up their highest score with a 70-0 defeat of Nottingham City.

WHITEHAVEN scored a club record 80-6 win over Nottingham City.

WIGAN achieved the highest score in any cup final with a 48-16 defeat of St. Helens in the Premiership Trophy final.

TRAFFORD BOROUGH suffered a club record 104-12 defeat at St. Helens.

LEEDS went down to a club record score with the 74-6 defeat at Wigan, which was also the biggest defeat for any side in the Premiership Trophy.

HULL KINGSTON ROVERS suffered a club record 76-8 defeat at Halifax.

WORKINGTON TOWN conceded a club record total with the 68-6 defeat at Leigh.

WIDNES achieved a Regal Trophy final record margin win with a 24-0 defeat of Leeds.

GREAT BRITAIN achieved their highest score against Papua New Guinea of 56-4.

WALES ran up their highest score with a 68-0 defeat of Papua New Guinea.

GREAT BRITAIN UNDER-21s gained record wins of 58-0 and 56-2 over Papua New Guinea and France respectively.

Bramley's Steve Carroll, the only play-a-match scorer in 1991-92.

NEW RECORDS IN DETAIL . . .

STEVE CARROLL of Bramley finished with club records of 138 goals and 288 points in a season. The scrum half also became only the 13th player to score in every one of his club's matches throughout the season.

The previous Bramley goals record was 130 by John Wilson in 1961-62. Carroll passed that figure with a goal in a 12-6 Division Three home defeat against Batley on 5 April.

Scrum half George Langfield held the old points record with 276 from 10 tries and 123 goals in 1956-57. Carroll broke the record with the first of three goals in an 18-18 Divisional Premiership home tie against Keighley Cougars on 21 April.

His total of 288 points was made up of five tries and 138 goals, including eight drop goals.

Carroll scored in all 33 of Bramley's matches as follows:

		T	G	Pts
Keighley C. .... (H)	0	7(1)	13
Trafford B. .... (A)	0	4	8
Keighley C. (YC) .... (A)	0	4	8
Huddersfield .... (H)	0	3(1)	5
Bradford N. (YC) .... (H)	0	4(1)	7
Dewsbury .... (A)	0	2	4
Nottingham C. .... (H)	0	7	14
Barrow .... (A)	0	4	8
Chorley B. .... (H)	1	6	16
Doncaster .... (A)	0	3	6
Dewsbury .... (H)	0	4	8
Huddersfield .... (A)	0	3	6
Featherstone R. (RT)...... (H)	0	6(2)	10
Featherstone R. (RT) ...... (A)	0	2	4
Whitehaven................... (H)	1	6	16
Chorley B. .... (A)	0	6	12
Barrow.......................... (H)	1	2	8
Hunslet......................... (H)	0	3	6
Hunslet .... (A)	0	3	6
Trafford B.................... (H)	0	6	12
Keighley C.................... (A)	0	3	6
Scarborough P.............. (H)	0	8(1)	15
Leeds (CC) .... (H)	1	2	8
Nottingham C................ (A)	0	5	10
Batley .... (A)	0	1	2
Doncaster...................... (H)	1	7	18
Highfield .... (A)	0	6	12
Scarborough P. .... (A)	0	7(1)	13
Highfield...................... (H)	0	4	8
Whitehaven................... (H)	0	2	4
Batley.......................... (H)	0	1	2
Keighley C. (DP)........... (H)	0	3	6
Keighley C. (DP) .... (A)	0	4(1)	7

Totals

33 appearances................. 5 138(8) 288

() drop goals included in total.

IVA ROPATI scored a Sheffield Eagles record of 30 tries in a season, despite not making his debut until their fourth match and being transferred to Oldham with seven matches remaining.

The previous record of 28 was set by Daryl Powell in 1988-89. Ropati broke the record with the first of two tries in a 51-6 Division Two home win over Leigh on 22 March. It was to be his last match for Sheffield.

The New Zealand centre scored two tries on his debut for them in a 44-22 Division Two win at London Crusaders on 22 September.

Ropati played in all 27 matches before moving in an exchange deal with Oldham's New Zealand centre Charlie McAlister.

Ropati's match-by-match record after signing for Sheffield is as follows:

London C.	(A)	2
Ryedale-York	(A)	1
Workington T.	(H)	1
Leigh	(A)	0
Rochdale H.	(H)	0
Oldham	(A)	1
Scarborough P. (RT)	(H)	1
Carlisle	(H)	0
London C.	(A)	1
Ryedale-York (RT)	(A)	0
Bradford N. (RT)	(A)	1
Workington T.	(A)	2
Leigh	(H)	1
Ryedale-York	(A)	1
Ryedale-York	(H)	2
Oldham	(A)	2
Rochdale H.	(A)	2
Carlisle	(A)	2
Whitehaven (CC)	(A)	0
Hull (CC)	(H)	0
Workington T.	(H)	2
Leigh	(A)	1
London C.	(H)	4
Oldham	(H)	0
Rochdale H.	(H)	0
Workington T.	(A)	1
Leigh	(H)	2
27 appearances		**30**

VINCE GRIBBIN of Whitehaven broke the club record for tries in a season by scoring five in the last match on 12 April to take his total to 31 in 27 appearances.

Needing three tries against Nottingham City to equal the old record of 29 in 40 appearances by winger Billy Smith in 1956-57, Gribbin scored five in the club record 80-6 Division Three home win.

A former Great Britain Test centre, Gribbin scored 17 of his record-breaking tries in nine matches on the wing including 10 in the last three.

He also holds the club match record of six, playing in the centre against Doncaster in 1984.

Gribbin's match-by-match record for 1991-92 is as follows:

Batley	(A)	0
Highfield	(H)	3
Carlisle (LC)	(H)	0
Scarborough P.	(A)	0
Chorley B.	(H)	1
Huddersfield	(H)	2
Nottingham C.	(A)	2
Doncaster	(H)	2
Dewsbury	(A)	1
Hunslet	(A)	0
Trafford B.	(H)	2
Doncaster (RT)	(A)	NA
Bramley	(A)	2
Keighley C.	(H)	0
Doncaster	(A)	NA
Barrow	(A)	1
Batley	(H)	1
Sheffield E. (CC)	(H)	0
Highfield	(A)	1
Dewsbury	(H)	1
Hunslet	(H)	0
Chorley B.	(A)	0
Barrow	(H)	1
Huddersfield	(A)	1
Scarborough P.	(H)	0
Bramley	(H)	0
Trafford B.	(A)[1]	2
Keighley C.	(A)	3
Nottingham C.	(H)	5
27 appearances		**31**

[1] At Huddersfield

JOHN WOODS of Leigh equalled the club and Division Two match record of 38 points in the 70-0 home defeat of Ryedale-York on 12 January. Playing at stand off, he scored 11 goals and four tries. Woods was at full back when he set the records with 38 points from 13 goals and four three-point tries in the 62-15 home win over Blackpool Borough on 11 September 1977.

JOHN WASYLIW of Keighley Cougars scored club records of 11 goals and 26 points in two different matches.

The winger broke the points record with seven goals and three tries in the 42-14 Division Three home defeat of Highfield. It was his first match of the season and only his third since signing from Halifax RU club eight months earlier. The old record of 24 points was set by Joe Phillips, the full back from New Zealand, who scored nine goals and two tries in a 39-20 home League defeat of Halifax on 5 October 1957.

Wasyliw equalled the club goals in a match record with

11 in a 70-0 Division Three home victory over Nottingham City on 23 February.

Others who kicked 11 were Rob Walker in a 67-0 home League win over the old Castleford side on 13 January 1906 and Bert Cook in a 49-10 home League defeat of Hull Kingston Rovers on 31 October 1953.

FRANO BOTICA of Wigan scored Premiership final records of 10 goals and 20 points in the 48-16 defeat of St. Helens at Old Trafford on 17 May. The 10 goals also equalled the most kicked in any cup final and set a new record at any stage of the Premiership.

Kevin Dick of Leeds held the previous Premiership final goals record with eight in a 24-2 defeat of Bradford Northern at Huddersfield in 1979. St. Helens full back Geoff Pimblett set the points record with 17 from seven goals and a try in a 32-20 defeat of Warrington at Swinton in 1977.

The only other player to kick 10 goals in any final was Austin Rhodes of St. Helens in a 44-22 Championship final defeat of Hunslet at Bradford in 1959.

Botica had twice equalled the previous Premiership competition record of nine goals in the two earlier rounds in 1992. He kicked nine in a 42-16 first round home defeat of Widnes and added a try for a then competition record-equalling 22 points.

The points record was beaten by Martin Offiah's 40 from 10 tries in the 74-6 semi-final thrashing of Leeds when Botica again kicked nine goals.

MARTIN OFFIAH of Wigan shattered the club record for tries in a match with 10 in the 74-6 Stones Bitter Premiership semi-final home defeat of Leeds. His 10 tries and 40 points were also records for any stage of the competition.

The old Wigan record of seven tries was shared by:

Johnny Ring (three times) — v. Flimby and Fothergill amateurs in a 116-0 Challenge Cup victory on 14 February 1925; v. Salford in a 57-19 home League win on 13 April 1925; v. Pemberton Rovers amateurs in a 51-11 Challenge Cup home win on 12 February 1927.

Billy Boston (twice) — v. Dewsbury in a 52-5 home League win on 20 August 1955 and at Salford in a 49-8 League victory on 30 April 1962.

Gordon Ratcliffe v. Liverpool Stanley in a 39-5 home League win on 23 August 1947.

Green Vigo v. St. Helens in a 37-5 Lancashire Cup first round home victory on 21 August 1976.

The previous Premiership competition record of four tries, all in first round ties, was shared by David Hall (Hull K.R.) v. Castleford; Phil Ford (Wigan) v. Hull in 1985 and Ellery Hanley (Wigan) v. Hull K.R. in 1986.

Offiah's 10 tries equalled the record against a professional side set by Australian winger Lionel Cooper in Huddersfield's 48-3 home League defeat of Keighley on 17 November 1951.

The most tries scored in any competitive match in Britain was 11 by Hull Kingston Rovers winger George West in a 73-5 Challenge Cup home tie win over Brookland Rovers amateurs on 4 March 1905. West added 10 goals for a record points total of 53.

Offiah's 40 points beat the Premiership competition record of 22 by John Dorahy (Hull K.R.) v. Leeds in 1984 and Wigan's Frano Botica at home to Widnes in first round of 1992.

MARK ROACHE and TONY ZELEI both broke Doncaster records in the club's 88-6 record defeat of Nottingham City in a Division Three home match on 1 September.

Winger Roache's four tries equalled the match record shared by five others: Vernon Grace v. Rochdale Hornets on 4 October 1952; Brian Tasker v. Leeds on 26 October 1963; John Buckton v. Rochdale Hornets on 30 August 1981; Tony Kemp v. Carlisle on 23 November 1986 and Neil Turner v. Keighley on 22 October 1989.

Zelei beat two Doncaster match records with 12 goals and 32 points. The full back's 12 goals beat the nine by David Towle in a 33-14 League win at York on 9 September 1967 and by Dean Carroll in the 58-2 defeat of Bramley on 6 January 1991.

Zelei's 32 points, including two tries, beat the 20 points (six goals, two tries) by Kevin Jones in a 40-12 Division Two home win over Whitehaven on 13 March 1988 and by David Noble (eight goals, one try) in a 48-19 Division Two home defeat of Dewsbury on 2 October 1988.

Roache's four tries also took him past the club career record of 72 by winger Neil Turner between 1985 and 1990. It is the only time he has scored more than two in a match.

At the end of the season Roache's career record stood at 83 tries since his debut in 1985. Roache also holds the Doncaster record of tries in a season with 21 in 1989-90. A former Rossington Hornets amateur, Roache began his professional career with Castleford in 1980. He scored five tries before signing for Doncaster in an exchange deal with David Plange. Roache made his debut for Doncaster while on loan, playing right wing in a 17-14 win at Southend Invicta on 3 March 1985. He had a spell in the centre before settling back on the wing. His season-by-season totals for Doncaster are as follows:

1984-85	4
1985-86	3
1986-87	6
1987-88	8
1988-89	14
1989-90	21
1990-91	15
1991-92	12
Total	**83**

JONATHAN DAVIES of Widnes broke goals and points records for both Wales and Great Britain in matches against Papua New Guinea. The centre's eight goals and 24 points, including two tries, for Wales at Swansea FC's Vetch Field beat the seven goals and 14 points by Johnny Thomas (Wigan) v. England at Tonypandy in 1908 and Paul Woods (Widnes) v. France at Widnes in 1978. Davies's eight goals and 16 points for Great Britain at Wigan two weeks later were records for a British player against Papua New Guinea.

MARTIN PEARSON of Featherstone Rovers scored Great Britain Under-21 records for tries, goals and points in a match. The stand off's eight goals in the 58-0 defeat of the touring Papua New Guinea senior squad at Leeds on 30 October equalled the record of Chris Rudd of Warrington in the 48-2 defeat of France Under-21s at Limoux in 1991.

Pearson broke the points record with 24 in the 56-2 win over France Under-21s at Halifax on 6 March and equalled the tries record with three. The previous points record of 22 was held by Paul Loughlin of St. Helens with seven goals and two tries in the 54-6 defeat of France in 1987.

Three Great Britain Under-21 hat-tricks for David Myers.

DAVID MYERS of Wigan three times equalled the Great Britain Under-21s record of three tries in a match. The winger scored hat-tricks against the senior Papua New Guinea tourists and in the two matches against France Under-21s. Hull prop Neil Puckering set the record with three tries against France Under-21s at St. Helens in 1987.

GRAHAM STEADMAN of Castleford scored a Yorkshire Cup final record of 16 points with two tries and four goals in the 28-6 defeat of Bradford Northern at Elland Road, Leeds. His total beat Castleford forward Martin Ketteridge's 14 points from five goals and a try in the 31-24 defeat of Hull at Leeds in 1986.

STEVE PARRISH of Batley kicked a club record 10 goals in a 64-0 Division Three win at Nottingham City on 10 November. It beat the nine goals by Wattie Davies in a 52-8 home League defeat of Widnes on 27 March 1909 and by Stan Thompson in a 30-4 home League win over Keighley on 20 September 1958.

MARK ASTON of Sheffield Eagles equalled the club match record of 12 goals in a home tie against Keighley Cougars, who were beaten 72-14 in the Divisional Premiership on 25 April. The record was set by Roy Rafferty with 12 in a 68-14 Division Two win at Fulham on 21 September 1986.

STEVE MAGUIRE of Whitehaven kicked a club record 12 goals in the 80-6 Division Three home defeat of Nottingham City on 12 April. Bill Holliday held the previous record with 11 in a 61-0 home League defeat of Hunslet on 31 March 1962. Holliday added a try for a club record 25 points.

BRADFORD NORTHERN scored a club record 76-0 victory in a 15-try rout of Leigh East amateurs in the Regal Trophy first round home tie on 17 November. It beat the 16-try, 72-9 Division Two home defeat of Doncaster on 4 November 1973 and the 12-try, 72-12 Division One home win over Hunslet on 7 October 1984.

DONCASTER achieved their highest score and winning margin with an 88-6 home defeat of Nottingham City on the first day of the new Division Three and it remained the division's record. The 16-try victory beat Doncaster's 58-2 Division Two home defeat of Bramley on 6 January 1991 when they scored 10 tries.

BATLEY gained a club record 64-0 victory at Nottingham City on 10 November when they scored 11 tries in a Division Three match. It beat the 10-try, 52-8 home League defeat of Widnes on 27 March 1909.

KEIGHLEY COUGARS scored a club record 70-0 win, including 12 tries, in a Division Three home match against Nottingham City on 23 February, their best since 13 January 1906 when they scored 15 tries in a 67-0 home League defeat of the old Castleford side.

WHITEHAVEN ran up a club record 80-6 win in a Division Three home victory over Nottingham City on 12 April. Their previous biggest victory was 72-6 in a Lancashire Cup first round home tie against Fulham on 14 September 1986 when they scored 12 tries compared with 14 against Nottingham.

WIGAN'S 48-16 defeat of St. Helens at Old Trafford was not only their highest score for a Premiership final but also the biggest in any cup final during the game's near 100-year history. The previous highest Premiership final scores were Warrington's 38-10 defeat of Halifax in 1986 and Widnes's 38-14 defeat of St. Helens two years later. Wigan also beat the previous widest winning margin of 1986.

TRAFFORD BOROUGH went down to a club record defeat when they lost 104-12 at St. Helens in the first round of the Greenalls Lancashire Cup on 15 September. Their previous biggest defeat was at Blackpool Borough when they lost 77-8 to Wigan in the old Western Division on 26 October 1963. Trafford conceded 20 tries against St. Helens compared with the 17 against Wigan.

LEEDS conceded the most points in their history with a 14-try, 74-6 Stones Bitter Premiership semi-final defeat at Wigan on 10 May, which was also a record score for the competition. Wakefield Trinity ran up the previous highest score against Leeds with a 17-try, 71-0 home League win on 12 September 1945. Leeds had also suffered the previous biggest Premiership defeat when they conceded 10 tries in a 54-0 first round loss at Hull Kingston Rovers on 29 April 1984.

HULL KINGSTON ROVERS went down to their biggest-ever defeat when they lost 76-8 at Halifax in a Division One match on 20 October. Their previous heaviest defeat was also at Halifax, who beat them 68-0 in a League match on 3 April 1956, scoring 18 tries compared with the 14 last season.

WORKINGTON TOWN's 68-6 Division Two defeat at Leigh on 8 March equalled the most points they have conceded in a match. The 13-try loss matched the 68-0 defeat at Wigan in a Silk Cut Challenge Cup preliminary round tie on 18 January 1987 when they conceded 12 tries.

WIDNES scored a record Regal Trophy final margin win with their 24-0 defeat of Leeds at Wigan. The previous record was Wigan's 18-4 defeat of Warrington at Bolton in 1986-87.

GREAT BRITAIN's 56-4 defeat of Papua New Guinea in the British Coal Test and World Cup match at Wigan was their highest score against the Kumuls. It beat the 42-0 win at Wigan in 1987 and the 42-22 victory at Port Moresby the following year.

WALES ran up their highest-ever score against any opposition with the 13-try, 68-0 defeat of Papua New Guinea, who suffered their widest margin defeat, at Swansea City's soccer ground. It was also the first time Wales had nilled any team. Their previous highest score was the 41-7 defeat of France at Llanelli on 23 November 1935 when they scored 11 tries. Papua's previous widest margin defeat was a 14-try, 70-8 thrashing by Australia at Wagga Wagga on 20 July 1988.

GREAT BRITAIN Under-21s gained record wins of 58-0 against Papua New Guinea and 56-2 over France. The 10-try defeat of Papua's senior national side at Leeds was the young Britons' highest score against any opposition, beating the 10-try, 54-6 defeat of France Under-21s at St. Helens in 1987. Britain beat that highest score against France with an 11-try, 56-2 victory at Halifax.

MILESTONES . . .

DAVID HOBBS passed the 1,000-point mark in his career at Bradford Northern with 10 goals in their 60-0 Stones Bitter Championship home defeat of Swinton on 17 April.

The forward's total at the end of the season stood at 1,006 from 28 tries and 460 goals including 26 drop goals.

The former Great Britain forward has made 177 appearances for Bradford, including seven as a substitute.

Signed from Oldham after starting with Featherstone Rovers in 1978, Hobbs's Northern debut was in an 11-3 Division One home victory over Warrington on 5 April 1987.

His most prolific season for Northern brought him 263 points in 1988-89, while his best match tally is 20 points, achieved three times.

His season-by-season scoring totals for Bradford are as follows:

	T	G	Dr	Pts
1986-87	0	0	1	1
1987-88	6	76	4	180
1988-89	10	109	5	263
1989-90	5	95	5	215
1990-91	5	49	6	124
1991-92	2	105	5	223
TOTALS	**28**	**434**	**26**	**1,006**

MARK CONWAY reached his 1,000th career point with the first of three goals in Wakefield Trinity's 22-18 Stones Bitter Championship home defeat of Bradford Northern on 8 September.

At the end of the season the scrum half's total was 1,173, made up of 86 tries and 422 goals, including nine drop goals.

He has scored 779 points for Wakefield, plus 390 for Leeds and four for Great Britain Under-21s.

A former Stanley Rangers (Wakefield) amateur, Conway made his debut for Leeds as a substitute in a 33-10 Yorkshire Cup first round victory at Castleford on 5 September 1982. His full debut followed at stand off in a 35-3 Division One defeat at Hull on 13 October 1982.

Conway moved to Wakefield in a six-player exchange deal and made his debut for Trinity with two tries at scrum half in a 56-8 Division Two home defeat of Carlisle on 30 August 1987.

His best match tally is 20 points from eight goals and a try in Wakefield's 52-9 Yorkshire Cup second round win at Huddersfield on 25 September 1991.

Conway's season-by-season totals are as follows:

148

Breaking through the 1,000 points barrier, Wakefield Trinity scrum half Mark Conway.

PAUL EASTWOOD of Hull scored his 100th career try and 1,000th point during the season.

The winger reached a century of touchdowns with one in Hull's 28-14 Stones Bitter Championship win at Wakefield Trinity on 29 September.

His total at the end of the season was 114 made up of 99 for Hull and 15 in representative matches, including six Test tries for Great Britain.

Eastwood scored his 1,000th point in all matches with one goal in a 21-18 John Smiths Yorkshire Cup second round replay defeat at Featherstone Rovers on 1 October.

His 1,000th point for Hull came with a 16-point haul in a 24-8 Silk Cut Challenge Cup third round win at Workington Town on 23 February.

A former Hullensian RU player, Eastwood made his debut for Hull as a substitute in a 22-10 Division One win at Oldham on 3 February 1985. His full debut followed on 29 March 1985 when Hull won 17-14 at home to Wigan in a Division One match.

Eastwood has scored one hat-trick for Hull and another for the Great Britain tourists against the Kiwi Colts on the 1990 trip to New Zealand.

He has never finished in the top ten and his best season's tally is 22 in 1989-90. He has twice finished as the top scorer of Division One points with 238 in 1989-90 and 214 the following season, when he was also the leading goalscorer with 85.

Eastwood's best match tally is 28 points from eight goals and three tries in a 48-0 Division One home defeat of Barrow on 7 January 1990.

His season-by-season totals are as follows:

Hull

	T	G	Pts	
1984-85	2	1	10	
1985-86	11	1	46	
1986-87	19	0	76	+GB Under-21s 1t
1987-88	13	0	52	
1988-89	7	39	106	
1989-90	22	101	290	
1990-91	11	101	246	+GB 3t, 18g
1991-92	14	101	258	+GB 1t, 6g; Humberside 1g

Totals

	T	G	Pts	
Hull	99	344	1,084	
Britain	6	24	72	
1990 tour	7	18	64	Not inc. 2 tries in 2 Tests
GB Under-21	2	0	8	
Yorkshire	0	0	0	
Humberside	0	1	2	
GRAND TOTALS	**114**	**387**	**1,230**	

	T	G	Pts	
Leeds				
1982-83	6	20	58	
1983-84	3	38	88	
1984-85	10	19	78	+GB U-21s 1t
1985-86	8	20	72	
1986-87	10	27	94	
Wakefield T.				
1987-88	20	19 (1)	117	
1988-89	10	22 (2)	82	
1989-90	6	107 (3)	235	
1990-91	6	72 (2)	166	
1991-92	6	78 (1)	179	

Totals

	T	G	Pts
Leeds	37	124	390
Wakefield T.	48	298 (9)	779
GB Under-21s	1	0	4

GRAND TOTALS 86 422 (9) 1,173
() Drop goals included in total.

DERYCK FOX of Featherstone Rovers took his club and representative career totals past the 1,000 mark during the season. He finished the campaign with 1,063 points, including 1,020 for Featherstone.

The scrum half passed his 1,000 points in all matches with six goals in a 36-20 Silk Cut Challenge Cup first round win at Batley on 26 January.

He reached 1,000 points in club matches alone with three goals in the 18-6 Stones Bitter Championship win at Swinton on 22 March.

Featherstone signed Fox from St. John Fisher (Dewsbury) amateurs after his return from BARLA's 1983 Great Britain youth tour of New Zealand. He made his senior debut as a substitute in a 24-8 Yorkshire Cup first round defeat at Hull on 4 September 1983. His full debut was 14 days later in an 18-14 Division One win at Whitehaven.

Last season was Fox's most prolific campaign, with 236 points in club and representative matches. His best match tally is 24 points from two tries and eight goals in a 52-10 Division One home defeat of Whitehaven on 13 November 1983.

Fox finished the season with a club total of 1,020 points from 78 tries and 380 goals, including 52 drop goals.

His season-by-season totals are:

	T	G	Pts	
1983-84................	6	26 (7)	69	
1984-85................	6	6 (4)	32	+ GB 2t, 1g
1985-86................	11	16 (3)	73	+ Yorks 5g
1986-87................	14	38 (5)	127	
1987-88................	16	16 (9)	87	+ Yorks 1g
1988-89................	9	28 (9)	83	
1989-90................	3	78 (8)	160	+ Yorks 1t
1990-91................	12	58 (2)	162	
1991-92................	1	114 (5)	227	+ GB 1t, Yorks 1t, 1dg

Totals

	T	G	Pts
Featherstone R.	78	380 (52)	1,020
Britain.................	3	1	14
1990 tour	2	0	8
Yorkshire	2	7 (1)	21
GRAND TOTALS	**85**	**388 (53)**	**1,063**

() drop goals included in total.

MIKE FLETCHER of Hull Kingston Rovers passed the 1,000 points mark in club and representative matches during the season.

He scored his 1,000th point in all matches with a goal in the 38-15 Stones Bitter Championship defeat at St. Helens on 9 November.

His total at the end of the season was 1,090, including

Featherstone Rovers skipper Deryck Fox, breaker of the 1,000-point barrier.

a representative haul of 10 points from four goals for Great Britain Under-21s and one goal for a Humberside XIII against Papua New Guinea.

Fletcher scored his 1,000th point for Rovers with the last of four goals in a 24-14 Stones Bitter Championship home victory over St. Helens on 15 December. His total for Rovers at the end of the season was 1,080 from 26 tries and 488 goals.

The centre or full back holds two club records for a season, with 199 goals and 450 points, including 13 tries, in 1989-90 when he headed two scoring lists. During that season he also equalled a club match record with 14 goals against Whitehaven.

He equalled his best points tally of 28 with 10 goals and two tries against Fulham that season and has kicked 10 goals in one other match.

The former Rovers Colt made his first team debut at full back on 23 April 1985 when they lost 32-0 at home to Widnes.

After failing to score in his one match in 1984-85, Fletcher's season-by-season totals are as follows:

	T	G	Pts	
1985-86	1	4	12	
1986-87	0	2	4	
1987-88	4	90	196	+GB Under-21 4g
1988-89	3	63	138	
1989-90	13	199	450	
1990-91	3	59	130	
1991-92	2	71	150	+ Humberside 1g

Totals

Hull K.R.	26	488	1,080
GB Under-21	0	4	8
Humberside	0	1	2
GRAND TOTALS	**26**	**493**	**1,090**

PHIL FORD of Leeds scored his 200th career try in the 27-10 Stones Bitter Championship win at Salford on 18 January.

The international winger's total at the end of the season was 203 made up of 50 for Leeds, 59 Bradford Northern, 16 Wigan, 57 Warrington and 21 in representative matches, including nine Test touchdowns for Great Britain.

A former Cardiff RU player, Ford made his Rugby League debut as an unnamed trialist when he scored Warrington's only try in the 10-9 home defeat of Featherstone Rovers on 11 January 1981.

The Welshman made another vital tryscoring debut when he moved to Wigan for what was then a record transfer fee for a winger of £40,000. His two tries included the last-minute winner in the 20-16 home defeat of Hull K.R. on 3 March 1985. Ford scored 16 tries in 15 appearances before being part of Wigan's player-exchange-plus-cash move to sign Ellery Hanley from Bradford in a £150,000 deal.

Ford went to Bradford with Steve Donlan and they made their debuts on 22 September 1985 in a 17-12 home defeat by Hull K.R. Ford scored 59 tries in just over three seasons before moving to Leeds in another cash-plus-player deal that took Mark Wilson to Bradford. Ford's value was said to be in excess of £55,000, which made him the game's costliest winger again.

He scored a hat-trick on his Leeds debut, a 48-4 home defeat of Oldham on 1 January 1989.

His most prolific season was 1986-87 when 30 Cup and League tries for Bradford gave him his highest position in the try chart of fifth, one of only two occasions he has finished in the top ten.

Ford's total tries include 142 in League matches, putting him fourth in the all-time list of Division One tryscorers, headed by club colleague Ellery Hanley with 208.

One of Ford's eight hat-tricks was a then record-equalling four tries in a 1985 Premiership first round tie for Wigan against Hull. He also scored a hat-trick playing full back for Wales against Papua New Guinea last season.

His season-by-season totals are:

Warrington

1980-81	4
1981-82	9
1982-83	20
1983-84	20
1984-85	4

Wigan

1984-85	13 + GB 2
1985-86	3

Bradford N.

1985-86	14
1986-87	30
1987-88	14 + GB 1; RL XIII 1
1988-89	1

Leeds

1988-89	10 + GB 3
1989-90	11 + GB 1
1990-91	17
1991-92	12 + Wales 4

Totals

Warrington	57	
Wigan	16	
Bradford N.	59	
Leeds	50	
Britain	9	
1988 tour	7	(Not inc. 2 in Tests)
RL XIII	1	
Wales	4	

GRAND TOTAL . 203

JONATHAN DAVIES of Widnes raced to the fastest-ever 1,000 career points just two years and 340 days after the former Wales RU international stand off played his first professional Rugby League match.

But his 109 matches were five more than it took Lewis Jones of Leeds, another former Wales RU international, to reach 1,000 points in just over three years during the 1950s.

Davies passed the 1,000 target with the last of three goals in Widnes's 18-10 Regal Trophy semi-final defeat of St. Helens at Wigan on 21 December.

He finished the season with a total of 1,071 points made up of 924 for Widnes and 147 in representative matches including the 1990 tour of Papua New Guinea and New Zealand.

The utility back has broken a number of records in his brief professional career. He holds the record for most points in a season for Widnes with 342 from 30 tries and 112 goals including two drop goals in 1990-91.

He shares the club match record of 34 points with Andy Currier, scoring four tries and nine goals in a 70-6 Lancashire Cup first round win at Whitehaven on 26 August 1990.

On his debut for Wales last season he broke two records with eight goals and 24 points in the 68-0 defeat of Papua New Guinea at Swansea.

Davies has scored three hat-tricks of tries, including two four-try feats, with a personal best goals tally of nine in a match.

The former Llanelli RU player's signing for Widnes on 5 January 1989 made more headlines nationwide than any other single event in Rugby League history. His contract was officially reported as £150,000 for four years and he made his debut as a substitute in a 50-8 Stones Bitter Championship home defeat of Salford on 15 January 1989.

Davies made one other substitute appearance before making his full debut at stand off, when he scored a try and five goals in a 38-14 home League defeat of Oldham on 5 February.

His season-by-season totals are as follows:

	App	T	G	Pts
Widnes				
1988-89	12+4	7	48(1)	123
1989-90	29+1	16	98	260
1990-91	32+2	30	112(2)	342
1991-92	24	13	74(1)	199
	+ GB 8g; Wales 13g, 1dg, 3t			
Totals				
Widnes	97+7	66	332(4)	924
Britain	6+1	2	23	54
1990 tour	5+1	4	19	54
	(Not inc. 2t, 15g in 5 Tests)			
Wales	2	3	14(1)	39
GRAND TOTALS	110+9	75	388(5)	1,071

Fastest-ever 1,000 career points for Jonathan Davies.

ANDY CURRIER of Widnes scored the 100th try of his career with the first of two in the 38-14 Stones Bitter Championship win at Swinton on 23 February.

His total at the end of the season was made up of 98 for Widnes and six in representative matches including the 1988 tour of Australia and New Zealand.

Currier holds the joint Widnes match record with five tries against Featherstone Rovers on 25 September 1988. Playing in the centre, he also kicked seven goals for a joint club record 34 points.

Formerly with Halton Hornets (Widnes) amateurs, Currier made a tryscoring debut for Widnes as a substitute in a 28-4 Division One home defeat of Salford on 18 September 1983. He made his full debut on the wing when Widnes lost 21-4 in a Division One match at Featherstone Rovers on 4 December 1983.

In addition to his record five-try feat, Currier has scored four tries in a match once and two other hat-tricks. His most prolific season was 1990-91, with 23 tries putting him 10th in the try chart — the only time he has finished in the top ten.

Currier's season-by-season try totals are as follows:

Widnes

1983-84	4	
1984-85	17	+ GB Under-21s 1
1985-86	2	
1986-87	1	
1987-88	11	
1988-89	18	+ Lancs 1
1989-90	13	
1990-91	23	
1991-92	9	+ Lancs 1

Totals

Widnes	98
1988 tour	3
Lancashire	2
GB Under-21s	1
GRAND TOTAL	**104**

LEADING SCORERS 1895-1974

	TRIES	GOALS	POINTS
1895-96	Hurst (Oldham) 28	Lorimer (Manningham) 35	Cooper (Bradford)..........106
			Lorimer (Manningham)...106
1896-97	Hannah (Hunslet)............19	Goldthorpe (Hunslet) 26	Rigg (Halifax) 112
		Sharpe (Liversedge) 26	
1897-98	Hoskins (Salford) 30	Goldthorpe (Hunslet) 66	Goldthorpe (Hunslet)......135
1898-99	Williams (Oldham) 39	Goldthorpe (Hunslet) 67	Jaques (Hull) 169
1899-00	Williams (Oldham) 36	Cooper (Bradford) 39	Williams (Oldham)........108
1900-01	Williams (Oldham) 47	Goldthorpe (Hunslet) 44	Williams (Oldham)........141
1901-02	Wilson (Broughton R.).....38	James (Broughton R.) 75	Lomas (Salford).............172
1902-03	Evans (Leeds).................27	Goldthorpe (Hunslet) 48	Davies (Batley)..............136
1903-04	Hogg (Broughton R.).......34	Lomas (Salford) 66	Lomas (Salford).............222
1904-05	Dechan (Bradford)..........31	Ferguson (Oldham)..........50	Lomas (Salford).............146
1905-06	Leytham (Wigan) 40	Ferguson (Oldham)..........49	Leytham (Wigan)...........160
1906-07	Eccles (Halifax)...............41	Lomas (Salford) 86	Lomas (Salford).............280
1907-08	Leytham (Wigan) 44	Goldthorpe (Hunslet)......101	Goldthorpe (Hunslet)......217
1908-09	Miller (Wigan)................49	Lomas (Salford) 88	Lomas (Salford).............272
	Williams (Halifax)...........49		
1909-10	Leytham (Wigan) 48	Carmichael (Hull K.R.)....78	Leytham (Wigan)...........232
1910-11	Kitchen (Huddersfield).....40	Carmichael (Hull K.R.)...129	Carmichael (Hull K.R.)...261
	Rosenfeld (Huddersfield) ..40		
	Miller (Wigan)................40		
1911-12	Rosenfeld (Huddersfield) ..78	Carmichael (Hull K.R.)...127	Carmichael (Hull K.R.)...254
1912-13	Rosenfeld (Huddersfield) ..56	Carmichael (Hull K.R.) 93	Thomas (Wigan)............198
1913-14	Rosenfeld (Huddersfield) ..80	Holland (Huddersfield) ...131	Holland (Huddersfield) ...268
1914-15	Rosenfeld (Huddersfield) ..56	Gronow (Huddersfield) ...136	Gronow (Huddersfield) ...284
● Competitive matches suspended during war years			
1918-19	Francis (Hull)................25	Kennedy (Hull) 54	Kennedy (Hull) 135
1919-20	Moorhouse (Huddersfield).39	Gronow (Huddersfield) ...148	Gronow (Huddersfield) ...332
1920-21	Stone (Hull) 41	Kennedy (Hull)..............108	Kennedy (Hull).............264
1921-22	Farrar (Oldham) 49	Sullivan (Wigan)...........100	Farrar (Oldham) 213
1922-23	Ring (Wigan) 41	Sullivan (Wigan)...........161	Sullivan (Wigan)...........349
1923-24	Ring (Wigan) 49	Sullivan (Wigan)...........158	Sullivan (Wigan)...........319
1924-25	Ring (Wigan) 54	Sullivan (Wigan)...........138	Sullivan (Wigan)...........282
1925-26	Ring (Wigan) 63	Sullivan (Wigan)...........131	Sullivan (Wigan)...........274
1926-27	Ellaby (St. Helens) 55	Sullivan (Wigan)...........149	Sullivan (Wigan)...........322
1927-28	Ellaby (St. Helens) 37	Thompson (Leeds).........106	Thompson (Leeds).........233
1928-29	Brown (Wigan) 44	Sullivan (Wigan)...........107	Sullivan (Wigan)...........226
	Mills (Huddersfield).........44		
1929-30	Ellaby (St. Helens) 39	Thompson (Leeds).........111	Thompson (Leeds).........243
1930-31	Harris, E. (Leeds) 58	Sullivan (Wigan)...........133	Sullivan (Wigan)...........278
1931-32	Mills (Huddersfield).........50	Sullivan (Wigan)...........117	Sullivan (Wigan)...........249
1932-33	Harris, E. (Leeds) 57	Sullivan (Wigan)...........146	Sullivan (Wigan)...........307
1933-34	Brown (Salford) 45	Sullivan (Wigan)...........193	Sullivan (Wigan)...........404
1934-35	Morley (Wigan) 49	Sullivan (Wigan)...........165	Sullivan (Wigan)...........348
1935-36	Harris, E. (Leeds) 63	Sullivan (Wigan)...........117	Sullivan (Wigan)...........246

	TRIES	GOALS	POINTS
1936-37	Harris, E. (Leeds) 40	Sullivan (Wigan) 120	Sullivan (Wigan) 258
1937-38	Harris, E. (Leeds) 45	Sullivan (Wigan) 135	Sullivan (Wigan) 285
1938-39	Markham (Huddersfield) ...39	Sullivan (Wigan) 124	Risman (Salford) 267

● For the next six seasons emergency war-time competitions resulted in a reduction of matches and players were allowed to 'guest' for other clubs

	TRIES	GOALS	POINTS
1939-40	Batten (Hunslet) 38	Hodgson (Swinton) 98	Hodgson (Swinton) 208
1940-41	Walters (Bradford N.) 32	Lockwood (Halifax) 70	Belshaw (Warrington) 174
1941-42	Francis (Barrow) 30	Lockwood (Halifax) 91	Lockwood (Halifax)........185
1942-43	Batten (Hunslet) 24	Lockwood (Halifax) 65	Lockwood (Halifax)........136
1943-44	Lawrenson (Wigan) 21	Horne (Barrow) 57	Horne (Barrow) 144
1944-45	Batten (Bradford N.)........41	Stott (Wakefield T.).......51	Stott (Wakefield T.) 129

● Normal peace-time rugby resumed

	TRIES	GOALS	POINTS
1945-46	Batten (Bradford N.)........35	Ledgard (Dewsbury) 89	Bawden (Huddersfield) ...239
1946-47	Bevan (Warrington) 48	Miller (Hull) 103	Bawden (Huddersfield) ...243
1947-48	Bevan (Warrington) 57	Ward (Wigan) 141	Ward (Wigan) 312
1948-49	Cooper (Huddersfield) 60	Ward (Wigan) 155	Ward (Wigan) 361
1949-50	Nordgren (Wigan) 57	Gee (Wigan) 133	Palin (Warrington) 290
		Palin (Warrington) 133	
1950-51	Bevan (Warrington) 68	Cook (Leeds) 155	Cook (Leeds) 332
1951-52	Cooper (Huddersfield) 71	Ledgard (Leigh) 142	Horne (Barrow) 313
1952-53	Bevan (Warrington) 72	Bath (Warrington)..........170	Bath (Warrington)..........379
1953-54	Bevan (Warrington) 67	Metcalfe (St. Helens)......153	Metcalfe (St. Helens)......369
		Bath (Warrington)..........153	
1954-55	Cooper (Huddersfield) 66	Ledgard (Leigh) 178	Ledgard (Leigh) 374
1955-56	McLean (Bradford N.) 61	Ledgard (Leigh) 155	Bath (Warrington)..........344
1956-57	Boston (Wigan)...............60	Jones (Leeds)................194	Jones (Leeds)................496
1957-58	Sullivan (Wigan) 50	Ganley (Oldham) 219	Ganley (Oldham) 453
1958-59	Vollenhoven (St. Helens) ..62	Ganley (Oldham) 190	Griffiths (Wigan) 394
1959-60	Vollenhoven (St. Helens) ..54	Rhodes (St. Helens) 171	Fox (Wakefield T.) 453
		Fox (Wakefield T.) 171	
1960-61	Vollenhoven (St. Helens) ..59	Rhodes (St. Helens) 145	Rhodes (St. Helens) 338
1961-62	Boston (Wigan)...............51	Fox (Wakefield T.) 183	Fox (Wakefield T.) 456
1962-63	Glastonbury (Work'ton T.)41	Coslett (St. Helens) 156	Coslett (St. Helens) 321
1963-64	Stopford (Swinton) 45	Coslett (St. Helens) 138	Fox (Wakefield T.) 313
1964-65	Lake (Wigan) 40	Kellett (Hull K.R.) 150	Killeen (St. Helens)........360
1965-66	Killeen (St. Helens) 32	Killeen (St. Helens)........120	Killeen (St. Helens)........336
	Lake (Wigan) 32		
1966-67	Young (Hull K.R.) 34	Risman (Leeds) 163	Killeen (St. Helens).......353
	Howe (Castleford) 34		
1967-68	Millward (Hull K.R.)........38	Risman (Leeds) 154	Risman (Leeds) 332
1968-69	Francis (Wigan) 40	Risman (Leeds) 165	Risman (Leeds) 345
1969-70	Atkinson (Leeds).............38	Tyrer (Wigan)...............167	Tyrer (Wigan)...............385
1970-71	Haigh (Leeds) 40	Coslett (St. Helens) 183	Coslett (St. Helens) 375
1971-72	Atkinson (Leeds).............36	Coslett (St. Helens) 214	Watkins (Salford)..........473
	Lamb (Bradford N.) 36		
1972-73	Atkinson (Leeds).............39	Watkins (Salford)..........221	Watkins (Salford)..........493
1973-74	Fielding (Salford) 49	Watkins (Salford)..........183	Watkins (Salford)..........438

LEADING SCORERS 1974-91

TRIES

1974-75

Dunn (Hull K.R.)	42
Fielding (Salford)	35
Bevan (Warrington)	31
A. Smith (Leeds)	30
Millward (Hull K.R.)	30
Atkinson (Leeds)	29
Richards (Salford)	28
Sullivan (Hull K.R.)	28
Mathias (St. Helens)	27
Dyl (Leeds)	26

1975-76

Richards (Salford)	37
Fielding (Salford)	33
Jones (St. Helens)	31
Briggs (Leigh)	27
D. Smith (Wakefield T.)	26
Burton (Castleford)	25
Clark (Hull)	23
Wright (Workington T.)	22
Barends (York)	21
Boxall (Hull)	21
Holmes (Leeds)	21
Mathias (St. Helens)	21
Butler (Salford)	21

1976-77

Wright (Widnes)	31
Burton (Castleford)	29
D. Smith (Leeds)	28
Fielding (Salford)	27
Dunn (Hull K.R.)	26
Cunningham (St. Helens)	26
Topliss (Wakefield T.)	24
Richards (Salford)	23
Mathias (St. Helens)	23
Barends (York)	22

1977-78

Wright (Widnes)	33
Fielding (Salford)	31
Cunningham (St. Helens)	30
Bevan (Warrington)	30
Fenton (Castleford)	30
Vigo (Wigan)	29
Glynn (St. Helens)	28
D. Smith (Leeds)	28
T. Morgan (York)	27
Burton (Castleford)	27

1978-79

Hartley (Hull K.R.)	35
Wright (Widnes)	28
Barends (Bradford N.)	25
Lowe (Hull K.R.)	25
Prendiville (Hull)	25
Fielding (Salford)	24
D. Redfearn (Bradford N.)	23
Mathias (St. Helens)	22
Bray (Hull)	21
O'Loughlin (Wigan)	21
Sullivan (Hull K.R.)	21

1979-80

Fielding (Salford)	30
Hubbard (Hull K.R.)	30
Munro (Oldham)	29
Ball (Barrow)	27
Bentley (Widnes)	27
Glynn (St. Helens)	27
Mathias (St. Helens)	27
Bevan (Warrington)	26
D. Redfearn (Bradford N.)	26
D. Smith (Leeds)	24

1980-81

Crossley (York)	35
Richardson (Castleford)	28
Hubbard (Hull K.R.)	25
Hartley (Hull K.R.)	23
McDermott (York)	23
Slater (Huddersfield)	23
Drummond (Leigh)	20
Ball (Barrow)	19
Bevan (Warrington)	19
Cramp (Huddersfield)	19
Hyde (Castleford)	19

1981-82

Jones (Workington T.)	31
Drummond (Leigh)	26
Basnett (Widnes)	26
Ashton (Oldham)	26
Morgan (Carlisle)	25
Hartley (Hull K.R.)	23
Hopkins (Workington T.)	23
Day (Hull)	23
Evans (Hull)	22
D. Hobbs (Featherstone R.)	21
Moll (Keighley)	21

1982-83

Eccles (Warrington)	37
Evans (Hull)	28
Crossley (Fulham)	27
David (Cardiff C.)	26
Topliss (Hull)	24

M'Barki (Fulham)..23
Hyde (Castleford) 22
McDermott (York)..22
Leuluai (Hull)...21
Phil Ford (Warrington) 20
Clark (Hull K.R.)...20

1983-84
Schofield (Hull)..38
Lydon (Widnes) 28
King (Hunslet)..28
Woods (Leigh)..27
Basnett (Widnes)..26
Gibson (Batley) 26
Herbert (Barrow)..25
Steadman (York) 25
Prohm (Hull K.R.)..25
Clark (Hull K.R.)...24

1984-85
Hanley (Bradford N.) 55
Prohm (Hull K.R.)..45
Gill (Wigan) 34
Ledger (St. Helens)...30
Meninga (St. Helens)...28
Gibbin (Whitehaven) 27
Gibson (Batley) 26
G. Peacham (Carlisle)..25
Byrne (Salford)...25
Evans (Hull)...24
Ferguson (Wigan) 24

1985-86
Halliwell (Leigh) 49
Hanley (Wigan)...38
Lister (Bramley) 34
Henderson (Leigh) 31
Frodsham (Blackpool B.)....................................30
Fox (Leigh) 29
Williams (Barrow)...27
Garrity (Runcorn H.) 24
Gibson (Leeds)..23
Beck (Workington T.) 23

1986-87
Hanley (Wigan)...63
Schofield (Hull)..37
Gill (Wigan) 32
Bate (Swinton) 31
Ford (Bradford N.) 30
Henderson (Leigh)...27
Edwards (Wigan)..26
Johnson (Warrington)..25
Lydon (Wigan)..24
Dunn (Rochdale H.) 23
Ledger (St. Helens)..23
McCormack (St. Helens) 23

1987-88
Offiah (Widnes)..44
Hanley (Wigan) 36
Schofield (Leeds)...25
Gibson (Leeds)..24
Goodway (Wigan) 23
Pape (Carlisle)..23
Edwards (Wigan)..21
Foy (Oldham)...21
Smith (Featherstone R.) 21
Bibb (Featherstone R.) 20
M. Conway (Wakefield T.) 20
Elia (St. Helens)..20
Quirk (St. Helens) 20

1988-89
Offiah (Widnes)..60
Ledger (Leigh)..34
Bate (Swinton) 32
Hanley (Wigan) 29
Lister (Bramley)..28
Powell (Sheffield E.) 28
Lewis (Bramley)..26
Quirk (St. Helens) 24
Anderson (Castleford) 24
Burns (Barrow) 24

1989-90
Offiah (Widnes)..45
Austin (Hull K.R.) 38
Sullivan (Hull K.R.) 35
Preston (Wigan)..33
Cordle (Bradford N.)...32
Larder (Castleford)..29
P. Lord (Oldham)..29
Edwards (Wigan)..26
Goodway (Wigan) 26
Cogger (Oldham)..24
Ellis (Castleford)...24
George (Halifax) 24
M. Lord (Rochdale H.) 24
Simpson (Keighley)..24

1990-91
Offiah (Widnes)..49
Austin (Halifax)..47
Wood (Halifax)...31
Hadley (Salford)..31
Davies (Widnes)..30
Hanley (Wigan) 29
Quirk (St. Helens) 26
Hunte (St. Helens)...26
Schofield (Leeds)...25
Steadman (Castleford)..23
Currier (Widnes) 23
Devereux (Widnes) 23

GOALS
(including drop goals)

1974-75

Fox (Hull K.R.)	146
Coslett (St. Helens)	129
Dutton (Widnes)	122
Lloyd (Castleford)	112
Quinn (York)	112
Hartley (Huddersfield)	110
MacCorquodale (Workington T.)	107
Marshall (Leeds)	107
Mumby (Bradford N.)	96
Fiddler (Salford, Leigh)	85

1975-76

Watkins (Salford)	175
Pimblett (St. Helens)	149
Lloyd (Castleford)	149
Dutton (Widnes)	148
Fairbairn (Wigan)	146
Stacey (Leigh)	137
MacCorquodale (Workington T.)	130
Fox (Hull K.R., York)	102
Marshall (Leeds)	101
Gaitley (New Hunslet)	100

1976-77

Lloyd (Castleford)	163
Quinn (Featherstone R.)	152
Pimblett (St. Helens)	152
Hesford (Warrington)	132
MacCorquodale (Workington T.)	128
Watkins (Salford)	125
Stephenson (Dewsbury)	106
Fairbairn (Wigan)	105
Dutton (Widnes)	97
Woods (Leigh)	90

1977-78

Pimblett (St. Helens)	178
Hesford (Warrington)	158
Woods (Leigh)	149
MacCorquodale (Workington T.)	138
Woods (Widnes)	122
Watkins (Salford)	110
Mumby (Bradford N.)	107
Lloyd (Castleford)	104
Fox (Bradford N.)	95
Oulton (Leeds)	80

1978-79

Lloyd (Hull)	172
Hesford (Warrington)	170
Burke (Widnes)	140
MacCorquodale (Workington T.)	114
Pimblett (St. Helens)	105
Beale (Keighley)	96
Woods (Leigh)	96
Birts (Halifax)	86
Fairbairn (Wigan)	86
Norton (Castleford)	82

1979-80

Quinn (Featherstone R.)	163
Hubbard (Hull K.R.)	138
Rule (Salford)	134
Hesford (Warrington)	128
Burke (Widnes)	127
Ball (Barrow)	119
Diamond (Wakefield T.)	116
Fitzsimons (Oldham)	108
Parrish (Hunslet)	98
Birts (Halifax)	97

1980-81

Hesford (Warrington)	147
Quinn (Featherstone R.)	123
Diamond (Wakefield T.)	112
Burke (Widnes)	110
Hubbard (Hull K.R.)	109
Ball (Barrow)	104
Birts (Halifax)	100
Beale (Keighley)	97
Parrish (Oldham)	95
Fairbairn (Wigan)	94

1981-82

Hopkins (Workington T.)	190
Fairbairn (Hull K.R.)	168
Parrish (Oldham)	164
Woods (Leigh)	158
Rule (Salford)	130
Dick (Leeds)	125
Quinn (Featherstone R.)	120
Agar (Halifax)	119
Crooks (Hull)	118
Hesford (Warrington)	116

1982-83

Diamond (Fulham)	136
Fitzsimons (Hunslet)	121
Crooks (Hull)	120
R. Beardmore (Castleford)	117
Hesford (Warrington)	113
Fenwick (Cardiff C.)	111
Jones (Swinton)	110
Whitfield (Wigan)	104
Kilner (Bramley)	104
Quinn (Featherstone R.)	98

1983-84
Hesford (Warrington)......................................142
R. Beardmore (Castleford)..........................142
Hallett (Cardiff C.)....................................140
Fitzsimons (Hunslet).................................131
Woods (Leigh)...124
Whitfield (Wigan)......................................122
Ball (Barrow)..104
Parrish (Oldham) 101
Agar (Halifax) 94
Tickle (Barrow) 91

1984-85
Day (St. Helens).......................................157
Fairbairn (Hull K.R.) 141
Wood (Runcorn H.) 126
Steadman (York).......................................122
Griffiths (Salford).....................................118
Parrish (Oldham)......................................117
Schofield (Hull) 105
Creasser (Leeds).......................................102
Agar (Halifax) 87
Jones (Swinton) 87

1985-86
C. Johnson (Leigh)....................................173
Stephenson (Wigan)..................................128
Noble (Doncaster).....................................118
Harcombe (Rochdale H.) 115
Kilner (Bramley).......................................110
Dorahy (Hull K.R.)...................................101
Woods (Bradford N.) 98
Creasser (Leeds).. 84
Carroll (Carlisle)....................................... 83
Smith (Workington T.).............................. 83

1986-87
Loughlin (St. Helens) 190
Bishop (Warrington) 117
Noble (Doncaster).....................................114
Whitfield (Halifax)....................................109
Platt (Hunslet)..102
Topping (Swinton) 100
C. Johnson (Leigh) 86
Ketteridge (Castleford) 80
Wood (Rochdale H.)................................... 80
Quinn (Featherstone R.) 77

1987-88
Woods (Warrington) 152
Quinn (Featherstone R.).............................128
Harcombe (Wakefield T.) 116
Loughlin (St. Helens) 114
Pearce (Hull)..111
Smith (Springfield B.)................................ 98
Stephenson (Leeds).................................... 95
M. Fletcher (Hull K.R.).............................. 94
Hobbs (Bradford N.) 83
Jones (Salford)... 79

1988-89
Aston (Sheffield E.)...................................148
Ketteridge (Castleford) 129
Hobbs (Bradford N.) 118
C. Johnson (Leigh).....................................117
Marwood (Barrow) 115
Loughlin (St. Helens) 113
Noble (Doncaster).....................................110
Woods (Warrington) 107
Currier (Widnes).......................................107
Turner (Rochdale H.) 104

1989-90
M. Fletcher (Hull K.R.).............................199
Loughlin (St. Helens) 145
Platt (Oldham)..126
Maskill (Leeds)...114
M. Conway (Wakefield T.) 107
Hobbs (Bradford N.) 104
Eastwood (Hull)..101
Aston (Sheffield E.).................................... 99
Davies (Widnes).. 98
Turner (Rochdale H.) 98

1990-91
Kerry (Salford)...177
Botica (Wigan)...126
Eastwood (Hull)..119
Davies (Widnes)..112
Irving (Leeds)... 99
Sullivan (Ryedale-York) 94
Loughlin (St. Helens) 94
Platt (Halifax) 91
Vickers (Carlisle)....................................... 88
Lumb (Hunslet)... 85

DROP GOALS

1974-75 Seabourne (Bradford N.) 10
1975-76 Hancock (Hull).................................10
1976-77 N. Stephenson (Dewsbury) 16
1977-78 Fiddler (Bramley, Leigh) 10
1978-79 Turley (Blackpool B.) 18
1979-80 Dean (Hunslet)..................................18
1980-81 Walker (Whitehaven) 22
1981-82 Agar (Halifax) 17
        Donlan (Leigh).....................................17
1982-83 Pinner (St. Helens)..............................13
1983-84 Hallett (Cardiff C.)..............................29
1984-85 Wood (Runcorn H.) 28
1985-86 Bishop (Warrington) 13
1986-87 Platt (Mansfield M.) 18
1987-88 W. Parker (Hull K.R.)...........................15
1988-89 Pearce (Hull)....................................16
1989-90 Harkin (Bradford N.).............................12
1990-91 Ashton (Workington T.) 13
        Carroll (Doncaster) 13

POINTS

1974-75	Fox (Hull K.R.)	333
1975-76	Watkins (Salford)	385
1976-77	Lloyd (Castleford)	341
1977-78	Pimblett (St. Helens)	381
1978-79	Lloyd (Hull)	373
1979-80	Quinn (Featherstone R.)	375
1980-81	Hesford (Warrington)	310
1981-82	Hopkins (Workington T.)	446
1982-83	Diamond (Fulham)	308
1983-84	Woods (Leigh)	355
1984-85	Day (St. Helens)	362
1985-86	C. Johnson (Leigh)	400
1986-87	Loughlin (St. Helens)	424
1987-88	Woods (Warrington)	351
1988-89	Aston (Sheffield E.)	307
1989-90	M. Fletcher (Hull K.R.)	450
1990-91	Kerry (Salford)	427

ALL-TIME RECORDS

Most goals in a match:
22 by Jim Sullivan (Wigan) v. Flimby & Fothergill (Challenge Cup), 14 February 1925

Most goals in a season:
DAVID WATKINS holds the record for most goals in a season with 221 — all for Salford — in 1972-73. Watkins played and scored a goal in every match that season as follows:

1972

Aug.	19	Leeds ....(H)	5
	23	Featherstone R. ....(A)	3
	26	Whitehaven ....(A)	4
	28	Swinton ....(H)	1
Sep.	1	Oldham ....(LC) (H)	10
	9	Leeds.......................................(A)	2
	15	Rochdale H. ....(LC) (H)	11
	17	Leigh......................................(A)	6
	24	Barrow...........................(JP) (A)	4
	29	Huyton ....(H)	10
Oct.	3	Oldham..........................(FT) (A)	4
	6	Wigan.........................(LC) (A)	4
	8	Blackpool B. ....(A)	5
	13	Blackpool B. ....(H)	8
	21	Swinton.............................(LCF)	5
Nov.	5	Huyton ....(A)	8
	10	Rochdale H. ....(H)	6
	17	Warrington ....(A)	4
	19	New Zealand.........................(H)	10
	24	Dewsbury ....(JP) (H)	6
	26	Workington T. ....(H)	6
Dec.	1	Barrow.....................................(H)	9
	10	Bradford N. ....(JP) (H)	9
	13	Oldham...................................(A)	4
	15	Leigh ....(H)	3
	24	Bradford N. ....(A)	5

	26	Workington T. ....(A)		3
	30	Hull K.R. ....(JP) (A)		5
1973				
Jan.	3	Bradford N............................(H)		6
	7	Rochdale H. ....(A)		2
	12	Featherstone R. ....(H)		4
	28	Featherstone R..........(RL Cup) (A)		4
Feb.	2	Whitehaven..............................(H)		4
	11	Barrow.....................................(A)		5
	23	St. Helens ....(H)		3
Mar.	7	Widnes....................................(A)		3
	9	Dewsbury ....(H)		3
	16	St. Helens ....(A)		2
	24	Leeds..........................(JP Final)		2
	30	Warrington ....(H)		1
Apr.	6	Widnes ....(H)		4
	13	Oldham...................................(H)		3
	15	Dewsbury ....(A)		2
	17	Wigan ....(A)		3
	20	Swinton...................................(A)		7
	23	Wigan......................................(H)		3
	29	Rochdale H. ....(top 16) (H)		2

	App	Gls
League	34	147
Lancs Cup...............................	4	30
John Player.............................	5	24
Tour match	1	10
RL Cup	1	4
Floodlit Cup	1	4
Top 16	1	2
Totals	**47**	**221**

Fastest goals century:
Three players share the record of scoring the fastest 100 goals from the start of a season in terms of number of matches played. They are Bernard Ganley, David Watkins and Steve Quinn, who achieved the century in 18 matches.

Ganley reached 100 goals on 16 November 1957, after playing 17 matches for Oldham and one for Great Britain.

Watkins scored his 100th goal on 17 November 1972, all for Salford.

Quinn scored his 100th goal on 16 December 1979, all for Featherstone Rovers.

Most goals in a career:
JIM SULLIVAN holds the record for most goals in a career with 2,867 between 1921-22 and 1945-46. He scored a century of goals in every season after leaving Welsh Rugby Union for Wigan until the War interrupted the 1939-40 campaign. The Test full back played all of his club rugby for Wigan apart from War-time appearances with Bradford Northern, Dewsbury and Keighley.

Sullivan's total includes 441 in representative matches, including three tours of Australasia. These figures are accepted by the Record Keepers' Club following research by James Carter and Malcolm Bentley.

159

Most one-point drop goals in a match:
5 by Danny Wilson (Swinton) v. Hunslet (John Player
Special), 6 November 1983
Peter Wood (Runcorn H.) v.Batley, 21 October 1984
Paul Bishop (Warrington) at Wigan (Premiership
semi-final), 11 May 1986

Most one-point drop goals in a season:
29 by Lyn Hallett (Cardiff C.).....................1983-84

Most one-point drop goals in a career:
97 by Norman Turley (Warrington, Runcorn H.,
Swinton, Blackpool B., Rochdale H., Barrow,
Workington T., Trafford B.,
Whitehaven).....................................1974-91

Most tries in a match:
11 by George West (Hull K.R.) v Brookland Rovers
Challenge Cup, 4 March 1905

Most tries in a career:
BRIAN BEVAN holds the record for most tries in a career
with 796 between 1946 and 1964. His season-by-season
record is:

1946-47	48
1947-48	57
1948-49	56
1949-50	33
1950-51	68
1951-52	51
1952-53	72
1953-54	67
1954-55	63
1955-56	57
1956-57	17
1957-58	46
1958-59	54
1959-60	40
1960-61	35
1961-62	15
1962-63	10
1963-64	7

Totals

Warrington	740
Blackpool Borough	17
Other Nationalities	26
Other representative matches	13
Grand Total	**796**

The Australian winger played his first game for
Warrington on 17 November 1945 and his last on 23 April
1962 before having two seasons at Blackpool Borough.
His last match for Borough was on 22 February 1964.

Most tries in a season:
ALBERT ROSENFELD holds the record for most tries
in a season with 80 — all for Huddersfield — in 1913-14.

Rosenfeld's match-by-match record:

1913			
Sep. 6	York	(A)	4
8	Warrington	(H)	2
13	Leeds	(H)	5
20	Halifax	(A)	1
27	Batley	(A)	0
Oct. 4	Oldham	(H)	2
11	Rochdale H.	(A)	0
18	Bramley	(YC) (H)	4
25	Dewsbury	(A)	4
Nov. 1	Halifax	(YC) (A)	2
8	Wigan	(A)	1
15	Dewsbury	(YC) (H)	3
19	Bradford N.	(H)	3
22	Leeds	(A)	3
29	Bradford N.	(Halifax, YCF)	1
Dec. 3	Halifax	(H)	3
6	Hunslet	(A)	2
13	Rochdale H.	(H)	3
20	Hull K.R.	(A)	2
25	Hull	(A)	1
26	Wakefield T.	(H)	3
27	Hunslet	(H)	0
1914			
Jan. 1	St. Helens	(A)	0
3	Warrington	(A)	0
10	York	(H)	3
17	Keighley	(A)	2
24	Dewsbury	(H)	1
31	Batley	(H)	0
Feb. 7	Oldham	(A)	0
14	Bramley	(H)	5
21	Wigan	(H)	3
28	Swinton Park R.	(RL Cup) (H)	7
Mar. 7	Wakefield T.	(A)	2
14	Hull K.R.	(RL Cup) (H)	2
18	Bramley	(A)	3
21	Widnes	(RL Cup) (H)	0
25	Keighley	(H)	3
28	Hull K.R.	(H)	1
30	Bradford N.	(A)	1
Apr. 4	Hull	(Leeds, RL Cup SF)	0
11	Hull	(H) did not play	
13	St. Helens	(H)	0
20	Hull	(Play-off) (H) did not play	
25	Salford	(Leeds, Championship final)	0

	App	Tries
League	33	63
Yorks Cup	4	8
RL Cup	4	9
Play-off	1	0
Totals	**42**	**80**

Most points in a season:

LEWIS JONES holds the record for most points in a season with 496 from 194 goals and 36 tries for Leeds and representative teams in 1956-57.

Jones's match-by-match record:

For Leeds

1956			Gls	Tries	Pts
Aug. 17	Halifax	(H)	3	0	6
22	Bradford N.	(A)	11	3	31
25	Wigan	(A)	4	0	8
27	Featherstone R.	(H)	4	1	11
Sep. 1	Wakefield T.	(YC) (A)	3	1	9
8	Dewsbury	(A)	6	0	12
15	Warrington	(H)	7	0	14
22	Huddersfield	(A)	3	0	6
29	York	(H)	6	0	12
Oct. 6	Batley	(A)	4	2	14
13	Australia	(H)	Did not play		
20	Hull K.R.	(A)	Did not play		
27	Wigan	(H)	2	0	4
Nov. 3	Hunslet	(A)	1	0	2
10	Barrow	(H)	3	2	12
17	Halifax	(A)	4	0	8
24	Keighley	(H)	3	3	15
Dec. 1	Barrow	(A)	4	0	8
8	Bramley	(A)	5	0	10
15	Doncaster	(H)	1	2	8
22	Bradford N.(abandoned)	(H)	1	1	5
25	Batley	(H)	8	1	19
29	Keighley	(A)	3	0	6
1957					
Jan. 5	Hull	(H)	5	2	16
12	Warrington	(A)	0	3	9
19	St. Helens	(H)	5	1	13
26	Doncaster	(A)	Did not play		
Feb. 2	Huddersfield	(H)	6	0	12
9	Wigan	(RL Cup) (H)	2	1	7
16	York	(A)	7	1	17
23	Warrington	(RL Cup) (H)	5	1	13
27	Castleford	(H)	4	1	11
Mar. 9	Halifax	(RL Cup) (A)	5	0	10
16	Wakefield T.	(H)	5	1	13
20	Bradford N	(H)	5	1	13
23	Hull	(A)	2	0	4
30	Whitehaven ....(Odsal, RL Cup SF)		1	0	2
Apr. 3	Wakefield T.	(A)	3	0	6
6	St. Helens	(A)	0	0	0
12	Hull K.R.	(H)	Did not play		
13	Dewsbury	(H)	6	2	18
19	Hunslet	(H)	5	2	16
20	Featherstone R.	(A)	2	0	4
22	Castleford	(A)	2	0	4
23	Bramley	(H)	7	1	17
May 4	Oldham	(Play-off) (A)	3	0	6
11	Barrow ...(Wembley, RL Cup final)		0	0	0

Representative matches
For Great Britain:

Jan. 26	France	(at Leeds)	9	1	21
Mar. 3	France	(at Toulouse)	5	1	13
Apr. 10	France	(at St. Helens)	7	1	17

For The Rest:

| Oct. 3 | Britain XIII | (at Bradford) | 4 | 0 | 8 |

For RL XIII:

| Oct. 29 | Australia | (Leigh) | 3 | 0 | 6 |

	App	Gls	Tries	Pts
League	36	147	30	384
RL Cup	5	13	2	32
Yorks Cup	1	3	1	9
Play-off	1	3	0	6
Representative	5	28	3	65
Totals	**48**	**194**	**36**	**496**

Most points in a match:

53 (11t,10g) by George West (Hull K.R.) v. Brookland Rovers (RL Cup), 4 March 1905

Most points in a career:

NEIL FOX holds the record for most points in a career with 6,220 between 1956 and 1979. This total does not include points scored during a spell of club rugby in New Zealand.

Fox was a month short of his 17th birthday when he made his debut for Wakefield Trinity on 10 April 1956. Apart from a brief time at Bradford Northern, Fox had 19 seasons at Wakefield before moving to a succession of clubs in later years.

After a long career as an international centre Fox moved into the forwards and played his last professional match for Bradford in their opening fixture of the 1979-80 season, on 19 August. That match enabled him to join the elite few who have played first team rugby at 40 years of age.

Fox's season-by-season tally is as follows:

	Gls	Tries	Pts
1955-56	6	0	12
1956-57	54	10	138
1957-58	124	32	344
1958-59	148	28	380
1959-60	171	37	453
1960-61	94	20	248
1961-62	183	30	456
1962 Tour			
Australasia	85	19	227
South Africa	19	4	50
1962-63	125	14	292
1963-64	125	21	313
1964-65	121	13	281
1965-66	98	11	229
1966-67	144	16	336
1967-68	98	18	250
1968-69	95	9	217
1969-70	17	5	49
1970-71	110	12	256
1971-72	84	6	186
1972-73	138	8	300
1973-74	62	8	148
1974-75	146(1)	14	333

1975-76.............................	102(1)	4	215
1976-77.............................	79(1)	6	175
1977-78.............................	95(1)	9	216
1978-79.............................	50	4	112
1979-80.............................	2	0	4

A breakdown of Fox's club and representative totals is as follows:

	App	Gls	Tries	Pts
Wakefield T.	574	1,836	272	4,488
Bradford N.	70	85(1)	12	205
Hull K.R.	59	212(2)	16	470
York.......................	13	42	2	90
Bramley....................	23	73	6	164
Huddersfield..............	21	73(1)	5	160
Club Totals	**760**	**2,321(4)**	**313**	**5,577**
				(cont)
Yorkshire.................	17	60	9	147
Britain v. Australia	8	26	3	61
New Zealand.	4	11	1	25
France.........	17	56	10	142
Other representative games including tour	22	101	22	268
Representative Totals.	**68**	**254**	**45**	**643**
Grand Totals	**828**	**2,575(4)**	**358**	**6,220**

( ) Figures in brackets are one-point drop goals included in total.

Score-a-match:
The following players have appeared and scored in all of their club's matches in one season:

Jim Hoey (Widnes)......................................1932-33
Billy Langton (Hunslet) 1958-59
Stuart Ferguson (Leigh) 1970-71
David Watkins (Salford)...............................1972-73
David Watkins (Salford)...............................1973-74
John Woods (Leigh).....................................1977-78
Steve Quinn (Featherstone R.) 1979-80
Mick Parrish (Hunslet) 1979-80
John Gorton (Swinton)................................1980-81
Mick Parrish (Oldham)................................1981-82
Peter Wood (Runcorn H.) 1984-85
David Noble (Doncaster)..............................1986-87
Mark Aston (Sheffield E.) 1988-89
Mike Fletcher (Hull K.R.) 1989-90
Steve Carroll (Bramley) 1991-92

Longest scoring run:
DAVID WATKINS holds the record for the longest scoring run, playing and scoring in 92 consecutive matches for Salford from 19 August 1972 to 25 April 1974. He totalled 403 goals, 41 tries and 929 points.

Longest run of appearances:
KEITH ELWELL holds the record for the longest run of appearances with one club with a total of 239 for Widnes. The consecutive run started at Wembley in the 1977 Challenge Cup final against Leeds on 7 May, and ended after he played in a Lancashire Cup-tie at home to St. Helens on 5 September 1982. He was dropped for the match at Featherstone Rovers a week later. Although he went on as a substitute the record refers to full appearances only. Elwell played as a substitute in the next match and then made a full appearance before his run of all appearances ended at 242.

TEAM
Highest score:
Huddersfield 119 v. Swinton Park 2 (RL Cup)
.......28 February 1914

Most points in all matches in a season:
1,436 by Leigh from 43 matches in 1985-86 as follows:
34 Division Two matches 1,156
2 Lancashire Cup 54
4 John Player Special Trophy 161
3 RL Challenge Cup 65

Most League points in a season:
1,156 by Leigh from 34 Division Two matches in 1985-86.

Longest winning run:
29 by Wigan from February to October 1987, as follows:
20 Division One, 3 Premiership, 4 Lancashire Cup, 1 Charity Shield and 1 World Club Challenge.

Longest unbeaten run:
43 Cup and League matches, including two draws, by Huddersfield in 1914-19.

They were unbeaten in the last 38 matches of 1914-15 and after the interruption of the First World War won their next five competitive matches — four Yorkshire Cup ties in 1918-19 and the first League match of 1919-20.

Longest winning run in the League:
31 matches by Wigan. Last 8 matches of 1969-70 and first 23 of 1970-71.
● In 1978-79 Hull won all of their 26 Division Two matches, the only time a club has won all its League matches in one season.

Longest losing run:
61 Cup and League matches by Runcorn Highfield from January 1989 to February 1991. Made up of 55 Division Two, 2 Challenge Cup, 2 Regal Trophy and 2 Lancs Cup.

Longest run without a win:
75 Cup and League matches by Runcorn Highfield from October 1988 to March 1991. Made up of 67 Division Two, 3 Challenge Cup, 3 Regal Trophy and 2 Lancs Cup.

Longest League losing run and run without a win:
Included in the above.
● Only three teams have lost all their matches in a season: Liverpool City (1906-07), Runcorn Highfield (1989-90) and Nottingham City (1991-92).

Wigan skipper Dean Bell hoists aloft the 1992 Silk Cut Challenge Cup.

CUPS

RUGBY LEAGUE CHALLENGE CUP

1992 Final

World-record buy Martin Offiah marked his Challenge Cup final debut by scoring two tries for Wigan, spectacularly preventing a Castleford touchdown and being awarded the Lance Todd Trophy as Man of the Match...only to be disappointed.

The Test winger had set his sights on registering the first hat-trick of tries in a Wembley final. He was denied the history-making feat by the intervention of a touch judge after touching down in the 53rd minute, having already recorded two first-half tries.

Leeds touch judge Michael Singer informed referee Robin Whitfield that Offiah had knocked on when the ball spun free from a Castleford player as the Great Britain wingman tackled him. Offiah scooped up the ball and raced 45 yards, leaving Australian second row man Graeme Bradley stranded. The ''score'' was announced over the public address system, flashed onto the television screen and noted in journalists' notebooks before Whitfield returned downfield to be told of the offence.

Although he was unable to rewrite the history books, Offiah's speed was the hallmark of the 1992 Silk Cut Challenge Cup final. The £440,000 January purchase from Widnes was able to deliver the stunning blows that repeatedly, if not permanently, knocked the fight out of Castleford whether it was by scoring tries or saving them.

Offiah chased kicks to score both of his tries and foiled the Yorkshiremen's attempt to capitalise on the same tactic when he out-sprinted St. John Ellis to tip the ball dead in the 55th minute. A try and goal then might have made the game more interesting at 19-12, but it could never be said that the score would have increased the pressure on Wigan.

Seeking their fifth successive Wembley triumph, and having just collected their third consecutive Championship title, Wigan appeared to be immune or even thrive on the sort of pressure which weighed heavily on Castleford despite pre-match insistence that they were confident of continuing their record of never having lost in four previous Wembley visits.

That confidence was shattered within five minutes. The spectre of the silverheeled Offiah seemed to unnerve Graham Steadman as he set about the seemingly simple task of fielding a speculative kick through by the winger. Offiah was a long way back when he put in the rather ambitious kick and the Great Britain full back was never under any pressure until he started to fumble the pick-up as Offiah sped in, kicking the ball from Stead-man's half-grasp to open the scoring. Botica added the first of his five goals in a faultless display with the boot.

Offiah timed his next unnatural appearance for just before the interval. Castleford players had yards' start on the Great Britain winger when stand off Shaun Edwards put in a long kick, but the Wigan flier ghosted past them all to force his way through two defenders to reach the ball first.

Edwards had touched down in the 21st minute, with Offiah at his side, after supporting a magnificent break by hooker Martin Dermott. A timely 37th-minute drop goal by the impressive Joe Lydon, who started at full back and finished in the centre, gave Wigan a comfortable 19-0 half-time lead, leaving Castleford to rue the loss of so much ball to Wigan and the speed of that man Offiah.

Castleford came out determined to make the second half more of a contest and, while they never seriously threatened Wigan's lead, they took satisfaction in winning the second period 12-9, scoring two tries to one. New Zealand centre Richard Blackmore scored the first touchdown within four minutes of the restart after Tawera Nikau and Dean Sampson had created the opportunity.

Kiwi Test forward Nikau continued to lead Castleford's fightback with a series of driving runs, setting a fine example in the absence of captain Lee Crooks, who went off with a groin strain in the 33rd minute.

With Steadman having recovered from his early jitters, Castleford became less guarded before Wigan put them back in their place with a well-worked try for substitute Steve Hampson to re-open a 19-point gap.

Nine minutes later Castleford bounced back with a diving try by Test prop Keith England off a superb back flip pass from Steadman. The touchdown was just reward for the hardworking England, while creator Steadman confirmed his return to form by brilliantly fielding a high kick under pressure and pulling off a try-saving tackle on Botica.

England's try put the score at 25-12 with 12 minutes left but Wigan never lost control and added a 72nd-minute penalty goal from Botica and a 78th-minute drop goal from the ever-cool Lydon to secure a 28-12 victory.

Offiah's display of stylish speed dominated the Press voting for the Lance Todd Trophy. He was awarded 20 votes, with five other Wigan players being nominated, though a long way behind. Dermott and Edwards both gained four votes, Botica and Andy Platt two each, with one for Australian centre Gene Miles.

The Wigan front row of Kelvin Skerrett, Dermott and Platt was the engine room of Wigan's Cup-winning machine, but the decisive turbo boost that left Castleford trailing came from Offiah. It was only the second time the Man of the Match award had gone to a winger, Len Killeen receiving the honour in 1966 mainly for his goalkicking.

Prop Platt, however, received praise from both coaches, driving in hard on attack and never easing up on defence. Test hooker Dermott was sharp at the play-the-ball and made valuable yardage with his short bursts, his snappy midfield break and by-pass of Steadman creating the 40-yard run-in for

Edwards' try.

A total of only six penalties, evenly shared, reflected the military discipline of both sides and the only incident of note was nothing more than a slap by Ellis on Offiah. Scrums went 13-9 to Wigan.

Wigan scrum half Andy Gregory made a record eighth appearance in a Wembley final after a week-long battle for fitness at a London clinic, registering another Wembley record with a seventh winners' medal. Having overcome a groin injury, he suffered a dead leg and was forced to retire in the 49th minute.

Castleford coach Darryl Van de Velde revealed he had received an offer of a post back in Australia. His post-match thoughts centred solely on a nightmare first-half performance in which his players tore up a no-errors gameplan.

Wigan, meanwhile, carried on rewriting Challenge Cup history with a record 13th success in a record 22nd final to earn a record £34,000 Silk Cut prize.

Andy Gregory, a record eighth Wembley and record seventh winner's medal.

SILK CUT CHALLENGE CUP FINAL

2 May   **Wembley**

WIGAN 28   CASTLEFORD 12

Wigan	No.	Castleford
Joe Lydon	1.	Graham Steadman
Frano Botica	2.	Jon Wray
Dean Bell, Capt.	3.	St. John Ellis
Gene Miles	4.	Richard Blackmore
Martin Offiah	5.	David Nelson
Shaun Edwards	6.	Grant Anderson
Andy Gregory	7.	Mike Ford
Kelvin Skerrett	8.	Lee Crooks, Capt.
Martin Dermott	9.	Graham Southernwood
Andy Platt	10.	Keith England
Denis Betts	11.	Graeme Bradley
Billy McGinty	12.	Martin Ketteridge
Phil Clarke	13.	Tawera Nikau
Steve Hampson	14.	Tony Smith
Neil Cowie	15.	Dean Sampson

T: Offiah (2), Edwards, Hampson
G: Botica (5), Lydon (2dg)
Substitutions:
Hampson for McGinty (27 min.)
Cowie for McGinty (63 min.)
Half-time: 19-0
Referee: Robin Whitfield (Widnes)

T: Blackmore, England
G: Ketteridge (2)
Substitutions:
Sampson for Crooks (33 min.)
Smith for Anderson (Half-time)
Attendance: 77,286
Receipts: £1,877,564

Scorechart

Minute	Score	Wigan	Castleford
5:	Offiah (T)		
	Botica (G)	6	0
21:	Edwards (T)		
	Botica (G)	12	0
37:	Lydon (DG)	13	0
39:	Offiah (T)		
	Botica (G)	19	0
44:	Blackmore (T)		
	Ketteridge (G)	19	6
59:	Hampson (T)		
	Botica (G)	25	6
68:	England (T)		
	Ketteridge (G)	25	12
72:	Botica (P)	27	12
78:	Lydon (DG)	28	12

	Wigan	Castleford
Scrums	13	9
Penalties	3	3

1992 Round by Round

In the six-tie preliminary round, Bramley entertained Leeds in a derby encounter, a hat-trick of tries by centre David Creasser and the scheming of Silk Cut Award-winner Garry Schofield being the foundations of a 36-12 Leeds victory. In another derby clash, Workington Town played hosts to Carlisle, who led 4-0 through two Barry Williams penalties before Town clinched an 11-4 success. An all-amateur meeting at Whitehaven saw visitors Hull Dockers race into a 14-6 lead before Kells rallied to secure a nailbiting 17-14 victory. Wakefield Trinity disposed of Huddersfield by 32-18 in a physical Belle Vue encounter, Trinity scoring six tries to three after the Fartowners had led 8-0 within 10 minutes. Batley travelled to Nottingham City to win 36-0, Steve Parrish taking the individual honours, while Salford won 64-13 at Chorley Borough.

In a first round disrupted by bad weather, Sheffield Eagles hammered Whitehaven 56-4 on their own ground, Mark Aston taking the Silk Cut Award after kicking nine goals. Barrow's Roy Haggerty scored an equalising 30-yard drop goal with the last kick of the home tie with Keighley Cougars for a 7-7 scoreline. Keighley pulled back from 14-2 in the replay to draw 14-14 with three second-half tries. The second replay at Widnes saw Barrow take command from the start, touching down three times in a 16-0 decider. Featherstone Rovers centre Paul Newlove showed his Test class with a hat-trick of tries at Batley. Deryck Fox added six goals in a 36-20 success, Third Division Batley having rallied from a 24-8 deficit at the interval. Halifax snatched a 12-8 victory which was hardly deserved at home to Hull K.R., who failed to take their chances, the clinching try coming from ex-Robin Dave Watson.

Trafford Borough hired Headingley, Leeds, for their home tie with Castleford, who won 50-0, full back Graham Steadman grab-bing four tries. A first-round shock came at Derwent Park, where Workington Town disposed of First Division Wakefield Trinity by 13-8, skipper Colin Armstrong leading a forceful pack. Another unexpected result was Dewsbury's 14-2 exclusion of Division Two title contenders Leigh, home skipper Paul Shuttleworth taking the Man of the Match award with a try and two goals. In the televised tie, Leeds gave a debut to former New Zealand Rugby Union international centre Craig Innes in a 48-6 defeat of Second Division Ryedale-York, but lost skipper Garry Schofield with a broken cheekbone. John Gallagher returned with a try and eight goals.

Hunslet visited amateurs Kells at Whitehaven and recorded a comfortable 32-14 success, the Cumbrians' Gary Burns taking the Silk Cut Award. In the tie of the round at Widnes, Kevin Ward was outstanding for St. Helens, who gained a 10-2 triumph through tries by Paul Bishop and Mike Riley. Doncaster became the first Third Division side to dispose of a First Division outfit in cup football by winning 14-4 at home, giving new coach Geoff Morris his third successive win. The match was marred by an accidental head injury to Swinton's Martin Leyland, who was put on the critical list at hospital, recovering within the month. Highfield's Willie Johnson hit the crossbar with a last-minute drop goal attempt to break the 12-12 deadlock with London Crusaders, who took the replay 24-10.

In a dramatic finish at Rochdale Hornets, visitors Hull clinched a 32-28 victory with a Paul Eastwood try after a failed interception by a home defender, Hull's Richard Gay having scored a hat-trick of tries. Having beaten Wigan at home in the Championship and the Regal Trophy, Salford failed in their bid for a hat-trick of victories, Shaun Edwards taking the Silk Cut Award as the Riversiders won 22-6 on the eve of departure for the inaugural World Sevens in Sydney. Bradford

Northern scored five first-half tries to destroy any hopes of a giant-killing act by Third Division hosts Scarborough Pirates, who were defeated 52-4. Warrington were restricted to a solitary try by Kevin Ellis at Second Division Oldham, who went down 8-3 after a tremendous battle.

In the second round, big-spending Leeds fell to St. Helens at Headingley by 32-12, the most points conceded by the Loiners at home in their 95-year Challenge Cup history. Following their World Sevens triumph in Sydney, Wigan continued their record Cup run by beating Warrington 14-0 at Central Park, tries coming from Kelvin Skerrett and Martin Offiah. Featherstone Rovers full back Chris Bibb scored two tries in their 23-10 defeat of Dewsbury at Mount Pleasant. Hosts Sheffield Eagles led 6-5 at home to Hull before the visitors' Welsh packman Mark Jones celebrated his call-up for Great Britain by scoring the winning try 14 minutes from time in an 11-6 success.

Third Division Hunslet made Castleford struggle for a 28-12 victory at Elland Road, Steadman claiming a hat-trick of tries. Halifax hammered visitors Doncaster 66-8, the Silk Cut Award going to reserve scrum half Chris Robinson, while Greg Pearce contributed 11 goals and a try. David Lowden scored the vital try in Workington Town's 9-2 home success over London Crusaders, while Barrow entertained Bradford Northern and, despite a Silk Cut Award performance from Neil Shaw, went down 30-13.

The highlight of the third round was the televised derby clash between St. Helens and Wigan at Knowsley Road. It was marked by erratic handling by the Saints and the bravery and commitment of a Wigan side wracked by injury to Martin Dermott, Steve Hampson and Martin Offiah. Wigan held on to a record 13-6 success. In a West Riding derby, Castleford disposed of Featherstone Rovers 19-12, home skipper Tawera Nikau producing two flashes of brilliance to seal success.

Yet another derby encounter saw Bradford Northern win 12-4 at Halifax despite losing Tony Marchant, sent off after only 13 minutes. Hull's formidable front row of Andy Dannatt, Lee Jackson and Peter Spring formed the base of their 24-8 victory at Workington Town, the Airlie Birds opting for a no-frills passage to the semi-finals.

Wigan reached Wembley for a fifth successive season with an astonishing 71-10 demolition of Bradford Northern at Bolton Wanderers FC's Burnden Park, doubling the previous record semi-final score. Martin Offiah grabbed five tries, centre partner Gene Miles adding two touchdowns in a Silk Cut Award performance as Wigan produced a near-perfect display against a Northern side lacking five injured regulars. Two weeks earlier at Leeds, Castleford held on to oust Hull 8-4, scrum half Mike Ford scoring the sole try of a tense encounter marred by crowd trouble. Australian Graeme Bradley took the Man of the Match award in a pack well led by skipper Lee Crooks.

Hull packman Mark Jones, scorer of the second round winning try at Sheffield.

1992 RESULTS

Preliminary Round

Bramley	12	Leeds	36
Chorley B.	13	Salford	64
Kells (Cumbria)	17	Hull Dockers	14
(at Whitehaven)			
Nottingham C.	0	Batley	36
Wakefield T.	32	Huddersfield	18
Workington T.	11	Carlisle	4

First Round

Barrow	7	Keighley C.	7
Batley	20	Featherstone R.	36
Dewsbury	14	Leigh	2
Doncaster	14	Swinton	4
Halifax	12	Hull K.R.	8
Highfield	12	London C.	12
Kells (Cumbria)	14	Hunslet	32
(at Whitehaven)			
Leeds	48	Ryedale-York	6
Oldham	3	Warrington	8
Rochdale H.	28	Hull	32
Salford	6	Wigan	22
Scarborough P.	4	Bradford N.	52
Trafford B.	0	Castleford	50
(at Leeds)			
Whitehaven	4	Sheffield E.	56
Widnes	2	St. Helens	10
Workington T.	13	Wakefield T.	8

Replays

Keighley C.	14	Barrow	14
London C.	24	Highfield	10

2nd Replay

Barrow	16	Keighley C.	0
(at Widnes)			

Second Round

Barrow	13	Bradford N.	30
Dewsbury	10	Featherstone R.	23
Halifax	66	Doncaster	8
Hunslet	12	Castleford	28
Leeds	12	St. Helens	32
Sheffield E.	6	Hull	11
Wigan	14	Warrington	0
Workington T.	9	London C.	2

Third Round

Castleford	19	Featherstone R.	12
Halifax	4	Bradford N.	12
St. Helens	6	Wigan	13
Workington T.	8	Hull	24

Semi-Finals

Castleford	8	Hull	4
(at Leeds)			
Wigan	71	Bradford N.	10
(at Bolton W. FC)			

Final

Wigan	28	Castleford	12
(at Wembley)			

Australian second row man Graeme Bradley, Silk Cut Award-winner for Castleford in their semi-final victory over Hull.

1992 PRIZES

Round	Per Team
Preliminary	£2,500 each club
First	£2,500 to losers
Second	£3,750 to losers
Third	£6,000 to losers
Semi-Finals	£9,500 to losers
Runners-up	£18,000
Winners	£34,000

Total Prize Money	£195,000
Capital Development Fund	£130,000
Grand Total	£325,000

CHALLENGE CUP ROLL OF HONOUR

Year	Winners		Runners-up		Venue	Attendance	Receipts
1897	Batley	10	St. Helens	3	Leeds	13,492	£624.17.7
1898	Batley	7	Bradford	0	Leeds	27,941	£1,586.3.0
1899	Oldham	19	Hunslet	9	Manchester	15,763	£946.16.0
1900	Swinton	16	Salford	8	Manchester	17,864	£1,100.0.0
1901	Batley	6	Warrington	0	Leeds	29,563	£1,644.16.0
1902	Broughton R.	25	Salford	0	Rochdale	15,006	£846.11.0
1903	Halifax	7	Salford	0	Leeds	32,507	£1,834.8.6
1904	Halifax	8	Warrington	3	Salford	17,041	£936.5.6
1905	Warrington	6	Hull K.R.	0	Leeds	19,638	£1,271.18.0
1906	Bradford	5	Salford	0	Leeds	15,834	£920.0.0
1907	Warrington	17	Oldham	3	Broughton	18,500	£1,010.0.0
1908	Hunslet	14	Hull	0	Huddersfield	18,000	£903.0.0
1909	Wakefield T.	17	Hull	0	Leeds	23,587	£1,490.0.0
1910	Leeds	7	Hull	7	Huddersfield	19,413	£1,102.0.0
Replay	Leeds	26	Hull	12	Huddersfield	11,608	£657.0.0
1911	Broughton R.	4	Wigan	0	Salford	8,000	£376.0.0
1912	Dewsbury	8	Oldham	5	Leeds	15,271	£853.0.0
1913	Huddersfield	9	Warrington	5	Leeds	22,754	£1,446.9.6
1914	Hull	6	Wakefield T.	0	Halifax	19,000	£1,035.5.0
1915	Huddersfield	37	St. Helens	3	Oldham	8,000	£472.0.0
1920	Huddersfield	21	Wigan	10	Leeds	14,000	£1,936.0.0
1921	Leigh	13	Halifax	0	Broughton	25,000	£2,700.0.0
1922	Rochdale H.	10	Hull	9	Leeds	32,596	£2,964.0.0
1923	Leeds	28	Hull	3	Wakefield	29,335	£2,390.0.0
1924	Wigan	21	Oldham	4	Rochdale	41,831	£3,712.0.0
1925	Oldham	16	Hull K.R.	3	Leeds	28,335	£2,879.0.0
1926	Swinton	9	Oldham	3	Rochdale	27,000	£2,551.0.0
1927	Oldham	26	Swinton	7	Wigan	33,448	£3,170.0.0
1928	Swinton	5	Warrington	3	Wigan	33,909	£3,158.1.11
1929	Wigan	13	Dewsbury	2	Wembley	41,500	£5,614.0.0
1930	Widnes	10	St. Helens	3	Wembley	36,544	£3,102.0.0
1931	Halifax	22	York	8	Wembley	40,368	£3,908.0.0
1932	Leeds	11	Swinton	8	Wigan	29,000	£2,479.0.0
1933	Huddersfield	21	Warrington	17	Wembley	41,874	£6,465.0.0
1934	Hunslet	11	Widnes	5	Wembley	41,280	£6,686.0.0
1935	Castleford	11	Huddersfield	8	Wembley	39,000	£5,533.0.0
1936	Leeds	18	Warrington	2	Wembley	51,250	£7,070.0.0
1937	Widnes	18	Keighley	5	Wembley	47,699	£6,704.0.0
1938	Salford	7	Barrow	4	Wembley	51,243	£7,174.0.0
1939	Halifax	20	Salford	3	Wembley	55,453	£7,681.0.0
1940	*No competition*						
1941	Leeds	19	Halifax	2	Bradford	28,500	£1,703.0.0
1942	Leeds	15	Halifax	10	Bradford	15,250	£1,276.0.0
1943	Dewsbury	16	Leeds	9	Dewsbury	10,470	£823.0.0
	Dewsbury	0	Leeds	6	Leeds	16,000	£1,521.0.0
	Dewsbury won on aggregate 16-15						
1944	Bradford	0	Wigan	3	Wigan	22,000	£1,640.0.0
	Bradford	8	Wigan	0	Bradford	30,000	£2,200.0.0
	Bradford won on aggregate 8-3						
1945	Huddersfield	7	Bradford N.	4	Huddersfield	9,041	£1,184.3.7
	Huddersfield	6	Bradford N.	5	Bradford	17,500	£2,050.0.0
	Huddersfield won on aggregate 13-9						

Year	Winners		Runners-up		Venue	Attendance	Receipts
1946	Wakefield T.	13	Wigan	12	Wembley	54,730	£12,013.13.6
1947	Bradford N.	8	Leeds	4	Wembley	77,605	£17,434.5.0
1948	Wigan	8	Bradford N.	3	Wembley	91,465	£21,121.9.9
1949	Bradford N.	12	Halifax	0	Wembley	*95,050	£21,930.5.0
1950	Warrington	19	Widnes	0	Wembley	94,249	£24,782.13.0
1951	Wigan	10	Barrow	0	Wembley	94,262	£24,797.19.0
1952	Workington T.	18	Featherstone R.	10	Wembley	72,093	£22,374.2.0
1953	Huddersfield	15	St. Helens	10	Wembley	89,588	£30,865.12.3
1954	Warrington	4	Halifax	4	Wembley	81,841	£29,706.7.3
Replay	Warrington	8	Halifax	4	Bradford	102,569	£18,623.7.0
1955	Barrow	21	Workington T.	12	Wembley	66,513	£27,453.16.0
1956	St. Helens	13	Halifax	2	Wembley	79,341	£29,424.7.6
1957	Leeds	9	Barrow	7	Wembley	76,318	£32,671.14.3
1958	Wigan	13	Workington T.	9	Wembley	66,109	£33,175.17.6
1959	Wigan	30	Hull	13	Wembley	79,811	£35,718.19.9
1960	Wakefield T.	38	Hull	5	Wembley	79,773	£35,754.16.0
1961	St. Helens	12	Wigan	6	Wembley	94,672	£38,479.11.9
1962	Wakefield T.	12	Huddersfield	6	Wembley	81,263	£33,390.18.4
1963	Wakefield T.	25	Wigan	10	Wembley	84,492	£44,521.17.0
1964	Widnes	13	Hull K.R.	5	Wembley	84,488	£44,840.19.0
1965	Wigan	20	Hunslet	16	Wembley	89,016	£48,080.4.0
1966	St. Helens	21	Wigan	2	Wembley	*98,536	£50,409.0.0
1967	Featherstone R.	17	Barrow	12	Wembley	76,290	£53,465.14.0
1968	Leeds	11	Wakefield T.	10	Wembley	87,100	£56,171.16.6
1969	Castleford	11	Salford	6	Wembley	*97,939	£58,848.1.0
1970	Castleford	7	Wigan	2	Wembley	95,255	£89,262.2.0
1971	Leigh	24	Leeds	7	Wembley	85,514	£84,452.15
1972	St. Helens	16	Leeds	13	Wembley	89,495	£86,414.30
1973	Featherstone R.	33	Bradford N.	14	Wembley	72,395	£125,826.40
1974	Warrington	24	Featherstone R.	9	Wembley	77,400	£132,021.05
1975	Widnes	14	Warrington	7	Wembley	85,098	£140,684.45
1976	St. Helens	20	Widnes	5	Wembley	89,982	£190,129.40
1977	Leeds	16	Widnes	7	Wembley	80,871	£241,488.00
1978	Leeds	14	St. Helens	12	Wembley	*96,000	£330,575.00
1979	Widnes	12	Wakefield T.	3	Wembley	94,218	£383,157.00
1980	Hull K.R.	10	Hull	5	Wembley	*95,000	£448,202.90
1981	Widnes	18	Hull K.R.	9	Wembley	92,496	£591,117.00
1982	Hull	14	Widnes	14	Wembley	92,147	£684,500.00
Replay	Hull	18	Widnes	9	Elland Rd., L'ds	41,171	£180,525.00
1983	Featherstone R.	14	Hull	12	Wembley	84,969	£655,510.00
1984	Widnes	19	Wigan	6	Wembley	80,116	£686,171.00
1985	Wigan	28	Hull	24	Wembley	*97,801	£760,322.00
1986	Castleford	15	Hull K.R.	14	Wembley	82,134	£806,676.00
1987	Halifax	19	St. Helens	18	Wembley	91,267	£1,009,206.00
1988	Wigan	32	Halifax	12	Wembley	*94,273	£1,102,247.00
1989	Wigan	27	St. Helens	0	Wembley	*78,000	£1,121,293.00
1990	Wigan	36	Warrington	14	Wembley	*77,729	£1,360,000.00
1991	Wigan	13	St. Helens	8	Wembley	75,532	£1,610,447.00
1992	Wigan	28	Castleford	12	Wembley	77,286	£1,877,564.00

*Indicates a capacity attendance, the limit being fixed annually taking into account variable factors.

RUGBY LEAGUE CHALLENGE CUP ....
A REVIEW
1969-70
Castleford 7 Edwards; Briggs, Thomas, Stenton, Lowndes (1t); Hardisty (Hargrave), Hepworth; Hartley, C. Dickinson, Redfearn (2g), Kirkbride, Lockwood, Reilly
Wigan 2 Tyrer (1g) (C. Hill); Jones, Francis, Rowe, Kevin O'Loughlin; D. Hill, Parr; Ashcroft, Burdell, Hogan, Ashurst, D. Robinson, Laughton
Referee: G.F. Lindop (Wakefield)
1970-71
Leigh 24 Eckersley (1t, 1g); Ferguson (5g), Dorrington (1t), Collins, Walsh; A. Barrow, Murphy (2g) (L. Chisnall); Watts, Ashcroft, Fiddler (1g), Grimes, Clarkson, Smethurst
Leeds 7 Holmes (2g); Langley, Hynes, Cowan (Dyl), Atkinson; Wainwright (1t), Seabourne; J. Burke, Fisher, Barnard, Hick, Haigh, Ramsey
Referee: W.H. Thompson (Huddersfield)
1971-72
St. Helens 16 G. Pimblett; L. Jones (1t), Benyon, Walsh, Wilson; K. Kelly, Heaton; Rees (1t), Greenall, J. Stephens, Mantle, E. Chisnall, Coslett (5g)
Leeds 13 Holmes; Alan Smith, Hynes (Langley), Dyl, Atkinson; Hardisty, Hepworth; Clawson (5g), Fisher, Ramsey, Cookson (1t), Haigh, Batten
Referee: E. Lawrinson (Warrington)
1972-73
Featherstone R. 33 C. Kellett (8g); Coventry, M. Smith (1t) (Hartley 1t), Newlove (2t), K. Kellett; Mason, Nash (1g); Tonks, Bridges, Farrar (1t), Rhodes (Hollis), Thompson, Stone
Bradford N. 14 Tees (4g); Lamb, Stockwell, Watson, D. Redfearn (1t); Blacker (Treasure), Seabourne; Hogan, Dunn, Earl (Long), Joyce, W. Pattinson, Fearnley (1t)
Referee: M.J. Naughton (Widnes)
1973-74
Warrington 24 Whitehead (7g); M. Philbin, Noonan, Whittle, Bevan; Murphy (2g) (Pickup), Gordon; D. Chisnall, Ashcroft (1t), Brady (Wanbon), Wright, Nicholas (1t), B. Philbin
Featherstone R. 9 Box (3g); Dyas, M. Smith, Hartley, Bray; Newlove (1t), Nash; Tonks, Bridges, Harris, Rhodes (Busfield), Thompson (Stone), Bell
Referee: S. Shepherd (Oldham)
1974-75
Widnes 14 Dutton (5g, 1dg); A. Prescott, George, Aspey, Anderson; Hughes, Bowden; Mills (1t), Elwell, Sheridan, Foran, Adams, Laughton
Warrington 7 Whitehead (2g); M. Philbin, Noonan, Reynolds (W. Briggs), Bevan (1t); Whittle, Gordon; D. Chisnall, Ashcroft, Wanbon, Conroy, Martyn (Nicholas), B. Philbin
Referee: P. Geraghty (York)

1975-76
St. Helens 20 G. Pimblett (3g, 2dg); L. Jones, Cunningham (1t), Noonan, Mathias; Benyon (Glynn 2t), Heaton (1t); Mantle (James), A. Karalius, Coslett, Nicholls, E. Chisnall, Hull
Widnes 5 Dutton (2g); A. Prescott (D. O'Neill), Hughes, George, Jenkins; Eckersley, Bowden; Nelson, Elwell (1dg), Wood, Foran (Sheridan), Adams, Laughton
Referee: R. Moore (Wakefield)
1976-77
Leeds 16 Murrell; Alan Smith (D. Smith), Hague, Dyl (1t), Atkinson (1t); Holmes, Dick (1t, 3g, 1dg); Harrison, Ward, Pitchford, Eccles, Cookson, Fearnley (Dickinson)
Widnes 7 Dutton (2g); S. Wright (George), Aspey (1t), Eckersley, D. O'Neill; Hughes, Bowden; Ramsey, Elwell, Mills, Dearden (Foran), Adams, Laughton
Referee: V. Moss (Manchester)
1977-78
Leeds 14 Oulton (1g); D. Smith (1t), Hague, Dyl, Atkinson (1t); Holmes (1dg), J. Sanderson (Dick); Harrison (Dickinson), Ward (2dg), Pitchford, Cookson (1t), Eccles, Crane
St. Helens 12 G. Pimblett (3g), L. Jones, Noonan, Glynn, Mathias; Francis (1t), K. Gwilliam; D. Chisnall, Liptrot, James, Nicholls, Cunningham, Pinner
Referee: W.H. Thompson (Huddersfield)
1978-79
Widnes 12 Eckersley (1dg); S. Wright (1t), Aspey, George (Hull), Burke (2g); Hughes (1t), Bowden; Mills, Elwell (1dg), Shaw, Adams, Dearden (M. O'Neill), Laughton
Wakefield T. 3 Sheard; Fletcher (1t), K. Smith, Diamond, Juliff; Topliss, Lampkowski; Burke, McCurrie, Skerrett, Ashurst, Keith Rayne, Idle
Referee: J.E. Jackson (Pudsey)
1979-80
Hull K.R. 10 Hall; Hubbard (1t, 3g) (Hogan), M. Smith, Hartley, Sullivan; Millward (1dg), Agar; Holdstock, Watkinson, Lockwood, Lowe, Rose (Millington), Casey
Hull 5 Woods; Bray, Walters, Wilby (1t), Prendiville; Newlove (Hancock), Pickerill; Tindall, Wileman, Stone (Farrar), Birdsall, Lloyd (1g), Norton
Referee: G.F. Lindop (Wakefield)
1980-81
Widnes 18 Burke (1t, 4g); S. Wright, George (1t), Cunningham (J. Myler), Bentley; Hughes, Gregory (1t); M. O'Neill (Shaw), Elwell, Lockwood, L. Gorley, E. Prescott, Adams (1dg)
Hull K.R. 9 Hall; Hubbard (3g), M. Smith, Hogan, Muscroft; Hartley, Harkin; Holdstock (Millington), Watkinson, Crooks (Proctor), Lowe, Burton (1t), Casey
Referee: D.G. Kershaw (Easingwold)

1981-82
Hull 14 Kemble; O'Hara (1t), Day, S. Evans,
Prendiville; Topliss, Harkin; Skerrett, Wileman,
Stone, Crane (Crooks), Lloyd (4g), Norton (1t)
Widnes 14 Burke (1g) (A. Myler); S. Wright (1t),
Keiron O'Loughlin, Cunningham (2t), Basnett;
Hughes, Gregory (1g); M. O'Neill, Elwell (1dg),
Lockwood (S. O'Neill), L. Gorley, E. Prescott,
Adams
Referee: G.F. Lindop (Wakefield)
Replay
Hull 18 Kemble (1t); Sullivan, Leuluai, S. Evans,
Prendiville; Topliss (2t), Dean; Tindall, Duke,
Stone, Skerrett, Crooks (1t, 3g), Norton (Crane)
Widnes 9 Burke (3g); S. Wright (1t), Keiron
O'Loughlin, Cunningham, Basnett; Hughes,
Gregory; M. O'Neill, Elwell, Lockwood,
L. Gorley, E. Prescott, Adams
Referee: G.F. Lindop (Wakefield)
1982-83
Featherstone R. 14 N. Barker; Marsden,
Quinn (4g), Gilbert (Lyman), K. Kellett;
A. Banks, Hudson; Gibbins, Handscombe,
Hankins, D. Hobbs (2t), Slatter (Siddall), Smith
Hull 12 Kemble; O'Hara, S. Evans, Leuluai (1t),
Prendiville; Topliss, Harkin (Day) (Crane);
Skerrett, Bridges, Stone, Rose, Crooks (1t, 3g),
Norton
Referee: M.R. Whitfield (Widnes)
1983-84
Widnes 19 Burke (3g); S. Wright, Hughes
(D. Hulme), Lydon (2t), Basnett;
Keiron O'Loughlin (1t), Gregory; S. O'Neill
(1dg), Elwell, K. Tamati, L. Gorley, M. O'Neill
(Whitfield), Adams
Wigan 6 Edwards; Ramsdale, Stephenson,
Whitfield (1g), (Elvin), Gill; Cannon, Stephens;
Hemsley (1t), H. Tamati, Case (Juliff), West,
Scott, Pendlebury
Referee: W.H. Thompson (Huddersfield)
1984-85
Wigan 28 Edwards (1t); Ferguson (2t),
Stephenson (1g), Donlan, Gill (1t, 3g);
Kenny (1t), M. Ford; Courtney, Kiss, Case
(Campbell), West, Dunn, Potter
Hull 24 Kemble; James (1t), S. Evans (1t),
Leuluai (2t), O'Hara (Schofield); Ah Kuoi,
Sterling; Crooks (2g), Patrick, Puckering
(Divorty 1t), Muggleton, Rose, Norton
Referee: R. Campbell (Widnes)
1985-86
Castleford 15 Lord (Roockley); Plange,
Marchant (1t), Hyde, Sandy (1t); Joyner,
R. Beardmore (1t, 1dg); Ward, K. Beardmore
(Horton), Johnson, England, Ketteridge (1g),
French

Hull K.R. 14 Fairbairn; Clark, M. Smith,
Prohm (2t), Laws; Dorahy (1g), Harkin; P.
Johnston, Watkinson, Ema, Kelly (G. Smith),
Des Harrison (Lydiat 1t), Miller
Referee: R. Whitfield (Widnes)
1986-87
Halifax 19 Eadie (1t); Wilson, Whitfield (3g),
Rix, George (1t); C. Anderson (Juliff), Stephens;
Beevers (James), McCallion (1t), Neller, Dixon,
Scott, Pendlebury (1dg)
St. Helens 18 Veivers; Ledger, Loughlin (1t, 3g),
Elia (1t), McCormack; Clark, Holding; Burke,
Liptrot, Fieldhouse, Platt, Haggerty (Round 1t),
Arkwright
Referee: J. Holdsworth (Kippax)
1987-88
Wigan 32 Lydon (1t, 1g); T. Iro (1t), K. Iro (2t),
Bell (1t), Gill (1t); Edwards (Byrne), Gregory
(1g); Case, Kiss, Shelford, Goodway, Potter
(Wane), Hanley (1t)
Halifax 12 Eadie; Meredith, T. Anderson (1t),
Wilkinson, Whitfield (2g); Grogan, Robinson
(Fairbank); James (1t), McCallion, Neller,
Holliday (Scott), Dixon, Pendlebury
Referee: G.F. Lindop (Wakefield)
1988-89
Wigan 27 Hampson (1t); T. Iro, K. Iro (2t),
Bell, Lydon (3g); Edwards, Gregory (1t, 1dg);
Lucas, Kiss (Betts), Shelford, Platt, Potter
(Goodway), Hanley (1t)
St. Helens 0 Connolly; O'Connor, Veivers,
Loughlin (Bloor), Quirk; Cooper, Holding;
Burke, Groves, Forber, Dwyer (Evans),
Haggerty, Vautin
Referee: R. Tennant (Castleford)
1989-90
Wigan 36 Hampson; Lydon (6g), K. Iro (2t),
Bell, Preston (2t) (Gildart); Edwards, Gregory;
Shelford, Dermott (Goulding), Platt, Betts (1t),
Goodway, Hanley (1t)
Warrington 14 Lyon (1t); Drummond, Mercer,
Darbyshire (1g), Forster; Crompton, Bishop (2g)
(McGinty); Burke, D. Mann, Harmon, Jackson
(Thomas), Sanderson, Gregory (1t)
Referee: J. Holdsworth (Kippax)
1990-91
Wigan 13 Hampson; Myers (1t), K. Iro, Bell,
Botica (1t, 2g); Edwards, Gregory (1dg); Lucas,
Dermott (Goulding), Platt, Betts, Clarke
(Goodway), Hanley
St. Helens 8 Veivers (Connolly); Hunte (1t),
T. Ropati, Loughlin, Quirk; Griffiths,
Bishop (2g); Neill (Groves), Dwyer, Ward,
Harrison, G. Mann, Cooper
Referee: J. Smith (Halifax)

THE LANCE TODD TROPHY

The Lance Todd Trophy is presented to the Man of the Match in the Rugby League Challenge Cup Final, the decision being reached by a ballot of members of the Rugby League Writers' Association present at the game.

Lance Todd made his name in Britain as a player with Wigan and as manager of Salford. His untimely death in a road accident on the return journey from a game at Oldham was commemorated by the introduction of the Lance Todd Trophy.

The award was instituted by Australian-born Harry Sunderland, Warrington director Bob Anderton and Yorkshire journalist John Bapty.

Around 1950, the Red Devils' Association at Salford, comprising players and officials who had worked with Todd, raised sufficient funds to provide a trophy and replica for each winner.

Hull's Tommy Harris is the only hooker to earn the title; and Ray Ashby and Brian Gabbitas the only players to share the honour.

Following the 1954 replay, it was decided by the Red Devils that in future the trophy would be awarded for the Wembley game. In 1954, Gerry Helme had received the trophy for his performance in the Odsal replay. In the 1982 replay at Elland Road, Leeds, the Man of the Match award went to Hull skipper David Topliss, the Lance Todd Trophy having been awarded to Eddie Cunningham, of Widnes, in the drawn Wembley tie.

In 1990 Andy Gregory, of Wigan, became the first player to win the trophy twice at Wembley, having also won it two years earlier.

The Lance Todd Trophy Roll of Honour

Year	Winner	Team	Position
1946	Billy Stott	Wakefield Trinity (v Wigan)	Centre
1947	Willie Davies	Bradford Northern (v Leeds)	Stand off
1948	Frank Whitcombe	Bradford Northern (v Wigan)	Prop
1949	Ernest Ward	Bradford Northern (v Halifax)	Centre
1950	Gerry Helme	Warrington (v Widnes)	Scrum half
1951	Cec Mountford	Wigan (v Barrow)	Stand off
1952	Billy Ivison	Workington T. (v Featherstone R.)	Loose forward
1953	Peter Ramsden	Huddersfield (v St. Helens)	Stand off
1954	Gerry Helme	Warrington (v Halifax)	Scrum half
1955	Jack Grundy	Barrow (v Workington Town)	Second row
1956	Alan Prescott	St. Helens (v Halifax)	Prop
1957	Jeff Stevenson	Leeds (v Barrow)	Scrum half
1958	Rees Thomas	Wigan (v Workington Town)	Scrum half
1959	Brian McTigue	Wigan (v Hull)	Second row
1960	Tommy Harris	Hull (v Wakefield Trinity)	Hooker
1961	Dick Huddart	St. Helens (v Wigan)	Second row
1962	Neil Fox	Wakefield Trinity (v Huddersfield)	Centre
1963	Harold Poynton	Wakefield Trinity (v Wigan)	Stand off
1964	Frank Collier	Widnes (v Hull K.R.)	Prop
1965	Ray Ashby	Wigan	Full back
	Brian Gabbitas	Hunslet	Stand off

1966	Len Killeen	St. Helens (v Wigan)	Winger
1967	Carl Dooler	Featherstone Rovers (v Barrow)	Scrum half
1968	Don Fox	Wakefield Trinity (v Leeds)	Prop
1969	Malcolm Reilly	Castleford (v Salford)	Loose forward
1970	Bill Kirkbride	Castleford (v Wigan)	Second row
1971	Alex Murphy	Leigh (v Leeds)	Scrum half
1972	Kel Coslett	St. Helens (v Leeds)	Loose forward
1973	Steve Nash	Featherstone R. (v Bradford N.)	Scrum half
1974	Derek Whitehead	Warrington (v Featherstone Rovers)	Full back
1975	Ray Dutton	Widnes (v Warrington)	Full back
1976	Geoff Pimblett	St. Helens (v Widnes)	Full back
1977	Steve Pitchford	Leeds (v Widnes)	Prop
1978	George Nicholls	St. Helens (v Leeds)	Second row
1979	David Topliss	Wakefield Trinity (v Widnes)	Stand off
1980	Brian Lockwood	Hull K.R. (v Hull)	Prop
1981	Mick Burke	Widnes (v Hull K.R.)	Full back
1982	Eddie Cunningham	Widnes (v Hull)	Centre
1983	David Hobbs	Featherstone Rovers (v Hull)	Second row
1984	Joe Lydon	Widnes (v Wigan)	Centre
1985	Brett Kenny	Wigan (v Hull)	Stand off
1986	Bob Beardmore	Castleford (v Hull K.R.)	Scrum half
1987	Graham Eadie	Halifax (v St. Helens)	Full back
1988	Andy Gregory	Wigan (v Halifax)	Scrum half
1989	Ellery Hanley	Wigan (v St. Helens)	Loose forward
1990	Andy Gregory	Wigan (v Warrington)	Scrum half
1991	Denis Betts	Wigan (v St. Helens)	Second row
1992	Martin Offiah	Wigan (v Castleford)	Winger

Lance Todd Trophy winner Martin Offiah beats Castleford duo Mike Ford (left) and Jon Wray to touch down for his second Wembley try.

175

CHALLENGE CUP RECORDS

ALL ROUNDS

TEAM
Highest score:
Huddersfield 119 v. *Swinton Park 2. 1914

INDIVIDUAL
Most goals in a match:
22 by Jim Sullivan (Wigan) v. *Flimby and Fothergill
. . . . 1925

Most tries in a match:
11 by George West (Hull K.R.) v. *Brookland Rovers
. . . . 1905

Most points in a match:
53 (11t,10g) by George West (Hull K.R.) as above.

*Amateur teams

FINAL RECORDS

TEAM

Most wins: 13 by Wigan

Most finals: 22 by Wigan

Highest score:
Wakefield T. 38 v. Hull 5. 1960

Widest margin:
Huddersfield 37 v. St. Helens 3. 1915

Biggest attendance:
102,569 Warrington v. Halifax (Replay) at Bradford
. . . . 1954

INDIVIDUAL
Most goals:
8 by Cyril Kellett (Featherstone R.) v. Bradford N.
. . . . 1973

Most tries:
3 by Bob Wilson (Broughton R.) v. Salford. 1902
Stan Moorhouse (Huddersfield) v. Warrington. 1913
Tom Holliday (Oldham) v. Swinton. 1927

Most points:
20 (7g,2t) by Neil Fox (Wakefield T.) v. Hull. . . 1960

WEMBLEY FACTS

WIGAN have made a record 18 appearances at Wembley and won there a record 12 times, including a record five successive appearances from 1988.

A RECORD 10 overseas players trod the Wembley turf in 1985. Hull fielded six — a record for one club. The Airlie Birds sextet were Australians Peter Sterling and John Muggleton, plus New Zealanders Gary Kemble, James Leuluai, Dane O'Hara and Fred Ah Kuoi. Wigan added Australians John Ferguson and Brett Kenny together with New Zealanders Graeme West and Danny Campbell, who went on as substitute. South African Nick Du Toit was substitute back but did not play.

THE 1985 aggregates of 10 tries and 52 points were both record totals for a Challenge Cup final with Hull's 24 points the most by a losing side. There were also 10 tries in the 1915 final when Huddersfield beat St. Helens 37-3, which is the widest margin. Wakefield Trinity ran up the highest Cup final score when they beat Hull 38-5 in 1960.

WORLD RECORD receipts of £1,877,564 were taken at the 1992 final between Wigan and Castleford from a crowd of 77,286.

ANDY GREGORY holds the record for most Cup-winning appearances at Wembley with seven. The scrum half has never been on a losing side in a record eight finals at the stadium, having also been in the Widnes side that drew with Hull in 1982 before losing the replay at Elland Road, Leeds.
Gregory's winning appearances were with Widnes (1981, 1984) and Wigan (1988, 1989, 1990, 1991, 1992).

ERIC ASHTON captained a record six teams at Wembley — Wigan in 1958, 1959, 1961, 1963, 1965 and 1966. His record of three wins (in 1958, 1959, 1965) is shared with Derek Turner (Wakefield Trinity 1960, 1962, 1963), Alex Murphy (St. Helens 1966, Leigh 1971 and Warrington 1974) and Ellery Hanley (Wigan 1989, 1990, 1991), this being the only three successive wins.

THE YOUNGEST player to appear in a Wembley Cup final was Shaun Edwards who was 17 years, 6 months and 19 days when he played full back for Wigan against Widnes in 1984. He was also the youngest captain at Wembley, leading Wigan to success in the 1988 final against Halifax at the age of 21 years, 6 months and 14 days.

ALEX MURPHY has been a record six times to Wembley as a coach. He was a winner as player-coach with Leigh (1971) and Warrington (1974), but losing each time when confined to the bench with Warrington (1975), Wigan (1984) and St. Helens (1987 and 1989). Murphy also went twice solely as a player, with St. Helens in 1961 and 1966.

MOST WINS as a coach at Wembley is three, by Jim Sullivan (Wigan 1948, 1951 and St. Helens 1956), Joe Egan (Wigan 1958, 1959 and Widnes 1964), Ken Traill (Wakefield T. 1960, 1962 and 1963) and John Monie (Wigan 1990, 1991 and 1992).

THE OLDEST player at Wembley was Gus Risman, who at 41 years 29 days led Workington Town to victory over Featherstone Rovers in 1952. He played full back.

THE TALLEST player at Wembley was St. Helens second row man John Harrison who appeared in the 1991 final against Wigan. He measured 6ft. 7in.

SCHOOLBOYS who have appeared in an Under-11 curtain-raiser at Wembley and gone on to play in the major final at the stadium are Joe Lydon, David Hulme, Mike Ford, Neil Puckering, David Plange, Denis Betts and Bobby Goulding. Lydon became the first to achieve the feat with Widnes in the 1984 final against Wigan, followed by teammate Hulme who went on as a 72nd-minute substitute. Both had played in the first schoolboys' curtain-raiser in 1975 — Lydon for Wigan, and Hulme for Widnes.

CYRIL KELLETT holds the record for most goals in a Challenge Cup final with his eight for Featherstone Rovers in 1973.

In the most remarkable exhibition of kicking seen at Wembley, the veteran full back was successful with every one of his attempts as Bradford Northern crashed 33-14.

Nine years earlier he scored only one for Hull Kingston Rovers in the 13-5 defeat by Widnes.

NEIL FOX — the record aggregate points scorer of all time — piled up the most points in a Challenge Cup final in 1960. His 20 points helped Wakefield Trinity to a 38-5 defeat of Hull. Fox's points came from two tries and seven goals.

His three drop goals for Trinity in the 12-6 victory over Huddersfield two years later was another extraordinary feat in the days when the drop goal was a rarity.

NO player has scored a hat-trick of tries at Wembley, the feat being achieved only three times in the preceding era.

The last to do it was Oldham winger Tom Holliday in the 26-7 defeat of Swinton in 1927.

Bob Wilson, the Broughton Rangers centre and captain, was the first to score three tries, in the 25-0 victory over Salford in 1902.

In between, Stan Moorhouse's three-try feat accounted for all of Huddersfield's points when they beat Warrington 9-5 in 1913.

MANY great players have gone through an entire career without achieving their ambition of playing at Wembley. Hull's Mike Smith achieved it in his first senior game.

Smith made one of the most remarkable debuts in sporting history when he played in the second row of an injury-hit Boulevard side against Wakefield Trinity in 1960.

In contrast, Freddie Miller signed for Hull in 1932 and did not play at Wembley until 1952...two years after joining Featherstone Rovers.

A NOTABLE Wembley captain was Gus Risman who led two clubs to victory...14 years apart.

He was captain of Salford when they beat Barrow in 1938. At 41, he led Workington Town to their triumph over Featherstone Rovers in 1952.

PROBABLY the unluckiest Challenge Cup finalist was Dai Davies who appeared in four finals and was on the losing side each time. Three of those occasions were at Wembley with different clubs. He was a loser with Warrington (1933), Huddersfield (1935) and Keighley (1937). Before the Wembley era he was also in Warrington's beaten team of 1928.

Steve Norton and Lee Crooks played at Wembley four times and were never on the winning side. Norton was in the beaten Hull teams of 1980, 1983 and 1985 in addition to playing in the 1982 drawn final. In 1970 he was a non-playing substitute for Castleford who won the Cup.

Crooks was in the beaten Hull sides of 1983 and 1985 plus the drawn final of 1982. He was then in Castleford's beaten 1992 team.

Norton and Crooks both won winners' medals in the 1982 replay.

Bill Ramsey was on the losing side in four Wembley finals but gained a winners' medal with Leeds in 1968. He picked up losers' medals with Hunslet (1965), Leeds (1971 and 1972) and Widnes (1977).

A TOTAL of 15 current clubs have yet to play at Wembley ...Batley, Bramley, Carlisle, Chorley Borough, Doncaster, Highfield, London Crusaders, Nottingham City, Oldham, Rochdale Hornets, Scarborough Pirates, Sheffield Eagles, Swinton, Trafford Borough and Whitehaven.

Fate seems to be against Swinton and Oldham. In the five years preceding the move to Wembley, one or the other appeared in the final, twice meeting each other. Oldham played in four successive finals in that period. Swinton's run of three finals ended when the first Wembley took place in 1929. They got through to the final three years later ...only for it to be played at Wigan!

WEMBLEY ERA SEMI-FINALS

It is generally felt that it is better to have played at Wembley and lost than never to have played there at all. This makes the semi-final stage of the RL Challenge Cup almost as important as the final with no consolation for the losers.

Of the 15 current clubs who have never appeared at Wembley, four have been beaten semi-finalists. They are Oldham (six times), Rochdale Hornets (twice), Swinton and Whitehaven.

Probably the unluckiest are Oldham. They have reached the penultimate stage six times without being able to realise their ambition. Oldham almost made it in 1964. After drawing 5-5 with Hull K.R., they were winning 17-14 in extra time of the replay when bad light stopped play and they were beaten in the third game.

Swinton did win a semi-final in 1932 but the final that year was switched from Wembley to Wigan!

There have been three occasions when Yorkshire has provided all four semi-finalists in one year — in 1962, 1973 and 1983. Four times have all four semi-finalists come from west of the Pennines — in 1930, 1989, 1990 and 1991.

Until 1962 the two semi-finals were always played on the same Saturday, but with four Yorkshire clubs competing for the first time it was decided to play one mid-week. Both matches were played at Odsal Stadium, Bradford. The first was on a Wednesday evening — without floodlights — when 43,625 saw Wakefield Trinity beat Featherstone Rovers and on the following Saturday there were 31,423 to see Huddersfield beat Hull K.R.

The following year both semi-finals were again played on the same Saturday, but since then they have been staged on different Saturdays.

Some semi-final facts during the Wembley era are:

Biggest attendance: 69,898 Warrington v. Leeds at Bradford in 1950

Biggest aggregate: 104,453 in 1939 (Only other six-figure aggregate was 102,080 in 1951)

Record receipts: £177,161 St. Helens v. Wigan at Old Trafford, Manchester in 1990

Lowest attendance: 7,971 Featherstone R. v. Leigh at Leeds in 1974

Highest score and widest margin: Wigan 71 v. Bradford N. 10 in 1992

CHALLENGE CUP SEMI-FINALS

Year	Winners		Runners-up		Venue	Attendance	Receipts
1929	Dewsbury	9	Castleford	3	Huddersfield	25,000	£1,562
	Wigan	7	St. Helens Recs.	7	Swinton	31,000	£2,209
Replay	Wigan	13	St. Helens Recs.	12	Leigh	21,940	£1,437
1930	Widnes	10	Barrow	3	Warrington	25,500	£1,630
	St. Helens	5	Wigan	5	Swinton	37,169	£2,666
Replay	St. Helens	22	Wigan	10	Leigh	24,000	£1,657
1931	Halifax	11	St. Helens	2	Rochdale	21,674	£1,498
	York	15	Warrington	5	Leeds	32,419	£2,329
1932	Leeds	2	Halifax	2	Huddersfield	31,818	£2,456
Replay	Leeds	9	Halifax	2	Wakefield	21,000	£1,417
	Swinton	7	Wakefield T.	4	Rochdale	21,273	£1,369
●	*Final was played at Wigan, not Wembley*						
1933	Huddersfield	30	Leeds	8	Wakefield	36,359	£2,299
	Warrington	11	St. Helens	5	Swinton	30,373	£2,055
1934	Hunslet	12	Huddersfield	7	Wakefield	27,450	£1,797
	Widnes	7	Oldham	4	Swinton	17,577	£1,050

Year	Winners		Runners-up		Venue	Attendance	Receipts
1935	Castleford	11	Barrow	5	Swinton	24,469	£1,534
	Huddersfield	21	Hull	5	Leeds	37,111	£2,753
1936	Leeds	10	Huddersfield	5	Wakefield	37,906	£2,456
	Warrington	7	Salford	2	Wigan	41,538	£2,796
1937	Keighley	0	Wakefield T.	0	Leeds	39,998	£2,793
Replay	Keighley	5	Wakefield T.	3	Huddersfield	14,400	£1,052
	Widnes	13	Wigan	9	Warrington	29,260	£1,972
1938	Barrow	4	Halifax	2	Huddersfield	31,384	£2,431
	Salford	6	Swinton	0	Belle Vue, Manchester	31,664	£2,396
1939	Halifax	10	Leeds	4	Bradford	64,453	£3,645
	Salford	11	Wigan	2	Rochdale	40,000	£2,154
●	*During the war the semi-finals were two-legged and the finals were not played at Wembley*						
1946	Wakefield T.	7	Hunslet	3	Leeds	33,000	£4,991
	Wigan	12	Widnes	5	Swinton	36,976	£4,746
1947	Bradford N.	11	Warrington	7	Swinton	33,474	£4,946
	Leeds	21	Wakefield T.	0	Huddersfield	35,136	£6,339
1948	Bradford N.	14	Hunslet	7	Leeds	38,125	£7,437
	Wigan	11	Rochdale H.	0	Swinton	26,004	£4,206
1949	Bradford N.	10	Barrow	0	Swinton	26,572	£4,646
	Halifax	11	Huddersfield	10	Bradford	61,875	£8,638
1950	Warrington	16	Leeds	4	Bradford	69,898	£9,861
	Widnes	8	Bradford N.	0	Wigan	25,390	£3,936
1951	Barrow	14	Leeds	14	Bradford	57,459	£8,248
Replay	Barrow	28	Leeds	13	Huddersfield	31,078	£5,098
	Wigan	3	Warrington	2	Swinton	44,621	£7,358
1952	Featherstone R.	6	Leigh	2	Leeds	35,621	£6,494
	Workington T.	5	Barrow	2	Wigan	31,206	£4,782
1953	Huddersfield	7	Wigan	0	Bradford	58,722	£10,519
	St. Helens	9	Warrington	3	Swinton	38,059	£7,768
1954	Halifax	18	Hunslet	3	Bradford	46,961	£8,243
	Warrington	8	Leeds	4	Swinton	36,993	£7,596
1955	Barrow	9	Hunslet	6	Wigan	25,493	£4,671
	Workington T.	13	Featherstone R.	2	Leeds	33,499	£7,305
1956	Halifax	11	Wigan	10	Bradford	51,889	£9,054
	St. Helens	5	Barrow	5	Swinton	38,897	£7,793
Replay	St. Helens	10	Barrow	5	Wigan	44,731	£7,750
1957	Barrow	2	Leigh	2	Wigan	34,628	£6,340
Replay	Barrow	15	Leigh	10	Swinton	28,081	£5,695
	Leeds	10	Whitehaven	9	Bradford	49,094	£8,987
1958	Wigan	5	Rochdale H.	3	Swinton	28,597	£6,354
	Workington T.	8	Featherstone R.	2	Bradford	31,517	£6,325
1959	Wigan	5	Leigh	0	Swinton	27,906	£6,068
	Hull	15	Featherstone R.	5	Bradford	52,131	£9,776
1960	Wakefield T.	11	Featherstone R.	2	Bradford	55,935	£10,390
	Hull	12	Oldham	9	Swinton	27,545	£6,093
1961	St. Helens	26	Hull	9	Bradford	42,935	£9,231
	Wigan	19	Halifax	10	Swinton	35,118	£7,557
1962	Wakefield T.	9	Featherstone R.	0	Bradford	43,625	£8,496
	Huddersfield	6	Hull K.R.	0	Bradford	31,423	£6,685

Year	Winners		Runners-up		Venue	Attendance	Receipts
1963	Wakefield T.	5	Warrington	2	Swinton	15,565	£3,530
	Wigan	18	Hull K.R.	4	Leeds	21,420	£6,029
1964	Widnes	7	Castleford	7	Swinton	25,603	£5,541
Replay	Widnes	7	Castleford	5	Wakefield	28,739	£5,313
	Hull K.R.	5	Oldham	5	Leeds	28,823	£7,411
Replay	Hull K.R.	14	Oldham	17	Swinton	27,209	£5,929

● *Score after 80 minutes was 14-14, then bad light caused match to be abandoned after 12 minutes of extra time with Oldham winning 17-14*

Year	Winners		Runners-up		Venue	Attendance	Receipts
Second Replay	Hull K.R.	12	Oldham	2	Huddersfield	28,732	£6,183
1965	Wigan	25	Swinton	10	St. Helens	26,658	£6,384
	Hunslet	8	Wakefield T.	0	Leeds	21,262	£6,090
1966	St. Helens	12	Dewsbury	5	Swinton	13,046	£3,102
	Wigan	7	Leeds	2	Huddersfield	22,758	£5,971
1967	Featherstone R.	16	Leeds	8	Huddersfield	20,052	£6,276
	Barrow	14	Dewsbury	9	Swinton	13,744	£4,560
1968	Leeds	25	Wigan	4	Swinton	30,058	£9,845
	Wakefield T.	0	Huddersfield	0	Bradford	21,569	£6,196
Replay	Wakefield T.	15	Huddersfield	10	Leeds	20,983	£6,425
1969	Castleford	16	Wakefield T.	10	Leeds	21,497	£8,477
	Salford	15	Warrington	8	Wigan	20,600	£7,738
1970	Castleford	6	St. Helens	3	Swinton	18,913	£7,171
	Wigan	19	Hull K.R.	8	Leeds	18,495	£7,862
1971	Leeds	19	Castleford	8	Bradford	24,464	£9,120
	Leigh	10	Huddersfield	4	Wigan	14,875	£5,670
1972	St. Helens	10	Warrington	10	Wigan	19,300	£8,250
Replay	St. Helens	10	Warrington	6	Wigan	32,380	£12,604
	Leeds	16	Halifax	3	Bradford	16,680	£6,851
1973	Featherstone R.	17	Castleford	3	Leeds	15,369	£9,454
	Bradford N.	23	Dewsbury	7	Leeds	14,028	£9,221
1974	Warrington	17	Dewsbury	7	Wigan	11,789	£6,821
	Featherstone R.	21	Leigh	14	Leeds	7,971	£4,461
1975	Widnes	13	Wakefield T.	7	Bradford	9,155	£5,856
	Warrington	11	Leeds	4	Wigan	13,168	£9,581
1976	Widnes	15	Featherstone R.	9	Swinton	13,019	£9,078
	St. Helens	5	Keighley	4	Huddersfield	9,829	£6,113
1977	Leeds	7	St. Helens	2	Wigan	12,974	£11,379
	Widnes	14	Hull K.R.	5	Leeds	17,053	£16,068
1978	Leeds	14	Featherstone R.	9	Bradford	12,824	£11,322
	St. Helens	12	Warrington	8	Wigan	16,167	£13,960
1979	Widnes	14	Bradford N.	11	Swinton	14,324	£16,363
	Wakefield T.	9	St. Helens	7	Leeds	12,393	£14,195
1980	Hull K.R.	20	Halifax	7	Leeds	17,910	£31,650
	Hull	10	Widnes	5	Swinton	18,347	£29,415
1981	Widnes	17	Warrington	9	Wigan	12,624	£20,673
	Hull K.R.	22	St. Helens	5	Leeds	17,073	£30,616
1982	Hull	15	Castleford	11	Leeds	21,207	£41,867
	Widnes	11	Leeds	8	Swinton	13,075	£25,796
1983	Featherstone R.	11	Bradford N.	6	Leeds	10,784	£22,579
	Hull	14	Castleford	7	Elland Rd., L'ds	26,031	£65,498
1984	Wigan	14	York	8	Elland Rd., L'ds	17,156	£52,888
	Widnes	15	Leeds	4	Swinton	14,046	£37,183

180

Year	Winners		Runners-up		Venue	Attendance	Receipts
1985	Wigan	18	Hull K.R.	11	Elland Rd., L'ds	19,275	£70,192
	Hull	10	Castleford	10	Leeds	20,982	£64,163
Replay	Hull	22	Castleford	16	Leeds	20,968	£65,005
1986	Castleford	18	Oldham	7	Wigan	12,430	£38,296
	Hull K.R.	24	Leeds	24	Elland Rd., L'ds	23,866	£83,757
Replay	Hull K.R.	17	Leeds	0	Elland Rd., L'ds	32,485	£113,345
1987	St. Helens	14	Leigh	8	Wigan	13,105	£48,627
	Halifax	12	Widnes	8	Leeds	16,064	£61,260
1988	Wigan	34	Salford	4	Bolton W. FC	20,783	£95,876
	Halifax	0	Hull	0	Leeds	20,534	£82,026
Replay	Halifax	4	Hull	3	Elland Rd., L'ds	25,117	£113,679
1989	St. Helens	16	Widnes	14	Wigan	17,119	£70,411
	Wigan	13	Warrington	6	Man. C. FC	26,529	£144,056
1990	Wigan	20	St. Helens	14	Man. U. FC	26,489	£177,161
	Warrington	10	Oldham	6	Wigan	15,631	£80,500
1991	Wigan	30	Oldham	16	Bolton W. FC	19,057	£116,937
	St. Helens	19	Widnes	2	Wigan	16,109	£81,342
1992	Castleford	8	Hull	4	Leeds	14,636	£91,225
	Wigan	71	Bradford N.	10	Bolton W. FC	18,027	£131,124

NON-LEAGUE CLUBS IN THE CHALLENGE CUP

AMATEUR clubs were invited to compete in the 1986 Rugby League Challenge Cup after a five-year break. The League asked for two of the three county cup competition winners to enter the preliminary round.

The League later decided that from 1987 the Silk Cut Challenge Cup campaign would feature 38 teams, amateur clubs joining the professionals for a preliminary round of six ties.

In the early years of the Northern Union Challenge Cup — as it was then called — the line between professional and amateur was less clearly defined.

A variety of Leagues also make it difficult to set non-League clubs apart. Fifty-six clubs appeared in the inaugurating first round of 1897 and four others received byes. The complications continued until 1904 when the League format settled down and non-League clubs had to qualify for the first round.

Between 1904 and 1907 there was a preliminary round of up to 14 ties involving mostly non-league clubs. In 1906-07 SAVILLE GREEN beat Bramley 10-0, and NEWINGTON ROVERS drew 3-3 and 13-13 with York before losing 14-5.

Not since 1909 when BEVERLEY beat Ebbw Vale 7-2 has a senior team been knocked out by a non-League club although amateur teams twice had victories in the two-leg era of 1946-54.

NON-LEAGUE CLUB VICTORIES OVER SENIOR CLUBS SINCE 1904
(Excluding preliminary rounds before 1908)
Non-League Clubs in Capitals

1905-06
*FEATHERSTONE ROVERS 23 v. Widnes 2
 (second round)

1907-08
WHITEHAVEN RECREATION 13 v. St. Helens 8
 (Lost 33-5 at Merthyr Tydfil in second round)

1908-09
BEVERLEY 7 v. Ebbw Vale 2
 (Lost 53-2 at Halifax in second round)

1945-46
SHARLSTON 12 v. Workington Town 7
 (1st leg) (Workington Town won 2nd leg 16-2)

1947-48
RISEHOW and GILLHEAD 10 v. Keighley 2 (2nd leg)
 (Keighley won 1st leg 11-0)

*FEATHERSTONE ROVERS are the only non-League club to appear in the third round when they lost 3-0 at Keighley. In the first round they beat BROOKLAND ROVERS 16-5.

There have been seven drawn clashes, with the professional club winning through each time. The last draw was in 1986-87 when KELLS drew 4-4 with Fulham at Whitehaven. Fulham won the replay 22-14 at Chiswick.

There have been several other instances of non-League clubs meeting in the first round. The last occasion was in 1960 when WALNEY CENTRAL beat LOCK LANE 10-5 before losing at Oldham 55-4 in the second round.

In 1964 THAMES BOARD MILLS received a bye when Bradford Northern disbanded, but lost 48-8 at Blackpool Borough in the second round.

CHALLENGE CUP PROGRESS CHART

A 20-year review ....

Key: W — Winners. F — Beaten finalists. SF — Semi-final. P — Preliminary round.

	1991-92	1990-91	1989-90	1988-89	1987-88	1986-87	1985-86	1984-85	1983-84	1982-83	1981-82	1980-81	1979-80	1978-79	1977-78	1976-77	1975-76	1974-75	1973-74	1972-73
BARROW	2	2	1	2	1	2	2	P	1	2	2	1	2	3	1	2	1	1	1	1
BATLEY	1	1	1	1	1	1	1	1	1	1	2	1	1	1	1	1	1	1	1	
BRADFORD N.	SF	3	3	2	1	2	3	3	3	SF	3	1	3	SF	3	3	2	3	3	F
BRAMLEY	P	1	1	P	P	1	2	3	1	1	1	1	1	2	1	1	1	1	2	1
CARLISLE	P	P	1	2	1	2	1	1	P	1	1									
CASTLEFORD	F	1	P	2	1	1	W	SF	3	SF	SF	2	2	3	3	3	1	1	1	SF
CHORLEY B.	P	1	1																	
DEWSBURY	2	1	2	1	1	1	1	1	1	1	1	2	1	2	1	3	1	1	SF	SF
DONCASTER	2	1	P	1	3	1	2	P	2	1	1	1	1	1	1	2	1	1	1	
FEATHERSTONE R.	3	1	1	3	2	1	1	P	1	W	P	3	1	1	SF	2	SF	1	F	W
HALIFAX	3	3	1	1	F	W	1	2	1	2	3	2	SF	1	1	1	1	1	1	1
HIGHFIELD	1	1	1	1	1	1	1	2	1	2	1	1	1	1	1	1	1	1	2	1
HUDDERSFIELD	P	P	P	1	P	1	1	1	1	1	1	1	2	3	3	1	1	1	1	1
HULL	SF	P	2	1	SF	3	1	F	2	F	W	2	F	3	2	2	1	2	1	2
HULL K.R.	1	1	1	3	3	3	F	SF	3	1	2	F	W	2	1	SF	2	3	2	2
HUNSLET	2	1	1	P	1	2	1	3	2	3	1	1	1	1	2	1	2	3	1	2
KEIGHLEY C.	1	2	2	2	2	2	1	1	1	1	2	2	1	1	SF	1	1	1		
LEEDS	2	2	P	3	2	3	SF	1	SF	2	SF	1	2	1	W	W	3	SF	3	1
LEIGH	1	1	1	1	1	SF	3	2	1	1	3	2	1	2	1	1	3	2	SF	2
LONDON C.	2	1	2	1	1	1	1	1	2	2	2	1								
NOTTINGHAM C.	P	1	1	1	2	2	P	1												
OLDHAM	1	SF	SF	3	1	2	SF	1	2	1	2	3	2	2	2	1	3	3	1	3
ROCHDALE H.	1	2	2	1	2	1	2	2	1	1	2	1	2	1	2	1	2	2	2	
RYEDALE-YORK	1	1	1	1	1	P	2	1	SF	1	1	2	2	1	1	1	2	2	1	1
ST. HELENS	3	F	SF	F	3	F	2	1	3	3	1	SF	2	SF	F	SF	W	2	3	2
SALFORD	1	3	2	1	SF	1	1	2	1	2	1	3	3	1	2	2	2	2	2	1
SCARBOROUGH P.	1																			
SHEFFIELD E.	2	2	2	2	2	1	1	1												
SWINTON	1	1	1	1	1	P	P	1	P	2	1	1	1	1	2	2	1	1	2	1
TRAFFORD B.	1	1	2	2	2	1	2	1	1	1	1	1	1	1	1	1	1	1		
WAKEFIELD T.	1	2	3	2	1	2	1	2	2	3	3	3	F	2	2	1	SF	1	3	
WARRINGTON	2	3	F	SF	2	1	2	2	2	3	1	SF	3	1	SF	1	3	F	W	3
WHITEHAVEN	1	2	3	1	P	3	1	1	1	1	1	1	1	1	1	1	1	1	1	1
WIDNES	1	SF	3	SF	3	SF	3	3	W	1	F	W	SF	W	3	F	F	W	2	2
WIGAN	W	W	W	W	W	1	3	W	F	1	2	1	1	2	2	2	2	2	3	3
WORKINGTON T.	3	2	1	P	1	P	1	2	2	3	2	2	1	1	2	3	2	2	2	

REGAL TROPHY

1991-92 Final

Underdogs Widnes lifted the Regal Trophy with a record winning margin, inspired by Les Holliday only 24 hours after the loose forward asked to come off the transfer list.

The £95,000-rated Great Britain and Cumbria packman earned the Man of the Match award, despite limping off on the hour, having scored a try and created two other touchdowns, plus opening the scoring with a drop goal.

Leeds coach Doug Laughton suffered at the hands of a side he built during his second reign at Widnes, his new charges entering the Wigan final as form favourites with 10 successive victories to their credit.

But the Chemics found the winning formula despite being without three injured star forwards in Esene Faimalo, Paul Moriarty and Emosi Koloto, plus Test half-back pairing Tony Myler and David Hulme. In addition, veteran coach Frank Myler made the controversial decision to axe Great Britain tour candidate Phil McKenzie, preferring Paul Hulme at hooker.

Leeds, lacking only long-term casualty Ellery Hanley, never looked like winning their first major open trophy since, ironically, beating Widnes in the same competition eight years ago.

On a heavily sanded Central Park pitch, the below-strength Widnes pack dominated the forward battle, laying the foundations for a four-try success, plus three disallowed efforts, in the widest winning margin in the 21 years of the tournament.

Widnes also gained supremacy at half back, despite utility back Barry Dowd making a rare appearance at scrum half, a replacement for flu victim David Hulme. Dowd overshadowed Bobby Goulding, who showed only flashes of his Test form.

The eagerly awaited stand-off duel between rival skippers Garry Schofield and Jonathan Davies was not the classic encounter anticipated. Both looked a degree under after suffering bouts of flu, Davies taking the honours by scoring a try and kicking three goals and a drop goal, collecting his first major trophy as skipper of the Chemics.

Winger John Bentley was the only Leeds back to cause Widnes much trouble and more should have been made of his ability to break tackles while in full stride.

It was unfair that the failure of New Zealand full back Morvin Edwards to field Holliday's towering kick which led to the loose forward's try overshadowed the two he successfully took under extreme pressure. Edwards could hardly be singled out for the Loiners conceding more points than in any match up to that point of the season.

The glaring weakness was up front, exposed alarmingly in the closing minutes when veteran Kiwi forwards Joe Grima and Kurt Sorensen charged through from halfway for the latter to get the final touchdown.

The Sorensen try came only a minute after Leeds had squandered their only scoring chance, centre David Creasser failing to ground the ball having been put through by ex-Widnes forward Mike O'Neill.

Big-spending Leeds failed to earn a dividend from their investment in the recruitment of coaching and playing talent, remaining a side of potential rather than achievement. Widnes confirmed that they were still a power in the battle for trophies — lifting a prize cheque for £32,000 — despite the absence of a quintet of star performers, plus ace winger Martin Offiah, freshly signed by Wigan.

The Chemics recorded their third Trophy success while extending their record number of appearances in the final to eight.

REGAL TROPHY FINAL

11 January		**Wigan**
WIDNES 24		**LEEDS 0**

Alan Tait	1.	Morvin Edwards
John Devereux	2.	Phil Ford
Andy Currier	3.	David Creasser
Darren Wright	4.	Simon Irving
Mark Sarsfield	5.	John Bentley
Jonathan Davies, Capt.	6.	Garry Schofield, Capt.
Barry Dowd	7.	Bobby Goulding
Kurt Sorensen	8.	Shaun Wane
Paul Hulme	9.	Richard Gunn
David Smith	10.	Mike O'Neill
Harvey Howard	11.	Roy Powell
Richard Eyres	12.	Paul Dixon
Les Holliday	13.	Gary Divorty
Paul Atcheson	14.	Carl Gibson
Joe Grima	15.	Steve Molloy

T: Davies, Holliday, Tait, Sorensen
G: Davies (3, 1dg), Holliday (dg)
Substitutions:
Atcheson for Sarsfield (73 min.)
Grima for Holliday (59 min.)
Referee: Brian Galtress (Bradford)

Substitutions:
Molloy for Wane (46 min.)
Gibson for Irving (53 min.)
Half-time: 7-0
Attendance: 15,070

Widnes celebrate their third Regal Trophy haul, by a record winning margin.

Meeting of rival skippers, Garry Schofield of Leeds (upper) and Jonathan Davies, the Widnes captain eventually coming out on top with an 11-point tally.

1991-92 Round by Round

Amateurs Leigh East provided the shock of the six-tie preliminary round by beating Third Division strugglers Chorley 20-10 at Leigh, despite having two players sent off, one in each half. The other amateur entrants, Saddleworth Rangers, went out 30-0 to Second Division Workington Town at Oldham, the visitors scoring five tries. Weakened Wigan were held to a 12-10 interval lead by Third Division pacesetters Dewsbury at Central Park before stepping up a gear to run in a further four tries in a 34-14 success. Underdogs Rochdale Hornets entertained Widnes and opened the scoring after four minutes, the Chemics not taking the lead until after the break en route to a 24-14 victory. Leigh travelled to Hull lacking seven first-team regulars and led 7-6 after 48 minutes, but then the Airlie Birds rallied and scored three tries in 18 minutes to secure a 22-7 win. Despite a below-par performance, Sheffield Eagles ran in six tries against visitors Scarborough Pirates, making their debut in the Regal Trophy with a 36-8 defeat.

In the first round, Leeds skipper Ellery Hanley returned from injury to play a significant role in their 17-8 victory at Warrington in a televised tie marred by the sending off of Wire winger Mark Forster for a late high tackle on visiting Kiwi full back Morvin Edwards. Amateurs Leigh East crashed 76-0 at Bradford Northern, who topped the previous club record by four points with 15 tries and eight goals in their first win since the arrival of manager Peter Fox. Doncaster defied a 17-strong injury list to beat visitors Whitehaven 21-20 in a see-saw encounter, the lead changing hands five times. Third Division Barrow defended well to trail only 10-0 at half-time at Halifax, who scored two tries in two minutes after the break on the way to a 46-4 success.

Highfield led Carlisle 10-2 at the break with two Simon Ashcroft tries before the Cumbrian visitors ran in four tries in 13 minutes in a 28-10 victory. Alex Murphy could be proud of his Third Division Huddersfield charges against his former club St. Helens, holding the First Division leaders to 10-0 at half-time before superior pace and class produced a final score of 32-10. The marksmanship of five-goal Castleford forward Martin Ketteridge was a major factor in their 22-10 success at Hull K.R. Third Division leaders Hunslet went down 25-10 at Keighley, for whom Man of the Match Johnny Walker, the ex-Otley RU winger, scored a hat-trick of tries.

Visitors Wakefield Trinity scored 22 points in as many minutes at Nottingham before the side with the worst defensive record in the league made the First Division outfit work hard for a 42-11 victory. Oldham struggled before clinching a 16-10 victory over London Crusaders with two tries in the last 10 minutes at the Watersheddings. A powerful forward display embodied by Kiwi duo Des Maea and Tony Tuimavave gave Sheffield Eagles a 13-6 success at fog-bound Ryedale-York. Australian full back Steve Gibson notched four tries in Salford's 14-touchdown tally against lowly Third Division visitors Trafford Borough, who crashed 74-10.

Wigan recorded a 34-8 triumph at Swinton, Man of the Match Andy Platt sealing victory with the creation of a try for Shaun Edwards in the 52nd minute. Widnes gained revenge for a Lancashire Cup exit at the hands of Workington Town by registering a 26-8 home success over the Cumbrians, who took the lead with a Martin Oglanby try. Veteran props Jeff Grayshon and Neil Kellett were the stars of Third Division Batley's creditable performance at waterlogged Hull, the Boulevarders scraping home 12-8. Third Division Bramley came within inches of a shock home win over First Division Featherstone

Rovers, a Steve Carroll drop goal attempt dropping just below the crossbar with three minutes left and the score level at 18-18. In the replay two days later, Rovers outclassed Bramley in an eight-try 44-8 spree, their first win in nine outings.

The second round was blighted by Ellery Hanley's jaw being broken in three places during the televised Leeds tie at Hull. No one was sent off for the off-the-ball incident, Man of the Match Garry Schofield inspiring a 12-4 Loiners success, his first win at the Boulevard since leaving Hull four years earlier. Playing their third cup-tie in six days, Featherstone Rovers were reduced to 12 men but still ran in nine tries in a 28-minute spell en route to a surprising 64-18 success over visitors Halifax. Bradford Northern's back row of David Hobbs, Karl Fairbank and John Pendlebury took the honours in a 44-10 home victory over Second Division pacesetters Sheffield Eagles, Hobbs contributing 20 points with a try and eight goals. Widnes full back Alan Tait scored a try after only 40 seconds as the Chemics won 30-16 at Carlisle, Man of the Match Jonathan Davies sealing success with a try on the hour.

Oldham wasted two clear-cut chances in the last quarter to go down 24-18 to First Division leaders St. Helens in an entertaining Watersheddings encounter. Salford recorded their seventh win in eight matches with a 30-10 victory at Wakefield Trinity, who never recovered from the dismissal of centre Chris Perry for an alleged trip in the 10th minute. Keighley's hopes of a shock win at Wigan lasted only half an hour after opening up an 8-0 lead in seven minutes, the home side's recovery being highlighted by a hat-trick of tries for Man of the Match, debutant winger Stuart Turner in the 32-8 win. Full back Graham Steadman returned from a two-match ban to claim a hat-trick of tries in the 38-6 defeat of visitors Doncaster, who provided the Man of the Match in

centre Vila Matautia.

In the third round, Leeds stormed to a 24-4 home success over Castleford in front of a crowd of over 15,400. Leading only 6-0 at the break, the Loiners opened up in the second half with superb attacking raids down both flanks, Paul Dixon taking the Man of the Match award with two tries. Salford earned a semi-final place for the first time in 12 years with a magnificent second-half fightback in the home tie against Wigan. The Red Devils came back from 12-4 down to record their second victory over Wigan in three weeks with a 24-14 success. Widnes disposed of visitors Featherstone Rovers 34-22, but only after Rovers had rocked them with two powerful recoveries, two points separating the sides with only seven minutes left. Tries from David Hulme and Jonathan Davies clinched victory. St. Helens centre Alan Hunte scored a hat-trick of tries in their 30-12 defeat of Bradford Northern at Knowsley Road, the visitors' misery being completed when skipper David Hobbs was sent off for an alleged high tackle in the 74th minute.

Bradford City FC's Valley Parade hosted its first representative fixture with the semi-final tie between Leeds and Salford, who dominated the first half to lead 11-2 at the break. Flu victim Garry Schofield inspired an impressive Leeds comeback, Simon Irving's new boots kicking five goals from five attempts in a 22-15 Leeds victory. Two weeks later, Widnes avenged the previous season's Silk Cut Challenge Cup semi-final defeat by St. Helens with an 18-10 win at Wigan. First Widnes, then St. Helens, defied the heavy rain and strong wind to serve up high-speed, open football, the Chemics building a 16-0 lead in half an hour before Saints rallied with a brace of Gary Connolly tries. Widnes skipper Davies passed the 1,000-point mark, less than three years after turning professional.

Les Holliday, 1992 Regal final Man of the Match.

1991-92 RESULTS

Preliminary Round

Hull	22	Leigh	7
Leigh East (at Leigh)	20	Chorley B.	10
Rochdale H.	14	Widnes	24
Saddleworth R. (at Oldham)	0	Workington T.	30
Sheffield E.	36	Scarborough P.	8
Wigan	34	Dewsbury	14

First Round

Bradford N.	76	Leigh East	0
Bramley	18	Featherstone R.	18
Doncaster	21	Whitehaven	20
Halifax	46	Barrow	4
Highfield	10	Carlisle	28
Huddersfield	10	St. Helens	32
Hull	12	Batley	8
Hull K.R.	10	Castleford	22
Keighley C.	25	Hunslet	10
Nottingham C.	11	Wakefield T.	42
Oldham	16	London C.	10
Ryedale-York	6	Sheffield E.	13
Salford	74	Trafford B.	10
Swinton	8	Wigan	34
Warrington	8	Leeds	17
Widnes	26	Workington T.	8

Replay

Featherstone R.	44	Bramley	8

Second Round

Bradford N.	44	Sheffield E.	10
Carlisle	16	Widnes	30
Castleford	38	Doncaster	6
Featherstone R.	64	Halifax	18
Hull	4	Leeds	12
Oldham	18	St. Helens	24
Wakefield T.	10	Salford	30
Wigan	32	Keighley	8

Third Round

Leeds	24	Castleford	4
St. Helens	30	Bradford N.	12
Salford	24	Wigan	14
Widnes	34	Featherstone R.	22

Semi-Finals

Leeds (at Bradford C. FC)	22	Salford	15
Widnes (at Wigan)	18	St. Helens	10

Final

Widnes (at Wigan)	24	Leeds	0

1991-92 PRIZES

Preliminary Round	£2,250 each club
First Round	£2,250 to losers
Second Round	£3,500 to losers
Third Round	£5,500 to losers
Semi-Finals	£9,000 to losers
Runners-up	£17,000
Winners	£32,000

Total Prize Money	£180,000
Capital Development Fund	£120,000
Grand Total	£300,000

REGAL TROPHY ROLL OF HONOUR

Season	Winners		Runners-up		Venue	Attendance	Receipts
1971-72	Halifax	22	Wakefield T.	11	Bradford	7,975	£2,545
1972-73	Leeds	12	Salford	7	Huddersfield	10,102	£4,563
1973-74	Warrington	27	Rochdale H.	16	Wigan	9,347	£4,380
1974-75	Bradford N.	3	Widnes	2	Warrington	5,935	£3,305
1975-76	Widnes	19	Hull	13	Leeds	9,035	£6,275
1976-77	Castleford	25	Blackpool B.	15	Salford	4,512	£2,919
1977-78	Warrington	9	Widnes	4	St. Helens	10,258	£8,429
1978-79	Widnes	16	Warrington	4	St. Helens	10,743	£11,709
1979-80	Bradford N.	6	Widnes	0	Leeds	9,909	£11,560
1980-81	Warrington	12	Barrow	5	Wigan	12,820	£21,020
1981-82	Hull	12	Hull K.R.	4	Leeds	25,245	£42,987
1982-83	Wigan	15	Leeds	4	Elland Rd, Leeds	19,553	£49,027
1983-84	Leeds	18	Widnes	10	Wigan	9,510	£19,824
1984-85	Hull K.R.	12	Hull	0	Hull City FC	25,326	£69,555
1985-86	Wigan	11	Hull K.R.	8	Elland Rd, Leeds	17,573	£66,714
1986-87	Wigan	18	Warrington	4	Bolton W. FC	21,144	£86,041
1987-88	St. Helens	15	Leeds	14	Wigan	16,669	£62,232
1988-89	Wigan	12	Widnes	6	Bolton W. FC	20,709	£94,874
1989-90	Wigan	24	Halifax	12	Leeds	17,810	£73,688
1990-91	Warrington	12	Bradford N.	2	Leeds	11,154	£57,652
1991-92	Widnes	24	Leeds	0	Wigan	15,070	£90,453

REGAL TROPHY FINAL ....
A REVIEW
1971-72
Halifax 22 Hepworth; Rayner, Davies (1t), Willicombe (1t), Kelly (1t); Burton (5g), Baker (Sanderson); Dewhirst, Hawksley, Callon (1t), (Reeves), Fogerty, J. Martin, Halmshaw
Wakefield T. 11 Wraith (Ward); Slater (1t), Marston, Hegarty, Major; Topliss (1t), Harkin; Jeanes, Morgan, Lyons, Harrison (Spencer), Valentine (1t), N. Fox (1g)
Referee: S. Shepherd (Oldham)
1972-73
Leeds 12 Holmes (1g); Alan Smith, Hynes, Dyl, Atkinson (2t); Hardisty, Hepworth; Clawson (2g) (Ward), Fisher (Pickup), Jeanes, Haigh, Cookson, Eccles
Salford 7 Charlton; Colloby, Watkins (2g), Hesketh, Richards; Gill (P. Ward), Banner; Ramshaw, J. Ward, Mackay, Grice (Davies), Kirkbride, Dixon (1t)
Referee: W.H. Thompson (Huddersfield)

1973-74
Warrington 27 Whitehead (6g, 1t); M. Philbin, Noonan (2t), Reynolds (Pickup), Bevan (1t); Whittle, Gordon; D. Chisnall, (Nicholas 1t), Ashcroft, Brady, Wright, Wanbon, B. Philbin
Rochdale H. 16 Crellin; Brelsford (2t), Brophy (1t), Taylor (1t), Aspinall; Butler (Wood), Gartland; Holliday (2g), Harris, Whitehead, Fogerty, Sheffield, Halmshaw
Referee: D.G. Kershaw (York)
1974-75
Bradford N. 3 Carlton (1t); Francis, Ward, Gant, D. Redfearn; Blacker, Seabourne; Earl, Jarvis, Jackson, Joyce, Trotter, Fearnley
Widnes 2 Dutton (1g); A. Prescott, D.O'Neill, Aspey, Anderson; Hughes, Bowden; Mills, Elwell, Sheridan, Adams, Blackwood, Laughton
Referee: G.F. Lindop (Wakefield)

189

1975-76
Widnes 19 Dutton (3g); A. Prescott, George,
Aspey, Jenkins (2t); Hughes, Bowden (1t, 1dg);
Mills, Elwell, Wood, Foran, Sheridan,
Adams (1t)
Hull 13 Stephenson; A. Macklin, Clark, Portz,
Hunter (1t); Hancock, Foulkes (Davidson);
Ramsey, Flanagan, Wardell, Boxall (2g),
Walker, Crane (2t)
Referee: J.V. Moss (Manchester)
1976-77
Castleford 25 Wraith (1t); Fenton, Joyner (1t),
P. Johnson (1t), Briggs; Burton (1t), Stephens
(1t); Khan, Spurr, A. Dickinson, Reilly, Lloyd
(5g), S. Norton
Blackpool B. 15 Reynolds; Robinson, Heritage,
Machen (1t), Pitman (Lamb); Marsh, Newall;
Hamilton, Allen (1t), Egan (3g, 1t), Gamble,
Groves (Hurst), M. Pattinson
Referee: M.J. Naughton (Widnes)
1977-78
Warrington 9 Finnegan; Hesford (3g), Benyon,
Wilson, Bevan (1t); K. Kelly, Gordon; Lester,
Dalgreen, Nicholas, Martyn, B. Philbin, Potter
Widnes 4 Eckersley; Wright, Aspey, George,
Woods (2g); Hughes, Bowden; Ramsey, Elwell,
Shaw (Dearden), Adams, Hull, Laughton
Referee: W.H. Thompson (Huddersfield)
1978-79
Widnes 16 Eckersley; Wright (1t), Aspey,
Hughes, Burke (3g); Moran, Bowden; Mills,
Elwell (2dg), Shaw, Dearden, Hull (1t), Adams
(2dg)
Warrington 4 Finnegan; M. Kelly, Hesford
(2g), Benyon, Sutton; K. Kelly, (Hunter),
Gordon; Lester, Waller, Nicholas, Case,
Martyn, A. Gwilliam
Referee: G.F. Lindop (Wakefield)
1979-80
Bradford N. 6 Mumby (1g); Barends, D.
Redfearn, D. Parker (1t), Gant; Stephenson
(1dg), A. Redfearn; Thompson, Bridges,
Forsyth (I. Van Bellen), Grayshon, G. Van
Bellen (Ferres), Casey
Widnes 0 Eckersley; Wright, Aspey, George,
Burke; Hughes, Bowden; Hogan (Mills),
Elwell, Shaw, L. Gorley, Hull, Adams
Referee: W.H. Thompson (Huddersfield)
1980-81
Warrington 12 Hesford (2g, 2dg); Thackray,
I. Duane, Bevan (2t), M. Kelly; K. Kelly,
A. Gwilliam; Courtney, Waller, Case, Martyn,
Potter, Hunter (Eccles)

Barrow 5 Elliott; McConnell, French, Ball (1g),
Wainwright; Mason (1t), Cairns; D. Chisnall,
Allen (Szymala), Flynn, K. James, Kirkby,
Hadley
Referee: W.H. Thompson (Huddersfield)
1981-82
Hull 12 Banks; O'Hara, Harrison, Leuluai,
Prendiville; Day, Dean (1dg) (K. Harkin);
Skerrett, Wileman (1t), Stone, Crane, L.
Crooks (4g), Norton
Hull K.R. 4 Fairbairn (2g); Hubbard, M.
Smith, Hogan, Muscroft; Hartley, P. Harkin
(Burton); Holdstock (Millington), Watkinson,
S. Crooks, Lowe, Casey, Hall
Referee: G.F. Lindop (Wakefield)
1982-83
Wigan 15 Williams; Ramsdale, Stephenson,
Whitfield (4g, 1dg), Gill (1t) (Juliff 1t); M.
Foy, Fairhurst; Shaw, Kiss, Campbell, West
(Case), Scott, Pendlebury
Leeds 4 Hague; Campbell, Wilkinson, Dyl,
Andy Smith; Holmes, Dick (2g); Dickinson,
Ward, Burke, Sykes, W. Heron, D. Heron
Referee: R. Campbell (Widnes)
1983-84
Leeds 18 Wilkinson; Prendiville, Creasser (5g),
D. Bell, Andy Smith; Holmes (1t), Dick (1t);
Keith Rayne, Ward (Squire), Kevin Rayne,
Moorby, Laurie, Webb
Widnes 10 Burke (1g); Wright, Keiron
O'Loughlin, Lydon (1t), Linton (1t); Hughes,
Gregory; S. O'Neill, Elwell, K. Tamati,
L. Gorley, Whitfield, Adams
Referee: W.H. Thompson (Huddersfield)
1984-85
Hull K.R. 12 Fairbairn; Clark (1t), Robinson,
Prohm (1t), Laws; M. Smith, Harkin;
Broadhurst, Watkinson, Ema, Burton, Hogan
(1t), Miller
Hull 0 Kemble (Schofield); S. Evans, Ah Kuoi,
Leuluai, O'Hara; Topliss, Sterling; Edmonds
(Dannatt), Patrick, Rose, L. Crooks, Proctor,
Divorty
Referee: S. Wall (Leigh)
1985-86
Wigan 11 Hampson; Mordt, Stephenson (1g),
Hanley, Gill (Edwards); Ella, M. Ford (1t);
Dowling (1dg), Kiss, Wane (1t), West,
Goodway, Potter (Du Toit)
Hull K.R. 8 Lydiat (1t); Clark, M. Smith,
Dorahy, Laws (1t); G. Smith, Harkin;
P. Johnston (Robinson), Watkinson, Ema,
Burton, Kelly, Miller
Referee: J. Holdsworth (Kippax)

1986-87
Wigan 18 Hampson; Stephenson, Lydon, Bell
(1t), Gill (2t, 1g); Hanley, Edwards; West,
Dermott, Case, Roberts, Potter, Goodway (1t)
Warrington 4 Johnson; Meadows, Cullen,
Ropati, Forster (1t); K. Kelly, Peters (Duane);
Boyd, K. Tamati (Rathbone), Jackson,
Sanderson, Roberts, M. Gregory
Referee: J. Holdsworth (Kippax)
1987-88
St. Helens 15 Veivers; Tanner, Loughlin
(2t, 3g), Elia, Quirk; Cooper, Holding (1dg);
Burke, Groves, Souto (Evans), Forber,
Haggerty, Platt
Leeds 14 Gurr; Morris, Schofield, Jackson (1t),
Basnett (Gibson); Creasser (1t, 3g), Ashton;
Tunks, Maskill, Kevin Rayne (Fairbank),
Powell, Medley, D. Heron
Referee: G.F. Lindop (Wakefield)
1988-89
Wigan 12 Hampson; Bell, K. Iro (1t), Lydon
(2g) (Gregory), T. Iro; Byrne, Edwards;
Shelford (Goodway), Dermott, Wane, Betts,
Potter, Hanley (1t)

Widnes 6 Tait; Thackray, Currier (1g), Wright
(1t), Offiah; T. Myler, D. Hulme; Sorensen,
McKenzie, Grima, M. O'Neill, Koloto
(P. Hulme), Eyres
Referee: J. Holdsworth (Kippax)
1989-90
Wigan 24 Lydon (2g); Marshall, K. Iro, Bell,
Preston; Edwards (1t), A. Gregory; Lucas
(Wane), Dermott, Platt, Betts, Gildart
(Goodway 1t), Hanley (3t)
Halifax 12 Whitfield (Smith) (Scott);
Riddlesden, Anderson, Hetherington, George;
Dorahy, Lyons; Hill (1t), McCallion, Johnston,
Bell, Milner, Holliday (4g)
Referee: D.G. Kershaw (Easingwold)
1990-91
Warrington 12 Lyon (4g); Drummond,
Bateman, Thorniley, Forster; O'Sullivan, Ellis;
Harmon (Phillips), D. Mann, Chambers
(Thomas 1t), Mercer, McGinty, Cullen
Bradford N. 2 Wilkinson; Cordle, Shelford,
Simpson, Marchant (Hellewell); Summers, Iti;
Hobbs (1g), Noble, Hamer, Medley, Croft,
Pendlebury
Referee: J. Smith (Halifax)

REGAL TROPHY MAN OF THE MATCH

Season	Winner	Team	Position
1971-72	Bruce Burton	Halifax (v. Wakefield T.)	Stand off
1972-73	Keith Hepworth	Leeds (v. Salford)	Scrum half
1973-74	Kevin Ashcroft	Warrington (v. Rochdale H.)	Hooker
1974-75	Barry Seabourne	Bradford N. (v. Widnes)	Scrum half
1975-76	Reg Bowden	Widnes (v. Hull)	Scrum half
1976-77	Gary Stephens	Castleford	Scrum half
	Howard Allen	Blackpool B.	Hooker
1977-78	Steve Hesford	Warrington (v. Widnes)	Winger
1978-79	David Eckersley	Widnes (v. Warrington)	Full back
1979-80	Len Casey	Bradford N. (v. Widnes)	Loose forward
1980-81	Tommy Martyn	Warrington (v. Barrow)	Second row
1981-82	Trevor Skerrett	Hull (v. Hull K.R.)	Prop
1982-83	Martin Foy	Wigan (v. Leeds)	Stand off
1983-84	Mark Laurie	Leeds (v. Widnes)	Second row
1984-85	Paul Harkin	Hull K.R. (v. Hull)	Scrum half
1985-86	Paul Harkin	Hull K.R. (v. Wigan)	Scrum half
1986-87	Andy Goodway	Wigan (v. Warrington)	Loose forward
1987-88	Paul Loughlin	St. Helens (v. Leeds)	Centre
1988-89	Ellery Hanley	Wigan (v. Widnes)	Loose forward
1989-90	Ellery Hanley	Wigan (v. Halifax)	Loose forward
1990-91	Billy McGinty	Warrington (v. Bradford N.)	Second row
1991-92	Les Holliday	Widnes (v. Leeds)	Loose forward

REGAL TROPHY RECORDS

ALL ROUNDS

TEAM
Highest score: Wigan 92 v. Runcorn H. 2 (1988-89)
Biggest attendance: 25,326 Hull v. Hull K.R.
(at Hull C. FC)....... Final 1984-85

INDIVIDUAL
Most tries: 6 by Vince Gribbin (Whitehaven) v. Doncaster 1984-85
*Most goals: 17 by Sammy Lloyd (Castleford)
*Most points: 43 (17g,3t) by Sammy Lloyd (Castleford)
*The above records were achieved in the Castleford v. Millom first round tie in 1973-74.

REGAL TROPHY FINAL RECORDS

Most final appearances: 8 by Widnes
Most wins: 5 by Wigan
Most tries: 3 by Ellery Hanley (Wigan) v. Halifax
.... 1989-90
Most goals: 6 by Derek Whitehead (Warrington) v.
Rochdale H............................. 1973-74
Most points: 15 (6g,1t) by Derek Whitehead (Warrington)
v. Rochdale H......................... 1973-74
Highest score: Warrington 27 v. Rochdale H. 16 1973-74
Widest margin win: Widnes 24 v. Leeds 0..... 1991-92
Biggest attendance: 25,326 Hull v. Hull K.R.
(at Hull C. FC)............... 1984-85
Biggest receipts: £94,874 Widnes v. Wigan
(at Bolton W. FC)............... 1988-89

Jonathan Davies lifts his first trophy as skipper of Widnes.

●*BEFORE 1977-78 the competition was known as the Player's No. 6 Trophy, then the John Player Trophy. In 1983-84 it became the John Player Special Trophy, renamed the Regal Trophy in 1989-90. It was not until 1979-80 that semi-finals were played at neutral venues.*

NON-LEAGUE CLUBS IN THE REGAL TROPHY

Amateur clubs have entered the Regal tournament in every season apart from a period between 1981 and 1984. Two figured in the first round up to 1979-80 and one the following season. They were then left out from 1981-82

because the number of professional clubs had grown beyond the mathematically suitable 32.

But the amateurs returned in 1984-85 with two clubs joining the professionals in a small preliminary round, the number being increased to three in 1989-90.

The fate of the amateurs has varied from the record 88-5 hammering Millom received at Castleford to victories by Cawoods over Halifax, Myson over Batley and Leigh East over Chorley.

The full list of amateur clubs' results — all first round matches except where stated (P) Preliminary (2) Second Round — is:

Season							Attendance
1971-72		Wigan	33	v	Ace Amateurs (Hull)	9	2,678
		Thames Board Mill (Warr.)	7	v	Huddersfield	27	1,175
1972-73		Bramley	26	v	Pilkington Recs. (St. Helens)	5	616
		Dewsbury	22	v	Dewsbury Celtic	4	1,897
1973-74		Whitehaven	26	v	Dewsbury Celtic	3	1,276
		Castleford	88	v	Millom (Cumbria)	5	1,031
1974-75		Whitehaven	32	v	Lock Lane (Castleford)	6	537
		Doncaster	15	v	Kippax White Swan	6	453
1975-76		Salford	57	v	Mayfield (Rochdale)	3	3,449
		Barrow	16	v	Pilkington Recs. (St. Helens)	9	612
1976-77		Halifax	24	v	Ovenden (Halifax)	4	3,680
		Salford	39	v	Ace Amateurs (Hull)	15	3,037
1977-78		N.D.L.B. (Hull)	4	v	New Hunslet	18	3,845
		Halifax	8	v	Cawoods (Hull)	9	1,168
	(2)	Wakefield T.	31	v	Cawoods (Hull)	7	3,380
1978-79		Leigh Miners Welfare	9	v	Halifax	21	1,621
		Milford (Leeds)	5	v	Dewsbury	38	3,129
1979-80		Pilkington Recs. (St. Helens)	9	v	Wigan	18	6,707
		Blackpool B.	6	v	West Hull	3	555
1980-81		Castleford	30	v	Pilkington Recs. (St. Helens)	17	2,823
1984-85	(P)	Myson (Hull)	2	v	Dewsbury	8	1,572
	(P)	Keighley	24	v	Dudley Hill (Bradford)	10	1,570
1985-86	(P)	Keighley	24	v	Jubilee (Featherstone)	6	1,007
	(P)	West Hull	10	v	Castleford	24	2,500
1986-87	(P)	Batley	2	v	Myson (Hull)	8	687
	(P)	Millom (Cumbria)	4	v	Wakefield T.	18	2,000
		Myson (Hull)	11	v	Swinton	18	1,648
1987-88	(P)	Featherstone R.	34	v	Thatto Heath (St. Helens)	16	1,045
	(P)	Heworth (York)	5	v	Swinton	32	1,063
1988-89	(P)	Wigan St. Patricks	36	v	Elland (Halifax)	2	2,510
		Sheffield E.	80	v	Wigan St. Patricks	8	621
1989-90	(P)	Batley	28	v	West Hull	14	844
	(P)	Crosfields (Warrington)	14	v	Workington T.	19	942
	(P)	Kells (Whitehaven)	2	v	Doncaster	28	2,127
1990-91	(P)	Dudley Hill (Bradford)	18	v	Dewsbury	24	970
	(P)	Saddleworth R. (Oldham)	35	v	Egremont (Cumbria)	18	900
		Rochdale H.	30	v	Saddleworth R. (Oldham)	10	2,434
1991-92	(P)	Saddleworth R.	0	v	Workington T.	30	1,650
	(P)	Leigh East	20	v	Chorley	10	1,393
		Bradford N.	76	v	Leigh East	0	1,613

REGAL TROPHY PROGRESS CHART

Key: W — Winners. F — Beaten finalists. SF — Semi-final. P — Preliminary round.

	1991-92	1990-91	1989-90	1988-89	1987-88	1986-87	1985-86	1984-85	1983-84	1982-83	1981-82	1980-81	1979-80	1978-79	1977-78	1976-77	1975-76	1974-75	1973-74	1972-73	1971-72
BARROW	1	1	1	1	1	3	2	1	2	3	3	F	1	1	1	1	2	1	1	1	3
BATLEY	1	3	1	1	2	P	1	1	P	1	1	1	1	1	1	1	2	1	1	2	1
BRADFORD N.	3	F	2	SF	1	3	2	2	1	3	2	1	W	SF	SF	2	1	W	1	3	1
BRAMLEY	1	2	1	2	P	1	1	3	*	1	1	1	2	1	1	2	1	2	SF	2	2
CARLISLE	2	P	1	1	1	2	P	P	2	2	2										
CASTLEFORD	3	3	SF	2	2	2	1	2	1	1	2	SF	3	3	2	W	SF	1	2	1	2
CHORLEY B.	P	1	1																		
DEWSBURY	P	1	2	1	2	1	1	3	1	1	1	1	1	2	1	1	1	1	3	2	1
DONCASTER	2	2	1	2	1	2	2	1	1	1	1	1	1	1	1	1	1	2	1	1	1
FEATHERSTONE R.	3	2	3	1	1	2	P	2	3	1	2	2	2	2	3	2	1	1	1	2	1
HALIFAX	2	P	F	2	2	2	1	SF	1	1	1	3	1	2	1	2	1	1	2	1	W
HIGHFIELD	1	1	1	1	1	1	1	2	2	P	1	1	1	1	1	1	1	2	1	1	1
HUDDERSFIELD	1	1	2	1	1	P	1	1	1	2	2	2	1	1	3	1	3	1	1	2	2
HULL	2	1	1	2	3	SF	3	F	2	2	W	SF	1	2	1	3	F	1	1	3	3
HULL K.R.	1	1	1	3	2	1	F	W	2	3	F	2	1	SF	1	1	3	SF	1	SF	2
HUNSLET	1	1	2	P	1	1	2	P	1	1	2	1	1	2	1	1	1	2	1	1	1
KEIGHLEY C.	2	2	1	1	1	1	2	1	2	1	2	1	2	3	2	1	1	2	3	1	2
LEEDS	F	2	3	1	F	1	1	SF	W	F	3	1	2	1	1	3	2	3	3	W	SF
LEIGH	P	2	1	3	2	3	SF	1	SF	2	1	3	3	3	3	SF	2	1	2	2	1
LONDON C.	1	1	1	P	P	1	1	1	1	1	1	2									
NOTTINGHAM C.	1	1	1	2	1	1	1														
OLDHAM	2	2	3	1	SF	1	2	2	1	1	SF	1	1	1	2	2	2	2	1	1	1
ROCHDALE H.	P	SF	1	2	1	1	1	2	1	2	1	1	1	1	1	1	1	1	F	1	2
RYEDALE-YORK	1	P	P	1	1	P	3	1	1	2	1	2	2	1	3	1	2	2	2	2	
ST. HELENS	SF	3	SF	SF	W	3	SF	3	SF	2	1	1	2	2	2	2	3	1	SF	SF	SF
SALFORD	SF	1	2	1	3	1	2	1	2	3	3	2	SF	2	2	2	SF	3	2	F	1
SCARBOROUGH P.	P																				
SHEFFIELD E.	2	P	3	2	1	2	1	1													
SWINTON	1	1	2	1	1	2	1	1	3	1	SF	1	1	1	1	1	1	3	1	3	1
TRAFFORD B.	1	1	1	2	3	2	1	1	1	2	P	2	2	1	1	F	1	1	1	1	3
WAKEFIELD T.	2	2	P	3	2	2	2	P	1	1	1	1	SF	3	SF	1	2	2	3	2	F
WARRINGTON	1	W	P	3	3	F	3	1	2	SF	2	W	3	F	W	1	1	3	W	1	1
WHITEHAVEN	1	1	2	1	1	1	1	2	P	1	1	3	1	1	1	1	1	SF	2	1	2
WIDNES	W	SF	2	F	1	SF	3	3	F	SF	3	3	F	W	F	SF	W	F	1	3	1
WIGAN	3	3	W	W	SF	W	W	2	3	W	1	1	2	2	3	2	2	2	2	1	3
WORKINGTON T.	1	1	1	P	1	1	1	1	1	1	2	1	3	2	2	3	3	1	2	1	1

*Bramley withdrew from the Trophy while in liquidation, opponents Hull K.R. receiving a bye.

PREMIERSHIP TROPHY

1992 Final

All-conquering Wigan laid claim to being classed as the best team in Rugby League history by lifting the first-ever treble of Championship, Challenge Cup and Premiership in the same season.

St. Helens arrived at Old Trafford as Britain's second best team and for 50 minutes provided formidable opposition, deservedly leading 12-10.

After 24 successive wins, Wigan looked ready to be taken as the sun scorched down, giving credence to the theory that the Riversiders might be burnt out. Then Wigan found, not so much a second wind, but a hurricane force that blew away their derby opposition.

It struck with devastating suddenness and brought six tries in 25 stunning minutes for a final scoreline of 48-16, leaving a host of records in its wake:

● The score was not only the highest for a Stones Bitter Premiership final, but also the biggest in any cup final during the game's 97-year history.

● Frano Botica's 10 goals, a Premiership competition record, also equalled the record for any cup final — set by Austin Rhodes, of St. Helens, in the old-style Championship final of 1959.

● Botica's 20-point haul was a record for a Stones Bitter Premiership final.

The statistics are as impressive as Wigan were in the second half of a first-rate contest. Australian centre Gene Miles sparked the explosion which smashed St. Helens into submission. With Saints leading 12-10 shortly after the break, the Kangaroo broke from outside his 25 to halfway and found the inevitable Martin Offiah. Even from 50 yards out, the touchdown was a formality.

Confidence rapidly flowed through the Wigan ranks, five tries followed until

Anthony Sullivan added his second touchdown for St. Helens in the final minute.

Wigan had raced to a 36-12 lead when Offiah appeared from nowhere to waft through clutching hands for a try behind the posts. After his 10-try humiliation of Leeds in the semi-finals, the pressure was on Offiah to produce something special again and he had struggled to get into the game throughout the first half.

Once he got into his stride after the break, Offiah took his tally of tries to 30 in 16 matches, or 25 in the last nine games. However the figures are presented they only indicate that Offiah is a phenomenon.

New Zealander Botica also continued a streak of excellence. Playing at stand off, he followed up his five out of five goalkicking success at Wembley with another 100 per cent strike rate from 10 attempts.

Although scrum half Shaun Edwards did not add to his leading tryscoring total of 40, he was a key figure in Wigan's late onslaught which brought two tries from Denis Betts, and one each from David Myers and Miles.

Centre Paul Loughlin was the star of St. Helens' first-half supremacy, scoring a try and two goals and creating Sullivan's first touchdown. Wigan had taken a 10-2 lead inside 22 minutes with three Botica goals and a smart try from prop Andy Platt, who dummied his way through from close range.

That try, added to his usual high workrate, helped the 1992 British Lion to the Harry Sunderland Trophy as man of the match.

The score was 2-2 when St. Helens captain Shane Cooper was sent to the sin bin for kicking out in the 18th minute. When he returned his side were 10-8 ahead. Penalties went 9-7 to St. Helens, who won the scrums 8-2.

With the Stretford End being prepared for demolition as part of an all-seater stadium project, the ground capacity was limited to 33,157, the sell-out crowd still producing competition record receipts of £389,988.

STONES BITTER PREMIERSHIP FINAL

17 May   **Old Trafford, Manchester**

WIGAN 48   **ST. HELENS 16**

Wigan	No.	St. Helens
Steve Hampson	1.	Phil Veivers
Joe Lydon	2.	Alan Hunte
Dean Bell, Capt.	3.	Gary Connolly
Gene Miles	4.	Paul Loughlin
Martin Offiah	5.	Anthony Sullivan
Frano Botica	6.	Tea Ropati
Shaun Edwards	7.	Paul Bishop
Neil Cowie	8.	Jonathan Neil
Martin Dermott	9.	Bernard Dwyer
Andy Platt	10.	Kevin Ward
Denis Betts	11.	Sonny Nickle
Billy McGinty	12.	George Mann
Phil Clarke	13.	Shane Cooper, Capt.
David Myers	14.	Jonathan Griffiths
Sam Panapa	15.	Paul Groves

T: Offiah (2), Betts (2), Platt
Myers, Miles
G: Botica (10)
Substitutions:
Panapa for McGinty (28 min.)
Myers for Hampson (62 min.)
Referee: John Holdsworth (Kippax)
Attendance: 33,157

T: Sullivan (2), Loughlin
G: Loughlin (2)
Substitutions:
Griffiths for Connolly (Half-time)
Groves for Neil (55 min.)
Half-time: 10-12
Receipts: £389,988

1992 Round by Round

Wigan's 42-16 first round success at home to Widnes was highlighted by two Martin Offiah tries and Frano Botica passing the 300 points mark for the season, but marred by a groin injury for scrum half Andy Gregory to put him in doubt for the following weekend's Silk Cut Challenge Cup final.

Garry Schofield dropped a last-minute goal for Leeds to snatch an 18-18 draw at Warrington, who had established a lead despite having winger Des Drummond sent off. Playing at loose forward for the first time, Schofield inspired Leeds to a 22-8 success in the Headingley replay, scoring two tries. Visitors Halifax trailed only 14-0 at the interval before St. Helens built a 10-try tally to run out 52-6 victors, tour replacement candidate Alan Hunte notching a hat-trick of tries. Wembley finalists Castleford recorded a 28-18 confidence-boosting victory over neighbours Wakefield Trinity, the visitors trailing 18-12 when Michael Jackson was dismissed only 13 minutes after coming on as substitute.

In the semi-finals, Wigan rewrote a host of records with a 74-6 hammering of Leeds at Central Park. The highest score in Premiership history was also a club record score against for Leeds. It was a personal triumph for winger Martin Offiah, his club record 10 tries being just one short of the British record of 11 by Hull K.R.'s George West 87 years earlier. Leeds had Bobby Goulding sent off in the 56th minute. St. Helens set up a derby Premiership final by beating Castleford 30-14 at Knowsley Road, the Wembley losers being hit by an 11th-minute injury to Graham Steadman and a crucial second-half try by oldboy Kevin Ward.

1992 Results

First Round

Castleford	28	Wakefield T.	18
St. Helens	52	Halifax	6
Warrington	18	Leeds	18
Wigan	42	Widnes	16

Replay

Leeds	22	Warrington	8

Semi-Finals

St. Helens	30	Castleford	14
Wigan	74	Leeds	6

Final

Wigan	48	St. Helens	16

(at Old Trafford, Manchester)

1992 Prizes

Winners: £17,500
Runners-up: £7,000

History

With the reintroduction of two divisions in 1973-74 there was no longer a need for a play-off to decide the championship.

However, it was decided to continue the tradition of an end-of-season play-off, the winners to receive the newly instituted Premiership Trophy.

In the first season of the Premiership, 1974-75, the top 12 Division One clubs and the top four from Division Two went into a first round draw, the luck of the draw operating through to the final, played on a neutral venue.

The following season the play-off was reduced to the top eight clubs in the First Division, the ties being decided on a merit basis i.e. 1st v. 8th, 2nd v. 7th etc. At the semi-final stage the highest placed clubs had the option of when to play at home in the two-legged tie.

In 1978-79 the two-leg system was suspended because of fixture congestion and the higher placed clubs had home advantage right through to the neutrally staged final.

Two legs returned the following season, but were finally abolished from 1980-81.

A Second Division Premiership tournament was introduced for the first time in 1986-87, Manchester United's Old Trafford being selected as a new fixed venue for a doubleheader final. With the introduction of a Third Division in 1991-92, the top eight Division Three clubs played off to visit the top four Second Division clubs, the second tier event being renamed the Divisional Premiership.

PREMIERSHIP ROLL OF HONOUR

Year	Winners	Runners-up	Venue	Attendance	Receipts
1975	Leeds (3) 26	St. Helens (1) 11	Wigan 14,531		£7,795
1976	St. Helens (4) 15	Salford (1).......... 2	Swinton 18,082		£13,138
1977	St. Helens (2) 32	Warrington (5) 20	Swinton 11,178		£11,626
1978	Bradford N. (2)...17	Widnes (1) 8	Swinton 16,813		£18,677
1979	Leeds (4) 24	Bradford N. (8)... 2	Huddersfield 19,486		£21,291
1980	Widnes (2) 19	Bradford N. (1)... 5	Swinton 10,215		£13,665
1981	Hull K.R. (3) 11	Hull (7)............. 7	Leeds 29,448		£47,529
1982	Widnes (3) 23	Hull (2)............. 8	Leeds 12,100		£23,749
1983	Widnes (5) 22	Hull (1)............10	Leeds 17,813		£34,145
1984	Hull K.R. (1) 18	Castleford (4)......10	Leeds 12,515		£31,769
1985	St. Helens (2) 36	Hull K.R. (1) 16	Elland Rd, Leeds...........15,518		£46,950
1986	Warrington (4) 38	Halifax (1)..........10	Elland Rd, Leeds...........13,683		£50,879
1987	Wigan (1)........... 8	Warrington (3).... 0	Old Trafford, Man'r.......38,756		£165,166
1988	Widnes (1) 38	St. Helens (2) 14	Old Trafford, Man'r.......35,252		£202,616
1989	Widnes (1) 18	Hull (4).............10	Old Trafford, Man'r.......40,194		£264,242
1990	Widnes (3) 28	Bradford N. (4)... 6	Old Trafford, Man'r.......40,796		£273,877
1991	Hull (3) 14	Widnes (2) 4	Old Trafford, Man'r.......42,043		£384,300
1992	Wigan (1)...........48	St. Helens (2) 16	Old Trafford, Man'r.......33,157		£389,988

() denotes final league position

PREMIERSHIP FINAL . . . . A REVIEW

1974-75
Leeds 26 Holmes (2g) (Marshall 3g); Alan Smith
(1t), Hynes (1t, 1dg) (Eccles), Dyl, Atkinson
(2t), Mason (1t), Hepworth; Dickinson, Ward,
Pitchford, Cookson, Batten, Haigh
St. Helens 11 G. Pimblett; L. Jones (1t),
Wilson, Hull, Mathias (1t); Walsh, Heaton (1t);
Warlow (Cunningham), A. Karalius, Mantle
(K. Gwilliam), E. Chisnall, Nicholls, Coslett (1g)
Referee: W.H. Thompson (Huddersfield)
1975-76
St. Helens 15 G. Pimblett (3g); L. Jones, Glynn
(1t), Noonan, Mathias; Benyon, Heaton
(K. Gwilliam); Mantle, A. Karalius (1t), James,
Nicholls, E. Chisnall (1t), Coslett
Salford 2 Watkins (2dg); Fielding, Richards,
Hesketh, Graham; Butler, Nash; Coulman,
Raistrick, Sheffield, Knighton (Turnbull),
Dixon, E. Prescott
Referee: M.J. Naughton (Widnes)
1976-77
St. Helens 32 G. Pimblett (7g, 1t); L. Jones,
Benyon (1t), Cunningham (1t), Mathias (1t);
Glynn (Ashton), K. Gwilliam (1t); D. Chisnall,
Liptrot, James (1t), Nicholls (A. Karalius),
E. Chisnall, Pinner
Warrington 20 Finnegan; Curling, Bevan
(Cunliffe), Hesford (4g), M. Kelly; A. Gwilliam
(1t), Gordon (1t); Weavill (1t), Price, Case,
Martyn (Peers), Lester, B. Philbin (1t)
Referee: G.F. Lindop (Wakefield)
1977-78
Bradford N. 17 Mumby (2g); Barends (1t),
Roe (1t), Austin, D. Redfearn (1t); Wolford (1dg),
A. Redfearn; I. Van Bellen (Fox), Raistrick,
Thompson, Joyce (Forsyth), Trotter, Haigh (1t)
Widnes 8 Eckersley; Wright, Hughes, Aspey (2t),
Woods (1g); Gill, Bowden; Mills, Elwell, Shaw
(Ramsey) (George), Adams, Hull, Laughton
Referee: J.E. Jackson (Pudsey)
1978-79
Leeds 24 Hague; Alan Smith (1t), D. Smith (1t),
Dyl (Fletcher), Atkinson; Dick (7g, 1dg),
J. Sanderson; Harrison, Ward (1t), Pitchford,
Joyce, Eccles (Adams), Cookson
Bradford N. 2 Mumby; D. Parker, Okulicz,
Gant, Spencer; Ferres (1g), A. Redfearn;
Thompson, Bridges, Forsyth (I. Van Bellen),
Trotter (Mordue), Grayshon, Casey
Referee: W.H. Thompson (Huddersfield)
1979-80
Widnes 19 Burke (1g); Wright (1t), George,
Aspey (1t), Bentley (1t); Eckersley (1dg),
Bowden; Shaw, Elwell (1t, 1dg), M. O'Neill,
L. Gorley (1t), Hull (Hogan), Adams

Bradford N. 5 Mumby (1g); MacLean (Ferres),
D. Redfearn (1t), D. Parker, Gant; Stephenson,
A. Redfearn; Thompson, Bridges, Forsyth,
Clarkson (G. Van Bellen), Grayshon, Hale
Referee: W.H. Thompson (Huddersfield)
1980-81
Hull K.R. 11 Proctor; Hubbard (1g), M. Smith
(1t), Hogan (1t), Muscroft; Hartley (1t), Harkin;
Holdstock, Watkinson, Millington, Lowe, Casey,
Hall (Burton)
Hull 7 Woods (2g); Peacham, Elliott, Wilby,
Prendiville; Banks, Dean; Tindall, Wileman,
Stone, Skerrett (Madley), Crane (1t), Norton
Referee: J. Holdsworth (Leeds)
1981-82
Widnes 23 Burke (4g, 1t); Wright (1t), Kieron
O'Loughlin, Cunningham (A. Myler), Basnett
(1t); Hughes (1t), Gregory; M. O'Neill, Elwell,
Lockwood (Whitfield), L. Gorley, E. Prescott,
Adams (1t)
Hull 8 Kemble; O'Hara (Day), Leuluai,
S. Evans, Prendiville; Topliss, Harkin; Tindall,
Wileman (Lloyd), Stone, Skerrett, Crooks
(1t, 2g, 1dg), Norton
Referee: S. Wall (Leigh)
1982-83
Widnes 22 Burke; Linton, Hughes, Lydon (5g),
Basnett (2t); A. Myler (1t), Gregory (1t) (Hulme);
M. O'Neill, Elwell, L. Gorley, Whitfield
(S. O'Neill), Prescott, Adams
Hull 10 Kemble; O'Hara (1t), Day (Solal),
Leuluai, S. Evans; Topliss (1t), Dean; Skerrett,
Bridges, Stone, Rose, Crooks (2g), Norton
(Crane)
Referee: F. Lindop (Wakefield)
1983-84
Hull K.R. 18 Fairbairn; Clark, M. Smith (1t),
Prohm (1t), Laws (1t); Dorahy (1t, 1g), Harkin;
Holdstock, Rudd, Millington (Robinson),
Burton (Lydiat), Broadhurst, Hall
Castleford 10 Roockley; Coen, Marchant, Hyde,
Kear (1t); Robinson, R. Beardmore (3g); Ward,
Horton, Connell, Crampton, Atkins, Joyner
Referee: R. Campbell (Widnes)
1984-85
St. Helens 36 Veivers (1t); Ledger (2t), Peters,
Meninga (2t) (Allen), Day (4g); Arkwright,
Holding; Burke (Forber), Ainsworth (1t),
P. Gorley, Platt, Haggerty, Pinner (1t)
Hull K.R. 16 Fairbairn (1t, 2g); Clark,
Robinson (1t), Prohm, Laws (1t); M. Smith,
G. Smith (Harkin); Broadhurst, Watkinson,
Ema (Lydiat), Kelly, Hogan, Hall
Referee: S. Wall (Leigh)
1985-86
Warrington 38 Paul Ford (Johnson 1t);
Forster (1t), Cullen, R. Duane, Carbert;

Bishop (1t, 5g), A. Gregory; Boyd (2t),
Tamati (1t), Jackson (1t), Sanderson (McGinty),
Roberts, M. Gregory
Halifax 10 Whitfield (3g) (Smith); Riddlesden,
T. Anderson, C. Anderson (1t), Wilson;
Crossley, Stephens; Scott, McCallion, Robinson,
Juliff, James (Bond), Dixon
Referee: F. Lindop (Wakefield)
1986-87
Wigan 8 Hampson; Gill (1g), Stephenson (1g),
Bell, Lydon (1t) (Russell); Edwards, Gregory;
Case, Kiss, Wane (West), Goodway, Potter,
Hanley
Warrington 0 Johnson; Drummond, Ropati, B.
Peters, Forster; Cullen, Bishop; Tamati, Roberts
(Eccles), Jackson, Humphries (M. Gregory),
Sanderson, Duane
Referee: K. Allatt (Southport)
1987-88
Widnes 38 Platt (1g); Thackray (Tait 1t), Currier
(4g), Wright (2t), Offiah; Dowd, D. Hulme (2t);
Sorensen (1t), McKenzie (1t), Grima
(S. O'Neill), M. O'Neill, P. Hulme, R. Eyres
St. Helens 14 Loughlin (3g); Ledger (1t),
Tanner, Elia, Quirk; Bailey, Holding; Burke,
Groves, Evans (Dwyer), Forber, Fieldhouse
(Allen), Haggerty (1t)
Referee: J. Holdsworth (Kippax)
1988-89
Widnes 18 Tait; Davies (3g), Currier (1t) (Pyke),
Wright (1t), Offiah (1t); D. Hulme (A. Myler),
P. Hulme; Sorensen, McKenzie, Grima,
M. O'Neill, Koloto, R. Eyres
Hull 10 Fletcher; Eastwood, Blacker, Price
(Wilby), O'Hara; Pearce (3g), Windley (Nolan);
Dannatt, Jackson, S. Crooks, Welham (1t),
Sharp, Divorty
Referee: J. Holdsworth (Kippax)
1989-90
Widnes 28 Tait (2t); Davies (4g), Currier (2t),
Wright, Offiah; D. Hulme, P. Hulme; Sorensen
(A. Myler), McKenzie, M. O'Neill, Koloto
(Grima), Eyres, Holliday (1t)
Bradford N. 6 Wilkinson; Cordle, McGowan
(Cooper), Marchant (1t), Francis; Simpson,
Harkin; Skerrett, Noble (Richards), Hobbs,
Medley, Fairbank, Mumby (1g)
Referee: C. Morris (Huddersfield)
1990-91
Hull 14 Gay (1t); Eastwood (1g), McGarry
(G. Nolan 1t), Webb, Turner; Mackey, Entat;
Harrison, L. Jackson, Dannatt, Marlow
(D. Busby), Walker (1t), Sharp
Widnes 4 Tait; Devereux, Currier, Davies,
Offiah (1t); Dowd, D. Hulme; Sorensen,
McKenzie (Wright), Grima, P. Hulme, Koloto
(Howard), McCurrie
Referee: J. Holdsworth (Kippax)

THE HARRY SUNDERLAND TROPHY

The trophy, in memory of the famous
Queenslander, a former Australian Tour
Manager, broadcaster and journalist, is
presented to the Man of the Match in the end
of season Championship or Premiership final.

The award is donated and judged by the
Rugby League Writers' Association and is
sponsored by Stones Bitter.

*Wigan skipper Dean Bell lets the Stones Bitter
Premiership Trophy go to his head.*

The Harry Sunderland Trophy Roll of Honour

Year	Winner	Team	Position
1965	Terry Fogerty	Halifax (v. St. Helens)	Second row
1966	Albert Halsall	St. Helens (v. Halifax)	Prop
1967	Ray Owen	Wakefield T. (v. St. Helens)	Scrum half
1968	Gary Cooper	Wakefield T. (v. Hull K.R.)	Full back
1969	Bev Risman	Leeds (v. Castleford)	Full back
1970	Frank Myler	St. Helens (v. Leeds)	Stand off
1971	Bill Ashurst	Wigan (v. St. Helens)	Second row
1972	Terry Clawson	Leeds (v. St. Helens)	Prop
1973	Mick Stephenson	Dewsbury (v. Leeds)	Hooker
1974	Barry Philbin	Warrington (v. St. Helens)	Loose forward
1975	Mel Mason	Leeds (v. St. Helens)	Stand off
1976	George Nicholls	St. Helens (v. Salford)	Second row
1977	Geoff Pimblett	St. Helens (v. Warrington)	Full back
1978	Bob Haigh	Bradford N. (v. Widnes)	Loose forward
1979	Kevin Dick	Leeds (v. Bradford N.)	Stand off
1980	Mal Aspey	Widnes (v. Bradford N.)	Centre
1981	Len Casey	Hull K.R. (v. Hull)	Second row
1982	Mick Burke	Widnes (v. Hull)	Full back
1983	Tony Myler	Widnes (v. Hull)	Stand off
1984	John Dorahy	Hull K.R. (v. Castleford)	Stand off
1985	Harry Pinner	St. Helens (v. Hull K.R.)	Loose forward
1986	Les Boyd	Warrington (v. Halifax)	Prop
1987	Joe Lydon	Wigan (v. Warrington)	Winger
1988	David Hulme	Widnes (v. St. Helens)	Scrum half
1989	Alan Tait	Widnes (v. Hull)	Full back
1990	Alan Tait	Widnes (v. Bradford N.)	Full back
1991	Greg Mackey	Hull (v. Widnes)	Stand off
1992	Andy Platt	Wigan (v. St. Helens)	Prop

PREMIERSHIP RECORDS First staged 1975

ALL ROUNDS

TEAM

Highest score: Wigan 74 v. Leeds 6 1992
(Also widest margin)
Biggest attendance: 42,043 Hull v. Widnes
..........Final at Old Trafford 1991

INDIVIDUAL

Most goals:
10 by Frano Botica (Wigan) v. St. Helens...Final 1992
Most tries:
10 by Martin Offiah (Wigan) v. Leeds
..........Semi-Final 1992
Most points:
40 (10t) by Martin Offiah (Wigan) v. Leeds
..........Semi-Final 1992

PREMIERSHIP FINAL

TEAM

Most appearances: 8 by Widnes
Most wins: 6 by Widnes
Highest score:
Wigan 48 v. St. Helens 16 (also widest margin) ...1992
Biggest attendance:
42,043 Hull v. Widnes
(at Old Trafford, Man'r) 1991

INDIVIDUAL

Most tries:
No player has scored 3 or more
Most goals:
10 by Frano Botica (Wigan) v. St. Helens...........1992
Most points:
20 (10g) by Frano Botica (Wigan) v. St. Helens ...1992

DIVISIONAL PREMIERSHIP TROPHY

1992 Final

Test centre Daryl Powell returned after a four-match suspension to inspire Sheffield Eagles to a 34-20 victory over Oldham in the inaugural Stones Bitter Divisional Premiership final at Old Trafford.

Although hooker Mick Cook retained the captaincy, it was club skipper Powell who stamped his international class on a thrilling contest as he scored the Eagles' first three tries and sent David Mycoe away for the fourth when Oldham threatened to stage a comeback.

Powell was the runaway winner of the Tom Bergin Trophy as Man of the Match for a first-class all-round performance highlighted by his hat-trick of tries, a repeat of his three-try feat in the 1989 doubleheader.

The Great Britain tourist had already powered in for his first two tries to help Sheffield to a 12-4 lead before Oldham were reduced to 12 men when prop Ian Sherratt was sent off in the 25th minute for a high tackle on Powell.

The Eagles centre resumed after treatment and within three minutes had completed his genuine hat-trick with a 40-yard charge that left Oldham full back Duncan Platt flat-footed.

Powell had taken only five minutes to show that his enforced break had probably done him good as he timed a short, sharp burst perfectly to go in off Richard Price's pass, scrum half Mark Aston adding the goal.

Although Oldham, who had finished third in the Second Division, hit back almost immediately, with Platt completing a 50-yard raid down the left, Price and Powell repeated their double act in the 15th minute for the centre to touch down. Aston added the goal and then produced the pass that sent Powell away for his third try.

But never-say-die Oldham drew level at 16-16 in the 58th minute as tries from the enterprising Ged Byrne and Keith Newton, both goaled by scrum half Tommy Martyn, epitomised their fighting spirit.

The Roughyeds snapped back when Mycoe's try edged Sheffield in front again and with only 10 minutes left it was 20-20 after former Swinton winger Scott Ranson raced 30 yards for another try.

But the Eagles' extra pair of legs began to tell in the sapping heat, substitutes Tim Lumb and Keith Mumby crashing through for late tries. Mumby's last-minute touchdown came 14 years after gaining a winners' medal with Bradford Northern in the major Premiership final.

Sheffield, who would have broken their own Second Division Premiership final record score of 43 in 1989 with better finishing, had three tryscoring efforts disallowed.

Oldham, making their third appearance in five years in the opening event of the Stones Bitter doubleheader, were well served by Under-21 duo Martyn and second row man Chris Joynt.

Penalties went 10-5 to Sheffield, with Oldham winning the scrums 8-6.

Outstanding Sheffield Eagles stand off Richard Price.

STONES BITTER DIVISIONAL PREMIERSHIP FINAL

17 May   Old Trafford, Manchester

SHEFFIELD EAGLES 34   **OLDHAM 20**

David Mycoe	1.	Duncan Platt
Mark Gamson	2.	Scott Ranson
Charlie McAlister	3.	Vince Nicklin
Daryl Powell	4.	Iva Ropati
David Plange	5.	Sean Tyrer
Richard Price	6.	Richard Russell, Capt.
Mark Aston	7.	Tommy Martyn
Paul Broadbent	8.	Ian Sherratt
Mick Cook, Capt.	9.	Richard Pachniuk
Hugh Waddell	10.	Keith Newton
Dale Laughton	11.	Chris Joynt
Ian Hughes	12.	Shane Tupaea
Anthony Farrell	13.	Ged Byrne
Tim Lumb	14.	Steve Warburton
Keith Mumby	15.	Tim Street

T: Powell (3), Mycoe, Lumb, Mumby
G: Aston (5)
Substitutions:
Mumby for Hughes (35 min.)
Lumb for Laughton (51 min.)
Referee: Stuart Cummings (Widnes)

T: Platt, Byrne, Newton, Ranson
G: Martyn (2)
Substitutions:
Street for Tupaea (20 min.)
Warburton for Russell (30 min.)
Half-time: 16-4

1992 Round by Round

In a new-style Stones Bitter Divisional Premiership, the top eight Third Division clubs played off in the first round on a merit basis. Champions Huddersfield beat Hunslet 13-6, seven points in the last four minutes denying the visitors a deserved draw. Keighley Cougars led 18-0 at Bramley on the hour before the home side staged a tremendous three-try comeback to snatch an 18-18 draw. In the replay at Lawkholme Lane, Keighley beat the Third Division runners-up 26-23, with winger Johnny Walker scoring a hat-trick of tries. Doncaster rounded off a disappointing season with a 24-6 defeat at Dewsbury, who were inspired by half backs Paul Delaney and Chris Squires. Batley put on a superb display of support play to register a 46-0 trouncing of visitors Barrow, hooker Mick Scott grabbing a hat-trick of tries, the afternoon being marred by the dismissal of three players, Steve Morrison and Steve Mossop from Barrow, plus Batley's Scott Rawlinson.

In the second round, the top four in the Second Division had home advantage against Third Division opposition. Second Division champions Sheffield Eagles recorded a 72-14 hammering of Keighley, playing their third game in five days. The visitors scored three tries but conceded 12, with hat-tricks for David Mycoe and Charlie McAlister, Mark Aston adding a club record-equalling 12 goals. Title runners-up Leigh suffered a shock defeat by Batley, the visitors gaining a well deserved 15-6 success. Four players were sent off, Paul Topping and Adrian Earner from Leigh, plus Batley's Steve Parrish and Mark Scott. Full back Duncan Platt earned Man of the Match rating with two tries and six goals in Oldham's 36-18 defeat of Dewsbury, who contributed two top-class touchdowns from wingers Eddie Rombo and Dennis

Bailey. Huddersfield lodged an appeal against London Crusaders' 14-4 passage to the semi-finals on the grounds that the home side fielded more than their permitted quota of overseas players. The Londoners scored two tries to nil, from Shane Buckley and Gary Deaker.

In the semi-finals, Sheffield Eagles reached their second Old Trafford final by beating Third Division Batley 36-22 after a 70-minute scare. With nine consecutive victories under their belt, Batley refused to be overawed, holding on to a two-point lead until the final minutes when the Eagles ran in three tries. Oldham qualified for a third Old Trafford visit in five years with a 22-14 home success over London Crusaders, their fifth victory against them in six 1991-92 meetings. Half back Tommy Martyn was outstanding with a try and two goals.

1992 Results

First Round

Batley	46	Barrow	0
Bramley	18	Keighley C.	18
Dewsbury	24	Doncaster	6
Huddersfield	13	Hunslet	6

Replay

Keighley C.	26	Bramley	23

Second Round

Leigh	6	Batley	15
London C.	14	Huddersfield	4
Oldham	36	Dewsbury	18
Sheffield E.	72	Keighley C.	14

Semi-Finals

Oldham	22	London C.	14
Sheffield E.	36	Batley	22

Final

Sheffield E.	34	Oldham	20

(at Old Trafford, Manchester)

1992 Prizes

Winners: £9,500   Runners-up: £3,750

SECOND DIVISION PREMIERSHIP. . . . A REVIEW

1986-87
Swinton 27 Viller; Bate (1t), Topping (Ratcliffe), Brown, Rippon (3g); Snape, Lee (1t); Grima (1t), Ainsworth (1t), Muller, Derbyshire (1t), M. Holliday (Allen), L. Holliday (1dg)
Hunslet 10 Kay; Tate, Penola, Irvine, Wilson; Coates, King; Sykes, Gibson (Senior), Bateman (2t), Platt (1g) (Mason), Bowden, Jennings
Referee: J. McDonald (Wigan)

1987-88
Oldham 28 Burke (Irving); Round, D. Foy (2t), McAlister (4g), Meadows (1t); Walsh (1t), Ford; Sherratt (Warnecke), Sanderson, Waddell, Hawkyard, Graham, Flanagan (1t)
Featherstone R. 26 Quinn (5g); Bannister (1t), Sykes (1t), Banks, Marsh (Crossley); Steadman (2t), Fox; Siddall (Bastian), K. Bell, Harrison, Hughes, Smith, Lyman
Referee: R. Whitfield (Widnes)

1988-89
Sheffield E. 43 Gamson; Cartwright, Dickinson, Powell (3t), Young; Aston (1t, 7g, 1dg), Close (Evans); Broadbent (1t), Cook (1t), Van Bellen, Nickle, Fleming (McDermott 1t), Smiles
Swinton 18 Topping; Ranson (1t), Viller (Maloney), Snape, Bate; Frodsham (1t), Hewitt; Mooney, Melling (1t), S. O'Neill, Ainsworth, Allen (Horrocks), J. Myler (3g)
Referee: R. Whitfield (Widnes)

1989-90
Oldham 30 Platt (1g) (Martyn 1t); Irving (1t), Hyde (2g), Henderson (1t), Lord (1t); Clark, Ford (1t); Casey (Newton), Ruane (1t), Fieldhouse, Round, McAlister, Russell
Hull K.R. 29 Lightfoot; Clark (1t), M. Fletcher (4g), Austin, Sullivan; Parker (2t, 1dg), Bishop (Irvine); Niebling, Rudd, Ema, D. Harrison (1t) (Armstrong), Thompson, Lyman (1t)
Referee: R. Whitfield (Widnes)

1990-91
Salford 27 Gibson; Evans (1t), Gilfillan (1t), Birkett, Hadley (Dean); Cassidy (1dg), Kerry (2t, 4g, 1dg); Worrall, Lee (1dg), Hansen, Bradshaw (Sherratt), Blease, Burgess
Halifax 20 Smith; Wood (1t), Wilson (1t), Austin, Silva (Platt 2g); Lyons, R. Southernwood (1t); Hill (1t), Ramshaw, Bell (Scott), Brown, Milner, Keebles
Referee: B. Galtress (Bradford)

ROLL OF HONOUR
SECOND DIVISION PREMIERSHIP

Year	Winners	Runners-up	Venue
1987	Swinton (2) 27	Hunslet (1) 10	Old Trafford, Manchester
1988	Oldham (1) 28	Featherstone R. (2)...26	Old Trafford, Manchester
1989	Sheffield E. (3)........43	Swinton (5)............18	Old Trafford, Manchester
1990	Oldham (3) 30	Hull K.R. (1)..........29	Old Trafford, Manchester
1991	Salford (1) 27	Halifax (2) 20	Old Trafford, Manchester

DIVISIONAL PREMIERSHIP

Year	Winners	Runners-up	Venue
1992	Sheffield E. (1)........34	Oldham (3)............20	Old Trafford, Manchester

( ) Denotes Second Division position

THE TOM BERGIN TROPHY

The trophy, in honour of the President of the Rugby League Writers' Association and former Editor of the *Salford City Reporter*, is presented to the Man of the Match in the end of season Second Division, later Divisional, Premiership final. The award is donated and judged by the Association and sponsored by Stones Bitter.

Year	Winner	Team	Position
1987	Gary Ainsworth	Swinton (v. Hunslet)	Hooker
1988	Des Foy	Oldham (v. Featherstone R.)	Centre
1989	Mark Aston	Sheffield E. (v. Swinton)	Stand off
1990	Mike Ford	Oldham (v. Hull K.R.)	Scrum half
1991	Steve Kerry	Salford (v. Halifax)	Scrum half
1992	Daryl Powell	Sheffield E. (v. Oldham)	Centre

Sheffield Eagles centre Daryl Powell, 1992 Tom Bergin Trophy winner, outstrips Oldham full back Duncan Platt.

LANCASHIRE CUP

1991 Final

Second Division outfit Rochdale Hornets entered their first Lancashire Cup final for 26 years as clear underdogs, having last won a major final in 1922 when they lifted the Challenge Cup. Their spirited performance in a 24-14 defeat by current joint league-leaders St. Helens dispelled the theory that the gap between the top tiers was growing wider.

Hornets, who had disposed of First Division Salford en route to the final at Warrington, produced endeavour and enthusiasm, leading 10-8 at the interval and providing the Man of the Match in former Oldham prop forward Bob Marsden, an inspirational leader.

St. Helens, anxious for a trophy success after two recent Wembley defeats at the hands of arch rivals Wigan, followed the form book by lifting the Greenalls Lancashire Cup for the 11th time, their first cup since winning the John Player Trophy in January 1988.

St. Helens scrum half Paul Bishop marred the celebrations with his dismissal after the final whistle, being involved in an incident with former Saints half back Brett Clark, who had to receive treatment. Widnes referee David Campbell, in charge of his first major final, reported that he had sent Bishop off for stamping.

The late incident was the only blemish on an exciting and intriguing contest with high-flying St. Helens, the clear pre-match favourites, never able to relax against a lower echelon side packed with experience.

Marsden and Bishop, apart from the latter's dismissal, were the game's outstanding figures. Marsden set up tries for centre Darren Abram and loose forward Mike Kuiti in an impressive all-round display. Diminutive scrum half Bishop tormented Rochdale with precision kicking and distributive passing skills, contributing a try and two goals.

New Zealand duo Kuiti and Paul Okesene were impressive for Hornets, as was skipper and full back Colin Whitfield before being helped off with a dislocated shoulder. Whitfield and Kuiti were involved in the build-up for the first try, by 1984 tourist Ronnie Duane, after 13 minutes.

Kuiti and Marsden then combined to produce Abram's touchdown to make it 10-4, before Saints pulled back to produce a half-time scoreline of 10-8, the Knowsley Road side's tryscorers being Veivers and Bishop.

An increasingly nervous St. Helens went ahead for the first time five minutes after the break when the irrepressible Bishop created a try for Australian stand off Veivers. Then Hornets scrum half Steve Gartland fumbled at a scrum and Kiwi Test forward George Mann took advantage to touch down. Bishop added both goals to open a 20-10 lead.

Rochdale bounced back with Kuiti's try, but the Second Division outfit's valiant efforts ended when Veivers, the sole survivor from Saints' last Lancashire Cup triumph in 1984, put Mann through for his second touchdown and the match clincher.

Goalkicking Rochdale Hornets skipper Colin Whitfield.

GREENALLS LANCASHIRE CUP FINAL

20 October   **Warrington**

ST. HELENS 24   **ROCHDALE HORNETS 14**

David Tanner	1.	Colin Whitfield, Capt
Mike Riley	2.	Phil Fox
Gary Connolly	3.	Darren Abram
Tea Ropati	4.	Ronnie Duane
Anthony Sullivan	5.	Tony Garritty
Phil Veivers	6.	Brett Clark
Paul Bishop	7.	Steve Gartland
Jonathan Neill	8.	Tony Humphries
Paul Groves	9.	Martin Hall
Kevin Ward	10.	Bob Marsden
John Harrison	11.	Cliff Eccles
George Mann	12.	Paul Okesene
Shane Cooper, Capt.	13.	Mike Kuiti
Mark Bailey	14.	Matt Calland
Paul Forber	15.	Simon Bamber

T: Veivers (2), Mann (2), Bishop
G: Bishop (2)
Substitutions:
Forber for Neill (46 min.)
Bailey for Connolly (74 min.)
Half-time: 8-10
Attendance: 9,269

T: Duane, Abram, Kuiti
G: Whitfield
Substitutions:
Bamber for Eccles (63 min.)
Calland for Fox (72 min.)
Referee: David Campbell (Widnes)

Prop Kevin Ward leads the St. Helens Lancashire Cup celebrations.

Two-try hero George Mann leaves stranded Rochdale Hornets centre Ronnie Duane (left).

St. Helens second row man John Harrison prepares to off-load, Kiwi Tea Ropati in support.

1991 Round by Round

Holders Widnes were knocked out at the preliminary-round stage at Second Division Workington Town in the shock result of the tournament. Each side scored three tries, Town's seven goals from Steve Wear clinching the 27-18 Cumbrian triumph.

In the first round, Trafford Borough suffered a club record defeat, 104-12 at St. Helens, only eight points short of Saints' highest tally. Hat-tricks of tries were claimed by Alan Hunte, Anthony Sullivan and Les Quirk. London Crusaders' hopes of a giant-killing act over mighty Wigan were dashed in the opening quarter with four tries for the visitors en route to a comfortable 38-10 success. Having disposed of holders Widnes, Workington Town struggled to beat Third Division Barrow 12-6 at Derwent Park, packman Martin Oglanby clinching victory with a 67th-minute try. In the other Cumbrian derby, Carlisle travelled to Whitehaven to register a 44-12 success after the scores were locked 12-12 at the interval. Carlisle's eight-try tally featured a brace for Steve Brierley, plus six goals from Dave Vickers.

Salford gained revenge for defeat at Warrington on the opening day of the season by winning 22-16 at the Willows, overcoming a 16-2 deficit with the inspiration of David Cruickshank's first try for the club. Neighbours Swinton went down to a last-minute goal from Oldham's Tommy Martyn in a 22-21 thriller at Station Road, Swinton having held a 14-0 lead after 16 minutes. Leigh ran in 12 tries in a 59-12 hammering of Chorley at Hilton Park, David Ruane claiming a hat-trick. Rochdale Hornets gained a 34-11 victory at Highfield, Brett Clark and Phil Fox each grabbing two tries, Colin Whitfield contributing five goals.

The highlight of the second round was Second Division Rochdale Hornets' defeat of First Division Salford at Spotland.

Hornets built a 21-0 half-time lead before running out 25-18 victors, centre Darren Abram grabbing two tries, Whitfield contributing four goals and a drop goal. Half back Paul Bishop was the star of St. Helens' 39-26 home win over Oldham, scoring two of their seven touchdowns in a 12-try encounter. Wigan ran up a 26-2 half-time lead over neighbours Leigh, going on to win 42-12 inspired by two-try Shaun Edwards, Frano Botica adding seven goals. More than 4,000 watched the Cumbrian derby between Workington Town and Carlisle, Town going down 11-2 with the visitors scoring the only try of the tie through Kiwi scrum half Clayton Friend.

In the semi-finals, St. Helens soaked up tremendous Wigan pressure to go in at the interval with a 14-0 lead, prop forward Kevin Ward defying an ankle injury to lead the home side to a spectacular 28-16 victory in front of more than 17,000 fans. Underdogs Rochdale Hornets continued their giant-killing act by disposing of Carlisle 19-6 at Spotland. The Hornets reached the Lancashire Cup final for the first time in 26 years, with packman Bob Marsden celebrating his Man of the Match award by scoring the last of their four tries.

Rochdale Hornets centre Ronnie Duane, tryscorer in the 1991 final.

Saints skipper Shane Cooper with the 1991 Greenalls Lancashire Cup.

1991 RESULTS

Preliminary Round

Workington T.	27	Widnes	18

First Round

Highfield	11	Rochdale H.	34
Leigh	59	Chorley B.	12
London C.	10	Wigan	38
St. Helens	104	Trafford B.	12
Salford	22	Warrington	16
Swinton	21	Oldham	22
Whitehaven	12	Carlisle	44
Workington T.	12	Barrow	6

Second Round

Rochdale H.	25	Salford	18
St. Helens	39	Oldham	26
Wigan	42	Leigh	12
Workington T.	2	Carlisle	11

Semi-Finals

Rochdale H.	19	Carlisle	6
St. Helens	28	Wigan	16

Final

St. Helens	24	Rochdale H.	14
(at Warrington)			

LANCASHIRE CUP ROLL OF HONOUR

Season	Winners		Runners-up		Venue	Attendance	Receipts
1905-06	Wigan	0	Leigh	0	Broughton	16,000	£400
(replay)	Wigan	8	Leigh	0	Broughton	10,000	£200
1906-07	Broughton R.	15	Warrington	6	Wigan	14,048	£392
1907-08	Oldham	16	Broughton R.	9	Rochdale	14,000	£340
1908-09	Wigan	10	Oldham	9	Broughton	20,000	£600
1909-10	Wigan	22	Leigh	5	Broughton	14,000	£296
1910-11	Oldham	4	Swinton	3	Broughton	14,000	£418
1911-12	Rochdale H.	12	Oldham	5	Broughton	20,000	£630
1912-13	Wigan	21	Rochdale H.	5	Salford	6,000	£200
1913-14	Oldham	5	Wigan	0	Broughton	18,000	£610
1914-15	Rochdale H.	3	Wigan	2	Salford	4,000	£475
1915-16 to 1917-18 *Competition suspended*							
1918-19	Rochdale H.	22	Oldham	0	Salford	18,617	£1,365
1919-20	Oldham	7	Rochdale H.	0	Salford	19,000	£1,615
1920-21	Broughton R.	6	Leigh	3	Salford	25,000	£1,800
1921-22	Warrington	7	Oldham	5	Broughton	18,000	£1,200
1922-23	Wigan	20	Leigh	2	Salford	15,000	£1,200
1923-24	St. Helens Recs.	17	Swinton	0	Wigan	25,656	£1,450
1924-25	Oldham	10	St. Helens Recs.	0	Salford	15,000	£1,116
1925-26	Swinton	15	Wigan	11	Broughton	17,000	£1,115
1926-27	St. Helens	10	St. Helens Recs.	2	Warrington	19,439	£1,192
1927-28	Swinton	5	Wigan	2	Oldham	22,000	£1,275
1928-29	Wigan	5	Widnes	4	Warrington	19,000	£1,150
1929-30	Warrington	15	Salford	2	Wigan	21,012	£1,250
1930-31	St. Helens Recs.	18	Wigan	3	Swinton	16,710	£1,030
1931-32	Salford	10	Swinton	8	Broughton	26,471	£1,654
1932-33	Warrington	10	St. Helens	9	Wigan	28,500	£1,675
1933-34	Oldham	12	St. Helens Recs.	0	Swinton	9,085	£516
1934-35	Salford	21	Wigan	12	Swinton	33,544	£2,191
1935-36	Salford	15	Wigan	7	Warrington	16,500	£950
1936-37	Salford	5	Wigan	2	Warrington	17,500	£1,160
1937-38	Warrington	8	Barrow	4	Wigan	14,000	£800
1938-39	Wigan	10	Salford	7	Swinton	27,940	£1,708

Season	Winners		Runners-up		Venue	Attendance	Receipts
1939-40*	Swinton	5	Widnes	4	Widnes	5,500	£269
	Swinton	16	Widnes	11	Swinton	9,000	£446
	Swinton won on aggregate 21-15						
1940-41 to 1944-45 *Competition suspended during war-time*							
1945-46	Widnes	7	Wigan	3	Warrington	28,184	£2,600
1946-47	Wigan	9	Belle Vue R.	3	Swinton	21,618	£2,658
1947-48	Wigan	10	Belle Vue R.	7	Warrington	23,110	£3,043
1948-49	Wigan	14	Warrington	8	Swinton	39,015	£5,518
1949-50	Wigan	20	Leigh	7	Warrington	33,701	£4,751
1950-51	Wigan	28	Warrington	5	Swinton	42,541	£6,222
1951-52	Wigan	14	Leigh	6	Swinton	33,230	£5,432
1952-53	Leigh	22	St. Helens	5	Swinton	34,785	£5,793
1953-54	St. Helens	16	Wigan	8	Swinton	42,793	£6,918
1954-55	Barrow	12	Oldham	2	Swinton	25,204	£4,603
1955-56	Leigh	26	Widnes	9	Wigan	26,507	£4,090
1956-57	Oldham	10	St. Helens	3	Wigan	39,544	£6,274
1957-58	Oldham	13	Wigan	8	Swinton	42,497	£6,918
1958-59	Oldham	12	St. Helens	2	Swinton	38,780	£6,933
1959-60	Warrington	5	St. Helens	4	Wigan	39,237	£6,424
1960-61	St. Helens	15	Swinton	9	Wigan	31,755	£5,337
1961-62	St. Helens	25	Swinton	9	Wigan	30,000	£4,850
1962-63	St. Helens	7	Swinton	4	Wigan	23,523	£4,122
1963-64	St. Helens	15	Leigh	4	Swinton	21,231	£3,857
1964-65	St. Helens	12	Swinton	4	Wigan	17,383	£3,393
1965-66	Warrington	16	Rochdale H.	5	St. Helens	21,360	£3,800
1966-67	Wigan	16	Oldham	13	Swinton	14,193	£3,558
1967-68	St. Helens	2	Warrington	2	Wigan	16,897	£3,886
(replay)	St. Helens	13	Warrington	10	Swinton	7,577	£2,485
1968-69	St. Helens	30	Oldham	2	Wigan	17,008	£4,644
1969-70	Swinton	11	Leigh	2	Wigan	13,532	£3,651
1970-71	Leigh	7	St. Helens	4	Swinton	10,776	£3,136
1971-72	Wigan	15	Widnes	8	St. Helens	6,970	£2,204
1972-73	Salford	25	Swinton	11	Warrington	6,865	£3,321
1973-74	Wigan	19	Salford	9	Warrington	8,012	£2,750
1974-75	Widnes	6	Salford	2	Wigan	7,403	£2,833
1975-76	Widnes	16	Salford	7	Wigan	7,566	£3,880
1976-77	Widnes	16	Workington T.	11	Wigan	8,498	£6,414
1977-78	Workington T.	16	Wigan	13	Warrington	9,548	£5,038
1978-79	Widnes	15	Workington T.	13	Wigan	10,020	£6,261
1979-80	Widnes	11	Workington T.	0	Salford	6,887	£7,100
1980-81	Warrington	26	Wigan	10	St. Helens	6,442	£8,629
1981-82	Leigh	8	Widnes	3	Wigan	9,011	£14,029
1982-83	Warrington	16	St. Helens	0	Wigan	6,462	£11,732
1983-84	Barrow	12	Widnes	8	Wigan	7,007	£13,160
1984-85	St. Helens	26	Wigan	18	Wigan	26,074	£62,139
1985-86	Wigan	34	Warrington	8	St. Helens	19,202	£56,030
1986-87	Wigan	27	Oldham	6	St. Helens	20,180	£60,329
1987-88	Wigan	28	Warrington	16	St. Helens	20,237	£67,339
1988-89	Wigan	22	Salford	17	St. Helens	19,154	£71,879
1989-90	Warrington	24	Oldham	16	St. Helens	9,990	£41,804
1990-91	Widnes	24	Salford	18	Wigan	7,485	£36,867
1991-92	St. Helens	24	Rochdale H.	14	Warrington	9,269	£44,278
*Emergency War-time competition							

211

LANCASHIRE CUP FINAL .... A REVIEW
1969-70
Swinton 11 Gowers; Gomersall, Fleet, Buckley,
M. Philbin (1t); Davies, Kenny (4g); Bate,
D. Clarke, Mackay, Holliday, Smith, Robinson
Leigh 2 Grainey; Tickle, Warburton, Collins,
Stringer (Brown); Eckersley, Murphy (1g);
D. Chisnall, Ashcroft, Watts, Welding, Lyon,
Fiddler
Referee: E. Clay (Leeds)
1970-71
Leigh 7 Ferguson (2g); Tickle (Canning),
L. Chisnall, Collins, Walsh; Eckersley (1t),
Murphy; D. Chisnall, Ashcroft, Watts, Grimes,
Clarkson, Mooney
St. Helens 4 F. Barrow; L. Jones, Benyon,
Walsh, Wilson; Myler, Whittle; Halsall,
A. Karalius, Rees (Prescott), Mantle,
E. Chisnall, Coslett (2g)
Referee: W.H. Thompson (Huddersfield)
1971-72
Wigan 15 Tyrer (3g); Eastham (1t), Francis (1t),
Fuller, Wright (Gandy); D. Hill, Ayres (1t);
Ashcroft, Clarke, Fletcher, Ashurst, Kevin
O'Loughlin, Laughton
Widnes 8 Dutton; Brown, McLoughlin, Aspey
(1g), Gaydon (1t); D. O'Neill (1t), Bowden;
Warlow, Foran, Doughty, Kirwan, Walsh
(Lowe), Nicholls
Referee: W.H. Thompson (Huddersfield)
1972-73
Salford 25 Charlton (1t); Eastham (1t),
Watkins (1t, 5g), Hesketh, Richards (1t); Gill,
Banner (1t); Mackay, Walker, Ward,
Whitehead, Dixon, Prescott
Swinton 11 Jackson; Fleay (1t), Cooke,
Buckley, Gomersall; Kenny (1g) (M. Philbin),
Gowers (3g); Halsall, Evans, Bate, R. Smith
(Holliday), Hoyle, W. Pattinson
Referee: W.H. Thompson (Huddersfield)
1973-74
Wigan 19 Francis; Vigo, D. Hill, Keiron
O'Loughlin (2t), Wright (1t); Cassidy,
Ayres (1g); Smethurst, Clarke, Gray (4g),
Irving, D. Robinson, Cunningham
Salford 9 Charlton; Fielding, Watkins (1t, 3g),
Hesketh, Holland; Gill, Banner; Mackay,
Walker, Davies (Grice), Dixon, Kear
(Knighton), E. Prescott
Referee: W.H. Thompson (Huddersfield)
1974-75
Widnes 6 Dutton (1g); George (1t),
D. O'Neill, Aspey, A. Prescott; Hughes (1dg),
Bowden; Mills, Elwell, J. Stephens, Adams,
Blackwood, Laughton

Salford 2 Charlton; Fielding (1g), Dixon,
Graham, Richards; Taylor, Banner; Mackay,
Devlin, Grice, Knighton, Coulman, E. Prescott
Referee: G.F. Lindop (Wakefield)
1975-76
Widnes 16 Dutton (3g, 1dg); A. Prescott (1t),
George (1t), Aspey (1t), Jenkins; Hughes,
Bowden; Mills, Elwell, Nelson, Foran,
Fitzpatrick (Sheridan), Adams
Salford 7 Watkins (2g); Fielding, Butler,
Hesketh, Richards (1t); Gill, Nash; Fiddler,
Hawksley, Dixon (Mackay), Turnbull,
Knighton, E. Prescott
Referee: W.H. Thompson (Huddersfield)
1976-77
Widnes 16 Dutton (4g, 1dg); Wright (1t),
Aspey, George (1t), A. Prescott; Eckersley,
Bowden (1dg); Ramsey, Elwell, Nelson,
Dearden, Adams, Laughton
Workington T. 11 Charlton; Collister,
Wilkins (1t), Wright, MacCorquodale (4g);
Lauder, Walker; Mills, Banks, Calvin,
Bowman, L. Gorley, W. Pattinson (P. Gorley)
Referee: W.H. Thompson (Huddersfield)
1977-78
Workington T. 16 Charlton (Atkinson);
Collister, Risman, Wright (1t), MacCorquodale
(4g); Wilkins (1t), Walker (2dg); Watts, Banks,
Bowman, L. Gorley, W. Pattinson, P. Gorley
Wigan 13 Swann; Vigo, Davies (Burke 1g),
Willicombe (1t), Hornby; Taylor, Nulty (1t, 1g);
Hogan, Aspinall, Irving, Ashurst (1t),
Blackwood, Melling (Regan)
Referee: W.H. Thompson (Huddersfield)
1978-79
Widnes 15 Eckersley; Wright (1t), Aspey,
George, Burke (3g); Hughes, Bowden; Mills,
Elwell, Shaw, Adams, Dearden (Hull),
Laughton (2t)
Workington T. 13 Charlton; Collister, Risman,
Wilkins (1t), MacCorquodale (1t, 2g); McMillan,
Walker; Beverley, Banks, Bowman, Blackwood,
P. Gorley, W. Pattinson (L. Gorley 1t)
Referee: W.H. Thompson (Huddersfield)
1979-80
Widnes 11 Eckersley; Wright, Aspey, Hughes
(George), Burke (2g); Moran (1t), Bowden;
Hogan, Elwell (1dg), Shaw, L. Gorley, Dearden,
Adams (1t)
Workington T. 0 Charlton; MacCorquodale,
Maughan, Thompson, Beck; Rudd, Walker
(Roper); Beverley, Banks, Wallbanks (Varty),
W. Pattinson, Lewis, Dobie
Referee: W.H. Thompson (Huddersfield)

1980-81
Warrington 26 Finnegan; Thackray (1t),
I. Duane, Bevan (1t), Hesford (7g, 1t);
K. Kelly, A. Gwilliam; Courtney, Waller, Case,
Martyn (1t), Eccles (Potter), Hunter
Wigan 10 Fairbairn (1t, 2g); Ramsdale (1t),
Willicombe, Davies, Hornby; M. Foy, Bolton
(Coyle); Breheny, Pendlebury (M. Smith),
S. O'Neill, Melling, Clough, Hollingsworth
Referee: D.G. Kershaw (York)
1981-82
Leigh 8 Hogan; Drummond, Bilsbury (1t),
Donlan (1dg), Worgan; Woods (2g), Green;
Wilkinson, Tabern, Cooke, Martyn (Platt),
Clarkson, McTigue
Widnes 3 Burke; George, Hughes,
Cunningham, Bentley (1t); Moran, Gregory;
M. O'Neill, Elwell, Lockwood, L. Gorley,
E. Prescott, Adams
Referee: W.H. Thompson (Huddersfield)
1982-83
Warrington 16 Hesford (2g); Fellows (1t),
R. Duane, Bevan, M. Kelly (1t); Cullen,
K. Kelly (1t); Courtney, Webb, Cooke
(D. Chisnall), Eccles (1t), Fieldhouse, Gregory
St. Helens 0 Parkes (Smith); Ledger,
Arkwright, Haggerty, Litherland; Peters,
Holding; James, Liptrot, Bottell (Mathias),
Moorby, P. Gorley, Pinner
Referee: J. Holdsworth (Leeds)
1983-84
Barrow 12 Tickle (1dg); Moore, Whittle,
Ball (3g, 1dg), Milby; McConnell (1t), Cairns;
Hodkinson, Wall, McJennett, Herbert, Szymala,
Mossop
Widnes 8 Burke; Lydon (1t, 2g), Hughes,
Keiron O'Loughlin, Basnett; A. Myler,
Gregory; S. O'Neill, Elwell, K. Tamati,
Whitfield, E. Prescott, Adams
Referee: K. Allatt (Southport)
1984-85
St. Helens 26 Veivers (Haggerty 1t); Ledger,
Allen, Meninga (2t), Day (1t, 5g); Arkwright,
Holding; Burke, Liptrot, P. Gorley, Platt,
Round, Pinner
Wigan 18 Edwards; Ferguson, Stephenson,
Whitfield (3g), Gill (1t) (Pendlebury); Cannon,
Fairhurst; Courtney, Kiss (1t), Case, West (1t),
Wane, Potter
Referee: R. Campbell (Widnes)
1985-86
Wigan 34 Edwards (1t); Henley-Smith
(Hampson), Stephenson (7g), Hanley (1t),
Whitfield; Ella (2t), M. Ford; Dowling, Kiss
(1t), Wane (Case), Du Toit, Goodway, Potter

Warrington 8 Johnson (1t); Carbert (2g), Cullen,
Blake (Forster), Thackray; Kelly, A. Gregory;
Eccles, Webb, Jackson, Boyd (Tamati),
M. Gregory, Rathbone
Referee: J. Holdsworth (Kippax)
1986-87
Wigan 27 Edwards (2t); Lydon (1t, 1dg),
Stephenson, Bell, Gill (5g); Hanley, M. Ford
(1t); West, Dermott, Case, Roberts (Louw),
Potter, Goodway
Oldham 6 M'Barki; Sherman, Bridge (1t),
Warnecke, Taylor; Topliss, Kirwan; Clark,
Flanagan, Hobbs (1g), Nadiole, Worrall, Raper
(Hawkyard)
Referee: J.E. Smith (Halifax)
1987-88
Wigan 28 Hampson; Russell, Stephenson (1g)
(Bell), Lydon (5g), Gill (1t); Edwards, A.
Gregory; Case, Kiss, Wane (West 1t),
Goodway, Potter, Hanley (2t)
Warrington 16 Johnson; Drummond, Forster
(2t), Peters, Carbert; Woods (2g), Holden;
K. Tamati, Webb (Harmon), Humphries,
Sanderson, Roberts, M. Gregory (1t)
Referee: G.F. Lindop (Wakefield)
1988-89
Wigan 22 Hampson; T. Iro, K. Iro (2t, 3g),
Bell (1t), Lydon (Byrne); Edwards, Gregory;
Lucas (Betts), Dermott, Shelford (1t), Platt,
Goodway, Hanley
Salford 17 Williams (Blease); Evans (1t).
Bentley (1t), Jones, Hadley; Shaw, Cairns;
Herbert (1t), Moran, Brown (2g), Gormley,
M. Worrall (1dg), Horo (McTigue)
Referee: K. Allatt (Southport)
1989-90
Warrington 24 Lyon (Darbyshire); Drummond,
J. Ropati (1t), Thorniley, Forster (1t); Turner
(4g), Mackey; Burke, Roskell, Molloy, Jackson
(2t), Sanderson (Duane), M. Gregory
Oldham 16 Platt (1g) (Russell); Robinson (1t),
Hyde (1g), Irving (1t), Lord (1t); Clark,
M. Ford; Casey (J. Fairbank), A. Ruane,
Fieldhouse, Allen, Newton, Cogger
Referee: R. Tennant (Castleford)
1990-91
Widnes 24 Tait; Wright, Currier (1t), Davies
(4g), Offiah (1t); A. Myler (1t), D. Hulme;
Sorensen, McKenzie, Ashurst (Smith 1t),
Eyres, Koloto, Holliday
Salford 18 Gibson; Evans, Birkett, Williams
(1t), Hadley; Fell (1t), Kerry (3g) (Cassidy);
Sherratt, Lee, Whiteley (Hansen), Bradshaw,
Blease (1t), Burgess
Referee: A. Burke (Oldham)

213

MAN OF THE MATCH AWARDS

An award for the adjudged man of the match in the Lancashire Cup final was first presented in 1974-75. For four years the award was sponsored by the *Rugby Leaguer* newspaper. From 1978-85 the trophy was presented by Burtonwood Brewery, then from 1986 by Greenall Whitley, as part of their sponsorship of the Lancashire Cup. Under the auspices of the *Rugby Leaguer*, the choice was made by the Editor, while the breweries invited a panel of the Press to make the decision.

Season	Winner	Team	Position
1974-75	Mike Coulman	Salford (v. Widnes)	Second row
1975-76	Mick George	Widnes (v. Salford)	Centre
1976-77	David Eckersley	Widnes (v. Workington T.)	Stand off
1977-78	Arnold Walker	Workington T. (v. Wigan)	Scrum half
1978-79	Arnold Walker	Workington T. (v. Widnes)	Scrum half
1979-80	Mick Adams	Widnes (v. Workington T.)	Loose forward
1980-81	Tony Waller	Warrington (v. Wigan)	Hooker
1981-82	Ray Tabern	Leigh (v. Widnes)	Hooker
1982-83	Steve Hesford	Warrington (v. St. Helens)	Full back
1983-84	David Cairns	Barrow (v. Widnes)	Scrum half
1984-85	Mal Meninga	St. Helens (v. Wigan)	Centre
1985-86	Steve Ella	Wigan (v. Warrington)	Stand off
1986-87	Mike Ford	Wigan (v. Oldham)	Scrum half
1987-88	Shaun Edwards	Wigan (v. Warrington)	Stand off
1988-89	Paul Shaw	Salford (v. Wigan)	Stand off
1989-90	Bob Jackson	Warrington (v. Oldham)	Second row
1990-91	David Fell	Salford (v. Widnes)	Stand off
1991-92	Bob Marsden	Rochdale H. (v. St. Helens)	Prop

LANCASHIRE CUP FINAL RECORDS

TEAM

Most appearances: 34 by Wigan
Most wins: 20 by Wigan
Highest score: Wigan 34 v. Warrington 8 1985
Widest margin: St. Helens 30 v. Oldham 2 1968
Biggest attendance:
42,793 St. Helens v. Wigan (at Swinton) 1953

INDIVIDUAL

Most tries:
4 by Brian Nordgren (Wigan) v. Leigh 1949
Most goals:
7 by Jim Ledgard (Leigh) v. Widnes 1955
Steve Hesford (Warrington) v. Wigan 1980
David Stephenson (Wigan) v. Warrington .. 1985
Most points:
17 (7g,1t) by Steve Hesford (Warrington) v. Wigan 1980

Workington Town scrum half Arnold Walker, the only player to win the Man of the Match award twice.

YORKSHIRE CUP

1991 Final

Utility back Graham Steadman produced a record-breaking performance from full back to earn the Man of the Match award and inspire Castleford to a 28-6 demolition of Bradford Northern in the John Smiths Yorkshire Cup final at Elland Road, Leeds.

The 1990 British Lion destroyed Northern in front of their newly-appointed team manager Peter Fox with two tries and four goals for a Yorkshire Cup final record tally of 16 points.

Although there were several other outstanding performances, Steadman, who enjoyed a series of attacking runs and had a hand in another of Castleford's five tries, was a unanimous winner of the White Rose Trophy.

The former York and Featherstone Rovers back made his first impact with a glorious try in the 14th minute, moving smoothly onto Shaun Irwin's smart pass and veering away from the cover on a 50-yard glide to the line. His second touchdown came on the hour as he timed his link-up perfectly to slip effortlessly off hooker Graham Southernwood's pass and add a fourth goal that gave him his record 16-point haul.

The previous best was 14 points by Martin Ketteridge in Castleford's 1986 final defeat of Hull. He was a 72nd-minute substitute for Dean Sampson in this encounter.

Steadman had been allocated the goalkicking role only three days earlier when skipper Lee Crooks was ruled out with a neck injury, his withdrawal not being made public until an hour before kick-off. The full back put in a stint of extra kicking practice on the eve of the final and it paid off as part of a superb all-round performance that included two mighty touch finders.

Steadman made his last major contribution in the 73rd minute, linking up yet again to send second row man Neil Battye charging over for the final try. But Castleford's runaway success was far from being a one-man show. New Zealand Test loose forward Tawera Nikau set a great example as stand-in skipper, while their half backs were in total control.

This was clearly shown in the 45th minute, when scrum half Mike Ford moved the ball sharply from a scrum and stand off Tony Smith burst onto the pass to sidestep his way behind the posts for a touchdown. Ford had scored the second Castleford try just before the interval, finishing off the move he started and which also involved Keith England and Kiwi threequarter Richard Blackmore. Steadman's goal gave the county cup-holders a 12-6 half-time lead, adding to his 18th-minute penalty goal.

Northern had taken an early lead with a penalty goal by David Hobbs. Trailing 6-2 after 34 minutes, Bradford hit back with a marvellous equalising try, carried out with the sort of precision that escaped them for most of the match. Paul Medley and Darrall Shelford combined down the right for the latter to hook a brilliant pass inside to wing partner Daio Powell, who pushed off two defenders on his way to the line.

It was an isolated piece of teamwork from Northern, although they produced individual bursts. Roger Simpson was their biggest single threat, with a succession of raids that would have pushed him close to match honours but for Steadman's exceptional display.

Packmen Jon Hamer and Karl Fairbank worked hard, but player-coach David Hobbs was well below his best in his last match in sole control before the takeover as team manager of Fox, a spectator in the Elland Road stand.

JOHN SMITHS YORKSHIRE CUP FINAL

20 October   Elland Road, Leeds

CASTLEFORD 28		BRADFORD NORTHERN 6
Graham Steadman	1.	Roger Simpson
St. John Ellis	2.	Daio Powell
Graeme Bradley	3.	Darrall Shelford
Richard Blackmore	4.	Steve McGowan
David Nelson	5.	Tony Marchant
Tony Smith	6.	Tony Anderson
Mike Ford	7.	Brett Iti
Dean Sampson	8.	David Hobbs
Graham Southernwood	9.	Brian Noble
Keith England	10.	Jon Hamer
Neil Battye	11.	Paul Medley
Shaun Irwin	12.	Karl Fairbank, Capt.
Tawera Nikau, Capt.	13.	Steve Barnett
Grant Anderson	14.	David Croft
Martin Ketteridge	15.	Craig Richards

T: Steadman (2), Ford, Battye, Smith
G: Steadman (4)
Substitution:
Ketteridge for Sampson (72 min.)
Half-time: 12-6
Referee: John Holdsworth (Kippax)

T: Powell
G: Hobbs
Substitutions:
Croft for Iti (62 min.)
Richards for Medley (62 min.)
Attendance: 8,916

1991 Round by Round

In the three-tie preliminary round, newcomers Scarborough Pirates made an impressive debut with a well-deserved 14-10 success at Doncaster, three goals from Welshman Gary Pearce proving vital. Simon Kenworthy starred in Huddersfield's 36-7 success at Nottingham City with a hat-trick of tries and six goals. Ryedale-York ran in six tries, plus six Graham Sullivan goals, in a 36-8 home victory over Hunslet, who replied with two Andy Raw touchdowns.

In the first round, Leeds handed the captaincy to Ellery Hanley and went down 16-11 at Hull, who were inspired by Australian skipper Greg Mackey, scorer of a try and creator of another. Castleford took only nine seconds to score the first of six tries in a 36-12 triumph at Third Division Batley. Having come under fire from Northern fans, Bradford player-coach David Hobbs turned hero by creating a try, kicking a 50-yard penalty goal and dropping a goal as the visitors snatched a dramatic 15-13 success at Sheffield Eagles. Scarborough led 7-0 shortly before the interval, but Featherstone Rovers' class told, the home side running out 30-7 victors.

Wakefield Trinity secured a last-minute win at Halifax, with a try from former Hunslet back row man Michael Jackson providing a final scoreline of 24-18. Visitors Ryedale-York enjoyed a 10-0 half-time lead before Alex Murphy gave Huddersfield a pep talk pending his coaching appointment, the Fartowners responding with a second-half rally to win 28-10. Third Division pacesetters Dewsbury trailed only 8-3 at Hull K.R. at the interval before a Paul Lyman try and two Mike Fletcher goals sealed a home victory by 18-5. The reliable boot of Steve Carroll earned him the Man of the Match award and gave Bramley a 20-8 victory at Keighley.

In the second round, nearly 5,000 fans turned up at Fartown to mark Alex Murphy's arrival as the new coach of Huddersfield. Wakefield Trinity spoilt the party by registering a 52-9 victory after the Fartowners had opened a 5-0 lead, Andy Wilson grabbing a hat-trick of tries. Visitors Hull K.R. trailed only 14-10 at half-time before Castleford stepped up a gear to run in a further three tries, Lee Crooks contributing seven goals in a 34-12 victory. Bradford Northern won 38-15 at Third Division Bramley, Daio Powell and Brian Noble both scoring two tries after the Villagers built a 7-2 surprise lead. Hull entertained

Featherstone Rovers and opened up a 14-2 lead before winger Ikram Butt inspired a revival to draw 16-16. Rovers took the replay 21-18. Both sides collected four tries, Eastwood managing only one successful kick for Hull, while Fox added two goals and a drop goal.

Castleford reached their eighth county final in 11 years by inflicting an 18-10 semi-final defeat on neighbours Featherstone Rovers. Bouncing back from three successive league defeats, the home side were well served by hooker Graham Southernwood, a tryscorer on his return from a six-match ban. Embattled player-coach Hobbs steered Bradford Northern to their third county final in five years by kicking five goals from five attempts in the 14-10 home success over Wakefield Trinity, full back Ian Wilkinson taking the Man of the Match award in his first appearance of the season.

Castleford's Kiwi captain Tawera Nikau hoists aloft the 1991 John Smiths Yorkshire Cup.

217

1991 RESULTS

Preliminary Round

Doncaster	10	Scarborough P.	14
Nottingham C.	7	Huddersfield	36
Ryedale-York	36	Hunslet	8

First Round

Batley	12	Castleford	36
Featherstone R.	30	Scarborough P.	7
Halifax	18	Wakefield T.	24
Huddersfield	28	Ryedale-York	10
Hull	16	Leeds	11
Hull K.R.	18	Dewsbury	5
Keighley C.	8	Bramley	20
Sheffield E.	13	Bradford N.	15

Second Round

Bramley	15	Bradford N.	38
Castleford	34	Hull K.R.	12
Huddersfield	9	Wakefield T.	52
Hull	16	Featherstone R.	16

Replay

Featherstone R.	21	Hull	18

Semi-Finals

Bradford N.	14	Wakefield T.	10
Castleford	18	Featherstone R.	10

Final

Castleford	28	Bradford N.	6

(at Elland Road, Leeds)

Bradford Northern wingman Daio Powell outstrips Castleford duo Keith England and Dean Sampson (right).

Castleford full back Graham Steadman, 1991 White Rose Trophy winner.

YORKSHIRE CUP ROLL OF HONOUR

Year	Winners		Runners-up		Venue	Attendance	Receipts
1905-06	Hunslet	13	Halifax	3	Bradford P.A.	18,500	£465
1906-07	Bradford	8	Hull K.R.	5	Wakefield	10,500	£286
1907-08	Hunslet	17	Halifax	0	Leeds	15,000	£397
1908-09	Halifax	9	Hunslet	5	Wakefield	13,000	£356
1909-10	Huddersfield	21	Batley	0	Leeds	22,000	£778
1910-11	Wakefield T.	8	Huddersfield	2	Leeds	19,000	£696
1911-12	Huddersfield	22	Hull K.R.	10	Wakefield	20,000	£700
1912-13	Batley	17	Hull	3	Leeds	16,000	£523
1913-14	Huddersfield	19	Bradford N.	3	Halifax	12,000	£430
1914-15	Huddersfield	31	Hull	0	Leeds	12,000	£422
1918-19	Huddersfield	14	Dewsbury	8	Leeds	21,500	£1,309
1919-20	Huddersfield	24	Leeds	5	Halifax	24,935	£2,096
1920-21	Hull K.R.	2	Hull	0	Leeds	20,000	£1,926
1921-22	Leeds	11	Dewsbury	3	Halifax	20,000	£1,650
1922-23	York	5	Batley	0	Leeds	33,719	£2,414
1923-24	Hull	10	Huddersfield	4	Leeds	23,300	£1,728
1924-25	Wakefield T.	9	Batley	8	Leeds	25,546	£1,912
1925-26	Dewsbury	2	Huddersfield	0	Wakefield	12,616	£718
1926-27	Huddersfield	10	Wakefield T.	3	Leeds	11,300	£853
1927-28	Dewsbury	8	Hull	2	Leeds	21,700	£1,466
1928-29	Leeds	5	Featherstone R.	0	Wakefield	13,000	£838
1929-30	Hull K.R.	13	Hunslet	7	Leeds	11,000	£687
1930-31	Leeds	10	Huddersfield	2	Halifax	17,812	£1,405
1931-32	Huddersfield	4	Hunslet	2	Leeds	27,000	£1,764
1932-33	Leeds	8	Wakefield T.	0	Huddersfield	17,685	£1,183
1933-34	York	10	Hull K.R.	4	Leeds	22,000	£1,480
1934-35	Leeds	5	Wakefield T.	5	Dewsbury	22,598	£1,529
Replay	Leeds	2	Wakefield T.	2	Huddersfield	10,300	£745
Replay	Leeds	13	Wakefield T.	0	Hunslet	19,304	£1,327
1935-36	Leeds	3	York	0	Halifax	14,616	£1,113
1936-37	York	9	Wakefield T.	2	Leeds	19,000	£1,294
1937-38	Leeds	14	Huddersfield	8	Wakefield	22,000	£1,508
1938-39	Huddersfield	18	Hull	10	Bradford	28,714	£1,534
1939-40	Featherstone R.	12	Wakefield T.	9	Bradford	7,077	£403
1940-41	Bradford N.	15	Dewsbury	5	Huddersfield	13,316	£939
1941-42	Bradford N.	24	Halifax	0	Huddersfield	5,989	£635
1942-43	Dewsbury	7	Huddersfield	0	Dewsbury	11,000	£680
	Huddersfield	2	Dewsbury	0	Huddersfield	6,252	£618
	Dewsbury won on aggregate 7-2						
1943-44	Bradford N.	5	Keighley	2	Bradford	10,251	£757
	Keighley	5	Bradford N.	5	Keighley	8,993	£694
	Bradford N. won on aggregate 10-7						
1944-45	Hunslet	3	Halifax	12	Hunslet	11,213	£744
	Halifax	2	Hunslet	0	Halifax	9,800	£745
	Halifax won on aggregate 14-3						
1945-46	Bradford N.	5	Wakefield T.	2	Halifax	24,292	£1,934
1946-47	Wakefield T.	10	Hull	0	Leeds	34,300	£3,718

Year	Winners		Runners-up		Venue	Attendance	Receipts
1947-48	Wakefield T.	7	Leeds	7	Huddersfield	24,344	£3,461
Replay	Wakefield T.	8	Leeds	7	Bradford	32,000	£3,251
1948-49	Bradford N.	18	Castleford	9	Leeds	31,393	£5,053
1949-50	Bradford N.	11	Huddersfield	4	Leeds	36,000	£6,365
1950-51	Huddersfield	16	Castleford	3	Leeds	28,906	£5,152
1951-52	Wakefield T.	17	Keighley	3	Huddersfield	25,495	£3,347
1952-53	Huddersfield	18	Batley	8	Leeds	14,705	£2,471
1953-54	Bradford N.	7	Hull	2	Leeds	22,147	£3,833
1954-55	Halifax	22	Hull	14	Leeds	25,949	£4,638
1955-56	Halifax	10	Hull	10	Leeds	23,520	£4,385
Replay	Halifax	7	Hull	0	Bradford	14,000	£2,439
1956-57	Wakefield T.	23	Hunslet	5	Leeds	30,942	£5,609
1957-58	Huddersfield	15	York	8	Leeds	22,531	£4,123
1958-59	Leeds	24	Wakefield T.	20	Bradford	26,927	£3,833
1959-60	Featherstone R.	15	Hull	14	Leeds	23,983	£4,156
1960-61	Wakefield T.	16	Huddersfield	10	Leeds	17,456	£2,937
1961-62	Wakefield T.	19	Leeds	9	Bradford	16,329	£2,864
1962-63	Hunslet	12	Hull K.R.	2	Leeds	22,742	£4,514
1963-64	Halifax	10	Featherstone R.	0	Wakefield	13,238	£2,471
1964-65	Wakefield T.	18	Leeds	2	Huddersfield	13,527	£2,707
1965-66	Bradford N.	17	Hunslet	8	Leeds	17,522	£4,359
1966-67	Hull K.R.	25	Featherstone R.	12	Leeds	13,241	£3,482
1967-68	Hull K.R.	8	Hull	7	Leeds	16,729	£5,515
1968-69	Leeds	22	Castleford	11	Wakefield	12,573	£3,746
1969-70	Hull	12	Featherstone R.	9	Leeds	11,089	£3,419
1970-71	Leeds	23	Featherstone R.	7	Bradford	6,753	£1,879
1971-72	Hull K.R.	11	Castleford	7	Wakefield	5,536	£1,589
1972-73	Leeds	36	Dewsbury	9	Bradford	7,806	£2,659
1973-74	Leeds	7	Wakefield T.	2	Leeds	7,621	£3,728
1974-75	Hull K.R.	16	Wakefield T.	13	Leeds	5,823	£3,090
1975-76	Leeds	15	Hull K.R.	11	Leeds	5,743	£3,617
1976-77	Leeds	16	Featherstone R.	12	Leeds	7,645	£5,198
1977-78	Castleford	17	Featherstone R.	7	Leeds	6,318	£4,528
1978-79	Bradford N.	18	York	8	Leeds	10,429	£9,188
1979-80	Leeds	15	Halifax	6	Leeds	9,137	£9,999
1980-81	Leeds	8	Hull K.R.	7	Huddersfield	9,751	£15,578
1981-82	Castleford	10	Bradford N.	5	Leeds	5,852	£10,359
1982-83	Hull	18	Bradford N.	7	Leeds	11,755	£21,950
1983-84	Hull	13	Castleford	2	Elland Rd, Leeds	14,049	£33,572
1984-85	Hull	29	Hull K.R.	12	Hull C. FC	25,237	£68,639
1985-86	Hull K.R.	22	Castleford	18	Leeds	12,686	£36,327
1986-87	Castleford	31	Hull	24	Leeds	11,132	£31,888
1987-88	Bradford N.	12	Castleford	12	Leeds	10,947	£40,283
Replay	Bradford N.	11	Castleford	2	Elland Rd, Leeds	8,175	£30,732
1988-89	Leeds	33	Castleford	12	Elland Rd, Leeds	22,968	£76,658
1989-90	Bradford N.	20	Featherstone R.	14	Leeds	12,607	£50,775
1990-91	Castleford	11	Wakefield T.	8	Elland Rd, Leeds	12,420	£61,432
1991-92	Castleford	28	Bradford N.	6	Elland Rd, Leeds	8,916	£54,183

221

YORKSHIRE CUP FINAL .... A REVIEW

1970-71
Leeds 23 Holmes; Alan Smith (2t), Hynes (4g), Cowan, Atkinson (1t); Wainwright (Langley), Shoebottom; J. Burke, Dunn (1t), Cookson, Ramsey (1t), Haigh, Batten
Featherstone R. 7 C. Kellett (2g); M. Smith, Cotton, Newlove, Hartley (1t); Harding (Coventry), Hudson; Windmill, D. Morgan, Lyons, Rhodes, Thompson, Farrar
Referee: D.S. Brown (Preston)
1971-72
Hull K.R. 11 Markham; Stephenson, Coupland, Kirkpatrick, Longstaff (1t); Millward (4g), Daley; Wiley, Flanagan, Millington, Wallis, Palmer (Cooper), Brown
Castleford 7 Edwards; Foster (1t), S. Norton, Worsley, Lowndes; Hargrave, Stephens; Hartley, Miller, I. Van Bellen (Ackroyd 2g), A. Dickinson, Lockwood, Blakeway
Referee: A. Givvons (Oldham)
1972-73
Leeds 36 Holmes (3t); Alan Smith, Hynes (1g), Dyl (2t), Atkinson (1t); Hardisty (1t), Hepworth (Langley); Clawson (5g) (Fisher), Ward, Ramsey, Cookson, Eccles (1t), Batten
Dewsbury 9 Rushton; Ashcroft (1t), Childe, Day, Yoward; Agar (3g), A. Bates; Bell (Beverley), M. Stephenson, Lowe, Grayshon, J. Bates (Lee), Hankins
Referee: M.J. Naughton (Widnes)
1973-74
Leeds 7 Holmes; Langley (1t) (Marshall 1g), Hynes (1g), Dyl, Atkinson; Hardisty, Hepworth; Jeanes (Ramsey), Ward, Clarkson, Eccles, Cookson, Batten
Wakefield T. 2 Wraith (Sheard); D. Smith, Crook (1g), Hegarty, B. Parker; Topliss, Bonnar; Valentine, Morgan, Bratt, Knowles (Ballantyne), Endersby, Holmes
Referee: M.J. Naughton (Widnes)
1974-75
Hull K.R. 16 Smithies; Sullivan (Dunn 1t), Watson (2t), Coupland, Kirkpatrick (1t); Millward, Stephenson; Millington, Heslop, Rose, Wallis, N. Fox (2g) (Madley), Brown
Wakefield T. 13 Sheard; D. Smith (1t), Crook (2g), Hegarty (1t), Archer; Topliss, Bonnar; Ballantyne, Handscombe, Bratt (1t), Skerrett, A. Tonks (Goodwin), (Holmes), Morgan
Referee: M.J. Naughton (Widnes)
1975-76
Leeds 15 Marshall; Alan Smith, Hague, Dyl (1t), Atkinson; Holmes (4g, 1dg), Hynes; Harrison, Payne, Pitchford, (Dickinson), Eccles, Batten, Cookson (1t)

Hull K.R. 11 Wallace; Dunn, A. Burwell, Watson, Sullivan (1t); Turner, Millward (1dg); Millington, Dickinson, Lyons, Rose, N. Fox (2g, 1t), Hughes (Holdstock)
Referee: J.V. Moss (Manchester)
1976-77
Leeds 16 Marshall (2g); Hague, Hynes, Dyl (2t), D. Smith; Holmes, Banner; Dickinson, Ward, Pitchford, Eccles (1t), Burton, Cookson (1t)
Featherstone R. 12 Box; Bray (1t), Coventry, Quinn (3g), K. Kellett; Newlove, Fennell; Gibbins, Bridges, Farrar, Stone, P. Smith (1t), Bell (Spells)
Referee: M.J. Naughton (Widnes)
1977-78
Castleford 17 Wraith; Richardson, Joyner, P. Johnson, Fenton; Burton (2t, 1dg), Pickerill (Stephens); Fisher (Woodall), Spurr, Weston, Huddlestone, Reilly, Lloyd (5g)
Featherstone R. 7 Marsden; Evans, Gilbert, Quinn (1g) (N. Tuffs), K. Kellett; Newlove, Butler; Townend (1g), Bridges, Farrar, Gibbins, Stone (P. Smith 1t), Bell
Referee: M.J. Naughton (Widnes)
1978-79
Bradford N. 18 Mumby; Barends, Gant (1t), D. Parker (1t), D. Redfearn; Slater (Wolford), A. Redfearn (1t); Thompson, Fisher, Forsyth (Joyce), Fox (3g), Trotter, Haigh (1t)
York 8 G. Smith (1t); T. Morgan, Day (Crossley), Foster, Nicholson; Banks (2g), Harkin; Dunkerley, Wileman, Harris, Rhodes, Hollis (1dg) (Ramshaw), Cooper
Referee: M.J. Naughton (Widnes)
1979-80
Leeds 15 Hague; Alan Smith (2t), D. Smith (1t), Dyl, Atkinson; Holmes (J. Sanderson), Dick (3g); Dickinson, Ward, Pitchford, Eccles, D. Heron (Adams), Cookson
Halifax 6 Birts (3g); Howard (Snee), Garrod, Cholmondeley, Waites; Blacker, Langton; Jarvis (Callon), Raistrick, Wood, Scott, Sharp, Busfield
Referee: M.J. Naughton (Widnes)
1980-81
Leeds 8 Hague; Alan Smith (1t), D. Smith, Atkinson, Oulton; Holmes, Dick (2g, 1dg); Harrison, Ward, Pitchford, Eccles, Cookson (Carroll), D. Heron
Hull K.R. 7 Robinson; McHugh (1t), M. Smith, Hogan (2g), Youngman; Hall, Harkin; Holdstock, Price, Crooks (Rose), Lowe, Casey, Crane
Referee: R. Campbell (Widnes)

222

1981-82
Castleford 10 Claughton; Richardson, Fenton, Hyde (1t), Morris; Joyner (1t), R. Beardmore; Hardy (P. Norton), Spurr, B. Johnson, Finch (2g), Ward, Timson
Bradford N. 5 Mumby; Barends, Hale, A. Parker (1t), Gant; Hanley (1g), A. Redfearn; Grayshon, Noble, Sanderson (D. Redfearn), G. Van Bellen (Jasiewicz), Idle, Rathbone
Referee: M.R. Whitfield (Widnes)
1982-83
Hull 18 Kemble; S. Evans (1t), Day, Leuluai, Prendiville (1t); Topliss, Harkin; Skerrett, Bridges, Stone, Rose (2t), L. Crooks (2g, 2dg), Crane (Norton)
Bradford N. 7 Mumby; Barends, Gant, A. Parker, Pullen (Smith); Whiteman (1t), Carroll (1g, 2dg); Grayshon, Noble, G. Van Bellen (Sanderson), Idle, Jasiewicz, Hale
Referee: S. Wall (Leigh)
1983-84
Hull 13 Kemble; Solal, Schofield, Leuluai, O'Hara (1t); Topliss, Dean; Edmonds, Wileman, Skerrett, Proctor (1t), L. Crooks, Crane (1t, 1dg)
Castleford 2 Coen; Fenton, Marchant, Hyde (Orum), Kear; Joyner, R. Beardmore (1g); Connell, Horton, Reilly, Timson, James, England
Referee: W.H. Thompson (Huddersfield)
1984-85
Hull 29 Kemble (2t); Leuluai, Schofield (4g, 1dg), S. Evans (1t), O'Hara; Ah Kuoi, Sterling; Edmonds, Patrick, L. Crooks (1t), Norton (1t), Proctor, Divorty (Rose)
Hull K.R. 12 Fairbairn (1t); Clark, Robinson (1t), Prohm, Laws; M. Smith, Harkin (Rudd); Broadhurst, Watkinson, Ema (Hartley), Burton, Kelly, Hall (1t)
Referee: G.F. Lindop (Wakefield)
1985-86
Hull K.R. 22 Fairbairn (Lydiat); Clark (1t), Dorahy (5g), Prohm, Laws; G. Smith, Harkin; Des Harrison, Watkinson, Ema, Burton, Hogan (Kelly), Miller (2t)
Castleford 18 Lord; Plange, Marchant (2t), Hyde, Spears; Diamond (1g), R. Beardmore (1t, 2g); Ward, K. Beardmore, B. Johnson, England, Ketteridge, Joyner
Referee: R. Campbell (Widnes)
1986-87
Castleford 31 Scott; Plange, Marchant, Johns, Hyde (Lord); Joyner, R. Beardmore (1dg); Ward (1t), K. Beardmore (2t), B. Johnson, Ketteridge (1t, 5g), Atkins (1t) (Shillito), England

Hull 24 Kemble; Brand (2t), Schofield, O'Hara (2t), Eastwood; Ah Kuoi, Windley; Brown (Puckering), S. Patrick, Dannatt, Norton (Divorty), L. Crooks (4g), Sharp
Referee: J. McDonald (Wigan)
1987-88
Bradford N. 12 Mercer; Ford, McGowan, Simpson, Francis; Mumby (2g), Harkin; Grayshon (Hobbs 2g), Noble, Hill, Skerrett, Fairbank (1t), Holmes (Roebuck)
Castleford 12 Roockley; Plange (1t), Marchant, Beattie, Hyde; Joyner, R. Southernwood; Shillito (R. Beardmore), K. Beardmore (Sampson), Ward, Ketteridge (2g), Fifita, Lindner (1t)
Referee: K. Allatt (Southport)
Replay
Bradford N. 11 Mumby; Ford, McGowan, Mercer, Simpson; Stewart, Harkin; Hobbs (1g, 1dg), Noble, Hill (1t), Skerrett, Fairbank, Heron (1t)
Castleford 2 Roockley; Plange, Marchant, Beattie, Hyde; R. Southernwood, R. Beardmore; Ward, Hill, Fifita (Sampson), Ketteridge (1g), England (Boothroyd), Joyner
Referee: K. Allatt (Southport)
1988-89
Leeds 33 Spencer; Ettingshausen, Schofield (2t, 1dg), Stephenson (6g), Gibson (2t); C. Lyons, Ashton; Crooks, Maskill, Waddell (Backo), Powell, Brooke-Cowden (Medley 1t), Heron
Castleford 12 Belcher; Plange, Marchant, Boothroyd (1t), Chapman (Roockley) (Sampson); Anderson, R. Beardmore; Ward, K. Beardmore, England, Ketteridge (2g), Gibbs, Joyner (1t)
Referee: R. Whitfield (Widnes)
1989-90
Bradford N. 20 Wilkinson; Cordle (2t), McGowan, Simpson, Francis; Henjak (Mumby), Harkin (2t); Skerrett, Barraclough, Hamer (Medley), Hobbs (2g), Fairbank, Pendlebury
Featherstone R. 14 Bibb; Drummond, I. Ropati (1t), Newlove, Banks; Smales, Fox (3g); Grayshon, Clark, G. Bell (Dakin), Price, Booth (Fisher), Smith (1t)
Referee: R. Whitfield (Widnes)
1990-91
Castleford 11 Larder; Ellis, Irwin, Anderson, Plange (1t); Steadman, Atkins (1t) (England); Crooks (1g), G. Southernwood, Sampson, Battye (Ketteridge); Hardy, Roebuck (1dg)
Wakefield T. 8 Harcombe (2g); Jones, Mason (1t), Eden, Wilson; Lazenby, M. Conway; Shelford, B. Conway (Slater), Thompson, Kelly (Perry), G. Price, Bell
Referee: J. Smith (Halifax)

THE WHITE ROSE TROPHY

First awarded in 1966, the trophy is presented to the adjudged man of the match in the Yorkshire Cup final.

Donated by the late T.E. Smith, of York, the award is organised by the Yorkshire Federation of Rugby League Supporters' Clubs and judged by a panel of the Press.

The trophy is not awarded in replays, although Bradford Northern's Brendan Hill was named Man of the Match in the second game against Castleford in 1987.

Season	Winner	Team	Position
1966-67	Cyril Kellett	Hull K.R. (v. Featherstone R.)	Full back
1967-68	Chris Davidson	Hull (v. Hull K.R.)	Scrum half
1968-69	Barry Seabourne	Leeds (v. Castleford)	Scrum half
1969-70	Joe Brown	Hull (v. Featherstone R.)	Loose forward
1970-71	Syd Hynes	Leeds (v. Featherstone R.)	Centre
1971-72	Ian Markham	Hull K.R. (v. Castleford)	Full back
1972-73	John Holmes	Leeds (v. Dewsbury)	Full back
1973-74	Keith Hepworth	Leeds (v. Wakefield T.)	Scrum half
1974-75	Roger Millward	Hull K.R. (v. Wakefield T.)	Stand off
1975-76	Neil Fox	Hull K.R. (v. Leeds)	Second row
1976-77	Les Dyl	Leeds (v. Featherstone R.)	Centre
1977-78	Bruce Burton	Castleford (v. Featherstone R.)	Stand off
1978-79	Bob Haigh	Bradford N. (v. York)	Loose forward
1979-80	Alan Smith	Leeds (v. Halifax)	Winger
1980-81	Kevin Dick	Leeds (v. Hull K.R.)	Scrum half
1981-82	Barry Johnson	Castleford (v. Bradford N.)	Prop
1982-83	Keith Mumby	Bradford N. (v. Hull)	Full back
1983-84	Mick Crane	Hull (v. Castleford)	Loose forward
1984-85	Peter Sterling	Hull (v. Hull K.R.)	Scrum half
1985-86	Gavin Miller	Hull K.R. (v. Castleford)	Loose forward
1986-87	Kevin Beardmore	Castleford (v. Hull)	Hooker
1987-88	Paul Harkin	Bradford N. (v. Castleford)	Scrum half
1988-89	Cliff Lyons	Leeds (v. Castleford)	Stand off
1989-90	Paul Harkin	Bradford N. (v. Featherstone R.)	Scrum half
1990-91	Tracy Lazenby	Wakefield T. (v. Castleford)	Stand off
1991-92	Graham Steadman	Castleford (v. Bradford N.)	Full back

YORKSHIRE CUP FINAL RECORDS

TEAM

Most appearances: 21 Leeds
Most wins: 17 Leeds
Highest score: Leeds 36 v. Dewsbury 9............ 1972
Widest margin win: Huddersfield 31 v. Hull 0... 1914
Biggest attendance:
36,000 Bradford N. v. Huddersfield (at Leeds).. 1949

INDIVIDUAL

Most tries:
4 by Stan Moorhouse (Huddersfield) v. Leeds.... 1919
Most goals:
6 by David Stephenson (Leeds) v. Castleford..... 1988
Most points:
16 (4g, 2t) by Graham Steadman (Castleford)
    v. Bradford N. 1991

1991 CHARITY SHIELD

Wigan showed that there was life after Ellery Hanley by registering a comfortable 22-8 victory over a weakened Hull side in a pioneering CIS Insurance Charity Shield encounter at Gateshead.

Without Leeds-bound Hanley, their main inspiration in the previous season's League-Cup double, Wigan recorded their third Charity Shield success after a hat-trick of defeats at the hands of Widnes.

Half backs Andy Gregory — appointed the new skipper — and fellow Test man Shaun Edwards provided the mainspring for Wigan, who were forced to adapt to the loss of Hanley's replacement, Andy Goodway, with a broken arm.

Hull, making their debut in the Charity Shield having won the Stones Bitter Premiership to qualify, fielded an understrength side lacking half of the players who had beaten favourites Widnes in the previous May's memorable Old Trafford final.

Missing from the Gateshead line-up were the injured Richard Gay, Andy Dannatt, Ian Marlow and Jon Sharp; Test prop Karl Harrison, transferred to Halifax; Australian centre pairing Damien McGarry and Brad Webb, returned Down Under and scrum half Patrick Entat, back in France.

Skipper Greg Mackey took the honours for the Airlie Birds, although the Australian scrum half was always struggling to find the right support.

The pipe-opener to the season provided only light entertainment for the near-capacity crowd of 10,248, nearly 75 per cent of whom were from the North East, the event also being televised live on local regional television.

With Gregory's promptings helping to establish early supremacy, Wigan looked set to romp away with the game, leading 16-2 on the half hour. Winger David Myers opened their account after only five minutes, centre Dean Bell adding a couple of touchdowns on his way to being awarded the Jack Bentley Memorial Trophy as Man of the Match.

New Zealand wingman Frano Botica added his third goal four minutes before the break, Hull's solitary reply being a 10th-minute penalty goal from Test winger Paul Eastwood.

After the interval, Hull showed the fighting spirit which had brought the Stones Bitter Premiership Trophy to the Boulevard, taking the second half 6-4. Edwards took only two minutes to claim a try before Hull closed defensive ranks and claimed their sole touchdown on the hour, Gary Nolan's efforts being goalled by Eastwood.

Nearly a year after switching codes, former Welsh Rugby Union international forward Mark Jones finally made his debut for Hull. It was a doubly notable event as the tall packman came onto the field in the 27th minute to temporarily replace Steve McNamara, who became the first player to go to the blood bin — the new international law to force a bleeding player to receive treatment off the field without his replacement counting towards the substitute quota.

McNamara returned after 10 minutes and, though Jones had to go off, he returned five minutes after the break to confirm his early impressive form.

Penalties went 12-5 to Hull, with the only foul coming in the last minute when Wigan's Kelvin Skerrett threw a punch.

Receipts for the first-ever professional Rugby League encounter at the Gateshead International Stadium amounted to £59,753. Wigan received the CIS Insurance Charity Shield and a £12,000 prize cheque to crown a pioneering afternoon which had kicked off with 80 North East youngsters taking part in a mini-rugby tournament, Newcastle beating Gateshead in the final.

CIS INSURANCE CHARITY SHIELD

25 August   Gateshead International Stadium

WIGAN 22   **HULL 8**

Steve Hampson	1.	Steve Feather
David Myers	2.	Paul Eastwood
Dean Bell	3.	Brian Blacker
Joe Lydon	4.	Gary Nolan
Frano Botica	5.	Neil Turner
Shaun Edwards	6.	Lee Hanlan
Andy Gregory, Capt.	7.	Greg Mackey, Capt.
Ian Lucas	8.	Steve Durham
Martin Dermott	9.	Lee Jackson
Kelvin Skerrett	10.	Ian Marlow
Denis Betts	11.	Steve McNamara
Andy Platt	12.	Russ Walker
Andy Goodway	13.	Dean Busby
Mike Forshaw	14.	Mike Dixon
Ian Gildart	15.	Mark Jones

T: Bell (2), Myers, Edwards   T: Nolan
G: Botica (3)   G: Eastwood (2)
Substitutions: Substitutions:
Gildart for Lucas (29 min.)   Jones for McNamara (27 min.)
Forshaw for Platt (57 min.)   Dixon for Durham (51 min.)
Half-time: 18-2   Attendance: 10,248
Referee: Robin Whitfield (Widnes)

● The Charity Shield is contested between the previous season's Challenge Cup winners and Division One Champions. When Wigan won both trophies in 1990 and 1991 they met the previous season's Premiership final winners.

CHARITY SHIELD ROLL OF HONOUR

Year	Winners		Runners-up		Venue	Attendance
1985-86	Wigan	34	*Hull K.R.	6	Isle of Man	4,066
1986-87	*Halifax	9	Castleford	8	Isle of Man	3,276
1987-88	*Wigan	44	Halifax	12	Isle of Man	4,804
1988-89	*Widnes	20	Wigan	14	Isle of Man	5,044
1989-90	*Widnes	27	Wigan	22	Liverpool FC	17,263
1990-91	†Widnes	24	*Wigan	8	Swansea C. FC	11,178
1991-92	*Wigan	22	†Hull	8	Gateshead	10,248

*Denotes previous season's Champions; † Premiership winners; unmarked, Challenge Cup winners

CHARITY SHIELD .... A REVIEW

1985-86
Wigan 34 Hampson; P. Ford, Stephenson (7g),
Donlan (2t), Gill (2t); Edwards, M. Ford (1t);
Courtney (Mayo), Kiss, Campbell, West
(Lucas), Du Toit, Wane
Hull K.R. 6 Fairbairn (Lydiat 1g); Clark (1t),
Robinson, Prohm, Laws; M. Smith, G. Smith;
Des Harrison, Watkinson, Ema, Kelly (Rudd),
Burton, Hogan
Referee: R. Campbell (Widnes)

1986-87
Halifax 9 Smith (Wilson); Riddlesden,
Whitfield (1t), Hague (1dg), George (1t);
C. Anderson, Stephens; Dickinson, McCallion,
Juliff, Scott (James), Bell, Dixon
Castleford 8 Roockley; Plange, Lord (1t),
Irwin (R. Southernwood), Spears; Joyner
(Fletcher), R. Beardmore; Ward,
K. Beardmore, Johnson, Ketteridge (2g),
Mountain, England
Referee: G.F. Lindop (Wakefield)

1987-88
Wigan 44 Hampson (2t); Stephenson (8g),
Byrne (Russell), Bell (2t), Gill (1t); Edwards
(2t), Gregory; West, Kiss, Case, Gildart
(Wane), Potter, Goodway
Halifax 12 Eadie (2g); Taylor, Wilson,
T. Anderson, George; Simpson (Juliff 1t),
Stephens; Dickinson, Pendlebury, Beevers,
James, Scott (Bell), Dixon (1t)
Referee: J. Holdsworth (Kippax)

1988-89
Widnes 20 Tait; Thackray, Currier (4g),
Wright (1t), Offiah (1t); Dowd, D. Hulme;
Sorensen, McKenzie, Grima (Pyke),
M. O'Neill, P. Hulme, Eyres
Wigan 14 Hampson; Gill, Lydon (1t, 1g), Bell,
Preston (Lucas); Byrne, Gregory; Shelford
(Betts), Kiss, Case, T. Iro (2t), Wane,
Goodway
Referee: R. Tennant (Castleford)

1989-90
Widnes 27 Tait (1dg); Kebbie (1t), Davies
(1t, 5g), Wright, Offiah (1t); A. Myler,
D. Hulme (1t); Sorensen, P. Hulme, Grima
(Pyke), M. O'Neill, Koloto, Eyres
Wigan 22 Hampson; Bell (Gilfillan), K. Iro
(1t), Lydon (1t, 5g), Preston; Byrne, Gregory;
Lucas, Kiss, Platt (1t) (Stazicker), Betts,
Gildart, Goodway
Referee: J. Holdsworth (Kippax)

1990-91
Widnes 24 Tait; Devereux (1t), Currier, Davies
(3t, 2g), Offiah (1t); A. Myler, D. Hulme;
Ashurst (Wright), McKenzie, Grima, P. Hulme
(Sorensen), Koloto, Holliday
Wigan 8 Gilfillan; Myers, Bell, Byrne, Preston;
Botica (1t, 2g) (Edwards), Goulding; Skerrett,
Bridge, Wane, Gildart (Forshaw), Platt, Betts
Referee: C. Morris (Huddersfield)

CHARITY SHIELD RECORDS

TEAM
Most appearances: 6 Wigan
Most wins: 3 Widnes, Wigan
Highest score: Wigan 44 v. Halifax 12.............. 1987
(Also widest margin)
Biggest attendance:
17,263 Widnes v. Wigan (at Liverpool FC)....... 1989

INDIVIDUAL
Most tries:
3 by Jonathan Davies (Widnes) v. Wigan.......... 1990
Most goals:
8 by David Stephenson (Wigan) v. Halifax........ 1987
Most points:
16 (8g) by David Stephenson (Wigan) v. Halifax 1987
(3t,2g) Jonathan Davies (Widnes) v. Wigan... 1990

MAN OF THE MATCH AWARDS

Season	Winner	Team	Position
1985-86	Shaun Edwards	Wigan (v. Hull K.R.)	Stand off
1986-87	Chris Anderson	Halifax (v. Castleford)	Stand off
1987-88	Shaun Edwards	Wigan (v. Halifax)	Stand off
1988-89	Phil McKenzie	Widnes (v. Wigan)	Hooker
1989-90	Denis Betts	Wigan (v. Widnes)	Second row
1990-91	Jonathan Davies	Widnes (v. Wigan)	Centre
1991-92	Dean Bell	Wigan (v. Hull)	Centre

● From 1987 it became the Jack Bentley Trophy in memory of the former *Daily Express* Rugby
League journalist.

1991 WORLD CLUB CHALLENGE

The accurate boot of former New Zealand Rugby Union international Frano Botica helped Wigan to their second Foster's World Club Challenge success, beating a determined Penrith 21-4 at Liverpool FC's Anfield stadium.

Botica, fresh from debut Test series against France and Australia, kicked six goals from seven attempts to take the Man of the Match award and so provide Wigan with the biggest winning margin in the three-match history of the Anglo-Australia tournament.

Despite a low-key build-up to the world title event by Penrith, the newly-crowned Sydney Premiership winners, the Australians — missing 1990 Kangaroo tourists Brad Fittler and Mark Geyer — ensured that the British Champions were tested to the full, highlighted by a string of over-exuberant challenges.

Watched by a crowd of more than 20,000, the world club decider started in brutal fashion as the visitors tried unsuccessfully to knock Wigan out of their stride. French referee Alain Sablayrolles, who had taken charge of the 1990 Anglo-Australia Tests, penalised the intimidation and former All Black Botica punished them by kicking four penalties inside the first 13 minutes to give Wigan the cushion of an eight-point lead.

Penrith loose forward Colin Van Der Voort was the culprit for the first two penalty awards, for crude challenges on Test men Shaun Edwards and Philip Clarke. Then a kick-off straight over the dead ball line by skipper Greg Alexander, an 11th-hour inclusion after being ruled out of Australia's tour of Papua New Guinea through injury, enabled Botica to land his third goal, this time from halfway.

Stand off Steve Carter was lucky to escape with conceding a penalty after a nasty late challenge on Wigan mainspring Andy Gregory, Botica adding another two points.

But, in the 18th minute, Penrith showed the quality which had brought them the Australian title. Alexander, displaying world-class vision befitting a man who appeared in every match on the 1990 British Coal tour of Britain, calmly weighed up the situation when taking the ball on the sixth tackle. His kick picked out Darren Willis on the right wing and the pursuing Joe Lydon stood no chance of preventing a score.

The Panthers threatened to take control, and it needed a fine tackle from winger David Myers to halt full back Greg Barwick. Wigan captain Gregory stemmed the tide by unlocking the visiting defence with splendid improvisation in the 27th minute. With seemingly little scope, Gregory slipped a sweetly timed pass to New Zealand Test centre Sam Panapa, who crashed over from

Wigan skipper Andy Gregory shows off the 1991 Foster's World Club Challenge Trophy.

close range. Panapa was a last-minute stand-in for the injured Dean Bell, who was withdrawn after breaking down in the pre-match warm-up on the pitch. With Botica again on target, Wigan fully deserved their 10-point half-time advantage.

Ben Alexander came on at the start of the second period, allowing brother Greg to move to full back, Brad Izzard moving into the pack. Moving as a more purposeful unit, Penrith kept Wigan on the defensive for long periods, with Test forward John Cartwright outstanding despite an injury which had ruled him out of the Papuan tour.

Wigan sent on defence-orientated Ian Gildart to bolster their pressurised rearguard as Penrith belied the effects of their Premiership final celebrations and round-the-world travel. With 10 minutes left, full back Hampson was obstructed and Botica cracked home his sixth successful shot to rule out a Penrith revival.

Wigan sensed the Panthers' submission and Edwards broke their cover in the 77th minute with an interception which launched a 60-yard run supported by wingman Myers, who crashed over in the corner to leave Botica with his only unsuccessful kick of the night. Lydon rounded off the scoring and the action with a last-second drop goal for a resounding victory which gave Australian coach John Monie his seventh trophy in a two-year reign at Central Park.

FOSTER'S WORLD CLUB CHALLENGE

2 October   **Anfield, Liverpool**

WIGAN 21		PENRITH 4
Steve Hampson	1.	Greg Barwick
David Myers	2.	Darren Willis
Sam Panapa	3.	Graeme Bradley
Joe Lydon	4.	Brad Izzard
Frano Botica	5.	Graham Mackay
Shaun Edwards	6.	Steve Carter
Andy Gregory, Capt.	7.	Greg Alexander, Capt.
Kelvin Skerrett	8.	Brandon Lee
Martin Dermott	9.	Royce Simmons
Andy Platt	10.	Paul Dunn
Denis Betts	11.	Paul Clarke
Billy McGinty	12.	John Cartwright
Philip Clarke	13.	Colin Van Der Voort
Ian Lucas	14.	Ben Alexander
Ian Gildart	15.	Grant Izzard
Neil Cowie	16.	Tony Xuereb
Mike Forshaw	17.	Paul Smith

T: Panapa, Myers
G: Botica (6), Lydon (dg)
Substitutions:
Cowie for Skerrett (37 min.)
Gildart for McGinty (65 min.)
Forshaw for Clarke (75 min.)
Lucas for Cowie (75 min.)
Half-time: 14-4
Attendance: 20,152

T: Willis
Substitutions:
B. Alexander for Barwick (40 min.)
G. Izzard for Lee (40 min.)
Smith for Willis (50 min.)
Xuereb for Van Der Voort (60 min.)
Referee: Alain Sablayrolles (France)
Receipts: £179,797

WORLD CLUB CHALLENGE ROLL OF HONOUR

Year	Winners		Runners-up		Venue	Attendance	Receipts
1987	Wigan	8	Manly-Warringah	2	Wigan	36,895	£131,000
1989	Widnes	30	Canberra	18	Old Trafford, Man'r	30,786	£207,764
1991	Wigan	21	Penrith	4	Anfield, Liverpool	20,152	£179,797

WORLD CLUB CHALLENGE . . . .
A REVIEW
1987-88
Wigan 8 Hampson; Russell, Stephenson (4g), Lydon, Gill; Edwards, Gregory; Case (Lucas), Kiss, Wane, Goodway, Potter, Hanley
Manly 2 Shearer; Ronson, Williams (Ticehurst), O'Connor (1g), Davis; Lyons, Hasler; Daley, Cochrane, Gately (Brokenshire), Gibbs, Cunningham (Shaw), Vautin
Referee: J. Holdsworth (Kippax)
1989-90
Widnes 30 Tait; Currier, Davies (1t, 3g), Wright (1t), Offiah (2t); A. Myler (Dowd), D. Hulme; Grima (Moriarty), McKenzie, Pyke, Sorensen, P. Hulme (1t), Eyres (1t)
Canberra 18 Belcher; Wood (2g), Meninga (1t) (Martin), Daley, Ferguson; O'Sullivan (1t, 1g), Stuart; Jackson (Lowry), Walters (1t), Lazarus, Lance, Coyne, Clyde
Referee: F. Desplas (France)

MAN OF THE MATCH AWARDS
1987: Shaun Wane (Wigan)
1989: David Hulme (Widnes)
1991: Frano Botica (Wigan)

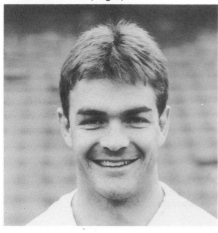

Penrith prop Paul Dunn.

Penrith captain Greg Alexander is halted by Wigan second row man Denis Betts.

In unfamiliar Penrith garb, Wigan celebrate their 1991 Foster's World Club success, the Trophy in the hands of hooker Martin Dermott (left) and coach John Monie.

BBC-2 FLOODLIT TROPHY

The BBC-2 Floodlit Trophy competition was launched in 1965. Eight clubs competed in the first year and the total had grown to 22 by 1980 when the competition was abolished as part of the BBC's financial cut-backs.

For 15 years the matches became a regular television feature on Tuesday evenings throughout the early winter months.

Although the format changed slightly over the years, it was basically a knockout competition on the lines of the Challenge Cup.

In 1966 the Floodlit Competition was used to introduce the limited tackle rule, then four tackles, which proved such a great success it was adopted in all other matches before the end of the year.

BBC-2 FLOODLIT TROPHY FINALS
(Only the 1967, at Leeds, and 1972, at Wigan, finals were played on neutral grounds)

Season	Winners		Runners-up		Venue	Attendance	Receipts
1965-66	Castleford	4	St. Helens	0	St. Helens	11,510	£1,548
1966-67	Castleford	7	Swinton	2	Castleford	8,986	£1,692
1967-68	Castleford	8	Leigh	5	Leeds	9,716	£2,099
1968-69	Wigan	7	St. Helens	4	Wigan	13,479	£3,291
1969-70	Leigh	11	Wigan	6	Wigan	12,312	£2,854
1970-71	Leeds	9	St. Helens	5	Leeds	7,612	£2,189
1971-72	St. Helens	8	Rochdale H.	2	St. Helens	9,300	£2,493
1972-73	Leigh	5	Widnes	0	Wigan	4,691	£1,391
1973-74	Bramley	15	Widnes	7	Widnes	4,422	£1,538
1974-75	Salford	0	Warrington	0	Salford	4,473	£1,913
Replay	Salford	10	Warrington	5	Warrington	5,778	£2,434
1975-76	St. Helens	22	Dewsbury	2	St. Helens	3,858	£1,747
1976-77	Castleford	12	Leigh	4	Leigh	5,402	£2,793
1977-78	Hull K.R.	26	St. Helens	11	Hull K.R.	10,099	£6,586
1978-79	Widnes	13	St. Helens	7	St. Helens	10,250	£7,017
1979-80	Hull	13	Hull K.R.	3	Hull	18,500	£16,605

BBC2 FLOODLIT TROPHY .... A REVIEW
1965-66
Castleford 4 Edwards; C. Battye, M. Battye, Willett (2g), Briggs; Hardisty, Millward; Terry, J. Ward, C. Dickinson, Bryant, Taylor, Small
St. Helens 0 F. Barrow; Vollenhoven, Wood, Benyon, Killeen; Murphy, Prosser; French, Dagnall, Watson, Hicks, Mantle, Laughton
Referee: L. Gant (Wakefield)
1966-67
Castleford 7 Edwards; Howe, Stenton, Willett (1g), Austin (1t); Hardisty, Hepworth (1g); Hartley, C. Dickinson, McCartney, Bryant, Small, Walker
Swinton 2 Gowers; Whitehead (1g), Gomersall, Buckley, Davies; Fleet, G. Williams; Halliwell, D. Clarke, Scott (Cummings), Rees, Simpson, Robinson
Referee: J. Manley (Warrington)
1967-68
Castleford 8 Edwards; Harris, Thomas, Stenton, Willett (4g); Hardisty, Hepworth; Hartley, J. Ward, Walton, Bryant (C. Dickinson), Redfearn, Reilly

Leigh 5 Grainey; Tickle (1t), Lewis, Collins, Walsh; Entwistle, A. Murphy; Whitworth, Ashcroft, Major, Welding, M. Murphy, Gilfedder (1g)
Referee: G.F. Lindop (Wakefield)
1968-69
Wigan 7 Tyrer (2g); Francis, Ashton, Ashurst, Rowe; C. Hill (1t), Jackson; J. Stephens, Clarke, Mills, Fogerty (Lyon), Kevin O'Loughlin
St. Helens 4 Williams; Wilson, Benyon, Myler, Wills; Whittle, Bishop; Warlow, Sayer, Watson, Mantle, Hogan, Coslett (2g)
Referee: E. Clay (Leeds)
1969-70
Leigh 11 Ferguson (3g) (Lewis); Tickle (1t), Dorrington, Collins, Walsh; Eckersley, Murphy (1g); D. Chisnall, Ashcroft, Watts, Welding, Grimes, Lyon
Wigan 6 C. Hill; Wright, Francis (2g), Rowe, Kevin O'Loughlin; D. Hill (1g), Jackson; J. Stephens, Clarke, Ashcroft, Ashurst, Mills, Laughton
Referee: W.H. Thompson (Huddersfield)

1970-71
Leeds 9 Holmes (2g); Alan Smith, Hynes
(1t, 1g), Cowan, Atkinson; Wainwright,
Shoebottom; J. Burke, Fisher, Barnard, Haigh,
Ramsey, Batten
St. Helens 5 F. Barrow; L. Jones (1t), Benyon,
Walsh, Wilson; Whittle, Heaton; Rees,
A. Karalius, E. Chisnall, Mantle, E. Prescott,
Coslett (1g)
Referee: E. Lawrinson (Warrington)
1971-72
St. Helens 8 G. Pimblett; L. Jones, Benyon,
Walsh, Wilson; Kelly, Heaton; Rees,
A. Karalius, E. Chisnall, E. Prescott, Mantle,
Coslett (4g)
Rochdale H. 2 Chamberlain (1g); Brelsford,
Crellin, Taylor, Glover; Myler, Gartland;
Birchall, P. Clarke, Brown, Welding, Sheffield
(Hodkinson), Delooze
Referee: E. Clay (Leeds)
1972-73
Leigh 5 Hogan; Lawson (1t) (Lester), Atkin,
Collins, Stacey; A. Barrow, Sayer (Ryding);
Grimes, D. Clarke, Fletcher, Fiddler (1g),
F. Barrow, Martyn
Widnes 0 Dutton; A. Prescott, Aspey,
Blackwood, McDonnell; Lowe, Ashton;
Mills, Elwell, Warlow, Foran, Sheridan,
Nicholls
Referee: G.F. Lindop (Wakefield)
1973-74
Bramley 15 Keegan; Goodchild (1t), Bollon,
Hughes, Austin (1t); T. Briggs, Ward (1g)
(Ashman); D. Briggs, Firth, Cheshire,
D. Sampson (1t), Idle, Wolford (2g)
Widnes 7 Dutton (2g); D. O'Neill, Hughes,
Aspey, Macko (1t); Warburton, Bowden;
Hogan, Elwell, Nelson, Sheridan, Blackwood
(Foran) Laughton
Referee: D.G. Kershaw (York)
1974-75
Salford 0 Charlton; Fielding, Hesketh,
Graham, Richards; Brophy (Taylor), Banner;
Coulman, Devlin, Grice, Knighton, Dixon,
E. Prescott
Warrington 0 Whitehead; Sutton, Cunliffe
(Lowe), Whittle, Bevan; Briggs, Gordon;
D. Chisnall, Ashcroft, Wright, Gaskell, Conroy,
B. Philbin (Jewitt)
Referee: W.H. Thompson (Huddersfield)
Replay
Salford 10 Stead; Fielding (1t), Watkins (2g),
Hesketh, Richards (1t); Gill, Banner; Grice,
Walker, Mackay, Dixon, Knighton, E. Prescott

Warrington 5 Cunliffe; Whitehead (1g), Pickup,
Whittle, Bevan (1t); Noonan (Briggs), Gordon;
D. Chisnall, Ashcroft, Wanbon, Conroy,
Nicholas (Brady), B. Philbin
Referee: W.H. Thompson (Huddersfield)
1975-76
St. Helens 22 G. Pimblett (2g); L. Jones,
Benyon (1t), Hull (1t), Mathias (2t); Wilson
(1t), Heaton (1dg); Mantle, A. Karalius, James,
Nicholls, E. Chisnall, Coslett (1g)
Dewsbury 2 Langley; Hegarty, Chalkley,
Simpson, Mitchell; N. Stephenson (1g) (Lee),
A. Bates; Beverley, Price, Hankins, Halloran
(Artis), Bell, Grayshon
Referee: W.H. Thompson (Huddersfield)
1976-77
Castleford 12 Wraith; Fenton, Joyner, P.
Johnson, Walsh (1t); Burton (1t), Stephens;
Khan, Spurr, A. Dickinson, Reilly, Lloyd (3g),
S. Norton
Leigh 4 Hogan; A. Prescott, Stacey, Woods,
Walsh (1t); Taylor, Sayer; D. Chisnall, Ashcroft
(1dg), Fletcher, Macko, Grimes, Boyd
Referee: J.E. Jackson (Pudsey)
1977-78
Hull K.R. 26 Hall (4g); Dunn (2t), M. Smith
(1t), Watson, Sullivan (1t); Hartley (1t),
Millward; Millington, Watkinson, Cunningham
(Hughes), Lowe, Rose (1t), Casey
St. Helens 11 G. Pimblett (Platt); L. Jones
(Courtney), Noonan, Cunningham (1t), Glynn
(2t, 1g); Francis, K. Gwilliam; D. Chisnall,
Liptrot, James, Hope, A. Karalius, Pinner
Referee: M.J. Naughton (Widnes)
1978-79
Widnes 13 Eckersley; Wright (2t), Hughes,
Aspey, P. Shaw; Burke (2g, 1t), Bowden;
Hogan, Elwell, Mills, Adams, Dearden,
Laughton
St. Helens 7 G. Pimblett (2g); L. Jones,
Glynn, Cunningham, Mathias; Francis,
Holding; D. Chisnall (1t), Liptrot, James,
Nicholls, Knighton (E. Chisnall), Pinner
Referee: J. McDonald (Wigan)
1979-80
Hull 13 Woods; Bray, G. Evans (1t), Coupland,
Dennison (1t, 2g); Newlove, Hepworth;
Tindall, Wileman, Farrar, Stone, Boxall
(Birdsall 1t), Norton
Hull K.R. 3 Robinson; Hubbard (1t),
M. Smith, Watson, Sullivan; Hall, Agar;
Holdstock, Tyreman, Lockwood, Clarkson
(Hartley), Lowe, Hogan (Millington)
Referee: W.H. Thompson (Huddersfield)

CAPTAIN MORGAN TROPHY

This sponsored competition, with a winners' prize of £3,000, lasted only one season. Entry was restricted to the 16 clubs who won their Yorkshire and Lancashire Cup first round ties. The Lancashire contingent was made up to eight by including the side which lost their first round county Cup-tie by the narrowest margin. The first round of the Captain Morgan Trophy was zoned with clubs being drawn against those in their own county. The remainder of the competition was integrated. The final was on a neutral ground as follows:

1973-74   Warrington   4   Featherstone R.   0   Salford   5,259   £2,265

1973-74
Warrington 4 Whitehead (2g); M. Philbin, Noonan, Reynolds (Pickup), Bevan; Whittle, Gordon; D. Chisnall, Ashcroft, Brady, Wanbon (Price), Wright, Mather

Featherstone R. 0 Box; Coventry, M. Smith, Hartley, Bray; Mason, Wood; Tonks, Bridges, Harris, Gibbins (Stone), Rhodes, Bell
Referee: G.F. Lindop (Wakefield)

Dean Bell celebrates Wigan's third successive Stones Bitter Championship title, the Kiwi's first as skipper.

LEAGUE

1991-92 CHAMPIONSHIP

Record-breakers Wigan became the first club to lift the coveted Championship Trophy in three successive seasons, clinching the record Stones Bitter £45,000 prize cheque by winning their last 17 league games.

The Riversiders sealed the title with a 50-8 hammering of Bradford Northern at Central Park with two games left to play, completing the 26-match programme with only four defeats and an impressive eight-point margin over runners-up, arch-rivals St. Helens.

While securing champion status with a winning sequence dating back to a 24-10 reversal at Salford in mid-November, Wigan also reached Wembley for the fifth successive year to set up a third consecutive Cup and League double. In mid-May they made it a first-ever treble by adding the Stones Bitter Premiership.

They confirmed their number-one rating in the Stones Bitter Championship with the best scoring records, amassing most points — 27 ahead of seventh-placed Halifax — and conceding fewer than 12 points per match.

Wigan were slow starters to the eight-month campaign. St. Helens, serving up a typical brand of open football, led the table in September. Widnes took over in October before the Saints resumed leadership throughout November. Big-spending Leeds, with new recruits Doug Laughton as coach and Ellery Hanley as captain, took pole position in December while qualifying for the Regal Trophy final.

It was 5 January before Wigan emerged as table-toppers, with a one-point lead, having played one more game than Leeds. Neighbours St. Helens regained supremacy during February, capitalising on a two-game advantage over Wigan who were Britain's representatives in the inaugural World Sevens in Sydney. Wigan caught up their backlog to head the table from the start of March.

Wigan and St. Helens were heading for a classic title showdown at Knowsley Road on Good Friday, the penultimate match-day of the season, when the Saints blew their chances in their 24th Championship fixture, at Warrington.

Needing to remain unbeaten for the remainder of the campaign, the Saints went down 30-18 at Wilderspool, a contributory factor being the resting of the inspirational Kiwi import Tea Ropati to allow Great Britain tour candidates Anthony Sullivan, Alan Hunte and Paul Loughlin an opportunity to impress on the eve of squad selection.

St. Helens had the consolation of finishing as title runners-up to receive a £17,000 Stones Bitter prize cheque, Castleford securing third spot.

The fate of the clubs at the bottom end of the Stones Bitter Championship table was even more thrilling. Swinton were doomed to relegation well before the halfway stage of the campaign, but the second downward-bound club was not to be determined until the last day of the season.

Swinton, who replaced Australian player-coach Chris O'Sullivan with ex-Oldham and Warrington coach Tony Barrow mid-stream, hit the foot of the table in mid-October along with Bradford Northern, both having secured only one victory in the opening six matches. Northern were runners-up in the John Smiths Yorkshire Cup final, immediately after which Peter Fox was brought back to Odsal for a second stint, this time as team manager over player-coach David Hobbs. His arrival from Featherstone Rovers coincided with Northern dropping to last place during November.

From Christmas to the end of February, Swinton were joined at the bottom by Featherstone Rovers, now being coached for the second time by Allan Agar. By mid-March the candidates for the drop along with Swinton were Bradford Northern and Featherstone Rovers, now joined by Salford, Hull and Halifax. After 12 April, the five-club relegation battle from the bottom up was:

Bradford 24 played, 18 points; Hull 24, 20; Salford 25, 20; Featherstone 25, 22; Halifax 24, 22.

On the last but one match-day, Good Friday, three surprise results produced one of the most exciting relegation tussles, Bradford Northern hammering Swinton 60-0 at Odsal to boost their points difference, Hull winning 12-8 at derby rivals Hull K.R. and Halifax recording a 24-16 success at Leeds.

Four clubs entered the final day of the league season facing relegation along with Swinton, who ironically still had a major part to play by entertaining Salford in a Manchester derby. Of the four contenders — Bradford Northern and Salford on 20 points, and Featherstone Rovers and Hull on the 22-mark — only Hull were at home.

The permutations were intriguing. If all three other clubs won during the afternoon, then Hull would have to at least draw with Wembley finalists Castleford in an evening encounter, delayed due to the availability of police cover. Defeat for any one of the afternoon trio while the other two were winning would settle the issue without concerning Hull. That was to be the case.

Bradford Northern survived a comeback by a weakened Hull K.R. outfit to win 14-12 at Craven Park. Welsh winger Adrian Hadley scored a hat-trick of tries for Salford in a 26-18 success at Swinton. Featherstone Rovers were to become double victims, losing 28-10 at Wakefield Trinity and conceding their First Division status in the process, being relegated for the first time since 1987. Ironically, the Colliers had been third in the table after the first month of the season.

In the new-style Second Division, the eight clubs met each other twice home and away for a total of 28 league fixtures. The theory of producing a more competitive structure in preparation for promotion to the Stones Bitter Championship proved to be the case, though there were complaints of over-familiarity from both players and supporters.

Sheffield Eagles made an immediate return to the premier grade as Second Division Champions, earning a Stones Bitter prize of £22,000. Joining them after a two-year stay in the Second Division were Leigh, a club which had come to within hours of being wound up before the start of the season due to financial problems. The crisis club dispensed with the services of coach Alex Murphy, re-engaging Kevin Ashcroft to finish only one point behind the Eagles and four ahead of third-placed Oldham.

Rochdale Hornets, who reached the Greenalls Lancashire Cup final, and Carlisle were the pacesetters in September, with Sheffield and Oldham, coached by Australian Peter Tunks, taking over in October. From November, the Sheffield/Leigh duo took it in turns to share the leadership, signs of nervousness never allowing one to dominate the top spot. The Eagles clinched the Second Division Championship bowl with a 42-7 success over Ryedale-York at the Don Valley Stadium on Easter Sunday.

Ryedale-York were the first side to be relegated to the Third Division along with Workington Town, who had been among the sides fancied for promotion at the start of the campaign. Both sides had experienced off-the-field problems, Ryedale-York making a stand against the contract system which cost them the services of a host of better-class players for the early part of the season, and Town parting company with player-coach Ray Ashton in mid-season after a highly impressive first 12 months in the role.

The first-ever Third Division campaign was deemed a success, rekindling spectator and media interest in the lower region of the championship. The 14 clubs, including newcomers Scarborough Pirates, responded to the challenge of a £10,500 Stones Bitter prize.

Pre-season favourites Doncaster repaid the bookmakers' confidence by topping the table with a 100 per cent record after the opening three games, before Batley and Dewsbury mounted a Heavy Woollen domination throughout October. Hunslet took over leadership at the start of November through to mid-December, when a revitalised Huddersfield entered the title frame.

Joint coaches Mick Blacker and Francis Jarvis had been sacked with the season only a few weeks old, Alex Murphy being persuaded to take the helm. With former Great Britain loose forward Terry Flanagan as his assistant, the Murphy magic soon began to work and the destiny of the first-ever Third Division title became a two-horse race between the Fartowners and Maurice Bamford's Bramley.

Bramley gained supremacy at the top of the table for three weeks from mid-January and again in late March by virtue of having played more matches. The crunch came on 29 March when Bramley needed to win their last league match to force Huddersfield to win two of their three remaining games to secure the title. Bramley lost 12-6 at home to Batley while Murphy's men registered a resounding 42-10 home success over Barrow.

Nearly 4,000 fans turned up at Fartown, three times the previous season's average, for their final league match, a 30-20 defeat of Hunslet, after which Huddersfield received their first trophy for 17 years.

Bramley were promoted as runners-up, four points behind the Fartowners and three ahead of third-placed Dewsbury, who had played their home matches at fourth-placed Batley's Mount Pleasant.

All was not rosy in the Third Division. Newboys Scarborough Pirates were in the top three after the first week of October before a potential £1m sponsorship pay-out from a promotion wager and the sacking of coach Len Casey took their toll. The Pirates finished ninth under Trevor Bailey, 12 points adrift of eighth-placed Hunslet.

Three clubs did not reach double-figure points aggregates: Chorley Borough; Trafford

Borough, who left their Altrincham home with four matches remaining and had to seek sanctuary at Huddersfield before an impending move to Blackpool; and Nottingham City, creators of a number of unwanted records.

Nottingham, formerly Mansfield Marksman, became only the third team to lose all their matches in a season, going down in all 26 Third Division games, plus three cup ties to join Runcorn Highfield in 1989-90, and Liverpool City in 1906-07. Nottingham also conceded a record total of 1,323 points during a two or three division era, the previous worst being the 1,133 points conceded by First Division Barrow in 1989-90. City finished the campaign with the longest current losing run of 36 matches in all competitions.

Sheffield Eagles stand-in skipper Mark Aston with the Stones Bitter Second Division Championship Trophy.

FINAL TABLES 1991-92

STONES BITTER CHAMPIONSHIP

	P.	W.	D.	L.	Dr.	FOR Gls.	Trs.	Pts.	Dr.	AGAINST Gls.	Trs.	Pts.	Pts.
Wigan	26	22	0	4	3	107	107	645	5	39	56	307	44
St. Helens	26	17	2	7	6	76	98	550	2	59	67	388	36
Castleford	26	15	2	9	0	87	96	558	3	55	63	365	32
Warrington	26	15	0	11	5	71	90	507	7	64	74	431	30
Leeds	26	14	1	11	5	71	92	515	4	65	68	406	29
Wakefield T.	26	13	1	12	6	57	70	400	5	67	74	435	27
Halifax	26	12	0	14	2	86	111	618	0	87	98	566	24
Widnes	26	12	0	14	1	77	89	511	3	69	84	477	24
Hull K.R.	26	12	0	14	7	60	63	379	4	63	84	466	24
Salford	26	11	0	15	4	76	81	480	5	71	90	507	22
Bradford N.	26	11	0	15	2	65	86	476	1	74	91	513	22
Hull	26	11	0	15	0	84	75	468	4	89	86	526	22
Featherstone R.	26	11	0	15	3	67	78	449	2	88	98	570	22
Swinton	26	3	0	23	2	42	42	254	1	136	145	853	6

SECOND DIVISION

	P.	W.	D.	L.	Dr.	FOR Gls.	Trs.	Pts.	Dr.	AGAINST Gls.	Trs.	Pts.	Pts.
Sheffield E.	28	21	1	6	10	121	141	816	10	61	66	396	43
Leigh	28	21	0	7	17	92	104	617	9	62	67	401	42
Oldham	28	18	2	8	6	84	96	558	5	72	68	421	38
London C.	28	14	0	14	0	74	70	428	5	75	82	483	28
Rochdale H.	28	12	2	14	5	87	110	619	11	73	83	489	26
Carlisle	28	12	1	15	10	70	85	490	6	72	79	466	25
Ryedale-York	28	5	2	21	8	53	56	338	3	115	129	749	12
Workington T.	28	4	2	22	8	63	44	310	15	114	132	771	10

THIRD DIVISION

	P.	W.	D.	L.	Dr.	FOR Gls.	Trs.	Pts.	Dr.	AGAINST Gls.	Trs.	Pts.	Pts.
Huddersfield	26	23	0	3	5	124	154	869	5	44	41	257	46
Bramley	26	21	0	5	5	109	113	675	4	47	40	258	42
Dewsbury	26	19	1	6	4	113	141	794	7	46	45	279	39
Batley	26	18	2	6	3	97	111	641	9	43	46	279	38
Barrow	26	17	1	8	5	91	119	663	5	55	60	355	35
Doncaster	26	15	2	9	3	84	99	567	8	55	61	362	32
Keighley C.	26	15	2	9	7	94	98	587	6	65	71	420	32
Hunslet	26	16	0	10	10	100	111	654	1	86	95	553	32
Scarborough P.	26	10	0	16	3	72	84	483	9	71	87	499	20
Whitehaven	26	9	0	17	4	71	91	510	1	97	100	595	18
Highfield	26	9	0	17	2	54	74	406	2	94	114	646	18
Chorley B.	26	4	0	22	6	46	48	290	2	114	153	842	8
Trafford B.	26	2	0	24	4	49	51	306	5	130	169	941	4
Nottingham C.	26	0	0	26	4	22	29	164	1	179	241	1323	0

Corals pre-season betting for the 1991-92 Championship: 11-10 Wigan; 4-1 Leeds; 6-1 Castleford, St. Helens; 13-2 Widnes; 10-1 Hull; 33-1 Bradford N.; 100-1 Warrington; 150-1 Wakefield T.; 200-1 Featherstone R., Halifax; 500-1 Salford; 5,000-1 Hull K.R., Swinton.

Corals pre-season betting for the Second Division Championship: 10-11 Sheffield E.; 2-1 Oldham; 6-1 Workington T.; 8-1 Rochdale H.; 14-1 Leigh; 16-1 London C.; 33-1 Carlisle; 40-1 Ryedale-York.

Corals pre-season betting for the Third Division Championship: 15-8 Doncaster; 5-2 Hunslet; 5-1 Batley, Dewsbury; 10-1 Barrow; 12-1 Keighley C.; 14-1 Huddersfield; 33-1 Bramley, Whitehaven; 66-1 Highfield, Scarborough P.; 200-1 Chorley B., Trafford B.; 1,000-1 Nottingham C.

TWO DIVISION CHAMPIONSHIP ROLL OF HONOUR

	FIRST DIVISION	**SECOND DIVISION**
1902-03	Halifax	Keighley
1903-04	Bradford	Wakefield Trinity
1904-05	Oldham	Dewsbury
1962-63	Swinton	Hunslet
1963-64	Swinton	Oldham
1973-74	Salford	Bradford Northern
1974-75	St. Helens	Huddersfield
1975-76	Salford	Barrow
1976-77	Featherstone Rovers	Hull
1977-78	Widnes	Leigh
1978-79	Hull Kingston Rovers	Hull
1979-80	Bradford Northern	Featherstone Rovers
1980-81	Bradford Northern	York
1981-82	Leigh	Oldham
1982-83	Hull	Fulham
1983-84	Hull Kingston Rovers	Barrow
1984-85	Hull Kingston Rovers	Swinton
1985-86	Halifax	Leigh
1986-87	Wigan	Hunslet
1987-88	Widnes	Oldham
1988-89	Widnes	Leigh
1989-90	Wigan	Hull Kingston Rovers
1990-91	Wigan	Salford

THREE DIVISION CHAMPIONSHIP ROLL OF HONOUR

	FIRST DIVISION	**SECOND DIVISION**	**THIRD DIVISION**
1991-92	Wigan	Sheffield Eagles	Huddersfield

THE UPS AND DOWNS OF TWO DIVISION FOOTBALL
Since re-introduction of two divisions in 1973-74.

● Figure in brackets indicates position in division.

	RELEGATED	PROMOTED
1973-74	Oldham (13) Hull K.R. (14) Leigh (15) Whitehaven (16)	Bradford Northern (1) York (2) Keighley (3) Halifax (4)
1974-75	York (13) Bramley (14) Rochdale Hornets (15) Halifax (16)	Huddersfield (1) Hull K.R. (2) Oldham (3) Swinton (4)
1975-76	Dewsbury (13) Keighley (14) Huddersfield (15) Swinton (16)	Barrow (1) Rochdale Hornets (2) Workington T. (3) Leigh (4)
1976-77	Rochdale Hornets (13) Leigh (14) Barrow (15) Oldham (16)	Hull (1) Dewsbury (2) Bramley (3) New Hunslet (4)
1977-78	Hull (13) New Hunslet (14) Bramley (15) Dewsbury (16)	Leigh (1) Barrow (2) Rochdale Hornets (3) Huddersfield (4)
1978-79	Barrow (13) Featherstone Rovers (14) Rochdale Hornets (15) Huddersfield (16)	Hull (1) New Hunslet (2) York (3) Blackpool Borough (4)
1979-80	Wigan (13) Hunslet (14) York (15) Blackpool Borough (16)	Featherstone Rovers (1) Halifax (2) Oldham (3) Barrow (4)
1980-81	Halifax (13) Salford (14) Workington T. (15) Oldham (16)	York (1) Wigan (2) Fulham (3) Whitehaven (4)
1981-82	Fulham (13) Wakefield T. (14) York (15) Whitehaven (16)	Oldham (1) Carlisle (2) Workington T. (3) Halifax (4)

1982-83	Barrow (13)	Fulham (1)
	Workington T. (14)	Wakefield T. (2)
	Halifax (15)	Salford (3)
	Carlisle (16)	Whitehaven (4)
1983-84	Fulham (13)	Barrow (1)
	Wakefield T. (14)	Workington T. (2)
	Salford (15)	Hunslet (3)
	Whitehaven (16)	Halifax (4)
1984-85	Barrow (13)	Swinton (1)
	Leigh (14)	Salford (2)
	Hunslet (15)	York (3)
	Workington T. (16)	Dewsbury (4)
1985-86	York (14)	Leigh (1)
	Swinton (15)	Barrow (2)
	Dewsbury (16)	Wakefield T. (3)
1986-87	Oldham (13)	Hunslet (1)
	Featherstone Rovers (14)	Swinton (2)
	Barrow (15)	
	Wakefield T. (16)	
1987-88	Leigh (12)	Oldham (1)
	Swinton (13)	Featherstone Rovers (2)
	Hunslet (14)	Wakefield T. (3)
1988-89	Oldham (12)	Leigh (1)
	Halifax (13)	Barrow (2)
	Hull K.R. (14)	Sheffield E. (3)
1989-90	Leigh (12)	Hull K.R. (1)
	Salford (13)	Rochdale Hornets (2)
	Barrow (14)	Oldham (3)
1990-91	Oldham (12)	Salford (1)
	Sheffield E. (13)	Halifax (2)
	Rochdale Hornets (14)	Swinton (3)

THE UPS AND DOWNS OF THREE DIVISION FOOTBALL
Since introduction in 1991-92.

	FIRST DIVISION	SECOND DIVISION	THIRD DIVISION
1991-92	Down: Featherstone R. (13)	Up: Sheffield E. (1)	Up: Huddersfield (1)
	Swinton (14)	Leigh (2)	Bramley (2)
		Down: Ryedale-York (7)	
		Workington T. (8)	

FIRST DIVISION RECORDS
Since reintroduction in 1973

INDIVIDUAL

Match records

Most tries:
6 Shane Cooper (St. Helens) v. Hull, 17 February 1988

Most goals: 13 Geoff Pimblett (St. Helens) v. Bramley, 5 March 1978

Most points: 38 (11g,4t) Bob Beardmore (Castleford) v. Barrow, 22 March 1987

Season records

Most tries: 44 Ellery Hanley (Wigan) 1986-87

Most goals: 130 Steve Hesford (Warrington) 1978-79

Most points: 295 (101g,1dg,23t) John Woods (Leigh) 1983-84

TEAM

Highest score and widest margin: Leeds 90 v. Barrow 0,
11 February 1990

Highest away score: Rochdale H. 12 v. Castleford 76,
3 March 1991

Widest away margin: Wakefield T. 6 v. Wigan 72,
29 March 1987; Barrow 0 v. Wigan 66, 1 October 1989

Most points by losing team: Hunslet 40 v. Barrow 41,
9 September 1984

Scoreless draw: Wigan 0 v. Castleford 0, 26 January 1974

Highest score draw: Hunslet 32 v. Swinton 32,
20 September 1987

Best opening sequence: 13 wins then a draw by Widnes
1981-82

Longest winning run: 25 by St. Helens. Won last 13 of
1985-86 and first 12 of 1986-87 (Also longest unbeaten
run.)

Longest losing run: 20 by Whitehaven 1983-84;
Rochdale H. 1990-91

Longest run without a win: 23, including 3 draws, by
Whitehaven 1981-82 (Also worst opening sequence)

Biggest attendance: 29,763 Wigan v. Widnes, 9 April 1991

100 Division One career tries
208 Ellery Hanley (Bradford N., Wigan, Leeds)
165 Keith Fielding (Salford)
144 David Smith (Wakefield T., Leeds, Bradford N.)
142 Phil Ford (Warrington, Wigan, Bradford N., Leeds)
141 Garry Schofield (Hull, Leeds)
139 Stuart Wright (Wigan, Widnes)
136 Roy Mathias (St. Helens)
133 John Joyner (Castleford)
130 John Bevan (Warrington)
128 Des Drummond (Leigh, Warrington)
128 Martin Offiah (Widnes, Wigan)
126 Steve Hartley (Hull K.R.)
126 David Topliss (Wakefield T., Hull, Oldham)
125 John Woods (Leigh, Bradford N., Warrington)
122 Maurice Richards (Salford)
122 Steve Evans (Featherstone R., Hull, Wakefield T.,
    Bradford N.)
113 David Redfearn (Bradford N.)
111 Henderson Gill (Bradford N., Wigan)
106 Neil Holding (St. Helens, Rochdale H.)
106 Gary Hyde (Castleford, Oldham)
103 Keiron O'Loughlin (Wigan, Workington T.,
    Widnes, Salford)

Top four Division One career goals
854 John Woods (Leigh, Bradford N., Warrington)
845 Steve Hesford (Warrington)
818 Steve Quinn (Featherstone R.)
811 George Fairbairn (Wigan, Hull K.R.)

Top four Division One career points
2,130 John Woods (Leigh, Bradford N., Warrington)
1,814 George Fairbairn (Wigan, Hull K.R.)
1,768 Steve Quinn (Featherstone R.)
1,756 Steve Hesford (Warrington)

20 Division One tries in a season
1973-74	36	Keith Fielding (Salford)
	29	Roy Mathias (St. Helens)
	21	David Smith (Wakefield T.)
1974-75	21	Maurice Richards (Salford)
	21	Roy Mathias (St. Helens)
1975-76	26	Maurice Richards (Salford)
	20	David Smith (Wakefield T.)
1976-77	22	David Topliss (Wakefield T.)
	21	Keith Fielding (Salford)
	21	Ged Dunn (Hull K.R.)
	20	David Smith (Leeds)
	20	Stuart Wright (Widnes)
1977-78	26	Keith Fielding (Salford)
	25	Steve Fenton (Castleford)
	24	Stuart Wright (Widnes)
	20	David Smith (Leeds)
	20	Bruce Burton (Castleford)
	20	John Bevan (Warrington)
1978-79	28	Steve Hartley (Hull K.R.)
1979-80	24	Keith Fielding (Salford)
	21	Roy Mathias (St. Helens)
	21	Steve Hubbard (Hull K.R.)
	20	David Smith (Leeds)
1980-81	20	Steve Hubbard (Hull K.R.)
1981-82		David Hobbs (Featherstone R.) was top scorer with 19 tries.
1982-83	22	Bob Eccles (Warrington)
	20	Steve Evans (Hull)
1983-84	28	Garry Schofield (Hull)
	23	John Woods (Leigh)
	20	James Leuluai (Hull)
1984-85	40	Ellery Hanley (Bradford N.)
	34	Gary Prohm (Hull K.R.)
	23	Henderson Gill (Wigan)
	22	Barry Ledger (St. Helens)
	22	Mal Meninga (St. Helens)
1985-86	22	Ellery Hanley (Wigan)
1986-87	44	Ellery Hanley (Wigan)
	24	Phil Ford (Bradford N.)
	24	Henderson Gill (Wigan)
	23	Garry Schofield (Hull)
	21	John Henderson (Leigh)
1987-88	33	Martin Offiah (Widnes)
	22	Ellery Hanley (Wigan)
1988-89	37	Martin Offiah (Widnes)
	20	Grant Anderson (Castleford)
1989-90	28	Martin Offiah (Widnes)
	25	Mark Preston (Wigan)
	20	Steve Larder (Castleford)
1990-91	22	Martin Offiah (Widnes)
	22	Les Quirk (St. Helens)
	20	Ellery Hanley (Wigan)
1991-92	31	John Devereux (Widnes)
	27	Greg Austin (Halifax)
	25	Shaun Edwards (Wigan)
	23	Mark Preston (Halifax)

Top Division One goalscorers
1973-74	126	David Watkins (Salford)
1974-75	96	Sammy Lloyd (Castleford)
1975-76	118	Sammy Lloyd (Castleford)
1976-77	113	Steve Quinn (Featherstone R.)
1977-78	116	Steve Hesford (Warrington)
1978-79	130	Steve Hesford (Warrington)

1979-80	104	Steve Hubbard (Hull K.R.)
1980-81	96	Steve Diamond (Wakefield T.)
1981-82	110	Steve Quinn (Featherstone R.)
		John Woods (Leigh)
1982-83	105	Bob Beardmore (Castleford)
1983-84	106	Steve Hesford (Warrington)
1984-85	114	Sean Day (St. Helens)
1985-86	85	David Stephenson (Wigan)
1986-87	120	Paul Loughlin (St. Helens)
1987-88	95	John Woods (Warrington)
1988-89	95	David Hobbs (Bradford N.)
1989-90	96	Paul Loughlin (St. Helens)
1990-91	85	Paul Eastwood (Hull)
1991-92	86	Frano Botica (Wigan)

Top Division One points-scorer 1991-92
199 (85g,1dg,7t) Frano Botica (Wigan)

SECOND DIVISION RECORDS
Since reintroduction in 1973

INDIVIDUAL

Match records
Most tries: 6 Ged Dunn (Hull K.R.) v. New Hunslet, 2 February 1975; David Kettlestring (Ryedale-York) at Keighley, 11 March 1990; Greg Austin (Halifax) v. Trafford B., 7 April 1991
Most goals: 15 Mick Stacey (Leigh) v. Doncaster, 28 March 1976
Most points: 38 (13g,4t) John Woods (Leigh) v. Blackpool B., 11 September 1977; 38 (11g,4t) John Woods (Leigh) v. Ryedale-York, 12 January 1992

Season records
Most tries: 48 Steve Halliwell (Leigh) 1985-86
Most goals: 167 Mike Fletcher (Hull K.R.) 1989-90
Most points: 395 (163g,3dg,22t) Lynn Hopkins (Workington T.) 1981-82

TEAM

Highest score: Leigh 92 v. Keighley 2, 30 April 1986; Hull K.R. 92 v. Whitehaven 10, 18 March 1990; Rochdale H. 92 v. Runcorn H. 0, 5 November 1989 (Also widest margin)
Highest away: Runcorn H. 2 v. Leigh 88, 15 January 1989 (Also widest margin)
Most points by losing team: Dewsbury 36 v. Rochdale H. 34, 9 October 1988; Oldham 50 v. Keighley 34, 12 November 1989
Highest score draw: Huddersfield B. 32 v. Keighley 32, 17 April 1986
Scoreless draw: Dewsbury 0 v. Rochdale H. 0, 30 January 1983
Longest winning run: 30 by Leigh in 1985-86. Hull won all 26 matches in 1978-79

Longest losing run: 55 by Runcorn H. (9 in 1988-89, all 28 in 1989-90 and 18 in 1990-91)
Longest run without a win: 67, inc 2 draws, by Runcorn H. (19 in 1988-89, all 28 in 1989-90 and 20 in 1990-91)
Biggest attendance: 12,424 Hull v. New Hunslet, 18 May 1979

1991-92 Top Division Two scorers
Most tries: 31 Iva Ropati (Oldham & Sheffield E.)
Most goals: 74 John Woods (Leigh)
Most points: 178 (72g,2dg,8t) John Woods (Leigh)

THIRD DIVISION RECORDS
Introduced in 1991

INDIVIDUAL

Match records
Most tries: 5 Eddie Rombo (Dewsbury) v. Highfield, 1 March 1992; Vince Gribbin (Whitehaven) v. Nottingham C., 12 April 1992
Most goals: 12 Tony Zelei (Doncaster) v. Nottingham C., 1 September 1991; Steve Maguire (Whitehaven) v. Nottingham C., 12 April 1992
Most points: 32 (12g,2t) Tony Zelei (Doncaster) v. Nottingham C., 1 September 1991

Season records
Most tries: 31 Vince Gribbin (Whitehaven) 1991-92
Most goals: 113 Steve Carroll (Bramley) 1991-92
Most points: 238 (109g,4dg,4t) Steve Carroll 1991-92

TEAM

Highest score: Doncaster 88 v. Nottingham C. 6, 1 September 1991 (Also widest margin win with Nottingham C. 0 v. Huddersfield 82, 29 March 1992)
Highest away: Nottingham C. 0 v. Huddersfield 82, 29 March 1992
Most points by losing team: Hunslet 33 v. Doncaster 32, 16 February 1992
Highest score draw: None of 20-20 or more
Scoreless draw: None
Longest winning run: 11 by Huddersfield 1991-92 (Also longest unbeaten run)
Longest losing run: 26 by Nottingham C. 1991-92 all matches
Biggest attendance: 4,119 Batley v. Dewsbury, 26 December 1991

● League match records do not include scores in abandoned matches that were replayed.

Huddersfield's Australian captain Greg Shuttleworth with the inaugural Stones Bitter Third Division Championship Trophy.

Studious Fartown coaching duo Alex Murphy (right) and assistant Terry Flanagan.

NINETEEN-SEASON TABLE

Widnes continue as the most successful Division One club since the reintroduction of two divisions in 1973 in terms of most points gained. The three times champions head a 19-season table with 720 points from 550 matches.

Although St. Helens have won the title just once, in 1974-75, they are the only club to have finished in the top eight throughout the 19 seasons. In addition to St. Helens, only Widnes, Leeds, Warrington and Castleford have remained in Division One.

Bradford Northern, Hull and Leigh were all Division Two champions who went on to win the Division One title a few years after being promoted, while Hull Kingston Rovers, Halifax and Wigan are other former lower grade clubs who later won the major championship.

The highest place gained by a newly-promoted club is third by Hull in 1979-80 after winning the Division Two title with a 100 per cent record the previous season.

Division One champions who were relegated a few seasons after winning the Division One title were Salford, Featherstone Rovers, Leigh, Halifax and Hull K.R.

The records of the five clubs who have appeared in Division One throughout the 19 seasons are as follows:

FIRST DIVISION SCORING

The following table shows the scoring totals for each season since the inauguration of two divisions in 1973-74:

DIVISION ONE

Season	Matches each club played	Goals	1-Point drop goals	Tries	Pts
1973-74	30	1,508	—	1,295	6,901
1974-75	30	1,334	48	1,261	6,499
1975-76	30	1,498	53	1,331	7,042
1976-77	30[1]	1,435	91	1,423	7,230
1977-78	30[2]	1,402	99	1,443	7,232
1978-79	30	1,367	119	1,448	7,197
1979-80	30	1,389	131	1,349	6,956
1980-81	30	1,439	147	1,342	7,051
1981-82	30	1,486	132	1,354	7,166
1982-83	30	1,369	64	1,386	6,960
1983-84	30	1,472	108	1,479	8,968
1984-85	30	1,464	84	1,595	9,392
1985-86	30	1,296	80	1,435	8,412
1986-87	30	1,412	90	1,607	9,342
1987-88	26	1,070	75	1,170	6,895
1988-89	26	1,107	80	1,154	6,910
1989-90	26	1,198	80	1,295	7,656
1990-91	26	1,115	58	1,189	7,044
1991-92	26	1,026	46	1,178	6,810

[1] Salford & Leeds played 29 matches — their final match was abandoned and not replayed. This match was expunged from league records.
[2] Featherstone R. & Bradford N. played 29 matches — their final match was cancelled following Featherstone's strike.

	P.	W.	D.	L.	F.	A.	Pts
1. Widnes	550	350	20	180	10,342	7,219	720
2. St. Helens	550	348	22	180	11,540	7,819	718
3. Leeds	549	318	22	209	10,462	8,165	658
4. Warrington	550	298	20	232	9,357	8,052	616
5. Castleford	550	287	27	236	10,493	8,799	601

● Although Wigan have had only 18 seasons in Division One they have totalled 670 points from 520 matches.

CHAMPIONSHIP PLAY-OFFS

Following the breakaway from the English Rugby Union, 22 clubs formed the Northern Rugby Football League. Each club played 42 matches and Manningham won the first Championship as league leaders in 1895-96.

This format was then abandoned and replaced by the Yorkshire Senior and Lancashire Senior Combination leagues until 1901-02 when 14 clubs broke away to form the Northern Rugby League with Broughton Rangers winning the first Championship.

The following season two divisions were formed with the Division One title going to Halifax (1902-03), Bradford (1903-04), who won a play-off against Salford 5-0 at Halifax after both teams tied with 52 points, and Oldham (1904-05).

In 1905-06 the two divisions were merged with Leigh taking the Championship as league leaders. They won the title on a percentage basis as the 31 clubs did not play the same number of matches. The following season the top four play-off was introduced as a fairer means of deciding the title.

The top club played the fourth-placed, the second meeting the third, with the higher club having home advantage. The final was staged at a neutral venue.

It was not until 1930-31 that all clubs played the same number of league matches, but not all against each other, the top four play-off being a necessity until the reintroduction of two divisions in 1962-63.

This spell of two division football lasted only two seasons and the restoration of the one-league Championship table brought about the introduction of a top-16 play-off, this format continuing until the reappearance of two divisions in 1973-74.

Since then the Championship Trophy has been awarded to the leaders of the First Division, with the Second Division champions receiving a silver bowl. A Third Division was introduced from 1991-92.

Slalom Lager launched a three-year sponsorship deal of the Championship and the Premiership in 1980-81 in a £215,000 package, extending the deal for another three years from 1983-84 for £270,000. From 1986-87, the sponsorship was taken over by brewers Bass, under the Stones Bitter banner, in a new £400,000 three-year deal, renewed for a further three years from 1989-90 for £750,000.

CHAMPIONSHIP PLAY-OFF FINALS

Season	Winners		Runners-up		Venue	Attendance	Receipts
Top Four Play-Offs							
1906-07	Halifax	18	Oldham	3	Huddersfield	13,200	£722
1907-08	Hunslet	7	Oldham	7	Salford	14,000	£690
Replay	Hunslet	12	Oldham	2	Wakefield	14,054	£800
1908-09	Wigan	7	Oldham	3	Salford	12,000	£630
1909-10	Oldham	13	Wigan	7	Broughton	10,850	£520
1910-11	Oldham	20	Wigan	7	Broughton	15,543	£717
1911-12	Huddersfield	13	Wigan	5	Halifax	15,000	£591
1912-13	Huddersfield	29	Wigan	2	Wakefield	17,000	£914
1913-14	Salford	5	Huddersfield	3	Leeds	8,091	£474
1914-15	Huddersfield	35	Leeds	2	Wakefield	14,000	£750
COMPETITION SUSPENDED DURING WAR TIME							
1919-20	Hull	3	Huddersfield	2	Leeds	12,900	£1,615
1920-21	Hull	16	Hull K.R.	14	Leeds	10,000	£1,320
1921-22	Wigan	13	Oldham	2	Broughton	26,000	£1,825
1922-23	Hull K.R.	15	Huddersfield	5	Leeds	14,000	£1,370
1923-24	Batley	13	Wigan	7	Broughton	13,729	£968
1924-25	Hull K.R.	9	Swinton	5	Rochdale	21,580	£1,504
1925-26	Wigan	22	Warrington	10	St. Helens	20,000	£1,100
1926-27	Swinton	13	St. Helens Recs.	8	Warrington	24,432	£1,803
1927-28	Swinton	11	Featherstone R.	0	Oldham	15,451	£1,136
1928-29	Huddersfield	2	Leeds	0	Halifax	25,604	£2,028
1929-30	Huddersfield	2	Leeds	2	Wakefield	32,095	£2,111
Replay	Huddersfield	10	Leeds	0	Halifax	18,563	£1,319
1930-31	Swinton	14	Leeds	7	Wigan	31,000	£2,100
1931-32	St. Helens	9	Huddersfield	5	Wakefield	19,386	£943
1932-33	Salford	15	Swinton	5	Wigan	18,000	£1,053
1933-34	Wigan	15	Salford	3	Warrington	31,564	£2,114
1934-35	Swinton	14	Warrington	3	Wigan	27,700	£1,710
1935-36	Hull	21	Widnes	2	Huddersfield	17,276	£1,208

Season	Winners		Runners-up		Venue	Attendance	Receipts
1936-37	Salford	13	Warrington	11	Wigan	31,500	£2,000
1937-38	Hunslet	8	Leeds	2	Elland Rd., Leeds	54,112	£3,572
1938-39	Salford	8	Castleford	6	Man. C. FC	69,504	£4,301

WAR-TIME EMERGENCY PLAY-OFFS
For the first two seasons the Yorkshire League and Lancashire League champions met in a two-leg final as follows:

1939-40	Swinton	13	Bradford N.	21	Swinton	4,800	£237
	Bradford N.	16	Swinton	9	Bradford	11,721	£570

Bradford N. won 37-22 on aggregate

1940-41	Wigan	6	Bradford N.	17	Wigan	11,245	£640
	Bradford N.	28	Wigan	9	Bradford	20,205	£1,148

Bradford N. won 45-15 on aggregate
For the remainder of the War the top four in the War League played-off as follows:

1941-42	Dewsbury	13	Bradford N.	0	Leeds	18,000	£1,121
1942-43	Dewsbury	11	Halifax	3	Dewsbury	7,000	£400
	Halifax	13	Dewsbury	22	Halifax	9,700	£683

Dewsbury won 33-16 on aggregate but the Championship was declared null and void because they had played an ineligible player

1943-44	Wigan	13	Dewsbury	9	Wigan	14,000	£915
	Dewsbury	5	Wigan	12	Dewsbury	9,000	£700

Wigan won 25-14 on aggregate

1944-45	Halifax	9	Bradford N.	2	Halifax	9,426	£955
	Bradford N.	24	Halifax	11	Bradford	16,000	£1,850

Bradford N. won 26-20 on aggregate

1945-46	Wigan	13	Huddersfield	4	Man. C. FC	67,136	£8,387
1946-47	Wigan	13	Dewsbury	4	Man. C. FC	40,599	£5,895
1947-48	Warrington	15	Bradford N.	5	Man. C. FC	69,143	£9,792
1948-49	Huddersfield	13	Warrington	12	Man. C. FC	75,194	£11,073
1949-50	Wigan	20	Huddersfield	2	Man. C. FC	65,065	£11,500
1950-51	Workington T.	26	Warrington	11	Man. C. FC	61,618	£10,993
1951-52	Wigan	13	Bradford N.	6	Huddersfield Town FC	48,684	£8,215
1952-53	St. Helens	24	Halifax	14	Man. C. FC	51,083	£11,503
1953-54	Warrington	8	Halifax	7	Man. C. FC	36,519	£9,076
1954-55	Warrington	7	Oldham	3	Man. C. FC	49,434	£11,516
1955-56	Hull	10	Halifax	9	Man. C. FC	36,675	£9,179
1956-57	Oldham	15	Hull	14	Bradford	62,199	£12,054
1957-58	Hull	20	Workington T.	3	Bradford	57,699	£11,149
1958-59	St. Helens	44	Hunslet	22	Bradford	52,560	£10,146
1959-60	Wigan	27	Wakefield T.	3	Bradford	83,190	£14,482
1960-61	Leeds	25	Warrington	10	Bradford	52,177	£10,475
1961-62	Huddersfield	14	Wakefield T.	5	Bradford	37,451	£7,979

TWO DIVISIONS 1962-63 and 1963-64

Top Sixteen Play-Offs

1964-65	Halifax	15	St. Helens	7	Swinton	20,786	£6,141
1965-66	St. Helens	35	Halifax	12	Swinton	30,634	£8,750
1966-67	Wakefield T.	7	St. Helens	7	Leeds	20,161	£6,702
Replay	Wakefield T.	21	St. Helens	9	Swinton	33,537	£9,800
1967-68	Wakefield T.	17	Hull K.R.	10	Leeds	22,586	£7,697
1968-69	Leeds	16	Castleford	14	Bradford	28,442	£10,130
1969-70	St. Helens	24	Leeds	12	Bradford	26,358	£9,791
1970-71	St. Helens	16	Wigan	12	Swinton	21,745	£10,200
1971-72	Leeds	9	St. Helens	5	Swinton	24,055	£9,513
1972-73	Dewsbury	22	Leeds	13	Bradford	18,889	£9,479

CHAMPIONSHIP FINAL . . . . A 10-YEAR REVIEW

1961-62 HUDDERSFIELD 14 Dyson (4g); Breen, Deighton, Booth, Wicks (1t); Davies, Smales (1t); Slevin, Close, Noble, Kilroy, Bowman, Ramsden
WAKEFIELD T. 5 Round; F. Smith, Skene, N. Fox (1t, 1g), Hirst; Poynton, Holliday; Wilkinson, Kosanovic, Firth, Briggs, Vines, Turner
Referee: N. T. Railton (Wigan)
TWO DIVISIONS — NO PLAY-OFFS 1963 and 1964

1964-65 HALIFAX 15 James (3g); Jackson (1t), Burnett (2t), Kellett, Freeman; Robinson, Daley; Roberts, Harrison, Scroby, Fogerty, Dixon, Renilson
ST. HELENS 7 F. Barrow; Harvey, Vollenhoven, Northey, Killeen (1t, 2g); Murphy, Smith; Tembey (Warlow), Dagnall, Watson, French, Mantle, Laughton
Referee: D. S. Brown (Dewsbury)

1965-66 ST. HELENS 35 F. Barrow; A. Barrow (1t), Murphy (1g), Benyon, Killeen (3t, 6g); Harvey; Bishop; Halsall (3t), Sayer, Watson, French, Warlow (Hitchen), Mantle
HALIFAX 12 Cooper (3g); Jones, Burnett, Dixon, Freeman; Robinson, Baker (1t); Roberts, Harrison, Scroby, Ramshaw (Duffy), Fogerty (1t), Renilson
Referee: J. Manley (Warrington)

1966-67 WAKEFIELD T. 7 Cooper; Hirst, Brooke, N. Fox (2g), Coetzer; Poynton, Owen (1t); Bath, Prior, Campbell, Clarkson, Haigh, D. Fox
ST. HELENS 7 F. Barrow; Vollenhoven, A. Barrow, Smith, Killeen (2g); Douglas, Bishop; Warlow, Sayer, Watson (1t), French, Hogan (Robinson), Mantle
Referee: G. Philpott (Leeds)

Replay: WAKEFIELD T. 21 Cooper; Hirst (1t), Brooke (2t), N. Fox (3g), Coetzer; Poynton (1t), Owen (1t); Bath, Prior, Campbell, Clarkson, Haigh, D. Fox
ST. HELENS 9 F. Barrow; Vollenhoven (1t), A. Barrow, Smith, Killeen (2g); Douglas, Bishop (1g); Warlow, Sayer, Watson, French, Hogan, Mantle
Referee: J. Manley (Warrington)

1967-68 WAKEFIELD T. 17 G. Cooper; Coetzer, Brooke, N. Fox (1t, 2g), Batty; Poynton (1g), Owen (1t); Jeanes (1t), Shepherd, D. Fox (1g), Haigh, McLeod, Hawley
HULL K.R. 10 Wainwright; C. Young, Moore (1t), A. Burwell, Longstaff (1t); Millward (2g), C. Cooper; L. Foster, Flanagan, Mennell, Lowe, Major, F. Foster
Referee: D. S. Brown (Preston)

1968-69 LEEDS 16 Risman (4g); Cowan (1t), Hynes, Watson, Atkinson (1t); Shoebottom, Seabourne (Langley); Clark (Hick), Crosby, K. Eyre, Joyce, Ramsey (1g), Batten
CASTLEFORD 14 Edwards; Briggs, Howe, Thomas, Lowndes; Hardisty (1t, 1g), Hepworth; Hartley, C. Dickinson (1t), J. Ward, Redfearn (3g), Lockwood, Reilly (Fox)
Referee: W. H. Thompson (Huddersfield)

1969-70 ST. HELENS 24 F. Barrow; L. Jones, Benyon, Walsh (1t, 2g), E. Prescott (2t), Myler, Heaton; Halsall, Sayer (1t), Watson, Mantle, E. Chisnall, Coslett (4g)
LEEDS 12 Holmes (3g); Alan Smith (1t), Hynes, Cowan (1t), Atkinson; Shoebottom, Seabourne; J. Burke, Crosby, A. Eyre, Ramsey (Hick), Eccles, Batten
Referee: W. H. Thompson (Huddersfield)

1970-71 ST. HELENS 16 Pimblett; L. Jones, Benyon (1t), Walsh, Blackwood (1t); Whittle, Heaton; J. Stephens, A. Karalius, Rees (Wanbon), Mantle, E. Chisnall, Coslett (5g)
WIGAN 12 Tyrer (1g); Kevin O'Loughlin; Francis, Rowe, Wright; D. Hill, Ayres; Hogan, Clarke, Fletcher, Ashurst (1t, 2g), Robinson (1t) (Cunningham), Laughton
Referee: E. Lawrinson (Warrington)

1971-72 LEEDS 9 Holmes (Hick); Alan Smith, Langley, Dyl, Atkinson (1t); Hardisty, Barham; Clawson (3g), Ward, Fisher (Pickup), Cookson, Eccles, Batten
ST. HELENS 5 Pimblett; L. Jones (Whittle), Benyon, Walsh (1g), Wilson; Kelly, Heaton; Rees, Greenall (1t), J. Stephens, Mantle, E. Chisnall, Coslett
Referee: S. Shepherd (Oldham)

1972-73 DEWSBURY 22 Rushton; Ashcroft, Clark, N. Stephenson (5g, 1t), Day; Agar (1t), A. Bates; Beverley (Taylor), M. Stephenson (2t), Lowe, Grayshon, J. Bates, Whittington
LEEDS 13 Holmes; Alan Smith, Hynes (1g), Dyl (1t), Atkinson; Hardisty, Hepworth; Clawson (1g), Fisher (Ward), Clarkson (Langley), Cookson (1t), Eccles (1t), Haigh
Referee: H. G. Hunt (Prestbury)

LEAGUE LEADERS TROPHY

While the top 16 play-off decided the Championship between 1964 and 1973 it was decided to honour the top club in the league table with a League Leaders Trophy. The winners were:

1964-65   St. Helens
1965-66   St. Helens
1966-67   Leeds
1967-68   Leeds
1968-69   Leeds
1969-70   Leeds
1970-71   Wigan
1971-72   Leeds
1972-73   Warrington

CLUB CHAMPIONSHIP (Merit Table)

With the reintroduction of two divisions, a complicated merit table and Division Two preliminary rounds system produced a 16-club play-off with the Club Championship finalists as follows:

Season	Winners		Runners-up		Venue	Attendance	Receipts
1973-74	Warrington	13	St. Helens	12	Wigan	18,040	£10,032

This format lasted just one season and was replaced by the Premiership.

CLUB CHAMPIONSHIP FINAL . . . . A REVIEW

1973-74   WARRINGTON 13   Whitehead (2g); M. Philbin (1t), Noonan (1t), Pickup (Lowe), Bevan; Whittle, A. Murphy; D. Chisnall, Ashcroft, Brady (1t), Wanbon (Gaskell), Mather, B. Philbin
ST. HELENS 12   Pimblett; Brown, Wills, Wilson (2t), Mathias; Eckersley, Heaton; Mantle, Liptrot, M. Murphy, E. Chisnall (Warlow), Nicholls, Coslett (3g)
Referee: P. Geraghty (York)

PREMIERSHIP

With the further reintroduction of two divisions in 1973-74, it was declared that the title of Champions would be awarded to the leaders of the First Division.

However, it was also decided to continue the tradition of an end-of-season competition, the winners to receive the newly instituted Premiership Trophy.

*For full details of the Premiership Trophy see the CUPS section.

David Eckersley, stand off for 1974 Club Championship runners-up St. Helens.

COUNTY LEAGUE

In the early seasons of the code the Lancashire Senior and Yorkshire Senior Competitions, not to be confused with the later reserve leagues, were major leagues. The winners were:

	Lancashire SC	Yorkshire SC
1895-96	Runcorn	Manningham
1896-97	Broughton Rangers	Brighouse Rangers
1897-98	Oldham	Hunslet
1898-99	Broughton Rangers	Batley
1899-00	Runcorn	Bradford
1900-01	Oldham	Bradford
1901-02	Wigan	Leeds

With the introduction of two divisions in 1902-03, the county league competitions were scrapped until they reappeared as the Lancashire League and Yorkshire League in 1907-08. Clubs from the same county played each other home and away to decide the titles. These games were included in the main championship table along with inter-county fixtures. The county leagues continued until 1970, with the exception of war-time interruptions and two seasons when regional leagues with play-offs operated during the 1960s two-division era. They were then abolished when a more integrated fixture formula meant clubs did not play all others from the same county, this system later being replaced by the two-division structure.

LEAGUE LEADERS .... A REVIEW

The following is a list of the League leaders since the formation of the Northern Union, with the exception of the three eras of two-division football. From 1896 to 1901, the League was divided into a Lancashire Senior Competition and a Yorkshire Senior Competition, winners of both leagues being listed for those seasons.
From 1905 to 1930 not all the clubs played each other, the League being determined on a percentage basis.

LSC — Lancashire Senior Competition
LL — Lancashire League
YSC — Yorkshire Senior Competition
YL — Yorkshire League
WEL — War Emergency League
* Two points deducted for breach of professional rules
† Decided on a percentage basis after Belle Vue Rangers withdrew shortly before the start of the season.

		P.	W.	D.	L.	F.	A.	Pts.	
1895-96	Manningham	42	33	0	9	367	158	66	
1896-97	Broughton R.	26	19	5	2	201	52	43	LSC
	Brighouse R.	30	22	4	4	213	68	48	YSC
1897-98	Oldham	26	23	1	2	295	94	47	LSC
	Hunslet	30	22	4	4	327	117	48	YSC
1898-99	Broughton R.	26	21	0	5	277	74	42	LSC
	Batley	30	23	2	5	279	75	48	YSC
1899-00	Runcorn	26	22	2	2	232	33	46	LSC
	Bradford	30	24	2	4	324	98	50	YSC
1900-01	Oldham	26	22	1	3	301	67	45	LSC
	Bradford	30	26	1	3	387	100	51*	YSC
1901-02	Broughton R.	26	21	1	4	285	112	43	
1902-05	Two Divisions								
1905-06	Leigh	30	23	2	5	245	130	48	80.00%
1906-07	Halifax	34	27	2	5	649	229	56	82.35%
1907-08	Oldham	32	28	2	2	396	121	58	90.62%
1908-09	Wigan	32	28	0	4	706	207	56	87.50%
1909-10	Oldham	34	29	2	3	604	184	60	88.23%
1910-11	Wigan	34	28	1	5	650	205	57	83.82%
1911-12	Huddersfield	36	31	1	4	996	238	63	87.50%
1912-13	Huddersfield	32	28	0	4	732	217	56	87.50%
1913-14	Huddersfield	34	28	2	4	830	258	58	85.29%
1914-15	Huddersfield	34	28	4	2	888	235	60	88.24%
1915-18	Competitive matches suspended during First World War								
1918-19	Rochdale H.	12	9	0	3	92	52	18	75.00% LL
	Hull	16	13	0	3	392	131	26	81.25% YL
1919-20	Huddersfield	34	29	0	5	759	215	58	85.29%
1920-21	Hull K.R.	32	24	1	7	432	233	49	76.56%
1921-22	Oldham	36	29	1	6	521	201	59	81.94%
1922-23	Hull	36	30	0	6	587	304	60	83.33%
1923-24	Wigan	38	31	0	7	824	228	62	81.57%
1924-25	Swinton	36	30	0	6	499	224	60	83.33%
1925-26	Wigan	38	29	3	6	641	310	61	80.26%
1926-27	St. Helens R.	38	29	3	6	544	235	61	80.26%
1927-28	Swinton	36	27	3	6	439	189	57	79.16%

		P.	W.	D.	L.	F.	A.	Pts.	
1928-29	Huddersfield	38	26	4	8	476	291	56	73.68%
1929-30	St. Helens	40	27	1	12	549	295	55	68.75%
1930-31	Swinton	38	31	2	5	504	156	64	
1931-32	Huddersfield	38	30	1	7	636	368	61	
1932-33	Salford	38	31	2	5	751	165	64	
1933-34	Salford	38	31	1	6	715	281	63	
1934-35	Swinton	38	30	1	7	468	175	61	
1935-36	Hull	38	30	1	7	607	306	61	
1936-37	Salford	38	29	3	6	529	196	61	
1937-38	Hunslet	36	25	3	8	459	301	53	
1938-39	Salford	40	30	3	7	551	191	63	
1939-40	Swinton	22	17	0	5	378	158	34	WEL LL
	Bradford N.	28	21	0	7	574	302	42	WEL YL
1940-41	Wigan	16	15	1	0	297	71	31	WEL LL
	Bradford N.	25	23	1	1	469	126	47	WEL YL
1941-42	Dewsbury	24	19	1	4	431	172	39	81.25% WEL
1942-43	Wigan	16	13	0	3	301	142	26	81.25% WEL
1943-44	Wakefield T.	22	19	0	3	359	97	38	86.36% WEL
1944-45	Bradford N.	20	17	0	3	337	69	34	85.00% WEL
1945-46	Wigan	36	29	2	5	783	219	60	
1946-47	Wigan	36	29	1	6	567	196	59	
1947-48	Wigan	36	31	1	4	776	258	63	
1948-49	Warrington	36	31	0	5	728	247	62	
1949-50	Wigan	36	31	1	4	853	320	63	
1950-51	Warrington	36	30	0	6	738	250	60	
1951-52	Bradford N.	36	28	1	7	758	326	57	
1952-53	St. Helens	36	32	2	2	769	273	66	
1953-54	Halifax	36	30	2	4	538	219	62	
1954-55	Warrington	36	29	2	5	718	321	60	
1955-56	Warrington	34	27	1	6	712	349	55	80.88% †
1956-57	Oldham	38	33	0	5	893	365	66	
1957-58	Oldham	38	33	1	4	803	415	67	
1958-59	St. Helens	38	31	1	6	1,005	450	63	
1959-60	St. Helens	38	34	1	3	947	343	69	
1960-61	Leeds	36	30	0	6	620	258	60	
1961-62	Wigan	36	32	1	3	885	283	65	
1962-64	Two Divisions								
1964-65	St. Helens	34	28	0	6	621	226	56	
1965-66	St. Helens	34	28	1	5	521	275	57	
1966-67	Leeds	34	29	0	5	704	373	58	
1967-68	Leeds	34	28	0	6	720	271	56	
1968-69	Leeds	34	29	2	3	775	358	60	
1969-70	Leeds	34	30	0	4	674	314	60	
1970-71	Wigan	34	30	0	4	662	308	60	
1971-72	Leeds	34	28	2	4	750	325	58	
1972-73	Warrington	34	27	2	5	816	400	56	

Veteran coach Peter Fox, who in October 1991 left Featherstone Rovers to join Bradford Northern for a second spell as coaching supremo.

COACHES

INDEX OF COACHES

The following is an index of the 242 coaches who have held first team coaching posts since the start of the 1974-75 season to the end of May 1992.

It includes the alphabetical listing of British clubs they coached in the period.

Eleven new coaches were added to the list during the past 12 months when 16 clubs made at least one change.

Although some clubs appoint team managers with a coach as his assistant, the list refers only to the man generally recognised as being in overall charge of team affairs.

A caretaker coach, who stands in while the club is seeking a permanent appointment, is only listed if he takes charge for more than a few matches.

For a list of each club's appointments since 1974 see CLUBS section.

Ray Abbey (Dewsbury)
Jack Addy (Dewsbury, Huddersfield B.)
Allan Agar (Bramley, Carlisle, Featherstone R., Rochdale H.)
Gary Ainsworth (Trafford B.)
Dave Alred (Bridgend)
Chris Anderson (Halifax)
Harry Archer (Workington T.)
Chris Arkwright (Highfield)
Kevin Ashcroft (Leigh, Salford, Warrington)
Eric Ashton (St. Helens)
Ray Ashton (Workington T.)
Bill Ashurst (Runcorn H., Wakefield T.)
Mal Aspey (Salford)
John Atkinson (Carlisle)
Jack Austin (Hunslet)

Trevor Bailey (Scarborough P., Wakefield T.)
Maurice Bamford (Bramley, Dewsbury, Halifax, Huddersfield, Leeds, Wigan, Workington T.)
Frank Barrow (Oldham, Swinton)
Tony Barrow (Oldham, Swinton, Warrington)
Ray Batten (Wakefield T.)
Jeff Bawden (Whitehaven)
Mel Bedford (Huddersfield)
Cameron Bell (Carlisle)
Billy Benyon (Leigh, St. Helens, Warrington)
Les Bettinson (Salford)
Charlie Birdsall (Rochdale H.)

Alan Bishop (Runcorn H.)
Tommy Bishop (Barrow, Leigh, Workington T.)
Mick Blacker (Halifax, Huddersfield, Mansfield M.)
Tommy Blakeley (Blackpool B.)
Dick Bonser (Rochdale H.)
Reg Bowden (Fulham, Warrington)
Drew Broatch (Hunslet)
Ian Brooke (Bradford N., Huddersfield, Wakefield T.)
Arthur Bunting (Hull, Hull K.R.)
Mark Burgess (Nottingham C.)
Dave Busfield (Dewsbury)

Len Casey (Hull, Scarborough P., Wakefield T.)
Jim Challinor (Oldham)
Paul Charlton (Workington T.)
Eddie Cheetham (Leigh)
Dave Chisnall (Runcorn H.)
Colin Clarke (Leigh, Wigan)
Terry Clawson (Featherstone R.)
Noel Cleal (Hull)
Malcolm Clift (Leeds)
Joe Coan (Wigan)
John Cogger (Runcorn H.)
Gary Cooper (York)
Kel Coslett (Rochdale H., St. Helens, Wigan)
Keith Cotton (Featherstone R.)
Mike Coulman (Salford)
Les Coulter (Keighley)
Dave Cox (Batley, Castleford, Dewsbury, Huyton, Oldham, Workington T.)
Jim Crellin (Blackpool B., Halifax, Mansfield M., Rochdale H., Swinton)
Terry Crook (Batley, Dewsbury)

Arthur Daley (Runcorn H.)
Paul Daley (Batley, Featherstone R., Hunslet, York)
Jackie Davidson (Whitehaven, Workington T.)
Keith Davies (Workington T.)
Tommy Dawes (Barrow, Carlisle, Whitehaven)
Harry Dawson (Widnes)
Tony Dean (Hull, Wakefield T.)
Henry Delooze (Rochdale H.)
Steve Dennison (Mansfield M.)
Robin Dewhurst (Leeds)
Bakary Diabira (Blackpool B., Keighley)
Tommy Dickens (Blackpool B., Leigh)
Roy Dickinson (Bramley)
Colin Dixon (Halifax, Keighley, Salford)
Mal Dixon (York)
John Dorahy (Halifax)

Australian Noel Cleal, sacked as coach of Hull in April 1992 with two league games left to play.

David Doyle-Davidson (Hull, York)
Ray Dutton (Whitehaven)

Graham Eadie (Halifax)
Bob Eccles (Chorley)
Derek Edwards (Doncaster)
Joe Egan Jnr. (Blackpool B.)

George Fairbairn (Hull K.R., Wigan)
Vince Farrar (Featherstone R.)
Albert Fearnley (Batley, Blackpool B., Keighley)
John Fieldhouse (Oldham)
Tony Fisher (Bramley, Keighley)
Eric Fitzsimons (Oldham, Rochdale H., Whitehaven)
Bob Fleet (Swinton)
Geoff Fletcher (Huyton, Runcorn H.)
Terry Fogerty (Rochdale H.)
Chris Forster (Bramley, Huddersfield B.)
Derek Foster (Ryedale-York)
Frank Foster (Barrow, Whitehaven)
Kenny Foulkes (Hull)
Don Fox (Batley)
Harry Fox (Halifax)
Neil Fox (Huddersfield)
Peter Fox (Bradford N., Bramley, Featherstone R., Leeds, Wakefield T.)
Bill Francis (Oldham)
Roy Francis (Bradford N., Leeds)

Brian Gartland (Oldham)
Stan Gittins (Blackpool B., Chorley, Rochdale H., Springfield B.)
Bill Goodwin (Fulham, Kent Invicta)
Terry Gorman (Huyton, Swinton)
Keith Goulding (Featherstone R., Huddersfield, York)
Mal Graham (Oldham)
Tom Grainey (Leigh, Swinton)
Jeff Grayshon (Dewsbury)
Lee Greenwood (Keighley, Mansfield M./ Nottingham C.)
Geoff Gunney (Wakefield T.)

Bob Haigh (Wakefield T.)
Derek Hallas (Halifax)
Ken Halliwell (Swinton)
Alan Hardisty (Dewsbury, Halifax, York)
Arnold Hema (Nottingham C.)
Graham Heptinstall (Doncaster)
Alan Hepworth (Batley)
Keith Hepworth (Bramley, Hull)
Gary Hetherington (Sheffield E.)
Ron Hill (Dewsbury)
David Hobbs (Bradford N.)
Neil Holding (Rochdale H.)
Bill Holliday (Swinton)
Eric Hughes (Rochdale H., Widnes)
Syd Hynes (Leeds)

Bob Irving (Blackpool B.)
Keith Irving (Workington T.)

Dennis Jackson (Barrow)
Francis Jarvis (Huddersfield)
Peter Jarvis (Bramley, Hunslet)
Graeme Jennings (Hunslet)
Barry Johnson (Bramley)
Brian Johnson (Warrington)
Willie Johnson (Highfield)
Allen Jones (Huddersfield B.)
Lewis Jones (Dewsbury)

Vince Karalius (Widnes, Wigan)
Paul Kavanagh (Barrow)
John Kear (Bramley)
Arthur Keegan (Bramley)
Ivor Kelland (Barrow)
Alan Kellett (Carlisle, Halifax, Keighley)
Bill Kenny (Doncaster)
Bill Kindon (Leigh)

255

Bill Kirkbride (Mansfield M., Rochdale H.,
 Wakefield T., York)
Phil Kitchin (Whitehaven, Workington T.)

Dave Lamming (Wakefield T.)
Steve Lane (Kent Invicta)
Phil Larder (Widnes)
Doug Laughton (Leeds, Widnes)
Roy Lester (Carlisle, Fulham)
Alan Lockwood (Dewsbury)
Brian Lockwood (Batley, Huddersfield,
 Wakefield T.)
Paul Longstaff (Rochdale H.)
Graham Lowe (Wigan)
Phil Lowe (York)
Trevor Lowe (Batley, Doncaster)
Ken Loxton (Bramley)
Geoff Lyon (Blackpool B.)

Mike McClennan (St. Helens)
Stan McCormick (Salford)
John McFarlane (Whitehaven)
Alan McInnes (Salford, Wigan)
John Mantle (Blackpool B., Cardiff C., Leigh)
Roger Millward (Halifax, Hull K.R.)
John Monie (Wigan)
Mick Morgan (Carlisle)
Geoff Morris (Doncaster)
David Mortimer (Huddersfield)
Alex Murphy (Huddersfield, Leigh, St. Helens,
 Salford, Warrington, Wigan)
Frank Myler (Oldham, Rochdale H., Swinton,
 Widnes)

Steve Nash (Mansfield M.)
Steve Norton (Barrow)

Chris O'Sullivan (Swinton)

Les Pearce (Bramley, Halifax)
Mike Peers (Chorley B./Trafford B., Swinton)
Geoff Peggs (Keighley)
George Pieniazek (Batley, Featherstone R.)
Billy Platt (Mansfield M.)
Harry Poole (Hull K.R.)

Bill Ramsey (Hunslet)
Terry Ramshaw (Oldham)
Keith Rayne (Batley)
Rod Reddy (Barrow)
Graham Rees (Blackpool B.)
Malcolm Reilly (Castleford, Leeds)
Alan Rhodes (Doncaster, Sheffield E.)
Austin Rhodes (Swinton)

*John Monie, Stones Bitter Coach of the Year
for a record third successive season.*

Bev Risman (Fulham)
Ken Roberts (Halifax)
Don Robinson (Bramley)
Don Robson (Doncaster)
Peter Roe (Halifax, Keighley)
Sol Roper (Workington T.)

Roy Sabine (Keighley)
Dave Sampson (Castleford, Doncaster,
 Nottingham C.)
Barry Seabourne (Bradford N., Huddersfield,
 Keighley)
Les Sheard (Huddersfield)
Danny Sheehan (York)
John Sheridan (Doncaster)
Tommy Smales [*Scrum half*] (Featherstone R.)
Tommy Smales [*Forward*] (Batley, Bramley,
 Dewsbury, Doncaster, Featherstone R.)
Peter Smethurst (Leigh, Oldham)
Barry Smith (Whitehaven)
Bill Smith (Whitehaven, Workington T.)
Brian Smith (Huddersfield)
Brian Smith [*Australian*] (Hull)
Ike Southward (Whitehaven, Workington T.)
Graham Starkey (Oldham, Rochdale H.)
Gary Stephens (York)
Nigel Stephenson (Huddersfield, Hunslet)
Dave Stockwell (Batley, Bramley)
John Stopford (Swinton)
Ted Strawbridge (Doncaster)
Ross Strudwick (Fulham/London C., Halifax)
Clive Sullivan (Doncaster, Hull)
Phil Sullivan (Fulham)

Kevin Tamati (Salford)
John Taylor (Chorley B.)
Bob Tomlinson (Huddersfield)
Ted Toohey (Wigan)
David Topliss (Wakefield T.)
Peter Tunks (Oldham)
Norman Turley (Trafford B., Whitehaven,
  Workington T.)
Derek Turner (Wakefield T.)
Colin Tyrer (Widnes)

Darryl Van de Velde (Castleford)
Don Vines (Doncaster)

Arnold Walker (Whitehaven)
Trevor Walker (Batley)
Peter Walsh (Workington T.)
David Ward (Batley, Hunslet, Leeds)
John Warlow (Bridgend)
David Watkins (Cardiff C.)
Bernard Watson (Dewsbury)
Neil Whittaker (Huddersfield B.)
Mel Wibberley (Nottingham C.)
Ron Willey (Bradford N.)
Dean Williams (Workington T.)
Frank Wilson (Runcorn H.)
John Wolford (Hunslet)
Jeff Woods (Bridgend)
John Woods (Leigh)
Paul Woods (Runcorn H.)
Geoff Wraith (Wakefield T.)

Billy Yates (Doncaster)

*Darryl Van de Velde, who agreed a new one-year
contract for 1992-93*

DOSSIER OF 1991-92 COACHES

The following is a dossier of the British coaching and playing careers of coaches holding first team posts from June 1991 to the end of May 1992. Overseas details are not included.

● BF — beaten finalist.

JACK ADDY
Dewsbury: Feb. 84 - Jan. 87 (Promotion)
Huddersfield B: Jan. 87 - Mar. 88
Dewsbury: Dec. 90 -
Played for: Dewsbury

ALLAN AGAR
Carlisle: May 81 - June 82 (Promotion)
Featherstone R.:   Dec. 82 - Oct. 85
                   (RL Cup winners)
Bramley: Dec. 85 - Apr. 87
Rochdale H.:   July 89 - Jan. 91 (Promotion)
Featherstone R.:   Oct. 91 -
Played for: Featherstone R., Dewsbury, New Hunslet, Hull K.R., Wakefield T., Carlisle, Bramley

GARY AINSWORTH
Trafford B.:   Dec. 91 - May 92
Played for: Leigh, Swinton, St. Helens, Trafford B., Workington T.

CHRIS ARKWRIGHT
Highfield: Apr. 91 - Aug. 91
Played for: St. Helens, Highfield

KEVIN ASHCROFT
Leigh: June 75 - Jan. 77 (Promotion)
                   Floodlit Trophy (BF)
Salford: Nov. 80 - Mar. 82
Warrington: Mar. 82 - May 84
                   (Lancs. Cup winners & BF)
Salford: May 84 - Oct. 89 (Promotion)
Leigh: Sep. 91 - (Promotion)
Played for: Dewsbury, Rochdale H., Leigh, Warrington, Salford

RAY ASHTON
Workington T.:   June 90 - Dec. 91
Lancashire: 1991-92
Played for: Oldham, Leeds, Workington T.

TREVOR BAILEY
Wakefield T.:   Dec. 86 - Apr. 87
Scarborough P.:   Dec. 91 -
Played for: non-professional player

MAURICE BAMFORD
Dewsbury:	Aug. 74 - Oct. 74
Halifax:	Feb. 78 - May 80
	(Yorks. Cup BF, Promotion)
Huddersfield:	May 80 - May 81
Wigan:	May 81 - May 82
Bramley:	May 82 - Oct. 83
Leeds:	Nov. 83 - Feb. 85
	(John Player winners)
Leeds:	Dec. 86 - Apr. 88
	(John Player BF)
Workington T.:	July 88 - Dec. 88
Dewsbury:	Dec. 88 - Dec. 90
Bramley:	Apr. 92 - (Promotion)
Great Britain &	
Under-21s:	Oct. 84 - Dec. 86

Played for: Dewsbury, Batley

TONY BARROW
Warrington:	Mar. 86 - Nov. 88 (Premier winners & BF, John Player BF, Lancs. Cup BF)
Oldham:	Nov. 88 - Jan. 91 (Promotion, Lancs. Cup BF, Div. 2 Premier winners)
Swinton:	Jan. 92 -

Played for: St. Helens, Leigh

CAMERON BELL (New Zealander)
Carlisle:	Feb. 90 -

ALAN BISHOP
Runcorn H.:	Oct. 90 - Apr. 91

Played for: Huyton

MICK BLACKER
Halifax:	June 80 - June 82 (Promotion)
Mansfield M.:	May 84 - Oct. 85
Huddersfield:	Feb. 91 - Sep. 91

Played for: Bradford N., Halifax, Warrington, Mansfield M.

MARK BURGESS
Nottingham C.:	June 91 - May 92

Played for: Rochdale H., Hunslet, Dewsbury, Nottingham C.

LEN CASEY
Wakefield T.:	Apr. 85 - June 86 (Promotion)
Hull:	June 86 - Mar. 88 (Yorks. Cup BF)
Scarborough P.:	Feb. 91 - Dec. 91

Played for: Hull, Hull K.R., Bradford N., Wakefield T.

NOEL CLEAL (Australian)
Hull:	Sep. 90 - Apr. 92 (Premier winners, Charity Shield BF)

Played for: Widnes, Hull

JIM CRELLIN
Blackpool B.:	May 76 - Mar. 77 (John Player BF)
Halifax:	June 77 - Oct. 77
Swinton:	Nov. 83 - May 86 (Div. 2 champs)
Mansfield M.:	Dec. 86 - June 88
Rochdale H.:	June 88 - June 89
Swinton:	July 89 - July 91 (Promotion)

Played for: Workington T., Oldham, Rochdale H.

PAUL DALEY
New Hunslet:	Apr. 74 - Aug. 78 (Promotion)
York:	Jan. 79 - May 79 (Promotion)
Featherstone R.:	May 79 - Jan. 81 (Div. 2 champs)
Hunslet:	Apr. 81 - Nov. 85 (Promotion)
Featherstone R.:	Nov. 86 - Apr. 87
Batley:	July 87 - Apr. 90
Hunslet:	May 90 -

Played for: Halifax, Bradford N., Hull K.R., Hunslet

JACKIE DAVIDSON
Workington T.:	Apr. 85 - Jan. 86
Whitehaven:	May 91 -
Cumbria:	1985-86

Played for: Whitehaven

ROY DICKINSON
Bramley:	Jan. 91 - Apr. 92

Played for: Leeds, Halifax, Bramley

BOB ECCLES
Chorley B.:	May 90 - Sep. 91

Played for: Warrington, Springfield B./Chorley B./Trafford B.

GEORGE FAIRBAIRN
Wigan:	Apr. 80 - May 81 (Promotion)
Hull K.R.:	May 91 -

Played for: Wigan, Hull K.R.

TONY FISHER
Bramley:	Nov. 87 - Feb. 89
Keighley:	June 90 - Sep. 91

Played for: Bradford N., Leeds, Castleford

DEREK FOSTER
Ryedale-York: July 91 -
Played for: Castleford, York

PETER FOX
Featherstone R.: Jan. 71 - May 74
           (RL Cup winners & BF)
Wakefield T.:   June 74 - May 76
           (Yorks. Cup BF)
Bramley: Sep. 76 - Apr. 77 (Promotion)
Bradford N.: Apr. 77 - May 85 (Div. 1
           champs (2), Yorks. Cup winners
           & BF (2), Premier winners
           & BF (2), John Player winners)
Leeds: May 85 - Dec. 86
Featherstone R.: May 87 - Oct. 91 (Promotion,
           Div. 2 Premier BF, Yorks.
           Cup BF)
Bradford N.: Oct. 91 -
England: 1977 (2 matches)
Great Britain: 1978 (3 Tests v. Australia)
Yorkshire: 1985-86 to 1991-92
Played for: Featherstone R., Batley, Hull K.R.,
Wakefield T.

STAN GITTINS
Blackpool B./
Springfield B.: Nov. 85 - June 88
Chorley: June 89 - Apr. 90
Rochdale H.: Apr. 91 - (Lancs. Cup BF)
Played for: Batley, Swinton, Chorley

ARNOLD HEMA (New Zealander)
Nottingham C.: Feb. 91 - June 91
Played for: Nottingham C.

GARY HETHERINGTON
Sheffield E.: July 86 - (Promotion (2),
           Div. 2 Premier winners,
           Divisional Premier winners)
Played for: York, Leeds, Kent I., Sheffield E.

DAVID HOBBS
Bradford N.: Mar. 90 - Oct. 91 (Premier BF,
           Regal BF, Yorks. Cup BF)
Played for: Featherstone R., Oldham, Bradford N.

FRANCIS JARVIS
Huddersfield: Feb. 91 - Sep. 91
Played for: Bradford N., Featherstone R., Hunslet,
Halifax

BRIAN JOHNSON (Australian)
Warrington: Nov. 88 - (Lancs. Cup winners,
           RL Cup BF, Regal winners)
Played for: Warrington

WILLIE JOHNSON
Highfield: Aug. 91 -
Played for: Dewsbury, Swinton, Highfield

PAUL KAVANAGH
Barrow: Feb. 91 -
Played for: Barrow, Workington T.

PHIL LARDER
Widnes: May 92 -
Played for: Oldham, Whitehaven

DOUG LAUGHTON
Widnes: May 78 - Mar. 83
           (RL Cup winners (2) & BF,
           Lancs. Cup winners (2) & BF,
           John Player winners & BF,
           Premier winners (2), Floodlit
           Trophy winners)
Widnes: Jan. 86 - May 91 (Div. 1
           champs (2), Premier winners
           (3) & BF, Charity Shield
           winners (3), John Player BF,
           Lancs. Cup winners, World
           Club Challenge winners)
Leeds: May 91 - (Regal Trophy BF)
Lancashire: 1982-83, 1988-89, 1989-90
Played for: Wigan, St. Helens, Widnes

MIKE McCLENNAN (New Zealander)
St. Helens: Feb. 90 - (RL Cup BF, Lancs.
           Cup winners, Premier BF)

First-ever club coaching appointment for Phil Larder,
appointed by Widnes in May 1992.

ROGER MILLWARD

Hull K.R.: Mar. 77 - May 91 (Div. 1 champs (3), RL Cup winners & BF (2), John Player winners & BF (2), Premier winners (2) & BF, Yorks. Cup winners & BF (2), Floodlit Trophy winners & BF, Charity Shield BF, Div. 2 champs, Div. 2 Premier BF)

Halifax: May 91 -

Played for: Castleford, Hull K.R.

JOHN MONIE (Australian)

Wigan: Sep. 89 - (Div. 1 champs (3), RL Cup winners (3), Regal winners, Premier winners, Charity Shield winners & BF, World Club Challenge winners)

GEOFF MORRIS

Doncaster: Jan. 92 -

Played for: Castleford, Rochdale H., Doncaster

ALEX MURPHY

Leigh: Nov. 66 - May 71 (RL Cup winners, Lancs. Cup winners & BF, Floodlit Trophy winners & BF)

Warrington: May 71 - May 78 (League Leaders, Club Merit winners, RL Cup winners & BF, John Player winners (2), Floodlit Trophy BF, Capt. Morgan winners, Premier BF)

Salford: May 78 - Nov. 80

Leigh: Nov. 80 - June 82 (Div. 1 champs, Lancs. Cup winners)

Wigan: June 82 - Aug. 84 (John Player winners, RL Cup BF)

Leigh: Feb. 85 - Nov. 85

St. Helens: Nov. 85 - Jan. 90 (RL Cup BF (2), John Player winners, Premier BF)

Leigh: Mar. 90 - Aug. 91

Huddersfield: Sep. 91 - (Div. 3 champs)

Lancashire: 1973-74 to 1977-78 Champions (2); 1985-86 to 1987-88

England: 1975 (including World Championship (European Champions))

Played for: St. Helens, Leigh, Warrington

FRANK MYLER

Rochdale H.: May 71 - Oct. 74 (John Player BF, Floodlit Trophy BF)

Widnes: May 75 - May 78 (Div. 1 champs, RL Cup BF (2), Lancs. Cup winners (2), John Player winners & BF, Premier BF)

Swinton: Jan. 80 - May 81

Oldham: May 81 - May 83 (Div. 2 champs)

Oldham: June 84 - Apr. 87 (Lancs. Cup BF)

Widnes: June 91 - May 92 (Regal Trophy winners)

GB Under-24s: 1983

England: 1977-78 (European champs)

Great Britain: 1983-84 and 1984 tour

Played for: Widnes, St. Helens, Rochdale H.

CHRIS O'SULLIVAN (Australian)

Swinton: July 91 - Dec. 91

Played for: Warrington, Swinton

MIKE PEERS

Swinton: June 86 - Oct. 87 (Promotion, Div. 2 Premier winners)

Springfield B./
Chorley B./
Trafford B.: Aug. 87 - May 91

Played for: Warrington, Swinton

PETER ROE

Keighley: Sep. 85 - July 86

Halifax: Aug. 90 - May 91 (Promotion, Div. 2 Premier BF)

Keighley C.: Sep. 91 -

Played for: Keighley, Bradford N., York, Hunslet

DAVE SAMPSON

Castleford: Apr. 87 - Apr. 88 (Yorks. Cup BF)

Doncaster: May 89 - Jan. 92

Nottingham C.: May 92 -

Played for: Wakefield T., Bramley, Castleford

ROYCE SIMMONS (Australian)

Hull: May 92 -

GARY STEPHENS

York: Apr. 88 - June 91

Played for: Castleford, Wigan, Leigh, Halifax, Leeds, York

ROSS STRUDWICK (Australian)
Halifax: Aug. 88 - Feb. 89
Fulham/
London C.:   June 89 -

KEVIN TAMATI (New Zealander)
Salford: Oct. 89 -(Lancs. Cup BF, Div.
                2 champs, Div. 2 Premier
                winners)
Played for: Widnes, Warrington, Salford

JOHN TAYLOR
Chorley B.:   Sep. 91 -
Played for: Salford, Leigh, Widnes

DAVID TOPLISS
Wakefield T.:   May 87 - (Promotion, Yorks.
                Cup BF)
GB Under-21s: 1988-89
Played for: Wakefield T., Hull, Oldham

PETER TUNKS (Australian)
Oldham: Apr. 91 - (Div. 2 Premier BF)
Played for: Leeds, Salford, Sheffield E.

NORMAN TURLEY
Workington T.: Mar. 87 - Apr. 88
Whitehaven: June 90 - Apr. 91
Trafford B.:   June 91 - Dec. 91
Played for: Warrington, Rochdale H.,
Blackpool B., Trafford B., Swinton, Runcorn H.,
Barrow, Workington T., Whitehaven

DARRYL VAN DE VELDE (Australian)
Castleford: July 88 - (Yorks. Cup winners
                (2) & BF, Challenge Cup BF)

PETER WALSH (Australian)
Workington T.: Apr. 92 -
Played for: Oldham

DAVID WARD
Hunslet: July 86 - Apr. 88 (Div. 2
                champs, Div. 2 Premier BF)
Hunslet: Jan. 89 - May 89
Leeds: Sep. 89 - May 91
Batley: May 91 -
Played for: Leeds, Workington T.

DEAN WILLIAMS (New Zealander)
Workington T.: Dec. 91 - Apr. 92
Played for: Workington T.

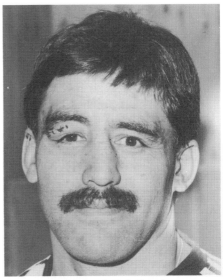

Salford coach Kevin Tamati.

Batley and former Hunslet and Leeds coach, David Ward.

REPRESENTATIVE REGISTER

The following is a list of international and county coaches since 1974-75.

GREAT BRITAIN
Jim Challinor	Dec. 71 - Aug. 74
	(Inc. tours)
David Watkins	1977 World Championship
Peter Fox	1978
Eric Ashton	1979 tour
Johnny Whiteley	Aug. 80 - Nov. 82
Frank Myler	Dec. 82 - Aug. 84
	(Inc. tour)
Maurice Bamford	Oct. 84 - Dec. 86
Malcolm Reilly	Jan. 87 -
	(Inc. tours)

ENGLAND
Alex Murphy	Jan. 75 - Nov. 75
	(Inc. World Championship tour)
Peter Fox	1976-77
Frank Myler	1977-78
Eric Ashton	1978-79 & 1979-80
Johnny Whiteley	1980-81 & 1981-82
Reg Parker	1984-85
(Mgr)	

WALES
Les Pearce	Jan. 75 - Nov. 75
	(Inc. World Championship tour)
David Watkins Bill Francis	} 1976-77
Kel Coslett Bill Francis	} 1977-78
Kel Coslett	1978-79 to 1981-82
David Watkins	1982-83, 1984-85
Clive Griffiths	1991-92

GREAT BRITAIN UNDER-24s
Johnny Whiteley	1976-82
Frank Myler	1983-84

GREAT BRITAIN UNDER-21s
Maurice Bamford	Oct. 84 - Dec. 86
Malcolm Reilly	1986-87, 1987-88, 1989-90, 1991-92
David Topliss	1988-89
Phil Larder	1990-91, 1991-92

CUMBRIA
Ike Southward	1975-76
Frank Foster	1976-77 & 1977-78
Sol Roper	1978-79
Frank Foster	1979-80
Phil Kitchin	1980-81 to 1981-82
Frank Foster	1982-83
Jackie Davidson	1985-86
Phil Kitchin	1986-87 to 1991-92

LANCASHIRE
Alex Murphy	1973-74 to 1977-78
Eric Ashton	1978-79 to 1979-80
Tom Grainey	1980-81 to 1981-82
Doug Laughton	1982-83
Alex Murphy	1985-86 to 1987-88
Doug Laughton	1988-89 to 1989-90
Ray Ashton	1991-92

YORKSHIRE
Johnny Whiteley	1970-71 to 1979-80
Arthur Keegan	1980-81
Johnny Whiteley	1981-82 to 1982-83
Peter Fox	1985-86 to 1991-92

OTHER NATIONALITIES
Dave Cox	1974-75 to 1975-76

Record-breaking 1991-92 Wales captain Jonathan Davies.

ENGLAND AND WALES

1991-92 WALES REVIEW

Now bring on England ... that was the Welsh rally call after celebrating their rebirth by hammering Papua New Guinea 68-0 and disposing of a more formidable French challenge by 35-6.

They totalled 19 tries to none to set up the ultimate prize — an encounter with England, scheduled for the autumn of 1992.

Wales returned to the international scene at the end of October after a seven-year absence, entertaining the 1991 Kumuls at Vetch Field, Swansea, in front of 11,422 passion-filled supporters.

The homecoming was marked by the highest-ever score in their 83-year history, skipper Jonathan Davies contributing a record eight goals and 24 points. The opening game of the five-match Papuan tour is fully chronicled in the section 1991 KUMULS.

Four months later, the Dragons returned to Swansea FC's home to meet France for the first time since 1981 and the first occasion on Welsh soil for 17 years. The Tricolours had just suffered a double defeat by Great Britain, 30-12 in Perpignan and 36-0 at Hull.

Making only two changes from the born-again side which demolished Papua — Ian Marlow replacing the injured Paul Moriarty and fit-again Gerald Cordle coming in for in-dispute Matthew Silva — Wales showed character and commitment to overcome a tough French outfit.

Wales were soon on the scoreboard and Widnes winger John Devereux touched down after only four minutes, finishing off a diagonal sweep by stand off Jonathan Griffiths. While the Kumul contest turned into a festival, this Gallic clash became physical. The 10,000-plus crowd were spell-bound as the French pack, particularly Yves Viloni, refused to lie down.

The Welsh responded, led by the relent-less charges of props Mark Jones and David Young, who won the British Coal Man of the Match award. Hooker Barry Williams completed an impressive front row, forming the base for an encouraging home display which belied the lack of match practice of many of the squad, in particular Kevin Ellis, Marlow and David Bishop.

As half-time approached, Wales bagged their second score, half backs Griffiths and Ellis combining to send Warrington's newly-capped Great Britain centre Allan Bateman in at the corner. Skipper Davies, not as lethal as of late, contributed two goals and a drop goal for a first-half lead of 13-0. He also spent 10 minutes in the sin bin with opposite number Patrick Marginet for fighting.

The first 20 minutes of the second half belonged to the French, skipper Gilles Dumas setting the pace with three penalty goals and a show of astute tactical kicking to peg Wales in their own territory.

The Welsh weathered the storm and then cut loose in a devastating finish to the British Coal international. The highly effective Williams claimed a close-range try before full back Phil Ford added to his hat-trick against Papua. Then substitute Rowland Phillips took great delight in burrowing his way over.

Griffiths, Marlow and Davies combined brilliantly deep in the Welsh half to send Anthony Sullivan flying down the left flank. When the cover looked to have him cornered, Davies backed up to put the final touch to a magical evening.

John Devereux, Welsh tryscorer against France.

BRITISH COAL INTERNATIONAL

22 March   **Vetch Field, Swansea**

WALES 35		FRANCE 6
Phil Ford (Leeds)	1.	Patrick Limongi (Carcassonne)
John Devereux (Widnes)	2.	Philippe Chiron (Avignon)
Allan Bateman (Warrington)	3.	Patrick Marginet (St. Esteve)
Jonathan Davies (Widnes), Capt.	4.	Philippe Sokolow (Limoux)
Anthony Sullivan (St. Helens)	5.	Cyrille Pons (St. Gaudens)
Jonathan Griffiths (St. Helens)	6.	Gilles Dumas (St. Gaudens), Capt.
Kevin Ellis (Warrington)	7.	Patrick Entat (Carcassonne)
Mark Jones (Hull)	8.	Gerard Boyals (St. Gaudens)
Barry Williams (Carlisle)	9.	Thierry Valero (Lezignan)
David Young (Salford)	10.	Yves Viloni (Carpentras)
Rob Ackerman (Carlisle)	11.	Christophe Grandjean (Lezignan)
Ian Marlow (Hull)	12.	Christophe Bonnafous (Albi)
David Bishop (Hull K.R.)	13.	Jacques Pech (Limoux)
Adrian Hadley (Salford)	14.	Frank Romano (Carpentras)
Rowland Phillips (Warrington)	15.	Francis Lope (Albi)
Gerald Cordle (Bradford N.)	16.	Jean-Pierre Mater (Villeneuve)
Gary Pearce (Ryedale-York)	17.	Jean Frison (Villefranche)

T: Devereux, Bateman, Williams, Ford, Phillips, Davies
G: Davies (5, 1dg)
Substitutions:
Phillips for Bishop (55 min.)
Cordle for Bateman (70 min.)
Hadley for Sullivan (73 min.)
Pearce for Williams (75 min.)
Manager: Jim Mills
Coach: Clive Griffiths

G: Dumas (3)
Substitutions:
Frison for Sokolow (39 min.)
Mater for Marginet (Half-time)
Romano for Bonnafous (55 min.)
Lope for Boyals (72 min.)
Half-time: 13-0
Referee: Colin Morris
(Huddersfield)
Attendance: 10,133

Wales prop Mark Jones powers past French skipper Gilles Dumas, supported by hooker Barry Williams (right).

EUROPEAN CHAMPIONSHIP

● The following is a list of European Championship matches since the tournament was introduced in 1935, the year that France emerged as an International competitor.

E — England, Fr — France, ON — Other Nationalities, W — Wales

1934-35 *Winners:* England on points average

1 Jan.	Fr	18	W	11	Bordeaux
28 Mar.	Fr	15	E	15	Paris
10 Apr.	E	24	W	11	Liverpool

1935-36 *Winners:* Wales

23 Nov.	W	41	Fr	7	Llanelli
1 Feb.	E	14	W	17	Hull K.R.
16 Feb.	Fr	7	E	25	Paris

1936-37 *Winners:* Wales

7 Nov.	W	3	E	2	Pontypridd
6 Dec.	Fr	3	W	9	Paris
10 Apr.	E	23	Fr	9	Halifax

1937-38 *Winners:* Wales

29 Jan.	E	6	W	7	Bradford
20 Mar.	Fr	15	E	17	Paris
2 Apr.	W	18	Fr	2	Llanelli

1938-39 *Winners:* France

5 Nov.	W	17	E	9	Llanelli
25 Feb.	E	9	Fr	12	St. Helens
16 Apr.	Fr	16	W	10	Bordeaux

1945-46 *Winners:* England on points average

24 Nov.	W	11	E	3	Swansea
23 Feb.	E	16	Fr	6	Swinton
24 Mar.	Fr	19	W	7	Bordeaux

1946-47 *Winners:* England

12 Oct.	E	10	W	13	Swinton
16 Nov.	W	5	E	19	Swansea
8 Dec.	Fr	0	E	3	Bordeaux
18 Jan.	Fr	14	W	5	Marseilles
12 Apr.	W	17	Fr	15	Swansea
17 May	E	5	Fr	2	Leeds

1947-48 *Winners:* England

20 Sep.	E	8	W	10	Wigan
25 Oct.	E	20	Fr	15	Huddersfield
23 Nov.	Fr	29	W	21	Bordeaux
6 Dec.	W	7	E	18	Swansea
20 Mar.	W	12	Fr	20	Swansea
11 Apr.	Fr	10	E	25	Marseilles

1948-49 *Winners:* France

22 Sep.	E	11	W	5	Wigan
23 Oct.	W	9	Fr	12	Swansea
28 Nov.	Fr	5	E	12	Bordeaux
5 Feb.	W	14	E	10	Swansea
12 Mar.	E	5	Fr	12	Wembley
10 Apr.	Fr	11	W	0	Marseilles

1949-50 *Winners:* England on points average

19 Sep.	E	7	ON	13	Workington
22 Oct.	W	5	ON	6	Abertillery
12 Nov.	W	16	Fr	8	Swansea
4 Dec.	Fr	5	E	13	Bordeaux
15 Jan.	Fr	8	ON	3	Marseilles
1 Mar.	E	11	W	6	Wigan

1950-51 *Winners:* France on points average

14 Oct.	W	4	E	22	Abertillery
11 Nov.	E	14	Fr	9	Leeds
10 Dec.	Fr	16	ON	3	Bordeaux
31 Mar.	W	21	ON	27	Swansea
11 Apr.	E	10	ON	35	Wigan
15 Apr.	Fr	28	W	13	Marseilles

1951-52 *Winners:* France on points average

19 Sep.	E	35	W	11	St. Helens
3 Nov.	ON	17	Fr	14	Hull
25 Nov.	Fr	42	E	13	Marseilles
1 Dec.	W	11	ON	22	Abertillery
6 Apr.	Fr	20	W	12	Bordeaux
23 Apr.	E	31	ON	18	Wigan

1952-53 *Winners:* Other Nats on points average

17 Sep.	E	19	W	8	Wigan
18 Oct.	E	12	ON	31	Huddersfield
25 Oct.	W	22	Fr	16	Leeds
23 Nov.	Fr	10	ON	29	Marseilles
11 Apr.	Fr	13	E	15	Paris
15 Apr.	W	18	ON	16	Warrington

1953-54 *Winners:* England

16 Sep.	E	24	W	5	St. Helens
7 Oct.	ON	30	W	5	Bradford
18 Oct.	Fr	10	ON	15	Bordeaux
7 Nov.	E	7	Fr	5	Bradford
28 Nov.	E	30	ON	22	Wigan
13 Dec.	Fr	23	W	22	Marseilles

● Championship suspended in 1954-55 because of World Cup

1955-56   *Winners:* Other Nationalities

12 Sep.	E	16	ON	33	Wigan
19 Oct.	ON	32	Fr	19	Leigh
10 May	Fr	23	E	9	Lyons

1969-70   *Winners:* England on points average

18 Oct.	E	40	W	23	Leeds
23 Oct.	W	2	Fr	8	Salford
25 Oct.	E	11	Fr	11	Wigan
25 Jan.	Fr	11	W	15	Perpignan
24 Feb.	E	26	W	7	Leeds
15 Mar.	Fr	14	E	9	Toulouse

1974-75   *Winners:* England

19 Jan.	Fr	9	E	11	Perpignan
16 Feb.	W	21	Fr	8	Swansea
25 Feb.	E	12	W	8	Salford

● Championship suspended in 1975-76 because of World Cup

1976-77   *Winners:* France

29 Jan.	E	2	W	6	Leeds
20 Feb.	Fr	13	W	2	Toulouse
20 Mar.	Fr	28	E	15	Carcassonne

1977-78   *Winners:* England

15 Jan.	W	29	Fr	7	Widnes
5 Mar.	Fr	11	E	13	Toulouse
28 May	E	60	W	13	St. Helens

1978-79   *Winners:* England

4 Feb.	Fr	15	W	8	Narbonne
16 Mar.	E	15	W	7	Widnes
24 Mar.	E	12	Fr	6	Warrington

1979-80   *Winners:* England

26 Jan.	W	7	Fr	21	Widnes
29 Feb.	E	26	W	9	Hull K.R.
16 Mar.	Fr	2	E	4	Narbonne

1980-81   *Winners:* France

31 Jan.	Fr	23	W	5	Narbonne
21 Feb.	E	1	Fr	5	Leeds
18 Mar.	E	17	W	4	Hull K.R.

1975 WORLD CHAMPIONSHIP
Winners: Australia (home and away basis)

Date	Match and Result				Venue	Attendance
2 Mar.	France	14	Wales	7	Toulouse	7,563
16 Mar.	England	20	France	2	Leeds	10,842
1 June	Australia	36	New Zealand	8	Brisbane	10,000
10 June	Wales	12	England	7	Brisbane	6,000
14 June	Australia	30	Wales	13	Sydney	25,386
15 June	New Zealand	27	France	0	Christchurch	2,500
21 June	New Zealand	17	England	17	Auckland	12,000
22 June	Australia	26	France	6	Brisbane	9,000
28 June	New Zealand	13	Wales	8	Auckland	18,000
28 June	Australia	10	England	10	Sydney	33,858
20 Sep.	England	22	Wales	16	Warrington	5,034
27 Sep.	New Zealand	8	Australia	24	Auckland	18,000
11 Oct.	France	2	England	48	Bordeaux	1,581
17 Oct.	France	12	New Zealand	12	Marseilles	18,000
19 Oct.	Wales	6	Australia	18	Swansea	11,112
25 Oct.	England	27	New Zealand	12	Bradford	5,507
26 Oct.	France	2	Australia	41	Perpignan	10,440
1 Nov.	England	16	Australia	13	Wigan	9,393
2 Nov.	Wales	25	New Zealand	24	Swansea	2,645
6 Nov.	Wales	23	France	2	Salford	2,247

Final Table

	P.	W.	D.	L.	F.	A.	Pts
Australia	8	6	1	1	198	69	13
England	8	5	2	1	167	84	12
Wales	8	3	0	5	110	130	6
New Zealand	8	2	2	4	121	149	6
France	8	1	1	6	40	204	3

1975 World Championship squads for Australasian section

ENGLAND
R. Millward (Hull KR)
J. Atkinson (Leeds)
J. Bridges (Featherstone R)
D. Chisnall (Warrington)
E. Chisnall (St. Helens)
P. Cookson (Leeds)
M. Coulman (Salford)
G. Dunn (Hull KR)
L. Dyl (Leeds)
G. Fairbairn (Wigan)
K. Fielding (Salford)
K. Gill (Salford)
P. Gordon (Warrington)
T. Martyn (Warrington)
M. Morgan (Wakefield T)
S. Nash (Featherstone R)
G. Nicholls (St. Helens)
D. Noonan (Warrington)
S. Norton (Castleford)
J. Walsh (St. Helens)
Manager: W. Oxley (Barrow)
Coach: A. J. Murphy (Warrington)

WALES
D. Watkins (Salford)
P. Banner (Salford)
B. Butler (Swinton)
K. Coslett (St. Helens)
E. Cunningham (St. Helens)
C. Dixon (Salford)
R. Evans (Swinton)
T. Fisher (Leeds)
W. Francis (Wigan)
J. Mantle (St. Helens)
R. Mathias (St. Helens)
J. Mills (Widnes)
M. Nicholas (Warrington)
P. Rowe (Blackpool B)
C. Sullivan (Hull KR)
D. Treasure (Oldham)
G. Turner (Hull KR)
R. Wanbon (Warrington)
D. Willicombe (Wigan)
F. Wilson (St. Helens)
Manager: R. Simpson (Castleford)
Coach: L. Pearce (Halifax)

ENGLAND — OTHER INTERNATIONAL MATCHES

● W-Won, D-Drawn, L-Lost refer to England.

v. WALES

20 Apr. 1908	L	18-35	Tonypandy
28 Dec. 1908	W	31-7	Broughton
4 Dec. 1909	W	19-13	Wakefield
9 Apr. 1910	L	18-39	Ebbw Vale
10 Dec. 1910	W	39-13	Ebbw Vale
1 Apr. 1911	W	27-8	Ebbw Vale
20 Jan. 1912	W	31-5	Oldham
15 Feb. 1913	W	40-16	Plymouth
14 Feb. 1914	W	16-12	St. Helens

v. FRANCE

*15 Apr. 1934	W	32-21	Paris
17 Nov. 1962	W	18-6	Leeds

*Included Welsh players.

v. OTHER NATIONALITIES

5 Apr. 1904	L	3-9	Wigan
2 Jan. 1905	W	26-11	Bradford
			(Park Avenue)
1 Jan. 1906	D	3-3	Wigan

v. WALES (cont.)

21 Jan. 1921	W	35-9	Leeds
11 Dec. 1922	W	12-7	London, Herne Hill
7 Feb. 1923	L	2-13	Wigan
1 Oct. 1923	W	18-11	Huddersfield
7 Feb. 1925	W	27-22	Workington
30 Sep. 1925	W	18-14	Wigan
12 Apr. 1926	W	30-22	Pontypridd
6 Apr. 1927	W	11-8	Broughton
11 Jan. 1928	W	20-12	Wigan
14 Nov. 1928	W	39-15	Cardiff
18 Mar. 1931	W	23-18	Huddersfield
27 Jan. 1932	W	19-2	Salford
30 Nov. 1932	W	14-13	Leeds
23 Dec. 1939	L	3-16	Bradford
9 Nov. 1940	W	8-5	Oldham
18 Oct. 1941	D	9-9	Bradford
27 Feb. 1943	W	15-9	Wigan
26 Feb. 1944	D	9-9	Wigan
10 Mar. 1945	W	18-8	Wigan
7 Nov. 1968	L	17-24	Salford
8 Nov. 1981	W	20-15	Cardiff
14 Oct. 1984	W	28-9	Ebbw Vale

v. OTHER NATIONALITIES (cont.)

*5 Feb. 1921	W	33-16	Workington
15 Oct. 1924	L	17-23	Leeds
4 Feb. 1926	W	37-11	Whitehaven
20 Mar. 1929	W	27-20	Leeds
7 Apr. 1930	L	19-35	Halifax
1 Oct. 1930	W	31-18	St. Helens
30 Mar. 1933	W	34-27	Workington

*Other Nationalities side all-Welsh.

v. AUSTRALIA

2 Jan. 1909	W	14-9	Huddersfield
3 Feb. 1909	D	17-17	Glasgow
3 Mar. 1909	W	14-7	Everton
18 Oct. 1911	L	6-11	Fulham
6 Dec. 1911	W	5-3	Nottingham
10 Oct. 1921	W	5-4	Arsenal
*31 Dec. 1933	L	13-63	Paris
*13 Jan. 1934	W	19-14	Gateshead
12 Nov. 1975	L	0-25	Leeds

*Included Welsh players.

v. NEW ZEALAND

11 Jan. 1908	W	18-16	Wigan

v. PAPUA NEW GUINEA

6 July 1975	W	40-12	Port Moresby

ENGLAND RECORDS

Highest score:	60-13 v. Wales at St. Helens, 28 May 1978 (Also widest margin win)
Highest score against:	63-13* v. Australia at Paris, 31 December 1933

*England included Welshmen. Highest score against All-England side 42-13 v. France at Marseilles, 25 November 1951 (Also widest margin defeat)

Most tries in a match:	4 by J. Leytham (Wigan) v. Other Nationalities at Bradford, 2 January 1905
	4 by S. Moorhouse (Huddersfield) v. Wales at Plymouth, 15 February 1913
	4 by P. Norburn (Swinton) v. Other Nationalities at Wigan, 28 November 1953
	4 by K. Fielding (Salford) v. France at Bordeaux, 11 October 1975
	4 by S. Wright (Widnes) v. Wales at St. Helens, 28 May 1978
Most goals and points in a match:	9g-21pts by G. Pimblett (St. Helens) v. Wales at St. Helens, 28 May 1978
Biggest home attendance:	27,500 v. Wales at Wigan, 1 March 1950

269

WALES — OTHER INTERNATIONAL MATCHES

● W-Won, D-Drawn,
L-Lost refer to Wales.

v. FRANCE
*19 May 1955	L	11-24	Nantes
1 Mar. 1959	L	8-25	Toulouse
17 Feb. 1963	L	3-23	Toulouse
9 Mar. 1969	L	13-17	Paris
22 Mar. 1992	W	35-6	Swansea FC

*v. France 'B'

v. NEW ZEALAND
1 Jan. 1908	W	9-8	Aberdare
4 Dec. 1926	W	34-8	Pontypridd
18 Oct. 1947	L	20-28	Swansea
7 Dec. 1951	L	3-15	Bradford

v. AUSTRALIA
7 Oct. 1911	L	20-28	Ebbw Vale
10 Dec. 1921	L	16-21	Pontypridd
18 Jan. 1930	L	10-26	Wembley
30 Dec. 1933	L	19-51	Wembley
20 Nov. 1948	L	5-12	Swansea
15 Oct. 1978	L	3-8	Swansea
24 Oct. 1982	L	7-37	Cardiff

A Welsh League XIII beat Australia 14-13 at Merthyr on 16 January 1909.

v. PAPUA NEW GUINEA
27 Oct. 1991	W	68-0	Swansea FC

v. NORTHERN RL
17 Apr. 1937	W	15-12	Newcastle

v. EMPIRE XIII
19 May 1951	L	16-29	Llanelli

1991 Welsh debutant Paul Moriarty.

WALES RECORDS

Highest score:	68-0 v. Papua New Guinea at Swansea FC, 27 October 1991 (Also widest margin win)
Highest score against:	60-13 v. England at St. Helens, 28 May 1978 (Also widest margin defeat)
Most tries in a match:	4 by W. T. Davies (Halifax) v. Australia at Ebbw Vale, 7 October 1911
Most goals and points in a match:	8g-24pts by Jonathan Davies (Widnes) v. Papua New Guinea at Swansea FC, 27 October 1991
Biggest home attendance:	30,000 v. England at Swansea, 24 November 1945

MISCELLANEOUS

1908	November	18	Northern RL	9	v.	Australia	10	Everton
1909	January	16	Welsh League	14	v.	Australia	13	Merthyr Tydfil
1910	September	17	Wales & the West	27	v.	England	25	Plymouth
1910	September	19	Tourists	15	v.	Colonials	31	Leeds
1910	December	27	Tourists	40	v.	Colonials	22	Wigan
1911	September	23	Midlands & South	11	v.	Australia	20	Coventry
1911	October	25	Northern RL	3	v.	Australia	16	Everton
1911	December	20	Wales & the West	3	v.	Australia	23	Bristol
1912	January	31	Northern RL	12	v.	Australia	20	Wigan
1929	December	4	Northern RL	18	v.	Australia	5	Wigan
1929	December	18	Northern RL	22	v.	Australia	32	Newcastle
1933	November	1	Northern RL	7	v.	Australia	5	York
1934	March	17	Northern RL	32	v.	France	16	Warrington
1935	April	28	French XIII	12	v.	Northern RL	32	Paris
1935	May	6	Northern RL	25	v.	France	18	Leeds
1936	April	26	France	8	v.	Dominions XIII	5	Paris
1937	March	21	France	3	v.	Dominions XIII	6	Lyons
1937	November	1	France	0	v.	Empire XIII	15	Paris
1938	April	28	French XIII	13	v.	Northern RL	25	Pau
1940	March	23	Lancs League	10	v.	Yorks League	13	Barrow
1940	May	4	Tour Probables	29	v.	1936 Tourists	21	Salford
1942	March	21	RL XIII	18	v.	N. Command	22	Halifax
1942	October	10	RL XIII	10	v.	N. Command	14	Hull
1943	December	18	RL XIII	11	v.	Army XIII	4	Halifax
1944	October	7	RL XIII	27	v.	N. Command	23	Huddersfield
1946	January	6	French XIII	6	v.	British XIII	19	Paris
1946	April	28	Paris XIII	19	v.	RL XIII	36	Paris
1949	May	26	French XIII	23	v.	Empire XIII	10	Bordeaux
1949	May	29	French XIII	12	v.	Empire XIII	38	Albi
1950	October	4	Tourists	23	v.	Rest of League	16	Wigan
1951	May	3	French XIII	10	v.	U.K. XIII	13	Paris
1951	May	19	Great Britain	20	v.	Australasia	23	Leeds
1952	January	23	Empire XIII	26	v.	New Zealand	2	Chelsea
1954	January	3	France	19	v.	Internat. XIII	15	Lyons
1954	November	17	RL XIII	13	v.	Australasia	25	Bradford
1955	December	7	RL XIII	24	v.	New Zealand	11	Bradford
1956	October	3	Great Britain	26	v.	Rest of League	23	Bradford
1956	October	21	France	17	v.	RL XIII	18	Marseilles
1956	October	29	RL XIII	15	v.	Australia	19	Leigh
1957	July	6	British XIII	26	v.	French XIII	12	Auckland
1957	July	20	British XIII	61	v.	French XIII	41	Benoni (S. Africa)
1957	July	24	British XIII	32	v.	French XIII	11	Durban (S. Africa)
1957	July	27	British XIII	69	v.	French XIII	11	East London (S. Africa)
1958	April	16	RL XIII	19	v.	France	8	Leeds
1958	November	22	RL XIII	8	v.	France	26	St. Helens
1960	September	12	Great Britain	21	v.	Rest of League	16	St. Helens
1960	October	10	Great Britain	33	v.	Rest of World	27	Bradford
1961	September	20	RL XIII	22	v.	New Zealand	20	White City, Manchester
1961	October	12	French XIII	21	v.	RL XIII	20	Paris
1962	August	23	South Africa	30	v.	Great Britain	49	Pretoria (S. Africa)
1962	August	26	South Africa	35	v.	Great Britain	39	Durban (S. Africa)
1962	August	28	South Africa	23	v.	Great Britain	45	Johannesburg (S. Africa)
1962	November	1	France	16	v.	Eastern Div.	23	Carcassonne
1965	August	18	Other Nats.	7	v.	New Zealand	15	Crystal Palace
1966	May	5	Paris XIII	20	v.	RL XIII	0	Paris
1966	November	6	Tourists	31	v.	Rest of League	38	Leeds

ENGLAND TEAMS ● From 1975 to 1982 and revived in 1984 for one game.

1975 France
Perpignan: 19 Jan

Won 11-9

Murphy (Oldham) 1t
Fielding (Salford) 1t
Walsh (St. Helens)
Dyl (Leeds) 1t
Redfearn, D (Bradford)
Topliss (Wakefield)
*Millward (Hull KR)
Coulman (Salford)
Gray (Wigan) 1g
Millington (Hull KR)
Cunningham, J (Barrow)
Chisnall, E (St. Helens)
Nicholls (St. Helens)
Sub: Eckersley (St. Helens)
 Morgan (Wakefield)

1975 Wales
Salford: 25 Feb

Won 12-8

Sheard (Wakefield)
Dunn (Hull KR)
Noonan (Warrington) 1t
Dyl (Leeds)
Atkinson (Leeds) 1t
Gill, K (Salford)
*Millward (Hull KR)
Coulman (Salford)
Gray (Wigan) 3g
Jackson (Bradford)
Martyn (Warrington)
Cunningham, J (Barrow)
Morgan (Wakefield)
Sub: Chisnall, D (Warrington)

1975 France (WC)
Leeds: 16 Mar

Won 20-2

Charlton (Salford)
Fielding (Salford) 2t
Noonan (Warrington)
Dyl (Leeds)
Atkinson (Leeds)
Gill, K (Salford)
*Millward (Hull KR) 1t
Chisnall, D (Warrington)
Gray (Wigan) 4g
Jackson (Bradford)
Martyn (Warrington)
Nicholls (St. Helens)
Philbin, B (Warrington)
Sub: Morgan (Wakefield) 1t

1975 Wales (WC)
Brisbane: 10 June

Lost 7-12

Fairbairn (Wigan) 2g
Fielding (Salford)
Noonan (Warrington)
Dyl (Leeds)
Atkinson (Leeds)
*Millward (Hull KR)
Nash (Featherstone)
Chisnall, D (Warrington)
Morgan (Wakefield)
Coulman (Salford)
Chisnall, E (St. Helens)
Nicholls (St. Helens)
Norton (Castleford)
Sub: Gill, K (Salford)
 Martyn (Warrington) 1t

1975 New Zealand (WC)
Auckland: 21 June

Drew 17-17

Fairbairn (Wigan) 2t,4g
Fielding (Salford)
Walsh (St. Helens)
Dyl (Leeds)
Atkinson (Leeds) 1t
Gill, K (Salford)
Nash (Featherstone)
Chisnall, D (Warrington)
Bridges (Featherstone)
Chisnall, E (St. Helens)
*Nicholls (St. Helens)
Cookson (Leeds)
Norton (Castleford)
Sub: Morgan (Wakefield)

1975 Australia (WC)
Sydney: 28 June

Drew 10-10

Fairbairn (Wigan) 2g
Fielding (Salford)
Walsh (St. Helens)
Dyl (Leeds)
Dunn (Hull KR) 1t
*Millward (Hull KR)
Nash (Featherstone)
Coulman (Salford)
Bridges (Featherstone)
Morgan (Wakefield)
Nicholls (St. Helens)
Cookson (Leeds)
Norton (Castleford)
Sub: Gill, K (Salford) 1t
 Chisnall, E (St. Helens)

1975 Wales (WC)
Warrington: 20 Sept

Won 22-16

Fairbairn (Wigan) 6g
Fielding (Salford) 1t
Hughes (Widnes) 1t
Holmes (Leeds) 1t
Atkinson (Leeds)
Gill, K (Salford)
*Millward (Hull KR)
Hogan, B (Wigan)
Bridges (Featherstone) 1dg
Forsyth (Bradford)
Grayshon (Dewsbury)
Irving (Wigan)
Norton (Castleford)
Sub: Eckersley (St. Helens)
 Nicholls (St. Helens)

1975 France (WC)
Bordeaux: 11 Oct

Won 48-2

Fairbairn (Wigan) 4g
Fielding (Salford) 4t
Hughes (Widnes) 1t
Holmes (Leeds) 2t
Dunn (Hull KR) 2t
Gill, K (Salford) 1t
*Millward (Hull KR) 2g
Hogan, B (Wigan) 1t
Bridges (Featherstone)
Forsyth (Bradford) 1t
Grayshon (Dewsbury)
Irving (Wigan)
Norton (Castleford)
Sub: Eckersley (St. Helens)
 Nicholls (St. Helens)

1975 New Zealand (WC)
Bradford: 25 Oct

Won 27-12

Fairbairn (Wigan) 3g
Wright (Wigan) 1t
Hughes (Widnes) 1t
Holmes (Leeds)
Dunn (Hull KR) 1t
Gill, K (Salford) 3t
*Millward (Hull KR)
Hogan, B (Wigan)
Bridges (Featherstone)
Forsyth (Bradford)
Grayshon (Dewsbury)
Adams (Widnes)
Norton (Castleford) 1t
Sub: Dyl (Leeds)
 Nicholls (St. Helens)

1975 Australia (WC)
Wigan: 1 Nov
Won 16-13
Fairbairn (Wigan) 5g
Dunn (Hull KR)
Holmes (Leeds) 1t
Dyl (Leeds)
Redfearn, D (Bradford)
Gill, K (Salford)
*Millward (Hull KR)
Hogan, B (Wigan)
Bridges (Featherstone)
Thompson (Featherstone)
Grayshon (Dewsbury) 1t
Irving (Wigan)
Norton (Castleford)
Sub: Hughes (Widnes)
　　 Adams (Widnes)

1978 France
Toulouse: 5 Mar
Won 13-11
Fairbairn (Wigan) 2g
Wright (Widnes)
Hughes (Widnes) 2t
Dyl (Leeds)
Atkinson (Leeds)
*Millward (Hull KR)
Nash (Salford)
Harrison (Leeds)
Elwell (Widnes)
Nicholls (St. Helens)
Lowe (Hull KR)
Adams (Widnes)
Casey (Hull KR)
Sub: Holmes (Leeds) 1t
　　 Thompson (Bradford)

1979 France
Warrington: 24 Mar
Won 12-6
Mumby (Bradford)
Wright (Widnes)
Glynn (St. Helens)
Woods (Leigh) 3g
Hughes (Widnes) 1t
Evans (Featherstone)
Redfearn, A (Bradford)
Tindall (Hull)
Liptrot (St. Helens)
*Lockwood (Hull KR)
Martyn (Warrington) 1t
Grayshon (Bradford)
Hogan, P (Hull KR)
Sub: Banks (York)
　　 Szymala (Barrow)

1977 Wales
Leeds: 29 Jan
Lost 2-6
Fairbairn (Wigan) 1g
Wright (Widnes)
Holmes (Leeds)
Dyl (Leeds)
Jones (St. Helens)
Gill, K (Salford)
*Millward (Hull KR)
Hogan, B (Wigan)
Bridges (Featherstone)
Thompson (Featherstone)
Grayshon (Dewsbury)
Gorley, L (Workington)
Laughton (Widnes)
Sub: Eckersley (St. Helens)
　　 Reilly (Castleford)

1978 Wales
St. Helens: 28 May
Won 60-13
Pimblett (St. Helens) 1t,9g
Wright (Widnes) 4t
Hughes (Widnes) 2t
Dyl (Leeds) 1t
Atkinson (Leeds) 2t
*Millward (Hull KR) 1t
Nash (Salford) 1t
Harrison (Leeds)
Elwell (Widnes)
Nicholls (St. Helens)
Rose (Hull KR)
Casey (Hull KR) 1t
Norton (Hull) 1t
Sub: Eckersley (St. Helens)
　　 Thompson (Bradford)

1980 Wales
Hull KR: 29 Feb
Won 26-9
Fairbairn (Wigan) 1t,6g
Wright (Widnes)
Joyner (Castleford) 1t
Smith, M (Hull KR)
Drummond (Leigh)
Evans (Featherstone)
Holding (St. Helens)
Holdstock (Hull KR) 1t
*Ward (Leeds)
Rayne, Keith (Wakefield) 1t
Casey (Hull KR)
Gorley, P (St. Helens)
Pinner (St. Helens) 2dg
Sub: Woods (Leigh)
　　 Grayshon (Bradford)

1977 France
Carcassonne: 20 Mar
Lost 15-28
Fairbairn (Wigan) 3g
Dunn (Hull KR)
Hughes (Widnes)
Dyl (Leeds)
Smith, D (Leeds) 1t
Gill, K (Salford)
*Millward (Hull KR)
Coulman (Salford)
Ward (Leeds)
Farrar (Featherstone)
Lowe (Hull KR) 1t
Rose (Hull KR)
Norton (Castleford)
Sub: Holmes (Leeds)
　　 Nicholls (St. Helens) 1t

1979 Wales
Widnes: 16 Mar
Won 15-7
Mumby (Bradford) 1t,1g
Wright (Widnes)
Glynn (St. Helens)
Smith, K (Wakefield) 1t
Hughes (Widnes)
Kelly (Warrington)
Stephens (Castleford)
Beverley (Workington)
Liptrot (St. Helens)
*Lockwood (Hull KR)
Martyn (Warrington)
Grayshon (Bradford)
Adams (Widnes)
Sub: Woods (Leigh) 1t,2g
　　 Watkinson (Hull KR)

1980 France
Narbonne: 16 Mar
Won 4-2
Fairbairn (Wigan)
Drummond (Leigh)
Smith, M (Hull KR)
Joyner (Castleford)
Evans (Featherstone) 1t
Woods (Leigh)
Redfearn, A (Bradford) 1dg
Holdstock (Hull KR)
*Ward (Leeds)
Rayne, Keith (Wakefield)
Grayshon (Bradford)
Smith, P (Featherstone)
Pinner (St. Helens)
Sub: Gorley, P (St. Helens)

273

1981 France
Leeds: 21 Feb
Lost 1-5
*Fairbairn (Wigan) 1dg
Drummond (Leigh)
Joyner (Castleford)
Smith, M (Hull KR)
Fenton (Castleford)
Kelly (Warrington)
Walker (Whitehaven)
O'Neill, S (Wigan)
Ward (Leeds)
Case (Warrington)
Casey (Hull KR)
Potter (Warrington)
Pinner (St. Helens)
Sub: Woods (Leigh)
Pattinson (Workington)

1981 Wales
Hull KR: 18 Mar
Won 17-4
*Fairbairn (Wigan) 4g
Richardson (Castleford)
Joyner (Castleford) 1t
Smith (Hull KR)
Fenton (Castleford)
Kelly (Warrington) 1t
Nash (Salford)
Holdstock (Hull KR)
Ward (Leeds)
Casey (Hull KR)
Potter (Warrington)
Pattinson (Workington)
Norton (Hull)
Sub: Woods (Leigh) 1t
Adams (Widnes)

1981 Wales
Cardiff: 8 Nov
Won 20-15
Fairbairn (Hull KR) 1g
Drummond (Leigh) 1t
Smith, M (Hull KR)
Dyl (Leeds)
Gill, H (Wigan) 1t
Woods (Leigh) 3g
Nash (Salford)
Grayshon (Bradford) 1t
*Ward (Leeds)
Millington (Hull KR)
Lowe (Hull KR)
Gorley, P (St. Helens) 1t
Norton (Hull)
Sub: Gorley, L (Widnes)

1984 Wales
Ebbw Vale: 14 Oct
Won 28-9
Burke (Widnes) 1t,4g
Drummond (Leigh)
Schofield (Hull)
Hanley (Bradford) 1t
Clark (Hull KR) 3t
*Donlan (Leigh)
Cairns (Barrow)
Hobbs (Featherstone)
Beardmore, K (Castleford)
Waddell (Blackpool)
Kelly (Hull KR)
Goodway (Oldham)
Huddart (Whitehaven)
Sub: Ledger (St. Helens)
Arkwright (St. Helens)

Kevin Beardmore, capped once for England in 1984.

Prop Brian Case, a 1981 England cap.

ENGLAND REGISTER
● Since reintroduction in 1975

The following is a register of England appearances since the reintroduction of European and World Championship matches in 1975, but does not include the challenge match against Australia played after the 1975 World Championship.

Figures in brackets are the total appearances for England since 1975, with the plus sign indicating substitute appearances, e.g. (7 + 3).

A few players also played in the 1969-70 European Championship and this is shown as an additional total outside bracket, e.g. (11)2.

World Championship matches are in bold letters. Substitute appearances are in lower case letters.

A - Australia, F - France,
NZ - New Zealand, W - Wales.

ADAMS, M. (3 + 2) Widnes: 1975 **NZ, a**; 1978 F; 1979 W; 1981 w
ARKWRIGHT, C. (+ 1) St. Helens: 1984 w
ATKINSON, J. (7)4 Leeds: 1975 **W, F, W, NZ, W**; 1978 F, W

BANKS, B. (+ 1) York: 1979 f
BEARDMORE, K. (1) Castleford: 1984 **W**
BEVERLEY, H. (1) Workington T: 1979 **W**
BRIDGES, K. (7) Featherstone R: 1975 **NZ, A, W, F, NZ, A**; 1977 **W**
BURKE, M. (1) Widnes: 1984 **W**

CAIRNS, D. (1) Barrow: 1984 **W**
CASE, B. (1) Warrington: 1981 F
CASEY, L. (5) Hull KR: 1978 F, W; 1980 W; 1981 F, W
CHARLTON, P. (1) Salford: 1975 **F**
CHISNALL, D. (3 + 1) Warrington: 1975 w, **F, W, NZ**
CHISNALL, E. (3 + 1) St. Helens: 1975 F, **W, NZ, a**
CLARK, G. (1) Hull KR: 1984 **W**
COOKSON, P. (2) Leeds: 1975 **NZ, A**
COULMAN, M. (5) Salford: 1975 F, W, **W, A**; 1977 F
CUNNINGHAM, J. (2) Barrow: 1975 F, **W**

DONLAN, S. (1) Leigh: 1984 **W**
DRUMMOND, D. (5) Leigh: 1980 W, F; 1981 F, W; 1984 **W**
DUNN, G. (6) Hull KR: 1975 W, **A, F, NZ, A**; 1977 F
DYL, L. (12 + 1) Leeds: 1975 F, **W, F, W, NZ, A, nz,** a; 1977 W, F; 1978 F, W; 1981 W

ECKERSLEY, D. (+ 5) St. Helens: 1975 f, w, f; Widnes: 1977 w; 1978 w
ELWELL, K. (2) Widnes: 1978 F, W
EVANS, S. (3) Featherstone R: 1979 F; 1980 W, F

FAIRBAIRN, G. (15) Wigan: 1975 **W, NZ, A, W, F, NZ, A**; 1977 W, F; 1978 F; 1980 W, F; 1981 F, W; Hull KR: 1981 W
FARRAR, V. (1) Featherstone R: 1977 F
FENTON, S. (2) Castleford: 1981 F, W
FIELDING, K. (7) Salford: 1975 F, **F, W, NZ, A, W, F**
FORSYTH, C. (3) Bradford N: 1975 **W, F, NZ**

GILL, H. (1) Wigan: 1981 W
GILL, K. (9 + 2) Salford: 1975 W, **F, w, NZ, a, W, F, NZ, A**; 1977 W, F
GLYNN, P. (2) St. Helens: 1979 W, F
GOODWAY, A. (1) Oldham: 1984 **W**
GORLEY, L. (1 + 1) Workington T: 1977 W; Widnes: 1981 w
GORLEY, P. (2 + 1) St. Helens: 1980 W, f; 1981 W
GRAY, J. (3) Wigan: 1975 F, W, **F**
GRAYSHON, J. (9 + 1) Dewsbury: 1975 **W, F, NZ, A**; 1977 W; Bradford N: 1979 W, F; 1980 w, F; 1981 W

HANLEY, E. (1) Bradford N: 1984 **W**
HARRISON, M. (2) Leeds: 1978 F, W
HOBBS, D. (1) Featherstone R: 1984 **W**
HOGAN, B. (5) Wigan: 1975 **W, F, NZ, A**; 1977 W
HOGAN, P. (1) Hull KR: 1979 F
HOLDING, N. (1) St. Helens: 1980 W
HOLDSTOCK, R. (3) Hull KR: 1980 W, F; 1981 W
HOLMES, J. (5 + 2) Leeds: 1975 **W, F, NZ, A**; 1977 W, f; 1978 f
HUDDART, M. (1) Whitehaven: 1984 **W**
HUGHES, E. (8 + 1) Widnes: 1975 **W, F, NZ, a**; 1977 F; 1978 F, W; 1979 W, F

IRVING, R. (3) Wigan: 1975 **W, F, A**

JACKSON, P. (2) Bradford N: 1975 W, **F**
JONES, L. (1) St. Helens: 1977 W
JOYNER, J. (4) Castleford: 1980 W, F; 1981 F, W

KELLY, A. (1) Hull KR: 1984 **W**
KELLY, K. (3) Warrington: 1979 W; 1981 F, W
LAUGHTON, D. (1) Widnes: 1977 W
LEDGER, B. (+ 1) St. Helens: 1984 w
LIPTROT, G. (2) St. Helens: 1979 W, F
LOCKWOOD, B. (2) + 1 Hull KR: 1979 W, F
LOWE, P. (3)2 Hull KR: 1977 F; 1978 F; 1981 W

MARTYN, T. (4 + 1) Warrington: 1975 W, **F, w**; 1979 W, F
MILLINGTON, J. (2) Hull KR: 1975 F; 1981 W
MILLWARD, R. (13)3 + 1 Hull KR: 1975 F, W, **F, W, A, W, F, NZ, A**; 1977 W, F; 1978 F, W
MORGAN, M. (3 + 3) Wakefield T: 1975 f, W, f, **W, nz, A**
MUMBY, K. (2) Bradford N: 1979 W, F
MURPHY, M. (1) Oldham: 1975 F

NASH, S. (7) Featherstone R: 1975 **W, NZ, A**; Salford: 1978 F, W; 1981 W, **W**
NICHOLLS, G. (7 + 4) St. Helens: 1975 F, **F, W, NZ, A, w, nz, f**; 1977 f; 1978 F, W
NOONAN, D. (3) Warrington: 1975 W, **F, W**
NORTON, S. (11) Castleford: 1975 **W, NZ, A, W, F, NZ, A**; 1977 F; Hull: 1978 W; 1981 W, **W**

O'NEILL, S. (1) Wigan: 1981 F

PATTINSON, W. (1 + 1) Workington T: 1981 f, W
PHILBIN, B. (1) Warrington: 1975 **F**
PIMBLETT, G. (1) St. Helens: 1978 W
PINNER, H. (3) St. Helens: 1980 W, F; 1981 F
POTTER, I. (2) Warrington: 1981 F, W

RAYNE, Keith (2) Wakefield T: 1980 W, F
REDFEARN, A. (2) Bradford N: 1979 F; 1980 F
REDFEARN, D. (2) Bradford N: 1975 F, **A**
REILLY, M. (+ 1)2 Castleford: 1977 w
RICHARDSON, T. (1) Castleford: 1981 W
ROSE, P. (2) Hull KR: 1977 F; 1978 W

SCHOFIELD, G. (1) Hull: 1984 W
SHEARD, L. (1) Wakefield T: 1975 W
SMITH, D. (1) Leeds: 1977 F
SMITH, K. (1) Wakefield T: 1979 W
SMITH, M. (5) Hull KR: 1980 W, F; 1981 F, W, W
SMITH, P. (1) Featherstone R: 1980 F
STEPHENS, G. (1) Castleford: 1979 W
SZYMALA, E. (+1) Barrow: 1979 f

THOMPSON, J. (2+1)1 Featherstone R: 1975 A;
1977 W; Bradford N: 1978 w
TINDALL, K. (1) Hull: 1979 F
TOPLISS, D. (1) Wakefield T: 1975 F

WADDELL, H. (1) Blackpool B: 1984 W
WALKER, A. (1) Whitehaven: 1981 F
WALSH, J. (3) St. Helens: 1975 F, NZ, A
WARD, D. (6) Leeds: 1977 F; 1980 W, F;
1981 F, W, W
WATKINSON, D. (+1) Hull KR: 1977 w
WOODS, J. (3+4) Leigh: 1979 w, F; 1980 w, F;
1981 f, w, W
WRIGHT, S. (7) Wigan: 1975 NZ; Widnes: 1977 W;
1978 F, W; 1979 W, F; 1980 W

WALES TEAMS ● From 1975, when it revived after a gap of five years and continued until 1982 and on to 1984, folding again. Revived in 1991.

1975 France	1975 England	1975 France (WC)
Swansea: 16 Feb	Salford: 25 Feb	Toulouse: 2 Mar
Won 21-8	Lost 8-12	Lost 7-14
Francis (Wigan)	Francis (Wigan)	Francis (Wigan)
Mathias (St. Helens) 1t	Mathias (St. Helens)	Mathias (St. Helens)
Willicombe (Wigan)	Willicombe (Wigan)	Willicombe (Wigan)
Wilson, F (St. Helens)	Wilson, F (St. Helens)	Wilson, F (St. Helens) 1t
Bevan (Warrington) 2t	Bevan (Warrington)	Richards (Salford)
*Watkins (Salford) 1dg	*Watkins (Salford) 1t,1g,1dg	*Watkins (Salford)
Banner (Salford)	Banner (Salford)	Banner (Salford)
Mills (Widnes) 1t	Mills (Widnes)	Murphy (Bradford)
Fisher (Leeds)	Evans (Swinton)	Evans (Swinton)
Mantle (St. Helens)	Mantle (St. Helens)	Butler (Swinton)
Nicholas (Warrington)	Dixon (Salford)	Dixon (Salford)
Dixon (Salford)	Gallacher (Keighley)	Mantle (St. Helens)
Coslett (St. Helens) 4g	Coslett (St. Helens) 1g	Coslett (St. Helens) 2g
Sub: Gallacher (Keighley)	Sub: Turner (Hull KR)	Sub: Wallace (York)
	Nicholas (Warrington)	

1975 England (WC)	1975 Australia (WC)	1975 New Zealand (WC)
Brisbane: 10 June	Sydney: 14 June	Auckland: 28 June
Won 12-7	Lost 13-30	Lost 8-13
Francis (Wigan)	Francis (Wigan)	Francis (Wigan) 1t
Sullivan (Hull KR) 1t	Sullivan (Hull KR)	Sullivan (Hull KR)
*Watkins (Salford) 3g	*Watkins (Salford) 5g	*Watkins (Salford) 1g
Willicombe (Wigan)	Willicombe (Wigan)	Willicombe (Wigan)
Mathias (St. Helens)	Mathias (St. Helens)	Mathias (St. Helens)
Treasure (Oldham) 1t	Turner (Hull KR)	Treasure (Oldham)
Banner (Salford)	Treasure (Oldham)	Banner (Salford)
Mills (Widnes)	Mills (Widnes)	Mills (Widnes) 1t
Fisher (Leeds)	Fisher (Leeds) 1t	Fisher (Leeds)
Wanbon (Warrington)	Wanbon (Warrington)	Wanbon (Warrington)
Dixon (Salford)	Mantle (St. Helens)	Mantle (St. Helens)
Cunningham, E (St. Helens)	Cunningham, E (St. Helens)	Dixon (Salford)
Coslett (St. Helens)	Coslett (St. Helens)	Coslett (St. Helens)
Sub: Wilson, F (St. Helens)	Sub: Wilson (St. Helens)	Sub: Butler (Swinton)
Mantle (St. Helens)	Rowe (Blackpool)	

1975 England (WC)
Warrington: 20 Sept
Lost 16-22
Francis (Wigan)
Sullivan (Hull KR)
*Watkins (Salford) 5g
Wilson, F (St. Helens)
Bevan (Warrington)
Treasure (Oldham)
Banner (Salford) 1t
Mantle (St. Helens)
Fisher (Castleford)
James (St. Helens)
Cunningham, E (St. Helens)
Gregory (Wigan)
Coslett (St. Helens) 1t
Sub: Turner (Hull KR)
    Rowe (Blackpool)

1975 Australia (WC)
Swansea: 19 Oct
Lost 6-18
*Watkins (Salford) 3g
Mathias (St. Helens)
Francis (Wigan)
Wilson, F (St. Helens)
Bevan (Warrington)
Turner (Hull KR)
Banner (Featherstone)
Mills (Widnes)
Fisher (Castleford)
Mantle (St. Helens)
Cunningham, E (St. Helens)
Dixon (Salford)
Coslett (St. Helens)
Sub: Rowe (Blackpool)

1975 New Zealand (WC)
Swansea: 2 Nov
Won 25-24
*Watkins (Salford) 5g
Mathias (St. Helens)
Wilson, F (St. Helens)
Willicombe (Wigan) 1t
Bevan (Warrington) 1t
Francis (Wigan) 2t
Banner (Featherstone)
Mills (Widnes)
Fisher (Castleford)
Murphy (Bradford)
Mantle (St. Helens) 1t
Gallacher (Keighley)
Gregory (Wigan)
Sub: Jones (Leigh)

1975 France (WC)
Salford: 6 Nov
Won 23-2
*Watkins (Salford) 4g
Mathias (St. Helens)
Wilson, F (St. Helens)
Willicombe (Wigan) 1t
Bevan (Warrington) 1t
Francis (Wigan) 1t
Banner (Featherstone) 1t
Mantle (St. Helens)
Evans (Swinton)
Murphy (Bradford)
Gregory (Wigan) 1t
Gallacher (Keighley)
Jones (Leigh)
Sub: Turner (Hull KR)
    Butler (Warrington)

1977 England
Leeds: 29 Jan
Won 6-2
*Watkins (Salford)
Mathias (St. Helens)
Bevan (Warrington)
Cunningham, E (St. Helens) 1t
Richards (Salford)
Francis (Wigan)
Woods (Widnes) 1g
Mills (Workington)
Fisher (Castleford)
Mantle (Salford)
Nicholas (Warrington)
Dixon (Salford)
Rowe (Huddersfield) 1dg
Sub: Wilkins (Workington)

1977 France
Toulouse: 20 Feb
Lost 2-13
Wilkins (Workington)
Mathias (St. Helens)
Bevan (Warrington)
Treasure (Oldham)
Sullivan (Hull KR)
*Francis (Wigan)
Woods (Widnes) 1g
Mills (Widnes)
Fisher (Castleford)
Butler (Warrington)
Nicholas (Warrington)
Dixon (Salford)
Rowe (Huddersfield)
Sub: Curling (Warrington)
    Murphy (Bradford)

1978 France
Widnes: 15 Jan
Won 29-7
Risman (Workington)
Mathias (St. Helens) 1t
Willicombe (Wigan)
Cunningham, E (St. Helens) 1t
Sullivan (Hull KR) 1t
*Francis (St. Helens) 1t
Woods (Widnes) 7g
Mills (Widnes) 1t
Evans (Salford)
James (St. Helens)
Nicholas (Warrington)
Shaw (Widnes)
Dixon (Salford)
Sub: Pritchard (Barrow)
    Jones (Leigh)

1978 England
St. Helens: 28 May
Lost 13-60
Watkins (Salford) 1g
Mathias (St. Helens)
Turner (Hull)
Willicombe (Wigan) 1t
Sullivan (Hull KR) 1t
*Francis (St. Helens)
Woods (Widnes) 1g
Mills (Widnes)
Evans (Salford)
James (St. Helens) 1t
Davies, F (New Hunslet)
Mantle (Leigh)
Cunningham, E (St. Helens)
Sub: Pritchard (Barrow)
    Jones (Leigh)

1978 Australia
Swansea: 15 Oct
Lost 3-8
*Watkins (Salford) 1g,1dg
Sullivan (Hull KR)
Willicombe (Wigan)
Cunningham, E (St. Helens)
Bevan (Warrington)
Francis (St. Helens)
Woods (Widnes)
Mills (Widnes)
Fisher (Bradford)
James (St. Helens)
Shaw (Widnes)
Skerrett (Wakefield)
Mathias (St. Helens)

277

1979 France
Narbonne: 4 Feb
Lost 8-15

Box (Featherstone)
Sullivan (Hull KR)
*Watkins (Salford) 2g,1dg
Bevan (Warrington)
Juliff (Wakefield)
Francis (St. Helens)
Woods (Rochdale)
Murphy (St. Jacques)
Cunningham, T (Warrington)
James (St. Helens)
Skerrett (Wakefield)
Rowe (Huddersfield) 1t
Mathias (St. Helens)
Sub: Johns (Salford)
　　　Risman (Workington)

1979 England
Widnes: 16 Mar
Lost 7-15

Box (Featherstone) 1t,2g
Sullivan (Hull KR)
Risman (Workington)
Bevan (Warrington)
Juliff (Wakefield)
*Francis (St. Helens)
Woods (Rochdale)
Mills (Widnes)
Cunningham, T (Warrington)
James (St. Helens)
Skerrett (Wakefield)
Rowe (Huddersfield)
Mathias (St. Helens)
Sub: Prendiville (Hull)
　　　Nicholas (Warrington)

1980 France
Widnes: 26 Jan
Lost 7-21

Box (Featherstone)
Juliff (Wakefield)
Diamond (Wakefield) 2g
Bevan (Warrington) 1t
Camilleri (Barrow)
*Francis (Oldham)
Flowers (Wigan)
James (St. Helens)
Parry (Blackpool)
Shaw (Widnes)
McJennett (Barrow)
Skerrett (Wakefield)
Mathias (St. Helens)
Sub: Griffiths (St. Helens)
　　　Seldon (St. Helens)

1980 England
Hull KR: 29 Feb
Lost 9-26

Box (Featherstone)
Prendiville (Hull)
Walters (Hull)
*Francis (Oldham)
Juliff (Wakefield) 1t
Woods (Hull) 3g
Flowers (Wigan)
James (St. Helens)
Parry (Blackpool)
Shaw (Widnes)
Seldon (St. Helens)
Bevan (Warrington)
Mathias (St. Helens)
Sub: Diamond (Wakefield)

1981 France
Narbonne: 31 Jan
Lost 5-23

Box (Wakefield)
Cambriani (Fulham)
Diamond (Wakefield)
*Bevan (Warrington)
Prendiville (Hull)
Wilson, D (Swinton) 1g
Woods (Hull)
James (St. Helens)
Parry (Blackpool) 1t
Owen, G (Oldham)
Skerrett (Hull)
Juliff (Wakefield)
Mathias (St. Helens)
Sub: Griffiths (St. Helens)
　　　Owen, R (St. Helens)

1981 England
Hull KR: 18 Mar
Lost 4-17

Rule (Salford) 2g
Cambriani (Fulham)
Walters (Hull)
*Bevan (Warrington)
Juliff (Wakefield)
Wilson, D (Swinton)
Woods (Hull)
James (St. Helens)
Parry (Blackpool)
Owen, G (Oldham)
Skerrett (Hull)
Dixon (Hull KR)
Mathias (St. Helens)
Sub: Herdman (Fulham)

1981 England
Cardiff: 8 Nov
Lost 15-20

Pritchard (Cardiff)
Cambriani (Fulham)
Bayliss (St. Helens)
Fenwick (Cardiff) 4g
*Bevan (Warrington)
Wilson, D (Swinton) 1dg
Flowers (Wigan) 1t
James (St. Helens)
Parry (Blackpool)
David (Cardiff)
Shaw (Widnes)
Herdman (Fulham)
Ringer (Cardiff)
Sub: Prendiville (Hull) 1t
　　　Owen, R (St. Helens)

1982 Australia
Cardiff: 24 Oct
Lost 7-37

Hopkins (Workington) 1g
Camilleri (Widnes)
Fenwick (Cardiff) 1g
*Bevan (Warrington)
Prendiville (Hull)
Hallett (Cardiff)
Williams (Cardiff) 1t
Shaw (Wigan)
Parry (Blackpool)
David (Cardiff)
Herdman (Fulham)
Juliff (Wigan)
Ringer (Cardiff)
Sub: McJennett (Barrow)

1984 England
Ebbw Vale: 14 Oct
Lost 9-28

Hallett (Bridgend) 2g
Camilleri (Bridgend)
Prendiville (Hull)
Davies, M (Bridgend)
Ford (Warrington)
Wilson, D (Swinton) 1t,1dg
Flowers (Bridgend)
*Skerrett (Hull)
Preece (Bradford)
Shaw (Wigan)
McJennett (Barrow)
O'Brien (Bridgend)
Juliff (Bridgend)
Sub: Johns (Blackpool)
　　　Walters (Bridgend)

1991 Papua New Guinea
Swansea FC: 27 Oct
Won 68-0
Ford (Leeds) 3t
Devereux (Widnes)
Bateman (Warrington) 1t
*Davies (Widnes) 2t,8g
Sullivan (St. Helens) 2t
Griffiths (St. Helens) 1t
Ellis (Warrington) 1t
Jones (Hull)
Williams (Carlisle)
Young (Salford)
Ackerman (Carlisle) 1t
Moriarty (Widnes)
Bishop (Hull KR) 1t
Sub: Hadley (Salford) 1t
    Phillips (Warrington)
    Silva (Halifax)
    Pearce (Scarborough)

1992 France
Swansea FC: 22 Mar
Won 35-6
Ford (Leeds) 1t
Devereux (Widnes) 1t
Bateman (Warrington) 1t
*Davies (Widnes) 1t,5g,1dg
Sullivan (St. Helens)
Griffiths (St. Helens)
Ellis (Warrington)
Jones (Hull)
Williams (Carlisle) 1t
Young (Salford)
Ackerman (Carlisle)
Marlow (Hull)
Bishop (Hull KR)
Sub: Hadley (Salford)
    Phillips (Warrington) 1t
    Cordle (Bradford)
    Pearce (Ryedale-York)

Two-cap David Bishop.

WALES REGISTER
● Since 1975

Figures in brackets are the total appearances for Wales since 1975, with the plus sign indicating substitute appearances, e.g. (7+3).

A few players also played in the 1969-70 European Championship and this is shown as an additional total outside bracket, e.g. (11)2.

World Championship matches are in bold letters. Substitute appearances are in lower case letters. A - Australia, E - England, F - France, NZ - New Zealand, P - Papua New Guinea.

ACKERMAN, R (2) Carlisle: 1991 P; 1992 F

BANNER, P (9) Salford: 1975 F, E, **F, E, NZ;**
Featherstone R: 1975 **E, A, NZ, F**
BATEMAN, A (2) Warrington: 1991 P; 1992 F
BAYLISS, S (1) St. Helens: 1981 E
BEVAN, J (17) Warrington: 1975 F, E, **E, A, NZ, F;**
1977 E, F; 1978 A; 1979 F, E; 1980 F, E;
1981 F, E, E; 1982 A
BISHOP, D (2) Hull KR: 1991 P; 1992 F
BOX, H (5) Featherstone R: 1979 F, E; 1980 F, E;
Wakefield T: 1981 F
BUTLER, B (2+2) Swinton: 1975 **F, nz;** Warrington:
1975 f; 1977 F

CAMBRIANI, A (3) Fulham: 1981 F, E, E
CAMILLERI, C (3) Barrow: 1980 F; Widnes:
1982 A; Bridgend: 1984 E
CORDLE, G (+1) Bradford N: 1991 p
COSLETT, K (8)2 St. Helens: 1975 F, E, **F, E, A,
NZ, E, A**
CUNNINGHAM, E (8) St. Helens: 1975 **E, A, E, A;**
1977 E; 1978 F, E, A

CUNNINGHAM, T (2) Warrington: 1979 F, E
CURLING, D (+1) Warrington: 1977 f

DAVID, T (2) Cardiff C: 1981 E; 1982 A
DAVIES, F (1) New Hunslet: 1978 E
DAVIES, J (2) Widnes: 1991 P; 1992 F
DAVIES, M (1) Bridgend: 1984 E
DEVEREUX, J (2) Widnes: 1991 P; 1992 F
DIAMOND, S (2+1) Wakefield T: 1980 F, e; 1981 F
DIXON, C (10)3 Salford: 1975 F, E, **F, E, NZ, A;**
1977 E, F; 1978 F; Hull KR: 1981 E

ELLIS, K (2) Warrington: 1991 P; 1992 F
EVANS, R (5) Swinton: 1975 E, **F, F;** 1978 F;
Salford: 1978 E

FENWICK, S (2) Cardiff C: 1981 E; 1982 A
FISHER, T (10)4 Leeds: 1975 F, **E, A, NZ;**
Castleford: 1975 **E, A, NZ;** 1977 E, F;
Bradford N: 1978 A
FLOWERS, N (4) Wigan: 1980 F, E; 1981 E;
Bridgend: 1984 E

279

FORD, Phil (3) Warrington: 1984 E; Leeds: 1991 P; 1992 F
FRANCIS, W (19) Wigan: 1975 F, E, **F, E, A, NZ, E, A, NZ, F**; 1977 E, F; St. Helens: 1978 F, E, A; 1979 F, E; Oldham: 1980 F, E

GALLACHER, S (3+1) Keighley: 1975 f, E, **NZ, F**
GREGORY, B (3) Wigan: 1975 **E, NZ, F**
GRIFFITHS, C (+2) St. Helens: 1980 f; 1981 f
GRIFFITHS, J (2) St. Helens: 1991 P; 1992 F

HADLEY, A (+2) Salford: 1991 p; 1992 f
HALLETT, L (2) Cardiff C: 1982 A; Bridgend: 1984 E
HERDMAN, M (2+1) Fulham: 1981 e, E; 1982 A
HOPKINS, L (1) Workington T: 1982 A

JAMES, M (11) St. Helens: 1975 E; 1978 F, E, A; 1979 F, E; 1980 F, E; 1981 F, E, E
JOHNS, G (+2) Salford: 1979 f; Blackpool B: 1984 e
JONES, C (1+3) Leigh: 1975 **nz, F**; 1978 f, e
JONES, M (2) Hull: 1991 P; 1992 F
JULIFF, B (8) Wakefield T: 1979 F, E; 1980 F, E; 1981 F, E; Wigan: 1982 A; 1984 E

McJENNETT, M (2+1) Barrow: 1980 F; 1982 a; 1984 E
MANTLE, J (11+1)3 St. Helens: 1975 F, E, **F, e, A, NZ, E, A, NZ, F**; 1977 E; 1978 E
MARLOW, I (1) Hull: 1992 F
MATHIAS, R (20) St. Helens: 1975 F, E, **F, E, A, NZ, A, NZ, F**; 1977 E, F; 1978 F, E, A; 1979 F, E; 1980 F, E; 1981 F, E
MILLS, J (13)4 Widnes: 1975 F, E, **E, A, NZ, A, NZ**; 1977 E, F; 1978 F, E, A; 1979 E
MORIARTY, P (1) Widnes: 1991 P
MURPHY, M (4+1) Bradford N: 1975 **F, NZ, F**; 1977 f; St. Jacques, France: 1979 F

NICHOLAS, M (4+2) Warrington: 1975 F, e; 1977 E, F; 1978 F; 1979 e

O'BRIEN, C (1) Bridgend: 1984 E
OWEN, G (2) Oldham: 1981 E, F
OWEN, R (+2) St. Helens: 1981 f, e

PARRY, D (6) Blackpool B: 1980 F, E; 1981 F, E, E; 1982 A
PEARCE, G (+2) Scarborough P: 1991 p; Ryedale-York: 1992 f
PHILLIPS, R (+2) Warrington: 1991 p; 1992 f
PREECE, C (1) Bradford N: 1984 E
PRENDIVILLE, P (4+2) Hull: 1979 e; 1980 E; 1981 F, e; 1982 A; 1984 E
PRITCHARD, G (1+2) Barrow: 1978 f, e; Cardiff C: 1981 E

RICHARDS, M (2)1 Salford: 1975 **F**; 1977 E
RINGER, P (2) Cardiff C: 1981 E; 1982 A
RISMAN, J (2+1) Workington T: 1978 F; 1979 f, E
ROWE, P (4+3)2 Blackpool B: 1975 **a, e, a**; Huddersfield: 1977 E, F; 1979 F, E
RULE, S (1) Salford: 1981 E

SELDON, C (1+1) St. Helens: 1980 f, E
SHAW, G (7) Widnes: 1978 F, A; 1980 F, E; 1981 E; Wigan: 1982 A; 1984 E
SILVA, M (+1) Halifax: 1991 p
SKERRETT, T (7) Wakefield T: 1978 A; 1979 F, E; 1980 F; Hull: 1981 F, E; 1984 E
SULLIVAN, A (2) St. Helens: 1991 P; 1992 F
SULLIVAN, C (10)4 Hull KR: 1975 **E, A, NZ, E**; 1977 F; 1978 F, E, A; 1979 F, E

TREASURE, D (5) Oldham: 1975 **E, A, NZ, E**; 1977 F
TURNER, G (3+3) Hull KR: 1975 e, **A, e, A, f**; Hull: 1978 E

WALLACE, R (+1) York: 1975 **f**
WALTERS, G (2+1) Hull: 1980 E; 1981 E; Bridgend 1984 e
WANBON, R (3)3+1 Warrington: 1975 **E, A, NZ**
WATKINS, D (14) Salford: 1975 F, E, **F, E, A, NZ, E, A, NZ, F**; 1977 E; 1978 E, A; 1979 F
WILKINS, R (1+1) Workington T: 1977 e, F
WILLIAMS, Barry (2) Carlisle: 1991 P; 1992 F
WILLIAMS, Brynmor (1) Cardiff C: 1982 A
WILLICOMBE, D (11)+2 Wigan: 1975 F, E, **F, E, A, NZ, NZ, F**; 1978 F, E, A
WILSON, D (4) Swinton: 1981 F, E, E; 1984 E
WILSON, F (7+2)4 St. Helens: 1975 F, E, **F, e, a, E, A, NZ, F**
WOODS, P (10) Widnes: 1977 E, F; 1978 F, E, A; Rochdale H: 1979 F, E; Hull: 1980 E; 1981 F, E

YOUNG, D (2) Salford: 1991 P; 1992 F

Kumul second row man Max Tiri distributes the ball in the 1991 British Coal international against Wales in Swansea.

1991 KUMULS

1991 KUMULS

TOUR REVIEW

Papua New Guinea's second professional tour of Britain started — and virtually finished — in South Wales. The rebirth of the Wales side heralded the premature death of the five-match tour as the Welshmen inflicted a 68-0 hammering on a Papuan squad still reeling from two crushing Test defeats on home soil by Australia earlier in the month.

A euphoric crowd of nearly 11,500 at Swansea City FC's Vetch Field witnessed the emotional return of Wales in a record-breaking spree, the Welsh registering their highest-ever score, with skipper Jonathan Davies creating goals and points records.

The post-match celebrations of a Wales revival, amid demands for fixtures against France and England, doubled as a wake for the British Coal tour. Mindful of the inaugural tour of 1987, featuring victories over Featherstone Rovers and Fulham and a draw with Lancashire, plus the shock 20-18 Test victory over Great Britain in the summer of 1990, the League had devised a tour of solely representative fixtures.

The 13-try drubbing was shown live on nationwide satellite television. Attendances for the remaining four tour matches, including a World Cup-rated British Coal Test, did not total the Swansea gate.

Great Britain Under-21s, keen to impress national coach Malcolm Reilly in a tour season, ran in 10 tries at Leeds only three days after the South Wales debacle.

Having experienced the wintry conditions of two evening matches, the Papuans warmed to the early afternoon fixture at the Boulevard, Hull, registering their first points of the tour and coming within minutes of a shock victory over a strong Humberside XIII, a touchdown by Hull K.R. winger Bright Sodje securing a fortunate 16-14 home victory.

Fewer than 1,600 fans turned out at Workington for the Bonfire Night meeting with Cumbria, debutant Alan Tait pressing home a claim for a Great Britain Test recall with a two-try Man of the Match display.

For the third time in the five-match programme, the score passed the half-century mark when Great Britain earned two World Cup points in the British Coal Test at Wigan. The 56-4 victory was also a triumph for Wakefield Trinity second row man Michael Jackson, who scored two tries to take the British Coal Man of the Match award on his Test debut.

The crowd of 4,193 was the lowest Test attendance for 20 years.

Lacking stalwarts such as Bal Numapo and Arnold Krewanty in the backs, and Michael Matmillo and Arebo Taumaku in the pack, the Kumuls proved to be too light-weight for the demanding, albeit short, tour. The five matches produced a tally of only 30 points, with 232 conceded.

Ever-present utility back Philip Boge scored most goals and points on the three-week tour with five and 10 respectively.

The Papuans made little impact, only centre Richard Wagambie capturing the public's imagination, Huddersfield being the leaders of a pack of clubs considering an approach. Tour skipper Stanley Haru did not possess the leadership qualities of his predecessor, Numapo — called up as a replacement on the French leg of the tour — although his deputy, front row forward Kes Paglipari, was one of the better performers.

The 1991 Kumuls secured their only victory of a nine-match European tour with a 26-20 success over a weak Provence Selection at Carpentras. France won the World Cup-rated Test encounter 28-14 at Carcassonne. Boge continued his record of playing in every match, stand off Tuksy Karu becoming top scorer with a final tally of nine goals and 18 points, while Wagambie topped the tryscoring chart with four touchdowns, three registered in France.

BRITISH TOUR RESULTS

Date	Result	Score	Opposition	Venue	Attendance
Oct 27	L	0-68	Wales	Swansea F.C.	11,422
30	L	0-58	Great Britain U-21s	Leeds	2,027
Nov 3	L	14-16	Humberside XIII	Hull	2,800
5	L	12-34	Cumbria	Workington	1,588
9	L	4-56	GREAT BRITAIN*	Wigan	4,193

*World Cup-rated

BRITISH TOUR SUMMARY

						FOR				AGAINST		
P	W	D	L	T	G	Dr	Pts	T	G	Dr	Pts
5	0	0	5	4	7	0	30	42	32	0	232

BRITISH TEST SUMMARY

						FOR				AGAINST		
P	W	D	L	T	G	Dr	Pts	T	G	Dr	Pts
1	0	0	1	0	2	0	4	10	8	0	56

BRITISH TOUR RECORDS

Biggest attendance: 11,422 v. Wales

Highest score: 14 v. Humberside XIII 16

Highest score against: Lost to Wales 68-0

Most tries in a match: No player scored more than one

Most goals in a match:
3 by Philip Boge v. Humberside XIII

Most points in match: 6 by Philip Boge
v. Humberside XIII

Most tries on tour: 2 by Chris Itam

Most goals on tour: 5 by Philip Boge

Most points on tour: 10 by Philip Boge

Most appearances: 5 by Philip Boge,
Leslee Hoffman (3+2), Chris Itam (3+2),
Ngala Lapan (2+3)

Sin bin: Danny Moi v. Great Britain U-21s;
James Naipao v. Great Britain

Opponents' sin bin: Colin Armstrong (Cumbria)

Centre Richard Wagambie, scorer of four tries in Europe.

FRENCH TOUR RESULTS

Date	Result	Score	Opposition	Venue
Nov 13	L	4-35	**Midi-Pyrénées Selection**	Toulouse

T: Gispe

17	L	16-32	**President's XIII**	Villeneuve

T: Wagambie, Daki, Kola
G: Karu (2)

20	W	26-20	**Provence Selection**	Carpentras

T: Wagambie (2), Boge, Kouoru, Naipao
G: Karu (3)

24	L	14-28	**FRANCE (World Cup-rated)**	Carcassonne

France: Balleroy; Garcia (1t), Despin, Bienes, Pons (1t); Dumas (Capt) (1t, 4g), Entat; Viloni, Lope, Ailleres, Montgaillard, Divet (1t), Bonnafous (1t). Subs: Fages, Alesina, Storer, Baba (all played)

Papua New Guinea: Wanega; Itam (1t), Wagambie, Boge, Kouoru; Karu (2g), Haru (Capt) (1t, 1g); Naipao, Matmillo, Ngaffin, Tiri, Paglipari, Gispe. Subs: Palangat, Lapan, Angra, Hoffman (all played)
Referee: Colin Morris (England)
Attendance: 1,440

FRENCH TOUR SUMMARY

				FOR				AGAINST			
P	W	D	L	T	G	Dr	Pts	T	G	Dr	Pts
4	1	0	3	11	8	0	60	20	17	1	115

Thomas Daki, Kumul tryscorer in Villeneuve.

James Naipao, scorer of a Kumul try in Carpentras.

TOUR PARTY

Managers: Tau Peruka, Rod Pearce and Joe Keviame
Coach: Skerry Palanga
Doctor: Gideon Kendino
Physiotherapist: Michael Wilson
Trainer: Lester Manuai

Player	IN BRITAIN App	Sub	T	G	Pts	IN FRANCE App	Sub	T	G	Pts	IN TOTAL App	Sub	T	G	Pts
ANGRA, Michael	1	1	–	5	10	4	4	1	–	4	5	5	1	5	14
BOGE, Philip	5	–	–	–	–	1	–	1	–	4	6	–	1	–	4
DAKI, Thomas	2	2	–	–	–	1	–	1	–	4	3	2	1	–	4
GISPE, Joe	3	–	–	–	–	3	1	1	–	4	6	1	1	–	4
HARU, Stanley	4	–	–	–	–	2	2	1	1	6	6	2	1	1	6
HOFFMAN, Leslee	3	2	2	–	8	1	1	1	–	4	4	3	3	–	12
ITAM, Chris	3	2	–	–	–	3	1	–	–	–	6	3	–	–	–
KARARA, Sam	2	–	–	–	–	3	–	–	–	–	5	2	–	–	–
KARU, Tuksy	2	2	–	2	4	3	–	–	7	14	5	2	–	9	18
KOLA, Johannes	1	1	–	–	–	1	1	1	–	4	2	2	1	–	4
KOUORU, Joshua	4	–	–	–	–	3	2	1	–	4	7	2	1	–	4
LAPAN, Ngala	2	3	–	–	–	1	2	–	–	–	3	5	–	–	–
*MOI, Danny	3	1	–	–	–	3	1	1	–	4	6	1	1	–	4
NAIPAO, James	3	1	–	–	–	4	–	–	–	–	7	1	–	–	–
NGAFFIN, Kera	4	–	–	–	–	3	1	–	–	–	7	1	–	–	–
PAGLIPARI, Kes	2	1	–	–	–	3	–	–	–	–	5	2	–	–	–
PALANGAT, Lipirin	2	1	–	–	–	–	–	–	–	–	2	1	–	–	–
*SINEMAU, Korul	2	2	–	–	–	–	–	–	–	–	2	3	–	–	–
TIRI, Max	2	1	–	–	–	3	1	–	–	–	3	2	–	–	–
UNAGI, John	3	1	–	–	–	–	–	–	–	–	3	–	–	–	–
*URADOK, Jack	3	1	1	–	4	4	–	3	–	12	7	1	4	–	16
WAGAMBIE, Richard	3	1	–	–	–	1	–	–	–	–	4	1	–	–	–
WANEGA, Ipisa	3	–	–	–	–	1	–	–	–	–	4	–	–	–	–
YAWING, John	2	–	1	–	4	1	1	–	–	–	3	1	1	–	4

*Returned home after British leg: Michael Matmillo (4 app.) and Bal Numapo (1 app.) joined the tour in France, being non-scorers.

Ngala Lapan.

Chris Itam.

Leslee Hoffman.

MATCH BY MATCH

WALES INTERNATIONAL

Born-again Wales, returning to the international scene after a seven-year absence, roared into the record books with a 68-0 humiliation of a woefully inadequate Papua New Guinea at Vetch Field, Swansea.

Thirteen-try Wales registered the highest-ever score in their 83-year history. By leading 46-0 at the interval, the re-formed Welshmen had already topped the previous best tally of 41-7 against France at Llanelli in 1935.

Inevitably, inspirational skipper Jonathan Davies rewrote a chapter in the record book, amassing 24 points from two tries and eight goals, easily surpassing the seven goals and 14 points of Johnny Thomas in 1908 and Paul Woods in 1978.

But the bare statistics cannot capture the passion generated by the return of Wales to the Valleys. Nearly 11,500 Welsh patriots trooped into Swansea City FC's compact ground to welcome back a host of former Rugby Union heroes, the national pride evident in a stirring rendition of the anthem.

While the free-flowing Welshmen generated euphoria, the Papuans set alarm bells ringing. The Kumuls never got to grips with the home side's powerful forwards and were bemused by the backs, particularly the mercurial Davies and full back Phil Ford. After showing glimpses of their renowned support play in the opening minutes, the Papuans rarely made an impression, with covering and tackling both well below international standard.

It took only two minutes for Wales to open their account. Davies kicked a penalty goal and by the 28th minute he had equalled the Welsh points-scoring record with a further four goals and a touchdown. But the Widnes captain also took the spotlight with his leadership of the Welsh XIII, all desperate to impress their fellow-countrymen.

And impress they did. Leeds utility back Ford took the British Coal Man of the Match award, completing his hat-trick of tries in the 66th minute before being substituted seven minutes from the end.

A springboard for the wave of attacks was the half-back combination of Warrington scrum half Kevin Ellis and St. Helens stand off Jonathan Griffiths, until the latter retired after 52 minutes with a serious knee injury. St. Helens winger Anthony Sullivan grabbed two spectacular tries to emerge from the shadow of his late father Clive, the holder of 14 Welsh caps.

Props David Young and Mark Jones, classed as students of the professional game, passed the test of international football by combining strength with skill. Second row man Paul Moriarty returned to his home town to further his claims for a Great Britain call-up after a brave fight to recover from the rebuilding of a knee cap.

Carlisle duo Barry Williams, a revelation in the hooking role, and second row man Rob Ackerman comfortably made the transition from the Second Division to the international arena, while loose forward David Bishop overcame a lack of match fitness to catch the eye with a forceful performance highlighted by a 56th-minute touchdown.

Other tries in the Welsh landslide came from Ackerman, Griffiths, Ellis, Allan Bateman and Adrian Hadley, who came on as a substitute along with Rowland Phillips, Matthew Silva and Gary Pearce.

When the Kumuls, who suffered in the wintry evening weather, did try to throw the ball about, they found the home cover up to international standard, boosting the post-match Welsh demands for future international fixtures against France and England in the spring and autumn, respectively, of 1992.

BRITISH COAL INTERNATIONAL

27 October   Vetch Field, Swansea

WALES 68   **PAPUA NEW GUINEA 0**

Phil Ford (Leeds)	1.	Philip Boge
John Devereux (Widnes)	2.	Joshua Kouoru
Allan Bateman (Warrington)	3.	Korul Sinemau
Jonathan Davies (Widnes), Capt.	4.	Richard Wagambie
Anthony Sullivan (St. Helens)	5.	Jack Uradok
Jonathan Griffiths (St. Helens)	6.	Tuksy Karu
Kevin Ellis (Warrington)	7.	Stanley Haru, Capt.
David Young (Salford)	8.	John Unagi
Barry Williams (Carlisle)	9.	Kes Paglipari
Mark Jones (Hull)	10.	James Naipao
Rob Ackerman (Carlisle)	11.	Thomas Daki
Paul Moriarty (Widnes)	12.	Max Tiri
David Bishop (Hull K.R.)	13.	Joe Gispe
Adrian Hadley (Salford)	14.	Ngala Lapan
Rowland Phillips (Warrington)	15.	Chris Itam
Matthew Silva (Halifax)	16.	Michael Angra
Gary Pearce (Scarborough P.)	17.	Leslee Hoffman

T: Ford (3), Davies (2), Sullivan (2),
Ackerman, Griffiths, Bateman, Hadley,
Bishop, Ellis
G: Davies (8)
Substitutions:
Phillips for Moriarty (Half-time)
Hadley for Griffiths (52 min.)
Pearce for Williams (66 min.)
Silva for Ford (73 min.)

Substitutions:
Itam for Kouoru (Half-time)
Lapan for Haru (49 min.)
Hoffman for Gispe (66 min.)
Angra for Wagambie (73 min.)
Half-time: 46-0
Referee: Bill Harrigan (Australia)
Attendance: 11,422

Kumul Test stand off Tuksy Karu.

Kumul skipper Stanley Haru.

30 October
Leeds

GREAT BRITAIN U-21s	58
PAPUA NEW GUINEA	0

1. Wanega
2. Palangat (Wagambie)
3. Uradok
4. Boge
5. Itam
6. Lapan
7. Karara (Karu)
8. Ngaffin
9. Moi
10. Yawing (Naipao)
11. Kola (Unagi)
12. Paglipari, Capt.
13. Hoffman

Great Britain Under-21s:
Mycoe (Sheffield E.); Myers (Wigan), Connolly (St. Helens), P. Newlove (Featherstone R.), Hallas (Hull K.R.); Pearson (Featherstone R.), Goulding (Leeds), Capt.; Sumner (Warrington), Dixon (Hull), Parr (Huddersfield), D. Busby (Hull), McNamara (Hull), McCurrie (Widnes). Substitutes: Martyn (Oldham) for Newlove, Pinkney (Ryedale-York) for Hallas, Precious (Hunslet) for Parr, Joynt (Oldham) for McNamara

T: Myers (3), McCurrie (2), Newlove (2), Connolly, Goulding, Pearson
G: Pearson (8), Goulding

Half-time: 30-0

Referee: Bill Harrigan (Australia)
Attendance: 2,027

Great Britain Under-21s carried on where Wales had left off by hammering a sub-standard Papuan second string in a 10-try rout. Well led by scrum half Goulding, the young Lions combined effectively with current top try-scorer Myers grabbing a hat-trick.

Featherstone Rovers centre Paul Newlove marked his return to the international scene with two touchdowns, a feat repeated by British Coal Man of the Match McCurrie, the Widnes loose forward.

Stand off Pearson marked his Under-21 debut with a 20-point haul from a try and a record eight goals, while other impressive performances came from centre Connolly and second row man McNamara.

3 November
Boulevard, Hull

HUMBERSIDE XIII	16
PAPUA NEW GUINEA	14

1. Wanega
2. Kouoru
3. Wagambie
4. Boge
5. Itam
6. Haru, Capt.
7. Lapan (Karu)
8. Unagi
9. Moi (Hoffman)
10. Ngaffin (Sinemau)
11. Naipao
12. Angra (Tiri)
13. Gispe

T: Wagambie, Itam
G: Boge (3)

Humberside XIII:
M. Fletcher (HKR); Eastwood (Hull), Blacker (Hull), McCarthy (HKR), Sodje (HKR); Portlock (Hull), Bishop (HKR); Dannatt (Hull), L. Jackson (Hull), Vannett (HKR), P. Fletcher (HKR), Sharp (Hull), D. Busby (Hull). Substitutes: Ronson (Hull) for Portlock, Lyman (HKR) for Jackson, Jones (Hull) for Vannett, Chatfield (HKR) for Bishop

T: Jackson, P. Fletcher, Sodje
G: M. Fletcher, Eastwood

Half-time: 12-4

Referee: John Holdsworth (Kippax)
Attendance: 2,800

Papua came within seconds of snatching their first victory, which was stolen from them by a fluke try by Hull K.R. winger Sodje. Kumul loose forward Gispe could only watch in horror as his attempted interception rebounded from his hands straight to Sodje, who touched down.

It was a heartbreaking end to a match in which the visitors put behind them the nightmares of the Welsh and Under-21 hammerings. A defence which had conceded 126 points in two games looked much more organised and the attack, which had failed to produce a point in 160 minutes, showed flair and pace.

Stand off Haru and prop Ngaffin, voted Man of the Match, were the inspiration, while centre Wagambie displayed pace and class, his 60-yard solo try putting the Papuans back in the game with 10 minutes to go. Itam's try in the corner four minutes later seemed to have clinched a well-deserved victory, but it was not to be.

5 November
Workington
CUMBRIA   34
PAPUA NEW GUINEA   12

1. Boge
2. Uradok
3. Sinemau (Itam)
4. Kouoru
5. Palangat (Lapan)
6. Haru, Capt.
7. Karara
8. Yawing
9. Moi (Kola)
10. Daki (Angra)
11. Paglipari
12. Tiri
13. Hoffman

T: Yawing, Itam
G: Boge (2)

Cumbria:
Tait (Widnes); Rudd (Warrington), Kay (Barrow),
Birkett (Salford), Quirk (St. Helens); Wear
(Workington T.), Cameron (Whitehaven); D. Kendall
(Barrow), Roskell (Workington T.), C. Armstrong
(Workington T.), Chambers (Warrington), Walker
(Hull), Capt., Maguire (Whitehaven). Substitutes:
Beckwith (Whitehaven) for Kay, Gribbin
(Whitehaven) for Quirk, Oglanby (Workington T.) for
Kendall, Riley (Workington T.) for Roskell

T: Tait (2), Maguire, Rudd, Birkett, Armstrong
G: Wear (5)

Half-time: 18-6

Referee: Colin Morris (Huddersfield)
Attendance: 1,588

Ignored by the Great Britain selectors, full back Tait
proved a point by scoring two tries in a Man of the Match
performance on his debut for Cumbria. The Widnes 1990
British Lion inspired the Cumbrians to a six-try victory,
Workington Town stand off Wear adding five goals.

The Papuans scored the first and last tries, prop Yawing
racing 40 yards in only the fifth minute and substitute Itam
diving over in the corner in the last minute.

The Kumuls' attempts at free-flowing football were
marred by spilled possession, while their concentration in
defence was again subject to long lapses.

*Papuan full back Philip Boge, most appearances, goals
and points in Britain.*

TEST MATCH

It was a situation where Great Britain just could not win. Malcolm Reilly's charges registered a 52-point winning margin and picked up two valuable World Cup points, but provided only light entertainment for the lowest home Test crowd for 20 years.

Papua New Guinea had already been hammered 68-0 by Wales and 58-0 by Great Britain Under-21s, to be classed as a shadow of the side which had toured four years earlier and still been beaten 42-0 in the Test arena.

Skippered for the first time by Garry Schofield, in the absence of the injured Ellery Hanley, Britain's problem was how to put the Kumuls out of their misery without causing too much suffering. They managed it by not being completely ruthless and limiting the variety of their play.

The result was a low-key afternoon in the afterglow of the much-hyped Rugby Union World Cup. A 56-4 British Coal Test victory for the Lions also produced two points and a scoring margin boost in the bid to qualify to meet Australia in the 1992 World Cup final.

Ironically, the Wigan encounter was hailed as the Kumuls' best performance of their five-match tour of Britain in which they had not won a game and conceded 232 points. Even their defence was judged to have improved as they restricted Britain to just 10 touchdowns, the first being probably the fastest in Test history — 47 seconds. Four forward drives from as many play-the-balls took them to the halfway line to open up play for centre Jonathan Davies to sidestep through and give Schofield an easy run-in for his 26th Test try.

There were encouraging displays from the home side's three Test debutants. Wakefield Trinity back row forward Michael Jackson and Widnes second row man Paul Moriarty each collected two touchdowns, Anthony Sullivan slipping easily through for another. Jackson's rapid rise from Second Division football with Hunslet gathered momentum as the Trinity packman took the British Coal Man of the Match award with a splendid all-round performance. He scored the best solo touchdown, ripping past two defenders on a 40-yard curving run to the posts, plus heading Britain's official tackle count with prop Karl Harrison. Unfortunately, an ankle wound became infected and kept Jackson out of action for several weeks.

Featherstone Rovers centre Paul Newlove made a return to Test football on the right wing after a two-year absence. The Great Britain Under-21 threequarter marked the occasion with a 57th-minute try.

Schofield, playing in his 32nd Test, was as enthusiastic as any of the newcomers and marked his Test captaincy debut with a quietly commanding display. The Leeds stand off ignored the temptation to go for personal records after his quick try and made a major contribution to five other touchdowns.

As Britain's chances of breaking world scoring records diminished, they increased their resolve not to let the tourists cross their line and desperate tackling kept them out when centre Richard Wagambie inspired a late rally.

Twelve of Britain's second-half points came while James Naipao was in the sin bin for a foul, but this was generally a well-disciplined display by the Papuans, with penalties only 11-4 against them. Hooker Kes Paglipari won the scrums 9-4 for the Kumuls and was the only tourist to outshine his opposite number.

Britain's 56-point tally was their highest in six Tests against Papua, while Davies continued to rewrite the record books, his eight goals and 16 points being British records against them.

BRITISH COAL TEST (World Cup-rated)

9 November   **Wigan**

GREAT BRITAIN 56		PAPUA NEW GUINEA 4
Steve Hampson (Wigan)	1.	Ipisa Wanega
Paul Newlove (Featherstone R.)	2.	Joshua Kouoru
Daryl Powell (Sheffield E.)	3.	Richard Wagambie
Jonathan Davies (Widnes)	4.	Philip Boge
Anthony Sullivan (St. Helens)	5.	Chris Itam
Garry Schofield (Leeds), Capt.	6.	Tuksy Karu
Shaun Edwards (Wigan)	7.	Stanley Haru, Capt.
Karl Harrison (Halifax)	8.	John Unagi
Martin Dermott (Wigan)	9.	Kes Paglipari
Andy Platt (Wigan)	10.	Kera Ngaffin
Denis Betts (Wigan)	11.	James Naipao
Paul Moriarty (Widnes)	12.	Leslee Hoffman
Michael Jackson (Wakefield T.)	13.	Joe Gispe
Deryck Fox (Featherstone R.)	14.	Ngala Lapan
Karl Fairbank (Bradford N.)	15.	Lipirin Palangat
Gary Connolly (St. Helens)	16.	Max Tiri
Gary Price (Wakefield T.)	17.	Thomas Daki

T: Jackson (2), Moriarty (2),
Schofield, Powell, Sullivan, Betts,
Newlove, Fairbank
G: Davies (8)
Substitutions:
Connolly for Hampson (52 min.)
Fairbank for Platt (64 min.)
Fox for Edwards (70 min.)
Price for Moriarty (74 min.)

G: Karu (2)
Substitutions:
Tiri for Naipao (64 min.)
Lapan for Karu (69 min.)
Daki for Ngaffin (69 min.)
Palangat for Wanega (74 min.)
Half-time: 20-4
Referee: Bill Harrigan (Australia)
Attendance: 4,193

Scorechart

Minute	Score	GB	PNG	Minute	Score	GB	PNG
1:	Schofield (T)			57:	Newlove (T)		
	Davies (G)	6	0		Davies (G)	36	4
12:	Moriarty (T)	10	0	63:	Jackson (T)		
17:	Karu (PG)	10	2		Davies (G)	42	4
28:	Moriarty (T)	14	2	66:	Betts (T)		
32:	Powell (T)				Davies (G)		
	Davies (G)	20	2		Davies (PG)★	50	4
39:	Karu (PG)	20	4	78:	Fairbank (T)		
42:	Jackson (T)				Davies (G)	56	4
	Davies (G)	26	4		Scrums	4	9
49:	Sullivan (T)	30	4		Penalties	11	4

★Penalty awarded after try

The 1991 Kumuls, left to right: Back Row: Wanega, Wagambie, Kola, Hoffman, Moi, Uradok, Kouoru, Yauving, Sineman, Lapan, Gispe. Middle Row: Wilson (Physiotherapist), Palangat, Karu, Ngaffin, Boge, Naipao, Daki, Angra, Unagi, Manuai (Trainer), Keviame (Finance Manager). Front Row: Paruka (Tour Manager), Tiri, Itam, Haru (Captain), Palanga (Coach), Paglipari, Karara, Kendino (Doctor), Pearce (Team Manager).

Greg Alexander, captain of 1991 Australian Grand Final victors Penrith Panthers.

DOWN UNDER

WINFIELD CUP
1991 Sydney Premiership Grand Final

Penrith won Australia's major trophy for the first time in their 25-year history with a 19-12 defeat of Canberra at the Sydney Football Stadium to gain revenge for an 18-14 defeat in the previous year's final. They had finished at the top of the Winfield Cup table, while Canberra reached the final from fourth place.

The victory was a fitting finale for Royce Simmons, Penrith's Test hooker, who had already announced he would retire after the match, although he played against Wigan in the Foster's World Club Challenge the following month.

Simmons scored two of Penrith's three tries, breaking tackles to go in for the first after only six minutes and clinching victory two minutes from the end with another.

Despite Simmons's outstanding contribution, the Clive Churchill Medal for the Man of the Match went, rather controversially, to Canberra loose forward Bradley Clyde.

Winger Matthew Wood scored both of the losers' tries and added a goal, while Mal Meninga was an outstanding captain for Canberra, who seemed to be heading for victory when they led 12-6 at half-time.

But it was Penrith's captain, Greg Alexander, who took control in the second half and landed a vital drop goal at a crucial stage. Brad Izzard added impetus to the Panthers' attack when he went on as a 30th-minute substitute and crashed over for a second-half try.

The attendance of 41,815 produced a ground record for the fourth successive season since the Grand Final was taken to the new Sydney Football Stadium, which continues to expand its capacity gradually.

Neither side included British players, although both fielded a number who had played for varying spells with English clubs.

WINFIELD CUP GRAND FINAL

22 September 1991 — Sydney Football Stadium

PENRITH 19		CANBERRA 12
Greg Barwick	1.	Gary Belcher
Graham Mackay	2.	Paul Martin
Brad Fittler	3.	Mal Meninga, Capt.
Col Bentley	4.	Mark Bell
Paul Smith	5.	Matthew Wood
Steve Carter	6.	Laurie Daley
Greg Alexander, Capt.	7.	Ricky Stuart
Paul Clarke	8.	Brent Todd
Royce Simmons	9.	Steve Walters
Paul Dunn	10.	Glenn Lazarus
Mark Geyer	11.	David Barnhill
Barry Walker	12.	Gary Coyne
Colin Van Der Voort	13.	Bradley Clyde

T: Simmons (2), Izzard
G: Alexander (3, 1dg)
Substitutions:
Brad Izzard for Bentley
John Cartwright for Walker
Coach: Phil Gould
Half-time: 6-12
Referee: Bill Harrigan
Scrums: 7-7
Penalties: 5-7

T: Wood (2)
G: Meninga, Wood
Substitutions:
Darren Fritz for Clyde
Michael Twigg for Barnhill
Scott Gale for Stuart
Coach: Tim Sheens
Clive Churchill Medal for Man of the Match: Bradley Clyde (Canberra)
Attendance: 41,815

1991 WINFIELD CUP

	P.	W.	D.	L.	F.	A.	Pts
Penrith	22	17	1	4	483	250	35
Manly-Warringah	22	14	1	7	391	299	29
North Sydney	22	14	1	7	345	303	29
Canberra	22	14	0	8	452	327	28
Canterbury-Bankstown	22	13	1	8	424	374	27
Western Suburbs	22	13	1	8	359	311	27
Brisbane Broncos	22	13	0	9	470	326	26
Illawarra	22	12	1	9	451	291	25
St. George	22	11	3	8	388	320	25
Cronulla-Sutherland	22	8	3	11	384	441	19
Eastern Suburbs	22	9	1	12	337	487	19
Balmain	22	8	1	13	351	412	17
Newcastle	22	6	3	13	308	424	15
South Sydney	22	7	0	15	370	513	14
Parramatta	22	6	0	16	351	534	12
Gold Coast	22	2	1	19	240	492	5

WINFIELD CUP PLAY-OFF
Fifth place play-off
Western Suburbs 19 v. Canterbury 14
Minor preliminary semi-final
Canberra 22 v. Western Suburbs 8
Major preliminary semi-final
North Sydney 28 v. Manly 16
Minor semi-final
Canberra 34 v. Manly 26
Major semi-final
Penrith 16 v. North Sydney 14
Preliminary final
Canberra 30 v. North Sydney 14
Grand Final
Penrith 19 v. Canberra 12

● All matches played at the
Sydney Football Stadium except for
the fifth place play-off at the
Parramatta Stadium.

LEADING SCORERS
● Not including play-offs

Tries
19 Alan McIndoe (Illawarra)
Goals (inc. drop goals)
78 Jason Taylor (Western Suburbs)
Points
172 Daryl Halligan (North Sydney)

*Penrith hooker Royce Simmons, who bade
farewell to the Sydney Premiership with a
two-try Grand Final performance.*

BRITISH PLAYERS IN GRAND FINALS

British players who have appeared in the Sydney Grand Final are:

Dick Huddart (St. George) 1966 winners, 1 try
Dave Bolton (Balmain) 1966 losers; 1969 winners, 2 drop goals
Mervyn Hicks (Canterbury) 1967 losers
Ken Batty (St. George) 1971 losers
Malcolm Reilly (Manly) 1972 winners, 1973 winners
Tommy Bishop (Cronulla) 1973 losers
Bob Wear (Cronulla) 1973 losers
Cliff Watson (Cronulla) 1973 losers
Brian Lockwood (Canterbury) 1974 losers
Gary Stephens (Manly) 1976 winners
Steve Norton (Manly) 1976 winners
Phil Lowe (Manly) 1976 winners, 1 try
Kevin Ward (Manly) 1987 winners
Ellery Hanley (Balmain) 1988 losers
Andy Currier (Balmain) 1989 losers, 3 goals
Shaun Edwards (Balmain) 1989 losers, sub

Apart from Hicks and Currier, all the above also appeared in a Challenge Cup final at Wembley. In addition Len Killeen, the South African winger who began his league career with St. Helens, also played at Wembley and got a Grand Final winners' medal with Balmain in 1969 when he kicked two goals.

Australians who have achieved the big double since the Grand Final became mandatory in 1954 are: Chris Anderson, Harry Bath, Graham Eadie, John Ferguson, Kerry Hemsley, Brett Kenny, John Muggleton, Peter Sterling, Michael O'Connor and Paul Vautin.

There were a record four British players in the 1973 Grand Final. Reilly got a winners' medal with Manly, while Bishop, Watson and Wear were in the beaten Cronulla side.

Three British players — Stephens, Norton and Lowe — were also in the Manly side which won the final in 1976.

Ellery Hanley was the first player to appear in both major finals in the same year. In 1988 he led Wigan to success at Wembley and four months later was in Balmain's beaten Grand Final team.

Shaun Edwards is the only other player to play in both finals in the same year. He was stand off when Wigan beat St. Helens at Wembley in 1989 and made a late substitute appearance for Balmain when they were beaten by Canberra at Sydney.

Sheffield Eagles skipper Daryl Powell, who made 13 appearances for Gold Coast in 1991.

BRITISH PLAYERS IN 1991 WINFIELD CUP SYDNEY PREMIERSHIP

A total of five players appeared in the Winfield Cup competition during 1991. They included four Test players — Paul Dixon (Leeds) and Daryl Powell (Sheffield Eagles), who joined Gold Coast; Martin Offiah (Widnes) to St George and Jonathan Davies (Widnes) to Canterbury-Bankstown.

All did well, with the Widnes pair outstanding. Despite his late start and early departure to the season, Offiah challenged strongly for the tryscoring leadership and finished eighth with 11 tries in 14 matches.

Davies was 10th in the Winfield Cup points chart, with 94, and reached a century after adding six points in a play-off match.

Great Britain scrum half Bobby Goulding joined Eastern Suburbs, but failed to make First Grade and suddenly returned to Wigan. Easts claimed he had broken his contract and left outstanding debts. The matter was cleared up and Goulding was transferred to Leeds before the start of the new season.

British players' records in the 1991 Winfield Cup, including play-off matches:

	App	T	G	Pts
Jonathan Davies (Widnes-Canterbury Bankstown)...........	14	7	36	100
Paul Dixon (Leeds-Gold Coast).................................	10	1	—	4
David Myers (Wigan-Manly Warringah).......................	2 + 2	1	—	4
Martin Offiah (Widnes-St. George)...........................	14	11	—	44
Daryl Powell (Sheffield Eagles-Gold Coast)..................	12 + 1	1	—	4

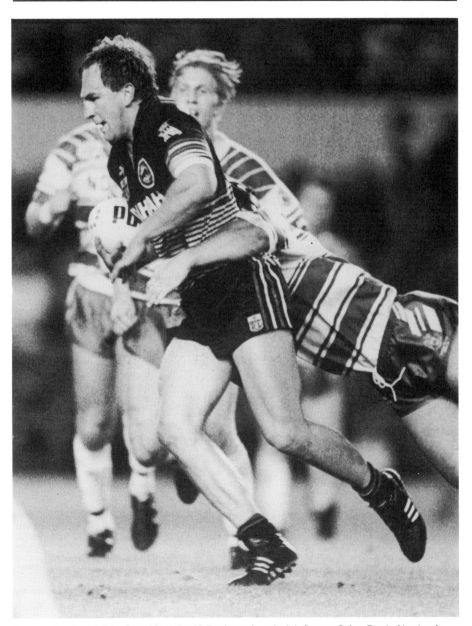

Kangaroo Test forward John Cartwright, a Penrith Panthers stalwart in their first-ever Sydney Premiership triumph.

STATE OF ORIGIN

The State of Origin matches between New South Wales and Queensland began in 1980 and are now established as a major part of the Australian Rugby League scene.

Their introduction revived interest in the inter-state matches which had been dominated by New South Wales, who had won the last 15 matches by mainly wide margins.

Under the old system players appeared for the state in which they were playing club rugby at the time and this gave a big advantage to New South Wales because many of Queensland's best players were with Sydney clubs.

But in State of Origin matches players appear for the state in which they first played senior rugby and this has resulted in the matches becoming more fiercely and evenly fought before increased attendances.

NEW SOUTH WALES v. QUEENSLAND RESULTS

State of Origin only.

Date	Winner	Score	Venue	Attendance
8 July 1980	Queensland	20-10	Brisbane	31,000
28 July 1981	Queensland	22-15	Brisbane	25,613
1 June 1982	New South Wales	20-16	Brisbane	27,326
8 June 1982	Queensland	11-7	Brisbane	19,435
22 June 1982	Queensland	10-5	Sydney	20,242
7 June 1983	Queensland	24-12	Brisbane	29,412
21 June 1983	New South Wales	10-6	Sydney	21,620
28 June 1983	Queensland	43-22	Brisbane	26,084
29 May 1984	Queensland	29-12	Brisbane	33,662
19 June 1984	Queensland	14-2	Sydney	29,088
17 July 1984	New South Wales	22-12	Brisbane	16,599
28 May 1985	New South Wales	18-2	Brisbane	33,011
11 June 1985	New South Wales	21-14	Sydney	39,068
23 July 1985	Queensland	20-6	Brisbane	18,825
27 May 1986	New South Wales	22-16	Brisbane	33,000
10 June 1986	New South Wales	24-20	Sydney	40,707
1 July 1986	New South Wales	18-16	Brisbane	21,097
2 June 1987	New South Wales	20-16	Brisbane	33,411
16 June 1987	Queensland	12-6	Sydney	42,048
15 July 1987	Queensland	10-8	Brisbane	33,000
*6 Aug. 1987	New South Wales	30-18	California	12,349
17 May 1988	Queensland	26-18	Sydney	26,441
31 May 1988	Queensland	16-6	Brisbane	31,817
21 June 1988	Queensland	38-22	Sydney	16,910
23 May 1989	Queensland	36-6	Brisbane	33,000
14 June 1989	Queensland	16-12	Sydney	40,000
28 June 1989	Queensland	36-16	Brisbane	33,000
9 May 1990	New South Wales	8-0	Sydney	41,235
30 May 1990	New South Wales	12-6	Melbourne	25,800
13 June 1990	Queensland	14-10	Brisbane	31,000
8 May 1991	Queensland	6-4	Brisbane	31,500
29 May 1991	New South Wales	14-12	Sydney	41,520
12 June 1991	Queensland	14-12	Brisbane	32,500

*Not part of 1987 series.

SUMMARY
New South Wales won 13; Queensland won 20. Since it became a three-match series in 1982, Queensland have won seven series to New South Wales' three.

ENGLISH REFEREES English referees who have taken charge of State of Origin matches are: Billy Thompson on 8 July 1980 and Robin Whitfield on 28 June 1983.

1991 STATE OF ORIGIN MATCHES *Denotes captain

8 May	29 May	12 June
Brisbane	**Sydney**	**Brisbane**
New South Wales 4	**New South Wales 14**	**New South Wales 12**
Alexander (Penrith)	Ettingshausen (Cronulla)	Alexander (Penrith)
Johns (Brisbane B.)	Johns (Brisbane B.) 1t	Johns (Brisbane B.) 1t
Ettingshausen (Cronulla)	Daley (Canberra)	McGaw (Cronulla)
Daley (Canberra) 1t	O'Connor (Manly) 3g	O'Connor (Manly) 1t
O'Connor (Manly)	Wishart (Illawarra)	Wishart (Illawarra)
C. Lyons (Manly)	C. Lyons (Manly)	Fittler (Penrith)
Stuart (Canberra)	Stuart (Canberra)	Stuart (Canberra)
Roach (Balmain)	Roach (Balmain)	Roach (Balmain)
*Elias (Balmain)	*Elias (Balmain)	*Elias (Balmain)
Roberts (Manly)	Gillespie (Wests)	Gillespie (Wests)
Geyer (Penrith)	Roberts (Manly)	Cartwright (Penrith)
Sironen (Balmain)	Geyer (Penrith)	Clyde (Canberra)
Hasler (Manly)	Clyde (Canberra)	Mackay (St. George)
Subs: Lazarus (Canberra)	Subs: Hasler (Manly)	Subs: Hasler (Manly) 1t
Gillespie (Wests)	McGaw (Cronulla) 1t	Izzard (Penrith)
McGaw (Cronulla)	Mackay (St. George)	Salvatori (Easts)
Fittler (Penrith)	Cartwright (Penrith)	Fairleigh (Norths)

Queensland 6	**Queensland 12**	**Queensland 14**
Hauff (Brisbane B.)	Hauff (Brisbane B.)	Hauff (Brisbane B.) 1t
Hancock (Brisbane B.)	Hancock (Brisbane B.)	Hancock (Brisbane B.) 1t
P. Jackson (Norths)	P. Jackson (Norths)	P. Jackson (Norths)
Meninga (Canberra) 1t, 1g	Meninga (Canberra) 2g	Meninga (Canberra) 1g
Carne (Brisbane B.)	Carne (Brisbane B.) 1t	Carne (Brisbane B.)
*Lewis (Gold Coast)	*Lewis (Gold Coast)	*Lewis (Gold Coast)
Langer (Brisbane B.)	Langer (Brisbane B.)	Langer (Brisbane B.)
Bella (Manly)	Bella (Manly)	Bella (Manly)
S. Walters (Canberra)	S. Walters (Canberra)	S. Walters (Canberra)
S. Jackson (Wests)	S. Jackson (Wests)	S. Jackson (Wests)
Gee (Brisbane B.)	Gee (Brisbane B.)	Gee (Brisbane B.)
McLean (Newcastle)	McLean (Newcastle)	McLean (Newcastle)
Larson (Norths)	Larson (Norths)	Larson (Norths)
Subs: Kevin Walters (Brisbane B.)	Subs: Kevin Walters (Brisbane B.)	Subs: Shearer (Brisbane B.) 1t
Renouf (Brisbane B.)	Shearer (Brisbane B.) 1t	G. Coyne (Canberra)
G. Coyne (Canberra)	G. Coyne (Canberra)	Lindner (Wests)
Allen (Brisbane B.)	Allen (Brisbane B.)	
Referee: Bill Harrigan	Referee: David Manson	Referee: Bill Harrigan
Man of the Match: Lewis	Man of the Match: S. Walters	Man of the Match: Bella

NEW SOUTH WALES v. QUEENSLAND RECORDS
State of Origin only

NEW SOUTH WALES

Highest score:	30-18 at California, 6 August 1987
Widest margin:	18-2 at Brisbane, 28 May 1985
Most full appearances:	19 by Michael O'Connor (St. George, Manly)
Most tries in a match:	3 by Chris Anderson (Canterbury), 28 June 1983
Most goals in a match:	No player has kicked more than five
Most points in a match:	18 (2t,5g) Michael O'Connor (Manly), 28 May 1985
Biggest home attendance:	42,048, 16 June 1987

QUEENSLAND

Highest score:	43-22 at Brisbane, 28 June 1983
Widest margin:	36-6 at Brisbane, 23 May 1989
Most full appearances:	31 by Wally Lewis (Fortitude Valley, Wynnum Manly, Brisbane Broncos, Gold Coast)
Most tries in a match:	3 by Kerry Boustead (Manly), 29 May 1984
Most goals in a match:	7 by Mal Meninga (Souths, B), 8 July 1980
Most points in a match:	16 (2t,4g) by Mal Meninga (Canberra), 23 May 1989 and Dale Shearer (Manly),, 28 June 1989
Biggest home attendance:	33,662, 29 May 1984

Coaches:

New South Wales:	Ted Glossop (1980, 1981, 1983); Frank Stanton (1982, 1984); Terry Fearnley (1985); Ron Willey (1986, 1987); John Peard (1988); Jack Gibson (1989, 1990); Tim Sheens (1991)
Queensland:	John McDonald (1980); Arthur Beetson (1981, 1982, 1983, 1984, 1989, 1990); Des Morris (1985); Wayne Bennett (1986, 1987, 1988); Graham Lowe (1991)

QUEENSLAND REGISTER

The following is a register of players who have appeared for Queensland in the State of Origin series plus the match against New South Wales in the United States of America, up to and including 1991. + indicates number of matches played as a substitute. B-Brisbane, S-Sydney.

ALLEN, Gavin (+2) Brisbane Broncos
ASTILL, Bruce (+1) Souths, B

BACKER, Brad (3) Easts, B
BACKO, Sam (7) Canberra 3; Brisbane Broncos 4
BEETSON, Arthur (1) Parramatta
BELCHER, Gary (15) Canberra
BELLA, Martin (14) Norths, S 8; Manly 6
BOUSTEAD, Kerry (6) Easts, S 3; Manly 3
BRENNAN, Mitch (4) Souths, S 3; Redcliffe 1
BROHMAN, Darryl (2) Penrith
BROWN, Dave (9+1) Manly 5+1; Easts, S 4
BUTLER, Terry (1) Wynnum Manly

CARNE, Willy (4) Brisbane Broncos
CARR, Norm (2) Wests, B
CLOSE, Chris (9) Manly 7; Redcliffe 2
CONESCU, Greg (20) Norths, B 4; Redcliffe 10; Gladstone Brothers 3; Brisbane Broncos 3
COYNE, Gary (2+7) Canberra
COYNE, Mark (+2) St. George
CURRIE, Tony (8+3) Wests, B +1; Redcliffe +1; Canterbury 5+1; Brisbane Broncos 3

DOWLING, Greg (11) Wynnum Manly 7; Norths, B 4
DOWLING, John (3) St. George

FRENCH, Brett (1+3) Wynnum Manly; Norths, S +3
FRENCH, Ian (3+6) Wynnum Manly 2+3; Norths, S 1+3
FULLERTON-SMITH, Wally (12) Redcliffe 8; St. George 4

GEE, Andrew (3+1) Brisbane Broncos
GILLMEISTER, Trevor (5+5) Easts, S

HAGAN, Michael (2+3) Newcastle
HANCOCK, Michael (6) Brisbane Broncos
HANCOCK, Rohan (5) Easts, B 1; Toowoomba Wattles 4
HAUFF, Paul (3) Brisbane Broncos

HENRICK, Ross (2) Norths, B 1; Fortitude Valley 1
HEUGH, Cavill (2+1) Easts, B

JACKSON, Peter (11+2) Canberra 7; Souths, B +1; Brisbane Broncos 1+1; Norths, S 3
JACKSON, Steve (3+1) Wests, S
JONES, Gavin (3) Norths, S

KELLAWAY, Bob (+1) Souths, B
KHAN, Paul (4) Easts, B 3; Cronulla 1
KILROY, Joe (2) Brisbane Broncos
KISS, Les (4) Norths, S

LANG, John (1) Easts, S
LANGER, Allan (15) Ipswich 4, Brisbane Broncos 11
LARSON, Gary (3) Norths, S
LEWIS, Wally (31) Wynnum Manly 13; Fortitude Valley 8; Brisbane Broncos 7; Gold Coast 3
LINDNER, Bob (17+1) Souths, B 1; Wynnum Manly 5; Parramatta 6; Gold Coast 2; Wests, S 3+1

McCABE, Paul (5) Easts, S 1; Manly 4
McINDOE, Alan (9) Illawarra 3; Penrith 6
McLEAN, Mike (3) Newcastle
MENINGA, Mal (23) Souths, B 13; Canberra 10
MILES, Gene (19) Wynnum Manly 14; Brisbane Broncos 5
MORRIS, Rod (4) Balmain 2; Wynnum Manly 2
MURRAY, Mark (14) Fortitude Valley 3, Redcliffe 11

NIEBLING, Bryan (9) Fortitude Valley 3; Redcliffe 6

OLIPHANT, Greg (1) Balmain

PHELAN, Chris (2) Souths, B 1; Parramatta 1

QUINN, Graham (1) St. George

REDDY, Rod (1) St. George
RENOUF, Steve (+1) Brisbane Broncos
RIBOT, John (8) Manly 5; Redcliffe 3

SCOTT, Colin (16+1) Wynnum Manly 15+1; Easts, B 1
SHEARER, Dale (14+4) Manly 11+2; Brisbane Broncos 3+2
SMITH, Allan (1) Norths, S
SMITH, Gary (+1) Brothers
STACEY, Steve (2) Easts, B
STAINS, Danny (4) Cronulla

TESSMAN, Brad (4+1) Souths, B 3; Easts, S 1+1
TRONC, Scott (+1) Wests, S

VAUTIN, Paul (20+1) Manly 19+1; Easts, S 1
WALKER, Bruce (1) Manly
WALTERS, Kerrod (5) Brisbane Broncos
WALTERS, Kevin (+5) Canberra +1; Brisbane Broncos +4
WALTERS, Steve (4) Canberra

NEW SOUTH WALES REGISTER

The following is a register of players who have appeared for New South Wales in the State of Origin series plus the match against Queensland in the United States of America, up to and including 1991. + indicates number of matches played as a substitute. B-Brisbane, S-Sydney.

ALEXANDER, Greg (4+2) Penrith
ANDERSON, Chris (4) Canterbury
AYLIFFE, Royce (1+2) Easts, S

BLAKE, Phil (+1) Souths, S
BOWDEN, Steve (1) Newtown
BOYD, Les (3) Manly
BOYLE, David (2+2) Souths, S
BRENTNALL, Greg (4) Canterbury
BROOKS, David (1) Balmain
BROWN, Ray (1+2) Manly
BUGDEN, Geoff (2) Parramatta

CARTWRIGHT, John (2+3) Penrith
CLEAL, Noel (11+1) Manly
CLYDE, Bradley (7) Canberra
CONLON, Ross (3) Canterbury
COOPER, Bob (1) Wests, S
COVENEY, John (2) Canterbury
CRONIN, Mick (6) Parramatta

DALEY, Laurie (5) Canberra
DALEY, Phil (3) Manly
DAVIDSON, Les (5) Souths, S
DOCKING, Jonathan (2) Cronulla
DUKE, Phillip (1) Moree
DUNN, Paul (2+1) Canterbury

EADIE, Graham (1) Manly
EDGE, Steve (1) Parramatta
ELIAS, Ben (11) Balmain
ELLA, Steve (3+4) Parramatta
ETTINGSHAUSEN, Andrew (12+1) Cronulla

FAHEY, Terry (2) Easts, S
FAIRLEIGH, David (+1) Norths, S
FARRAR, Andrew (5+2) Canterbury
FENECH, Mario (2) Souths, S
FERGUSON, John (8) Easts, S 3; Canberra 5
FIELD, Paul (2) Cootamundra
FITTLER, Brad (1+2) Penrith
FLORIMO, Greg (+1) Norths, S
FOLKES, Steve (8+1) Canterbury

GERARD, Geoff (2) Manly
GEYER, Mark (3) Penrith
GILLESPIE, David (5+4) Canterbury 3+3, Wests 2+1
GROTHE, Eric (9) Parramatta
GURR, Marty (2) Easts, S

HAMBLY, Gary (1) Souths, S
HANSON, Steve (1) Norths, S
HASLER, Des (6+6) Manly
HASTINGS, Kevin (+1) Easts, S
HETHERINGTON, Brian (1+1) Illawarra
HILDITCH, Ron (1) Parramatta
HUNT, Neil (2) Parramatta

IZZARD, Brad (2+2) Penrith

JACK, Garry (17) Balmain
JARVIS, Pat (6+2) St. George 4+2, Canterbury 2
JENSEN, Barry (1) Newtown
JOHNS, Chris (6) Brisbane Broncos
JOHNSTON, Brian (8) St. George
JOHNSTON, Lindsey (2) Norths, S
JURD, Stan (1+1) Parramatta

KELLY, Peter (2) Penrith
KENNY, Brett (16+1) Parramatta
KRILICH, Max (5) Manly

LAMB, Terry (4+3) Canterbury 3+3, Wests, S 1
LANGMACK, Paul (3+1) Canterbury
LAZARUS, Glenn (1+4) Canberra
LEIS, Jim (1) Wests, S
LYONS, Cliff (6) Manly
LYONS, Graham (2+1) Souths, S

McGAW, Mark (10+3) Cronulla
McGUIRE, Bruce (5) Balmain
MACKAY, Brad (4+1) St. George
McKINNON, Don (1) Norths, S
MATTERSON, Terry, (+1) Brisbane Broncos
MELROSE, Tony (1) Souths, S
MERLO, Paul (1) Wests, S
MILLER, Gavin (5) Cronulla
MORRIS, Steve (2) St. George
MORTIMER, Chris (8+1) Canterbury 7, Penrith 1+1
MORTIMER, Steve (8) Canterbury
MUGGLETON, John (2) Parramatta

NISZCOTT, Ziggy (2) Souths, S

O'CONNOR, Michael (19) St. George 6, Manly 13

PEARCE, Wayne (15) Balmain
POTTER, Michael (+1) Canterbury
PRICE, Ray (8) Parramatta

RAMPLING, Tony (2 + 1) Souths, S
RAUDONIKIS, Tom (1) Newtown
ROACH, Steve (17) Balmain
ROBERTS, Ian (5) Manly
ROGERS, Steve (4) Cronulla

SALVATORI, Craig (+ 1) Easts, S
SARGENT, Mark (+ 1) Newcastle
SIGSWORTH, Phil (3) Newtown 2, Manly 1
SIMMONS, Royce (10) Penrith
SIRONEN, Paul (2 + 3) Balmain
STERLING, Peter (13) Parramatta
STONE, Robert (+ 1) St. George
STUART, Ricky (6) Canberra

THOMPSON, Alan (5 + 1) Manly
TOOVEY, Geoff (+ 1) Manly
TREWHELLA, David (1 + 1) Easts, S
TUNKS, Peter (7 + 1), Souths 1, Canterbury 6 + 1

WALFORD, Ricky (1) St. George
WALSH, Chris (1) St. George
WILSON, Alan (+ 2) Cronulla
WISHART, Rod (5) Illawarra
WRIGHT, Rex (1) N. Newcastle
WYNN, Graeme (1) St. George
WYNN, Peter (4) Parramatta

YOUNG, Craig (4 + 1) St. George

AUSTRALIA TOUR OF PAPUA NEW GUINEA 1991

Date	Result	Score	Opposition	Venue	Attendance
29 Sept.	W	40-6	**Northern Zone** T: Clyde (2), Belcher, Meninga, Toovey, Kevin Walters, Lyons, Gourley G: Meninga (4)	Lae	10,290
2 Oct.	W	42-25	**Islands Zone** T: Fittler (2), Jackson (2), Carne, Johns, Lyons, Gourley G: Belcher (5)	Rabaul	9,000
6 Oct.	W	58-2	**PAPUA NEW GUINEA** **Papua New Guinea:** Wanega (1g); Palangat, Itam, Wagambie, Sinemau; Haru (Capt), Karara; Ben-Moide, Moi, Unagi, Daki, Tiri, Gispe. Subs: Kouoru, Lapan, Naipao, Paglipari (all played) **Australia:** Belcher (5g); Wishart (3t), Meninga (Capt), Ettingshausen (2t), Carne (3t); Lyons (1t), Toovey; Lazarus, Kerrod Walters, Bella, Roberts (1t), Clyde, Fittler (2t). Subs: Gourley, Johns, Coyne, Kevin Walters (all played) Referee: Dennis Hale (New Zealand)	Goroka	13,000
9 Oct.	W	28-3	**Highlands Zone** T: Belcher, Carne, Johns, Gourley, Lazarus G: Wishart (4)	Mt Hagen	9,000
13 Oct.	W	40-6	**PAPUA NEW GUINEA** **(World Cup-rated)** **Papua New Guinea:** Boge (1g); Palangat, Kouoru, Sinemau, Wagambie; Haru (Capt) (1t), Karara; Unagi, Moi, Naipao, Daki, Paglipari, Gispe. Subs: Uradok, Lapan, Ngaffin, Hoffman (all played) **Australia:** Belcher (1t); Wishart (1t), Meninga (Capt) (1t, 2g), Ettingshausen (1t), Carne (3t); Jackson (1t), Toovey; Lazarus, Kerrod Walters, Bella, Roberts, Clyde (1t), Fittler. Subs: Lyons, Johns, Coyne, Kevin Walters (all played) Referee: Dennis Hale (New Zealand)	Port Moresby	14,500

TOUR SUMMARY

P	W	L	F	A
5	5	0	208	42

TOUR REGISTER

Captain: Mal Meninga
Coach: Bobby Fulton
Manager: Kevin Brasch

N = New South Wales, Q = Queensland

Player	Club	State	App	Sub	T	G	Pts
BELCHER, Gary	Canberra	Q	5	—	3	10	32
BELLA, Martin	Manly	Q	3	2	—	—	—
CARNE, Willie	Brisbane Broncos	Q	5	—	8	—	32
CLYDE, Bradley	Canberra	N	4	—	3	—	12
COYNE, Gary	Canberra	Q	2	2	—	—	—
ETTINGSHAUSEN, Andrew	Cronulla	N	3	1	3	—	12
FITTLER, Brad	Penrith	N	3	2	4	—	16
GEE, Andrew	Brisbane Broncos	Q	1	—	—	—	—
GOURLEY, Scott	St. George	N	2	2	3	—	12
JACKSON, Peter	North Sydney	Q	3	1	3	—	12
JOHNS, Chris	Brisbane Broncos	N	2	3	2	—	8
LAZARUS, Glenn	Canberra	N	5	—	1	—	4
LYONS, Cliff	Manly	N	3	2	3	—	12
*McGAW, Mark	Cronulla	N	1	—	—	—	—
*McGUIRE, Bruce	Canterbury	N	1	—	—	—	—
MENINGA, Mal	Canberra	Q	3	—	2	6	20
*ROACH, Steve	Balmain	N	1	—	—	—	—
ROBERTS, Ian	Manly	N	3	1	1	—	4
SALVATORI, Craig	Eastern Suburbs	N	1	—	—	—	—
TOOVEY, Geoff	Manly	N	4	1	1	—	4
*WALTERS, Kerrod	Brisbane Broncos	Q	3	1	—	—	—
WALTERS, Kevin	Brisbane Broncos	Q	3	2	1	—	4
WALTERS, Steve	Canberra	Q	Injured before tour began				
WISHART, Rod	Illawarra	N	4	—	4	4	24
TOTALS					**42**	**20**	**208**

*Replacements due to injuries: Roach for Salvatori, Kerrod Walters for Steve Walters, McGaw for Ettingshausen, McGuire for Gee.

Chris Johns.

Glenn Lazarus.

Kevin Walters.

AUSTRALIA v NEW ZEALAND TEST SERIES in 1991

Date		Venue	Attendance
3 July	**AUSTRALIA 8 NEW ZEALAND 24**	Melbourne	26,900

Australia: Hauff; Ettingshausen, Meninga (Capt) (2g), Johns, Shearer; Lewis, Langer; Roach, S. Walters (1t), Bella, Roberts, Lindner, Clyde. Subs: Gillespie, Cartwright (both played). Hasler, P. Jackson (not used)

New Zealand: Botica (4g); Blackmore (1t), McCracken (1t), Watson, Williams; Kemp, Freeman (Capt); Todd, D. Mann, Brown, Koloto, Lonergan, Nikau (1t). Subs: Friend (1t), G. Mann, Mercer, Patton (all played)
Referee: John Holdsworth (England)

24 July	**AUSTRALIA 44 NEW ZEALAND 0**	Sydney	34,911

Australia: Ettingshausen; Carne (1t), Meninga (Capt) (6g), Daley (2t), Wishart (1t); P. Jackson, Langer; Salvatori, S. Walters, Bella, Gillespie (1t), Geyer (1t), Clyde (1t). Subs: Hasler (1t), Johns, Roberts, Cartwright (all played)

New Zealand: Botica; Blackmore, McCracken, K. Iro, Williams; Watson, Freeman (Capt); Todd, D. Mann, Brown, Koloto, Lonergan, Nikau. Subs: Friend, G. Mann, Mercer, Patton (all played)
Referee: John Holdsworth (England)

31 July	**NEW ZEALAND 12 AUSTRALIA 40** (World Cup-rated)	Auckland	29,139

New Zealand: Botica (2g); Blackmore (1t), McCracken (1t), K. Iro, Watson; Freeman (Capt), Friend; Todd, D. Mann, Brown, G. Mann, Mercer, Nikau. Subs: Patton, Williams, Koloto, Faimalo (all played)

Australia: Ettingshausen (1t); Carne (1t), Meninga (Capt) (1t, 6g), Daley (1t), Wishart (1t); P. Jackson, Langer; Salvatori, S. Walters (1t), Bella, Gillespie, Geyer, Clyde (1t). Subs: Johns, Roberts, Hasler, Cartwright (all played)
Referee: John Holdsworth (England)

FRANCE TOUR OF NEW ZEALAND AND PAPUA NEW GUINEA 1991
NEW ZEALAND

Date	Result	Score	Opposition	Venue	Attendance
9 June	L	8-28	**Kiwi Colts** T: Dumas G: Dumas 2	Rotorua	
13 June	L	6-60	**NEW ZEALAND** New Zealand:	Auckland	7,000

Botica (8g); Panapa (1t), McCracken (2t), Watson, Blackmore (2t); K. Shelford (1t), Freeman (Capt) (1t); Todd (1t), D. Mann (1t), Brown, Koloto, Lonergan (1t), Nikau (1t). Subs: Patton, Friend, G. Mann, Mercer (all played)

France:
Auroy; Despin, Chamorin, Bienes, Pons; Dumas (Capt)
(1t, 1g), Entat; Storer, Valero, Buttignol, Cabestany, Verdes,
Plante. Subs: Romano, Tisseyre, Campana (all played). Fages
(not used)
Referee: Graham Ainui (Papua New Guinea)

16 June	L	2-54	**President's XIII** G: Dumas	Palmerston North	
19 June	W	14-6	**West Coast** T: Garcia 2, Pons G: Tisseyre	Greymouth	
23 June	L	10-32	**NEW ZEALAND** **(World Cup-rated)**	Christchurch	2,000

New Zealand:
Botica (6g); Panapa (1t), McCracken, Watson (1t), Blackmore
(1t); K. Shelford (1t), Freeman (Capt); Todd, D. Mann,
Brown, Koloto, Lonergan, Nikau. Subs: Friend (1t), Patton,
G. Mann, Mercer (all played)
France:
Fages; Garcia, Despin, Bienes, Pons; Dumas (Capt) (3g),
Entat; Storer, Valero, Buttignol, Boyals, Cabestany, Verdes
(1t). Subs: Bernabe, Palisses, Romano, Viscay (all played)
Referee: Graham Ainui (Papua New Guinea)

NZ SUMMARY

P	W	L	F	A
5	1	4	40	180

PAPUA NEW GUINEA

Date	Result	Score	Opposition	Venue	Attendance
27 June	L	22-24	**Southern Zone** T: Verdes (2), Palisses, Garcia G: Tisseyre (2), Fages	Port Moresby	4,556
30 June	L	24-28	**Islands Zone** T: Garcia (2), Pons, Sirvent, Chamorin G: Torreilles (2)	Rabaul	5,272
3 July	W	16-15	**Northern Zone** T: Valero, Garcia, Plante G: Fages, Dumas	Madang	3,664
7 July	W	20-18	**PAPUA NEW GUINEA**	Goroka	11,485

Papua New Guinea:
Wanega (5g); Krewanty, Gela (1t), Kamiak, Rena; Haru
(Capt), Ongugo; Naipao (1t), Bate, Unagi, Daki, Tiri, Gispe.
Subs: J. Kouoru, Kola, Soga, Paglipari (all played)
France:
Auroy; Garcia (1t), Despin (1t), Bienes (1t), Pons; Fages,
Entat; Boyals, Torreilles (4g), Buttignol (Capt), Plante,
Cabestany, Verdes. Subs: Chamorin, Delpech (both played).
Tisseyre, Viscay (not used)
Referee: Colin Morris (England)

PNG SUMMARY

P	W	L	F	A
4	2	2	82	85

TOUR SUMMARY

P	W	L	F	A
9	3	6	122	265

TOUR REGISTER

Captain: Gilles Dumas
Coach: Carlos Zalduendo
Manager: Louis Bonnery

Player	Club	App	Sub	T	G	Pts
AUROY, Christophe	XIII Catalan	5	—	—	—	—
BERNABE, Thierry	Carcassonne	3	1	—	—	—
BIENES, Denis	St. Gaudens	6	2	1	—	4
BOYALS, Gerard	St. Gaudens	5	1	—	—	—
BUTTIGNOL, Thierry	Avignon	5	1	—	—	—
CABESTANY, Didier	St. Esteve	6	1	—	—	—
CAMPANA, Patrice	Villeneuve	1	1	—	—	—
CHAMORIN, Pierre	St. Esteve	4	1	1	—	4
DELPECH, Guy	Pamiers	4	1	—	—	—
DESPIN, David	Villeneuve	6	1	1	—	4
DUMAS, Gilles	St. Gaudens	5	—	2	8	24
ENTAT, Patrick	Hull	6	1	—	—	—
FAGES, Pascal	Pia	7	1	—	2	4
GARCIA, Jean-Marc	St. Esteve	7	1	7	—	28
PALISSES, Roger	St. Esteve	4	2	1	—	4
PLANTE, Bertrand	Villeneuve	5	—	1	—	4
PONS, Cyrille	St. Gaudens	7	—	2	—	8
ROMANO, Franck	Carpentras	2	4	—	—	—
SAUMITOU, Jean-Bernard	Villeneuve	1	—	—	—	—
SIRVENT, Claude	St. Gaudens	2	1	1	—	4
STORER, Yves	St. Gaudens	5	1	—	—	—
TISSEYRE, Marc	Pamiers	3	1	—	3	6
TORREILLES, Patrick	Pia	4	—	—	6	12
VALERO, Thierry	Lezignan	5	1	1	—	4
VERDES, Daniel	Villeneuve	6	2	3	—	12
VISCAY, Robert	St. Gaudens	3	3	—	—	—
TOTALS				**21**	**19**	**122**

Prop Lee Crooks on Great Britain duty in Perpignan in February 1992, recalled to the Test scene after a three-year absence.

GREAT BRITAIN

GREAT BRITAIN

In a season of three Test encounters building up to a British Coal tour Down Under, Great Britain coach Malcolm Reilly called up a total of 34 players, including 12 debutants.

The international supremo was forced to spread his net because of the desire to experiment, injuries and a controversial League ruling that an inaugural world seven-a-side competition should take precedence over Test football.

The newcomers to the Test scene included six of the Wales side which had returned to the international scene in record-breaking fashion, beating Papua New Guinea 68-0 after a seven-year absence. They were Allan Bateman, John Devereux, Jonathan Griffiths, Mark Jones, Paul Moriarty and Anthony Sullivan.

Other new caps were John Bentley, Gary Connolly, Alan Hunte, Michael Jackson, Steve McNamara and Gary Price.

Injury victims included Ellery Hanley, named as the original skipper for the November encounter with the Kumuls; replacement captain Garry Schofield, who missed the French double; and the free-scoring Martin Offiah, in dispute with Widnes for the Papuan Test and injured with Wigan for the meetings with France.

The bizarre sevens-versus-country controversy arose in February when Britain were scheduled to meet France in Perpignan. The League's Board of Directors had earlier selected Wigan to be the British representatives in the first-ever Nissan World Sevens, rescheduling their Silk Cut Challenge Cup commitments to allow the Riversiders to travel to Sydney and return in time for their Test contingent to join the trip across the Channel.

Heavy snow then played havoc with the tight timetable, forcing a fixture pile-up, and the Board were faced with the choice of disrupting the sevens, the Cup or the Test.

The Board, including Great Britain manager and Wigan chairman Maurice Lindsay, took what they considered to be the line of least disruption and ordered Wigan to undertake the sevens and then play their delayed Silk Cut tie on the day of the British Coal Test in France. Britain would be left without six Wigan players, although it was felt that for a non-World Cup Test in a tour season, the forced experimentation would not be detrimental.

Despite the backcloth of trial and tribulation, Great Britain achieved a 100 per cent record, collecting valuable World Cup points against Papua and France at home.

In November, the Lions ran up a record score against Papua New Guinea at Wigan, Jonathan Davies contributing a record eight goals. Debutant packmen Michael Jackson and Paul Moriarty each scored two tries as the Kumuls rounded off a disastrous five-match tour. The British Coal Test is fully chronicled in the section 1991 KUMULS.

Three months later Britain went to Perpignan to face France, with Davies becoming the first former Wales Rugby Union international captain to lead a Test side.

There were 13 changes from the 17-man squad on duty against Papua, with no Wigan players available. Britain included four players making their debuts and struggled for long periods.

It was 12-12 when substitute forward Richard Eyres touched down in the 64th minute and Davies's goal took them six points ahead. But it was the introduction of two back substitutes immediately after Eyres' try that saved Britain's blushes, as Graham Steadman replaced full back Alan Tait and Daryl Powell took over at stand off from debutant Jonathan Griffiths. The pair soon worked in perfect harmony for Steadman to score tries with his first two touches of the ball, receiving each time from Powell after a scrum.

Five minutes after going on, Steadman linked up at a set piece 30 yards out to take

Powell's pass on the burst, a couple of quick sidesteps leaving the French in disarray before using his power to force a way over as two defenders closed in.

Davies tagged on the second of his three goals, and five minutes later the substitute duo had done it again to seal a flattering 30-12 scoreline. This time the scrum was near their own 25-yard line and, in another well-planned move, Powell immediately booted the ball downfield. Steadman was 15 yards clear of the chase before slowing down to gather the ball and go over near the posts.

Great Britain had made a nervous start, as France opened up a six-point lead after 15 minutes before debutant touchdowns from Griffiths, Bentley and Devereux. Widnes forward Eyres went on as Britain's first substitute in the 51st minute. Loose forward Les Holliday, the creator of two first-half tries, took the British Coal Man of the Match award.

Three weeks later, five Wigan players returned to Test duty, including Shaun Edwards as skipper for the second time. Seeking two World Cup points and a healthy scoring margin to stave off the challenge of New Zealand for second place in the table, Britain won 36-0 with Wigan hooker Martin Dermott taking the British Coal individual award.

Britain's new half-back pairing of Powell and Edwards provided the directness missing in Perpignan, Powell using his power to make big dents in the French defence, while Edwards teased it open with dummies and twinkling footwork. On defence, the duo shared evenly an impressive tally of 38 tackles.

As in Perpignan, Lee Crooks was the cornerstone of the pack, while Hull wingman Paul Eastwood justified his debatable return with a try and goals to all six touchdowns. Debutant winger Hunte impressed with an enterprising display including a classically-taken touchdown.

1992 TOUR SQUAD

Great Britain's biggest-ever tour squad of 32 players was announced on 6 April, highlighted by the selection of a record 13 Wigan players, beating the previous record of eight — also by Wigan — set in 1950. Garry Schofield, appointed as vice-captain, was chosen for a record fourth tour Down Under — three full tours of Australasia and one to Papua New Guinea and New Zealand only.

Jonathan Davies, skipper of Great Britain and Wales during 1991-92, and a 1990 tourist, withdrew on 24 April with a pelvic bone injury, being replaced by Alan Hunte of St. Helens. On 17 May, Leeds scrum half Bobby Goulding, having been suspended for four matches, was withdrawn and replaced by Featherstone Rovers skipper Deryck Fox. The original squad was:

BACKS
CONNOLLY, Gary (St. Helens)
DAVIES, Jonathan (Widnes)
DEVEREUX, John (Widnes)
EASTWOOD, Paul (Hull)
EDWARDS, Shaun (Wigan)
ELLIS, Kevin (Warrington)
GREGORY, Andy (Wigan)
GOULDING, Bobby (Leeds)
HALLAS, Graeme (Hull K.R.)
HAMPSON, Steve (Wigan)
LOUGHLIN, Paul (St. Helens)
LYDON, Joe (Wigan)
NEWLOVE, Paul (Featherstone R.)
OFFIAH, Martin (Wigan)
POWELL, Daryl (Sheffield E.)
SCHOFIELD, Garry (Leeds) *Vice-Capt*
STEADMAN, Graham (Castleford)

FORWARDS
BETTS, Denis (Wigan)
CLARKE, Phil (Wigan)
COWIE, Neil (Wigan)
CROOKS, Lee (Castleford)
DERMOTT, Martin (Wigan)
FAIRBANK, Karl (Bradford N.)
HANLEY, Ellery (Leeds) *Captain*
HOLLIDAY, Les (Widnes)
JACKSON, Lee (Hull)
JACKSON, Michael (Wakefield T.)
LUCAS, Ian (Wigan)
McGINTY, Billy (Wigan)
NICKLE, Sonny (St. Helens)
PLATT, Andy (Wigan)
SKERRETT, Kelvin (Wigan)

16 February   **Perpignan**

GREAT BRITAIN 30

Alan Tait (Widnes)	1.	Patrick Limongi (Carcassonne)
John Devereux (Widnes)	2.	Jean-Marc Garcia (St. Esteve)
Gary Connolly (St. Helens)	3.	Pierre Chamorin (St. Esteve)
Jonathan Davies (Widnes), Capt.	4.	Pascal Fages (Pia)
John Bentley (Leeds)	5.	Claude Sirvent (St. Gaudens)
Jonathan Griffiths (St. Helens)	6.	Gilles Dumas (St. Gaudens), Capt.
Bobby Goulding (Leeds)	7.	Patrick Entat (Carcassonne)
Lee Crooks (Castleford)	8.	Bernard Llong (Carcassonne)
Lee Jackson (Hull)	9.	Thierry Valero (Lezignan)
Paul Dixon (Leeds)	10.	Yves Viloni (Carpentras)
Karl Fairbank (Bradford N.)	11.	Guy Delpech (Villeneuve)
Michael Jackson (Wakefield T.)	12.	Christophe Bonnafous (Albi)
Les Holliday (Widnes)	13.	Jacques Pech (Limoux)
Daryl Powell (Sheffield E.)	14.	Thierry Matteo (Villeneuve)
Mark Jones (Hull)	15.	Pascal Bomati (XIII Catalan)
Graham Steadman (Castleford)	16.	Patrick Torreilles (Pia)
Richard Eyres (Widnes)	17.	Lilian Hebert (Cahors)

FRANCE 12

T: Steadman (2), Griffiths, Bentley, Devereux, Eyres
G: Davies (3)
Substitutions:
Eyres for Dixon (51 min.)
Powell for Griffiths (64 min.)
Steadman for Tait (64 min.)
Jones for Fairbank (70 min.)
Manager: Maurice Lindsay
Coach: Malcolm Reilly

T: Pech, Garcia
G: Dumas (2)
Substitutions:
Torreilles for Pech (Half-time)
Bomati for Garcia (55 min.)
Hebert for Bonnafous (59 min.)
Matteo for Fages (65 min.)
Half-time: 8-8
Referee: Eddie Ward (Australia)
Attendance: 5,688

Scorechart

Minute	Score	GB	France
15:	Pech (T)		
	Dumas (G)	0	6
23:	Griffiths (T)	4	6
33:	Dumas (P)	4	8
36:	Bentley (T)	8	8
45:	Devereux (T)	12	8
47:	Garcia (T)	12	12
64:	Eyres (T)		
	Davies (G)	18	12
69:	Steadman (T)		
	Davies (G)	24	12
74:	Steadman (T)		
	Davies (G)	30	12
	Scrums	12	14
	Penalties	9	7

Debutant tryscorer John Bentley.

7 March   **Hull**

GREAT BRITAIN 36   **FRANCE 0**

Graham Steadman (Castleford)	1.	Patrick Limongi (Carcassonne)
Paul Eastwood (Hull)	2.	Claude Sirvent (St. Gaudens)
Gary Connolly (St. Helens)	3.	Pierre Chamorin (St. Esteve)
Allan Bateman (Warrington)	4.	Pascal Fages (Pia)
Alan Hunte (St. Helens)	5.	Cyrille Pons (St. Gaudens)
Daryl Powell (Sheffield E.)	6.	Gilles Dumas (St. Gaudens), Capt.
Shaun Edwards (Wigan), Capt.	7.	Patrick Entat (Carcassonne)
Lee Crooks (Castleford)	8.	Pierre Aillieres (Toulouse)
Martin Dermott (Wigan)	9.	Thierry Valero (Lezignan)
Kelvin Skerrett (Wigan)	10.	Yves Viloni (Carpentras)
Denis Betts (Wigan)	11.	Bernard Llong (Carcassonne)
Karl Fairbank (Bradford N.)	12.	Christophe Bonnafous (Albi)
Les Holliday (Widnes)	13.	Jacques Pech (Limoux)
John Devereux (Widnes)	14.	Francis Lope (Albi)
Andy Platt (Wigan)	15.	Patrick Torreilles (Pia)
Deryck Fox (Featherstone R.)	16.	Pascal Bomati (XIII Catalan)
Steve McNamara (Hull)	17.	Patrick Marginet (St. Esteve)

T: Eastwood, Holliday, Platt, Hunte, Dermott, Fox
G: Eastwood (6)
Substitutions:
Platt for Skerrett (31 min.)
McNamara for Fairbank (58 min.)
Fox for Bateman (66 min.)
Manager: Maurice Lindsay
Coach: Malcolm Reilly

Substitutions:
Torreilles for Llong (47 min.)
Lope for Bonnafous (71 min.)
Bomati for Chamorin (75 min.)
Marginet for Pons (75 min.)
Half-time: 12-0
Referee: Eddie Ward (Australia)
Attendance: 5,250

Scorechart

Minute	Score	GB	France
5:	Holliday (T)		
	Eastwood (G)	6	0
26:	Eastwood (T)		
	Eastwood (G)	12	0
49:	Platt (T)		
	Eastwood (G)	18	0
56:	Hunte (T)		
	Eastwood (G)	24	0
63:	Dermott (T)		
	Eastwood (G)	30	0
79:	Fox (T)		
	Eastwood (G)	36	0
	Scrums	11	14
	Penalties	2	10

Winger Paul Eastwood, a 16-point tally.

TESTS

● Although early Tests were played under the titles of Northern Union or England, it is acceptable to regard them as Great Britain.
W-Won, D-Drawn, L-Lost refer to Great Britain.

GREAT BRITAIN v. AUSTRALIA

Date	Result	Venue	Attendance
12 Dec. 1908	D 22-22	QPR, London	2,000
23 Jan. 1909	W 15-5	Newcastle	22,000
15 Feb. 1909	W 6-5	Birmingham	9,000
18 Jun. 1910	W 27-20	Sydney	42,000
2 Jul. 1910	W 22-17	Brisbane	18,000
8 Nov. 1911	L 10-19	Newcastle	6,500
16 Dec. 1911	D 11-11	Edinburgh	6,000
1 Jan. 1912	L 8-33	Birmingham	4,000
27 Jun. 1914	W 23-5	Sydney	40,000
29 Jun. 1914	L 7-12	Sydney	55,000
4 Jul. 1914	W 14-6	Sydney	34,420
26 Jun. 1920	L 4-8	Brisbane	28,000
3 Jul. 1920	L 8-21	Sydney	40,000
10 Jul. 1920	W 23-13	Sydney	32,000
1 Oct. 1921	W 6-5	Leeds	32,000
5 Nov. 1921	L 2-16	Hull	21,504
14 Jan. 1922	W 6-0	Salford	21,000
23 Jun. 1924	W 22-3	Sydney	50,000
28 Jun. 1924	W 5-3	Sydney	33,842
12 Jul. 1924	L 11-21	Brisbane	36,000
23 Jun. 1928	W 15-12	Brisbane	39,200
14 Jul. 1928	W 8-0	Sydney	44,548
21 Jul. 1928	L 14-21	Sydney	37,000
5 Oct. 1929	L 8-31	Hull K.R.	20,000
9 Nov. 1929	W 9-3	Leeds	31,402
4 Jan. 1930	D 0-0	Swinton	34,709
15 Jan. 1930	W 3-0	Rochdale	16,743
6 Jun. 1932	W 8-6	Sydney	70,204
18 Jun. 1932	L 6-15	Brisbane	26,500
16 Jul. 1932	W 18-13	Sydney	50,053
7 Oct. 1933	W 4-0	Belle Vue, Manchester	34,000
11 Nov. 1933	W 7-5	Leeds	29,618
16 Dec. 1933	W 19-16	Swinton	10,990
29 Jun. 1936	L 8-24	Sydney	63,920
4 Jul. 1936	W 12-7	Brisbane	29,486
18 Jul. 1936	W 12-7	Sydney	53,546
16 Oct. 1937	W 5-4	Leeds	31,949
13 Nov. 1937	W 13-3	Swinton	31,724
18 Dec. 1937	L 3-13	Huddersfield	9,093
17 Jun. 1946	D 8-8	Sydney	64,527
6 Jul. 1946	W 14-5	Brisbane	40,500
20 Jul. 1946	W 20-7	Sydney	35,294
9 Oct. 1948	W 23-21	Leeds	36,529
6 Nov. 1948	W 16-7	Swinton	36,354
29 Jan. 1949	W 23-9	Bradford	42,000
12 Jun. 1950	W 6-4	Sydney	47,215
1 Jul. 1950	L 3-15	Brisbane	35,000
22 Jul. 1950	L 2-5	Sydney	47,178
4 Oct. 1952	W 19-6	Leeds	34,505
8 Nov. 1952	W 21-5	Swinton	32,421
13 Dec. 1952	L 7-27	Bradford	30,509
12 Jun. 1954	L 12-37	Sydney	65,884
3 Jul. 1954	W 38-21	Brisbane	46,355
17 Jul. 1954	L 16-20	Sydney	67,577
17 Nov. 1956	W 21-10	Wigan	22,473
1 Dec. 1956	L 9-22	Bradford	23,634
15 Dec. 1956	W 19-0	Swinton	17,542
14 Jun. 1958	L 8-25	Sydney	68,777
5 Jul. 1958	W 25-18	Brisbane	32,965
19 Jul. 1958	W 40-17	Sydney	68,720
17 Oct. 1959	L 14-22	Swinton	35,224
21 Nov. 1959	W 11-10	Leeds	30,184
12 Dec. 1959	W 18-12	Wigan	26,089
9 Jun. 1962	W 31-12	Sydney	70,174
30 Jun. 1962	W 17-10	Brisbane	34,766
14 Jul. 1962	L 17-18	Sydney	42,104
16 Oct. 1963	L 2-28	Wembley	13,946
9 Nov. 1963	L 12-50	Swinton	30,833
30 Nov. 1963	W 16-5	Leeds	20,497
25 Jun. 1966	W 17-13	Sydney	57,962
16 Jul. 1966	L 4-6	Brisbane	45,057
23 Jul. 1966	L 14-19	Sydney	63,503
21 Oct. 1967	W 16-11	Leeds	22,293
3 Nov. 1967	L 11-17	White City, London	17,445
9 Dec. 1967	L 3-11	Swinton	13,615
6 Jun. 1970	L 15-37	Brisbane	42,807
20 Jun. 1970	W 28-7	Sydney	60,962
4 Jul. 1970	W 21-17	Sydney	61,258
3 Nov. 1973	W 21-12	Wembley	9,874
24 Nov. 1973	L 6-14	Leeds	16,674
1 Dec. 1973	L 5-15	Warrington	10,019
15 Jun. 1974	L 6-12	Brisbane	30,280
6 Jul. 1974	W 16-11	Sydney	48,006
20 Jul. 1974	L 18-22	Sydney	55,505
21 Oct. 1978	L 9-15	Wigan	17,644
5 Nov. 1978	W 18-14	Bradford	26,447
18 Nov. 1978	L 6-23	Leeds	29,627
16 Jun. 1979	L 0-35	Brisbane	23,051

30 Jun. 1979	L	16-24	Sydney	26,837
14 Jul. 1979	L	2-28	Sydney	16,844
30 Oct. 1982	L	4-40	Hull C. FC	26,771
20 Nov. 1982	L	6-27	Wigan	23,216
28 Nov. 1982	L	8-32	Leeds	17,318
9 Jun. 1984	L	8-25	Sydney	30,190
26 Jun. 1984	L	6-18	Brisbane	26,534
7 Jul. 1984	L	7-20	Sydney	18,756
25 Oct. 1986	L	16-38	Man U. FC	50,583
8 Nov. 1986	L	4-34	Elland Rd, Leeds	30,808

* 22 Nov. 1986	L	15-24	Wigan	20,169
11 Jun. 1988	L	6-17	Sydney	24,202
28 Jun. 1988	L	14-34	Brisbane	27,103
* 9 Jul. 1988	W	26-12	Sydney	15,994
27 Oct. 1990	W	19-12	Wembley	54,569
10 Nov. 1990	L	10-14	Man U. FC	46,615
* 24 Nov. 1990	L	0-14	Elland Rd, Leeds	32,500

* Also World Cup match.

	Played	Won	Drawn	Lost	Tries	Goals	Dr	Pts for
Great Britain	105	51	4	50	255	260	6	1313
Australia	105	50	4	51	301	325	6	1605

GREAT BRITAIN-AUSTRALIA TEST MATCH RECORDS

Britain

Highest score: 40-17 Third Test at Sydney, 19 July 1958 (Also widest margin win)

Most tries in a match: 4 by J. Leytham (Wigan) Second Test at Brisbane, 2 July 1910

Most goals in a match: 10 by B. L. Jones (Leeds) Second Test at Brisbane, 3 July 1954

Most points in a match: 20 by B. L. Jones (as above)
20 (7g, 2t) by R. Millward (Hull K.R.) Second Test at Sydney, 20 June 1970

Biggest attendance: 54,569 First Test at Wembley, London, 27 October 1990

Australia

Highest score: 50-12 Second Test at Swinton, 9 Nov 1963 (Also widest margin win)

Most tries in a match: 3 by J. Devereux, First Test at QPR, London, 12 December 1908
3 by R. Gasnier, First Test at Swinton, 17 October 1959
3 by R. Gasnier, First Test at Wembley, 16 October 1963
3 by K. Irvine, Second Test at Swinton, 9 November 1963
3 by K. Irvine, Third Test at Sydney, 23 July 1966
3 by G. Miles, First Test at Old Trafford, Manchester, 25 October 1986
3 by M. O'Connor, First Test at Old Trafford, Manchester, 25 October 1986

Most goals in a match: 10 by M. Cronin, First Test at Brisbane, 16 June 1979

Most points in a match: 22 (5g, 3t) by M. O'Connor First Test at Old Trafford, Manchester, 25 October 1986

Biggest attendance: 70,204 First Test at Sydney, 6 June 1932

● In a World Cup match at Perpignan, France, on 29 October 1972, R. Fulton scored 3 tries

GREAT BRITAIN v. NEW ZEALAND

Date		Score	Venue	Attendance
25 Jan. 1908	W	14-6	Leeds	8,182
8 Feb. 1908	L	6-18	Chelsea	14,000
15 Feb. 1908	L	5-8	Cheltenham	4,000
30 Jul. 1910	W	52-20	Auckland	16,000
1 Aug. 1914	W	16-13	Auckland	15,000
31 Jul. 1920	W	31-7	Auckland	34,000
7 Aug. 1920	W	19-3	Christchurch	10,000
14 Aug. 1920	W	11-10	Wellington	4,000
2 Aug. 1924	L	8-16	Auckland	22,000
6 Aug. 1924	L	11-13	Wellington	6,000
9 Aug. 1924	W	31-18	Dunedin	14,000
2 Oct. 1926	W	28-20	Wigan	14,500
13 Nov. 1926	W	21-11	Hull	7,000
15 Jan. 1927	W	32-17	Leeds	6,000
4 Aug. 1928	L	13-17	Auckland	28,000
18 Aug. 1928	W	13-5	Dunedin	12,000
25 Aug. 1928	W	6-5	Christchurch	21,000
30 Jul. 1932	W	24-9	Auckland	25,000
13 Aug. 1932	W	25-14	Christchurch	5,000
20 Aug. 1932	W	20-18	Auckland	6,500
8 Aug. 1936	W	10-8	Auckland	25,000
15 Aug. 1936	W	23-11	Auckland	17,000
10 Aug. 1946	L	8-13	Auckland	10,000
4 Oct. 1947	W	11-10	Leeds	28,445
8 Nov. 1947	L	7-10	Swinton	29,031
20 Dec. 1947	W	25-9	Bradford	42,680
29 Jul. 1950	L	10-16	Christchurch	10,000
12 Aug. 1950	L	13-20	Auckland	20,000
6 Oct. 1951	W	21-15	Bradford	37,475
10 Nov. 1951	W	20-19	Swinton	29,938
15 Dec. 1951	W	16-12	Leeds	18,649
24 Jul. 1954	W	27-7	Auckland	22,097
31 Jul. 1954	L	14-20	Greymouth	4,240
14 Aug. 1954	W	12-6	Auckland	6,186
8 Oct. 1955	W	25-6	Swinton	21,937
12 Nov. 1955	W	27-12	Bradford	24,443
17 Dec. 1955	L	13-28	Leeds	10,438
26 Jul. 1958	L	10-15	Auckland	25,000
9 Aug. 1958	W	32-15	Auckland	25,000
30 Sept. 1961	L	11-29	Leeds	16,540
21 Oct. 1961	W	23-10	Bradford	19,980
4 Nov. 1961	W	35-19	Swinton	22,536
28 Jul. 1962	L	0-19	Auckland	14,976
11 Aug. 1962	L	8-27	Auckland	16,411
25 Sept. 1965	W	7-2	Swinton	8,541
23 Oct. 1965	W	15-9	Bradford	15,740
6 Nov. 1965	D	9-9	Wigan	7,919
6 Aug. 1966	W	25-8	Auckland	14,494
20 Aug. 1966	W	22-14	Auckland	10,657
11 Jul. 1970	W	19-15	Auckland	15,948
19 Jul. 1970	W	23-9	Christchurch	8,600
25 Jul. 1970	W	33-16	Auckland	13,137
25 Sept. 1971	L	13-18	Salford	3,764
16 Oct. 1971	L	14-17	Castleford	4,108
6 Nov. 1971	W	12-3	Leeds	5,479
27 Jul. 1974	L	8-13	Auckland	10,466
4 Aug. 1974	W	17-8	Christchurch	6,316
10 Aug. 1974	W	20-0	Auckland	11,574
21 Jul. 1979	W	16-8	Auckland	9,000
5 Aug. 1979	W	22-7	Christchurch	8,500
11 Aug. 1979	L	11-18	Auckland	7,000
18 Oct. 1980	D	14-14	Wigan	7,031
2 Nov. 1980	L	8-12	Bradford	10,946
15 Nov. 1980	W	10-2	Leeds	8,210
14 Jul. 1984	L	0-12	Auckland	10,238
22 Jul. 1984	L	12-28	Christchurch	3,824
28 Jul. 1984	L	16-32	Auckland	7,967
19 Oct. 1985	L	22-24	Leeds	12,591
2 Nov. 1985	W	25-8	Wigan	15,506
*9 Nov. 1985	D	6-6	Elland Rd, Leeds	22,209
*17 Jul. 1988	L	10-12	Christchurch	8,525
21 Oct. 1989	L	16-24	Man U. FC	18,273
28 Oct. 1989	W	26-6	Elland Rd, Leeds	13,073
*11 Nov. 1989	W	10-6	Wigan	20,346
24 Jun. 1990	W	11-10	Palmerston N.	8,073
8 Jul. 1990	W	16-14	Auckland	7,843
*15 Jul. 1990	L	18-21	Christchurch	3,133

*Also World Cup match.

	Played	Won	Drawn	Lost	Tries	Goals	Dr	Pts for
Great Britain	77	47	3	27	273	220	4	1293
New Zealand	77	27	3	47	177	222	1	1009

GREAT BRITAIN-NEW ZEALAND TEST MATCH RECORDS

Britain

Highest score: 52-20 First Test at Auckland, 30 July 1910 (Also widest margin win)

Most tries in a match: 4 by W. Boston (Wigan) First Test at Auckland, 24 July 1954
4 by G. Schofield (Hull) Second Test at Wigan, 2 November 1985

Most goals in a match: 7 by N. Fox (Wakefield T.) Third Test at Swinton, 4 November 1961

7 by E. Fraser (Warrington) Second Test at Auckland, 9 August 1958

Most points in a match: 16 (4t) by G. Schofield (Hull) Second Test at Wigan, 2 November 1985

Biggest attendance: 42,680 Third Test at Bradford, 20 December 1947

● In a World Cup match at Pau, France, on 4 November 1972, Britain won 53-19 with J. Holmes (Leeds) scoring 26 points from 10 goals and two tries.

In a World Cup match at Sydney on 8 June 1968, Bev Risman scored 7 goals.

New Zealand

Highest score: 32-16 Third Test at Auckland, 28 July 1984

Widest margin win: 19-0 First Test at Auckland, 28 July 1962

27-8 Second Test at Auckland, 11 August 1962

No player has scored three tries or more in a Test.

Most goals and points: 7g-14pts by D. White, Second Test at Greymouth, 31 July 1954

J. Fagan, First Test at Headingley, 30 September 1961

E. Wiggs, Second Test at Auckland, 20 August 1966

Biggest attendance: 34,000 First Test at Auckland, 31 July 1920

● In a World Cup match at Sydney, Australia, on 25 June 1957, W. Sorensen also scored 7 goals, 14 points.

GREAT BRITAIN v. FRANCE
● **Results since France were given Test match status.**

Date		Result	Venue	Attendance
26 Jan. 1957	W	45-12	Leeds	20,221
3 Mar. 1957	D	19-19	Toulouse	16,000
10 Apr. 1957	W	29-14	St. Helens	23,250
3 Nov. 1957	W	25-14	Toulouse	15,000
23 Nov. 1957	W	44-15	Wigan	19,152
2 Mar. 1958	W	23-9	Grenoble	20,000
14 Mar. 1959	W	50-15	Leeds	22,000
5 Apr. 1959	L	15-24	Grenoble	8,500
6 Mar. 1960	L	18-20	Toulouse	15,308
26 Mar. 1960	D	17-17	St. Helens	14,000
11 Dec. 1960	W	21-10	Bordeaux	8,000
28 Jan. 1961	W	27-8	St. Helens	18,000
17 Feb. 1962	L	15-20	Wigan	17,277
11 Mar. 1962	L	13-23	Perpignan	14,000
2 Dec. 1962	L	12-17	Perpignan	5,000
3 Apr. 1963	W	42-4	Wigan	19,487
8 Mar. 1964	W	11-5	Perpignan	4,326
18 Mar. 1964	W	39-0	Leigh	4,750
6 Dec. 1964	L	8-18	Perpignan	15,000
23 Jan. 1965	W	17-7	Swinton	9,959
16 Jan. 1966	L	13-18	Perpignan	6,000
5 Mar. 1966	L	4-8	Wigan	14,004
22 Jan. 1967	W	16-13	Carcassonne	10,650
4 Mar. 1967	L	13-23	Wigan	7,448
11 Feb. 1968	W	22-13	Paris	8,000
2 Mar. 1968	W	19-8	Bradford	14,196
30 Nov. 1968	W	34-10	St. Helens	6,080
2 Feb. 1969	L	9-13	Toulouse	10,000
7 Feb. 1971	L	8-16	Toulouse	14,960
17 Mar. 1971	W	24-2	St. Helens	7,783
6 Feb. 1972	W	10-9	Toulouse	11,508
12 Mar. 1972	W	45-10	Bradford	7,313
20 Jan. 1974	W	24-5	Grenoble	5,500
17 Feb. 1974	W	29-0	Wigan	10,105
6 Dec. 1981	W	37-0	Hull	13,173
20 Dec. 1981	L	2-19	Marseilles	6,500
20 Feb. 1983	W	20-5	Carcassonne	3,826
6 Mar. 1983	W	17-5	Hull	6,055
29 Jan. 1984	W	12-0	Avignon	4,000
17 Feb. 1984	W	10-0	Leeds	7,646
1 Mar. 1985	W	50-4	Leeds	6,491
17 Mar. 1985	L	16-24	Perpignan	5,000
*16 Feb. 1986	D	10-10	Avignon	4,000
1 Mar. 1986	W	24-10	Wigan	8,112
*24 Jan. 1987	W	52-4	Leeds	6,567
8 Feb. 1987	W	20-10	Carcassonne	2,000
24 Jan. 1988	W	28-14	Avignon	6,500
6 Feb. 1988	W	30-12	Leeds	7,007
21 Jan. 1989	W	26-10	Wigan	8,266
5 Feb. 1989	W	30-8	Avignon	6,500
18 Mar. 1990	W	8-4	Perpignan	6,000
7 Apr. 1990	L	18-25	Leeds	6,554
*27 Jan. 1991	W	45-10	Perpignan	3,965
16 Feb. 1991	W	60-4	Leeds	5,284
16 Feb. 1992	W	30-12	Perpignan	5,688
*7 Mar. 1992	W	36-0	Hull	5,250

★Also World Cup match.

	Played	Won	Drawn	Lost	Tries	Goals	Dr	Pts for
Great Britain	56	39	3	14	258	240	1	1341
France	56	14	3	39	103	135	4	609

GREAT BRITAIN-FRANCE TEST MATCH RECORDS

Britain

Highest score: 60-4 at Leeds, 16 February 1991 (Also widest margin win)
Most tries in a match: 5 by M. Offiah (Widnes) at Leeds, 16 February 1991
Most goals in a match: 10 by B. Ganley (Oldham) at Wigan, 23 November 1957
Most points in a match: 21 (9g, 1t) by B.L. Jones (Leeds) at Leeds, 26 January 1957
21 (9g, 1t) by N. Fox (Wakefield T.) at Wigan, 3 April 1963
21 (9g, 1t) by N. Fox (Wakefield T.) at Leigh, 18 March 1964
Biggest attendance: 23,250 at St. Helens, 10 April 1957

France

Highest score: 25-18 at Leeds, 7 April 1990
Widest margin win: 19-2 at Marseilles, 20 December 1981
Most tries in a match: 3 by D. Couston at Perpignan, 17 March 1985
Most goals in a match: 7 by P. Lacaze at Wigan, 4 March 1967
Most points in a match: 14 by P. Lacaze (as above)
14 (4g, 2t) by G. Benausse at Wigan, 17 February 1962
Biggest attendance: 20,000 at Grenoble, 2 March 1958
●In a World Cup match at Toulouse on 7 November 1954, there were 37,471

Additional Great Britain v. France

Pre-Test status

22 May 1952	L	12-22	Paris	16,466
24 May 1953	L	17-28	Lyons	
27 Apr. 1954	W	17-8	Bradford	14,153
11 Dec. 1955	L	5-17	Paris	18,000
11 Apr. 1956	W	18-10	Bradford	10,453

Other match

31 July 1982	L	7-8	Venice	1,500

GREAT BRITAIN v. PAPUA NEW GUINEA

5 Aug. 1984	W	38-20	Mt. Hagen	7,510
*24 Oct. 1987	W	42-0	Wigan	9,121
*22 May 1988	W	42-22	Port Moresby	12,107
27 May 1990	L	18-20	Goroka	11,598
*2 Jun. 1990	W	40-8	Port Moresby	5,969
*9 Nov. 1991	W	56-4	Wigan	4,193

*Also World Cup match.

Martin Offiah, most tries in a match versus France.

	Played	Won	Lost	Tries	Goals	Dr	Pts for
Great Britain	6	5	1	41	36	0	236
Papua New Guinea	6	1	5	11	14	2	74

GREAT BRITAIN-PAPUA NEW GUINEA TEST MATCH RECORDS

Britain
Highest score: 56-4 at Wigan, 9 November 1991 (Also widest margin win)
Most tries in a match: No player has scored 3 or more
Most goals in a match: 8 by J. Davies (Widnes) at Wigan, 9 November 1991
Most points in a match: 16 by J. Davies (Widnes) as above
Biggest attendance: 9,121 at Wigan, 24 October 1987

Papua New Guinea
Highest score: 22-42 at Port Moresby, 22 May 1988
Only win: 20-18 at Goroka, 27 May 1990
Most tries in a match: No player has scored 3 or more
Most goals in a match: 6 by B. Numapo at Goroka, 27 May 1990
Most points in a match: 11 (5g, 1dg) by B. Numapo as above
Biggest attendance: 12,107 at Port Moresby, 22 May 1988

Halifax prop Karl Harrison drives into the Papuan defence in the 1991 British Coal Test at Wigan.

GREAT BRITAIN REPRESENTATION CLUB-BY-CLUB

Wigan beat their own record by fielding eight players in the Great Britain side which met Papua New Guinea at Wigan on 24 October 1987. The octet was backs Steve Hampson, David Stephenson, Joe Lydon, Shaun Edwards and Andy Gregory, plus forwards Brian Case, Andy Goodway and Ellery Hanley. The previous best of seven were backs Martin Ryan, Gordon Ratcliffe, Ernie Ashcroft, Jack Hilton and Tommy Bradshaw, plus forwards Ken Gee and Joe Egan in the 6-4 victory over Australia at Sydney on 12 June 1950. Wigan also hold the record for the total of players selected with a remarkable 78.

Mick Sullivan gained Test honours with four clubs — Huddersfield (16), Wigan (19), St. Helens (10) and York (1). Billy Boston gained the most Test honours with a single club, making all 31 of his appearances for Britain while with Wigan.

Only seven of last season's clubs have not had a player selected for Great Britain in Test or World Cup matches — Chorley Borough, Bramley, Doncaster, Carlisle, Nottingham City, Scarborough Pirates and Trafford Borough. Of the extinct clubs only Broughton Rangers (later Belle Vue Rangers), Merthyr Tydfil, St. Helens Recs and the old Runcorn had players selected for Britain.

● A register of each club's representation for Great Britain is featured in the section CLUBS.

GREAT BRITAIN TEAMS
...A 20-year review

The following is a compendium of Great Britain Test and World Cup teams since the start of the 1972-73 season.

Initials are included where more than one celebrated player shared a surname in the same era. Only playing substitutes are included on the teamsheet.

(WC): World Cup t: try g: goal dg: drop goal * captain

1972 Australia (WC)
Perpignan: 29 Oct
Won 27-21

Charlton (Salford)
*Sullivan, C (Hull) 1t
Hesketh (Salford)
Walsh, John (St. Helens)
Atkinson, J (Leeds) 1t
O'Neill, D (Widnes) 1t
Nash (Featherstone)
Clawson (Leeds) 6g
Stephenson, M (Dewsbury) 1t
Jeanes (Leeds)
Lockwood (Castleford)
Lowe, P (Hull KR) 1t
Nicholls (Widnes)
Sub: Holmes (Leeds)

1972 France (WC)
Grenoble: 1 Nov
Won 13-4
Charlton (Salford)
*Sullivan, C (Hull) 1t
Hesketh (Salford)
Walsh, John (St. Helens)
Atkinson, J (Leeds)
O'Neill, D (Widnes)
Nash (Featherstone)
Clawson (Leeds) 2g
Stephenson, M (Dewsbury)
Lockwood, B (Castleford)
Dixon, C (Salford)
Lowe, P (Hull KR) 2t
Nicholls (Widnes)

1972 New Zealand (WC)
Pau: 4 Nov
Won 53-19
Charlton (Salford) 1t
*Sullivan, C (Hull) 1t
Hesketh (Salford) 1t
Walsh, John (St. Helens)
Atkinson, J (Leeds) 2t
Holmes (Leeds) 10g,2t
Nash (Featherstone) 1t
Jeanes (Leeds) 1t
Stephenson, M (Dewsbury) 1t
Lockwood (Castleford)
Irving (Oldham)
Lowe, P (Hull KR)
Nicholls (Widnes) 1t
Sub: Redfearn, D (Bradford)
Karalius, A (St. Helens)

1972 Australia (WC)
Lyons: 11 Nov
Drew 10-10
Charlton (Salford)
*Sullivan, C (Hull) 1t
Hesketh (Salford)
Walsh, John (St. Helens)
Atkinson, J (Leeds)
Holmes (Leeds)
Nash (Featherstone)
Clawson (Leeds) 2g
Stephenson, M (Dewsbury) 1t
Jeanes (Leeds)
Lockwood, B (Castleford)
Lowe, P (Hull KR)
Nicholls (Widnes)
Sub: Irving (Oldham)

1973 Australia
Wembley: 3 Nov
Won 21-12
Charlton (Salford)
*Sullivan, C (Hull)
Hynes (Leeds)
Hesketh (Salford)
Atkinson, J (Leeds)
Topliss (Wakefield)
Nash (Featherstone) 1dg
Clawson (Oldham) 4g
Clarke (Wigan) 1t
Lockwood (Castleford) 1t
Nicholls (St. Helens)
Lowe, P (Hull KR) 2t
Batten, R (Leeds)

1973 Australia
Leeds: 24 Nov
Lost 6-14
Charlton (Salford)
*Sullivan, C (Hull)
Hynes (Leeds)
Hesketh (Salford)
Atkinson, J (Leeds)
Topliss (Wakefield)
Nash (Featherstone)
Clawson (Oldham) 3g
Clarke (Wigan)
Lockwood (Castleford)
Mantle (St. Helens)
Lowe, P (Hull KR)
Batten, R (Leeds)
Sub: Eckersley (St. Helens)
Dixon, C (Salford)

1973 Australia
Warrington: 1 Dec
Lost 5-15
Charlton (Salford)
Smith, A (Leeds)
Hynes (Leeds)
Hesketh (Salford)
*Sullivan, C (Hull)
Eckersley (St. Helens)
Millward (Hull KR) 1t,1g
Clawson (Oldham)
Clarke (Wigan)
Harrison, M (Hull)
Nicholls (St. Helens)
Lowe, P (Hull KR)
Laughton (Widnes)
Sub: Watkins, D (Salford)
Dixon, C (Salford)

1974 France
Grenoble: 20 Jan
Won 24-5
Charlton (Salford)
Fielding (Salford) 3t
Willicombe (Halifax) 1t
Hesketh (Salford)
Redfearn, D (Bradford)
Gill, K (Salford) 1t
Bates, A (Dewsbury)
Clawson (Oldham) 3g
Bridges (Featherstone)
Lockwood (Castleford)
Dixon, C (Salford)
Nicholls (St. Helens)
*Laughton (Widnes) 1t
Sub: Watkins, D (Salford)
Gray (Wigan)

1974 France
Wigan: 17 Feb
Won 29-0
Charlton (Salford) 2t
Fielding (Salford)
Willicombe (Wigan) 1t
Hesketh (Salford)
Redfearn, D (Bradford) 2t
Gill, K (Salford)
Bates, A (Dewsbury)
Clawson (Oldham) 2g
Bridges (Featherstone)
Fogerty (Rochdale)
Dixon, C (Salford)
Nicholls (St. Helens)
*Laughton (Widnes) 1t
Sub: Watkins, D (Salford) 1g
Gray (Wigan) 1t,1g

1974 Australia
Brisbane: 15 June
Lost 6-12
Charlton (Salford)
Redfearn, D (Bradford)
Watkins, D (Salford) 1g
*Hesketh (Salford)
Bevan, J (Warrington)
Millward (Hull KR)
Nash (Featherstone)
Clawson (Oldham) 2g
Bridges (Featherstone)
Mills (Widnes)
Dixon, C (Salford)
Thompson, J (Featherstone)
Nicholls (St. Helens)
Sub: Eckersley (St. Helens)
Gray (Wigan)

1974 Australia
Sydney: 6 July
Won 16-11
Charlton (Salford)
Dyl (Leeds)
Eckersley (St. Helens)
*Hesketh (Salford)
Millward (Hull KR)
Gill, K (Salford) 1t
Nash (Featherstone)
Mills (Widnes)
Gray (Wigan) 3g,1dg
Thompson, J (Featherstone)
Dixon, C (Salford) 1t
Chisnall, E (St. Helens) 1t
Nicholls (St. Helens)
Sub: Norton (Castleford)

1974 Australia
Sydney: 20 July
Lost 18-22
Charlton (Salford)
Richards (Salford) 1t
Dyl (Leeds) 1t
*Hesketh (Salford)
Bevan, J (Warrington)
Gill, K (Salford)
Nash (Featherstone)
Clawson (Oldham)
Gray (Wigan) 6g
Thompson, J (Featherstone)
Dixon, C (Salford)
Chisnall, E (St. Helens)
Nicholls (St. Helens)
Sub: Millward (Hull KR)
    Rose, P (Hull KR)

1974 New Zealand
Auckland: 27 July
Lost 8-13
Charlton (Salford)
Redfearn, D (Bradford)
Dyl (Leeds)
*Hesketh (Salford)
Bevan, J (Warrington) 1t
Gill, K (Salford)
Nash (Featherstone) 1t
Clawson (Oldham) 1g
Gray (Wigan)
Thompson, J (Featherstone)
Dixon, C (Salford)
Norton (Castleford)
Nicholls (St. Helens)
Sub: Ashcroft (Warrington)

1974 New Zealand
Christchurch: 4 Aug
Won 17-8
Charlton (Salford)
Redfearn, D (Bradford) 1t
Dyl (Leeds) 1t
Dixon, C (Salford)
Richards (Salford)
*Hesketh (Salford) 1t
Nash (Featherstone)
Mills (Widnes)
Gray (Wigan) 4g
Thompson, J (Featherstone)
Chisnall, E (St. Helens)
Norton (Castleford)
Nicholls (St. Helens)
Sub: Bates, A (Dewsbury)

1974 New Zealand
Auckland: 10 Aug
Won 20-0
Charlton (Salford)
Redfearn, D (Bradford) 1t
Willicombe (Wigan)
Dyl (Leeds) 1t
Bevan, J (Warrington) 2t
*Hesketh (Salford) 1t
Nash (Featherstone)
Clawson (Oldham)
Gray (Wigan) 4g
Thompson, J (Featherstone)
Chisnall, E (St. Helens)
Dixon, C (Salford)
Nicholls (St. Helens)
Sub: Bates, A (Dewsbury)
    Ramsey (Bradford)

1977 France (WC)
Auckland: 5 June
Won 23-4
Fairbairn (Wigan) 7g
Fielding (Salford)
Holmes (Leeds)
Dyl (Leeds) 1t
Wright, S (Widnes) 1t
*Millward (Hull KR) 1t
Nash (Salford)
Thompson, J (Featherstone)
Ward, D (Leeds)
Pitchford, S (Leeds)
Bowman, E (Workington)
Nicholls (St. Helens)
Hogan (Barrow)
Sub: Gill, K (Salford)
    Casey (Hull KR)

1977 New Zealand (WC)
Christchurch: 12 June
Won 30-12
Fairbairn (Wigan) 6g
Wright, S (Widnes) 2t
Holmes (Leeds)
Dyl (Leeds)
Francis, W (Wigan)
*Millward (Hull KR) 1t
Nash (Salford)
Thompson, J (Featherstone)
Ward, D (Leeds)
Pitchford, S (Leeds)
Bowman, E (Workington) 1t
Nicholls (St. Helens) 1t
Hogan (Barrow) 1t
Sub: Casey (Hull KR)

1977 Australia (WC)
Brisbane: 18 June
Lost 5-19
Fairbairn (Wigan) 1g
Wright, S (Widnes)
Francis, W (Wigan)
Dyl (Leeds)
Fielding (Salford)
*Millward (Hull KR) 1t
Nash (Salford)
Thompson, J (Featherstone)
Ward, D (Leeds)
Pitchford, S (Leeds)
Bowman, E (Workington)
Nicholls (St. Helens)
Hogan (Barrow)
Sub: Holmes (Leeds)
    Smith, P (Featherstone)

1977 Australia (WC)
Sydney: 25 June
Lost 12-13
Fairbairn (Wigan) 3g
Wright, S (Widnes)
Holmes (Leeds)
Dyl (Leeds)
Francis, W (Wigan)
*Millward (Hull KR)
Nash (Salford)
Thompson, J (Featherstone)
Elwell (Widnes)
Pitchford, S (Leeds) 1t
Bowman, E (Workington)
Casey (Hull KR)
Hogan (Barrow)
Sub: Gill, K (Salford) 1t
    Smith, P (Featherstone)

1978 Australia
Wigan: 21 Oct
Lost 9-15
Fairbairn (Wigan) 3g
Wright, S (Widnes)
Hughes (Widnes)
Cunningham (St. Helens)
Bevan, J (Warrington) 1t
*Millward (Hull KR)
Nash (Salford)
Thompson, J (Bradford)
Ward, D (Leeds)
Rose, P (Hull KR)
Nicholls (St. Helens)
Casey (Hull KR)
Norton (Hull)
Sub: Holmes (Leeds)
    Hogan (Barrow)

1979 Australia
Brisbane: 16 June
Lost 0-35
Woods, J (Leigh)
Barends (Bradford)
Joyner (Castleford)
Hughes (Widnes)
Mathias (St. Helens)
Holmes (Leeds)
Stephens (Castleford)
Mills (Widnes)
Ward, D (Leeds)
Skerrett (Wakefield)
Nicholls (St. Helens)
*Laughton (Widnes)
Norton (Hull)
Sub: Evans, S (Featherstone)
    Hogan (Hull KR)

1979 New Zealand
Auckland: 21 July
Won 16-8
Fairbairn (Wigan) 1t,2g
Evans, S (Featherstone) 1t
Joyner (Castleford)
Smith, M (Hull KR) 1t
Hughes (Widnes) 1t
Holmes (Leeds)
Stephens (Castleford)
Casey (Bradford)
Ward, D (Leeds)
*Nicholls (St. Helens)
Hogan (Hull KR)
Grayshon (Bradford)
Adams, M (Widnes)
Sub: Lockwood (Hull KR)

1978 Australia
Bradford: 5 Nov
Won 18-14
Fairbairn (Wigan) 6g
Wright, S (Widnes) 2t
Joyner (Castleford)
Dyl (Leeds)
Atkinson, J (Leeds)
*Millward (Hull KR)
Nash (Salford)
Mills (Widnes)
Fisher (Bradford)
Lockwood (Hull KR)
Nicholls (St. Helens)
Lowe, P (Hull KR)
Norton (Hull)
Sub: Holmes (Leeds)
    Rose, P (Hull KR)

1979 Australia
Sydney: 30 June
Lost 16-24
Fairbairn (Wigan)
Barends (Bradford)
Joyner (Castleford) 1t
Woods, J (Leigh) 5g
Hughes (Widnes) 1t
Holmes (Leeds)
Stephens (Castleford)
*Nicholls (St. Helens)
Ward, D (Leeds)
Skerrett (Wakefield)
Casey (Bradford)
Grayshon (Bradford)
Adams, M (Widnes)
Sub: Evans, S (Featherstone)
    Watkinson (Hull KR)

1979 New Zealand
Christchurch: 5 Aug
Won 22-7
Fairbairn (Wigan) 5g
Evans, S (Featherstone) 1t
Joyner (Castleford)
Smith, M (Hull KR)
Hughes (Widnes) 1t
Holmes (Leeds)
Stephens (Castleford)
*Nicholls (St. Helens)
Ward, D (Leeds)
Skerrett (Wakefield)
Casey (Bradford) 1t
Grayshon (Bradford) 1t
Adams, M (Widnes)

1978 Australia
Leeds: 18 Nov
Lost 6-23
Fairbairn (Wigan)
Wright, S (Widnes)
Joyner (Castleford)
Bevan, J (Warrington) 1t
Atkinson, J (Leeds)
*Millward (Hull KR) 1t
Nash (Salford)
Mills (Widnes)
Fisher (Bradford)
Farrar (Hull)
Nicholls (St. Helens)
Lowe, P (Hull KR)
Norton (Hull)
Sub: Holmes (Leeds)
    Rose, P (Hull KR)

1979 Australia
Sydney: 14 July
Lost 2-28
Fairbairn (Wigan) 1g
Evans, S (Featherstone)
Joyner (Castleford)
Woods, J (Leigh)
Hughes (Widnes)
Topliss (Wakefield)
Redfearn, A (Bradford)
*Nicholls (St. Helens)
Ward, D (Leeds)
Casey (Bradford)
Hogan (Hull KR)
Grayshon (Bradford)
Norton (Hull)
Sub: Holmes (Leeds)
    Adams, M (Widnes)

1979 New Zealand
Auckland: 11 Aug
Lost 11-18
Fairbairn (Wigan) 1g
Evans, S (Featherstone)
Joyner (Castleford)
Smith, M (Hull KR) 1t
Hughes (Widnes) 1t
Holmes (Leeds)
Stephens (Castleford) 1t
Skerrett (Wakefield)
Ward, D (Leeds)
*Nicholls (St. Helens)
Casey (Bradford)
Grayshon (Bradford)
Adams, M (Widnes)
Sub: Woods, J (Leigh)
    Hogan (Hull KR)

321

1980 New Zealand
Wigan: 18 Oct
Drew 14-14
*Fairbairn (Wigan) 4g
Camilleri (Barrow) 1t
Joyner (Castleford)
Smith, M (Hull KR) 1t
Bentley (Widnes)
Hartley, S (Hull KR)
Dick (Leeds)
Holdstock (Hull KR)
Watkinson (Hull KR)
Skerrett (Hull)
Gorley, L (Widnes)
Grayshon (Bradford)
Casey (Hull KR)
Sub: Pinner (St. Helens)

1980 New Zealand
Bradford: 2 Nov
Lost 8-12
*Fairbairn (Wigan) 4g
Drummond (Leigh)
Joyner (Castleford)
Smith, M (Hull KR)
Camilleri (Barrow)
Kelly (Warrington)
Dick (Leeds)
Holdstock (Hull KR)
Elwell (Widnes)
Shaw, G (Widnes)
Casey (Hull KR)
Grayshon (Bradford)
Pinner (St. Helens)
Sub: Evans, S (Featherstone)
    Gorley, L (Widnes)

1980 New Zealand
Leeds: 15 Nov
Won 10-2
Burke (Widnes) 2g
Drummond (Leigh) 2t
Joyner (Castleford)
Evans, S (Featherstone)
Atkinson, J (Leeds)
Woods, J (Leigh)
Walker (Whitehaven)
Skerrett (Hull)
Elwell (Widnes)
*Casey (Hull KR)
Gorley, P (St. Helens)
Adams, M (Widnes)
Norton (Hull)

1981 France
Hull: 6 Dec
Won 37-0
Fairbairn (Hull KR) 1g
Drummond (Leigh) 2t
Smith, M (Hull KR)
Woods, J (Leigh) 1t,7g
Gill (Wigan) 3t
Hartley (Hull KR) 1t
Gregory, A (Widnes)
Grayshon (Bradford)
*Ward, D (Leeds)
Skerrett (Hull)
Gorley, L (Widnes)
Gorley, P (St. Helens)
Norton (Hull)
Sub: Burke (Widnes)
    Szymala (Barrow)

1981 France
Marseilles: 20 Dec
Lost 2-19
Burke (Widnes)
Drummond (Leigh)
Smith, M (Hull KR)
Woods, J (Leigh) 1g
Gill (Wigan)
Hartley (Hull KR)
Gregory, A (Widnes)
*Grayshon (Bradford)
Watkinson (Hull KR)
Skerrett (Hull)
Gorley, L (Widnes)
Szymala (Barrow)
Norton (Hull)
Sub: Gorley, P (St. Helens)

1982 Australia
Hull City FC: 30 Oct
Lost 4-40
Fairbairn (Hull KR)
Drummond (Leigh)
Hughes (Widnes)
Dyl (Leeds)
Evans, S (Hull)
Woods, J (Leigh)
*Nash (Salford)
Grayshon (Bradford)
Ward, D (Leeds)
Skerrett (Hull)
Gorley, L (Widnes)
Crooks, L (Hull) 2g
Norton (Hull)
Sub: Heron, D (Leeds)

1982 Australia
Wigan: 20 Nov
Lost 6-27
Mumby (Bradford) 3g
Drummond (Leigh)
Smith, M (Hull KR)
Stephenson, D (Wigan)
Gill (Wigan)
Holmes (Leeds)
Kelly, K (Warrington)
*Grayshon (Bradford)
Dalgreen (Fulham)
Skerrett (Hull)
Eccles (Warrington)
Burton (Hull KR)
Heron, D (Leeds)
Sub: Woods, J (Leigh)
    Rathbone (Bradford)

1982 Australia
Leeds: 28 Nov
Lost 8-32
Fairbairn (Hull KR)
Drummond (Leigh)
Stephenson, D (Wigan)
Smith, M (Hull KR)
Evans (Hull) 1t
*Topliss (Hull)
Gregory, A (Widnes)
O'Neill, M (Widnes)
Noble (Bradford)
Rose (Hull)
Smith, P (Featherstone)
Crooks, L (Hull) 2g,1dg
Crane (Hull)
Sub: Courtney (Warrington)

1983 France
Carcassonne: 20 Feb
Won 20-5
Burke (Widnes) 1g
Drummond (Leigh)
Joyner (Castleford) 1t
Duane, R (Warrington)
Lydon (Widnes) 1t,3g
Myler, A (Widnes)
Gregory, A (Widnes)
O'Neill, M (Widnes)
Noble (Bradford) 1t
Goodway (Oldham) 1t
*Casey (Hull KR)
Rathbone (Bradford)
Flanagan (Oldham)
Sub: Woods, J (Leigh)
    Smith, P (Featherstone)

1983 France
Hull: 6 March
Won 17-5
Mumby (Bradford) 4g
Drummond (Leigh)
Joyner (Castleford)
Duane, R (Warrington) 1t
Lydon (Widnes)
Myler, A (Widnes)
Gregory, A (Widnes) 1t
O'Neill, M (Widnes)
Noble (Bradford)
Goodway (Oldham)
*Casey (Hull KR)
Rathbone (Bradford)
Flanagan (Oldham)
Sub: Smith, P (Featherstone) 1t

1984 France
Avignon: 29 Jan
Won 12-0
*Mumby (Bradford)
Drummond (Leigh)
Duane, R (Warrington)
Foy, D (Oldham) 1t
Clark (Hull KR)
Lydon (Widnes)
Cairns (Barrow)
Rayne, Keith (Leeds)
Watkinson (Hull KR)
Goodway (Oldham) 1t
Worrall, M (Oldham)
Hobbs, D (Featherstone)
Hall (Hull KR)
Sub: Hanley (Bradford)
    Crooks, L (Hull) 2g

1984 France
Leeds: 17 Feb
Won 10-0
Mumby (Bradford)
Clark (Hull KR)
Joyner (Castleford)
Schofield (Hull)
Basnett (Widnes)
Hanley (Bradford)
Cairns (Barrow)
Rayne, Keith (Leeds)
*Noble (Bradford)
Ward, K (Castleford)
Jasiewicz (Bradford)
Hobbs, D (Featherstone) 5g
Hall (Hull KR)
Sub: Smith, M (Hull KR)
    Smith, P (Featherstone)

1984 Australia
Sydney: 9 June
Lost 8-25
Burke (Widnes) 2g
Drummond (Leigh)
Schofield (Hull) 1t
Mumby (Bradford)
Hanley (Bradford)
Foy, D (Oldham)
Holding (St. Helens)
Crooks, L (Hull)
*Noble (Bradford)
Goodway (Oldham)
Burton (Hull KR)
Worrall, M (Oldham)
Adams (Widnes)
Sub: Lydon (Widnes)
    Hobbs, D (Featherstone)

1984 Australia
Brisbane: 26 June
Lost 6-18
Burke (Widnes) 1g
Drummond (Leigh)
Schofield (Hull) 1t
Mumby (Bradford)
Hanley (Bradford)
Myler, A (Widnes)
Holding (St. Helens)
Rayne, Keith (Leeds)
*Noble (Bradford)
Crooks, L (Hull)
Burton (Hull KR)
Goodway (Oldham)
Worrall (Oldham)
Sub: Gregory, A (Widnes)
    Adams (Widnes)

1984 Australia
Sydney: 7 July
Lost 7-20
Burke (Widnes) 1g
Drummond (Leigh)
Schofield (Hull)
Mumby (Bradford)
Hanley (Bradford) 1t
Myler, A (Widnes)
Holding (St. Helens) 1dg
Hobbs, D (Featherstone)
*Noble (Bradford)
Case (Wigan)
Burton (Hull KR)
Goodway (Oldham)
Adams (Widnes)

1984 New Zealand
Auckland: 14 July
Lost 0-12
Burke (Widnes)
Drummond (Leigh)
Schofield (Hull)
Mumby (Bradford)
Hanley (Bradford)
Smith, M (Hull KR)
Holding (St. Helens)
Hobbs, D (Featherstone)
*Noble (Bradford)
Case (Wigan)
Burton (Hull KR)
Goodway (Oldham)
Adams (Widnes)

1984 New Zealand
Christchurch: 22 July
Lost 12-28
Burke (Widnes) 2g
Drummond (Leigh)
Hanley (Bradford) 1t
Mumby (Bradford)
Lydon (Widnes)
Myler, A (Widnes) 1t
Gregory, A (Widnes)
Hobbs, D (Featherstone)
*Noble (Bradford)
Case (Wigan)
Burton (Hull KR)
Goodway (Oldham)
Adams (Widnes)
Sub: Joyner (Castleford)
    Beardmore, K (Castleford)

1984 New Zealand
Auckland: 28 July
Lost 16-32
Burke (Widnes) 4g
Drummond (Leigh)
Hanley (Bradford) 1t
Mumby (Bradford) 1t
Lydon (Widnes)
Myler, A (Widnes)
Gregory, A (Widnes)
Hobbs, D (Featherstone)
*Noble (Bradford)
Case (Wigan)
Adams (Widnes)
Goodway (Oldham)
Flanagan (Oldham)
Sub: Donlan (Leigh)
    Joyner (Castleford)

323

1984 Papua New Guinea
Mount Hagen: 5 Aug
Won 38-20
Burke (Widnes) 1t,5g
Drummond (Leigh) 2t
Hanley (Bradford) 1t
Mumby (Bradford) 1t
Lydon (Widnes)
Myler, A (Widnes)
Gregory, A (Widnes)
Rayne, Keith (Leeds) 1t
*Noble (Bradford)
Goodway (Oldham)
Flanagan (Oldham)
Hobbs, D (Featherstone) 1t
Adams (Widnes)
Sub: Donlan (Leigh)
    Proctor (Hull)

1985 France
Leeds: 1 March
Won 50-4
Edwards (Wigan)
Ledger (St. Helens)
Creasser (Leeds) 8g
Gribbin (Whitehaven) 1t
Gill (Wigan) 1t
Hanley (Bradford) 2t
Fox (Featherstone) 2t,1g
Dickinson (Leeds)
Watkinson (Hull KR) 1t
Dannatt (Hull)
*Goodway (Oldham)
Rathbone (Bradford)
Divorty (Hull) 1t
Sub: Gibson (Batley)
    Platt (St. Helens)

1985 France
Perpignan: 17 March
Lost 16-24
Johnson, C (Leigh)
Clark (Hull KR)
Creasser (Leeds) 1g
Foy, D (Oldham) 1t
Ford, P (Wigan) 2t
*Hanley (Bradford)
Fox (Featherstone)
Dickinson (Leeds)
Kiss (Wigan)
Wane (Wigan)
Dannatt (Hull)
Rathbone (Bradford)
Divorty (Hull) 1g
Sub: Harkin (Hull KR)
    Powell, R (Leeds)

1985 New Zealand
Leeds: 19 Oct
Lost 22-24
Burke (Widnes) 3g
Drummond (Leigh)
Schofield (Hull)
Hanley (Wigan) 1t
Lydon (Widnes) 1t,2g
Myler, A (Widnes)
Fox (Featherstone)
Crooks, L (Hull)
Watkinson (Hull KR)
Fieldhouse (Widnes)
Goodway (Wigan) 1t
Potter (Wigan)
*Pinner (St. Helens)
Sub: Arkwright (St. Helens)

1985 New Zealand
Wigan: 2 Nov
Won 25-8
Burke (Widnes)
Drummond (Leigh)
Schofield (Hull) 4t
Hanley (Wigan)
Lydon (Widnes) 4g
Myler, A (Widnes)
Fox (Featherstone)
Grayshon (Leeds)
Watkinson (Hull KR)
Fieldhouse (Widnes)
Goodway (Wigan)
Potter (Wigan)
*Pinner (St. Helens) 1dg
Sub: Edwards (Wigan)
    Burton (Hull KR)

1985 New Zealand (Also WC)
Elland Rd, Leeds: 9 Nov
Drew 6-6
Burke (Widnes)
Drummond (Leigh)
Schofield (Hull)
Edwards (Wigan)
Lydon (Widnes)
Hanley (Wigan)
Fox (Featherstone)
Grayshon (Leeds)
Watkinson (Hull KR)
Fieldhouse (Widnes)
Goodway (Wigan)
Potter (Wigan)
*Pinner (St. Helens)
Sub: Arkwright (St. Helens)
    Crooks, L (Hull) 3g

1986 France (Also WC)
Avignon: 16 Feb
Drew 10-10
Burke (Widnes)
Drummond (Leigh)
Schofield (Hull)
Hanley (Wigan) 1t
Gill (Wigan)
Myler, A (Widnes)
Fox (Featherstone)
Crooks, L (Hull) 3g
Watkinson (Hull KR)
Wane (Wigan)
Potter (Wigan)
Fieldhouse (Widnes)
*Pinner (St. Helens)
Sub: Platt (St. Helens)

1986 France
Wigan: 1 March
Won 24-10
Lydon (Wigan)
Drummond (Leigh) 1t
Schofield (Hull) 1t,2g
Marchant (Castleford) 1t
Laws (Hull KR)
Myler, A (Widnes)
Fox (Featherstone)
Crooks, L (Hull) 2g
*Watkinson (Hull KR)
Fieldhouse (Widnes)
Rayne, Kevin (Leeds)
James (Halifax) 1t
Potter (Wigan)
Sub: Platt (St. Helens)

1986 Australia
Man. U. FC: 25 Oct
Lost 16-38
Lydon (Wigan) 1t
Marchant (Castleford)
Schofield (Hull) 2t
Hanley (Wigan)
Gill (Wigan) 1g
Myler, A (Widnes)
Fox (Featherstone)
Ward (Castleford)
*Watkinson (Hull KR)
Fieldhouse (Widnes)
Crooks, L (Hull) 1g
Potter (Wigan)
Goodway (Wigan)

1986 Australia
Elland Rd, Leeds: 8 Nov
Lost 4-34
Lydon (Wigan)
Ledger (St. Helens)
Schofield (Hull) 1t
Marchant (Castleford)
Gill (Wigan)
Myler, A (Widnes)
Fox (Featherstone)
Ward (Castleford)
*Watkinson (Hull KR)
Fieldhouse (St. Helens)
Crooks, L (Hull)
Potter (Wigan)
Goodway (Wigan)
Sub: Edwards (Wigan)
      Platt (St. Helens)

1986 Australia (Also WC)
Wigan: 22 Nov
Lost 15-24
Lydon (Wigan) 2g
Gill (Wigan) 1g
Schofield (Hull) 2t,1dg
Stephenson (Wigan)
Basnett (Widnes)
Myler, A (Widnes)
Gregory, A (Warrington)
Ward (Castleford)
*Watkinson (Hull KR)
Crooks, L (Hull)
Burton (Hull KR)
Goodway (Wigan)
Pinner (Widnes)
Sub: Potter (Wigan)

1987 France (Also WC)
Leeds: 24 Jan
Won 52-4
Lydon (Wigan) 1t,8g
Forster (Warrington) 1t
Schofield (Hull)
Stephenson (Wigan)
Gill (Wigan)
*Hanley (Wigan) 2t
Edwards (Wigan) 2t
Hobbs (Oldham)
Beardmore, K (Castleford)
Crooks, L (Hull)
Goodway (Wigan) 1t
Haggerty (St. Helens)
Gregory, M (Warrington) 2t
Sub: Creasser (Leeds)
      England (Castleford)

1987 France
Carcassonne: 8 Feb
Won 20-10
Lydon (Wigan) 4g
Forster (Warrington)
Schofield (Hull)
*Hanley (Wigan) 1t
Gill (Wigan) 1t
Edwards (Wigan)
Gregory, A (Wigan)
Hobbs (Oldham)
England (Castleford)
Burton (Hull KR)
Haggerty (St. Helens)
Gregory, M (Warrington)
Sub: Dixon (Halifax)

1987 Papua New Guinea (Also WC)
Wigan: 24 Oct
Won 42-0
Hampson (Wigan)
Drummond (Warrington)
Stephenson (Wigan) 7g
Lydon (Wigan) 1t
Ford (Bradford) 1t
Edwards (Wigan) 2t
Gregory, A (Wigan) 1t
Ward (Castleford)
Groves (St. Helens)
Case (Wigan)
Medley (Leeds) 1t
Goodway (Wigan)
*Hanley (Wigan) 1t
Sub: Woods (Warrington)
      Fairbank (Bradford)

1988 France
Avignon: 24 Jan
Won 28-14
Hampson (Wigan)
Drummond (Warrington) 1t
Schofield (Leeds) 2t
Loughlin (St. Helens) 3g
Offiah (Widnes) 1t
*Hanley (Wigan) 1t
Edwards (Wigan)
Ward (Castleford)
Beardmore, K (Castleford)
Waddell (Oldham)
Powell, R (Leeds)
Medley (Leeds)
Platt (St. Helens)
Sub: Creasser (Leeds) 1g
      Dixon (Halifax)

1988 France
Leeds: 6 Feb
Won 30-12
Hampson (Wigan)
Plange (Castleford) 1t
Schofield (Leeds) 1t,5g
*Hanley (Wigan) 2t
Ford (Bradford)
Edwards (Wigan)
Gregory, A (Wigan) 1t
Ward (Castleford)
Beardmore, K (Castleford)
Waddell (Oldham)
Powell, R (Leeds)
Dixon (Halifax)
Platt (St. Helens)
Sub: Stephenson (Leeds)
      Medley (Leeds)

1988 Papua New Guinea (Also WC)
Port Moresby: 22 May
Won 42-22
Loughlin (St. Helens) 7g
Ford (Bradford)
Schofield (Leeds) 2t
Stephenson (Leeds) 1t
Gill (Wigan) 2t
Edwards (Wigan)
Gregory, A (Wigan)
Ward (Castleford)
Beardmore, K (Castleford)
Case (Wigan)
Medley (Leeds) 1t
Gregory, M (Warrington) 1t
*Hanley (Wigan)
Sub: Hulme, D (Widnes)
      Dixon (Halifax)

1988 Australia
Sydney: 11 June
Lost 6-17
Loughlin (St. Helens) 1g
Ford (Bradford)
Schofield (Leeds)
Stephenson (Leeds)
Offiah (Widnes)
Hulme, D (Widnes)
Gregory, A (Wigan)
Ward (Castleford)
Beardmore, K (Castleford)
Dixon (Halifax)
Gregory, M (Warrington)
Platt (St. Helens)
*Hanley (Wigan) 1t
Sub: Gill (Wigan)
      Powell, R (Leeds)

1988 Australia
Brisbane: 28 June
Lost 14-34
Loughlin (St. Helens) 3g
Gill (Wigan)
Ford (Bradford) 1t
*Hanley (Wigan)
Offiah (Widnes) 1t
Hulme, D (Widnes)
Gregory, A (Wigan)
Ward (Castleford)
Beardmore, K (Castleford)
Powell, R (Leeds)
Dixon (Halifax)
Platt (St. Helens)
Gregory, M (Warrington)
Sub: Wright (Widnes)
        Hulme, P (Widnes)

1988 Australia (Also WC)
Sydney: 9 July
Won 26-12
Ford (Bradford) 1t
Gill (Wigan) 2t
Stephenson (Leeds)
Loughlin (St. Helens) 3g
Offiah (Widnes) 1t
Hulme, D (Widnes)
Gregory, A (Wigan)
Ward (Castleford)
Hulme, P (Widnes)
Waddell (Oldham)
Gregory, M (Warrington) 1t
Powell, R (Leeds)
*Hanley (Wigan)
Sub: Case (Wigan)

1988 New Zealand (Also WC)
Christchurch: 17 July
Lost 10-12
Ford (Bradford)
Gill (Wigan)
Stephenson (Leeds)
Loughlin (St. Helens) 1t,1g
Offiah (Widnes)
Hulme, D (Widnes) 1t
Gregory, A (Wigan)
Ward (Castleford)
Beardmore, K (Castleford)
Waddell (Oldham)
Gregory, M (Warrington)
Powell, R (Leeds)
*Hanley (Wigan)
Sub: Hulme, P (Widnes)

1989 France
Wigan: 21 Jan
Won 26-10
Tait (Widnes)
Ford (Leeds) 1t
Loughlin (St. Helens) 3g
Lydon (Wigan) 1t
Offiah (Widnes) 1t
Edwards (Wigan) 1t
Gregory, A (Wigan)
Ward (Castleford)
Beardmore, K (Castleford)
Waddell (Leeds)
Gregory, M (Warrington)
Powell, R (Leeds)
*Hanley (Wigan) 1t
Sub: Williams (Salford)
        Eyres (Widnes)

1989 France
Avignon: 5 Feb
Won 30-8
Tait (Widnes) 1t
Ford (Leeds) 2t
Williams (Salford) 1t
Lydon (Wigan) 3g
Offiah (Widnes)
Edwards (Wigan) 1t
Gregory, A (Wigan)
Ward (Castleford)
Beardmore, K (Castleford)
Crooks, L (Leeds)
Gregory, M (Warrington)
Powell, R (Leeds)
*Hanley (Wigan) 1t
Sub: Hampson (Wigan)
        England (Castleford)

1989 New Zealand
Man. U. FC: 21 Oct
Lost 16-24
Tait (Widnes) 1t
Ford (Leeds) 1t
Currier (Widnes)
Loughlin (St. Helens) 2g
Offiah (Widnes) 1t
Hulme, D (Widnes)
Gregory, A (Wigan)
Skerrett (Bradford)
Beardmore, K (Castleford)
Hobbs (Bradford)
Goodway (Wigan)
Platt (Wigan)
*Gregory, M (Warrington)
Sub: Edwards (Wigan)
        Newlove, P (Featherstone)

1989 New Zealand
Elland Rd, Leeds: 28 Oct
Won 26-6
Hampson (Wigan)
Ford (Leeds)
Newlove, P (Featherstone)
Loughlin (St. Helens) 5g
Offiah (Widnes) 1t
Edwards (Wigan) 1t
Hulme, D (Widnes)
Skerrett (Bradford)
Hulme, P (Widnes)
Platt (Wigan)
Goodway (Wigan) 2t
Powell, R (Leeds)
*Gregory, M (Warrington)
Sub: Hobbs (Bradford)
        Fox (Featherstone)

1989 New Zealand (Also WC)
Wigan: 11 Nov
Won 10-6
Tait (Widnes) 1t
Ford (Leeds)
Newlove, P (Featherstone)
Loughlin (St. Helens) 1g
Offiah (Widnes) 1t
Edwards (Wigan)
Hulme, D (Widnes)
Skerrett (Bradford)
Hulme, P (Widnes)
Platt (Wigan)
Goodway (Wigan)
Powell, R (Leeds)
*Gregory, M (Warrington)
Sub: Lydon (Wigan)
        England (Castleford)

1990 France
Perpignan: 18 Mar
Won 8-4
Tait (Widnes)
Lydon (Wigan)
Schofield (Leeds) 2g
Loughlin (St. Helens)
Offiah (Widnes) 1t
Edwards (Wigan)
Gregory, A (Wigan)
Skerrett (Bradford)
Beardmore, K (Castleford)
Platt (Wigan)
Gregory, M (Warrington)
Goodway (Wigan)
*Hanley (Wigan)
Sub: Powell, D (Sheffield)
        Betts (Wigan)

1990 France

Leeds: 7 Apr

Lost 18-25

Tait (Widnes) 1t
Cordle (Bradford) 1t
Schofield (Leeds)
Gibson (Leeds)
Offiah (Widnes) 1t
Steadman (Castleford) 3g
*Edwards (Wigan)
Skerrett (Bradford)
Beardmore, K (Castleford)
England (Castleford)
Betts (Wigan)
Fairbank, K (Bradford)
Gregory, M (Warrington)
Sub: Irwin (Castleford)
    Bishop (Hull KR)

1990 Papua New Guinea

Goroka: 27 May

Lost 18-20

Tait (Widnes)
Eastwood (Hull) 1t
Powell, D (Sheffield)
Davies (Widnes) 1t,3g
Gibson (Leeds)
Schofield (Leeds)
Goulding (Wigan) 1t
Powell, R (Leeds)
Jackson (Hull)
Dixon (Leeds)
Betts (Wigan)
Fairbank, K (Bradford)
*Gregory, M (Warrington)
Sub: Irwin (Castleford)
    England (Castleford)

1990 Papua New Guinea (Also WC)

Port Moresby: 2 June

Won 40-8

Tait (Widnes)
Eastwood (Hull) 1t
Davies (Widnes) 6g
Powell, D (Sheffield) 1t
Gibson (Leeds) 2t
Schofield (Leeds) 1t
Goulding (Wigan) 1t
Powell, R (Leeds)
Jackson (Hull)
England (Castleford)
Betts (Wigan)
Dixon (Leeds) 1t
*Gregory, M (Warrington)
Sub: Fox (Featherstone)
    Clarke (Wigan)

1990 New Zealand

Palmerston North: 24 June

Won 11-10

Bibb (Featherstone)
Davies (Widnes) 1t,1g
Lydon (Wigan)
Gibson (Leeds) 1t
Offiah (Widnes)
Schofield (Leeds) 1dg
Goulding (Wigan)
Skerrett (Bradford)
Dermott (Wigan)
England (Castleford)
Betts (Wigan)
Dixon (Leeds)
*Gregory, M (Warrington)
Sub: Powell, D (Sheffield)
    Powell, R (Leeds)

1990 New Zealand

Auckland: 8 July

Won 16-14

Lydon (Wigan)
Davies (Widnes) 2g
Powell, D (Sheffield)
Gibson (Leeds)
Offiah (Widnes) 1t
Schofield (Leeds) 1t
Goulding (Wigan)
Skerrett (Bradford)
Jackson (Hull)
England (Castleford)
Betts (Wigan) 1t
Dixon (Leeds)
*Gregory, M (Warrington)
Sub: Irwin (Castleford)
    Powell, R (Leeds)

1990 New Zealand (Also WC)

Christchurch: 15 July

Lost 18-21

Lydon (Wigan)
Davies (Widnes) 3g
Gibson (Leeds)
Powell, D (Sheffield)
Offiah (Widnes) 1t
Schofield (Leeds) 1t
Goulding (Wigan)
Skerrett (Bradford)
Dermott (Wigan)
England (Castleford)
Betts (Wigan)
Powell, R (Leeds) 1t
*Gregory, M (Warrington)
Sub: Irwin (Castleford)
    Dixon (Leeds)

1990 Australia

Wembley: 27 Oct

Won 19-12

Hampson (Wigan)
Eastwood (Hull) 2t,3g
Powell, D (Sheffield)
Gibson (Leeds)
Offiah (Widnes) 1t
Schofield (Leeds) 1dg
Gregory, A (Wigan)
Harrison (Hull)
Jackson (Hull)
Dixon (Leeds)
Betts (Wigan)
Powell, R (Leeds)
*Hanley (Wigan)
Sub: Fairbank (Bradford)
    Ward (St. Helens)

1990 Australia

Man. U. FC: 10 Nov

Lost 10-14

Hampson (Wigan)
Eastwood (Hull) 1g
Powell, D (Sheffield)
Gibson (Leeds)
Offiah (Widnes)
Schofield (Leeds)
Gregory, A (Wigan)
Harrison (Hull)
Jackson (Hull)
Platt (Wigan)
Betts (Wigan)
Dixon (Leeds) 1t
*Hanley (Wigan)
Sub: Loughlin (St. Helens) 1t
    Ward (St. Helens)

Fourteen-cap Sheffield Eagles centre Daryl Powell.

1990 Australia (Also WC)
Elland Rd, Leeds: 24 Nov
Lost 0-14
Hampson (Wigan)
Eastwood (Hull)
Powell, D (Sheffield)
Gibson (Leeds)
Offiah (Widnes)
Schofield (Leeds)
Gregory, A (Wigan)
Harrison (Hull)
Jackson, L (Hull)
Platt (Wigan)
Betts (Wigan)
Dixon (Leeds)
*Hanley (Wigan)
Sub: Davies (Widnes)
    Gregory, M (Warrington)
    Powell, R (Leeds)

1991 France (Also WC)
Perpignan: 27 Jan
Won 45-10
Hampson (Wigan)
Eastwood (Hull) 6g
Powell, D (Sheffield)
Gibson (Leeds)
Offiah (Widnes) 2t
Schofield (Leeds) 2t,1dg
Edwards (Wigan) 2t
Lucas (Wigan)
Jackson, L (Hull)
Platt (Wigan) 1t
Betts (Wigan) 1t
Holliday (Widnes)
*Hanley (Wigan)
Sub: Aston (Sheffield)
    Ellis, S (Castleford)
    Eyres (Widnes)
    Fairbank (Bradford)

1991 France
Leeds: 16 Feb
Won 60-4
Hampson (Wigan) 1t
Eastwood (Hull) 1t,8g
Powell, D (Sheffield)
Loughlin (St. Helens)
Offiah (Widnes) 5t
Schofield (Leeds) 3t
Edwards (Wigan) 1t
Dannatt (Hull)
Jackson, L (Hull)
Platt (Wigan)
Eyres (Widnes)
Fairbank (Bradford)
*Hanley (Wigan)
Sub: Ellis, K (Warrington)
    Ellis, S (Castleford)
    England (Castleford)
    Powell, R (Leeds)

1991 Papua New Guinea (Also WC)
Wigan: 9 Nov
Won 56-4
Hampson (Wigan)
Newlove, P (Featherstone) 1t
Powell, D (Sheffield) 1t
Davies (Widnes) 8g
Sullivan (St. Helens) 1t
*Schofield (Leeds) 1t
Edwards (Wigan)
Harrison (Halifax)
Dermott (Wigan)
Platt (Wigan)
Betts (Wigan) 1t
Moriarty (Widnes) 2t
Jackson, M (Wakefield) 2t
Sub: Connolly (St. Helens)
    Fox (Featherstone)
    Fairbank (Bradford) 1t
    Price (Wakefield)

1992 France
Perpignan: 16 Feb
Won 30-12
Tait (Widnes)
Devereux (Widnes) 1t
Connolly (St. Helens)
*Davies (Widnes) 3g
Bentley (Leeds) 1t
Griffiths (St. Helens) 1t
Goulding (Leeds)
Crooks (Castleford)
Jackson, L (Hull)
Dixon (Leeds)
Fairbank (Bradford)
Jackson, M (Wakefield)
Holliday (Widnes)
Sub: Powell, D (Sheffield)
    Steadman (Castleford) 2t
    Jones (Hull)
    Eyres (Widnes) 1t

1992 France (Also WC)
Hull: 7 Mar
Won 36-0
Steadman (Castleford)
Eastwood (Hull) 1t,6g
Connolly (St. Helens)
Bateman (Warrington)
Hunte (St. Helens) 1t
Powell, D (Sheffield)
*Edwards (Wigan)
Crooks (Castleford)
Dermott (Wigan) 1t
Skerrett (Wigan)
Betts (Wigan)
Fairbank (Bradford)
Holliday (Widnes) 1t
Sub: Fox (Featherstone) 1t
    Platt (Wigan) 1t
    McNamara (Hull)

GREAT BRITAIN REGISTER

The following is a record of the 604 players who have appeared for Great Britain in 269 Test and World Cup matches.

It does not include matches against France before 1957, the year they were given official Test match status.

Figures in brackets are the total of appearances, with the plus sign indicating substitute appearances, e.g. (7 + 3).

For matches against touring teams, the year given is for the first half of the season.

World Cup matches are in bold letters except when also classified as Test matches. Substitute appearances are in lower case letters.

A - Australia, F - France, NZ - New Zealand, P - Papua New Guinea.

ACKERLEY, A (2) Halifax: 1952 A; 1958 NZ
ADAMS, L (1) Leeds: 1932 A
ADAMS, M (11+2) Widnes: 1979 Aa, NZ3; 1980
NZ; 1984 A2a, NZ3, P
ARKWRIGHT, C (+2) St. Helens: 1985 nz2
ARKWRIGHT, J (6) Warrington: 1936 A2, NZ;
1937 A3
ARMITT, T (8) Swinton: 1933 A; 1936 A2, NZ2;
1937 A3
ASHBY, R (2) Liverpool: 1964 F; Wigan: 1965 F
ASHCROFT, E (11) Wigan: 1947 NZ2; 1950 A3,
NZ; 1954 A3, NZ2
ASHCROFT, K (5+1) Leigh: **1968 A**; 1968 F; 1969
F; **1970 F,NZ**; Warrington: 1974 nz
ASHTON, E (26) Wigan: **1957 A,NZ**; 1958 A2,NZ2;
1959 F, A3; 1960 F2; **1960 NZ,A**; 1961 NZ3;
1962 F3,A3; 1963 F,A2
ASHURST, W (3) Wigan: 1971 NZ; 1972 F2
ASKIN, T (6) Featherstone R: 1928 A3,NZ3
ASPINALL, W (1) Warrington: 1966 NZ
ASTON, L (3) St. Helens: 1947 NZ3
ASTON, M (+1) Sheffield E: 1991 f
ATKINSON, A (11) Castleford: 1929 A3; 1932
A3,NZ3; 1933 A; 1936 A
ATKINSON, J (26) Leeds: **1968 F,NZ**; 1970
A3,NZ3; **1970 A2,F,NZ**; 1971 F2,NZ; 1972 F2;
1972 A2,F,NZ; 1973 A2; 1978 A2; 1980 NZ
AVERY, A (4) Oldham: 1910 A,NZ; 1911 A2

BACON, J (11) Leeds: 1920 A3,NZ3; 1921 A3; 1924
A; 1926 NZ
BARENDS, D (2) Bradford N: 1979 A2
BARTON, F (1) Wigan: 1951 NZ
BARTON, J (2) Wigan: 1960 F; 1961 NZ
BASNETT, J (2) Widnes: 1984 F; 1986 A
BASSETT, A (2) Halifax: 1946 A2
BATEMAN, A (1) Warrington: 1992 F
BATES, A (2+2) Dewsbury: 1974 F2,nz2
BATTEN, E (4) Bradford N: 1946 A2,NZ; 1947 NZ
BATTEN, R (3) Leeds: 1969 F; 1973 A2
BATTEN, W (10) Hunslet: 1907 NZ; 1908 A3; 1910
A2,NZ; 1911 A2; Hull: 1921 A
BAXTER, J (1) Rochdale H: 1907 NZ
BEAMES, J (2) Halifax: 1921 A2
BEARDMORE, K (13+1) Castleford: 1984 nz; 1987
F2; 1988 F2, P, A2, NZ; 1989 F2, NZ; 1990 F2
BELSHAW, W (8) Liverpool S: 1936 A3,NZ2; 1937
A; Warrington: A2
BENNETT, J (7) Rochdale H: 1924 A3,NZ3; Wigan:
1926 NZ
BENTHAM, N (10) Wigan H: 1928 A3,NZ3;
Halifax: 1929 A2; Warrington: 1929 A2
BENTHAM, W (2) Broughton R: 1924 NZ2
BENTLEY, J (1) Leeds: 1992 F
BENTLEY, K (1) Widnes: 1980 NZ
BENYON, W (5+1) St. Helens: 1971 F2,NZnz;
1972 F2

BETTS, D (12+1) Wigan: 1990 fF, P2, NZ3, A3;
1991 F, P; 1992 F
BEVAN, D (1) Wigan: 1952 A
BEVAN, J (6) Warrington: 1974 A2,NZ2; 1978 A2
BEVERLEY, H (6) Hunslet: 1936 A3; 1937 A;
Halifax: A2
BIBB, C (1) Featherstone R: 1990 NZ
BIRCH, J (1) Leeds: 1907 NZ
BISHOP, D (+1) Hull KR: 1990 f
BISHOP, T (15) St. Helens: 1966 A3,NZ2; 1967 A3;
1968 F3; **1968 A,F,NZ**; 1969 F
BLAN, W (3) Wigan: 1951 NZ3
BLINKHORN, T (1) Warrington: 1929 A
BOLTON, D (23) Wigan: 1957 F3; 1958 F,A2; 1959
F,A3; 1960 F2; 1961 NZ3; 1962 F2,A,NZ2;
1963 F,A2
BOSTON, W (31) Wigan: 1954 A2,NZ3; 1955 NZ;
1956 A3; 1957 F5; **1957 F,A**; 1958 F; 1959 A;
1960 F; **1960 A**; 1961 F,NZ3; 1962 F2,A3,NZ;
1963 F
BOTT, C (1) Oldham: 1966 F
BOWDEN, J (3) Huddersfield: 1954 A2,NZ
BOWEN, F (3) St. Helens Recs: 1928 NZ3
BOWERS, J (1) Rochdale H: 1920 NZ
BOWMAN, E (4) Workington T: **1977 F, NZ, A2**
BOWMAN, H (8) Hull: 1924 NZ2; 1926 NZ2; 1928
A2,NZ; 1929 A
BOWMAN, K (3) Huddersfield: 1962 F; 1963 F,A
BOYLEN, F (1) Hull: 1908 A
BRADSHAW, T (6) Wigan: 1947 NZ2; 1950 A3,NZ
BRIDGES, K (3) Featherstone R: 1974 F2,A
BRIGGS, B (1) Huddersfield: 1954 NZ
BROGDEN, S (16) Huddersfield: 1929 A; 1932 A3,
NZ3; 1933 A2; Leeds: 1936 A3,NZ2; 1937 A2
BROOKE, I (13) Bradford N: 1966 A3,NZ2;
Wakefield T: 1967 A3; 1968 F2; **1968 A,F,NZ**
BROOKS, E (3) Warrington: 1908 A3
BROUGH, A (2) Oldham: 1924 A,NZ
BROUGH, J (5) Leeds: 1928 A2,NZ2; 1936 A
BROWN, G (6) Leeds: **1954 F2,NZ,A**; 1955 NZ2
BRYANT, W (4+1) Castleford: 1964 F2; 1966 Aa;
1967 F
BUCKLEY, A (7) Swinton: 1963 A; 1964 F; 1965
NZ; 1966 F,A2
BURGESS, W (16) Barrow: 1924 A3,NZ3; 1926 NZ3;
1928 A3,NZ2; 1929 A2
BURGESS, W (14) Barrow: 1962 F; 1963 A; 1965 NZ2;
1966 F,A3,NZ2; 1967 F,A; 1968 F; Salford: 1969 F
BURGHAM, O (1) Halifax: 1911 A
BURKE, M (14+1) Widnes: 1980 NZ; 1981 fF; 1983 F;
1984 A3, NZ3, P; 1985 NZ3; 1986 F
BURNELL, A (3) Hunslet: 1951 NZ2; 1954 NZ
BURTON, C (8+1) Hull KR: 1982 A; 1984 A3, NZ2;
1985 nz; 1986 A; 1987 F
BURWELL, A (7+1) Hull KR: 1967 a; 1968 F3; **1968
A,F,NZ**; 1969 F
BUTTERS, F (2) Swinton: 1929 A2

CAIRNS, D (2) Barrow: 1984 F2
CAMILLERI, C (2) Barrow: 1980 NZ2
CARLTON, F (2) St. Helens: 1958 NZ; Wigan: 1962 NZ
CARR, C (7) Barrow: 1924 A2,NZ2; 1926 NZ3
CARTWRIGHT, J (7) Leigh: 1920 A,NZ3; 1921 A3
CASE, B (6+1) Wigan: 1984 A, NZ3; 1987 P; 1988 P, a
CASEY, L (12+2) Hull KR: **1977 f,nz,A**; 1978 A; Bradford N: 1979 A2,NZ3; Hull KR: 1980 NZ3; 1983 F2
CASTLE, F (4) Barrow: 1952 A3; 1954 A
CHALLINOR, J (3) Warrington: 1958 A,NZ; **1960 F**
CHARLTON, P (18+1) Workington T: 1965 NZ; Salford: **1970 nz**; 1972 F2; **1972 A2,F,NZ**; 1973 A3; 1974 F2,A3,NZ3
CHERRINGTON, N (1) Wigan: 1960 F
CHILCOTT, J (3) Huddersfield: 1914 A3
CHISNALL, D (2) Leigh: 1970 A; **1970 NZ**
CHISNALL, E (4) St. Helens: 1974 A2,NZ2
CLAMPITT, L (3) Broughton R: 1907 NZ; 1911 A; 1914 NZ
CLARK, D (11) Huddersfield: 1911 A2; 1914 A3; 1920 A3,NZ3
CLARK, G (3) Hull KR: 1984 F2; 1985 F
CLARK, M (5) Leeds: 1968 F2; **1968 A,F,NZ**
CLARKE, C (7) Wigan: 1965 NZ; 1966 F,NZ; 1967 F; 1973 A3
CLARKE, P (+1) Wigan: 1990 p
CLAWSON, T (14) Featherstone R: 1962 F2; Leeds: **1972 A2,F**; Oldham: 1973 A3; 1974 F2,A2,NZ2
CLOSE, D (1) Huddersfield: 1967 F
COLDRICK, A (4) Wigan: 1914 A3,NZ
COLLIER, F (2) Wigan: 1963 A; Widnes: 1964 F
CONNOLLY, G (2+1) St. Helens: 1991 p; 1992 F2
CORDLE, G (1) Bradford N: 1990 F
COULMAN, M (2+1) Salford: 1971 f,NZ2
COURTNEY, N (+1) Warrington: 1982 a
COVERDALE, R (4) Hull: **1954 F2,NZ,A**
CRACKNELL, R (2) Huddersfield: 1951 NZ2
CRANE, M (1) Hull: 1982 A
CREASSER, D (2+2) Leeds: 1985 F2; 1987 f; 1988 f
CROOKS, L (14+2) Hull: 1982 A2; 1984 f, A2; 1985 NZnz; 1986 F2, A3; 1987 F; Leeds: 1989 F; Castleford: 1992 F2
CROSTON, A (1) Castleford: 1937 A
CROWTHER, H (1) Hunslet: 1929 A
CUNLIFFE, J (4) Wigan: 1950 A,NZ; 1951 NZ; 1954 A
CUNLIFFE, W (11) Warrington: 1920 A,NZ2; 1921 A3; 1924 A3,NZ; 1926 NZ
CUNNIFFE, B (1) Castleford: 1937 A
CUNNINGHAM, E (1) St. Helens: 1978 A
CURRAN, G (6) Salford: 1946 A,NZ; 1947 NZ; 1948 A3
CURRIER, A (1) Widnes: 1989 NZ
CURZON, E (1) Salford: 1910 A

DAGNALL, R (4) St. Helens: 1961 NZ2; 1964 F; 1965 F
DALGREEN, J (1) Fulham: 1982 A
DANBY, T (3) Salford: 1950 A2,NZ
DANIELS, A (3) Halifax: 1952 A2; 1955 NZ
DANNATT, A (3) Hull: 1985 F2; 1991 F
DARWELL, J (5) Leigh: 1924 A3,NZ2
DAVIES, A (20) Oldham: 1955 NZ; 1956 A3; **1957 F,A**; 1957 F2; 1958 F,A2,NZ2; 1959 F2,A; **1960 NZ,F,A**; 1960 F
DAVIES, E (3) Oldham: 1920 NZ3
DAVIES, J (7+1) Widnes: 1990 P2, NZ3, a; 1991 P; 1992 F
DAVIES, J (2) Huddersfield: 1911 A2
DAVIES, W (1) Swinton: 1968 F
DAVIES, W.A (2) Leeds: 1914 A,NZ
DAVIES, W.J (1) Castleford: 1933 A
DAVIES, W.T (1) Halifax: 1911 A
DAVIES, W.T.H (3) Bradford N: 1946 NZ; 1947 NZ2
DAWSON, E (1) York: 1956 A
DERMOTT, M (4) Wigan: 1990 NZ2; 1991 P; 1992 F
DEVEREUX, J (1) Widnes: 1992 F
DICK, K (2) Leeds: 1980 NZ2
DICKENSON, G (1) Warrington: 1908 A
DICKINSON, R (2) Leeds: 1985 F2
DINGSDALE, W (3) Warrington: 1929 A2; 1933 A
DIVORTY, G (2) Hull: 1985 F2
DIXON, C (12+2) Halifax: 1968 F; Salford: 1969 F; 1971 NZ; **1972 F**; 1973 a2; 1974 F2,A3,NZ3
DIXON, M (2) Featherstone R: 1962 F; 1964 F
DIXON, P (11+4) Halifax: 1987 f; 1988 fF, p, A2; Leeds: 1990 P2, NZ2nz, A3; 1992 F
DOCKAR, A (1) Hull KR: 1947 NZ
DONLAN, S (+2) Leigh: 1984 nz, p
DRAKE, J (1) Hull: 1960 F
DRAKE, W (1) Hull: 1962 F
DRUMMOND, D (24) Leigh: 1980 NZ2; 1981 F2; 1982 A3; 1983 F2; 1984 F, A3, NZ3, P; 1985 NZ3; 1986 F2; Warrington: 1987 P;1988 F
DUANE, R (3) Warrington: 1983 F2; 1984 F
DUTTON, R (6) Widnes: 1970 NZ2; **1970 A2,F,NZ**
DYL, L (11) Leeds: 1974 A2,NZ3; **1977 F,NZ,A2**; 1978 A; 1982 A
DYSON, F (1) Huddersfield: 1959 A

EASTWOOD, P (8) Hull: 1990 P2, A3; 1991 F2; 1992 F
ECCLES, P (1) Halifax: 1907 NZ
ECCLES, R (1) Warrington: 1982 A
ECKERSLEY, D (2+2) St. Helens: 1973 Aa; 1974 Aa
EDGAR, B (11) Workington T: 1958 A,NZ; 1961 NZ; 1962 A3,NZ; 1965 NZ; 1966 A3
EDWARDS, A (7) Salford: 1936 A3,NZ2; 1937 A2
EDWARDS, D (3+2) Castleford: 1968 f; 1970 A; 1971 NZ2nz

EDWARDS, S (18+3) Wigan: 1985 F,nzNZ; 1986 a; 1987 F2, P; 1988 F2, P; 1989 F2, nzNZ2; 1990 F2; 1991 F2, P; 1992 F

EGAN, J (14) Wigan: 1946 A3; 1947 NZ3; 1948 A3; 1950 A3,NZ2

ELLABY, A (13) St. Helens: 1928 A3,NZ2; 1929 A2; 1932 A3,NZ2; 1933 A

ELLIS, K (+1) Warrington: 1991 f

ELLIS, S (+2) Castleford: 1991 f2

ELWELL, K (3) Widnes: **1977 A;** 1980 NZ2

ENGLAND, K (6+5) Castleford: 1987 fF; 1989 f, nz; 1990 F, pP, NZ3; 1991 f

EVANS, B (10) Swinton: 1926 NZ; 1928 NZ; 1929 A; 1932 A2,NZ3; 1933 A2

EVANS, F (4) Swinton: 1924 A2,NZ2

EVANS, J (4) Hunslet: 1951 NZ; 1952 A3

EVANS, J (3) Swinton: 1926 NZ3

EVANS, R (4) Wigan: 1961 NZ2; 1962 F,NZ

EVANS, S (7+3) Featherstone R: 1979 Aa2,NZ3; 1980 NZnz; Hull: 1982 A2

EYRE, K (1) Hunslet: 1965 NZ

EYRES, R (1+3) Widnes: 1989 f; 1991 fF; 1992 f

FAIRBAIRN, G (17) Wigan: **1977 F,NZ,A2;** 1978 A3; 1979 A2,NZ3; 1980 NZ2; Hull KR: 1981 F; 1982 A2

FAIRBANK, K (5+4) Bradford N: 1987 p; 1990 F, P, a; 1991 fF, p; 1992 F2

FAIRCLOUGH, L (6) St. Helens: 1926 NZ; 1928 A2,NZ2; 1929 A

FARRAR, V (1) Hull: 1978 A

FEATHERSTONE, J (6) Warrington: 1948 A; 1950 NZ2; 1952 A3

FEETHAM, J (8) Hull KR: 1929 A; Salford: 1932 A2,NZ2; 1933 A3

FIELD, H (3) York: 1936 A,NZ2

FIELD, N (1) Batley: 1963 A

FIELDHOUSE, J (7) Widnes: 1985 NZ3; 1986 F2, A; St. Helens: 1986 A

FIELDING, K (3) Salford: 1974 F2; **1977 F**

FILDES, A (15) St. Helens Recs: 1926 NZ2; 1928 A3,NZ3; 1929 A3; St. Helens: 1932 A,NZ3

FISHER, A (11) Bradford N: 1970 A2,NZ3; **1970 A;** Leeds: **1970 A;** 1971 F2; Bradford N: 1978 A2

FLANAGAN, P (14) Hull KR: 1962 F; 1963 F; 1966 A3,NZ; 1967 A3; 1968 F2; **1968 F,NZ;** 1970 A

FLANAGAN, T (4) Oldham: 1983 F2; 1984 NZ, P

FOGERTY, T (2+1) Halifax: 1966 nz; Wigan: 1967 F; Rochdale H: 1974 F

FORD, P (13) Wigan: 1985 F; Bradford N: 1987 P; 1988 F, P, A3, NZ; Leeds: 1989 F2, NZ3

FORSTER, M (2) Warrington: 1987 F2

FOSTER, F (1) Hull KR: 1967 A

FOSTER, P (3) Leigh: 1955 NZ

FOSTER, T (3) Bradford N: 1946 NZ; 1948 A2

FOX, Deryck (9+4) Featherstone R: 1985 F2, NZ3; 1986 F2, A2; 1989 nz; 1990 p; 1991 p; 1992 f

FOX, Don (1) Featherstone R: 1963 A

FOX, N (29) Wakefield T: 1959 F,A2; 1960 F3; 1961 NZ2; 1962 F3,A3,NZ2; 1963 A2,F; 1964 F; 1965 F; 1966 F; 1967 F2,A; 1968 F3; 1969 F

FOY, D (3) Oldham: 1984 F, A; 1985 F

FRANCIS, R (1) Barrow: 1947 NZ

FRANCIS, W (4) Wigan: 1967 A; **1977 NZ,A2**

FRASER, E (16) Warrington: 1958 A3,NZ2; 1959 F2,A; 1960 F3; **1960 F,NZ;** 1961 F,NZ2

FRENCH, R (4) Widnes: 1968 F2; **1968 A,NZ**

FRODSHAM, A (3) St. Helens: 1928 NZ2; 1929 A

GABBITAS, B (1) Hunslet: 1959 F

GALLAGHER, F (12) Dewsbury: 1920 A3; 1921 A; Batley: 1924 A3,NZ3; 1926 NZ2

GANLEY, B (3) Oldham: 1957 F2; 1958 F

GARDINER, D (1) Wigan: 1965 NZ

GEE, K (17) Wigan: 1946 A3,NZ; 1947 NZ3; 1948 A3; 1950 A3,NZ2; 1951 NZ2

GEMMELL, R (3) Leeds: 1964 F; Hull: 1968 F; 1969 F

GIBSON, C (10+1) Batley: 1985 f; Leeds: 1990 F, P2, NZ3, A3; 1991 F

GIFFORD, H (2) Barrow: 1908 A2

GILFEDDER, L (5) Warrington: 1962 A,NZ2,F; 1963 F

GILL, H (14+1) Wigan: 1981 F2; 1982 A; 1985 F; 1986 F, A3; 1987 F2; 1988 P, A2a, NZ

GILL, K (5+2) Salford: 1974 F2,A2,NZ; **1977 f,a**

GOODWAY, A (23) Oldham: 1983 F2; 1984 F, A3, NZ3, P; 1985 F; Wigan: 1985 NZ3; 1986 A3; 1987 F, P; 1989 NZ3; 1990 F

GOODWIN, D (5) Barrow: 1957 F2; 1958 F,NZ2

GORE, J (1) Salford: 1926 NZ

GORLEY, L (4+1) Widnes: 1980 NZnz; 1981 F2; 1982 A

GORLEY, P (2+1) St. Helens: 1980 NZ; 1981 Ff

GOULDING, R (6) Wigan: 1990 P2, NZ3; Leeds 1992 F

GOWERS, K (14) Swinton: 1962 F; 1963 F,A3; 1964 F2; 1965 NZ2; 1966 F2,A,NZ2

GRAY, J (5+3) Wigan: 1974 f2,A2a,NZ3

GRAYSHON, J (13) Bradford N: 1979 A2,NZ3; 1980 NZ2; 1981 F2; 1982 A2; Leeds: 1985 NZ2

GREENALL, D (6) St. Helens: 1951 NZ3; 1952 A2; 1954 NZ

GREENALL, J (1) St. Helens Recs: 1921 A

GREENOUGH, R (1) Warrington: **1960 NZ**

GREGORY, A (24+1) Widnes: 1981 F2; 1982 A; 1983 F2; 1984 a, NZ2, P; Warrington: 1986 A; Wigan: 1987 F, P; 1988 F, P, A3, NZ; 1989 F2, NZ; 1990 F, A3

GREGORY, M (19+1) Warrington: 1987 F2; 1988 P, A3, NZ; 1989 F2, NZ3; 1990 F2, P2, NZ3, a

GRIBBIN, V (1) Whitehaven: 1985 F

GRIFFITHS, J (1) St. Helens: 1992 F

GRONOW, B (7) Huddersfield: 1911 A2; 1920 A2, NZ3

GROVES, P (1) St. Helens: 1987 P

GRUNDY, J (12) Barrow: 1955 NZ3; 1956 A3; 1957 F3; **1957 F,A,NZ**

GUNNEY, G (11) Hunslet: 1954 NZ3; 1956 A; 1957 F3; **1957 F,NZ**; 1964 F; 1965 F

GWYNNE, T.E (3) Hull: 1928 A,NZ; 1929 A

GWYTHER, E (6) Belle Vue R: 1947 NZ2; 1950 A3; 1951 NZ

HAGGERTY, R (2) St. Helens: 1987 F2

HAIGH, R (5+1) Wakefield T: **1968 A,F**; Leeds: **1970 NZ,a**; 1971 F,NZ

HALL, D (2) Hull KR: 1984 F2

HALL, W (4) Oldham: 1914 A3,NZ

HALLAS, D (2) Leeds: 1961 F,NZ

HALMSHAW, A (1) Halifax: 1971 NZ

HALSALL, H (1) Swinton: 1929 A

HAMPSON, S (10+1) Wigan: 1987 P; 1988 F2; 1989 f, NZ; 1990 A3; 1991 F2, P

HANLEY, E (33+1) Bradford N: 1984 fF, A3, NZ3, P; 1985 F2; Wigan: 1985 NZ3; 1986 F, A; 1987 F2, P; 1988 F2, P, A3, NZ; 1989 F2; 1990 F, A3; 1991 F2

HARDISTY, A (12) Castleford: 1964 F3; 1965 F,NZ; 1966 A3,NZ; 1967 F2; 1970 A

HARE, I (1) Widnes: 1967 F

HARKIN, P (+1) Hull KR: 1985 f

HARRIS, T (25) Hull: 1954 NZ2; 1956 A3; 1957 F5; **1957 F,A**; 1958 A3,NZ,F; 1959 F2,A3; 1960 F2; **1960 NZ**

HARRISON, F (3) Leeds: 1911 A3

HARRISON, K (4) Hull: 1990 A3; Halifax: 1991 P

HARRISON, M (7) Hull: 1967 F2; 1971 NZ2; 1972 F2; 1973 A

HARTLEY, D (11) Hunslet: 1964 F2; Castleford: 1968 F; 1969 F; 1970 A2,NZ2; **1970 A2,F**

HARTLEY, S (3) Hull KR: 1980 NZ; 1981 F2

HELME, G (12) Warrington: 1948 A3; 1954 A3,NZ2; **1954 F2,A,NZ**

HEPWORTH, K (11) Castleford: 1967 F2; 1970 A3,NZ2; **1970 A2,F,NZ**

HERBERT, N (6) Workington T: 1961 NZ; 1962 F,A3,NZ

HERON, D (1+1) Leeds: 1982 aA

HESKETH, C (21+2) Salford: 1970 NZ; **1970 NZ,a**; 1971 Ff,NZ3; **1972 A2,F,NZ**; 1973 A3; 1974 F2,A3,NZ3

HICKS, M (1) St. Helens: 1965 NZ

HIGGINS, F (6) Widnes: 1950 A3,NZ2; 1951 NZ

HIGGINS, H (2) Widnes: 1937 A2

HIGSON, J (2) Hunslet: 1908 A2

HILL, C (1) Wigan: 1966 F

HILL, D (1) Wigan: 1971 F

HILTON, H (7) Oldham: 1920 A3,NZ3; 1921 A

HILTON, J (4) Wigan: 1950 A2,NZ2

HOBBS, D (10+2) Featherstone R: 1984 F2, Aa, NZ3, P; Oldham: 1987 F2; Bradford N: 1989 NZnz

HODGSON, M (16) Swinton: 1929 A2; 1932 A3,NZ3; 1933 A3; 1936 A3,NZ; 1937 A

HOGAN, P (6+3) Barrow: **1977 F,NZ,A2**; 1978 a; Hull KR: 1979 Aa,NZnz

HOGG, A (1) Broughton R: 1907 NZ

HOLDEN, K (1) Warrington: 1963 A

HOLDER, W (1) Hull: 1907 NZ

HOLDING, N (4) St. Helens: 1984 A3, NZ

HOLDSTOCK, R (2) Hull KR: 1980 NZ2

HOLLAND, D (4) Oldham: 1914 A3,NZ

HOLLIDAY, L (3) Widnes: 1991 F; 1992 F2

HOLLIDAY, W (9+1) Whitehaven: 1964 F; Hull KR: 1965 F,NZ3; 1966 Ff; 1967 A3

HOLLINDRAKE, T (1) Keighley: 1955 NZ

HOLMES, J (14+6) Leeds: 1971 NZ; 1972 F2; **1972 Aa,NZ**; **1977 F,NZ,Aa**; 1978 a3; 1979 A2a,NZ3; 1982 A

HORNE, W (8) Barrow: 1946 A3; 1947 NZ; 1948 A; 1952 A3

HORTON, W (14) Wakefield T: 1928 A3,NZ3; 1929 A; 1932 A3,NZ; 1933 A3

HOWLEY, T (6) Wigan: 1924 A3,NZ3

HUDDART, R (16) Whitehaven: 1958 A2,NZ2; St. Helens: 1959 A; 1961 NZ3; 1962 F2,A3,NZ2; 1963 A

HUDSON, B (8) Salford: 1932 NZ; 1933 A2; 1936 A,NZ2; 1937 A2

HUDSON, W (1) Wigan: 1948 A

HUGHES, E (8) Widnes: 1978 A; 1979 A3, NZ3; 1982 A

HULME, D (7+1) Widnes: 1988 p, A3, NZ; 1989 NZ3

HULME, P (3+2) Widnes: 1988 Aa, nz; 1989 NZ2

HUNTE, A (1) St. Helens: 1992 F

HURCOMBE, D (8) Wigan: 1920 A2,NZ; 1921 A; 1924 A2,NZ2

HYNES, S (12+1) Leeds: 1970 A2,NZ2nz; **1970 A2,F,NZ**; 1971 F; 1973 A3

IRVING, R (8+3) Oldham: 1967 F2,A3; 1970 a,NZ; 1971 NZ; 1972 f; **1972 NZ,a**

IRWIN, S (+4) Castleford: 1990 f, p, nz2

JACKSON, K (2) Oldham: 1957 F2

JACKSON, L (9) Hull: 1990 P2, NZ, A3; 1991 F2; 1992 F

JACKSON, M (2) Wakefield T: 1991 P; 1992 F

JACKSON, P (27) Barrow: 1954 A3,NZ3; **1954 F2,A,NZ**; 1955 NZ3; 1956 A3; **1957 F,NZ**; 1957 F5; 1958 F,A2,NZ

JAMES, N (1) Halifax: 1986 F

JARMAN, J.W (2) Leeds: 1914 A2

JASIEWICZ, R (1) Bradford N: 1984 F

JEANES, D (8) Wakefield T: 1971 F,NZ2; 1972 F2; Leeds: **1972 A2,NZ**

JENKINS, B (12) Wigan: 1907 NZ3; 1908 A3; 1910 A,NZ; 1911 A2, 1914 A,NZ

JENKINS, D (1) Hunslet: 1929 A
JENKINS, D (1) Leeds: 1947 NZ
JENKINS, E (9) Salford: 1933 A; 1936 A3,NZ2; 1937 A3
JENKINSON, A (2) Hunslet: 1911 A2
JOHNSON, A (4) Widnes: 1914 A,NZ; 1920 A2
JOHNSON, A (6) Warrington: 1946 A2,NZ; 1947 NZ3
JOHNSON, C (1) Leigh: 1985 F
JOLLEY, J (3) Runcorn: 1907 NZ3
JONES, B (3) Wakefield T: 1964 F; 1965 F; 1966 F
JONES, B.L (15) Leeds: 1954 A3,NZ3; 1955 NZ3; 1957 F3; **1957 F,A,NZ**
JONES, D (2) Merthyr: 1907 NZ2
JONES, E (4) Rochdale H: 1920 A,NZ3
JONES, J (1) Barrow: 1946 NZ
JONES, K (2) Wigan: **1970 F,NZ**
JONES, L (1) St. Helens: 1971 NZ
JONES, M (+1) Hull: 1992 f
JORDAN, G (2) Featherstone R: 1964 F; 1967 A
JOYNER, J (14+2) Castleford: 1978 A2; 1979 A3,NZ3; 1980 NZ3; 1983 F2; 1984 F, nz2
JUBB, K (2) Leeds: 1937 A2
JUKES, W (6) Hunslet: 1908 A3; 1910 A2,NZ

KARALIUS, A (4+1) St. Helens: 1971 NZ3; 1972 F; **1972 nz**
KARALIUS, V (12) St. Helens: 1958 A2,NZ2; 1959 F; **1960 NZ,F,A**; 1960 F; 1961 F; Widnes: 1963 A2
KEEGAN, A (9) Hull: 1966 A2; 1967 F2,A3; 1968 F; 1969 F
KELLY, K (4) St. Helens: 1972 F2; Warrington: 1980 NZ; 1982 A
KEMEL, G (2) Widnes: 1965 NZ2
KERSHAW, H (2) Wakefield T: 1910 A,NZ
KINNEAR, R (1) Wigan: 1929 A
KISS, N (1) Wigan: 1985 F
KITCHEN, F (2) Leigh: **1954 A,NZ**
KITCHIN, P (1) Whitehaven: 1965 NZ
KITCHING, J (1) Bradford N: 1946 A
KNAPMAN, E (1) Oldham: 1924 NZ
KNOWELDEN, B (1) Barrow: 1946 NZ

LAUGHTON, D (15) Wigan: 1970 A3,NZ2; **1970 A2,F,NZ**; 1971 F2; Widnes: 1973 A; 1974 F2; 1979 A
LAWRENSON, J (3) Wigan: 1948 A3
LAWS, D (1) Hull KR: 1986 F
LEDGARD, J (11) Dewsbury: 1947 NZ2; Leigh: 1948 A; 1950 A2,NZ; 1951 NZ; **1954 F2,A,NZ**
LEDGER, B (2) St. Helens: 1985 F; 1986 A
LEWIS, G (1) Leigh: 1965 NZ
LEYTHAM, J (5) Wigan: 1907 NZ2; 1910 A2,NZ
LITTLE, S (10) Oldham: 1956 A; 1957 F5; **1957 F,A,NZ**; 1958 F
LLEWELLYN, T (2) Oldham: 1907 NZ2

LLOYD, R (1) Halifax: 1920 A
LOCKWOOD, B (8+1) Castleford: **1972 A2,F,NZ**; 1973 A2; 1974 F; Hull KR: 1978 A; 1979 nz
LOMAS, J (7) Salford: 1908 A2; 1910 A2,NZ; Oldham: 1911 A2
LONGSTAFF, F (2) Huddersfield: 1914 A,NZ
LONGWORTH, W (3) Oldham: 1908 A3
LOUGHLIN, P (12+1) St. Helens: 1988 F, P, A3, NZ; 1989 F, NZ3; 1990 F, a; 1991 F
LOWE, J (1) Leeds: 1932 NZ
LOWE, P (12) Hull KR: 1970 NZ; 1972 F2; **1972 A2,F,NZ**; 1973 A3, 1978 A2
LOXTON, K (1) Huddersfield: 1971 NZ
LUCAS, I (1) Wigan: 1991 F
LYDON, J (22+2) Widnes: 1983 F2; 1984 F, a, NZ2, P; 1985 NZ3; Wigan: 1986 F, A3; 1987 F2, P; 1989 F2, nz; 1990 F, NZ3

McCORMICK, S (3) Belle Vue R: 1948 A2; St. Helens: A
McCUE, T (6) Widnes: 1936 A; 1937 A; 1946 A3,NZ
McINTYRE, L (1) Oldham: 1963 A
McKEATING, V (2) Workington T: 1951 NZ2
McKINNEY, T (11) Salford: 1951 NZ; 1952 A2; 1954 A3,NZ; Warrington: 1955 NZ3; St. Helens: **1957 NZ**
McNAMARA, S (+1) Hull: 1992 f
McTIGUE, B (25) Wigan: 1958 A2,NZ2; 1959 F2,A3; 1960 F2; **1960 NZ,F,A**; 1961 F,NZ3; 1962 F,A3,NZ2; 1963 F
MANN, A (2) Bradford N: 1908 A2
MANTLE, J (13) St. Helens: 1966 F2,A3; 1967 A2; 1969 F; 1971 F2,NZ2; 1973 A
MARCHANT, A (3) Castleford: 1986 F, A2
MARTIN, W (1) Workington T: 1962 F
MARTYN, M (2) Leigh: 1958 A; 1959 A
MATHIAS, R (1) St. Helens: 1979 A
MEASURES, J (2) Widnes: 1963 A2
MEDLEY, P (3+1) Leeds: 1987 P; 1988 Ff, P
MIDDLETON, A (1) Salford: 1929 A
MILLER, J (1) Wigan: 1911 A
MILLER, J (6) Warrington: 1933 A3; 1936 A,NZ2
MILLS, J (6) Widnes: 1974 A2,NZ; 1978 A2; 1979 A
MILLWARD, R (28+1) Castleford: 1966 F; Hull KR: 1967 A3; 1968 F2; **1968 A,F,NZ**; 1970 A2,NZ3; 1971 F,NZ3; 1973 A; 1974 A2a; **1977 F,NZ,A2**; 1978 A3
MILNES, A (2) Halifax: 1920 A2
MOONEY, W (2) Leigh: 1924 NZ2
MOORHOUSE, S (2) Huddersfield: 1914 A,NZ
MORGAN, A (4) Featherstone R: 1968 F2; **1968 F,NZ**
MORGAN, E (2) Hull: 1921 A2
MORGAN, R (2) Swinton: 1963 F,A
MORIARTY, P (1) Widnes: 1991 P
MORLEY, J (2) Wigan: 1936 A; 1937 A

MORTIMER, F (2) Wakefield T: 1956 A2
MOSES, G (9) St. Helens: 1955 NZ2; 1956 A; 1957 F3; **1957 F,A,NZ**
MUMBY, K (11) Bradford N: 1982 A; 1983 F; 1984 F2, A3, NZ3, P
MURPHY, A (27) St. Helens: 1958 A3,NZ; 1959 F2,A; **1960 NZ,F,A**; 1960 F; 1961 F,NZ3; 1962 F,A3; 1963 A2; 1964 F; 1965 F,NZ; 1966 F2; Warrington: 1971 NZ
MURPHY, H (1) Wakefield T: 1950 A
MYLER, A (14) Widnes: 1983 F2; 1984 A2, NZ2, P; 1985 NZ2; 1986 F2, A3
MYLER, F (23+1) Widnes: **1960 NZ,F,A**; 1960 F; 1961 F; 1962 F; 1963 A; 1964 F; 1965 F,NZ; 1966 A,NZnz; 1967 F2; St. Helens: 1970 A3,NZ3; **1970 A2,F**

NASH, S (24) Featherstone R: 1971 F,NZ; 1972 F2; **1972 A2,F,NZ**; 1973 A2; 1974 A3,NZ3; Salford: **1977 F,NZ,A2**; 1978 A3; 1982 A
NAUGHTON, A (2) Warrington: **1954 F2**
NEWBOULD, H (1) Wakefield T: 1910 A
NEWLOVE, P (3+1) Featherstone R: 1989 nzNZ2; 1991 P
NICHOLLS, G (29) Widnes: 1971 NZ; 1972 F2; **1972 A2,F,NZ**; St. Helens: 1973 A2; 1974 F2,A3,NZ2; **1977 F,NZ,A**; 1978 A3; 1979 A3,NZ3
NICHOLSON, R (3) Huddersfield: 1946 NZ; 1948 A2
NOBLE, B (11) Bradford N: 1982 A; 1983 F2; 1984 F, A3, NZ3, P
NORTON, S (11+1) Castleford: 1974 a,NZ2; Hull: 1978 A3; 1979 A2; 1980 NZ; 1981 F2; 1982 A

OFFIAH, M (20) Widnes: 1988 F, A3, NZ; 1989 F2, NZ3; 1990 F2, NZ3, A3; 1991 F2
O'GRADY, T (6) Oldham: 1954 A2,NZ3; Warrington: 1961 NZ
OLIVER, J (4) Batley: 1928 A3,NZ
O'NEILL, D (2+1) Widnes: 1971 nz; **1972 A,F**
O'NEILL, M (3) Widnes: 1982 A; 1983 F2
OSTER, J (1) Oldham: 1929 A
OWEN, J (1) St. Helens Recs: 1921 A
OWEN, S (1) Leigh: 1958 F
OWENS, I (4) Leeds: 1946 A3,NZ

PADBURY, R (1) Runcorn: 1908 A
PALIN, H (2) Warrington: 1947 NZ2
PARKER, D (2) Oldham: 1964 F2
PARKIN, J (17) Wakefield T: 1920 A2,NZ3; 1921 A2; 1924 A3,NZ; 1926 NZ2; 1928 A,NZ; 1929 A2
PARR, K (1) Warrington: 1968 F
PAWSEY, C (7) Leigh: 1952 A3; 1954 A2,NZ2
PEPPERELL, A (2) Workington T: 1950 NZ; 1951 NZ

PHILLIPS, D (4) Oldham: 1946 A3; Belle Vue R: 1950 A
PIMBLETT, A (3) Warrington: 1948 A3
PINNER, H (6+1) St. Helens: 1980 nzNZ; 1985 NZ3; 1986 F; Widnes: 1986 A
PITCHFORD, F (2) Oldham: 1958 NZ; 1962 F
PITCHFORD, S (4) Leeds: **1977 F,NZ,A2**
PLANGE, D (1) Castleford: 1988 F
PLATT, A (13+4) St. Helens: 1985 f; 1986 f, a; 1988 F2, A2; Wigan: 1989 NZ3; 1990 F, A2; 1991 F2, P; 1992 f
POLLARD, C (1) Wakefield T: 1924 NZ
POLLARD, E (2) Wakefield T: 1932 A2
POLLARD, R (1) Dewsbury: 1950 NZ
POOLE, H (3) Hull KR: 1964 F; Leeds: 1966 NZ2
POTTER, I (7+1) Wigan: 1985 NZ3; 1986 F2, A2a
POWELL, D (11+3) Sheffield E: 1990 f, P2, nzNZ2, A3; 1991 F2, P; 1992 fF
POWELL, R (13+6) Leeds: 1985 f; 1988 F2, A2a, NZ; 1989 F2, NZ2; 1990 P2, nz2NZ, Aa; 1991 f
POYNTON, H (3) Wakefield T: 1962 A2,NZ
PRESCOTT, A (28) St. Helens: 1951 NZ2; 1952 A3; 1954 A3,NZ3; 1955 NZ3; 1956 A3; 1957 F5; **1957 F,A,NZ**; 1958 F,A2
PRICE, G (+1) Wakefield T: 1991 p
PRICE, J (6) Broughton R: 1921 A2; Wigan: 1924 A2,NZ2
PRICE, M (2) Rochdale H: 1967 A2
PRICE, R (9) Warrington: 1954 A,NZ2; 1955 NZ; 1956 A3; 1957 F2
PRICE, T (1) Bradford N: 1970 A
PRIOR, B (1) Hunslet: 1966 F
PROCTOR, W (+1) Hull: 1984 p
PROSSER, D (1) Leeds: 1937 A
PROSSER, S (1) Halifax: 1914 A

RAE, J (1) Bradford N: 1965 NZ
RAMSDALE, R (8) Wigan: 1910 A2; 1911 A2; 1914 A3,NZ
RAMSEY, W (7+1) Hunslet: 1965 NZ2; 1966 F,A2,NZ2; Bradford N; 1974 nz
RATCLIFFE, G (3) Wigan: 1947 NZ; 1950 A2
RATHBONE, A (4+1) Bradford N: 1982 a; 1983 F2; 1985 F2
RAYNE, Keith (4) Leeds: 1984 F2, A, P
RAYNE, Kevin (1) Leeds: 1986 F
REDFEARN, A (1) Bradford N: 1979 A
REDFEARN, D (6+1) Bradford N: **1972 nz**; 1974 F2,A,NZ3
REES, D (1) Halifax: 1926 NZ
REES, T (1) Oldham: 1929 A
REES, W (11) Swinton: 1926 NZ2; 1928 A3,NZ3; 1929 A3
REILLY, M (9) Castleford: 1970 A3,NZ3; **1970 A2,F**
RENILSON, C (7+1) Halifax: 1965 NZ; 1967 a; 1968 F3; **1968 A,F,NZ**

RHODES, A (4) St. Helens: **1957 NZ**; **1960 F,A**; 1961 NZ
RICHARDS, M (2) Salford: 1974 A,NZ
RILEY, J (1) Halifax: 1910 A
RING, J (2) Wigan: 1924 A; 1926 NZ
RISMAN, A (17) Salford: 1932 A,NZ3; 1933 A3; 1936 A2,NZ2; 1937 A3; 1946 A3
RISMAN, B (5) Leeds: 1968 F2; **1968 A,F,NZ**
RIX, S (9) Oldham: 1924 A3,NZ3; 1926 NZ3
ROBERTS, K (10) Halifax: 1963 A; 1964 F2; 1965 F,NZ3; 1966 F,NZ2
ROBINSON, A (3) Halifax: 1907 NZ; 1908 A2
ROBINSON, Dave (13) Swinton: 1965 NZ; 1966 F2,A3,NZ2; 1967 F2,A2; Wigan: 1970 A
ROBINSON, Don (10) Wakefield T: **1954 F2,NZ,A**; 1955 NZ; Leeds: 1956 A2; 1959 A2; 1960 F
ROBINSON, J (2) Rochdale H: 1914 A2
ROBINSON, W (2) Leigh: 1963 F,A
ROGERS, J (7) Huddersfield: 1914 A; 1920 A3; 1921 A3
ROSE, D (4) Leeds: **1954 F2,A,NZ**
ROSE, P (2+3) Hull KR: 1974 a; 1978 Aa2; Hull: 1982 A
ROUND, G (8) Wakefield T: 1959 A; 1962 F2,A3,NZ2
RUDDICK, J (3) Broughton R: 1907 NZ2; 1910 A
RYAN, M (4) Wigan: 1947 NZ; 1948 A2; 1950 A
RYAN, R (5) Warrington: 1950 A,NZ2; 1951 NZ; 1952 A
RYDER, R (1) Warrington: 1952 A

SAYER, W (7) Wigan: 1961 NZ; 1962 F,A3,NZ; 1963 A
SCHOFIELD, D (1) Halifax: 1955 NZ
SCHOFIELD, G (32) Hull: 1984 F, A3, NZ; 1985 NZ3; 1986 F2, A3; 1987 F2; Leeds: 1988 F2,P,A; 1990 F2, P2, NZ3, A3; 1991 F2, P
SEABOURNE, B (1) Leeds: 1970 NZ
SENIOR, K (2) Huddersfield: 1965 NZ; 1967 F
SHARROCK, J (4) Wigan: 1910 A2,NZ; 1911 A
SHAW, B (6) Hunslet: 1956 A2; **1960 F,A**; 1960 F; Leeds: 1961 F
SHAW, G (1) Widnes: 1980 NZ
SHAW, J (5) Halifax: **1960 F,A**; 1960 F; 1961 F; 1962 NZ
SHELTON, G (7) Hunslet: 1964 F2; 1965 NZ3; 1966 F2
SHOEBOTTOM, M (10+2) Leeds: **1968 A,nz**; 1969 F; 1970 A2a,NZ; **1970 A2,F,NZ**; 1971 F
SHUGARS, F (1) Warrington: 1910 NZ
SILCOCK, N (12) Widnes: 1932 A2,NZ2; 1933 A3; 1936 A3; 1937 A2
SILCOCK, N (3) Wigan: 1954 A3
SILCOCK, R (1) Wigan: 1908 A
SIMMS, B (1) Leeds: 1962 F
SKELHORNE, G (7) Warrington: 1920 A,NZ3; 1921 A3

SKERRETT, K (9) Bradford N: 1989 NZ3; 1990 F2, NZ3; Wigan: 1992 F
SKERRETT, T (10) Wakefield T: 1979 A2,NZ2; Hull: 1980 NZ2; 1981 F2; 1982 A2
SLOMAN, R (5) Oldham: 1928 A3,NZ2
SMALES, T (8) Huddersfield: 1962 F; 1963 F,A; 1964 F2; Bradford N: 1965 NZ3
SMALL, P (1) Castleford: 1962 NZ
SMITH, A (6) Oldham: 1907 NZ3; 1908 A3
SMITH, A (10) Leeds: 1970 A2,NZ3; **1970 A2**; 1971 F2; 1973 A
SMITH, F (9) Hunslet: 1910 A,NZ; 1911 A3; 1914 A3,NZ
SMITH, G (3) York: 1963 A; 1964 F2
SMITH, H (2) Bradford N: 1926 NZ2
SMITH, M (10+1) Hull KR: 1979 NZ3; 1980 NZ2; 1981 F2; 1982 A2; 1984 f,NZ
SMITH, P (1+5) Featherstone R: **1977 a2;** 1982 A; 1983 f2; 1984 f
SMITH, S (11) Wakefield T: 1929 A; Leeds: 1929 A2; 1932 A3,NZ3; 1933 A2
SMITH, S (4) Hunslet: **1954 A,NZ,F2**
SOUTHWARD, I (11) Workington T: 1958 A3,NZ; Oldham: 1959 F2,A2; 1960 F2; 1962 NZ
SPENCER, J (1) Salford: 1907 NZ
STACEY, J.C (1) Halifax: 1920 NZ
STEADMAN, G (2+1) Castleford: 1990 F; 1992 fF
STEPHENS, G (5) Castleford: 1979 A2,NZ3
STEPHENSON, D (9+1) Wigan: 1982 A2; 1986 A; 1987 F, P; Leeds: 1988 f, P, A2, NZ
STEPHENSON, M (5+1) Dewsbury: 1971 nz; 1972 F; **1972 A2,F,NZ**
STEVENSON, J (19) Leeds: 1955 NZ3; 1956 A3; 1957 F5; **1957 F,A,NZ**; 1958 F; York: 1959 A2; 1960 F2
STOCKWELL, S (3) Leeds: 1920 A; 1921 A2
STONE, W (8) Hull: 1920 A3,NZ3; 1921 A2
STOPFORD, J (12) Swinton: 1961 F; 1963 F,A2; 1964 F2; 1965 F,NZ2; 1966 F,A
STOTT, J (1) St. Helens: 1947 NZ
STREET, H (4) Dewsbury: 1950 A3,NZ
SULLIVAN, A (1) St. Helens: 1991 P
SULLIVAN, C (17) Hull: 1967 F; **1968 A,F,NZ**; 1970 A; 1971 NZ3; 1972 F2; **1972 A2,F,NZ**; 1973 A3
SULLIVAN, J (25) Wigan: 1924 A3,NZ; 1926 NZ3; 1928 A3,NZ3; 1929 A3; 1932 A3,NZ3; 1933 A3
SULLIVAN, M (46) Huddersfield: **1954 F2,NZ,A**; 1955 NZ3; 1956 A3; 1957 F3; **1957 F,A,NZ**; Wigan: 1957 F2; 1958 F,A3,NZ2; 1959 F2,A3; 1960 F3; **1960 F,NZ,A**; St. Helens: 1961 F,NZ2; 1962 F3,A3,NZ; York: 1963 A
SZYMALA, E (1+1) Barrow: 1981 fF

TAIT, A (9) Widnes: 1989 F2, NZ2; 1990 F2, P2; 1992 F
TAYLOR, H (3) Hull: 1907 NZ3

335

TAYLOR, R (2) Hull: 1921 A; 1926 NZ
TEMBEY, J (2) St. Helens: 1963 A; 1964 F
TERRY, A (11) St. Helens: 1958 A2; 1959 F2,A3; 1960 F; 1961 F,NZ; Leeds: 1962 F
THOMAS, A (4) Leeds: 1926 NZ2; 1929 A2
THOMAS, G (1) Warrington: 1907 NZ
THOMAS, G (9) Wigan: 1914 A; Huddersfield: 1920 A3,NZ2; 1921 A3
THOMAS, J (8) Wigan: 1907 NZ; 1908 A3; 1910 A2,NZ; 1911 A
THOMAS, L (1) Oldham: 1947 NZ
THOMAS, P (1) Leeds: 1907 NZ
THOMPSON, C (2) Hunslet: 1951 NZ2
THOMPSON, J (12) Leeds: 1924 A,NZ2; 1928 A,NZ; 1929 A; 1932 A3,NZ3
THOMPSON, J (20+1) Featherstone R: 1970 A2,NZ2; **1970 A2,F,NZ**; 1971 Ff; 1974 A3,NZ3; **1977 F,NZ,A2**; Bradford N: 1978 A
THORLEY, J (4) Halifax: **1954 F2,NZ,A**
TOOHEY, E (3) Barrow: 1952 A3
TOPLISS, D (4) Wakefield T: 1973 A2; 1979 A; Hull: 1982 A
TRAILL, K (8) Bradford N: 1950 NZ2; 1951 NZ; 1952 A3; 1954 A,NZ
TROUP, L.A (2) Barrow: 1936 NZ2
TURNBULL, A (1) Leeds: 1951 NZ
TURNER, D (24) Oldham: 1956 A2; 1957 F5; **1957 F,A,NZ**; 1958 F; Wakefield T: 1959 A; 1960 F3; **1960 NZ,A**; 1961 F,NZ; 1962 A2,NZ2,F
TYSON, B (3) Hull KR: 1963 A; 1965 F; 1967 F
TYSON, G (4) Oldham: 1907 NZ; 1908 A3

VALENTINE, D (15) Huddersfield: 1948 A3; 1951 NZ; 1952 A2; 1954 A3,NZ2; **1954 F2,NZ,A**
VALENTINE, R (1) Huddersfield: 1967 A
VINES, D (3) Wakefield T: 1959 F2,A

WADDELL, H (5) Oldham: 1988 F2, A, NZ; Leeds: 1989 F
WAGSTAFF, H (12) Huddersfield: 1911 A2; 1914 A3,NZ; 1920 A2,NZ2; 1921 A2
WALKER, A (1) Whitehaven: 1980 NZ
WALLACE, J (1) St. Helens Recs: 1926 NZ
WALSH, Joe (1) Leigh: 1971 NZ
WALSH, John (4+1) St. Helens: 1972 f; **1972 A2,F,NZ**
WALTON, D (1) Castleford: 1965 F
WANE, S (2) Wigan: 1985 F; 1986 F
WARD, D (12) Leeds: **1977 F,NZ,A**; 1978 A; 1979 A3,NZ3;1981 F; 1982 A
WARD, Edward (3) Wigan: 1946 A2; 1947 NZ
WARD, Ernest (20) Bradford N: 1946 A3,NZ; 1947 NZ2; 1948 A3; 1950 A3,NZ2; 1951 NZ3; 1952 A3
WARD, J (4) Castleford: 1963 A; 1964 F2; Salford: 1970 NZ

WARD, K (14+2) Castleford: 1984 F; 1986 A3; 1987 P; 1988 F2, P, A3, NZ; 1989 F2; St. Helens: 1990 a2
WARD, W (1) Leeds: 1910 A
WARLOW, J (6+1) St. Helens: 1964 F; **1968 f,NZ**; 1968 F; Widnes: 1971 F2,NZ
WARWICK, S (2) Salford: 1907 NZ2
WATKINS, D (2+4) Salford: 1971 f,NZ; 1973 a; 1974 f2,A
WATKINS, W (7) Salford: 1933 A; 1936 A2,NZ2; 1937 A2
WATKINSON, D (12+1) Hull KR: 1979 a; 1980 NZ; 1981 F; 1984 F; 1985 F, NZ3; 1986 F2, A3
WATSON, C (29+1) St. Helens: 1963 A2; 1966 F2,A3,NZ2; 1967 F,A3; 1968 F2; **1968 A,F,nz**; 1969 F; 1970 A3,NZ3; **1970 A2,F,NZ**; 1971 F
WATTS, B (5) York: **1954 F2,NZ,A**; 1955 NZ
WEBSTER, F (3) Leeds: 1910 A2,NZ
WHITCOMBE, F (2) Bradford N: 1946 A2
WHITE, L (7) Hunslet: 1932 A3,NZ2; 1933 A2
WHITE, L (6) York: 1946 A3,NZ; Wigan: 1947 NZ2
WHITE, T (1) Oldham: 1907 NZ
WHITEHEAD, D (3) Warrington: 1971 F2,NZ
WHITELEY, J (15) Hull: **1957 A**; 1958 A3,NZ; 1959 F2,A2; 1960 F; **1960 NZ,F**; 1961 NZ2; 1962 F
WILKINSON, J (13) Halifax: 1954 A,NZ2; 1955 NZ3; Wakefield T: 1959 A; 1960 F2; **1960 NZ,F,A**; 1962 NZ
WILLIAMS, F (2) Halifax: 1914 A2
WILLIAMS, P (1+1) Salford: 1989 fF
WILLIAMS, R (12) Leeds: 1948 A2; 1950 A2,NZ2; 1951 NZ3; Hunslet: 1954 A2,NZ
WILLIAMS, W (2) Salford: 1929 A; 1932 A
WILLICOMBE, D (3) Halifax: 1974 F; Wigan: 1974 F,NZ
WILSON, G (3) Workington T: 1951 NZ3
WILSON, H (3) Hunslet: 1907 NZ3
WINSLADE, C (1) Oldham: 1959 F
WINSTANLEY, W (5) Leigh: 1910 A,NZ; Wigan: 1911 A3
WOOD, A (4) Oldham: 1911 A2; 1914 A,NZ
WOODS, H (6) Liverpool S: 1936 A3,NZ2; Leeds: 1937 A
WOODS, J (1) Barrow: 1933 A
WOODS, J (7+4) Leigh: 1979 A3,nz; 1980 NZ; 1981 F2; 1982 Aa; 1983 f; Warrington: 1987 p
WOODS, T (2) Rochdale H: 1911 A2
WORRALL, M (3) Oldham: 1984 F, A2
WRIGHT, D (+1) Widnes: 1988 a
WRIGHT, J (1) Swinton: 1932 NZ
WRIGHT, S (7) Widnes: **1977 F,NZ,A2**; 1978 A3
WRIGLESWORTH, G (5) Leeds: 1965 NZ; 1966 A2,NZ2

YOUNG, C (5) Hull KR: 1967 A3; 1968 F2
YOUNG, F (1) Leeds: 1908 A
YOUNG, H (1) Huddersfield: 1929 A

GREAT BRITAIN TOUR SUMMARIES

						For			Against	
1910	P	W	D	L	T	G	Pts	T	G	Pts
In Australia	14	9	1	4	76	56	340	51	47	247
In New Zealand	4	4	0	0	43	29	187	11	7	47
TOTAL	18	13	1	4	119	85	527	62	54	294
1914	P	W	D	L	T	G	Pts	T	G	Pts
In Australia	12	9	0	3	77	55	341	24	31	134
In New Zealand	6	6	0	0	46	28	194	12	13	62
TOTAL	18	15	0	3	123	83	535	36	44	196
1920	P	W	D	L	T	G	Pts	T	G	Pts
In Australia	15	12	0	3	83	64	377	48	42	228
In New Zealand	10	9	0	1	89	47	361	24	16	104
TOTAL	25	21	0	4	172	111	738	72	58	332
1924	P	W	D	L	T	G	Pts	T	G	Pts
In Australia	18	14	0	4	104	77	466	56	45	258
In New Zealand	9	7	0	2	64	40	272	25	21	117
TOTAL	27	21	0	6	168	117	738	81	66	375
1928	P	W	D	L	T	G	Pts	T	G	Pts
In Australia	16	11	1	4	67	60	321	43	45	219
In New Zealand	8	7	0	1	55	36	237	16	12	72
TOTAL	24	18	1	5	122	96	558	59	57	291
1932	P	W	D	L	T	G	Pts	T	G	Pts
In Australia	18	15	1	2	105	84	483	32	38	172
In New Zealand	8	8	0	0	65	52	299	17	18	87
TOTAL	26	23	1	2	170	136	782	49	56	259

Uncapped 1992 Great Britain tourists Billy McGinty (left) and Sonny Nickle.

	P	W	D	L	T	**For** G	Pts	T	**Against** G	Pts
1936										
In Australia	17	14	0	3	79	82	401	38	45	204
In New Zealand	8	8	0	0	52	27	210	8	16	56
TOTAL	25	22	0	3	131	109	611	46	61	260
1946	P	W	D	L	T	G	Pts	T	G	Pts
In Australia	20	16	1	3	146	100	638	36	45	198
In New Zealand	7	5	0	2	35	20	145	12	21	78
TOTAL	27	21	1	5	181	120	783	48	66	276
1950	P	W	D	L	T	G	Pts	T	G	Pts
In Australia	19	15	0	4	133	102	603	22	56	178
In New Zealand	6	4	0	2	37	25	161	16	20	88
TOTAL	25	19	0	6	170	127	764	38	76	266
1954	P	W	D	L	T	G	Pts	T	G	Pts
In Australia	*22	13	1	7	133	114	627	78	96	426
In New Zealand	10	8	0	2	60	56	292	14	32	106
TOTAL	*32	21	1	9	193	170	919	92	128	532

*One match abandoned. Scores included in points total.

	P	W	D	L	T	G	Pts	T	G	Pts
1958										
In Australia	21	19	1	1	184	129	810	64	93	378
In New Zealand	9	8	0	1	88	61	386	18	27	108
TOTAL	30	27	1	2	272	190	1,196	82	120	486
1962	P	W	D	L	T	G	Pts	T	G	Pts
In Australia	21	18	0	3	151	113	679	61	60	303
In New Zealand	9	6	0	3	73	50	319	35	28	161
TOTAL	30	24	0	6	224	163	998	96	88	464
1966	P	W	D	L	T	G	Pts	T	G	Pts
In Australia	22	13	0	9	112	85	506	47	83	307
In New Zealand	8	8	0	0	57	47	265	10	24	78
TOTAL	30	21	0	9	169	132	771	57	107	385
1970	P	W	D	L	T	G	Pts	T	G	Pts
In Australia	17	15	1	1	104	92	496	27	66	213
In New Zealand	7	7	0	0	61	37	257	9	24	75
TOTAL	24	22	1	1	165	129	753	36	90	288

	P	W	D	L	T	G	DG	Pts	T	G	DG	Pts
1974												
In Australia	20	15	0	5	104	93	2	500	38	59	3	235
In New Zealand	8	6	0	2	37	32	0	175	8	27	0	78
TOTAL	28	21	0	7	141	125	2	675	46	86	3	313
1979	P	W	D	L	T	G	DG	Pts	T	G	DG	Pts
In Australia	18	13	1	4	66	73	3	347	39	68		253
In New Zealand	9	8	0	1	48	34	0	212	15	12		69
TOTAL	27	21	1	5	114	107	3	559	54	80		332

1984	P	W	D	L	T	G	For DG	Pts	T	G	Against DG	Pts
In Australia	15	11	0	4	70	59	1	399	40	46	2	254
In New Zealand	8	4	0	4	32	25	1	179	21	21	0	126
In Papua New Guinea	1	1	0	0	7	5	0	38	4	2	0	20
TOTAL	24	16	0	8	109	89	2	616	65	69	2	400

1988	P	W	D	L	T	G	DG	Pts	T	G	DG	Pts
In Papua New Guinea	2	2	0	0	13	13	0	78	7	6	0	40
In Australia	13	8	0	5	59	47	0	330	42	36	1	241
In New Zealand	3	1	0	2	8	8	0	48	10	10	0	60
TOTAL	18	11	0	7	80	68	0	456	59	52	1	341

1990	P	W	D	L	T	G	DG	Pts	T	G	DG	Pts
In Papua New Guinea	5	4	0	1	31	24	0	172	7	15	2	60
In New Zealand	10	6	0	4	30	28	3	179	24	32	1	161
TOTAL	15	10	0	5	61	52	3	351	31	47	3	221

GREAT BRITAIN TOUR SQUADS TO AUSTRALIA AND NEW ZEALAND
Captains in bold

1910 Tour

J. Lomas (Salford)
A. Avery (Oldham)
J. Bartholomew (Huddersfield)
W. Batten (Hunslet)
F. Boylen (Hull)
E. Curzon (Salford)
J. Davies (Huddersfield)
F. Farrar (Hunslet)
T. Helm (Oldham)
B. Jenkins (Wigan)
T. Jenkins (Ebbw Vale)
W. Jukes (Hunslet)
H. Kershaw (Wakefield T.)
J. Leytham (Wigan)
T. Newbould (Wakefield T.)
R. Ramsdale (Wigan)
J. Riley (Halifax)
G. Ruddick (Broughton R.)
J. Sharrock (Wigan)
F. Shugars (Warrington)
F. Smith (Hunslet)
J. Thomas (Wigan)
W. Ward (Leeds)
F. Webster (Leeds)
W. Winstanley (Leigh)
F. Young (Leeds)

Managers: J. Clifford
(Huddersfield) and J.
Houghton (St. Helens)

1914 Tour

H. Wagstaff (Huddersfield)
J. Chilcott (Huddersfield)
J. Clampitt (Broughton R.)
D. Clark (Huddersfield)
A. Coldrick (Wigan)
W. Davies (Leeds)
A. Francis (Hull)
J. Guerin (Hunslet)
W. Hall (Oldham)
D. Holland (Oldham)
J. Jarman (Leeds)
B. Jenkins (Wigan)
A. Johnson (Widnes)
F. Longstaff (Huddersfield)
S. Moorhouse (Huddersfield)
J. O'Garra (Widnes)
W. Prosser (Halifax)
R. Ramsdale (Wigan)
J. Robinson (Rochdale H.)
J. Rogers (Huddersfield)
W. Roman (Rochdale H.)
J. Smales (Hunslet)
F. Smith (Hunslet)
G. Thomas (Wigan)
F. Williams (Halifax)
A. Wood (Oldham)

Managers: J. Clifford
(Huddersfield) and J.
Houghton (St. Helens)

1920 Tour

H. Wagstaff (Huddersfield)
J. Bacon (Leeds)
J. Bowers (Rochdale H.)
J. Cartwright (Leigh)
D. Clark (Huddersfield)
W. Cunliffe (Warrington)
E. Davies (Oldham)
J. Doyle (Barrow)
F. Gallagher (Dewsbury)
B. Gronow (Huddersfield)
H. Hilton (Oldham)
D. Hurcombe (Wigan)
A. Johnson (Widnes)
E. Jones (Rochdale H.)
R. Lloyd (Halifax)
A. Milnes (Halifax)
J. Parkin (Wakefield T.)
G. Rees (Leeds)
W. Reid (Widnes)
J. Rogers (Huddersfield)
G. Skelhorne (Warrington)
J. Stacey (Halifax)
S. Stockwell (Leeds)
W. Stone (Hull)
G. Thomas (Huddersfield)
A. Wood (Oldham)

Managers: S. Foster (Halifax)
and J. Wilson (Hull K.R.)

1924 Tour

J. Parkin (Wakefield T.)
J. Bacon (Leeds)
J. Bennett (Rochdale H.)
W. Bentham (Broughton R.)
H. Bowman (Hull)
A. Brough (Oldham)
W. Burgess (Barrow)
C. Carr (Barrow)
W. Cunliffe (Warrington)
J. Darwell (Leigh)
F. Evans (Swinton)
F. Gallagher (Batley)
B. Gronow (Huddersfield)
T. Howley (Wigan)
D. Hurcombe (Wigan)
E. Knapman (Oldham)
W. Mooney (Leigh)
C. Pollard (Wakefield T.)
J. Price (Wigan)
D. Rees (Halifax)
J. Ring (Wigan)
S. Rix (Oldham)
R. Sloman (Oldham)
J. Sullivan (Wigan)
J. Thompson (Leeds)
S. Whitty (Hull)

Managers: J.H. Dannatt
(Hull) and E. Osborne
(Warrington)

1928 Tour

J. Parkin (Wakefield T.)
T. Askin (Featherstone R.)
N. Bentham (Wigan Highfield)
F. Bowen (St. Helens Recs)
H. Bowman (Hull)
J. Brough (Leeds)
W. Burgess (Barrow)
O. Dolan (St. Helens Recs)
A. Ellaby (St. Helens)
B. Evans (Swinton)
J. Evans (Swinton)
L. Fairclough (St. Helens)
A. Fildes (St. Helens Recs)
A. Frodsham (St. Helens)
W. Gowers (Rochdale H.)
T. Gwynne (Hull)
B. Halfpenny (St. Helens)
W. Horton (Wakefield T.)
J. Oliver (Batley)
W. Rees (Swinton)
M. Rosser (Leeds)
R. Sloman (Oldham)
J. Sullivan (Wigan)
J. Thompson (Leeds)
W. Williams (Salford)
H. Young (Bradford N.)

Managers: G. Hutchins
(Oldham) and E. Osborne
(Warrington)

1932 Tour

J. Sullivan (Wigan)
A. Atkinson (Castleford)
L. Adams (Leeds)
S. Brogden (Huddersfield)
F. Butters (Swinton)
I. Davies (Halifax)
W. Dingsdale (Warrington)
A. Ellaby (St. Helens)
B. Evans (Swinton)
J. Feetham (Salford)
N. Fender (York)
A. Fildes (St. Helens)
M. Hodgson (Swinton)
W. Horton (Wakefield T.)
B. Hudson (Salford)
J. Lowe (Leeds)
E. Pollard (Wakefield T.)
A. Risman (Salford)
G. Robinson (Wakefield T.)
N. Silcock (Widnes)
S. Smith (Leeds)
J. Thompson (Leeds)
L. White (Hunslet)
W. Williams (Salford)
J. Woods (Barrow)
J. Wright (Swinton)

Managers: R. Anderton
(Warrington) and G. Hutchins
(Oldham)

1936 Tour

J. Brough (Leeds)
J. Arkwright (Warrington)
T. Armitt (Swinton)
A. Atkinson (Castleford)
W. Belshaw (Liverpool S.)
H. Beverley (Hunslet)
S. Brogden (Leeds)
E. Davies (Wigan)
A. Edwards (Salford)
H. Ellerington (Hull)
G. Exley (Wakefield T.)
H. Field (York)
F. Harris (Leeds)
M. Hodgson (Swinton)
B. Hudson (Salford)
E. Jenkins (Salford)
H. Jones (Keighley)
T. McCue (Widnes)
J. Miller (Warrington)
J. Morley (Wigan)
A. Risman (Salford)
N. Silcock (Widnes)
S. Smith (Leeds)
L. Troup (Barrow)
W. Watkins (Salford)
H. Woods (Liverpool S.)

Managers: R. Anderton
(Warrington) and
W. Popplewell (Bramley)

1946 Tour

A. Risman (Salford)
A. Bassett (Halifax) .
E. Batten (Bradford N.)
G. Curran (Salford)
W. Davies (Bradford N.)
J. Egan (Wigan)
T. Foster (Bradford N.)
K. Gee (Wigan)
W. Horne (Barrow)
F. Hughes (Workington T.)
D. Jenkins (Leeds)
A. Johnson (Warrington)

J. Jones (Barrow)
J. Kitching (Bradford N.)
B. Knowelden (Barrow)
J. Lewthwaite (Barrow)
T. McCue (Widnes)
H. Murphy (Wakefield T.)
R. Nicholson (Huddersfield)
I. Owens (Leeds)
D. Phillips (Oldham)
M. Ryan (Wigan)
Edward Ward (Wigan)
Ernest Ward (Bradford N.)
F. Whitcombe (Bradford N.)
L. White (York)

Managers: W. Popplewell
(Bramley) and W. Gabbatt
(Barrow)

1950 Tour

E. Ward (Bradford N.)
E. Ashcroft (Wigan)
T. Bradshaw (Wigan)
J. Cunliffe (Wigan)
T. Danby (Salford)
A. Daniels (Halifax)
J. Egan (Wigan)
J. Featherstone (Warrington)
K. Gee (Wigan)
E. Gwyther (Belle Vue R.)
F. Higgins (Widnes)
J. Hilton (Wigan)
W. Horne (Barrow)
J. Ledgard (Leigh)
H. Murphy (Wakefield T.)
D. Naughton (Widnes)
F. Osmond (Swinton)
A. Pepperell (Workington T.)
D. Phillips (Belle Vue R.)
R. Pollard (Dewsbury)
G. Ratcliffe (Wigan)
M. Ryan (Wigan)
R. Ryan (Warrington)
H. Street (Dewsbury)
K. Traill (Bradford N.)
R. Williams (Leeds)

Managers: G. Oldroyd
(Dewsbury) and T. Spedding
(Belle Vue R.)

1954 Tour

R. Williams (Hunslet)
E. Ashcroft (Wigan)
W. Boston (Wigan)
J. Bowden (Huddersfield)
B. Briggs (Huddersfield)
A. Burnell (Hunslet)
E. Cahill (Rochdale H.)
F. Castle (Barrow)
J. Cunliffe (Wigan)
D. Greenall (St. Helens)
G. Gunney (Hunslet)
T. Harris (Hull)
G. Helme (Warrington)
J. Henderson (Workington T.)
P. Jackson (Barrow)
B. L. Jones (Leeds)
T. McKinney (Salford)
T. O'Grady (Oldham)
C. Pawsey (Leigh)
A. Prescott (St. Helens)
R. Price (Warrington)
N. Silcock (Wigan)
K. Traill (Bradford N.)
A. Turnbull (Leeds)
D. Valentine (Huddersfield)
J. Wilkinson (Halifax)

Managers: T. Hesketh
(Wigan) and H. Rawson
(Hunslet)

1958 Tour

A. Prescott (St. Helens)
A. Ackerley (Halifax)
H. Archer (Workington T.)
E. Ashton (Wigan)
D. Bolton (Wigan)
F. Carlton (St. Helens)
J. Challinor (Warrington)
A. Davies (Oldham)
B. Edgar (Workington T.)
E. Fraser (Warrington)
D. Goodwin (Barrow)
T. Harris (Hull)
R. Huddart (Whitehaven)
K. Jackson (Oldham)
P. Jackson (Barrow)
V. Karalius (St. Helens)

B. McTigue (Wigan)
M. Martyn (Leigh)
G. Moses (St. Helens)
A. Murphy (St. Helens)
F. Pitchford (Oldham)
I. Southward (Workington T.)
M. Sullivan (Wigan)
A. Terry (St. Helens)
J. Whiteley (Hull)
W. Wookey (Workington T.)

Managers: B. Manson
(Swinton) and T. Mitchell
(Workington T.)
Coach: J. Brough
(Workington T.)

1962 Tour

E. Ashton (Wigan)
D. Bolton (Wigan)
W. Boston (Wigan)
F. Carlton (Wigan)
G. Cooper (Featherstone R.)
B. Edgar (Workington T.)
R. Evans (Wigan)
D. Fox (Featherstone R.)
N. Fox (Wakefield T.)
E. Fraser (Warrington)
L. Gilfedder (Warrington)
N. Herbert (Workington T.)
R. Huddart (St. Helens)
B. McTigue (Wigan)
A. Murphy (St. Helens)
K. Noble (Huddersfield)
H. Poynton (Wakefield T.)
G. Round (Wakefield T.)
W. Sayer (Wigan)
J. Shaw (Halifax)
P. Small (Castleford)
I. Southward (Workington T.)
M. Sullivan (St. Helens)
J. Taylor (Hull K.R.)
D. Turner (Wakefield T.)
J. Wilkinson (Wakefield T.)

Managers: S. Hadfield
(Wakefield T.) and A. Walker
(Rochdale H.)
Coach: C. Hutton (Hull K.R.)

1966 Tour

H. Poole (Leeds)
W. Aspinall (Warrington)
T. Bishop (St. Helens)
I. Brooke (Bradford N.)
W. Bryant (Castleford)
A. Buckley (Swinton)
W. Burgess (Barrow)
C. Clarke (Wigan)
G. Crewdson (Keighley)
C. Dooler (Featherstone R.)
B. Edgar (Workington T.)
P. Flanagan (Hull K.R.)
T. Fogerty (Halifax)
K. Gowers (Swinton)
A. Hardisty (Castleford)
B. Jones (Wakefield T.)
A. Keegan (Hull)
J. Mantle (St. Helens)
F. Myler (Widnes)
W. Ramsey (Hunslet)
K. Roberts (Halifax)
D. Robinson (Swinton)
G. Shelton (Hunslet)
J. Stopford (Swinton)
C. Watson (St. Helens)
G. Wriglesworth (Leeds)

Managers: W. Spaven (Hull
K.R.) and J. Errock (Oldham)

1970 Tour

F. Myler (St. Helens)
J. Atkinson (Leeds)
D. Chisnall (Leigh)
R. Dutton (Widnes)
D. Edwards (Castleford)
A. Fisher (Bradford N.)
P. Flanagan (Hull K.R.)
A. Hardisty (Castleford)
D. Hartley (Castleford)
K. Hepworth (Castleford)
C. Hesketh (Salford)
S. Hynes (Leeds)
R. Irving (Oldham)
D. Laughton (Wigan)
P. Lowe (Hull K.R.)
R. Millward (Hull K.R.)
T. Price (Bradford N.)

M. Reilly (Castleford)
D. Robinson (Wigan)
B. Seabourne (Leeds)
M. Shoebottom (Leeds)
A. Smith (Leeds)
C. Sullivan (Hull)
J. Thompson (Featherstone R.)
J. Ward (Salford)
C. Watson (St. Helens)

Manager: J. Harding (Leigh)
Coach: J. Whiteley (Hull)

1974 Tour

C. Hesketh (Salford)
K. Ashcroft (Warrington)
J. Atkinson (Leeds)
A. Bates (Dewsbury)
J. Bates (Dewsbury)
J. Bevan (Warrington)
J. Bridges (Featherstone R.)
J. Butler (Rochdale H.)
P. Charlton (Salford)
E. Chisnall (St. Helens)
T. Clawson (Oldham)
C. Dixon (Salford)
L. Dyl (Leeds)
D. Eckersley (St. Helens)
K. Gill (Salford)
J. Gray (Wigan)
J. Mills (Widnes)
R. Millward (Hull K.R.)
S. Nash (Featherstone R.)
G. Nicholls (St. Helens)
S. Norton (Castleford)
D. Redfearn (Bradford N.)
P. Rose (Hull K.R.)
J. Thompson (Featherstone R.)
D. Watkins (Salford)
D. Willicombe (Wigan)

Replacements during tour
W. Ramsey (Bradford N.) for
J. Bates; M. Richards
(Salford) for Atkinson

Manager: R. Parker
(Blackpool B.)
Coach: J. Challinor
(St. Helens)

1979 Tour

D. Laughton (Widnes)
M. Adams (Widnes)
D. Barends (Bradford N.)
L. Casey (Bradford N.)
S. Evans (Featherstone R.)
P. Glynn (St. Helens)
J. Grayshon (Bradford N.)
P. Hogan (Hull K.R.)
J. Holmes (Leeds)
E. Hughes (Widnes)
M. James (St. Helens)
J. Joyner (Castleford)
G. Liptrot (St. Helens)
B. Lockwood (Hull K.R.)
T. Martyn (Warrington)
R. Mathias (St. Helens)
J. Mills (Widnes)
R. Millward (Hull K.R.)
K. Mumby (Bradford N.)
S. Nash (Salford)
G. Nicholls (St. Helens)
S. Norton (Hull)
A. Redfearn (Bradford N.)
T. Skerrett (Wakefield T.)
M. Smith (Hull K.R.)
G. Stephens (Castleford)
C. Stone (Hull)
D. Ward (Leeds)
D. Watkinson (Hull K.R.)
J. Woods (Leigh)

Replacements during tour
J. Burke (Wakefield T.) for
Mills; G. Fairbairn (Wigan)
for Martyn; D. Topliss
(Wakefield T.) for Millward

Managers: H. Womersley
(Bradford N.) and
R. Gemmell (Hull)
Coach E. Ashton (St. Helens)

1984 Tour*

B. Noble (Bradford N.)
M. Adams (Widnes)
R. Ashton (Oldham)
K. Beardmore (Castleford)
M. Burke (Widnes)
C. Burton (Hull K.R.)
B. Case (Wigan)
G. Clark (Hull K.R.)
L. Crooks (Hull)
S. Donlan (Leigh)
D. Drummond (Leigh)
R. Duane (Warrington)
T. Flanagan (Oldham)
D. Foy (Oldham)
A. Goodway (Oldham)
A. Gregory (Widnes)
E. Hanley (Bradford N.)
D. Hobbs (Featherstone R.)
N. Holding (St. Helens)
J. Joyner (Castleford)
J. Lydon (Widnes)
K. Mumby (Bradford N.)
A. Myler (Widnes)
M. O'Neill (Widnes)
H. Pinner (St. Helens)
W. Proctor (Hull)
Keith Rayne (Leeds)
G. Schofield (Hull)
M. Smith (Hull K.R.)
M. Worrall (Oldham)

Replacement during tour
J. Basnett (Widnes) for Duane

Managers: R. Gemmell (Hull)
and R. Davis (RLHQ)
Coach: Frank Myler (Oldham)

*One match in Papua New
Guinea

1988 Tour*

E. Hanley (Wigan)
K. Beardmore (Castleford)
B. Case (Wigan)
L. Crooks (Leeds)
P. Dixon (Halifax)
S. Edwards (Wigan)
K. Fairbank (Bradford N.)
M. Ford (Oldham)
P. Ford (Bradford N.)
C. Gibson (Leeds)
H. Gill (Wigan)
A. Gregory (Wigan)
M. Gregory (Warrington)
P. Groves (St. Helens)
R. Haggerty (St. Helens)
D. Hulme (Widnes)
P. Loughlin (St. Helens)
P. Medley (Leeds)
M. Offiah (Widnes)
A. Platt (St. Helens)
R. Powell (Leeds)
G. Schofield (Leeds)
D. Stephenson (Leeds)
H. Waddell (Oldham)
K. Ward (Castleford)
I. Wilkinson (Halifax)

Replacements during tour
D. Wright (Widnes) for
Edwards; A. Currier (Widnes)
and P. Hulme (Widnes) for
Schofield and Medley; R.
Eyres (Widnes) and J. Joyner
(Castleford) for Crooks, Dixon
and Platt

Managers: L. Bettinson
(Salford) and D. Howes
(RLHQ)
Coach: M. Reilly

*Including Papua New Guinea

1990 Tour*

M. Gregory (Warrington)
D. Betts (Wigan)
C. Bibb (Featherstone R.)
D. Bishop (Hull K.R.)
P. Clarke (Wigan)
J. Davies (Widnes)
M. Dermott (Wigan)
P. Dixon (Leeds)
P. Eastwood (Hull)
K. England (Castleford)
K. Fairbank (Bradford N.)
D. Fox (Featherstone R.)
C. Gibson (Leeds)
R. Goulding (Wigan)
S. Irwin (Castleford)
L. Jackson (Hull)
I. Lucas (Wigan)
J. Lydon (Wigan)
M. Offiah (Widnes)
D. Powell (Sheffield E.)
R. Powell (Leeds)
G. Price (Wakefield T.)
G. Schofield (Leeds)
R. Simpson (Bradford N.)
K. Skerrett (Bradford N.)
I. Smales (Featherstone R.)
G. Steadman (Castleford)
A. Sullivan (Hull K.R.)
A. Tait (Widnes)

Replacements during tour
J. Devereux (Widnes) for
Sullivan; D. Lyon
(Warrington) for Tait.

Manager: M. Lindsay (Wigan)
Coach: M. Reilly

*Papua New Guinea and
New Zealand only

ALL TIME TOUR RECORDS
(not including 1992)

IN AUSTRALIA
Highest score: 101-0 v. South Australia in 1914

Biggest defeat: 42-6 v. New South Wales in 1920
(Also *widest margin*)

Fewest defeats: 1 (and 1 draw) from 21 matches in
1958 and from 17 matches in 1970

Most defeats: 9 from 22 matches in 1966

Biggest attendances: 70,419 v. New South Wales
(Sydney) in 1950

IN NEW ZEALAND
Highest score: 81-14 v. Bay of Plenty in 1962

Widest margin win: 72-3 v. Buller in 1928
72-3 v. North Island in 1958

Biggest defeat: 46-13 v. Auckland in 1962 (Also *widest margin*)

Fewest defeats: The tourists have won all their matches
in the following years: 1910 (4 matches), 1914 (6),
1932 (8), 1936 (8), 1966 (8), 1970 (7).

Most defeats: 4 from 8 matches in 1984

Biggest attendance: 35,000 v. Auckland in 1920

PLAYERS' FULL TOUR RECORDS
Most full appearances: 24 by Dick Huddart in 1958

Most tries: 38 by Mick Sullivan in 1958

Most goals and points: 127g, 278 pts by Lewis Jones in
1954

Most tours: 3 by Jonathan Parkin (1920, 1924, 1928)
Jim Sullivan (1924, 1928, 1932)
Joe Thompson (1924, 1928, 1932)
Augustus Risman (1932, 1936, 1946)
Brian Edgar (1958, 1962, 1966)
Roger Millward (1970, 1974, 1979)
John Joyner (1979, 1984, 1988 as
replacement)
Garry Schofield (1984, 1988, 1990)

Biggest club representation: 8 by Wigan in 1950 —
Ernie Ashcroft, Tommy Bradshaw, Jack Cunliffe, Joe
Egan, Ken Gee, Jack Hilton, Gordon Ratcliffe, Martin
Ryan

Brothers touring together: Bryn and Jack Evans (1928),
Don and Neil Fox (1962), Alan and John Bates
(1974), David and Paul Hulme (1988, Paul as
replacement)

GREAT BRITAIN IN THE WORLD CUP

A — Australia, Fr — France, GB — Great Britain, NZ — New Zealand, PNG — Papua New Guinea

1954 in France   *Winners:* Great Britain

30 Oct.	Fr	22	NZ	13	Paris	13,240
31 Oct.	GB	28	A	13	Lyons	10,250
7 Nov.	GB	13	Fr	13	Toulouse	37,471
7 Nov.	A	34	NZ	15	Marseilles	20,000
11 Nov.	GB	26	NZ	6	Bordeaux	14,000
11 Nov.	A	5	Fr	15	Nantes	13,000

Play off

13 Nov.	GB	16	Fr	12	Paris	30,368

Final Table

	P.	W.	D.	L.	F.	A.	Pts.
Great Britain	3	2	1	0	67	32	5
France	3	2	1	0	50	31	5
Australia	3	1	0	2	52	58	2
New Zealand	3	0	0	3	34	82	0

1957 in Australia   *Winners:* Australia

15 June	GB	23	Fr	5	Sydney	50,007
15 June	A	25	NZ	5	Brisbane	29,636
17 June	GB	6	A	31	Sydney	57,955
17 June	NZ	10	Fr	14	Brisbane	28,000
22 June	A	26	Fr	9	Sydney	35,158
25 June	GB	21	NZ	29	Sydney	14,263

Final Table

	P.	W.	D.	L.	F.	A.	Pts.
Australia	3	3	0	0	82	20	6
Great Britain	3	1	0	2	50	65	2
New Zealand	3	1	0	2	44	60	2
France	3	1	0	2	28	59	2

344

1960 in England   *Winners:* Great Britain

24 Sept.	GB	23	NZ	8	Bradford	20,577
24 Sept.	A	13	Fr	12	Wigan	20,278
1 Oct.	A	21	NZ	15	Leeds	10,773
1 Oct.	GB	33	Fr	7	Swinton	22,923
8 Oct.	A	3	GB	10	Bradford	32,773
8 Oct.	NZ	9	Fr	0	Wigan	2,876

Final Table

	P.	W.	D.	L.	F.	A.	Pts.
Great Britain	3	3	0	0	66	18	6
Australia	3	2	0	1	37	37	4
New Zealand	3	1	0	2	32	44	2
France	3	0	0	3	19	55	0

1968 in Australia   *Winners:* Australia
and New Zealand

25 May	A	25	GB	10	Sydney	62,256
25 May	Fr	15	NZ	10	Auckland	18,000
1 June	A	31	NZ	12	Brisbane	23,608
2 June	Fr	7	GB	2	Auckland	15,760
8 June	A	37	Fr	4	Brisbane	32,600
8 June	GB	38	NZ	14	Sydney	14,105

Final Table

	P.	W.	D.	L.	F.	A.	Pts.
Australia	3	3	0	0	93	26	6
France	3	2	0	1	26	49	4
Great Britain	3	1	0	2	50	46	2
New Zealand	3	0	0	3	36	84	0

Play off final

| 10 June | A | 20 | Fr | 2 | Sydney | 54,290 |

*Bev Risman, captain of the Great Britain
1968 World Cup squad in Australia and
New Zealand.*

1970 in England   *Winners:* Australia

21 Oct.	A	47	NZ	11	Wigan	9,586
24 Oct.	GB	11	A	4	Leeds	15,084
25 Oct.	NZ	16	Fr	15	Hull	3,824
28 Oct.	GB	6	Fr	0	Castleford	8,958
31 Oct.	GB	27	NZ	17	Swinton	5,609
1 Nov.	Fr	17	A	15	Bradford	6,215

Final Table

	P.	W.	D.	L.	F.	A.	Pts.
Great Britain	3	3	0	0	44	21	6
Australia	3	1	0	2	66	39	2
France	3	1	0	2	32	37	2
New Zealand	3	1	0	2	44	89	2

Play off final

| 7 Nov. | A | 12 | GB | 7 | Leeds | 18,776 |

1972 in France   *Winners:* Great Britain

28 Oct.	Fr	20	NZ	9	Marseilles	20,748
29 Oct.	GB	27	A	21	Perpignan	6,324
1 Nov.	A	9	NZ	5	Paris	8,000
1 Nov.	GB	13	Fr	4	Grenoble	5,321
4 Nov.	GB	53	NZ	19	Pau	7,500
5 Nov.	A	31	Fr	9	Toulouse	10,332

Final Table

	P.	W.	D.	L.	F.	A.	Pts.
Great Britain	3	3	0	0	93	44	6
Australia	3	2	0	1	61	41	4
France	3	1	0	2	33	53	2
New Zealand	3	0	0	3	33	82	0

Play off final

| 11 Nov. | GB | 10 | A | 10 | Lyons | 4,231 |

No further score after extra-time so Great Britain took the championship because they had scored the greatest number of points in the qualifying League table.

1977 in Australia   *Winners:* Australia
and New Zealand

29 May	A	27	NZ	12	Auckland	18,000
5 June	GB	23	Fr	4	Auckland	10,000
11 June	A	21	Fr	9	Sydney	13,231
12 June	GB	30	NZ	12	C'church	7,000
18 June	A	19	GB	5	Brisbane	27,000
19 June	NZ	28	Fr	20	Auckland	8,000

Final Table

	P.	W.	D.	L.	F.	A.	Pts.
Australia	3	3	0	0	67	26	6
Great Britain	3	2	0	1	58	35	4
New Zealand	3	1	0	2	52	77	2
France	3	0	0	3	33	72	0

Play off final

25 June A 13 GB 12 Sydney 24,457

1985-88 Series *Winners:* Australia

1985

7 July	NZ	18 A	0 Auckland	19,000
9 Nov.	GB	6 NZ	6 Leeds	22,209
7 Dec.	Fr	0 NZ	22 Perpignan	5,000

1986

16 Feb.	Fr	10 GB	10 Avignon	4,000
29 July	A	32 NZ	12 Brisbane	22,811
17 Aug.	PNG	24 NZ	22 Port Moresby	15,000
4 Oct.	PNG	12 A	62 Port Moresby	17,000
22 Nov.	GB	15 A	24 Wigan	20,169
13 Dec.	Fr	0 A	52 Carcassonne	3,000

1987

24 Jan.	GB	52 Fr	4 Leeds	6,567
24 Oct.	GB	42 PNG	0 Wigan	9,121
15 Nov.	Fr	21 PNG	4 Carcassonne	5,000

1988

22 May	PNG	22 GB	42 Port Moresby	12,077
9 July	A	12 GB	26 Sydney	15,994
10 July	NZ	66 PNG	14 Auckland	8,392
17 July	NZ	12 GB	10 Christchurch	8,525
20 July	A	70 PNG	8 Wagga Wagga	11,685

Final Table

	P.	W.	D.	L.	F.	A.	Pts.
Australia	7	5	0	2	252	91	12*
New Zealand	7	4	1	2	158	86	11*
Great Britain	8	4	2	2	203	90	10
P. N. Guinea	7	1	0	6	84	325	4*
France	5	1	1	3	35	140	3

*Awarded two points in lieu of France's non-fulfilment of fixtures Down Under.

Play off final

1988

9 Oct. A 25 NZ 12 Auckland 47,363

GREAT BRITAIN WORLD CUP SQUADS

Captains in bold

1954 IN FRANCE

D. Valentine (Huddersfield)
W. Banks (Huddersfield)
H. Bradshaw (Huddersfield)
G. Brown (Leeds)
R. Coverdale (Hull)
G. Helme (Warrington)
P. Jackson (Barrow)
F. Kitchen (Leigh)
J. Ledgard (Leigh)

A. Naughton (Warrington)
D. Robinson (Wakefield T)
D. Rose (Leeds)
R. Rylance (Huddersfield)
S. Smith (Hunslet)
M. Sullivan (Huddersfield)
J. Thorley (Halifax)
B. Watts (York)
J. Whiteley (Hull)

Manager: G. Shaw (Castleford)

1957 IN AUSTRALIA

A. Prescott (St. Helens)
E. Ashton (Wigan)
W. Boston (Wigan)
A. Davies (Oldham)
J. Grundy (Barrow)
G. Gunney (Hunslet)
T. Harris (Hull)
P. Jackson (Barrow)
L. Jones (Leeds)

S. Little (Oldham)
T. McKinney (St. Helens)
G. Moses (St. Helens)
R. Price (Warrington)
A. Rhodes (St. Helens)
J. Stevenson (Leeds)
M. Sullivan (Huddersfield)
D. Turner (Oldham)
J. Whiteley (Hull)

Managers: W. Fallowfield (RL Secretary) and H. Rawson (Hunslet)

1960 IN ENGLAND

E. Ashton (Wigan)
W. Boston (Wigan)
J. Challinor (Warrington)
A. Davies (Oldham)
E. Fraser (Warrington)
R. Greenough (Warrington)
T. Harris (Hull)
V. Karalius (St. Helens)
B. McTigue (Wigan)

A. Murphy (St. Helens)
F. Myler (Widnes)
A. Rhodes (St. Helens)
B. Shaw (Hunslet)
J. Shaw (Halifax)
M. Sullivan (Wigan)
D. Turner (Wakefield T)
J. Whiteley (Hull)
J. Wilkinson (Wakefield T)

Manager: W. Fallowfield (RL Secretary)

1968 IN AUSTRALIA AND NEW ZEALAND

B. Risman (Leeds)
K. Ashcroft (Leigh)
J. Atkinson (Leeds)
T. Bishop (St. Helens)
I. Brooke (Wakefield T)
A. Burwell (Hull KR)
M. Clark (Leeds)

D. Edwards (Castleford)
P. Flanagan (Hull KR)
R. French (Widnes)
R. Haigh (Wakefield T)
R. Millward (Hull KR)
A. Morgan (Featherstone R)
C. Renilson (Halifax)

M. Shoebottom (Leeds)
C. Sullivan (Hull)
J. Warlow (St. Helens)
C. Watson (St. Helens)
C. Young (Hull KR)

Manager: W. Fallowfield (RL Secretary)   Coach: C. Hutton (Hull KR)

1970 IN ENGLAND

F. Myler (St. Helens)
K. Ashcroft (Leigh)
J. Atkinson (Leeds)
P. Charlton (Salford)
D. Chisnall (Leigh)
R. Dutton (Widnes)
A. Fisher (Bradford N & Leeds)

R. Haigh (Leeds)
D. Hartley (Castleford)
K. Hepworth (Castleford)
C. Hesketh (Salford)
S. Hynes (Leeds)
K. Jones (Wigan)
D. Laughton (Wigan)

M. Reilly (Castleford)
M. Shoebottom (Leeds)
A. Smith (Leeds)
J. Thompson (Featherstone R)
C. Watson (St. Helens)

Manager: J. Harding (Leigh)   Coach: J. Whiteley (Hull KR)

1972 IN FRANCE

C. Sullivan (Hull)
J. Atkinson (Leeds)
P. Charlton (Salford)
T. Clawson (Leeds)
C. Dixon (Salford)
C. Hesketh (Salford)
J. Holmes (Leeds)

R. Irving (Oldham)
D. Jeanes (Leeds)
A. Karalius (St. Helens)
B. Lockwood (Castleford)
P. Lowe (Hull KR)
S. Nash (Featherstone R)
G. Nicholls (Widnes)

D. O'Neill (Widnes)
D. Redfearn (Bradford N)
M. Stephenson (Dewsbury)
D. Topliss (Wakefield T)
John Walsh (St. Helens)

Manager: W. Spaven (Hull KR)   Coach: J. Challinor (St. Helens)

1977 IN AUSTRALIA AND NEW ZEALAND

R. Millward (Hull KR)
E. Bowman (Workington T)
L. Casey (Hull KR)
L. Dyl (Leeds)
K. Elwell (Widnes)
G. Fairbairn (Wigan)
K. Fielding (Salford)

W. Francis (Wigan)
K. Gill (Salford)
A. Hodkinson (Rochdale H)
P. Hogan (Barrow)
J. Holmes (Leeds)
S. Lloyd (Castleford)
S. Nash (Salford)

G. Nicholls (St. Helens)
S. Pitchford (Leeds)
P. Smith (Featherstone R)
J. Thompson (Featherstone R)
D. Ward (Leeds)
S. Wright (Widnes)

Manager: R. Parker (Blackpool B)   Coach: D. Watkins (Salford)

Roger Millward, skipper of the 1977 Great Britain World Cup squad.

GREAT BRITAIN RECORDS

● In Test and World Cup matches.

MOST TRIES IN CAREER

*41 Mick Sullivan (Huddersfield, Wigan,
    St. Helens, York)............................... 1954-63
26 Garry Schofield (Hull, Leeds)................ 1984-
24 Billy Boston (Wigan).......................... 1954-63
19 Martin Offiah (Widnes)........................ 1988-
18 Ellery Hanley (Bradford N., Wigan)....... 1984-
17 Roger Millward (Cas'd, Hull K.R.)........ 1966-78
16 Alex Murphy (St. Helens, Warrington).... 1958-71
14 Eric Ashton (Wigan)............................ 1957-63
14 Neil Fox (Wakefield T.)....................... 1959-69
13 Clive Sullivan (Hull)........................... 1967-73
12 John Atkinson (Leeds)......................... 1968-80
10 Shaun Edwards (Wigan)....................... 1985-
10 Jim Leytham (Wigan).......................... 1907-10

*Mick Sullivan also scored two tries for Great Britain against France before the matches were given Test status.

● Most tries by a forward is eight by Derek Turner (Oldham, Wakefield T.) 1956-62; and Phil Lowe (Hull K.R.) 1970-78.

MOST GOALS IN CAREER

93 Neil Fox (Wakefield T.)......................... 1959-69
66 Lewis Jones (Leeds)............................. 1954-57
64 Jim Sullivan (Wigan)........................... 1924-33
53 Eric Fraser (Warrington)....................... 1958-61
44 George Fairbairn (Wigan, Hull K.R.)....... 1977-82
29 Paul Loughlin (St. Helens).................... 1988-
26 Jonathan Davies (Widnes)..................... 1990-
26 Joe Lydon (Widnes, Wigan)................... 1983-
25 Terry Clawson
    (Featherstone R., Leeds, Oldham)......... 1962-74
24 Paul Eastwood (Hull)........................... 1990-
22 Ray Dutton (Widnes)........................... 1970
22 John Holmes (Leeds)............................ 1971-82
22 Ernest Ward (Bradford N.).................... 1946-52
21 Mick Burke (Widnes)........................... 1980-86
21 Ken Gowers (Swinton)......................... 1962-66

MOST POINTS IN CAREER

228 Neil Fox (Wakefield T.)....................... 1959-69
147 Lewis Jones (Leeds)........................... 1954-57
128 Jim Sullivan (Wigan)......................... 1924-33
126 Garry Schofield (Hull, Leeds)............. 1984-
123 Mick Sullivan (Huddersfield, Wigan,
    St. Helens, York)............................... 1954-63
109 Eric Fraser (Warrington)..................... 1958-61
91 George Fairbairn (Wigan, Hull K.R.)..... 1977-82
81 Roger Millward (Castleford, Hull K.R.).. 1966-78
76 Martin Offiah (Widnes)....................... 1988-
75 Joe Lydon (Widnes, Wigan)................. 1983-

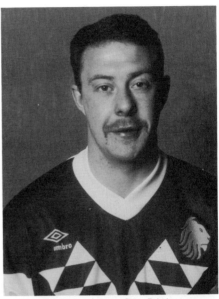

Garry Schofield, current top Great Britain tryscorer.

Paul Loughlin, current top Great Britain goalscorer.

MOST TRIES IN A MATCH

5 by Martin Offiah (Widnes) v. France at Leeds
16 February, 1991
4 by Jim Leytham (Wigan) v. Australia at Brisbane
2 July, 1910
Billy Boston (Wigan) v. New Zealand at Auckland
24 July, 1954
Alex Murphy (St. Helens) v. France at Leeds
14 March, 1959
Garry Schofield (Hull) v. New Zealand at Wigan
2 November, 1985
3 by Bill Jukes (Hunslet) v. Australia at Sydney
18 June, 1910
Bert Avery (Oldham) v. New Zealand at Auckland
30 July, 1910
Billy Stone (Hull) v. New Zealand at Auckland
31 July, 1920
Jonty Parkin (Wakefield T.) v. New Zealand at
Auckland 31 July, 1920
Charlie Carr (Barrow) v. New Zealand at Leeds
15 January, 1927
Stan Smith (Leeds) v. Australia at Sydney
16 July, 1932
Arthur Bassett (Halifax) v. Australia at Brisbane
6 July, 1946
George Wilson (Workington T.) v. New Zealand at
Bradford 6 October, 1951
Mick Sullivan (Huddersfield) v. New Zealand at
Bradford 12 November, 1955
Dave Bolton (Wigan) v. France at Wigan
23 November, 1957
Mick Sullivan (Wigan) v. Australia at Sydney
19 July, 1958
Mick Sullivan (Wigan) v. New Zealand at
Auckland 9 August, 1958
Mick Sullivan (Wigan) v. France at Leeds
14 March, 1959
Clive Sullivan (Hull) v. New Zealand at Sydney
(World Cup) 8 June, 1968
Bill Burgess (Barrow) v. France at St. Helens
30 November, 1968
Keith Fielding (Salford) v. France at Grenoble
20 January, 1974
Henderson Gill (Wigan) v. France at Hull
6 December, 1981
Garry Schofield (Leeds) v. France at Leeds
16 February, 1991

● Bill Jukes and Bert Avery are the only forwards to have
scored hat-tricks for Great Britain, both on tour in 1910.

MOST GOALS IN A MATCH

10 by Lewis Jones (Leeds) v. Australia at Brisbane
3 July, 1954
Bernard Ganley (Oldham) v. France at Wigan
23 November, 1957
John Holmes (Leeds) v. New Zealand at Pau
(World Cup) 4 November, 1972
9 by Lewis Jones (Leeds) v. France at Leeds
26 January, 1957
Neil Fox (Wakefield T.) v. France at Wigan
3 April, 1963
Neil Fox (Wakefield T.) v. France at Leigh
18 March, 1964
8 by Eric Fraser (Warrington) v. Australia at Sydney
19 July, 1958
David Creasser (Leeds) v. France at Leeds
1 March, 1985
Joe Lydon (Wigan) v. France at Leeds
24 January, 1987
Paul Eastwood (Hull) v. France at Leeds
16 February, 1991
Jonathan Davies (Widnes) v. Papua New Guinea
at Wigan 9 November, 1991
7 by Lewis Jones (Leeds) v. France at St. Helens
10 April, 1957
Eric Fraser (Warrington) v. New Zealand at
Auckland 9 August, 1958
Eric Fraser (Warrington) v. France at Leeds
14 March, 1959
Neil Fox (Wakefield T.) v. New Zealand at
Swinton 4 November, 1961
Neil Fox (Wakefield T.) v. France at Swinton
23 January, 1965
Bev Risman (Leeds) v. New Zealand at Sydney
(World Cup) 8 June, 1968
Roger Millward (Hull K.R.) v. Australia at
Sydney 20 June, 1970
George Fairbairn (Wigan) v. France at Auckland
(World Cup) 5 June, 1977
John Woods (Leigh) v. France at Hull
6 December, 1981
David Stephenson (Wigan) v. Papua New Guinea
at Wigan 24 October, 1987
Paul Loughlin (St. Helens) v. Papua New Guinea
at Port Moresby 22 May, 1988

MOST POINTS IN A MATCH

26 (10g, 2t) by John Holmes (Leeds) v. New Zealand
at Pau (World Cup)
4 November, 1972

21 (9g, 1t) by Lewis Jones (Leeds) v. France at
Leeds 26 January, 1957
Neil Fox (Wakefield T.) v. France at
Wigan 3 April, 1963
Neil Fox (Wakefield T.) v. France at
Leigh 18 March, 1964

20 (10g) by Lewis Jones (Leeds) v. Australia at
Brisbane 3 July, 1954

(10g) Bernard Ganley (Oldham) v. France at
Wigan 23 November, 1957

(7g, 2t) Roger Millward (Hull K.R.) v.
Australia at Sydney 20 June, 1970

(8g, 1t) Joe Lydon (Wigan) v. France at Leeds
24 February, 1987

(5t) Martin Offiah (Widnes) v. France at
Leeds 16 February, 1991

(8g, 1t) Paul Eastwood (Hull) v. France at
Leeds 16 February, 1991

Neil Fox.

MOST APPEARANCES

46	Mick Sullivan*
33 + 1	Ellery Hanley
32	Garry Schofield
31	Billy Boston
29 + 1	Cliff Watson
29	George Nicholls
29	Neil Fox
28 + 1	Roger Millward
28	Alan Prescott
27	Phil Jackson
27	Alex Murphy
26	Eric Ashton
26	John Atkinson
25	Brian McTigue
25	Jim Sullivan
25	Tommy Harris

*Mick Sullivan's record number of appear-
ances include a record run of 36 successive
matches. In addition he played in two
matches against France before they were
given Test status.

Lewis Jones.

LONGEST TEST CAREERS

14 years   —   Gus Risman
1932 to 1946 (17 appearances)
13 years 9 months — Billy Batten
1908 to 1921 (10 appearances)
13 years 6 months — Alex Murphy
1958 to 1971 (27 appearances)
12 years 9 months — Roger Millward
1966 to 1978 (28 + 1 appearances)
12 years 6 months — John Atkinson
1968 to 1980 (26 appearances)
12 years 6 months — Terry Clawson
1962 to 1974 (14 appearances)

YOUNGEST TEST PLAYER

Paul Newlove was 18 years 72 days old when he made his Great Britain Test debut as a 76th-minute substitute in the first Test against New Zealand at Old Trafford, Manchester, on 21 October 1989, making his full debut a week later. Born on 10 August 1971, he beat the previous record held by Shaun Edwards (born 17 October 1966) who was 18 years 135 days old when capped against France at Leeds on 1 March 1985.

Roger Millward (born 16 September 1947) was 18 years 37 days old when he was a non-playing substitute for the second Test against New Zealand at Bradford on 23 October 1965.

OLDEST TEST PLAYER

Jeff Grayshon (born 4 March 1949) was 36 years 8 months when he played in his last Test for Britain, against New Zealand at Elland Road, Leeds, on 9 November 1985.

RECORD TEAM CHANGES

The record number of team changes made by the Great Britain selectors is 10. This has happened on three occasions, all against Australia.

In 1929, Britain crashed 31-8 to Australia in the first Test at Hull KR and retained only three players for the second Test at Leeds, where they won 9-3.

After their biggest ever defeat of 50-12 in the 1963 second Test at Swinton, Britain dropped nine players and were forced to make another change when Vince Karalius was injured and replaced by Don Fox. Britain stopped Australia making a clean sweep of the series by winning 16-5 at Leeds in the last Test.

Following the 40-4 first Test defeat at Hull City's soccer ground in 1982, the selectors again made 10 changes, not including substitutes, Britain going down 27-6 in the second Test at Wigan.

Britain have never fielded the same team for three or more successive Tests.

Record-breaking Great Britain Under-21 goalkicker Martin Pearson, the Featherstone Rovers stand off.

UNDER-21s

1991-92 REVIEW

Wigan winger David Myers registered a hat-trick of try hat-tricks in a trio of Great Britain Under-21 encounters. Unable to command a regular first-team spot at Central Park, the former Widnes and Warrington back revelled in the scoring blitz by the young Lions.

The rampant Under-21s demolished the Papua New Guinea tourists 58-0 at Leeds, a record score for the juniors, before beating their French counterparts 56-2 at Halifax and 34-2 at Albi. Their final tally was 148 points, an average of 47 per match, with only four conceded.

While Myers dominated the tryscoring, Featherstone Rovers stand off Martin Pearson equalled the Under-21s goals record, with

eight on his debut against Papua. He then completed a hat-trick of records with three tries and 24 points at Halifax when he also kicked six goals.

Widnes loose forward Steve McCurrie took the British Coal Man of the Match award against Papua, his two-try tally being matched by centre Paul Newlove on his return to the international scene. Full details are chronicled in the section 1991 KUMULS.

Wigan's Phil Clarke returned from injury for the French double and skippered Britain to comfortable victories, earning the Man of the Match rating at Halifax and being a try-scorer on both occasions.

Great Britain coach Malcolm Reilly sprung a surprise for the Albi encounter by selecting St. Helens centre Gary Connolly and Hull

---

6 March		Halifax
GREAT BRITAIN 56		**FRANCE 2**
David Mycoe (Sheffield E.)	1.	Laurent Lucchese (Tarn Sud)
David Myers (Wigan)	2.	Philippe Ricard (Albi)
Mike Riley (St. Helens)	3.	Pascal Mons (Carcassonne)
Paul Newlove (Featherstone R.)	4.	David Despin (Villeneuve)
Richard Picksley (Sheffield E.)	5.	Eric Van Brussel (Carcassonne)
Martin Pearson (Featherstone R.)	6.	Alexandre Couttet (St. Gaudens)
Augustine O'Donnell (Wigan)	7.	Frederic Abadie (Lezignan)
Phil Sumner (Warrington)	8.	Sebastian Bouche (Toulouse Jules Julien)
Graham Southernwood (Castleford)	9.	Jean-Luc Vincent (St. Gaudens)
Paul Bonson (Featherstone R.)	10.	Lilian Hebert (Cahors)
Dean Busby (Hull)	11.	Pascal Jampy (XIII Catalan)
Chris Joynt (Oldham)	12.	Frederic Teixido (Limoux)
Phil Clarke (Wigan), Capt.	13.	Vincent Banet (XIII Catalan)
Jason Donohue (Leigh)	14.	Frederic Sana (St. Esteve)
Steve McCurrie (Widnes)	15.	Frederic Soulan (Ayguesvives)
Graeme Hallas (Hull K.R.)	16.	Stephane Tena (La Bacares)
Barrie-Jon Mather (Wigan)	17.	Christophe Canal (Villeneuve)

T: Myers (3), Pearson (3), Clarke, Joynt, Sumner, O'Donnell, McCurrie
G: Pearson (6)
Substitutions:
McCurrie for Sumner (41 min.)
Hallas for Picksley (53 min.)
Donohue for Newlove (71 min.)
Mather for Busby (77 min.)
Coach: Phil Larder

G: Abadie
Substitutions:
Sana for Jampy (35 min.)
Tena for Vincent (40 min.)
Soulan for Sana (73 min.)
Half-time: 30-2
Referee: Claude Alba (France)
Attendance: 2,638

second row man Steve McNamara only a fortnight after they had played for Great Britain in the British Coal Test at Hull, claiming it was part of their international education as tour candidates.

At Halifax, Great Britain's juniors ran in 11 tries without reply, featuring a touchdown by debutant Augustine O'Donnell, the Wigan utility man. Leigh half back Jason Donohue and Wigan's Barrie-Jon Mather came off the substitute bench for their first Under-21 caps.

In the return at Albi, Leeds prop Paul Anderson was drafted in as an 11th-hour debutant replacement for the injured Phil Sumner, while Wakefield's Richard Slater made his first appearance as a 69th-minute substitute.

Warrington prop Phil Sumner, a tryscorer at Halifax.

20 March   **Albi**

GREAT BRITAIN 34		**FRANCE 2**
David Mycoe (Sheffield E.)	1.	Olivier Bonnardel (Carpentras)
David Myers (Wigan)	2.	Claude Sirvent (St. Gaudens)
Gary Connolly (St. Helens)	3.	Patrice Rodriguez (Carpentras)
Paul Newlove (Featherstone R.)	4.	Pascal Mons (Carcassonne)
Mike Riley (St. Helens)	5.	Stephan Marc (St. Esteve)
Martin Pearson (Featherstone R.)	6.	Alex Couttet (St. Gaudens)
Augustine O'Donnell (Wigan)	7.	Laurent Zanchetti (Entraigues)
Paul Anderson (Leeds)	8.	Sebastian Marty (Villefranche)
Graham Southernwood (Castleford)	9.	Fabian Amador (Lezignan)
Paul Bonson (Featherstone R.)	10.	Lilian Hebert (Cahors)
Steve McNamara (Hull)	11.	Patrick Accrou (Avignon)
Chris Joynt (Oldham)	12.	Cyril Baudouin (Carpentras)
Phil Clarke (Wigan), Capt.	13.	Sebastian Balavoine (Pia)
Tommy Martyn (Oldham)	14.	Eric Garcia (Albi)
Dean Busby (Hull)	15.	Jean-Marc Vincent (St. Gaudens)
Graeme Hallas (Hull K.R.)	16.	Jean-Michel Baroni (Carpentras)
Richard Slater (Wakefield T.)	17.	Christophe Vela (Albi)

T: Myers (3), Clarke, Connolly
G: Pearson (5), O'Donnell, Martyn
Substitutions:
Hallas for Mycoe (37 min.)
Busby for Bonson (50 min.)
Martyn for Riley (62 min.)
Slater for McNamara (69 min.)
Coach: Malcolm Reilly

G: Rodriguez
Substitutions:
Vela for Couttet (44 min.)
Baroni for Accrou (44 min.)
Garcia for Marc (68 min.)
Vincent for Amador (71 min.)
Half-time: 14-0
Referee: Russell Smith (Castleford)
Attendance: 500

Sheffield Eagles full back David Mycoe, a 1991-92 ever-present Under-21.

Hull second row man Dean Busby off-loads against France at Halifax.

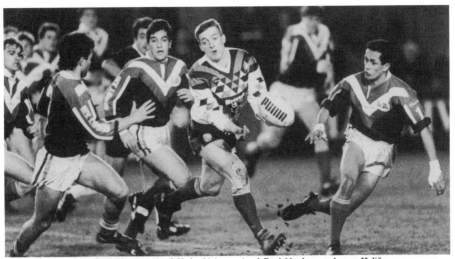

Great Britain's most-capped Under-21 international Paul Newlove on duty at Halifax.

GREAT BRITAIN UNDER-21s RESULTS

25 Nov.	1984	W 24-8	v.	F	Castleford
16 Dec.	1984	W 8-2	v.	F	Albi
9 Oct.	1985	L 12-16	v.	NZ	Bradford
19 Jan.	1986	L 6-19	v.	F	St. Esteve
2 Feb.	1986	W 6-2	v.	F	Whitehaven
8 Mar.	1987	W 40-7	v.	F	St. Jean de Luz
21 Mar.	1987	W 54-6	v.	F	St. Helens
6 Mar.	1988	L 13-14	v.	F	Ausillon
19 Mar.	1988	L 4-8	v.	F	St. Helens
20 Jan.	1989	W 30-0	v.	F	Leeds
4 Feb.	1989	L 8-16	v.	F	Carpentras
20 Jan.	1990	W 22-0	v.	F	Villeneuve
16 Feb.	1990	W 20-6	v.	F	Doncaster
26 Jan.	1991	W 48-2	v.	F	Limoux
15 Feb.	1991	L 6-16	v.	F	Wigan
30 Oct.	1991	W 58-0	v.	P	Leeds
6 Mar.	1992	W 56-2	v.	F	Halifax
20 Mar.	1992	W 34-2	v.	F	Albi

Key: F - France,
NZ - New Zealand
P - Papua New Guinea

GREAT BRITAIN UNDER-21s REGISTER

The following is a register of appearances for Great Britain Under-21s since this classification of match was introduced in 1984.

Figures in brackets are the total appearances, with the plus sign indicating substitute appearances, e.g. (3 + 1).

Away matches are in bold letters. Substitute appearances are in lower case letters.

ALLEN, S. (1) St. Helens: 1984 F
ANDERSON, G. (4) Castleford: 1989 F, **F**; 1990 **F**, F
ANDERSON, P. (1) Leeds: 1992 **F**

BECKWITH, M. (1 + 1) Whitehaven: 1986 f, F
BETTS, D. (4) Wigan: 1989 F, **F**; 1990 **F**, F
BIBB, C. (5) Featherstone R.: 1987 **F**, F; 1988 F; 1989 F, **F**
BISHOP, P. (1 + 1) Warrington: 1987 **F**, f
BONSON, P. (2) Featherstone R.: 1992 F, **F**
BOOTHROYD, G. (1) Castleford: 1989 F
BURGESS, A. (+1) Salford: 1991 f
BUSBY, D. (2 + 1) Hull: 1991 P; 1992 F, f

CARBERT, B. (3) Warrington: 1985 NZ; 1986 **F**, F
CASSIDY, F. (1 + 1) Swinton: 1988 f, **F**
CHAMBERS, G. (2) Warrington: 1991 **F**, F
CLARK, G. (2) Hull K.R.: 1984 F, **F**
CLARKE, P. (5) Wigan: 1990 **F**; 1991 **F**, F; 1992 F, **F**
CONNOLLY, G. (4) St. Helens: 1990 F; 1991 F, P; 1992 **F**
CONWAY, M. (1) Leeds: 1984 F
CREASSER, D. (5) Leeds: 1984 F, **F**; 1985 NZ; 1986 **F**, F
CRITCHLEY, J. (+1) Widnes: 1990 f
CROOKS, L. (2) Hull: 1984 F, **F**
CURRIER, A. (2) Widnes: 1984 F, **F**

DALTON, J. (3) Whitehaven: 1985 NZ; 1986 **F**, F
DANNATT, A. (6) Hull: 1984 F, **F**; 1985 NZ; 1986 **F**; 1987 **F**, F
DARBYSHIRE, P. (1 + 1) Warrington: 1991 f, **F**
DELANEY, P. (+2) Leeds: 1990 f, f
DERMOTT, M. (5) Wigan: 1987 **F**, F; 1988 **F**, F; 1989 F
DISLEY, G. (+1) Salford: 1987 f
DIVORTY, G. (6) Hull: 1984 F; 1985 NZ; 1986 **F**, F; 1987 **F**, F
DIXON, M. (1) Hull: 1991 P
DONOHUE, J. (+1) Leigh: 1992 f

EASTWOOD, P. (2) Hull: 1987 **F**, F
EDWARDS, S. (4) Wigan: 1984 F; 1985 NZ; 1987 **F**, F

FARRELL, A. (1 + 1) Huddersfield: 1989 f, **F**
FAWCETT, V. (3) Leeds: 1990 **F**, F; 1991 **F**
FLETCHER, M. (2) Hull K.R.: 1988 **F**, F
FORD, M. (3 + 1) Wigan: 1985 NZ; 1986 **F**; Leigh: 1987 f, **F**
FORSHAW, M. (+2) Wigan: 1991 f, f
FORSTER, M. (3) Warrington: 1985 NZ; 1986 **F**, F
FOX, D. (1) Featherstone R.: 1984 **F**

GILDART, I. (6) Wigan: 1988 **F**, F; 1989 F, **F**; 1990 **F**, F
GOULDING, R. (5) Wigan: 1990 **F**, F; 1991 **F**, F; Leeds: 1991 P
GREGORY, M. (1) Warrington: 1984 **F**
GRIBBIN, V. (1 + 1) Whitehaven: 1984 f, **F**
GROVES, P. (3) Salford: 1984 F, **F**; 1985 NZ

HALLAS, G. (1 + 2) Hull K.R.: 1991 P; 1992 f, f
HARCOMBE, K. (1) Rochdale H.: 1986 **F**
HARMON, N. (1 + 3) Warrington: 1988 f, F; 1989 f, f
HILL, B. (+1) Leeds: 1986 f
HILL, K. (3) Castleford: 1988 **F**, F; 1989 **F**
HUGHES, G. (1) Leigh: 1986 **F**
HULME, D. (2 + 1) Widnes: 1985 nz; 1986 **F**, F
HUNTE, A. (2) St. Helens: 1990 **F**, 1991 F

IRWIN, S. (4) Castleford: 1988 **F**; 1989 F, **F**; 1990 **F**

JACKSON, M. (+1) Hunslet: 1991 f
JOHNSON, E. (2) Leeds: 1988 **F**, F
JOYNT, C. (3) Oldham: 1991 P; 1992 F, **F**

LAY, S. (+1) Hunslet: 1989 f
LORD, G. (1) Castleford: 1988 **F**
LOUGHLIN, P. (2) St. Helens: 1987 **F**, F
LUCAS, I. (4) Wigan: 1988 **F**, F; 1989 **F**, F
LUMB, T. (+1) Hunslet: 1991 f
LYMAN, P. (3) Featherstone R.: 1985 NZ; 1986 **F**, F
LYON, D. (2) Widnes: 1985 NZ; 1986 **F**

McCORMACK, K. (2) St. Helens: 1987 **F**, F
McCURRIE, S. (1 + 1) Widnes: 1991 P; 1992 f
McNAMARA, S. (4) Hull: 1991 **F**, F, P; 1992 **F**
MARTYN, T. (1 + 3) Oldham: 1991 **F**, f, p; 1992 f
MATHER, B-J. (+1) Wigan: 1992 f
MEDLEY, P. (2) Leeds: 1987 **F**, F
MOLLOY, S. (2) Warrington: 1990 **F**, F
MOUNTAIN, D. (+1) Castleford: 1987 f
MOXON, D. (1) Bradford N.: 1991 **F**
MYCOE, D. (4) Sheffield E.: 1990 **F**; 1991 P; 1992 F, **F**
MYERS, D. (5) Wigan: 1991 **F**, F, P; 1992 F, **F**

NEWLOVE, P. (8) Featherstone R.: 1989 F, **F**; 1990 **F**, F; 1991 **F**, P; 1992 F, **F**
NICKLE, S. (1) Sheffield E.: 1990 **F**

O'DONNELL, A. (2) Wigan: 1992 F, **F**

PARKER, W. (2) Hull K.R.: 1988 **F**, F
PARR, C. (1) Huddersfield: 1991 P
PEARSON, M. (3) Featherstone R.: 1991 P; 1992 F, **F**
PICKSLEY, R. (1) Sheffield E.: 1992 F
PINKNEY, N. (+1) Ryedale-York: 1991 p
POWELL, R. (5) Leeds: 1984 F, **F**; 1985 NZ; 1986 **F**, F
PRATT, R. (2) Leeds: 1988 **F**, F
PRECIOUS, A. (+1) Hunslet: 1991 p
PRICE, G. (5 + 1) Wakefield T.: 1988 f; 1989 F, **F**; 1990 F; 1991 **F**, F
PRICE, R. (2) Hull: 1989 F, **F**
PROCTOR, W. (+1) Hull: 1984 f
PUCKERING, N. (4) Hull: 1986 **F**, F; 1987 **F**, F

RICHARDS, C. (2) Bradford N.: 1991 **F**, F
RILEY, M. (2) St. Helens: 1992 F, **F**
RIPPON, A. (1) Swinton: 1984 **F**
ROBINSON, S. (1) Halifax: 1988 F
ROEBUCK, N. (+1) Castleford: 1990 f
ROUND, P. (1 + 1) St. Helens: 1984 F, f
RUDD, C. (2) Warrington: 1991 **F**, F
RUSSELL, R. (1 + 1) Wigan: 1987 F; 1988 f

SAMPSON, D. (1) Castleford: 1988 **F**
SANDERSON, G. (4) Warrington: 1987 **F**, F;
1988 **F**, F
SCHOFIELD, G. (2) Hull: 1984 **F**, F
SLATER, R. (+1) Wakefield T.: 1992 f
SMITH, T. (1) Castleford: 1991 F
SOUTHERNWOOD, G. (6) Castleford: 1990 **F**, F;
1991 **F**, F; 1992 F, **F**
SOUTHERNWOOD, R. (2) Castleford: 1989 F, **F**
SPRUCE, S. (+1) Widnes: 1991 f
STREET, T. (2) Leigh: 1989 F, **F**
SULLIVAN, A. (1) Hull K.R.: 1990 F
SUMNER, P. (3) Warrington: 1990 F; 1991 P; 1992 **F**

TURNER, R. (1) Warrington: 1990 F

WANE, S. (3) Wigan: 1984 **F**; 1985 NZ; 1986 **F**
WESTHEAD, J. (1+2) Leigh: 1985 nz; 1986 f, **F**
WRIGHT, D. (2) Widnes: 1987 **F**; 1988 **F**

GREAT BRITAIN UNDER-21 RECORDS

Highest score:	58-0 v. Papua New Guinea at Leeds, 30 October 1991
Highest against:	6-19 v. France at St. Esteve, 19 January 1986
Most tries in a match:	3 by Neil Puckering (Hull) v. France at St. Helens, 21 March 1987 David Myers (Wigan) v. PNG at Leeds, 30 October 1991 David Myers (Wigan) v. France at Halifax, 6 March 1992 Martin Pearson (Featherstone R.) v. France at Halifax, 6 March 1992 David Myers (Wigan) v. France at Albi, 20 March 1992
Most goals in a match:	8 by Chris Rudd (Warrington) v. France at Limoux, 26 January 1991 Martin Pearson (Featherstone R.) v. PNG at Leeds, 30 October 1991
Most points in a match:	24 (3t,6g) by Martin Pearson (Featherstone R.) v. France at Halifax, 6 March 1992
Biggest attendance:	4,596 v. France at Doncaster, 16 February 1990

GREAT BRITAIN UNDER-24s RESULTS

3 Apr.	1965	W 17-9	v. F	Toulouse
20 Oct.	1965	W 12-5	v. F	Oldham
26 Nov.	1966	L 4-7	v. F	Bayonne
17 Apr.	1969	W 42-2	v. F	Castleford
14 Nov.	1976	W 19-2	v. F	Hull K.R.
5 Dec.	1976	W 11-9	v. F	Albi
12 Nov.	1977	W 27-9	v. F	Hull
18 Dec.	1977	W 8-4	v. F	Tonneins
4 Oct.	1978	L 8-30	v. A	Hull K.R.
14 Jan.	1979	W 15-3	v. F	Limoux
24 Nov.	1979	W 14-2	v. F	Leigh
13 Jan.	1980	W 11-7	v. F	Carcassonne
5 Nov.	1980	L 14-18	v. NZ	Fulham
10 Jan.	1981	W 9-2	v. F	Villeneuve
16 Jan.	1982	W 19-16	v. F	Leeds
21 Feb.	1982	W 24-12	v. F	Tonneins
16 Jan.	1983	W 19-5	v. F	Carpentras
11 Nov.	1983	W 28-23	v. F	Villeneuve
4 Dec.	1983	W 48-1	v. F	Oldham

GREAT BRITAIN UNDER-24s REGISTER
Since reintroduction in 1976

The following is a register of appearances for Great Britain Under-24s since this classification of match was reintroduced in 1976, until it was replaced by the new Under-21 level in 1984.

Figures in brackets are the total appearances, with the plus sign indicating substitute appearances, e.g. (7+3).

Away matches are in bold letters. Substitute appearances are in lower case letters.

ARKWRIGHT, C. (1) St. Helens: 1982 F
ASHTON, R. (3) Oldham: 1983 **F**, **F**, F

BANKS, B. (1) York: 1979 **F**
BELL, K. (2) Featherstone R.: 1977 F, **F**
BENTLEY, K. (+1) Widnes: 1980 nz
BURKE, M. (5) Widnes: 1979 F; 1980 **F**, NZ;
1982 F; 1983 **F**
BURTON, B. (2) Castleford: 1976 F, **F**

CAIRNS, D. (2) Barrow: 1979 F; 1982 **F**
CASE, B. (3 + 1) Warrington: 1979 **F**; 1980 NZ: 1981 **F**; 1982 f
CLARK, G. (3) Hull K.R.: 1983 **F**, **F**, F
CRAMPTON, J. (4) Hull: 1976 F, **F**; 1977 F, **F**
CROOKS, L. (1) Hull: 1983 F

DICKINSON, R. (5) Leeds: 1976 F, **F**; 1977 F, **F**; 1978 A
DRUMMOND, D. (5) Leigh: 1979 F; 1980 **F**; 1981 **F**; 1982 F, **F**
DUANE, R. (2) Warrington: 1983 **F**, **F**
DUNN, B. (2) Wigan: 1983 **F**, F

ECCLES, R. (2) Warrington: 1978 A; 1979 F
ENGLAND, K. (+ 1) Castleford: 1983 f
EVANS, S. (3) Featherstone R.: 1980 NZ; 1981 **F**; Hull: 1982 **F**

FENNELL, D. (1) Featherstone R.: 1978 A
FENTON, S. (6) Castleford: 1977 F, **F**; 1979 F; 1980 **F**, NZ; 1981 **F**
FIELDHOUSE, J. (1 + 1) Warrington: 1983 **F**, f
FLANAGAN, T. (5) Oldham: 1980 NZ; 1981 **F**; 1983 **F**, **F**, F
FORD, Phil (1) Warrington: 1982 **F**
FOX, V. (1) Whitehaven: 1980 NZ
FOY, D. (2) Oldham: 1983 **F**, F

GIBBINS, M. (2) Featherstone R.: 1977 F, **F**
GILBERT, J. (2 + 1) Featherstone R.: 1977 F; 1977 f; 1981 **F**
GILL, H. (1) Wigan: 1982 F
GOODWAY, A. (2) Oldham: 1983 **F**, F
GREGORY, A. (1) Widnes: 1982 F

HALL, D. (+ 1) Hull K.R.: 1976 f
HANLEY, E. (2) Bradford N.: 1982 **F**; 1983 F
HARKIN, P. (1) Hull K.R.: 1981 **F**
HARTLEY, I. (1) Workington T.: 1979 **F**
HOBBS, D. (2) Featherstone R.: 1982 F, **F**
HOGAN, P. (2) Barrow: 1978 A; Hull K.R.: 1979 **F**
HOLDING, N. (4) St. Helens: 1979 **F**; 1980 **F**, NZ; 1983 **F**
HOLDSTOCK, R. (3) Hull K.R.: 1978 A; 1979 F; 1980 **F**
HORNBY, J. (2) Wigan: 1978 A; 1979 **F**
HYDE, G. (1 + 1) Castleford: 1980 NZ; 1982 f

JAMES, K. (1) Bramley: 1980 **F**
JOHNSON, B. (2) Castleford: 1982 F, **F**
JOYNER, J. (4 + 1) Castleford: 1976 f; 1977 F, **F**; 1978 A; 1979 **F**

LEDGER, B. (2) St. Helens: 1983 **F**, F
LIPTROT, G. (4) St. Helens: 1977 F, **F**; 1978 A; 1979 **F**
LYDON, J. (3) Widnes: 1983 **F**, **F**, F

MASKILL, C. (1) Wakefield T.: 1983 **F**
MOLL, D. (1) Keighley: 1983 **F**
MUMBY, K. (6) Bradford N.: 1976 F, **F**; 1977 F, **F**; 1978 A; 1981 **F**
MUSCROFT, P. (3) New Hunslet: 1976 F, **F**; 1978 A
MYLER, A. (3) Widnes: 1982 **F**; 1983 **F**, F
MYLER, J. (1 + 1) Widnes: 1982 f, **F**

NOBLE, B. (4) Bradford N.: 1982 F, **F**; 1983 **F**, F
NULTY, J. (2) Wigan: 1976 F, **F**

O'NEILL, M. (3 + 2) Widnes: 1980 nz; 1982 F, f; 1983 **F**, **F**
O'NEILL, P. (3) Salford: 1980 **F**, NZ; 1981 **F**
O'NEILL, S. (2) Wigan: 1979 **F**; 1981 **F**

PINNER, H. (4 + 4) St. Helens: 1976 F, **F**; 1977 f, f; 1978 a; 1979 f, **F**; 1980 **F**
POTTER, I. (4) Warrington: 1979 **F**; 1981 **F**; Leigh: 1982 F, **F**
PROCTOR, W. (1) Hull: 1983 **F**

RATHBONE, A. (+ 1) Leigh: 1979 f
RAYNE, Keith (2) Wakefield T.: 1979 F; 1980 **F**
RICHARDSON, T. (1) Castleford: 1979 **F**
ROE, P. (4) Bradford N.: 1976 F, **F**; 1977 F, **F**
RUDD, I. (1 + 1) Workington T.: 1979 f; 1980 **F**

SCHOFIELD, G. (+ 2) Hull: 1983 f, f
SHEPHERD, M. (2) Huddersfield: 1977 F, **F**
SKERRETT, T. (1) Wakefield T.: 1977 **F**
SMITH, D. (2) Leeds: 1976 F, **F**
SMITH, Malcolm (1) Wigan: 1979 F
SMITH, Mike (7) Hull K.R.: 1976 F, **F**; 1977 **F**; 1978 A; 1979 F, **F**; 1980 **F**
SMITH, P. (1) Featherstone R.: 1978 A
SMITH, R. (+ 1) Salford: 1983 f
STEPHENSON, D. (5) Salford: 1979 F; 1980 **F**, NZ; 1982 **F**; Wigan: 1982 **F**
SWANN, M. (1) Leigh: 1979 F
SYZMALA, E. (2) Barrow: 1976 F, **F**

THACKRAY, R. (1) Warrington: 1980 NZ
TIMSON, A. (2) Castleford: 1982 F, **F**
TURNBULL, S. (2) Salford: 1976 F, **F**

VAN BELLEN, G. (2) Bradford N.: 1980 NZ; 1982 **F**

WARD, D. (+ 2) Leeds: 1976 f, f
WARD, K. (3) Castleford: 1980 **F**, NZ; 1981 **F**
WHITFIELD, C. (1) Salford: 1981 **F**
WILKINSON, A. (1) Leigh: 1977 **F**
WOOD, J. (2) Widnes: 1977 **F**
WOODS, J. (5) Leigh: 1977 F, **F**; 1978 A; 1979 **F**, F
WORRALL, M. (3) Oldham: 1983 **F**, **F**, F

Yorkshire second row man Karl Fairbank is halted by a double Red Rose rearguard of Ian Blease (left) and Shaun Wane.

WAR OF THE ROSES

WAR OF THE ROSES

1991 WAR OF THE ROSES

Yorkshire extended their run of Rodstock War of the Roses triumphs to six, but only after a new-look Lancashire went near to their first victory. The 17-12 scoreline produced the narrowest margin of the County of Origin series.

Goalkicking proved crucial in the Leeds encounter as both sides scored three tries, Lancashire failing to kick a goal while the home side registered two from Lee Crooks and a drop goal by Deryck Fox.

For Yorkshire, it was a triumph for the Featherstone Rovers club. Coach Peter Fox took his unbeaten record with the county to a total of eight games in six years and all three Yorkshire tries were claimed by Post Office Road players — Deryck Fox, Chris Bibb and Ian Smales.

For Lancashire, it was an impressive representative debut for Ray Ashton, then player-coach of Second Division Workington Town. Oldham-born Ashton adopted a policy of introducing new blood in a bold bid to end Yorkshire's domination, selecting eight new county caps in David Lyon, David Myers, Paul Topping, David Jones, Bobby Goulding, Denis Betts, Ian Blease and substitute Steve Kerry.

Ashton did better than his more illustrious predecessors, Alex Murphy and Doug Laughton, by reducing the final arrears to only five points, the scores having been level at 12-apiece after 44 minutes. The Red Rose side also had skipper Shaun Edwards named as Man of the Match.

With the scores deadlocked, it took a classic piece of tryscoring centre play by Smales to clinch victory for the home county in front of an 8,523 crowd, the best Yorkshire attendance since the launch of the War of the Roses series in 1985. The Featherstone utility forward, a late replacement for injured Sheffield Eagles Test centre Daryl Powell, pulled off a superb sweeping dummy on the hour, clubmate Fox adding his drop goal with 13 minutes left.

Castleford prop forward Crooks, recalled for his third county cap, opened the scoring with a penalty goal after only two minutes.

But Lancashire's Edwards revelled in the responsibility of captaincy. The Wigan stand off set up both of his side's first-half tries to give them an 8-2 lead inside 25 minutes. His first influence came in the 13th minute, leaving the Yorkshire defence standing with their backs to the line as he went on a searching run across the field before spotting the gap to send in Widnes centre Andy Currier for a well-worked touchdown.

Fourteen minutes later, Edwards again ran across from a scrum, taking the cover with him before pushing off Fox and putting in Myers near the corner flag.

Edwards faded a little in the second half, but stayed ahead in his stand off duel with Test rival Garry Schofield, whose main contribution was a strong defensive display.

Carl Gibson and Fox became the only players to maintain a 100 per cent appearance record in the Rodstock War of the Roses series, Fox having the double satisfaction of getting the better of opposite number Bobby Goulding, his Test rival on the 1990 tour Down Under.

Yorkshire scrum half Deryck Fox, scorer of a try and drop goal.

RODSTOCK WAR OF THE ROSES

18 September   Leeds

YORKSHIRE 17   LANCASHIRE 12

Chris Bibb (Featherstone R.)	1.	David Lyon (Warrington)
Carl Gibson (Leeds)	2.	David Myers (Wigan
Ian Smales (Featherstone R.)	3.	Andy Currier (Widnes)
Andy Mason (Wakefield T.)	4.	Paul Topping (Leigh)
Anthony Sullivan (St. Helens)	5.	David Jones (Wakefield T.)
Garry Schofield (Leeds)	6.	Shaun Edwards (Wigan), Capt.
Deryck Fox (Featherstone R.)	7.	Bobby Goulding (Leeds)
Kelvin Skerrett (Wigan)	8.	Shaun Wane (Leeds)
Lee Jackson (Hull)	9.	Martin Dermott (Wigan)
Lee Crooks (Castleford)	10.	Andy Platt (Wigan)
Paul Dixon (Leeds)	11.	Denis Betts (Wigan)
Karl Fairbank (Bradford N.)	12.	Ian Blease (Salford)
Ellery Hanley (Leeds), Capt.	13.	Richard Eyres (Widnes)
Graham Steadman (Castleford)	14.	Steve Kerry (Salford)
Roy Powell (Leeds)	15.	Paul Cullen (Warrington)

T: Fox, Bibb, Smales
G: Crooks (2), Fox (dg)
Substitutions:
Steadman for Mason (45 min.)
Powell for Skerrett (75 min.)
Referee: Colin Morris (Huddersfield)

T: Currier, Myers, Jones
Substitutions:
Cullen for Betts (53 min.)
Kerry for Goulding (75 min.)
Half-time: 8-8
Attendance: 8,523

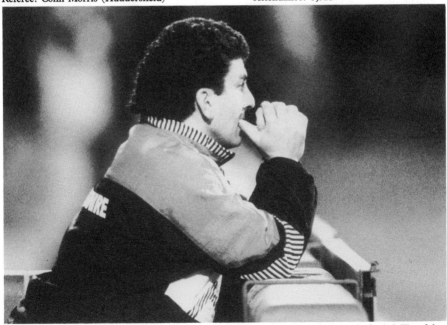

Lancashire's debutant coach Ray Ashton, who came closest to ending Yorkshire's dominance in the sixth War of the Roses clash.

LANCASHIRE v. YORKSHIRE RESULTS
All county championship matches except where stated.

Date	Result		Score	Venue	Attendance
7 Dec. 1895	Yorkshire	won	8-0	Oldham	9,059
29 Feb. 1896	Lancashire	won	8-3	Huddersfield	5,300
21 Nov. 1896	Lancashire	won	7-3	Oldham	15,000
20 Nov. 1897	Yorkshire	won	7-6	Bradford P.A.	11,000
5 Nov. 1898	Yorkshire	won	20-9	Salford	8,000
4 Nov. 1899	Lancashire	won	16-13	Halifax	9,000
3 Nov. 1900	Lancashire	won	24-5	Rochdale	18,000
15 Feb. 1902	Yorkshire	won	13-8	Hull	15,000
15 Nov. 1902	Lancashire	won	13-0	Salford	14,000
14 Nov. 1903	Lancashire	won	8-0	Leeds	11,000
12 Nov. 1904	Yorkshire	won	14-5	Oldham	8,500
4 Nov. 1905	Lancashire	won	8-0	Hull	8,000
3 Nov. 1906	Lancashire	won	19-0	Salford	5,000
2 Nov. 1907	Yorkshire	won	15-11	Halifax	7,000
31 Oct. 1908	Lancashire	won	13-0	Salford	5,000
4 Nov. 1909	Yorkshire	won	27-14	Hull	6,000
7 Nov. 1910	Lancashire	won	17-3	Wigan	2,000
25 Jan. 1912	Lancashire	won	13-12	Halifax	3,199
16 Dec. 1912	Yorkshire	won	20-8	Oldham	4,000
10 Dec. 1913	Yorkshire	won	19-11	Huddersfield	3,500
24 Sept. 1919	Lancashire	won	15-5	Broughton	5,000
21 Oct. 1920	Yorkshire	won	18-3	Hull	7,000
4 Oct. 1921	Yorkshire	won	5-2	Rochdale	4,000
7 Dec. 1922	Match drawn	—	11-11	Hull K.R.	8,000
8 Dec. 1923	Lancashire	won	6-5	Oldham	8,000
29 Nov. 1924	Lancashire	won	28-9	Halifax	6,000
12 Dec. 1925	Lancashire	won	26-10	St. Helens	13,000
30 Oct. 1926	Lancashire	won	18-13	Wakefield	9,000
29 Oct. 1927	Lancashire	won	35-19	Warrington	12,000
3 Nov. 1928	Lancashire	won	33-10	Halifax	6,520
22 Mar. 1930	Lancashire	won	18-3	Rochdale	4,000
18 Oct. 1930	Yorkshire	won	25-15	Wakefield	9,000
17 Oct. 1931	Lancashire	won	11-8	Warrington	10,049
*29 Oct. 1932	Yorkshire	won	30-3	Wakefield	4,000
25 Sept. 1933	Yorkshire	won	15-12	Oldham	2,000
*9 Jan. 1935	Match drawn	—	5-5	Leeds	1,500
12 Oct. 1935	Lancashire	won	16-5	Widnes	6,700
21 Oct. 1936	Lancashire	won	28-6	Castleford	7,648
12 Feb. 1938	Lancashire	won	10-9	Rochdale	3,653
*26 Oct. 1938	Match drawn	—	10-10	Leeds	3,000
10 Nov. 1945	Lancashire	won	17-16	Swinton	11,059
9 Nov. 1946	Yorkshire	won	13-10	Hunslet	5,000
12 Nov. 1947	Lancashire	won	22-10	Wigan	6,270
3 May 1949	Lancashire	won	12-3	Halifax	7,000
5 Oct. 1949	Lancashire	won	22-13	Warrington	15,000
18 Oct. 1950	Yorkshire	won	23-15	Huddersfield	6,547
10 Oct. 1951	Yorkshire	won	15-5	Leigh	11,573

Date	Result		Score	Venue	Attendance
28 Apr. 1953	Yorkshire	won	16-8	Hull	8,400
14 Oct. 1953	Lancashire	won	18-10	Leigh	12,870
6 Oct. 1954	Yorkshire	won	20-10	Bradford	8,500
26 Sept. 1955	Lancashire	won	26-10	Oldham	8,000
26 Sept. 1956	Lancashire	won	35-21	Hull	8,500
23 Sept. 1957	Yorkshire	won	25-11	Widnes	6,200
24 Sept. 1958	Yorkshire	won	35-19	Hull K.R.	5,000
29 Oct. 1958	Yorkshire	won	16-15	Leigh	8,500
11 Nov. 1959	Yorkshire	won	38-28	Leigh	6,417
31 Aug. 1960	Lancashire	won	21-20	Wakefield	15,045
9 Oct. 1961	Lancashire	won	14-12	Leigh	4,970
26 Sept. 1962	Yorkshire	won	22-8	Wakefield	7,956
11 Sept. 1963	Lancashire	won	45-20	St. Helens	11,200
23 Sept. 1964	Yorkshire	won	33-10	Hull	7,100
10 Nov. 1965	Yorkshire	won	16-13	Swinton	5,847
21 Sept. 1966	Lancashire	won	22-17	Leeds	10,528
24 Jan. 1968	Lancashire	won	23-17	Widnes	8,322
25 Sept. 1968	Yorkshire	won	10-5	Hull K.R.	6,656
3 Sept. 1969	Lancashire	won	14-12	Salford	4,652
13 Jan. 1971	Yorkshire	won	32-12	Castleford	2,000
24 Feb. 1971	Yorkshire	won	34-8	Castleford	4,400
29 Sept. 1971	Yorkshire	won	42-22	Leigh	4,987
11 Oct. 1972	Yorkshire	won	32-18	Castleford	2,474
19 Sept. 1973	Lancashire	won	17-15	Widnes	3,357
25 Sept. 1974	Yorkshire	won	20-14	Keighley	1,219
16 Oct. 1974	Lancashire	won	29-11	Widnes	3,114
20 Dec. 1975	Yorkshire	won	17-7	Wigan	700
1 Mar. 1977	Yorkshire	won	18-13	Castleford	2,730
††19 Oct. 1977	Lancashire	won	33-8	Widnes	5,056
27 Sept. 1978	Lancashire	won	23-7	Widnes	4,283
12 Sept. 1979	Yorkshire	won	19-16	Castleford	2,738
24 Sept. 1980	Lancashire	won	17-9	Widnes	1,593
9 Sept. 1981	Yorkshire	won	21-15	Castleford	1,222
26 May 1982	Yorkshire	won	22-21	Leigh	1,738
WR11 Sept. 1985	Yorkshire	won	26-10	Wigan	6,743
WR17 Sept. 1986	Yorkshire	won	26-14	Leeds	5,983
WR16 Sept. 1987	Yorkshire	won	16-10	Wigan	9,748
WR21 Sept. 1988	Yorkshire	won	24-14	Leeds	8,244
WR20 Sept. 1989	Yorkshire	won	56-12	Wigan	10,182
WR18 Sept. 1991	Yorkshire	won	17-12	Leeds	8,523

* Match abandoned but result stands   †† Queen's Jubilee match   WR War of the Roses

● There were also a few Lancashire-Yorkshire matches played during the war years but not of a competitive nature.

SUMMARY

Yorkshire won 43   Lancashire won 41   Drawn 3

LANCASHIRE v. YORKSHIRE RECORDS

LANCASHIRE

Highest score:	45-20 at St. Helens, 11 Sept. 1963
Widest margin win:	As above and 33-8 at Widnes, 19 Oct. 1977
Most tries in a match:	No player has scored more than 3
Most goals in a match:	9 by L. Gilfedder (Wigan) at St. Helens, 11 Sept. 1963
Most points in a match:	18 by L. Gilfedder (Wigan) as above
Biggest home attendance:	18,000 at Rochdale, 3 Nov. 1900

OTHER RECORDS (exceeding those against Yorkshire)

Highest score and widest margin win:	60-12 v. Cumberland at Wigan, 10 Sept. 1958
Most tries in a match:	4 by T. O'Grady (Oldham) v. Cumberland at Wigan, 6 Sept. 1956
	4 by W. Burgess (Barrow) v. Cumberland at Widnes, 12 Sept. 1962
Most goals in a match:	12 by E. Fraser (Warrington) v. Cumberland at Wigan, 10 Sept. 1958
Most points in a match:	24 by E. Fraser (Warrington) as above
Biggest home attendance:	24,000 v. Australia at Warrington, 26 Sept. 1929

YORKSHIRE

Highest score and widest margin win:	56-12 at Wigan, 20 Sept. 1989
Most tries in a match:	No player has scored more than 3
Most goals in a match:	10 by V. Yorke (York) at Hull K.R., 24 Sept. 1958
Most points in a match:	20 by V. Yorke (York) as above
Biggest home attendance:	15,045 at Wakefield, 31 Aug. 1960

OTHER RECORDS (exceeding those against Lancashire)

Highest against:	55-11 v. Australia at Huddersfield, 26 Nov. 1952
Most tries in a match:	5 by J. Parkin (Wakefield T.) v. Cumberland at Halifax, 14 Nov. 1921
Most goals in a match:	10 also by N. Fox (Wakefield T.) v. Australia at York, 28 Sept. 1959
Most points in a match:	23 by N. Fox (Wakefield T.) as above
Biggest home attendance:	19,376 v. Australia at Wakefield, 4 Oct. 1967

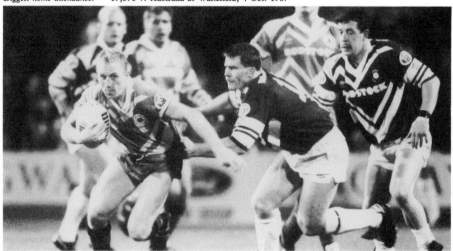

Lancashire skipper Shaun Edwards, Rodstock Man of the Match, outpaces Yorkshire duo Paul Dixon and Garry Schofield (right).

LANCASHIRE REGISTER

The following is a register of current players who have appeared for Lancashire, including fixtures other than the War of the Roses. Each played at least one first team game last season.

ARKWRIGHT, C. (4) St. Helens

BENTLEY, K. (4) Widnes
BETTS, D. (1) Wigan
BLEASE, I. (1) Salford
BYRNE, G. (1) Wigan

CASE, B. (3) Warrington 2, Wigan
COTTRELL, A. (+1) Leigh
CULLEN, P. (2+1) Warrington
CURRIER, A. (2) Widnes

DERMOTT, M. (2) Wigan
DOWD, B. (+1) Widnes
DRUMMOND, D. (4) Leigh 3, Warrington
DUANE, R. (1) Warrington

ECCLES, R. (3) Warrington
EDWARDS, S. (3+1) Wigan
EYRES, R. (2+1) Widnes

FIELDHOUSE, J. (2+2) Warrington +2, Widnes 2
FORBER, P. (1) St. Helens
FORSTER, M. (2) Warrington

GILDART, I. (+1) Wigan
GOULDING, R. (1) Leeds
GREGORY, A. (9) Widnes 3, Warrington 2, Wigan 4
GREGORY, M. (4) Warrington
GROVES, P. (1) St. Helens

HAGGERTY, R. (+1) St. Helens
HAMPSON, S. (3) Wigan
HENDERSON, J. (1+1) Leigh
HOLDING, N. (2) St. Helens
HULME, D. (1+1) Widnes
HULME, P. (2) Widnes
HUMPHRIES, A. (1) Warrington

JONES, D. (1) Wakefield T.

KERRY, S. (+1) Salford

LEDGER, B. (1) St. Helens
LOUGHLIN, P. (2) St. Helens
LYDON, J. (4) Widnes, Wigan 3
LYON, D. (1) Warrington

McCORMACK, K. (1) St. Helens
McCULLOCH, N. (+1) Leigh
McGINTY, W. (1+1) Warrington
MEADOWS, K. (1) St. Helens
MYERS, D. (1) Wigan
MYLER, A. (2) Widnes

OFFIAH, M. (1) Widnes
O'NEILL, M. (9) Widnes
O'NEILL, S. (3) Wigan

PENDLEBURY, J. (1) Salford
PLATT, A. (3) St. Helens, Wigan 2
POTTER, I. (5) Warrington 2, Leigh 2, Wigan
PRESTON, M. (2) Wigan

ROBERTS, M. (2) Warrington
ROUND, P. (2) Oldham

STEPHENSON, D. (6) Salford 2, Wigan 4

TOPPING, P. (1) Leigh

WANE, S. (2+1) Wigan 1+1, Leeds
WHITFIELD, C. (4+1) Salford 3, Wigan +1, Halifax
WILLIAMS, P. (+1) Salford
WOODS, J. (6) Leigh 5, Warrington
WRIGHT, D. (1) Widnes

Yorkshire substitute Graham Steadman is grounded by Red Rose right-wing pairing Andy Currier and David Myers (right).

LANCASHIRE TEAMS . . . A REVIEW
Lancashire team line-ups since the introduction of the Rodstock War of the Roses in September 1985, including opposition other than Yorkshire. * Denotes captain.

1985 Yorkshire

Wigan: 11 Sept

Lost 10-26

Burke (Widnes) 1g
Ledger (St. Helens)
Stephenson (Wigan)
Keiron O'Loughlin (Salford)
Lydon (Widnes)
A. Myler (Widnes)
*A. Gregory (Warrington) 1t
M. O'Neill (Widnes)
Webb (Warrington)
Forber (St. Helens)
Eccles (Warrington) 1t
Fieldhouse (Widnes)
Pendlebury (Salford)
Subs: Edwards (Wigan)
      Wane (Wigan)

1987 Papua New Guinea

St. Helens: 14 Oct

Drew 22-22

Hampson (Wigan)
Drummond (Warrington)
Lydon (Wigan) 1t, 1g
Henderson (Leigh) 1t
Offiah (Widnes)
Edwards (Wigan) 2t
*A. Gregory (Wigan)
Pyke (Leigh)
Groves (St. Helens)
Round (Oldham)
M. Gregory (Warrington)
Roberts (Warrington) 1t
Arkwright (St. Helens)
Subs: D. Hulme (Widnes)
      Cottrell (Leigh)

1989 Yorkshire

Wigan: 20 Sept

Lost 12-56

Hampson (Wigan)
Forster (Warrington)
Loughlin (St. Helens) 2g
Cullen (Warrington)
Preston (Wigan) 1t
Byrne (Wigan)
*A. Gregory (Wigan)
M. O'Neill (Widnes)
P. Hulme (Widnes)
Platt (Wigan)
McGinty (Warrington)
Eyres (Widnes)
M. Gregory (Warrington) 1t
Subs: Williams (Salford)
      Gildart (Wigan)

1986 Yorkshire

Leeds: 17 Sept

Lost 14-26

Lydon (Wigan)
Forster (Warrington)
R. Duane (Warrington)
Stephenson (Wigan) 1t, 3g
Basnett (Widnes) 1t
Edwards (Wigan)
*A. Gregory (Warrington)
Pyke (Leigh)
Liptrot (St. Helens)
Fieldhouse (Widnes)
Arkwright (St. Helens)
Platt (St. Helens)
M. Gregory (Warrington)
Subs: Henderson (Leigh)
      Haggerty (St. Helens)

1988 Yorkshire

Leeds: 21 Sept

Lost 14-24

Lydon (Wigan)
Thackray (Widnes) 1t
Currier (Widnes) 1t
Loughlin (St. Helens) 1g
Preston (Wigan)
D. Hulme (Widnes)
*A. Gregory (Wigan)
Pyke (Widnes)
Kiss (Wigan)
Wane (Wigan)
M. O'Neill (Widnes)
P. Hulme (Widnes)
Roberts (Warrington)
Subs: Dowd (Widnes) 1t
      R. Eyres (Widnes)

1991 Yorkshire

Leeds: 18 Sept

Lost 12-17

Lyon (Warrington)
Myers (Wigan) 1t
Currier (Widnes) 1t
Topping (Leigh)
Jones (Wakefield) 1t
*Edwards (Wigan)
Goulding (Leeds)
Wane (Leeds)
Dermott (Wigan)
Platt (Wigan)
Betts (Wigan)
Blease (Salford)
Eyres (Widnes)
Subs: Kerry (Salford)
      Cullen (Warrington)

1987 Yorkshire

Wigan: 16 Sept

Lost 10-16

Hampson (Wigan) 1t
McCormack (St. Helens)
Cullen (Warrington)
Whitfield (Halifax) 1g
D. Wright (Widnes)
Woods (Warrington)
*A. Gregory (Wigan)
Case (Wigan)
Dermott (Wigan)
Humphries (Warrington)
Round (Oldham) 1t
Potter (Wigan)
M. Gregory (Warrington)
Subs: McCulloch (Leigh)
      McGinty (Warrington)

Denis Betts, Lancashire 1991 debutant packman.

YORKSHIRE REGISTER

The following is a register of current players who have appeared for Yorkshire, including fixtures other than the War of the Roses. Each played at least one first team game last season.

BEARDMORE, K. (3) Castleford
BELL, K. (4) Featherstone R.
BIBB, C. (2) Featherstone R.
BURTON, C. (3) Hull K.R.

CREASSER, D. (1+1) Leeds
CROOKS, L. (3) Hull, Leeds, Castleford

DANNATT, A (+1) Hull
DICKINSON, R. (3+1) Leeds
DIXON, P. (4+1) Halifax 2+1, Leeds 2

EASTWOOD, P. (1) Hull

FAIRBANK, K. (2) Bradford N.
FLETCHER, A. (4) Wakefield T.
FOX, D. (8) Featherstone R.

GIBSON, C. (8) Batley 2, Leeds 6
GILL, H. (3) Wigan
GOODWAY, A. (4) Wigan
GRAYSHON, J. (14) Dewsbury 9, Bradford N. 5

HANLEY, E. (5) Wigan 4, Leeds
HERON, D. (2+4) Leeds
HILL, B. (1) Leeds
HOBBS, D. (6+1) Featherstone R. +1, Oldham 2, Bradford N. 4

IDLE, G. (1+1) Bramley +1, Bradford N.

JACKSON, L. (1) Hull
JOYNER, J. (12) Castleford

KELLY, A. (1) Hull K.R.

LYMAN, P. (1+2) Featherstone R.

McCALLION, S. (1) Halifax
MARCHANT, A. (4) Castleford
MASON, A. (5+2) Bramley 2+1, Wakefield T. 3+1
MEDLEY, P. (+2) Leeds, Bradford N.
MUMBY, K. (9) Bradford N.

NEWLOVE, P. (1) Featherstone R.
NOBLE, B. (2) Bradford N.

POWELL, D. (1) Sheffield E.
POWELL, R. (3+1) Leeds
PRICE, G. (1) York
PRYCE, G. (1) York

RAYNE, Keith (+1) Leeds
RAYNE, Kevin (2) Wakefield T.
ROE, Peter (3) Keighley 2, Bradford N.

SCHOFIELD, G. (4) Hull, Leeds 3
SKERRETT, K. (3) Bradford N. 2, Wigan
SMALES, I. (1) Featherstone R.
SMITH, M. (1) Hull K.R.
STEADMAN, G. (1+3) York +1, Featherstone R. 1+1 Castleford +1
SULLIVAN, A. (1) St. Helens

VAN BELLEN, G. (2) Bradford N.

WARD, K. (2) Castleford
WILKINSON, I. (2) Leeds, Halifax

Yorkshire captain Ellery Hanley outstrips former Wigan clubmate Martin Dermott.

369

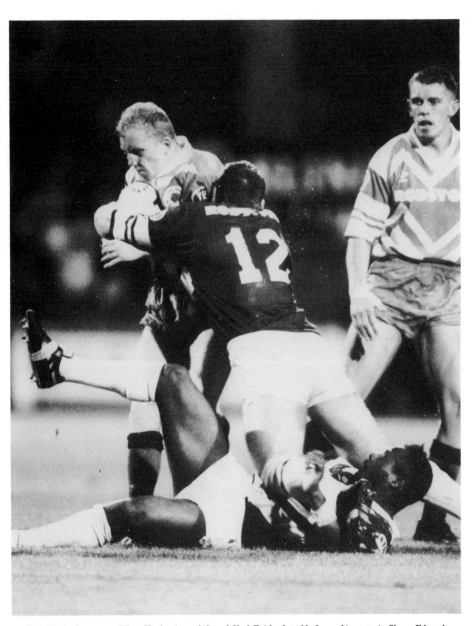

Yorkshire back row men Ellery Hanley (grounded) and Karl Fairbank tackle Lancashire captain Shaun Edwards.

YORKSHIRE TEAMS . . . A REVIEW
Yorkshire team line-ups since the introduction of the Rodstock War of the Roses in September 1985, including opposition other than Lancashire. * Denotes captain.

1985 Lancashire
Wigan: 11 Sept
Won 26-10

Kay (Hunslet)
Gibson (Batley)
Hyde (Castleford) 1t
Mason (Bramley) 2t
Laws (Hull K.R.)
*Joyner (Castleford)
Fox (Featherstone) 3g
Hill (Leeds)
Watkinson (Hull K.R.)
M. Morgan (Oldham)
Hobbs (Oldham) 1t
Burton (Hull K.R.)
D. Heron (Leeds) 1t
Subs: Lyman (Featherstone)
　　　Dannatt (Hull)

1987 Lancashire
Wigan: 16 Sept
Won 16-10

Wilkinson (Halifax)
Gibson (Leeds)
Marchant (Castleford) 1t
Mason (Wakefield)
Gill (Wigan) 1t
*Hanley (Wigan) 1t
Fox (Featherstone) 1g
Ward (Castleford)
K. Beardmore (Castleford)
Hobbs (Bradford) 1g
L. Crooks (Leeds)
Burton (Hull K.R.)
Goodway (Wigan)
Sub: Dixon (Halifax)

1989 Lancashire
Wigan: 20 Sept
Won 56-12

Bibb (Featherstone)
Gibson (Leeds)
Schofield (Leeds) 1t
D. Powell (Sheffield)
Newlove (Featherstone) 2t
Steadman (Castleford) 2t, 4g
Fox (Featherstone) 1t
K. Skerrett (Bradford)
K. Beardmore (Castleford)
Dixon (Leeds)
*Hobbs (Bradford) 1t, 4g
R. Powell (Leeds)
Goodway (Wigan) 2t
Subs: Mason (Wakefield)
　　　Medley (Bradford) 1t

1985 New Zealand
Bradford: 23 Oct
Won 18-8

Mumby (Bradford)
Gibson (Batley) 1t
Creasser (Leeds)
Schofield (Hull) 1dg
Mason (Bramley)
Hanley (Wigan) 1t, 1dg
Fox (Featherstone) 2g
*Grayshon (Bradford)
Noble (Bradford)
T. Skerrett (Hull)
L. Crooks (Hull)
Goodway (Wigan) 1t
D. Heron (Leeds)
Subs: Steadman (York)
　　　Lyman (Featherstone)

1987 Papua New Guinea
Leeds: 27 Oct
Won 28-4

Mumby (Bradford)
Eastwood (Hull)
Marchant (Castleford) 1t
Gibson (Leeds) 3t
Mason (Wakefield)
*Joyner (Castleford)
Fox (Featherstone)
Hobbs (Bradford) 2g
McCallion (Halifax)
Powell (Leeds)
Burton (Hull K.R.)
K. Fairbank (Bradford) 1t
Dixon (Halifax)
Subs: Creasser (Leeds) 1t
　　　D. Heron (Leeds)

1991 Lancashire
Leeds: 18 Sept
Won 17-12

Bibb (Featherstone)
Gibson (Leeds)
Smales (Featherstone)
Mason (Wakefield)
Sullivan (St. Helens)
Schofield (Leeds)
Fox (Featherstone)
K. Skerrett (Wigan)
L. Jackson (Hull)
L. Crooks (Castleford)
Dixon (Leeds)
K. Fairbank (Bradford)
*Hanley (Leeds)
Subs: Steadman (Castleford)
　　　R. Powell (Leeds)

1986 Lancashire
Leeds: 17 Sept
Won 26-14

Wilkinson (Leeds)
Gibson (Leeds)
Marchant (Castleford) 1t
Hanley (Wigan) 1t
Gill (Wigan) 1t
*Joyner (Castleford)
Fox (Featherstone)
Kelly (Hull K.R.)
Noble (Bradford)
Hobbs (Oldham) 5g
P. Smith (Featherstone)
Price (York)
Lyman (Featherstone) 1t
Subs: Mason (Bramley)
　　　Medley (Leeds)

1988 Lancashire
Leeds: 21 Sept
Won 24-14

Roockley (Castleford)
Gill (Wigan) 1t
Schofield (Leeds) 1t
Marchant (Castleford) 1t
Gibson (Leeds)
*Hanley (Wigan) 1t
Fox (Featherstone)
Hobbs (Bradford) 4g
K. Beardmore (Castleford)
K. Skerrett (Bradford)
Dixon (Halifax)
Powell (Leeds)
Goodway (Wigan)
Subs: Steadman (Featherstone)
　　　D. Heron (Leeds)

*Lee Jackson, Yorkshire 1991
debutant hooker.*

COUNTY CHAMPIONSHIP TITLES
(including joint titles)

Lancashire 34
Yorkshire 24
Cumbria 16
Cheshire 1

1895-96	Lancashire	1937-38	Lancashire
1896-97	Lancashire	1938-39	Lancashire
1897-98	Yorkshire	1945-46	Lancashire
1898-99	Yorkshire	1946-47	Yorkshire
1899-1900	Lancashire	1947-48	Lancashire
1900-01	Lancashire	1948-49	Cumberland
1901-02	Cheshire	1949-50	Undecided
1902-03	Lancashire	1950-51	Undecided
1903-04	Lancashire	1951-52	Yorkshire
1904-05	Yorkshire	1952-53	Lancashire
1905-06	Lancashire Cumberland	1953-54	Yorkshire
		1954-55	Yorkshire
1906-07	Lancashire	1955-56	Lancashire
1907-08	Cumberland	1956-57	Lancashire
1908-09	Lancashire	1957-58	Yorkshire
1909-10	Cumberland Yorkshire	1958-59	Yorkshire
		1959-60	Cumberland
1910-11	Lancashire	1960-61	Lancashire
1911-12	Cumberland	1961-62	Cumberland
1912-13	Yorkshire	1962-63	Yorkshire
1913-14	Undecided	1963-64	Cumberland
1919-20	Undecided	1964-65	Yorkshire
1920-21	Yorkshire	1965-66	Cumberland
1921-22	Yorkshire	1966-67	Cumberland
1922-23	Lancashire Yorkshire	1967-68	Lancashire
		1968-69	Yorkshire
1923-24	Lancashire	1969-70	Lancashire
1924-25	Lancashire	1970-71	Yorkshire
1925-26	Lancashire	1971-72	Yorkshire
1926-27	Lancashire	1972-73	Yorkshire
1927-28	Cumberland	1973-74	Lancashire
1928-29	Lancashire	1974-75	Lancashire
1929-30	Lancashire	1975-76	Yorkshire
1930-31	Yorkshire	1976-77	Yorkshire
1931-32	Lancashire	1977-78	Not Held
1932-33	Cumberland	1978-79	Lancashire
1933-34	Cumberland	1979-80	Lancashire
1934-35	Cumberland	1980-81	Cumbria
1935-36	Lancashire	1981-82	Cumbria
1936-37	Lancashire	1982-83	Yorkshire

World record signing Martin Offiah, a £440,000 recruit by Wigan from Widnes.

TRANSFERS

TRANSFERS

TRANSFER REVIEW
1 June 1991 to 31 May 1992

Two world record-shattering transfer deals dominated the period, with Wigan's Ellery Hanley moving to Leeds for £250,000 followed by Wigan signing Martin Offiah from Widnes for £440,000.

Hanley's move to Leeds on 6 September smashed the previous record transfer of £170,000 when stand off Graham Steadman left Featherstone Rovers for Castleford in 1989.

Although Hanley was not on Wigan's transfer list, the club had been asking up to £450,000 since their loose forward and skipper decided not to renew his contract at the start of the season.

Then aged 30, the Great Britain captain's three-year personal contract with Leeds was reckoned to be worth £250,000.

It was the second time Hanley had been involved in a world record transfer deal, having joined Wigan from Bradford Northern in 1985 for a cash plus two players package valued at £150,000.

Four months after Hanley's move to Leeds, the transfer record shot up to an amazing £440,000 when Wigan signed Offiah from Widnes on 3 January, a few days after his 26th birthday.

The Great Britain winger had been on the transfer list at £700,000 since November, after asking for a move at the end of the previous season and refusing to play for Widnes again.

A recent change in the bye-laws following the introduction of players' contracts meant Offiah could not appeal against the world record listing.

Offiah signed a four-year contract estimated to be worth nearly £600,000 which, with his transfer fee, earned him the title of Rugby League's first £1 million player.

The only other six-figure transfer during the period was Hull Test prop Karl Harrison's move to Halifax for £120,000.

There were 10 transfers adjudicated by the League's Tribunal. The following transfer fees were ruled: Sonny Nickle, Sheffield E. to St. Helens, £80,000 plus £25,000 when played two Tests against Australia and/or New Zealand; Garry Schubert, Carlisle to Workington T., £15,000; Neil Cowie, Rochdale H. to Wigan, £65,000 plus £15,000 on Great Britain Test debut; Mick Keebles, Halifax to Keighley C., £15,000; Dave Kendall, Carlisle to Barrow, £16,500; Brendan White, Keighley C. to Huddersfield, £500 and £500 after 15 first team games; Greg Pearce, London C. to Halifax, £40,000; Colin Atkinson, Halifax to London C., £4,000; Ben Beevers, Halifax to London C., £1,000; Stuart Turner, Widnes to Wigan, £6,000 and £4,000 after five first team games.

RUGBY UNION SIGNINGS

Leeds made the only signing of a major Rugby Union international during the period under review when they signed Craig Innes, the New Zealand All Black centre, a few months after he had played in the RU World Cup.

Innes, 22, who had been playing in England for Bedford, signed on 6 January for a five-year contract estimated at £300,000.

Leeds also clinched the biggest home Rugby Union capture of the season, with Bath and England B winger Jim Fallon, 27, signing on 19 May. His five-year contract was reported to be worth about £200,000.

Both players were signed by Doug Laughton in his first year as Leeds team manager after gaining a reputation as the best assessor of Rugby Union talent while at Widnes, where he signed a string of successful converts.

Andre Stoop, a South African-born Namibian international back, signed for Wigan in October after starring in two shock defeats of Ireland.

Innes and Fallon were the only major Rugby Union signings of the season after several internationals had switched codes in recent years, perhaps reflecting the 15-a-side code's relaxation of their laws on amateurism. For example, when Wales international centre Scott Gibbs was reported to be considering a £200,000 offer from Wigan, his Swansea club put together a financial package to keep him. It involved sponsorship, personal appearances and other so-called non-related rugby activities.

Among the lesser known converts were Carlisle's signing of Stirling and Scotland B forward George Graham, 25, and Hull's capture of Ian Stevens, 21, the South Wales Police and Wales Under-21 international stand off.

The total number of Rugby Union signings over the year was 21 compared with 35 in the previous 12 months, which was the most for more than a decade.

AMATEUR SIGNINGS

A total of 293 players were signed from amateur Rugby League clubs compared with 224 in the previous period.

OVERSEAS SIGNINGS

The number of overseas players making first-team appearances during 1991-92 was the lowest for three years, down from the previous season's record 168 to 151.

Although most came from New Zealand, their total dropped from a record 95 to 73. They included 21 Test players plus Tongan

Emosi Koloto, who has played for New Zealand.

Of the 65 Australians, only Gene Miles of Wigan was an international and his last Test appearance had been in 1987.

An historic breakthrough was the first appearance of Russians in a British club side, with Alexander Diatlov, Valeri Medwedj, Valeri Savikhine and Oleg Zotov playing for Trafford Borough.

London Crusaders were at the centre of a League investigation after Huddersfield accused them of fielding double their allotted number of overseas players in a Stones Bitter Divisional Premiership match. Huddersfield lost and claimed they should be awarded the tie because London's team included eight and possibly nine overseas players.

The League's Board of Directors rejected Huddersfield's claim because they "presented insufficient evidence", but said they would continue to investigate London's overseas register.

Huddersfield had named the eight Australians playing against them as: Andy Stevens, Gary Deaker, Shane Buckley, Bernie Wilkinson, Lachlan Churchill, Lee Tuson, Darryl Pitt and Steve Rosolen. Another player, Ben Olsen, was born of Australian parents but his grandfather was Danish.

As a development area team, London, along with Carlisle and Nottingham City, were allowed to register an unlimited number of overseas players but could only field four at one time. Other clubs are allowed three overseas players on their books plus any who have been in Britain for five years.

The following is a list of overseas players who made at least one first-team appearance during 1991-92. The New Zealand register includes a few Pacific island-born players.

OVERSEAS REGISTER 1991-92

*Test players as at 1 June 1992

AUSTRALIA (65)

Wayne Alberts	(Carlisle)
Peter Anderson	(Hull K.R.)
Tony Anderson	(Bradford N.)
Greg Austin	(Halifax)
Geoff Bagnall	(Wakefield T.)
Craig Bellamy	(Swinton)
James Black	(Carlisle)
Michael Booth	(Batley)
Graeme Bradley	(Castleford)
Russell Browning	(London C.)
Shane Buckley	(London C.)
Brendan Carey	(Trafford B.)
Paul Carr	(Hunslet)
Simon Chappell	(Highfield)
Jason Charlton	(Whitehaven)
Brett Clark	(Rochdale H.)
Mike Clements	(Oldham, Wakefield T., Ryedale-York)
Glen Coughlan	(Dewsbury)
David Cruickshank	(Salford)
Matthew Dray	(London C.)
Don Duffy	(Warrington)
Steve Georgallis	(Carlisle)
Steve Gibson	(Salford)
Wally Gibson	(Huddersfield)
Dane Grande	(Trafford B.)
Cavill Heugh	(Leeds)
Andy Hindricks	(Batley, Dewsbury)
Bob Jackson	(Warrington)
Ken Kerr	(Workington T.)
Mike Krause	(Batley)
Mark Lowry	(Swinton)
Troy McCarthy	(Hull K.R.)
Danny McKelvie	(Hunslet)
Phil McKenzie	(Widnes)
John Machon	(Keighley C.)
Greg Mackey	(Hull)
Tony Marshall	(Ryedale-York)
Paul May	(Bramley, Nottingham C.)
*Gene Miles	(Wigan)
Jim Moore	(Chorley B.)
Gary Morrisey	(Bramley, Nottingham C.)
Mark Mulligan	(Oldham)
Scott Neilson	(Huddersfield)
Ben Olsen	(London C.)
Chris O'Sullivan	(Swinton)
Ray Ovens	(London C.)
Greg Pearce	(Halifax)
Chris Perry	(Wakefield T.)
Darryl Pitt	(London C.)
John Plath	(London C.)
Wayne Portlock	(Hull)
Francis Rolls	(London C.)
David Ronson	(Hull)
Steve Rosolen	(London C.)
Danny Saltoon	(Whitehaven)
Gary Schubert	(Workington T.)
Greg Shuttleworth	(Huddersfield)
Peter Spring	(Hull)
Matthew Steele	(Hunslet, Ryedale-York)
Glen Tomlinson	(Batley)
Rodney Trayhurn	(Bramley)
Phil Veivers	(St. Helens)
Mark Wilkes	(Workington T.)
Bernie Wilkinson	(London C.)
Alan Wrice	(Bramley)

NEW ZEALAND (73)

Basil Ake	(Leigh)
*Dean Bell	(Wigan)
Glen Bell	(Dewsbury)
Karl Benson	(Chorley B.)
*Richard Blackmore	(Castleford)
*Frano Botica	(Wigan)
Mark Brooke-Cowden	(Halifax, Keighley C.)
Steve Carey	(Whitehaven)
*Dean Clark	(Hull K.R., Scarborough P.)
Trevor Clark	(Featherstone R.)
Aaron Conlon	(Barrow)
*Shane Cooper	(St. Helens)
Reg Dunn	(Barrow, Whitehaven)
Logan Edwards	(Oldham)
*Morvin Edwards	(Leeds)
*Esene Faimalo	(Widnes)
Joe Faimalo	(Oldham, Swinton, Workington T.)
Carl Findlay	(Carlisle)
*Clayton Friend	(Carlisle)
Jason Gilbert	(Huddersfield)
Joe Grima	(Widnes, Oldham)
Carl Hall	(Doncaster)
Shane Hansen	(Salford)
Bradley Hepi	(Carlisle)
Terry Hermansson	(Doncaster)

Greg Hiley	(Keighley C.)
Craig Innes	(Leeds)
Brett Iti	(Bradford N.)
Clarry Iti	(Featherstone R.)
Moses Keresoma	(Barrow)
*Mike Kuiti	(Rochdale H.)
Markish Langi	(Bramley)
Penieli "Ben" Lia	(Whitehaven, Workington T.)
Arnold Lomax	(Huddersfield)
John Lomax	(Workington T.)
Charlie McAlister	(Oldham, Sheffield E.)
Redvers McCabe	(Scarborough P.)
Des Maea	(Sheffield E.)
*Duane Mann	(Warrington)
*George Mann	(St. Helens)
Vila Matautia	(Doncaster)
*Gary Mercer	(Warrington)
Roby Muller	(Warrington)
Shane Ngataki	(Bramley, Swinton, Trafford B.)
Vince Nicklin	(Oldham)
*Tawera Nikau	(Castleford)
Dean Noble	(Scarborough P.)
*Dane O'Hara	(Doncaster)
Hitro Okesene	(Carlisle)
Paul Okesene	(Rochdale H.)
Aaron Palelei	(Keighley C.)
*Sam Panapa	(Wigan)
Dean Revell	(Ryedale-York)
Matthew Roiall	(Keighley C.)
Iva Ropati	(Oldham, Sheffield E.)
*Tea Ropati	(St. Helens)
*Adrian Shelford	(Wakefield T., Sheffield E.)
Darrall Shelford	(Bradford N.)
*Kelly Shelford	(Warrington)
Mani Solomona	(Trafford B.)
Se'e Solomona	(Widnes)
*Kurt Sorensen	(Widnes)
Peter Subritzky	(Salford)
Brad Tohitau	(Trafford B.)
Mike Toomata	(Whitehaven)
Tony Tuimavave	(Sheffield E.)
Shane Tupaea	(Oldham)
*Brendan Tuuta	(Featherstone R.)
Vaughan Watene	(Chorley B.)
*Dave Watson	(Halifax)
Sonny Whakarau	(Bramley)
Nigel White	(Carlisle)
Dean Williams	(Workington T.)

FRANCE (1)

Dazi Abderaman	(London C.)

KENYA (1)

Eddie Rombo	(Dewsbury)

MOROCCO (1)

Hussein M'Barki	(London C.)

RUSSIA (4)

Alexander Diatlov	(Trafford B.)
Valeri Medwedj	(Trafford B.)
Valeri Savikhine	(Trafford B.)
Oleg Zotov	(Trafford B.)

SOUTH AFRICA (1)

Andre Stoop	(Wigan)

TONGA (5)

Lee Hansen	(Leigh)
*[1]Emosi Koloto	(Widnes)
Patelesio Latu	(Highfield)
Bob Tuavao	(Highfield)
Harmon Tuavao	(Highfield)

*[1] New Zealand Test player

A one-season spell with Wigan for Kiwi Sam Panapa, scorer of 11 tries in 34 appearances.

RECORD TRANSFERS

The first £1,000 transfer came in 1921 when Harold Buck joined Leeds from Hunslet, although there were reports at the time that another player was involved in the deal to make up the four-figure transfer. Other claims for the first £1,000 transfer are attached to Stan Brogden's move from Bradford Northern to Huddersfield in 1929. The following list shows how transfer fees have grown this century in straight cash deals only:

Season	Player	Position	From	To	Fee
1901-02	Jim Lomas	Centre	Bramley	Salford	£100
1910-11	Jim Lomas	Centre	Salford	Oldham	£300
1912-13	Billy Batten	Centre	Hunslet	Hull	£600
1921-22	Harold Buck	Wing	Hunslet	Leeds	£1,000
1929-30	Stanley Smith	Wing	Wakefield T.	Leeds	£1,075
1933-34	Stanley Brogden	Wing/centre	Huddersfield	Leeds	£1,200
1937-38	Billy Belshaw	Full back	Liverpool S.	Warrington	£1,450
1946-47	Bill Davies	Full back/centre	Huddersfield	Dewsbury	£1,650
1947-48	Bill Hudson	Forward	Batley	Wigan	£2,000
1947-48	Jim Ledgard	Full back	Dewsbury	Leigh	£2,650
1948-49	Ike Owens	Forward	Leeds	Castleford	£2,750
1948-49	Ike Owens	Forward	Castleford	Huddersfield	£2,750
1948-49	Stan McCormick	Wing	Belle Vue R.	St. Helens	£4,000
1949-50	Albert Naughton	Centre	Widnes	Warrington	£4,600
1950-51	Bruce Ryan	Wing	Hull	Leeds	£4,750
1950-51	Joe Egan	Hooker	Wigan	Leigh	£5,000
1950-51	Harry Street	Forward	Dewsbury	Wigan	£5,000
1957-58	Mick Sullivan	Wing	Huddersfield	Wigan	£9,500
1958-59	Ike Southward	Wing	Workington T.	Oldham	£10,650
1960-61	Mick Sullivan	Wing	Wigan	St. Helens	£11,000
1960-61	Ike Southward	Wing	Oldham	Workington T.	£11,002 10s
1968-69	Colin Dixon	Forward	Halifax	Salford	£12,000
1969-70	Paul Charlton	Full back	Workington T.	Salford	£12,500
1972-73	Eric Prescott	Forward	St. Helens	Salford	£13,500
1975-76	Steve Nash	Scrum half	Featherstone R.	Salford	£15,000
1977-78	Bill Ashurst	Forward	Wigan	Wakefield T.	£18,000
1978-79	Clive Pickerill	Scrum half	Castleford	Hull	£20,000
1978-79	Phil Hogan	Forward	Barrow	Hull K.R.	£35,000
1979-80	Len Casey	Forward	Bradford N.	Hull K.R.	£38,000
1980-81	Trevor Skerrett	Forward	Wakefield T.	Hull	£40,000
1980-81	George Fairbairn	Full back	Wigan	Hull K.R.	£72,500
1985-86	Ellery Hanley	Centre/stand off	Bradford N.	Wigan	£85,000
1985-86	Joe Lydon	Centre	Widnes	Wigan	£100,000
1986-87	Andy Gregory	Scrum half	Warrington	Wigan	£130,000
1987-88	Lee Crooks	Forward	Hull	Leeds	£150,000

1987-88	Garry Schofield	Centre	Hull	Leeds	£155,000
1989-90	Graham Steadman	Stand off	Featherstone R.	Castleford	£170,000
1991-92	Ellery Hanley	Forward	Wigan	Leeds	£250,000
1991-92	Martin Offiah	Winger	Widnes	Wigan	£440,000

Great Britain skipper Ellery Hanley, world record transfer holder for only four months after his £250,000 move from Wigan to Leeds in September 1991.

MOST MOVES

Geoff Clarkson extended his record number of transfers to 12 when he left Leigh for Featherstone Rovers on 27 October 1983. He played for 10 different English clubs and had a brief spell in Australia.

Clarkson, born on 12 August 1943 was 40 years old when he finished playing regular first team rugby in 1983-84. He turned professional with Wakefield Trinity in 1966 after gaining Yorkshire County forward honours with Wakefield Rugby Union Club.

Clarkson's club career in England is as follows:

1966 — Wakefield T.
1968 — Bradford N.
1970 — Leigh
1971 — Warrington
1972 — Leeds
1975 — York
1976 — Bramley
1978 — Wakefield T. and Hull K.R.
1980 — Bradford N. and Oldham
1981 — Leigh
1983 — Featherstone R.

New Zealander Tea Ropati, the scorer of 17 tries in 27 games for St. Helens during 1991-92.

Wigan skipper Dean Bell, 1992 Stones Bitter Man of Steel.

AWARDS

AWARDS

THE 1992 MAN OF STEEL AWARDS

Launched in the 1976-77 season, the Rugby Football League's official awards are presented to the Man of Steel, the personality judged to have made the biggest contribution to the season; the First, Second and Third Division Players of the Year, decided by a ballot of the players; the Young Player of the Year, under-21 at the start of the season; the Coach of the Year and Referee of the Year, all chosen by a panel of judges, including Great Britain coach Malcolm Reilly.

The official award scheme was sponsored by Trumanns Steel from inception in 1977 to 1983, brewers Greenall Whitley taking over in 1984 until 1989. Stones Bitter introduced a three-year £50,000 sponsorship in 1990.

Stones Bitter Man of Steel

Wigan skipper **Dean Bell** became the first Kiwi to take the coveted title and a prize of £4,000 and a £300 silver champagne goblet. Enjoying his best season on the British club scene, Bell took over captaincy of the Riversiders for the first time in October 1991, as Wigan achieved the first-ever treble of Cup, League and Premiership, plus success in the CIS Insurance Charity Shield, the Foster's World Club Challenge and the inaugural Nissan World Sevens.

Stones Bitter First Division Player of the Year

Castleford full back **Graham Steadman** topped the poll of fellow Stones Bitter Championship players. Switched from stand off at the start of the season, he finished fifth in the try chart with 31 touchdowns. Steadman made two appearances for Great Britain, scoring two superb tries in France, plus one cap for Yorkshire, being selected for his second Lions tour. He was voted Man of the Match in the Yorkshire Cup final, scoring a final record of 16 points.

Stones Bitter Second Division Player of the Year

New Zealander **Iva Ropati** was the choice of the players in the eight-club Second Division. He scored a club record 30 tries for Sheffield Eagles before moving to Oldham to add another three touchdowns, finishing third in the try chart.

Stones Bitter Third Division Player of the Year

Australian full back **Wally Gibson,** of Huddersfield, became the first winner of the Third Division award as the choice of the players. He scored 20 tries and a drop goal in 26 appearances for the Third Division champions.

Stones Bitter Young Player of the Year

Gary Connolly switched from full back to centre with devastating effect, scoring 22 tries in 35 appearances for St. Helens. He made his Great Britain debut with three Test caps, playing twice for the Under-21s and being selected for his first British Lions tour Down Under.

Stones Bitter Referee of the Year

Widnes whistler **Robin Whitfield** collected his third Referee of the Year title. Top of the referees' marking chart, he took charge of the 1992 Silk Cut Challenge Cup final and the Charity Shield.

Stones Bitter Coach of the Year

Australian **John Monie** became the first to win three Coach of the Year titles. He masterminded Wigan's record-making triple success of Challenge Cup, Championship and Premiership. In addition, the Riversiders won the Charity Shield, World Club Challenge and the inaugural World Sevens.

● Each of the above six category winners received £1,000 and a £250 silver wine goblet.

THE MAN OF STEEL AWARDS ROLL OF HONOUR

	Man of Steel	1st Division Player	2nd Division Player	Young Player	Coach	Referee
1977	David Ward (Leeds)	Malcolm Reilly (Castleford)	Ged Marsh (Blackpool B.)	David Ward (Leeds)	Eric Ashton (St. Helens)	Billy Thompson (Huddersfield)
1978	George Nicholls (St. Helens)	George Nicholls (St. Helens)	John Woods (Leigh)	John Woods (Leigh)	Frank Myler (Widnes)	Billy Thompson (Huddersfield)
1979	Doug Laughton (Widnes)	Mick Adams (Widnes)	Steve Norton (Hull)	Steve Evans (Featherstone R.)	Doug Laughton (Widnes)	Mick Naughton (Widnes)
1980	George Fairbairn (Wigan)	Mick Adams (Widnes)	Steve Quinn (Featherstone R.)	Roy Holdstock (Hull K.R.)	Peter Fox (Bradford N.)	Fred Lindop (Wakefield)
1981	Ken Kelly (Warrington)	Ken Kelly (Warrington)	John Crossley (York)	Des Drummond (Leigh)	Billy Benyon (Warrington)	John Holdsworth (Kippax)
1982	Mick Morgan (Carlisle)	Steve Norton (Hull)	Mick Morgan (Carlisle)	Des Drummond (Leigh)	Arthur Bunting (Hull)	Fred Lindop (Wakefield)
1983	Allan Agar (Featherstone R.)	Keith Mumby (Bradford N.)	Steve Nash (Salford)	Brian Noble (Bradford N.)	Arthur Bunting (Hull)	Robin Whitfield (Widnes)
1984	Joe Lydon (Widnes)	Joe Lydon (Widnes)	David Cairns (Barrow)	Joe Lydon (Widnes)	Tommy Dawes (Barrow)	Billy Thompson (Huddersfield)
1985	Ellery Hanley (Bradford N.)	Ellery Hanley (Bradford N.)	Graham Steadman (York)	Lee Crooks (Hull)	Roger Millward (Hull K.R.)	Ron Campbell (Widnes)
1986	Gavin Miller (Hull K.R.)	Gavin Miller (Hull K.R.)	Derek Pyke (Leigh)	Shaun Edwards (Wigan)	Chris Anderson (Halifax)	Fred Lindop (Wakefield)
1987	Ellery Hanley (Wigan)	Andy Gregory (Wigan)	John Cogger (Runcorn H.)	Shaun Edwards (Wigan)	Graham Lowe (Wigan)	John Holdsworth (Kippax)
1988	Martin Offiah (Widnes)	Steve Hampson (Wigan)	Peter Smith (Featherstone R.)	Shaun Edwards (Wigan)	Doug Laughton (Widnes)	Fred Lindop (Wakefield)
1989	Ellery Hanley (Wigan)	David Hulme (Widnes)	Darryl Powell (Sheffield E.)	Paul Newlove (Featherstone R.)	Graham Lowe (Wigan)	John Holdsworth (Kippax)

	Man of Steel	1st Division Player	2nd Division Player	3rd Division Player	Young Player	Coach	Referee
1990	Shaun Edwards (Wigan)	Andy Goodway (Wigan)	John Woods (Rochdale H.)	—	Bobby Goulding (Wigan)	John Monie (Wigan)	Robin Whitfield (Widnes)
1991	Garry Schofield (Leeds)	Jonathan Davies (Widnes)	Tawera Nikau (Ryedale-York)	—	Denis Betts (Wigan)	John Monie (Wigan)	John Holdsworth (Kippax)
1992	Dean Bell (Wigan)	Graham Steadman (Castleford)	Iva Ropati (Oldham)	Wally Gibson (Huddersfield)	Gary Connolly (St. Helens)	John Monie (Wigan)	Robin Whitfield (Widnes)

NOMINEES:

1977 *1st Division Player:* Bruce Burton (Castleford), Vince Farrar (Featherstone R.), *2nd Division Player:* Jeff Grayshon (Dewsbury), Keith Hepworth (Hull). *Young Player:* Jimmy Crampton (Hull), Harry Pinner (St. Helens). *Coach:* Keith Cotton (Featherstone R.), Mal Reilly (Castleford). *Referee:* Joe Jackson (Pudsey), Mick Naughton (Widnes).

1978 *1st Division Player:* Roger Millward (Hull K.R.), Harry Pinner (St. Helens). *2nd Division Player:* Phil Hogan (Barrow), Mick Morgan (York). *Young Player:* Neil Hague (Leeds), Keith Mumby (Bradford N.). *Coach:* Eric Ashton MBE (St. Helens), John Mantle (Leigh). *Referee:* Ron Campbell (Widnes), Fred Lindop (Wakefield).

1979 *1st Division Player:* Brian Lockwood (Hull K.R.), Tommy Martyn (Warrington). *2nd Division Player:* Barry Banks (York), John Wolford (Dewsbury). *Young Player:* Mick Burke (Widnes), John Woods (Leigh). *Coach:* Billy Benyon (Warrington), Arthur Bunting (Hull). *Referee:* Fred Lindop (Wakefield), Billy Thompson (Huddersfield).

1980 *1st Division Player:* Len Casey (Hull K.R.), George Fairbairn (Wigan). *2nd Division Player:* Mick Blacker (Halifax), John Wolford (Dewsbury). *Young Player:* Steve Hubbard (Hull K.R.), Harry Pinner (St. Helens). *Coach:* Maurice Bamford (Halifax), Arthur Bunting (Hull). *Referee:* Ron Campbell (Widnes), Billy Thompson (Huddersfield).

1981 *1st Division Player:* Mick Adams (Widnes), Tommy Martyn (Warrington). *2nd Division Player:* Arnie Walker (Whitehaven), Danny Wilson (Swinton). *Young Player:* Paul Harkin (Hull K.R.), Keith Mumby (Bradford N.). *Coach:* Reg Bowden (Fulham), Peter Fox (Bradford N.). *Referee:* Ron Campbell (Widnes), Fred Lindop (Wakefield).

1982 *1st Division Player:* Jeff Grayshon (Bradford N.), Andy Gregory (Widnes). *2nd Division Player:* Denis Boyd (Carlisle), Alan Fairhurst (Swinton). *Young Player:* Lee Crooks (Hull), Andy Gregory (Widnes). *Coach:* Doug Laughton (Widnes), Alex Murphy/Colin Clarke (Leigh). *Referee:* Gerry Kershaw (York), Billy Thompson (Huddersfield).

1983 *1st Division Player:* Bob Eccles (Warrington), David Topliss (Hull). *2nd Division Player:* Tommy David (Cardiff C.), Mike Lampkowski (Wakefield T.). *Young Player:* Ronnie Duane (Warrington), Andy Goodway (Oldham). *Coach:* Alex Murphy (Wigan), Frank Myler (Oldham). *Referee:* John Holdsworth (Leeds), Fred Lindop (Wakefield).

1984 *1st Division Player:* Garry Schofield (Hull), John Woods (Leigh). *2nd Division Player:* Lynn Hopkins (Workington T.), John Wolford (Hunslet). *Young Player:* Gary Divorty (Hull), Garry Schofield (Hull). *Coach:* Arthur Bunting (Hull), Roger Millward (Hull K.R.). *Referee:* Derek Fox (Wakefield), Fred Lindop (Wakefield).

1985 *1st Division Player:* Harry Pinner (St. Helens), Gary Prohm (Hull K.R.). *2nd Division Player:* Terry Langton (Mansfield M.), Peter Wood (Runcorn H.). *Young Player:* Deryck Fox (Featherstone R.), Roy Powell (Leeds). *Coach:* Arthur Bunting (Hull), Colin Clarke/Alan McInnes (Wigan). *Referee:* Fred Lindop (Wakefield), Stan Wall (Leigh).

1986 *1st Division Player:* Steve Ella (Wigan), John Fieldhouse (Widnes). *2nd Division Player:* John Henderson (Leigh), Graham King (Hunslet). *Young Player:* Paul Lyman (Featherstone R.), Roy Powell (Leeds). *Coach:* Roger Millward (Hull K.R.), John Sheridan (Doncaster). *Referee:* John Holdsworth (Kippax), Robin Whitfield (Widnes).

1987   *1st Division Player:* Lee Crooks (Hull), Ellery Hanley (Wigan). *2nd Division Player:* Andy Bateman (Hunslet), Les Holliday (Swinton). *Young Player:* Paul Loughlin (St. Helens), Kevin McCormack (St. Helens). *Coach:* Chris Anderson (Halifax), Alex Murphy (St. Helens). *Referee:* Kevin Allatt (Southport), Fred Lindop (Wakefield).

1988   *1st Division Player:* Martin Offiah (Widnes), Kurt Sorensen (Widnes). *2nd Division Player:* Deryck Fox (Featherstone R.), Hugh Waddell (Oldham). *Young Player:* Paul Medley (Leeds), Steve Robinson (Halifax). *Coach:* Alex Murphy (St. Helens), Barry Seabourne (Bradford N.). *Referee:* John Holdsworth (Kippax), Ray Tennant (Castleford).

1989   *1st Division Player:* Andy Gregory (Wigan), Kelvin Skerrett (Bradford N.). *2nd Division Player:* Cavill Heugh (Barrow), Chris Johnson (Leigh). *Young Player:* Grant Anderson (Castleford), Denis Betts (Wigan). *Coach:* Peter Fox (Featherstone R.), Brian Smith (Hull). *Referee:* Ray Tennant (Castleford), Robin Whitfield (Widnes).

1990   *1st Division Player:* Deryck Fox (Featherstone R.), Andy Platt (Wigan). *2nd Division Player:* David Bishop (Hull K.R.), John Cogger (Oldham). *Young Player:* Denis Betts (Wigan), Anthony Sullivan (Hull K.R.). *Coach:* Tony Barrow (Oldham), Brian Johnson (Warrington). *Referee:* John Holdsworth (Kippax), Colin Morris (Huddersfield).

1991   *1st Division Player:* Andy Gregory (Wigan), George Mann (St. Helens). *2nd Division Player:* Steven Kerry (Salford), Peter Ropati (Leigh). *Young Player:* Phil Clarke (Wigan), Craig Richards (Bradford N.). *Coach:* Ray Ashton (Workington T.), Doug Laughton (Widnes). *Referee:* Brian Galtress (Bradford), Jim Smith (Halifax).

1992   *1st Division Player:* Dean Bell (Wigan), John Devereux (Widnes). *2nd Division Player:* Clayton Friend (Carlisle), Paul Topping (Leigh). *3rd Division Player:* Steve Carroll (Bramley), Paul Delaney (Dewsbury). *Young Player:* Paul Newlove (Featherstone R.), David Myers (Wigan). *Coach:* Alex Murphy (Huddersfield), Darryl Van de Velde (Castleford). *Referee:* Stuart Cummings (Widnes), John Holdsworth (Kippax).

STONES BITTER TEAM OF THE MONTH AWARDS 1991-92

Introduced in the 1979-80 season, the scheme acknowledges the adjudged Team of the Month in each division.

A panel of judges representing Stones Bitter and the Rugby League selected the three monthly winners, the First Division winners receiving £500, the Second Division £350, the Third Division £250, plus a framed citation.

The awards were sponsored for the first four seasons by Shopacheck before Lada Cars took over in the 1983-84 season and introduced the first-ever Team of the Year title. Stones Bitter took over the sponsorship in 1987-88, the 1992 Team of the Year, **Wigan,** receiving £1,500. A Third Division award was introduced in 1991-92.

	First Division	Second Division
Aug./Sept.	St. Helens	Rochdale H.
Oct.	Widnes	Sheffield E.
Nov.	Salford	Sheffield E.
Dec.	Leeds	Leigh
Jan.	Wigan	Sheffield E.
Feb.	Wigan	Oldham
Mar.	Wigan	Rochdale H.
Apr./May	Wigan	Sheffield E.

Third Division
Batley
Dewsbury
Huddersfield
Bramley
Dewsbury
Barrow
Bramley
Batley

Team of the Year
1983-84: Widnes
1984-85: Hull K.R.
1985-86: Halifax
1986-87: Wigan
1987-88: Widnes
1988-89: Wigan
1989-90: Wigan
1990-91: Wigan
1991-92: Wigan

WALLACE ARNOLD – SUNDAY MIRROR ENTERTAINER AWARDS 1991-92

Introduced in 1986-87, the scheme was sponsored by Wallace Arnold and promoted by the *Sunday Mirror.*

Each month a player was chosen as Entertainer of the Month to receive a Wallace Arnold holiday voucher for £400. The Entertainer of the Year was awarded a £1,500 holiday voucher, the 1992 winner being Great Britain and Wigan half back **Shaun Edwards.**

Entertainer of the Month

Sept.	Shaun Edwards (Wigan)
Oct.	Michael Jackson (Wakefield T.)
Nov.	Garry Schofield (Leeds)
Dec.	Alan Tait (Widnes)
Jan.	John Bentley (Leeds)
Feb.	Graham Steadman (Castleford)
Mar.	Gene Miles (Wigan)
Apr./May	Martin Offiah (Widnes)

Entertainer of the Year

1987:	Ellery Hanley (Wigan)
1988:	Martin Offiah (Widnes)
1989:	Martin Offiah (Widnes)
1990:	Deryck Fox (Featherstone R.)
1991:	Garry Schofield (Leeds)
1992:	Shaun Edwards (Wigan)

STONES BITTER TOP SCORERS AWARDS 1991-92

Launched in the 1976-77 season, the scheme was designed to reward the top try and goal scorers in the League. Sponsored by Stones Bitter, the 1992 awards were worth £30 a try and £10 a goal.

The top try merchant was Wigan half back **Shaun Edwards** who touched down 40 times to earn a prize cheque for £1,200.

The top marksman was Wigan utility man **Frano Botica** who hit the target 161 times to qualify for a prize pay out of £1,610.

Wigan utility back Frano Botica, 1991-92 top goalkicker.

REFEREES

REFEREES' HONOURS 1991-92

Silk Cut Challenge Cup final:
Robin Whitfield

Regal Trophy final:
Brian Galtress

Stones Bitter Premiership final:
John Holdsworth

Divisional Premiership final:
Stuart Cummings

Greenalls Lancashire Cup final:
David Campbell

John Smiths Yorkshire Cup final:
John Holdsworth

Australia v New Zealand (3):
John Holdsworth

Papua New Guinea v France:
Colin Morris

France v Papua New Guinea:
Colin Morris

Wales v France:
Colin Morris

War of the Roses:
Colin Morris

Under-21 France v Great Britain:
Russell Smith

CIS Insurance Charity Shield:
Robin Whitfield

SENIOR REFEREES 1992-93

DAVID ASQUITH (York)
Date of birth: 20.6.53
Grade One: 1989-90

DAVID ATKIN (Hull)
Date of birth: 19.12.64
Grade One: 1992-93

GEOFF BERRY (Batley)
Date of birth: 26.4.54
Grade Two: 1981-82
Grade One: 1983-84

ALAN BURKE (Oldham)
Date of birth: 21.1.57
Grade One: 1987-88
Lancashire Cup 1990-91

DAVID CAMPBELL (St. Helens)
Date of birth: 9.10.54
Grade One: 1989-90
Lancashire Cup 1991-92

DAVE CARTER (Widnes)
Date of birth: 29.11.55
Grade One: 1984-85
France v Great Britain Under-21s 1988-89

JOHN CONNOLLY (Wigan)
Date of birth: 30.9.59
Grade One: 1990-91

ROBERT CONNOLLY (Wigan)
Date of birth: 30.9.59
Grade One: 1990-91

PAUL CRASHLEY (Wakefield)
Date of birth: 1.8.50
Grade One: 1989-90

STEVE CROSS (Hull)
Date of birth: 23.3.50
Grade One: 1986-87

STUART CUMMINGS (Widnes)
Date of birth: 17.11.60
Grade One: 1991-92
Divisional Premiership 1991-92

BRIAN GALTRESS (Bradford)
Date of birth: 8.10.51
Grade One: 1988-89
Regal Trophy 1991-92
Second Division Premiership 1990-91
France v Great Britain Under-21s 1990-91

STEPHEN HAIGH (Ossett)
Date of birth: 5.4.45
Grade Two: 1980-81
Grade One: 1983-84

JOHN HOLDSWORTH (Kippax)
Date of birth: 25.1.47
Grade Two: 1979-80
Grade One: 1980-81
Challenge Cup 1986-87, 1989-90
John Player Trophy 1985-86, 1986-87, 1988-89
Premiership Trophy 1980-81, 1987-88, 1988-89,
    1990-91, 1991-92
Lancashire Cup 1982-83, 1985-86
Yorkshire Cup 1991-92
World Club Challenge 1987-88
Australia v New Zealand (3) 1991
France v Australia (2) 1990-91
Wales v England 1980-81
Great Britain v Rest of World 1988-89
RL Chairman's XIII v Papua New Guinea 1987-88
Cumbria v Yorkshire 1981-82
France v Great Britain Under-24s 1982-83
War of the Roses 1987-88
Charity Shield 1987-88, 1989-90

JOHN KENDREW (Castleford)
Date of birth: 22.4.50
Grade Two: 1982-83
Grade One: 1983-84
Lancashire v Papua New Guinea 1987-88

GERRY KERSHAW (Easingwold)
Date of birth: 24.10.43
Grade Two: 1969-70
Grade One: 1970-71
Challenge Cup 1980-81
Lancashire Cup 1980-81
Floodlit Trophy 1973-74
Regal Trophy 1973-74, 1989-90
Wales v England 1981-82
Wales v Australia 1982-83
France v Great Britain Under-24s 1981-82
Lancashire v Yorkshire 1971-72
Lancashire v Cumbria 1972-73
Cumbria v Other Nationalities 1974-75
Cumbria v Lancashire 1978-79, 1980-81
War of the Roses 1989-90

COLIN MORRIS (Huddersfield)
Date of birth: 14.3.57
Grade One: 1989-90
Premiership Trophy 1989-90
Papua New Guinea v France 1991
France v Papua New Guinea 1991-92
Wales v France 1991-92
France v Great Britain Under-21s 1989-90
Charity Shield 1990-91
War of the Roses 1991-92

STEVE NICHOLSON (Whitehaven)
Date of birth: 5.4.61
Grade One: 1992-93

IAN OLLERTON (Wigan)
Date of birth: 31.3.53
Grade One: 1990-91

JIM SMITH (Halifax)
Date of birth: 2.3.44
Grade Two: 1977-78
Grade One: 1983-84
Challenge Cup 1990-91
Regal Trophy 1990-91
Yorkshire Cup 1990-91
Lancashire Cup 1986-87

RUSSELL SMITH (Castleford)
Date of birth: 24.1.64
Grade One: 1991-92
France v Great Britain Under-21s 1991-92

COLIN STEELE (Dalton-in-Furness)
Date of birth: 11.9.60
Grade One: 1987-88
Cumbria v France 1988-89

CHARLIE TIDBALL (Wakefield)
Date of birth: 25.12.48
Grade One: 1987-88

PAUL VOLANTE (Birstall)
Date of birth: 30.6.52
Grade One: 1983-84

JOHN WHITELAM (Hull)
Date of birth: 11.5.53
Grade One: 1988-89

ROBIN WHITFIELD (Widnes)
Date of birth: 26.11.43
Grade Two: 1979-80
Grade One: 1980-81
Challenge Cup 1982-83, 1985-86, 1991-92
Yorkshire Cup 1981-82, 1988-89
Second Division Premiership 1987-88, 1988-89, 1989-90
France v Australia (2) 1982-83
France v New Zealand (2) 1989-90
New Zealand v Australia 1983
Australia v New Zealand (3) 1986
Yorkshire v Lancashire 1981-82
Charity Shield 1991-92
War of the Roses 1988-89

NEIL WOOD (Keighley)
Date of birth: 12.7.62
Grade One: 1992-93

Widnes whistler Robin Whitfield, 1991-92 Stones Bitter Referee of the Year.

THE ALLIANCE

FIRST DIVISION

	P.	W.	D.	L.	FOR	AGAINST	Pts.
Wigan	26	22	0	4	1004	318	44
Hull	26	17	1	8	625	413	35
Castleford	26	15	2	9	700	524	32
Leeds	26	15	0	11	759	524	30
Halifax	26	15	0	11	638	482	30
Widnes	26	14	0	12	752	714	28
St. Helens	26	13	1	12	724	584	27
Bradford N.	26	13	0	13	567	691	26
Wakefield T.	26	12	0	14	602	607	24
Warrington W.	26	12	0	14	546	580	24
Featherstone R.	26	10	1	15	438	583	21
Hull K.R.	26	10	1	15	428	616	21
Oldham	26	6	0	20	394	713	12
Workington T.	26	5	0	21	267	1095	10

● Bottom two clubs relegated

SECOND DIVISION EAST

	P.	W.	D.	L.	FOR	AGAINST	Pts.
Batley	18	14	0	4	369	196	28
Ryedale-York	18	12	0	6	440	238	24
Doncaster	18	11	0	7	362	266	22
Dewsbury	18	11	0	7	344	278	22
Bramley	18	11	0	7	345	307	22
Scarborough P.	18	8	1	9	315	388	17
Sheffield E.	18	8	0	10	424	355	16
Hunslet	18	7	1	10	295	329	15
London C.	18	5	0	13	291	487	10
Hemel Hempstead	18	2	0	16	273	614	4

SECOND DIVISION WEST

	P.	W.	D.	L.	FOR	AGAINST	Pts.
Rochdale H.	18	15	0	3	637	292	30
Salford	18	13	1	4	662	242	27
Leigh	18	12	0	6	493	320	24
Huddersfield	18	10	0	8	472	313	20
Swinton C.	18	9	0	9	433	385	18
Carlisle	18	9	0	9	428	392	18
Barrow	18	9	0	9	401	368	18
Keighley C.	18	7	1	10	322	428	15
Whitehaven	18	5	0	13	305	644	10
Chorley B.	18	0	0	18	133	902	0

● Top club in each Second Division promoted

YOUNGER'S CHALLENGE CUP 1992

Preliminary Round

Carlisle	28	Doncaster	8
Scarborough P.	12	Hull	34

First Round

Batley	7	Huddersfield	8
Castleford	12	Hull K.R.	16
Chorley B.	8	Featherstone R.	82
Hemel Hempst'd	20	Oldham	16
Hull	44	Keighley C.	0
Hunslet	10	Warrington W.	46
Leeds	30	Carlisle	14
Leigh	26	Dewsbury	6
Ryedale-York	30	Bramley	0
St. Helens	64	Workington	18
Salford	22	Bradford N.	18
Sheffield E.	36	London C.	22
Wakefield T.	44	Swinton C.	4
Widnes	24	Barrow	24
Wigan	38	Halifax	0

Bye: Rochdale H.

First Round Replay

Barrow	22	Widnes	30

Second Round

Huddersfield	14	Featherstone R.	12
Hull K.R.	56	Hemel Hempst'd	12
Leigh	18	Leeds	36
Rochdale H.	8	Warrington W.	26
Ryedale-York	14	Wigan	20
Salford	16	Widnes	40
Sheffield E.	21	St. Helens	51
Wakefield T.	30	Hull	12

Third Round

St. Helens	36	Hull K.R.	6
Wakefield T.	26	Widnes	32
Warrington W.	14	Leeds	38
Wigan	66	Huddersfield	0

Semi-Finals

Widnes	20	St. Helens	17
Wigan	18	Leeds	6

Final

Wigan	38	Widnes	14

SECOND DIVISION CUP

Semi-Finals

Batley	36	Keighley C.	16
Ryedale-York	18	Rochdale H.	17

Final

Batley	18	Ryedale-York	20

LANCASHIRE COMBINATION CHALLENGE SHIELD 1991-92

First Round

Barrow	9	Leigh	10
Carlisle	22	Salford	16
Chorley B.	5	Swinton C.	24
Hemel Hempstead	8	Oldham	46
London C.	14	Rochdale H.	25
Warrington W.	38	Wigan	14
Whitehaven	26	Widnes	18
Workington	20	St. Helens	32

Second Round

Leigh	22	Swinton C.	9
St. Helens	49	Oldham	10
Warrington W.	25	Carlisle	14
Whitehaven	16	Rochdale H.	13

Semi-Finals

*Warrington given bye.

Whitehaven	23	Leigh	2

Final

Warrington W.	32	Whitehaven	8

YORKSHIRE SENIOR COMPETITION CHALLENGE CUP 1991-92

Preliminary Round

Bramley	13	Huddersfield	10
Doncaster	4	Castleford	40

First Round

Batley	18	Hull	32
Bramley	6	Bradford N.	32
Featherstone R.	30	Sheffield E.	36
Hull K.R.	4	Dewsbury	21
Hunslet	4	Halifax	35
Leeds	26	Castleford	34
Ryedale-York	10	Scarborough P.	23
Wakefield T.	14	Keighley C.	26

Second Round

Bradford N.	24	Halifax	12
Castleford	10	Scarborough P.	30
Dewsbury	18	Sheffield E.	2
Keighley C.	10	Hull	24

Semi-Finals

Hull	46	Bradford N.	12
Scarborough P.	16	Dewsbury	20

Final

Dewsbury	2	Hull	10

YOUNGER'S PLAYER OF THE YEAR

1992: Robert Moules (Scarborough P.)

POT POURRI

DIARY OF LANDMARKS

1895   August 29... the beginning. The Northern Rugby Football Union formed at The George Hotel, Huddersfield, following the breakaway from the English RU by 21 clubs who wanted to pay players for taking time off work to play.

September 7... season opens with 22 clubs.

Joseph Platt appointed Rugby League Secretary.

1897   April 24... Batley won the first Northern Union — later Rugby League — Challenge Cup final.

Line-out abolished and replaced by punt from touch.

All goals to be worth two points.

1898   Professionalism allowed but players must be in full-time employment.

1899   Scrum if player cannot release the ball after a tackle.

1901   Punt from touch replaced by 10-yard scrum when ball is carried into touch.

1902   Two divisions introduced.

Punt from touch abolished completely. Touch-finding rule introduced with the ball having to bounce before entering touch.

1905   Two divisions scrapped.

Lancashire and Yorkshire County Cup competitions inaugurated.

1906   Thirteen-a-side introduced, from traditional 15.

Play-the-ball introduced.

1907   First tour — New Zealand to England. The tour party were RU 'rebels'.

First Top Four play-off for championship.

1908   Australia and New Zealand launch Rugby League.

First Australian tour of England.

1910   First British tour of Australia and New Zealand.

1915   Competitive rugby suspended for duration of First World War.

1919   Competitive rugby resumed in January.

1920   John Wilson appointed Rugby League Secretary.

1922   Title of Northern Rugby Football Union changed to Rugby Football League.

Goal from a mark abolished.

1927   First radio broadcast of Challenge Cup final — Oldham v. Swinton at Wigan.

1929   Wembley staged its first RL Challenge Cup final — Wigan v. Dewsbury.

1932   London exhibition match under floodlights at White City — Leeds v. Wigan.

1933   France staged its first Rugby League match — an exhibition between England and Australia in Paris.

London Highfield, formerly Wigan Highfield, became capital's first Rugby League team, also first to play regularly under floodlights.

1934   A French squad made a short tour of England before Rugby League was officially launched in France.

1935   European Championship introduced, contested by England, France and Wales.

1939   Second World War. Emergency war-time competitions introduced.

1945   War-time emergencies over.

Bill Fallowfield appointed Rugby League Secretary.

1946   First all-ticket match — Hull v. Hull K.R.

1948   King George VI became first reigning monarch to attend Rugby League match — Wigan v. Bradford Northern Cup final at Wembley.

First televised match — at Wembley — but shown only in London area.

Wembley's first all-ticket final.

International Board formed.

1949   Welsh League formed.

1950   Italian squad made brief tour of England.

1951   First televised match in the North — Britain v. New Zealand at Swinton.

First floodlights installation by Northern club, Bradford Northern.

1952   First nationally televised Challenge Cup final — Workington Town v. Featherstone Rovers.

1954   First World Cup, staged in France.

1955	London staged series of televised floodlit matches for the Independent Television Association Trophy.
	Welsh League disbanded.
1956	Sunday rugby for amateurs permitted by the Rugby Football League.
1962	Two divisions reintroduced, with Eastern and Western Divisions also formed.
1964	Substitutes allowed for injuries, but only up to half-time.
	Two division and regional leagues scrapped. One league system with Top-16 play-off for championship.
1965	BBC-2 Floodlit Trophy competition began with regular Tuesday night series.
	Substitutes allowed for any reason up to and including half-time.
	English Schools Rugby League formed.
1966	Four-tackle rule introduced for Floodlit Trophy competition in October, then for all games from December.
1967	First Sunday fixtures played, two matches on December 17.
1969	Substitutes allowed at any time.
	University Rugby League Association formed.
1971	John Player Trophy competition launched.
1972	Six-tackle rule introduced.
	Timekeepers with hooter system to signal end of match introduced.
	Colts League formed.
1973	Two divisions reintroduced.
	March 4... British Amateur Rugby League Association formed.
1974	Drop goal value halved to one point. Had been reduced earlier in international matches.
	David Oxley appointed Rugby League Secretary.
	David Howes appointed first full-time Public Relations Officer to the Rugby Football League.
	National Coaching Scheme launched.
1975	Premiership Trophy competition launched.

1976	Differential penalty introduced for technical scrum offences.
1977	County Championship not held for first time since 1895, excluding war years.
	Anglo-Australian transfer ban agreed.
1978	Papua New Guinea admitted as full members of International Board.
1981	Rugby League Professional Players' Association formed.
1982	County Championship scrapped.
1983	January 1... Sin bin introduced.
	Try value increased to four points.
	Handover after sixth tackle introduced, among several other new or amended laws following meeting of International Board.
	Anglo-Australian transfer ban lifted.
1984	Alliance League introduced in reserve grade reorganisation.
1985	First Charity Shield match played in Isle of Man.
	War of the Roses launched on Lancashire v. Yorkshire county of origin basis.
	Relegation-promotion reduced to three down, three up.
1986	Relegation-promotion altered for one year only to four down, two up to provide a 14-strong First Division for the 1987-88 season.
1987	Division Two Premiership Trophy competition launched.
	New players' contracts system introduced.
1988	Colts scrapped for new youth scheme.
	Six-man League Board of Directors appointed, plus first-ever Controller of Referees, ex-match official Fred Lindop.
1989	First-ever Sales Marketing Executive, Mike Turner, appointed by the League.
1990	Russia introduced Rugby League and sent 90-man squad of players and officials on three-match tour to Britain.
1991	Russian eight-club league launched.
	Three divisions introduced for 1991-92 season.
	Academy Under-18 league formed.
	Blood bin introduced.

DISCIPLINARY RECORDS

This sub-section is a compilation of sendings off and disciplinary verdicts for first team players.

The following information is based on the workings of the League's Disciplinary Committee which meets weekly during a season.

	1991-92	1990-91	1989-90	1988-89	1987-88
Barrow	6	5	5	4	4
Batley	7	4	1	2	1
Bradford N.	4	3	5	2	2
Bramley	2	5	4	2	4
Carlisle	2	4	0	4	9
Castleford	3	4	6	4	3
Chorley B.	5	7	3	—	—
Dewsbury	1	5	3	3	5
Doncaster	3	4	2	1	3
Featherstone R.	7	1	4	1	2
Halifax	2	3	8	1	1
Highfield	7	3	3	6	3
Huddersfield	2	1	7	3	0
Hull	2	1	3	1	2
Hull K.R.	1	3	3	3	1
Hunslet	2	6	6	5	2
Keighley C.	4	5	10	3	5
Leeds	2	5	3	0	2
Leigh	3	1	7	3	6
London C.	2	1	4	0	0
Nottingham C.	2	2	5	7	2
Oldham	5	3	6	3	4
Rochdale H.	4	5	3	3	5
Ryedale-York	1	3	7	3	4
St. Helens	6	1	6	3	1
Salford	0	5	4	2	2
Scarborough P.	1	—	—	—	—
Sheffield E.	7	2	3	4	0
Swinton	4	1	4	2	3
Trafford B.	6	2	9	2	2
Wakefield T.	3	2	6	1	5
Warrington	6	2	4	2	3
Whitehaven	5	3	6	3	3
Widnes	2	2	6	2	2
Wigan	2	7	8	3	5
Workington T.	6	4	8	3	5
Totals	**127**	**115**	**172**	**91**	**101**

DISMISSALS .... A five-year review

The following is a review of the number of first team dismissals in each season since 1987-88. The 1991-92 tally of 127 dismissals, 19 of whom were found not guilty, was 13 up on the previous season.

— indicates where a club was not in existence.

Two-match ban for Oldham's Tommy Martyn.

DISCIPLINARY ANALYSIS 1991-92

The following is a club-by-club disciplinary record for last season, showing the players sent off in first team matches and the findings of the League's Disciplinary Committee.

The committee's verdict is featured in the brackets after the player's name, each number indicating the match ban imposed. SOS stands for sending off sufficient and NG for not guilty. A suspension reduced or increased on appeal is shown as follows, 6 to 4.

During 1988-89 the totting-up system for sin-bin suspensions was abandoned. Previously two points were issued for a 10-minute temporary dismissal, a one-match ban being imposed when the total reached six. Instead, the sin bins were recorded and taken into account when considering a full dismissal.

The 1984-85 season was the first time video action other than official BBC or ITV tapes could be offered in evidence. Seven cases were considered by the committee after viewing a video, the player not having been dismissed.

Club	Total sent off	Dismissed Player	Number of Sin Bins
Barrow	6	D. Kendall (4 to SOS), G. Kendall (SOS), S. Morrison (6), S. Morrow (NG), S. Mossop (SOS), P. Trainor (NG)	14
Batley	7	J. Grayshon (3), N. Hartley (4), S. Parrish (SOS), S. Rawlinson (SOS), M. Scott (4, NG), A. Williams (NG)	14
Bradford N.	4	K. Fairbank (4 to NG), D. Hobbs (NG), T. Marchant (2), D. Moxon (SOS)	8
Bramley	2	A. Marson (SOS), C. Whitehead (4)	6
Carlisle	2	C. Friend (2), N. White (6)	10
Castleford	3	D. Sampson (6), G. Southernwood (6), G. Steadman (4 to 2)	10
Chorley B.	5	J. Carney (2, 2), K. Benson (NG), T. Hodson (4), J. Mayo (2 to SOS)	7
Dewsbury	1	D. Hall (6)	5
Doncaster	3	V. Matautia (4), R. Pell (6), K. Rayne (6)	5
Featherstone R.	7	T. Clark (SOS), A. Fisher (6, NG, 4), I. Smales (4), B. Tuuta (4, NG)	5
Halifax	2	G. Lord (6), R. Milner (2 to 1)	9
Highfield	7	G. Dean (4), T. Rawlinson (2), E. Tinsley (2), B. Tuavao (6), H. Tuavao (4, 6, 2)	6
Huddersfield	2	G. Coulter (4), F. Simpson (1)	19
Hull	2	S. McNamara (6 to 4, SOS)	12
Hull K.R.	1	P. Fletcher (4)	7
Hunslet	2	K. Bell (2), D. McKelvie (NG)	11
Keighley C.	4	A. Eyres (2 to NG), M. Fairbank (4, 8), P. Moses (4 to NG)	4
Leeds	2	B. Goulding (4), C. Heugh (SOS)	19
Leigh	3	A. Earner (6), M. Sheals (2), P. Topping (5 to 4)	12
London C.	2	B. Wilkinson (4), D. Winbourn (4)	8
Nottingham C.	2	T. Chappell (4), R. Trayhurn (SOS)	4
Oldham	5	T. Martyn (2), I. Sherratt (4), T. Street (SOS, 3, 6)	11
Rochdale H.	4	M. Calland (1), I. Gormley (4), R. Marsden (1), S. Ward (2)	8
Ryedale-York	1	C. Hammerton (NG)	15
St. Helens	6	P. Bishop (4 to 2), P. Forber (4), G. Mann (SOS, 4), S. Nickle (SOS), K. Ward (NG)	15
Salford	0		3
Scarborough P.	1	B. Carlyle (3)	7

Sheffield E.	7	M. Aston (SOS), M. Gamson (8), D. Laughton (SOS), D. Powell (4), R. Price (2, 2), T. Tuimavave (2)	5
Swinton	4	J. Allen (4), C. Bellamy (NG), S. Snape (3), C. Wilkinson (SOS)	16
Trafford B.	6	D. Grande (4), C. Johnson (2), K. Jones (6), J. Kerr (6), M. Meadows (SOS), M. Stewart (8)	15
Wakefield T.	3	M. Jackson (3 to 4), C. Perry (NG), G. Spencer (4)	8
Warrington	6	P. Darbyshire (3), D. Drummond (4), K. Ellis (NG, SOS), M. Forster (8), G. Sanderson (4 to 2)	8
Whitehaven	5	W. Fisher (8), B. Lia (6), J. Routledge (NG, 6), M. Toomata (NG)	14
Widnes	2	A. Currier (6), J. Grima (6)	12
Wigan	2	P. Clarke (2), A. Gregory (2)	8
Workington T.	6	W. Kitchin (2), J. Lomax (4), M. Oglanby (2), P. Penrice (4), M. Roskell (4), D. Williams (2)	13

In addition, the Disciplinary Committee carried out three *trials by video*, calling up after viewing a video tape players who had not been dismissed by the referee. Andy Dannatt of Hull was banned for eight matches, while Brendan Hill (Halifax) received a total of seven matches for two offences and Ian Sherratt (Swinton) three matches after the 1991 Second Division Premiership final.

SPONSORSHIP

This updated sub-section is a record of the sponsorship programme under the control of the Rugby Football League.

1991-92 COMPETITIONS:

Silk Cut Challenge Cup	£325,000
Regal Trophy	£300,000
Stones Bitter Championship and Premiership	£275,000
British Coal Tests	£190,000
CIS Insurance Charity Shield	£ 18,000

£1,108,000

Awards: £ 50,000

Miscellaneous: £ 75,000

GRAND TOTAL £1,258,000

COMPETITION SPONSORSHIP

The following is a review of sponsorship of the game's major competitions.

SILK CUT CHALLENGE CUP

	Prel. £	1st £	2nd £	3rd £	S.F. £	R.U. £	Winners £	Development Fund £	Total £
1979	—	750	1,160	2,000	3,555	6,555	12,555	4,500	60,000
1980	—	750	1,160	2,000	3,555	6,555	12,555	19,500	75,000
1981	—	750	1,160	2,000	3,555	6,555	12,555	29,500	85,000
1982	1,000	1,000	1,400	2,400	4,325	8,000	14,555	30,000	100,000
1983	1,000	1,000	1,400	2,400	4,325	8,000	14,555	40,000	110,000
1984	1,000	1,000	1,400	2,400	4,325	8,000	14,555	48,000	120,000
1985	1,100	1,100	1,500	2,500	4,500	9,000	16,000	47,600	130,000
1986	1,100	1,100	1,500	2,500	4,500	9,000	16,000	57,600	140,000
1987	1,200	1,200	1,650	2,750	4,500	9,000	16,000	58,200	150,000
1988	1,200	1,200	1,800	3,000	5,000	10,000	18,000	62,000	160,000
1989	1,300	1,300	2,000	3,250	5,500	11,000	20,000	62,600	170,000
1990	2,000	2,000	3,250	5,000	8,500	16,000	30,000	111,000	275,000
1991	2,250	2,250	3,500	5,500	9,000	17,000	32,000	120,000	300,000
1992	2,250	2,250	3,750	6,000	9,500	18,000	34,000	130,000	325,000

● Sponsored by State Express 1979-84

REGAL TROPHY

	Prel. £	1st £	2nd £	3rd £	S.F. £	R.U. £	Winners £	Development Fund £	Total £
1971-72	—	—	—	—	1,000	2,500	5,000	—	9,500
1972-73	—	150	300	450	1,000	2,500	5,000	—	16,100
1973-74	—	150	300	450	1,000	2,500	5,000	—	16,100
1974-75	—	150	300	450	1,000	2,500	5,000	—	16,100
1975-76	—	300	450	600	1,500	3,000	6,000	—	22,800
1976-77	—	400	550	700	1,500	3,000	6,000	—	25,600
1977-78	—	450	600	750	1,750	3,500	8,000	—	30,000
1978-79	—	550	700	900	1,750	3,500	8,000	—	33,000
1979-80	—	600	800	1,000	2,000	4,000	8,500	—	36,500
1980-81	—	600	800	1,000	2,000	4,000	8,500	3,500	40,000
1981-82	700	700	900	1,175	2,500	4,500	9,000	7,000	50,000
1982-83	700	700	900	1,175	2,500	5,000	10,000	10,500	55,000
1983-84	700	700	900	1,175	2,500	5,000	10,000	15,500	60,000
1984-85	750	750	1,000	1,500	2,500	5,000	10,000	20,000	75,000
1985-86	750	750	1,000	1,500	2,750	5,500	11,000	26,000	80,000
1986-87	800	800	1,100	1,700	3,000	6,000	12,000	26,200	85,000
1987-88	1,100	1,100	1,600	2,825	4,750	9,000	16,000	65,000	150,000
1988-89	1,250	1,250	1,850	3,175	5,250	10,000	18,000	74,000	170,000
1989-90	1,740	1,745	2,750	4,800	8,250	15,500	28,000	100,000	250,000
1990-91	2,000	2,000	3,250	5,000	8,500	16,000	30,000	110,000	275,000
1991-92	2,250	2,250	3,500	5,500	9,000	17,000	32,000	120,000	300,000

● Under the John Player banner from 1971-1989

STONES BITTER

	Championship winners	R.U.	Divisional winners	R.U.	Premiership winners	R.U.	Divisional Premiership winners	R.U.	Development Fund	Total
	£	£	£	£	£	£	£	£	£	£
1980-81	6,000	—	3,000	—	4,000	—	—	—	42,000	55,000
1981-82	10,000	—	6,000	—	6,000	—	—	—	48,000	70,000
1982-83	12,000	—	7,000	—	7,000	—	—	—	54,000	80,000
1983-84	12,000	—	7,000	—	7,000	—	—	—	59,000	85,000
1984-85	13,000	—	9,000	—	8,000	—	—	—	60,000	90,000
1985-86	13,000	—	9,000	—	8,000	—	—	—	65,000	95,000
1986-87	20,000	8,000	10,000	4,000	9,000	3,500	4,000	1,500	60,000	120,000
1987-88	20,000	8,000	10,000	4,000	9,000	3,500	4,000	1,500	70,000	123,000
1988-89	25,000	10,000	12,000	5,000	10,000	4,000	5,000	2,000	77,000	150,000
1989-90	40,000	15,000	18,000	7,500	15,000	6,000	8,000	3,000	112,500	225,000
1990-91	44,000	16,500	20,000	8,250	17,000	6,750	9,000	3,500	125,000	250,000
1991-92	45,000	17,000	22,000	8,500	17,500	7,000	9,500	3,750	130,000	275,000

- Sponsored by Slalom Lager from 1980-86
- 1991-92 prize money for Third Division: Winners £10,500, R.U. £4,250

GREENALLS LANCASHIRE CUP

	Winners	Total
	£	£
1976	1,000	4,000
1977	1,500	5,000
1978	1,800	5,500
1979	1,900	6,000
1980	2,530	10,000
1981	2,700	11,000
1982	3,000	11,500
1983	3,200	12,500
1984	3,400	13,250
1985	3,400	13,250
1986	4,300	17,000
1987	4,600	18,600
1988	5,000	19,000
1989	5,000	21,000
1990	6,000	25,000
1991	6,000	25,000

- Sponsored by Burtonwood Brewery 1976-85

YORKSHIRE CUP

	Sponsor	Winners	Total
		£	£
1972	Esso	800	4,000
1973	Esso	1,500	6,000
1974	Esso	1,400	6,000
1975	Esso	1,200	6,000
1976	Esso	1,200	6,000
1977	Esso	1,600	8,000
1978	Esso	2,000	9,000
1979	Esso	2,000	9,500
1980	Websters Brewery	2,750	13,000
1981	Websters Brewery	3,000	14,000
1982	Websters Brewery	2,500	15,000
1983	Philips Video	2,500	15,000
1984	Philips Video	2,500	15,000
1985	John Smiths	2,500	5,000
1986	John Smiths	2,500	12,500
1987	John Smiths	3,000	12,500
1988	John Smiths	3,500	27,500
1989	John Smiths	5,000	35,000
1990	John Smiths	5,000	35,000
1991	John Smiths	7,000	35,000

QUEEN'S HONOURS

Eight Rugby League players have been awarded the MBE by Her Majesty the Queen for their services to the game. Former Castleford player-coach Malcolm Reilly was awarded the OBE in June 1991, while Great Britain's full-time coach.

Player	Awarded MBE	GB Caps	Career	Clubs
Eric Ashton	June 1966	26	1955-69	Wigan
Geoff Gunney	June 1970	11	1951-73	Hunslet
Clive Sullivan	January 1974	17	1961-85	Hull, Hull K.R., Oldham, Doncaster
Chris Hesketh	January 1976	21 + 2	1963-79	Wigan, Salford
Roger Millward	January 1983	28 + 1	1963-80	Castleford, Hull K.R.
Neil Fox	June 1983	29	1956-79	Wakefield T., Bradford N., Hull K.R., York, Bramley, Huddersfield
David Watkins	January 1986	2 + 4	1967-82	Salford, Swinton, Cardiff C.
Ellery Hanley	January 1990	33 + 1	1978-	Bradford N., Wigan, Leeds
Awarded OBE				
Malcolm Reilly	June 1991	9	1967-87	Castleford

Ellery Hanley, MBE in 1990.

Malcolm Reilly, OBE in 1991.

ATTENDANCES

CLUB ATTENDANCE REVIEW

The following is a review of clubs' home attendances for league matches from 1983-84.

The main figure is the individual club's average gate for league games during that season. The figure in brackets indicates an upward or downward trend compared with the previous season.

Also indicated is the division the club competed in that season, i.e.

1 — First Division, 2 — Second Division, 3 — Third Division.

Club	83-84	84-85	85-86	86-87	87-88	88-89	89-90	90-91	91-92
Barrow	2 3218 (−450)	1 2728 (−490)	2 1926 (−802)	1 2664 (+738)	2 1624 (−1040)	2 1594 (−30)	1 1997 (+403)	2 962 (−1035)	3 1003 (+41)
Batley	2 864 (−52)	2 1015 (+151)	2 930 (−85)	2 744 (−186)	2 859 (+115)	2 924 (+65)	2 1506 (+582)	2 1188 (−318)	3 1145 (−43)
Bradford N.	1 5316 (+386)	1 4251 (−1065)	1 3975 (−276)	1 4312 (+377)	1 4723 (+411)	1 4969 (+246)	1 5584 (+615)	1 5274 (−310)	1 4725 (−549)
Bramley	2 759 (−50)	2 858 (+99)	2 831 (−27)	2 737 (−94)	2 858 (+121)	2 1004 (+146)	2 982 (−22)	2 805 (−177)	3 870 (+65)
Bridgend	2 581 (−273)	2 510 (−70)	—	—	—	—	—	—	—
Carlisle	2 752 (−1172)	2 986 (+234)	2 618 (−368)	2 789 (+171)	2 763 (−26)	2 678 (−85)	2 574 (−104)	2 781 (+207)	2 800 (+19)
Castleford	1 4288 (+740)	1 3217 (−1071)	1 3701 (+484)	1 4758 (+1057)	1 4520 (−238)	1 6580 (+2060)	1 6428 (−152)	1 6019 (−409)	1 6465 (+446)
Chorley B.	—	—	—	—	—	—	2 806 —	2 690 (−116)	3 394 (−296)
Dewsbury	2 706 (−73)	2 995 (+189)	1 1819 (+824)	2 669 (−1150)	2 658 (−11)	2 772 (+114)	2 1227 (+455)	2 955 (−272)	3 1140 (+185)
Doncaster	2 255 (−186)	2 266 (+11)	2 689 (+423)	2 1543 (+854)	2 1450 (−93)	2 1906 (+456)	2 1965 (+59)	2 1458 (−507)	3 1158 (−300)
Featherstone R.	1 3032 (+385)	1 2541 (−491)	1 2320 (−221)	1 2606 (+286)	2 1879 (−727)	1 4379 (+2500)	1 4269 (−110)	1 4722 (+453)	1 4001 (−721)
Halifax	2 1254 (−1016)	1 3497 (+2243)	1 4944 (+1447)	1 4891 (−53)	1 6521 (+1630)	1 8022 (+1501)	2 5921 (−2101)	2 4458 (−1463)	1 7181 (+2723)
Highfield	2 172 (−52)	2 509 (+337)	2 363 (−146)	2 331 (−32)	2 515 (+184)	2 298 (−217)	2 453 (+155)	2 632 (+179)	3 319 (−313)
Huddersfield	2 699 (−77)	2 905 (+206)	2 678 (−227)	2 524 (−154)	2 601 (+77)	2 1114 (+513)	2 1634 (+520)	2 1306 (−328)	3 2271 (+965)
Hull	1 10679 (−846)	1 8525 (−2154)	1 6245 (−2280)	1 5538 (−707)	1 5111 (−427)	1 6804 (+1693)	1 6218 (−586)	1 6699 (+481)	1 5892 (−807)
Hull K.R.	1 6966 (−413)	1 6715 (−251)	1 4855 (−1860)	1 4651 (−204)	1 4186 (−465)	1 5298 (+1112)	2 4851 (−447)	1 4952 (+101)	1 4752 (−200)
Hunslet	2 1338 (+143)	1 2246 (+908)	2 722 (−1524)	1 1050 (+328)	1 2678 (+1628)	2 947 (−1731)	2 1046 (+99)	2 767 (−279)	3 770 (+3)

Club	83-84	84-85	85-86	86-87	87-88	88-89	89-90	90-91	91-92
Keighley C.	2 734 (−351)	2 822 (+88)	2 685 (−137)	2 445 (−240)	2 958 (+513)	2 961 (+3)	2 936 (−25)	2 985 (+49)	3 1196 (+211)
Leeds	1 6542 (+649)	1 7330 (+788)	1 6928 (−402)	1 6393 (−535)	1 9911 (+3518)	1 12060 (+2149)	1 12251 (+191)	1 11102 (−1149)	1 12164 (+1062)
Leigh	1 4434 (−183)	1 3822 (−612)	2 2710 (−1112)	1 4232 (+1522)	1 4516 (+284)	2 2346 (−2170)	1 4568 (+2222)	2 1719 (−2849)	2 3014 (+1295)
London C.	1 2238 (−450)	2 949 (−1289)	2 817 (−132)	2 684 (−133)	2 615 (−69)	2 588 (−27)	2 841 (+253)	2 557 (−284)	2 724 (+167)
Nottingham C.	— —	2 1020 —	2 487 (−533)	2 368 (−119)	2 368 —	2 560 (+192)	2 577 (+17)	2 255 (−322)	3 270 (+15)
Oldham	1 4138 (+417)	1 4562 (+424)	1 4333 (−229)	1 3915 (−418)	2 3790 (−125)	1 5759 (+1969)	2 4401 (−1358)	1 5094 (+693)	2 3149 (−1945)
Rochdale H.	2 538 (−81)	2 542 (+4)	2 1267 (+725)	2 877 (−390)	2 1106 (+229)	2 1027 (−79)	2 2510 (+1483)	1 2542 (+32)	2 1415 (−1127)
Ryedale-York	2 1215 (−470)	2 1528 (+313)	1 2828 (+1300)	2 1520 (−1308)	2 1406 (−114)	2 2021 (+615)	2 2495 (+474)	2 1857 (−638)	2 1181 (−676)
St. Helens	1 4656 (+113)	1 7336 (+2680)	1 6022 (−1314)	1 7341 (+1319)	1 8417 (+1076)	1 9514 (+1097)	1 8555 (−959)	1 7391 (−1164)	1 8456 (+1065)
Salford	1 2399 (+471)	2 1795 (−604)	1 2520 (+725)	1 2826 (+306)	1 3747 (+921)	1 5470 (+1723)	1 3720 (−1750)	2 2314 (−1406)	1 3785 (+1471)
Scarborough P.	—	—	—	—	—	—	—	—	3 777
Sheffield E.	— —	2 885 —	2 698 (−187)	2 708 (+10)	2 847 (+139)	2 838 (−9)	1 4038 (+3200)	1 4031 (−7)	2 2435 (−1596)
Southend Invicta	2 731 —	2 216 (−515)	—	—	—	—	—	—	—
Swinton	2 1077 (−237)	2 1590 (+513)	1 2706 (+1116)	2 1622 (−1084)	1 2987 (+1365)	2 1435 (−1552)	2 1678 (+243)	2 1737 (+59)	1 2702 (+965)
Trafford B.	2 625 (−54)	2 555 (−70)	2 534 (−21)	2 475 (−59)	2 922 (+447)	2 512 (−410)	2 780 (+258)	2 638 (−142)	3 309 (−329)
Wakefield T.	1 3483 (+1139)	2 1568 (−1915)	2 1714 (+146)	1 2637 (+923)	2 2416 (−221)	1 5151 (+2735)	1 5428 (+277)	1 4848 (−580)	1 5022 (+174)
Warrington	1 4059 (+235)	1 3801 (−258)	1 3618 (−183)	1 4172 (+554)	1 4974 (+802)	1 4893 (−81)	1 5412 (+519)	1 5915 (+503)	1 5204 (−711)
Whitehaven	1 1639 (−103)	2 1540 (−99)	2 1878 (+338)	2 1800 (−78)	2 1772 (−28)	2 1310 (−462)	2 961 (−349)	2 1035 (+74)	3 632 (−403)
Widnes	1 4687 (−16)	1 4266 (−421)	1 4019 (−247)	1 3840 (−179)	1 6262 (+2422)	1 8648 (+2386)	1 7858 (−790)	1 6793 (−1065)	1 6291 (−502)
Wigan	1 7479 (+53)	1 10056 (+2577)	1 12515 (+2459)	1 12732 (+217)	1 13021 (+289)	1 14543 (+1522)	1 13973 (−570)	1 14493 (+520)	1 14040 (−453)
Workington T.	2 934 (−536)	1 920 (−14)	2 702 (−218)	2 653 (−49)	2 737 (+84)	2 774 (+37)	2 691 (−83)	2 1426 (+735)	2 1884 (+458)

COMPETITION ATTENDANCE REVIEW

		83-84	84-85	85-86	86-87	87-88	88-89	89-90	90-91	91-92
FIRST	Total	1,140,548	1,137,195	1,100,329	1,162,666	1,060,296	1,327,192	1,173,815	1,168,407	1,185,117
DIVISION	Av.	4,752	4,738	4,585	4,844	5,826	7,292	6,450	6,420	6,511
SECOND	Total	279,673	266,730	310,311	217,552	381,825	298,776	515,687	371,398	204,304
DIVISION	Av.	914	953	1,014	863	1,364	1,067	1,754	1,263	1,824
THIRD	Total	—	—	—	—	—	—	—	—	159,209
DIVISION	Av.									875
LEAGUE TOTALS (1st & 2nd) *plus 3rd	Total	1,420,221	1,403,925	1,410,640	1,380,218	1,442,121	1,625,968	1,689,502	1,539,805	1,548,630*
	Av.	2,601	2,700	2,584	2,805	3,121	3,519	3,549	3,235	3,253*
R.L. CUP	Av.	8,399	8,497	8,280	6,965	8,764	8,666	7,339	6,748	6,899
REGAL	Av.	3,893	4,881	4,232	4,122	3,570	4,987	4,876	3,515	4,007
PREMIER	Av.	8,136	10,115	9,273	15,154	13,462	15,856	16,796	12,483	13,513
10,000 + (No. of)		26	27	36	43	46	59	54	43	49

20,000-plus crowds . . . . A 10-year review
All matches except the Rugby League Challenge Cup final at Wembley

26,771	Britain v. Australia	First Test	Hull C. FC	30 Oct. 1982
23,216	Britain v. Australia	Second Test	Wigan	20 Nov. 1982
26,031	Hull v. Castleford	RL Cup semi-final	Elland Rd, Leeds	2 Apr. 1983
20,569	Hull v. Hull K.R.	Division One	Hull	8 Apr. 1983
20,077	St. Helens v. Wigan	RL Cup round 3	St. Helens	11 Mar. 1984
25,237	Hull v. Hull K.R.	Yorks Cup final	Hull C. FC	27 Oct. 1984
26,074	St. Helens v. Wigan	Lancs Cup final	Wigan	28 Oct. 1984
25,326	Hull v. Hull K.R.	John Player final	Hull C. FC	26 Jan. 1985
20,982	Hull v. Castleford	RL Cup semi-final	Leeds	6 Apr. 1985
20,968	Hull v. Castleford	RL Cup semi-final replay	Leeds	10 Apr. 1985
22,209	Britain v. New Zealand	Third Test	Elland Rd, Leeds	9 Nov. 1985
21,813	Wigan v. St. Helens	Division One	Wigan	26 Dec. 1985
23,866	Hull K.R. v. Leeds	RL Cup semi-final	Elland Rd, Leeds	29 Mar. 1986
32,485	Hull K.R. v. Leeds	RL Cup semi-final replay	Elland Rd, Leeds	3 Apr. 1986
28,252	Wigan v. St. Helens	Lancs Cup semi-final	Wigan	1 Oct. 1986
30,622	Wigan v. Australia	Tour	Wigan	12 Oct. 1986
20,180	Oldham v. Wigan	Lancs Cup final	St. Helens	19 Oct. 1986
50,583	Britain v. Australia	First Test	Manchester U. FC	25 Oct. 1986
30,808	Britain v. Australia	Second Test	Elland Rd, Leeds	8 Nov. 1986
20,169	Britain v. Australia	Third Test	Wigan	22 Nov. 1986
21,214	St. Helens v. Wigan	Division One	St. Helens	26 Dec. 1986
21,144	Warrington v. Wigan	John Player final	Bolton W. FC	10 Jan. 1987
20,355	Wigan v. St. Helens	Division One	Wigan	17 Apr. 1987
22,457	Wigan v. Halifax	Premiership semi-final	Wigan	10 May 1987
38,756	Warrington v. Wigan	Premiership final	Manchester U. FC	17 May 1987

(continued)

36,895	Wigan v. Manly	World Club Challenge	Wigan	7 Oct. 1987
20,234	Wigan v. Warrington	Lancs Cup final	St. Helens	11 Oct. 1987
23,809	Wigan v. St. Helens	Division One	Wigan	27 Dec. 1987
25,110	Wigan v. Leeds	RL Cup round 2	Wigan	14 Feb. 1988
20,783	Salford v. Wigan	RL Cup semi-final	Bolton W. FC	12 Mar. 1988
20,534	Halifax v. Hull	RL Cup semi-final	Leeds	26 Mar. 1988
25,117	Hull v. Halifax	RL Cup semi-final replay	Elland Rd, Leeds	30 Mar. 1988
21,812	St. Helens v. Wigan	Division One	St. Helens	1 Apr. 1988
35,252	St. Helens v. Widnes	Premiership final	Manchester U. FC	15 May 1988
22,968	Castleford v. Leeds	Yorks Cup final	Elland Rd, Leeds	16 Oct. 1988
20,709	Widnes v. Wigan	John Player final	Bolton W. FC	7 Jan. 1989
26,080	Leeds v. Widnes	RL Cup round 2	Leeds	26 Feb. 1989
26,529	Warrington v. Wigan	RL Cup semi-final	Manchester C. FC	25 Mar. 1989
21,076	Wigan v. St. Helens	Division One	Wigan	12 Apr. 1989
40,194	Hull v. Widnes	Premiership final	Manchester U. FC	14 May 1989
30,786	Widnes v. Canberra	World Club Challenge	Manchester U. FC	4 Oct. 1989
20,346	Britain v. New Zealand	Third Test	Wigan	11 Nov. 1989
27,075	Wigan v. St. Helens	Division One	Wigan	26 Dec. 1989
23,570	Leeds v. Wigan	Division One	Leeds	4 Mar. 1990
26,489	St. Helens v. Wigan	RL Cup semi-final	Manchester U. FC	10 Mar. 1990
24,462	Wigan v. Leeds	Division One	Wigan	10 Apr. 1990
40,796	Bradford N. v. Widnes	Premiership final	Manchester U. FC	13 May 1990
24,814	Wigan v. Australia	Tour	Wigan	14 Oct. 1990
54,569	Britain v. Australia	First Test	Wembley	27 Oct. 1990
46,615	Britain v. Australia	Second Test	Manchester U. FC	10 Nov. 1990
32,500	Britain v. Australia	Third Test	Elland Rd, Leeds	24 Nov. 1990
29,763	Wigan v. Widnes	Division One	Wigan	9 Apr. 1991
42,043	Hull v. Widnes	Premiership final	Manchester U. FC	12 May 1991
20,152	Wigan v. Penrith	World Club Challenge	Liverpool FC	2 Oct. 1991
26,307	Wigan v. St. Helens	Division One	Wigan	26 Dec. 1991
21,736	Wigan v. Warrington	RL Cup round 2	Wigan	16 Feb. 1992
20,821	Leeds v. Wigan	Division One	Leeds	15 Mar. 1992
33,157	St. Helens v. Wigan	Premiership final	Manchester U. FC	17 May 1992

1991-92 ATTENDANCE ANALYSIS

FIRST DIVISION

Total 1,185,117
Average 6,511

Wigan maintained a 14,000-plus home gate to top the attendance chart for the eighth successive season. Leeds strengthened their command of second place by adding 1,062 fans per home match for an average of 12,164. Half of the 14 clubs recorded an increase in gates, notably Salford, who celebrated a return to the First Division by attracting an extra 1,471 per home fixture. First Division gates rose by 1.4 per cent compared with the 1990-91 figures of 1,168,407 and 6,420.

SECOND DIVISION

Total 204,304
Average 1,824

The new-style eight-club Second Division, with every club playing each other four times, saw half of them recording an increase in gates. Leigh registered the biggest average increase of 1,295 a match, while Oldham topped the chart despite losing 1,945 fans per game following relegation from the First Division.

Shaun Wane of Leeds, who strengthened their claim to second place in the gates chart.

THIRD DIVISION

Total............................ 159,209
Average 875

The first-ever Third Division campaign saw seven of the 13 previous Second Division clubs record an increase in gates. Champions Huddersfield led the way, topping the chart with an average home gate of 2,271, an increase of 965 per match. Newcomers Scarborough Pirates were the eighth best supported club with an average home attendance of 777.

LEAGUE CHAMPIONSHIP

Aggregate..................... 1,548,630
Average 3,253

The new-style three-division format produced 476 matches, the same as the previous two-division set-up. There was a marginal increase of 18 fans per match compared with the 1990-91 average of 3,235, from an aggregate of 1,539,805.

SILK CUT CHALLENGE CUP

The 1992 Wembley campaign registered a 2.25 per cent increase in attendances, featuring the season's top gate of 77,386 for the Wigan-Castleford final. The 40 ties, including three replays, attracted a total of 275,953 spectators, an average of 6,899, compared with 1991 figures of 249,670 and 6,748.

REGAL TROPHY

An annual upsurge of 14 per cent was recorded in the Regal Trophy, celebrating the Silver Jubilee of the association between The Rugby Football League and Imperial Tobacco. The 38 ties, including a replay, were attended by a total of 154,568 fans, an average of 4,007 per match, compared with the previous season's figures of 137,066 and 3,515.

STONES BITTER PREMIERSHIP

The end-of-season top-eight tournament recorded an increase in turnout of 8.25 per cent, despite reduced capacity at the Old Trafford, Manchester, final due to demolition of the Stretford End. The seven ties attracted a total of 94,593 fans, an average of 13,513, compared with the 1991 figure of 12,483. The final attracted a capacity audience of 33,157, the previous year being a competition record of 42,043.

DIVISIONAL PREMIERSHIP

Staged for the first time, the Stones Bitter Divisional Premiership was contested by the top eight clubs in the Third Division playing off to visit the top four clubs in the Second Division. Excluding the Old Trafford final, the 11 ties, including a replay, attracted 18,007 fans, an average of 1,637.

GREENALLS LANCASHIRE CUP

Gates for the 16-tie Red Rose tournament fell by 7.5 per cent. The total turnout of 76,113 and average of 4,747 compared with the previous season's figures of 82,116 and 5,132.

JOHN SMITHS YORKSHIRE CUP

Attendances for the White Rose competition suffered a 25 per cent decrease, the 19 ties, including an extra preliminary round and a replay, attracting a total of 73,791 for an average of 3,803. The corresponding 1990-91 tallies were 86,431 and 5,084.

FIVE-FIGURE CROWDS

There was a total of 49 five-figure crowds, six more than in the previous season which featured an Australian tour. Wembley again topped the chart with a gate of 77,386 for the Silk Cut Challenge Cup final. Wigan attracted 19 10,000-plus crowds to Central Park, Leeds pulling in 10 five-figure gates at Headingley. Six gates exceeded 20,000 including Wembley, the Stones Bitter Premiership final and the World Club Challenge at Liverpool FC's Anfield. The 10,000-plus gates were divided into the following categories:

League 29
Challenge Cup 8
Regal Trophy 3
Premiership Trophy 3
Wales 2
Lancashire Cup 2
World Club Challenge 1
Charity Shield 1

Paul Medley of Bradford Northern, who suffered a downward trend in gates in 1991-92.

STONES BITTER CHAMPIONSHIP

	1991-92 Average	Annual Difference
Wigan	14040	(−453)
Leeds	12164	(+1062)
St. Helens	8456	(+1065)
*Halifax	7181	(+2723)
Castleford	6465	(+446)
Widnes	6291	(−502)
Hull	5892	(−807)
Warrington	5204	(−711)
Wakefield Trinity	5022	(+174)
Hull K.R.	4752	(−200)
Bradford Northern	4725	(−549)
Featherstone Rovers	4001	(−721)
*Salford	3785	(+1471)
*Swinton	2702	(+965)

*Promoted 1990-91

SECOND DIVISION

	1991-92 Average	Annual Difference
*Oldham	3149	(−1945)
Leigh	3014	(+1295)
*Sheffield Eagles	2435	(−1596)
Workington Town	1884	(+458)
*Rochdale Hornets	1415	(−1127)
Ryedale-York	1181	(−676)
Carlisle	800	(+19)
London Crusaders	724	(+162)

*Relegated 1990-91

THIRD DIVISION

	1991-92 Average	Annual Difference
Huddersfield	2271	(+965)
Keighley Cougars	1196	(+211)
Doncaster	1158	(−300)
Batley	1145	(−43)
Dewsbury	1140	(+185)
Barrow	1003	(+41)
Bramley	870	(+65)
Scarborough Pirates	777	—
Hunslet	770	(+3)
Whitehaven	632	(−403)
Chorley Borough	394	(−296)
Highfield	319	(−313)
Trafford Borough	309	(−329)
Nottingham City	270	(+15)

FIXTURES

PRINCIPAL DATES 1992-93

1992

23 August	CIS Insurance Charity Shield (at Gateshead)
30 August	Stones Bitter League campaign opens
13 September	County Cups Round 1
23 September	County Cups Round 2
7 October	County Cups Semi-Finals
17/18 October	County Cup Finals
24 October	World Cup Final (at Wembley)
	GREAT BRITAIN v. AUSTRALIA
7/8 November	Regal Trophy Round 1
5/6 December	Regal Trophy Round 2
13 December	FRANCE v. WALES
19/20 December	Regal Trophy Round 3

1993

2 January	Regal Trophy Semi-Final 1
9 January	Regal Trophy Semi-Final 2
16 January	Silk Cut Challenge Cup Preliminary Round
23 January	Regal Trophy Final
30/31 January	Silk Cut Challenge Cup Round 1
13/14 February	Silk Cut Challenge Cup Round 2
27/28 February	Silk Cut Challenge Cup Round 3
7 March	FRANCE v. GREAT BRITAIN
13 March	Silk Cut Challenge Cup Semi-Final 1
27 March	Silk Cut Challenge Cup Semi-Final 2
2 April	GREAT BRITAIN v. FRANCE
1 May	Silk Cut Challenge Cup Final
16 May	Stones Bitter Premiership Finals

STONES BITTER CHAMPIONSHIP 1992-93

SUNDAY, 30 AUGUST 1992

Hull	v.	Bradford N.	3.15
Leeds	v.	St. Helens	3.00
Leigh	v.	Warrington	3.00
Salford	v.	Hull K.R.	3.00
Sheffield E.	v.	Wigan	3.15
Wakefield T.	v.	Halifax	3.30
Widnes	v.	Castleford	3.00

SUNDAY, 6 SEPTEMBER 1992

Bradford N.	v.	Leigh	3.00
Castleford	v.	Salford	3.30
Halifax	v.	Leeds	3.00
Hull K.R.	v.	Widnes	3.15
St. Helens	v.	Wakefield T.	3.00
Warrington	v.	Sheffield E.	3.00
Wigan	v.	Hull	3.00

SUNDAY, 13 SEPTEMBER 1992
COUNTY CUPS — ROUND 1

SUNDAY, 20 SEPTEMBER 1992

Hull	v.	Warrington	3.15
Leeds	v.	Hull K.R.	3.00
Leigh	v.	Castleford	3.00
Salford	v.	Halifax	3.00
Sheffield E.	v.	St. Helens	3.15
Wakefield T.	v.	Wigan	3.30
Widnes	v.	Bradford N.	3.00

WEDNESDAY, 23 SEPTEMBER 1992
COUNTY CUPS — ROUND 2

SUNDAY, 27 SEPTEMBER 1992

Bradford N.	v.	Leeds	3.00
Castleford	v.	Hull	3.30
Halifax	v.	Leigh	3.00
Hull K.R.	v.	Sheffield E.	3.15
St. Helens	v.	Salford	3.00
Warrington	v.	Wakefield T.	3.00
Wigan	v.	Widnes	3.00

FRIDAY, 2 OCTOBER 1992

Bradford N.	v.	Salford	7.30

SUNDAY, 4 OCTOBER 1992

Hull	v.	Halifax	3.15
Leeds	v.	Warrington	3.00
Leigh	v.	Wigan	3.00
Sheffield E.	v.	Castleford	3.15
Wakefield T.	v.	St. Helens	3.30
Widnes	v.	Hull K.R.	3.00

WEDNESDAY, 7 OCTOBER 1992
COUNTY CUPS — SEMI FINALS

SUNDAY, 11 OCTOBER 1992

Castleford	v.	Widnes	3.30
Halifax	v.	Sheffield E.	3.00
Hull K.R.	v.	Leigh	3.15
St. Helens	v.	Hull	3.00
Salford	v.	Wakefield T.	3.00
Warrington	v.	Bradford N.	3.00
Wigan	v.	Leeds	3.00

SATURDAY/SUNDAY, 17/18 OCTOBER 1992
LANCASHIRE/YORKSHIRE COUNTY CUP FINALS

SUNDAY, 18 OCTOBER 1992

Bradford N.	v.	Hull K.R.	3.00
Hull	v.	Wigan	3.15
Leigh	v.	St. Helens	3.00
Salford	v.	Castleford	3.00
Sheffield E.	v.	Warrington	3.15
Wakefield T.	v.	Leeds	3.30
Widnes	v.	Halifax	3.00

SUNDAY, 25 OCTOBER 1992
NO GAMES — WORLD CUP FINAL (PROVISIONAL)

TUESDAY, 27 OCTOBER 1992
REGAL TROPHY — PRELIMINARY ROUND

SUNDAY, 1 NOVEMBER 1992

Castleford	v.	Leigh	3.30
Halifax	v.	Wakefield T.	3.00
Hull K.R.	v.	Salford	3.15
Leeds	v.	Widnes	3.00
St. Helens	v.	Bradford N.	3.00
Warrington	v.	Hull	3.00
Wigan	v.	Sheffield E.	3.00

SATURDAY/SUNDAY, 7/8 NOVEMBER 1992
REGAL TROPHY — ROUND 1

SUNDAY, 15 NOVEMBER 1992

Bradford N.	v.	Castleford	3.00
Hull	v.	Leeds	3.15
Leigh	v.	Halifax	3.00
Salford	v.	St. Helens	3.00
Sheffield E.	v.	Hull K.R.	3.15
Wakefield T.	v.	Warrington	3.30
Widnes	v.	Wigan	3.00

SUNDAY, 22 NOVEMBER 1992

Bradford N.	v.	St. Helens	3.00
Halifax	v.	Warrington	3.00
Hull K.R.	v.	Castleford	3.15
Leigh	v.	Leeds	3.00
Salford	v.	Wigan	3.00
Sheffield E.	v.	Widnes	3.15
Wakefield T.	v.	Hull	3.30

SUNDAY, 29 NOVEMBER 1992

Castleford	v.	Bradford N.	3.30
Hull	v.	Salford	3.15
Leeds	v.	Halifax	3.00
St. Helens	v.	Sheffield E.	3.00
Warrington	v.	Leigh	3.00
Widnes	v.	Wakefield T.	3.00
Wigan	v.	Hull K.R.	3.00

SATURDAY/SUNDAY, 5/6 DECEMBER 1992
REGAL TROPHY — ROUND 2

SUNDAY, 13 DECEMBER 1992

FRANCE	v.	WALES	
Halifax	v.	Wigan	3.00
Leigh	v.	Hull K.R.	3.00
Sheffield E.	v.	Leeds	3.15
Wakefield T.	v.	Bradford N.	3.30

SATURDAY, 19 DECEMBER 1992
REGAL TROPHY — ROUND 3

SUNDAY, 20 DECEMBER 1992

Bradford N.	v.	Hull	3.00
Castleford	v.	St. Helens	3.30
Hull K.R.	v.	Warrington	3.15
Salford	v.	Widnes	3.00

SATURDAY, 26 DECEMBER 1992

Halifax	v.	Bradford N.	3.00
Hull	v.	Sheffield E.	3.15
Leeds	v.	Castleford	11.30
St. Helens	v.	Wigan	3.00
Salford	v.	Leigh	3.00
Wakefield T.	v.	Hull K.R.	3.30
Warrington	v.	Widnes	3.00

FRIDAY, 1 JANUARY 1993

Castleford	v.	Wakefield T.	3.30
Hull K.R.	v.	Hull	3.15
Leeds	v.	Salford	3.00
Sheffield E.	v.	Halifax	3.15
Widnes	v.	St. Helens	3.00
Wigan	v.	Warrington	3.00

SATUDAY, 2 JANUARY 1993
REGAL TROPHY — SEMI-FINAL 1

SUNDAY, 3 JANUARY 1993

Hull	v.	Wakefield T.	3.15
St. Helens	v.	Leigh	3.00
Wigan	v.	Bradford N.	3.00

SATURDAY, 9 JANUARY 1993
REGAL TROPHY — SEMI-FINAL 2

SUNDAY, 10 JANUARY 1993

Bradford N.	v.	Wigan	3.00
Halifax	v.	Hull K.R.	3.00
Hull	v.	Widnes	3.15
Leigh	v.	Sheffield E.	3.00
St. Helens	v.	Castleford	3.00
Wakefield T.	v.	Salford	3.30
Warrington	v.	Leeds	3.00

SATURDAY, 16 JANUARY 1993
SILK CUT CHALLENGE CUP — PRELIMINARY
ROUND

SUNDAY, 17 JANUARY 1993

Castleford	v.	Warrington	3.30
Halifax	v.	Hull	3.00
Hull K.R.	v.	St. Helens	3.15
Leigh	v.	Bradford N.	3.00
Salford	v.	Leeds	3.00
Widnes	v.	Sheffield E.	3.00
Wigan	v.	Wakefield T.	3.00

SATURDAY, 23 JANUARY 1993
REGAL TROPHY FINAL

SUNDAY, 24 JANUARY 1993

Bradford N.	v.	Widnes	3.00
Hull	v.	Castleford	3.15
Leeds	v.	Wigan	3.00
St. Helens	v.	Halifax	3.00
Sheffield E.	v.	Salford	3.15
Wakefield T.	v.	Leigh	3.30
Warrington	v.	Hull K.R.	3.00

SATURDAY, 30 JANUARY 1993
SILK CUT CHALLENGE CUP — ROUND 1

SUNDAY, 7 FEBRUARY 1993

Castleford	v.	Sheffield E.	3.30
Halifax	v.	Salford	3.00
Hull K.R.	v.	Leeds	3.15
Leigh	v.	Wakefield T.	3.00
St. Helens	v.	Warrington	3.00
Widnes	v.	Hull	3.00

SATURDAY, 13 FEBRUARY 1993
SILK CUT CHALLENGE CUP — ROUND 2

FRIDAY, 19 FEBRUARY 1993

Salford	v.	Bradford N.	7.30

SUNDAY, 21 FEBRUARY 1993

Hull	v.	St. Helens	3.15
Sheffield E.	v.	Leigh	3.15
Wakefield T.	v.	Widnes	3.30
Warrington	v.	Castleford	3.00
Wigan	v.	Halifax	3.00

SATURDAY, 27 FEBRUARY 1993
SILK CUT CHALLENGE CUP — ROUND 3

SUNDAY, 7 MARCH 1993

FRANCE	v.	GREAT BRITAIN	
Bradford N.	v.	Wakefield T.	3.00
Halifax	v.	Castleford	3.00
Hull K.R.	v.	Wigan	3.15
Leeds	v.	Sheffield E.	3.00
Leigh	v.	Widnes	3.00
Salford	v.	Hull	3.00

FRIDAY, 12 MARCH 1993

Sheffield E.	v.	Bradford N.	7.30

SATURDAY, 13 MARCH 1993
SILK CUT CHALLENGE CUP — SEMI-FINAL 1

SUNDAY, 14 MARCH 1993

St. Helens	v.	Hull K.R.	3.00
Warrington	v.	Halifax	3.00
Widnes	v.	Leeds	3.00
Wigan	v.	Salford	3.00

SUNDAY, 21 MARCH 1993

Bradford N.	v.	Warrington	3.00
Castleford	v.	Hull K.R.	3.30
Halifax	v.	St. Helens	3.00
Hull	v.	Leigh	3.15
Leeds	v.	Wakefield T.	3.00
Salford	v.	Sheffield E.	3.00

SATURDAY, 27 MARCH 1993
SILK CUT CHALLENGE CUP — SEMI-FINAL 2

SUNDAY, 28 MARCH 1993

Castleford	v.	Halifax	3.30
Hull K.R.	v.	Bradford N.	3.15
Leeds	v.	Hull	3.00
Sheffield E.	v.	Wakefield T.	3.15
Warrington	v.	St. Helens	3.00
Widnes	v.	Salford	3.00
Wigan	v.	Leigh	3.00

FRIDAY, 2 APRIL 1993

GREAT BRITAIN	v.	FRANCE	7.30

SUNDAY, 4 APRIL 1993

Bradford N.	v.	Sheffield E.	3.00
Castleford	v.	Wigan	3.30
Halifax	v.	Widnes	3.00
Leigh	v.	Hull	3.00
St. Helens	v.	Leeds	3.00
Salford	v.	Warrington	3.00

FRIDAY, 9 APRIL 1993

Bradford N.	v.	Halifax	7.30
Hull	v.	Hull K.R.	3.15
Leeds	v.	Leigh	7.30
Wakefield T.	v.	Castleford	7.30
Widnes	v.	Warrington	3.00
Wigan	v.	St. Helens	3.00

SUNDAY, 11 APRIL 1993

Sheffield E.	v.	Hull	3.15

MONDAY, 12 APRIL 1993

Castleford	v.	Leeds	3.30
Hull K.R.	v.	Wakefield T.	3.15
Leigh	v.	Salford	3.00
St. Helens	v.	Widnes	3.00
Warrington	v.	Wigan	3.00

SUNDAY, 18 APRIL 1993

Hull K.R.	v.	Halifax	3.15
Leeds	v.	Bradford N.	3.00
Wakefield T.	v.	Sheffield E.	3.30
Warrington	v.	Salford	3.00
Widnes	v.	Leigh	3.00
Wigan	v.	Castleford	3.00

SECOND DIVISION

● **The fixture list below is subject to alteration. Neither the editors nor the publishers can take any responsibility for any subsequent changes or any inconvenience caused by such changes.**

SUNDAY, 30 AUGUST 1992

Carlisle	v.	Bramley
Huddersfield	v.	Featherstone R.
Oldham	v.	London C.
Swinton	v.	Rochdale H.

SUNDAY, 6 SEPTEMBER 1992

Bramley	v.	Huddersfield
Featherstone R.	v.	Swinton
London C.	v.	Rochdale H.
Oldham	v.	Carlisle

SUNDAY, 13 SEPTEMBER 1992
COUNTY CUPS — ROUND 1

SUNDAY, 20 SEPTEMBER 1992

Carlisle	v.	London C.
Huddersfield	v.	Oldham
Rochdale H.	v.	Featherstone R.
Swinton	v.	Bramley

WEDNESDAY, 23 SEPTEMBER 1992
COUNTY CUPS — ROUND 2

SUNDAY, 27 SEPTEMBER 1992

Bramley	v.	Rochdale H.
Featherstone R.	v.	Carlisle
London C.	v.	Huddersfield
Oldham	v.	Swinton

SUNDAY, 4 OCTOBER 1992

Carlisle	v.	Rochdale H.
London C.	v.	Bramley
Oldham	v.	Featherstone R.
Swinton	v.	Huddersfield

WEDNESDAY, 7 OCTOBER 1992
COUNTY CUPS — SEMI FINALS

SUNDAY, 11 OCTOBER 1992

Bramley	v.	Featherstone R.
Huddersfield	v.	Carlisle
Rochdale H.	v.	Oldham
Swinton	v.	London C.

SATURDAY/SUNDAY, 17/18 OCTOBER 1992
LANCASHIRE/YORKSHIRE COUNTY CUP FINALS

SUNDAY, 18 OCTOBER 1992

Bramley	v.	Oldham
Carlisle	v.	Swinton
Featherstone R.	v.	London C.
Huddersfield	v.	Rochdale H.

SUNDAY, 25 OCTOBER 1992
NO GAMES — WORLD CUP FINAL (PROVISIONAL)

TUESDAY, 27 OCTOBER 1992
REGAL TROPHY — PRELIMINARY ROUND

SUNDAY, 1 NOVEMBER 1992

Featherstone R.	v.	Huddersfield
London C.	v.	Carlisle
Oldham	v.	Swinton
Rochdale H.	v.	Bramley

SATURDAY/SUNDAY, 7/8 NOVEMBER 1992
REGAL TROPHY — ROUND 1

SUNDAY, 15 NOVEMBER 1992

Carlisle	v.	Oldham
Huddersfield	v.	Bramley
Rochdale H.	v.	London C.
Swinton	v.	Featherstone R.

SUNDAY, 22 NOVEMBER 1992

Bramley	v.	Carlisle
Featherstone R.	v.	Rochdale H.
London C.	v.	Swinton
Oldham	v.	Huddersfield

SUNDAY, 29 NOVEMBER 1992

Carlisle	v.	Featherstone R.
Huddersfield	v.	London C.
Rochdale H.	v.	Bramley
Swinton	v.	Oldham

SATURDAY/SUNDAY, 5/6 DECEMBER 1992
REGAL TROPHY — ROUND 2

SUNDAY, 13 DECEMBER 1992

FRANCE	v.	WALES
Bramley	v.	London C.
Featherstone R.	v.	Oldham
Huddersfield	v.	Swinton
Rochdale H.	v.	Carlisle

SATURDAY, 19 DECEMBER 1992
REGAL TROPHY — ROUND 3

SUNDAY, 20 DECEMBER 1992

Carlisle	v.	Huddersfield
London C.	v.	Featherstone R.
Oldham	v.	Bramley
Swinton	v.	Rochdale H.

SATURDAY, 26 DECEMBER 1992

Oldham	v.	Rochdale H.

SUNDAY, 27 DECEMBER 1992

Bramley	v.	Swinton
Featherstone R.	v.	Huddersfield

FRIDAY, 1 JANUARY 1993

Huddersfield	v.	London C.
Swinton	v.	Oldham

SATURDAY, 2 JANUARY 1993
REGAL TROPHY — SEMI-FINAL 1

SUNDAY, 3 JANUARY 1993

Bramley	v.	Carlisle
Huddersfield	v.	Featherstone R.
Rochdale H.	v.	London C.

SATURDAY, 9 JANUARY 1993
REGAL TROPHY — SEMI-FINAL 2

SUNDAY, 10 JANUARY 1993

Carlisle	v.	Rochdale H.
London C.	v.	Swinton
Oldham	v.	Bramley

SUNDAY, 17 JANUARY 1993

Bramley	v.	London C.
Carlisle	v.	Oldham
Featherstone R.	v.	Swinton

SATURDAY, 23 JANUARY 1993
REGAL TROPHY FINAL

SUNDAY, 24 JANUARY 1993

Huddersfield	v.	Carlisle
London C.	v.	Featherstone R.
Oldham	v.	Rochdale H.
Swinton	v.	Bramley

SATURDAY, 30 JANUARY 1993
SILK CUT CHALLENGE CUP — ROUND 1

SUNDAY, 7 FEBRUARY 1993

Bramley	v.	Huddersfield
Carlisle	v.	London C.
Featherstone R.	v.	Oldham
Rochdale H.	v.	Swinton

SATURDAY, 13 FEBRUARY 1993
SILK CUT CHALLENGE CUP — ROUND 2

SUNDAY, 21 FEBRUARY 1993

Huddersfield	v.	Rochdale H.
London C.	v.	Bramley
Oldham	v.	Carlisle
Swinton	v.	Featherstone R.

SATURDAY, 27 FEBRUARY 1993
SILK CUT CHALLENGE CUP — ROUND 3

SUNDAY, 28 FEBRUARY 1993

Bramley	v.	Swinton
Featherstone R.	v.	Carlisle
London C.	v.	Oldham
Rochdale H.	v.	Huddersfield

SUNDAY, 7 MARCH 1993

FRANCE	v.	GREAT BRITAIN
Carlisle	v.	Bramley
Huddersfield	v.	Oldham
Rochdale H.	v.	Featherstone R.
Swinton	v.	London C.

SATURDAY, 13 MARCH 1993
SILK CUT CHALLENGE CUP — SEMI-FINAL 1

SUNDAY, 14 MARCH 1993

Bramley	v.	Rochdale H.
London C.	v.	Huddersfield
Oldham	v.	Featherstone R.
Swinton	v.	Carlisle

SUNDAY, 21 MARCH 1993

Carlisle	v.	Huddersfield
Featherstone R.	v.	Bramley
Oldham	v.	London C.
Rochdale H.	v.	Swinton

SATURDAY, 27 MARCH 1993
SILK CUT CHALLENGE CUP — SEMI-FINAL 2

SUNDAY, 28 MARCH 1993

Featherstone R.	v.	Rochdale H.
Huddersfield	v.	Swinton
London C.	v.	Carlisle

FRIDAY, 2 APRIL 1993

GREAT BRITAIN	v.	FRANCE

411

SUNDAY, 4 APRIL 1993

Bramley	v.	Oldham
Carlisle	v.	Featherstone R.
Rochdale H.	v.	Huddersfield

FRIDAY, 9 APRIL 1993

Featherstone R.	v.	London C.
Huddersfield	v.	Bramley
Rochdale H.	v.	Oldham
Swinton	v.	Carlisle

MONDAY, 12 APRIL 1993

Bramley	v.	Featherstone R.
Carlisle	v.	Swinton
London C.	v.	Rochdale H.
Oldham	v.	Huddersfield

SUNDAY, 18 APRIL 1993

Featherstone R.	v.	Bramley
London C.	v.	Oldham
Rochdale H.	v.	Carlisle
Swinton	v.	Huddersfield

THIRD DIVISION

● **The fixture list below is subject to alteration. Neither the editors nor the publishers can take any responsibility for any subsequent changes or any inconvenience caused by such changes.**

SUNDAY, 30 AUGUST 1992

Batley	v.	Barrow
Chorley B.	v.	Ryedale-York
Highfield	v.	Dewsbury
Keighley C.	v.	Workington T.
Nottingham C.	v.	Blackpool G.
Scarborough P.	v.	Doncaster
Whitehaven	v.	Hunslet

SUNDAY, 6 SEPTEMBER 1992

Barrow	v.	Nottingham C.
Blackpool G.	v.	Scarborough P.
Dewsbury	v.	Whitehaven
Doncaster	v.	Highfield
Hunslet	v.	Keighley C.
Ryedale-York	v.	Batley
Workington T.	v.	Chorley B.

SUNDAY, 13 SEPTEMBER 1992
COUNTY CUPS — ROUND 1

SUNDAY, 20 SEPTEMBER 1992

Batley	v.	Doncaster
Chorley B.	v.	Blackpool G.
Highfield	v.	Workington T.
Hunslet	v.	Nottingham C.
Keighley C.	v.	Barrow
Scarborough P.	v.	Dewsbury
Whitehaven	v.	Ryedale-York

WEDNESDAY, 23 SEPTEMBER 1992
COUNTY CUPS — ROUND 2

SUNDAY, 27 SEPTEMBER 1992

Barrow	v.	Whitehaven
Blackpool G.	v.	Batley
Dewsbury	v.	Keighley C.
Doncaster	v.	Hunslet
Nottingham C.	v.	Chorley B.
Ryedale-York	v.	Highfield
Workington T.	v.	Scarborough P.

SUNDAY, 4 OCTOBER 1992

Batley	v.	Workington T.
Blackpool G.	v.	Barrow
Chorley B.	v.	Keighley C.
Hunslet	v.	Dewsbury
Nottingham C.	v.	Ryedale-York
Scarborough P.	v.	Highfield
Whitehaven	v.	Doncaster

WEDNESDAY, 7 OCTOBER 1992
COUNTY CUPS — SEMI-FINALS

SUNDAY, 11 OCTOBER 1992

Barrow	v.	Chorley B.
Blackpool G.	v.	Whitehaven
Dewsbury	v.	Nottingham C.
Highfield	v.	Batley
Keighley C.	v.	Scarborough P.
Ryedale-York	v.	Doncaster
Workington T.	v.	Hunslet

SATURDAY/SUNDAY, 17/18 OCTOBER 1992
LANCASHIRE/YORKSHIRE COUNTY CUP FINALS

SUNDAY, 18 OCTOBER 1992

Batley	v.	Ryedale-York
Chorley B.	v.	Dewsbury
Doncaster	v.	Barrow
Highfield	v.	Blackpool G.
Nottingham C.	v.	Workington T.
Scarborough P.	v.	Hunslet
Whitehaven	v.	Keighley C.

SUNDAY, 25 OCTOBER 1992
NO GAMES — WORLD CUP FINAL

TUESDAY, 27 OCTOBER 1992
REGAL TROPHY — PRELIMINARY ROUND

SUNDAY, 1 NOVEMBER 1992

Barrow	v.	Batley
Blackpool G.	v.	Doncaster
Dewsbury	v.	Scarborough P.
Hunslet	v.	Whitehaven
Keighley C.	v.	Nottingham C.
Ryedale-York	v.	Chorley B.
Workington T.	v.	Highfield

SATURDAY/SUNDAY, 7/8 NOVEMBER 1992
REGAL TROPHY — ROUND 1

SUNDAY, 15 NOVEMBER 1992

Batley	v.	Blackpool G.
Chorley B.	v.	Hunslet
Doncaster	v.	Workington T.
Highfield	v.	Ryedale-York
Nottingham C.	v.	Barrow
Whitehaven	v.	Dewsbury

SUNDAY, 22 NOVEMBER 1992

Barrow	v.	Ryedale-York
Blackpool G.	v.	Chorley B.
Dewsbury	v.	Doncaster
Hunslet	v.	Batley
Keighley C.	v.	Highfield
Scarborough P.	v.	Whitehaven
Workington T.	v.	Nottingham C.

SUNDAY, 29 NOVEMBER 1992

Batley	v.	Scarborough P.
Chorley B.	v.	Workington T.
Doncaster	v.	Blackpool G.
Highfield	v.	Hunslet
Nottingham C.	v.	Dewsbury
Ryedale-York	v.	Keighley C.
Whitehaven	v.	Barrow

SATURDAY/SUNDAY, 5/6 DECEMBER 1992
REGAL TROPHY — ROUND 2

SUNDAY, 13 DECEMBER 1992

FRANCE	v.	WALES
Barrow	v.	Doncaster
Chorley B.	v.	Batley
Dewsbury	v.	Highfield
Hunslet	v.	Blackpool G.
Keighley C.	v.	Whitehaven
Scarborough P.	v.	Nottingham C.
Workington T.	v.	Ryedale-York

SATURDAY, 19 DECEMBER 1992
REGAL TROPHY — ROUND 3

SUNDAY, 20 DECEMBER 1992

Batley	v.	Hunslet
Blackpool G.	v.	Workington T.
Doncaster	v.	Dewsbury
Highfield	v.	Scarborough P.
Nottingham C.	v.	Keighley C.
Ryedale-York	v.	Barrow
Whitehaven	v.	Chorley B.

SATURDAY, 26 DECEMBER 1992

Barrow	v.	Highfield
Dewsbury	v.	Batley
Doncaster	v.	Keighley C.
Hunslet	v.	Chorley B.
Scarborough P.	v.	Ryedale-York
Workington T.	v.	Whitehaven

SUNDAY, 27 DECEMBER 1992

Blackpool G.	v.	Nottingham C.

FRIDAY, 1 JANUARY 1993

Batley	v.	Dewsbury
Keighley C.	v.	Doncaster
Ryedale-York	v.	Scarborough P.

SATUDAY, 2 JANUARY 1993
REGAL TROPHY — SEMI-FINAL 1

SUNDAY, 3 JANUARY 1993

Barrow	v.	Workington T.
Chorley B.	v.	Highfield
Nottingham C.	v.	Hunslet
Whitehaven	v.	Blackpool G.

SATURDAY, 9 JANUARY 1993
REGAL TROPHY — SEMI-FINAL 2

SUNDAY, 10 JANUARY 1993

Blackpool G.	v.	Ryedale-York
Dewsbury	v.	Chorley B.
Doncaster	v.	Nottingham C.
Highfield	v.	Whitehaven
Scarborough P.	v.	Barrow
Workington T.	v.	Keighley C.

SATURDAY, 16 JANUARY 1993
SILK CUT CHALLENGE CUP — PRELIMINARY ROUND

SUNDAY, 17 JANUARY 1993

Barrow	v.	Dewsbury
Chorley B.	v.	Doncaster
Hunslet	v.	Highfield
Keighley C.	v.	Blackpool G.
Ryedale-York	v.	Nottingham C.
Whitehaven	v.	Scarborough P.

SATURDAY, 23 JANUARY 1993
REGAL TROPHY FINAL

SUNDAY, 24 JANUARY 1993

Barrow	v.	Hunslet
Batley	v.	Chorley B.
Doncaster	v.	Whitehaven
Highfield	v.	Keighley C.
Nottingham C.	v.	Scarborough P.
Ryedale-York	v.	Dewsbury
Workington T.	v.	Blackpool G.

SATURDAY, 30 JANUARY 1993
SILK CUT CHALLENGE CUP — ROUND 1

SUNDAY, 7 FEBRUARY 1993

Blackpool G.	v.	Highfield
Chorley B.	v.	Barrow
Dewsbury	v.	Workington T.
Hunslet	v.	Doncaster
Keighley C.	v.	Ryedale-York
Scarborough P.	v.	Batley
Whitehaven	v.	Nottingham C.

SATURDAY, 13 FEBRUARY 1993
SILK CUT CHALLENGE CUP — ROUND 2

SUNDAY, 21 FEBRUARY 1993

Batley	v.	Whitehaven
Highfield	v.	Doncaster
Hunslet	v.	Scarborough P.
Keighley C.	v.	Chorley B.
Ryedale-York	v.	Blackpool G.
Workington T.	v.	Dewsbury

SATURDAY, 27 FEBRUARY 1993
SILK CUT CHALLENGE CUP — ROUND 3

SUNDAY, 28 FEBRUARY 1993

Barrow	v.	Keighley C.
Dewsbury	v.	Hunslet
Doncaster	v.	Ryedale-York
Nottingham C.	v.	Batley
Scarborough P.	v.	Workington T.
Whitehaven	v.	Highfield

SUNDAY, 7 MARCH 1993

FRANCE	v.	GREAT BRITAIN
Blackpool G.	v.	Keighley C.
Doncaster	v.	Chorley B.
Highfield	v.	Nottingham C.
Hunslet	v.	Barrow
Workington T.	v.	Batley

SATURDAY, 13 MARCH 1993
SILK CUT CHALLENGE CUP — SEMI-FINAL 1

SUNDAY, 14 MARCH 1993

Batley	v.	Highfield
Blackpool G.	v.	Hunslet
Chorley B.	v.	Scarborough P.
Keighley C.	v.	Dewsbury
Nottingham C.	v.	Doncaster
Ryedale-York	v.	Workington T.

SUNDAY, 21 MARCH 1993

Barrow	v.	Blackpool G.
Dewsbury	v.	Ryedale-York
Doncaster	v.	Batley
Highfield	v.	Chorley B.
Hunslet	v.	Workington T.
Nottingham C.	v.	Whitehaven
Scarborough P.	v.	Keighley C.

SATURDAY, 27 MARCH 1993
SILK CUT CHALLENGE CUP — SEMI-FINAL 2

SUNDAY, 28 MARCH 1993

Chorley B.	v.	Nottingham C.
Dewsbury	v.	Barrow
Keighley C.	v.	Hunslet
Scarborough P.	v.	Blackpool G.
Whitehaven	v.	Batley
Workington T.	v.	Doncaster

FRIDAY, 2 APRIL 1993
GREAT BRITAIN v. FRANCE

SUNDAY, 4 APRIL 1993

Barrow	v.	Scarborough P.
Batley	v.	Nottingham C.
Blackpool G.	v.	Dewsbury
Ryedale-York	v.	Whitehaven

FRIDAY, 9 APRIL 1993

Dewsbury	v.	Blackpool G.
Highfield	v.	Barrow
Keighley C.	v.	Batley
Ryedale-York	v.	Hunslet
Scarborough P.	v.	Chorley B.
Whitehaven	v.	Workington T.

SUNDAY, 11 APRIL 1993

Nottingham C.	v.	Highfield

MONDAY, 12 APRIL 1993

Batley	v.	Keighley C.
Chorley B.	v.	Whitehaven
Doncaster	v.	Scarborough P.
Hunslet	v.	Ryedale-York
Workington T.	v.	Barrow

ROTHMANS FOOTBALL YEARBOOK 1992-93   Edited by Jack Rollin £14.99
ROTHMANS RUGBY UNION YEARBOOK 1992-93 Edited by Stephen Jones £14.99
PLAYFAIR FOOTBALL ANNUAL 1992-93   Edited by Jack Rollin £3.99
PLAYFAIR NON-LEAGUE FOOTBALL ANNUAL 1992-93   £3.99
   Edited by Bruce Smith
WILLIE CARSON: THE ILLUSTRATED BIOGRAPHY by Michael Seely   £9.99

Headline offers an exciting range of quality titles by both established and new authors, available from:
Headline Book Publishing PLC
Cash Sales Department,
P.O. Box 11,
Falmouth,
Cornwall,
TR10 9EN.

Alternatively you may fax your order to the above address. Fax No. 0326 376423.

Payments can be made as follows: cheque, postal order (payable to Headline Book Publishing PLC) or by credit cards, Visa/Access. Do not send cash or currency. UK and BFPO customers: please send a cheque or postal order (no currency) and allow £1.00 for postage and packing for the first book plus 50p for each additional book up to a maximum charge of £3.00.

Overseas customers, including Ireland, please allow £2.00 for postage and packing for the first book, £1.00 for the second book, and 50p for each additional book.

NAME (Block Letters) ....

ADDRESS ....

....

....

    I enclose my remittance for _____

    I wish to pay by Access/Visa Card

    Number ....

    Card Expiry Date ....